THE
GREAT
BRITISH
BED
AND
BREAKFAST

KGP Publishing
Penrith, Cumbria, England

All rights reserved. No part of the publication may be produced, stored in a retrievable system, or transmitted in any form or by any means - electronic, mechanical, photocopying, or otherwise - unless the written permission of the Publisher has been given beforehand.

Every effort is made to ensure accuracy, but the publishers do not hold themselves responsible for any consequences that may arise from errors or omissions. Whilst contents are believed to be correct at the time of going to press, changes may have occurred since that time or will occur during the currency of the book.

Published by: KGP Publishing, 54 Castlegate, Penrith, Cumbria CA11 7HY England

ACKNOWLEDGMENTS

Edited by: Ken Plant

Design and Layout by: Jennie Prior

Administration by: Joanne Cullen & Carole Douglas

Editorials: Karl Stedman

Maps and illustrations by: Jonathon Robinson & Jenny Walter

Picture Stories by: Jenny Walter

Photographs with poetry by: Val Corbett

Cover Picture
"Breakfast by the Window" by: Stephen Darbishire

ISBN Number 0-9522807-7-9

Distributed worldwide by: Portfolio

THE GREAT BRITISH BED & BREAKFAST
54 Castlegate
Penrith
Cumbria
CA11 7HY
England
Web Site: http://www.kgp-publishing.co.uk

CONTENTS

"Can you book us in for three nights please"

FOREWORD

Welcome to the 1999 edition of **The Great British Bed & Breakfast**.

Bed and Breakfasting has becomes more popular than ever. Gone, thank goodness, are the days of the dragon-like landladies, with all their terrifying restrictions, the butt of every seaside comedian's jokes - to be replaced by proprietors who are able to offer an individual service, of a quality envied by many of the top hotels...comfort and cossetting in surroundings quite impossible to match by larger and as consequence more impersonal establishments.

The range of properties in this publication is as diverse as the area it covers. There are thatched cottages and Georgian town houses, converted stables and former vicarages. Whether you're visiting a historic city, heading for the gentle countryside of a southern county or seeking solitude in a remote part of Scotland or Wales, you'll find a property offering good accommodation and good food at a good price. And you'll discover much more than a bed to rest in. There are properties with a history, others with literary connections and many with beautiful gardens. One of the great advantages in staying at an establishment which is proprietor run is the warmth of the welcome you receive. Another benefit is the wealth of knowledge that your hosts will have about the area.

What our hosts offer varies considerably, so if you have particular preferences it is advisable to check on booking...some offer vegetarian dishes...some, particularly in Scotland, offer high-tea instead of dinner. Some welcome dogs, some decidedly don't, some allow smoking only in designated rooms, some are licensed and others not...and it is well to ascertain if cheques or credit cards are acceptable.

Whether you are a visitor to Britain or one of the ever increasing number of people discovering the joys of the "short-break", our aim is to give you all the information you need to choose the establishment that is right for you. Details of properties have supplied by the owners themselves so you can rely on their accuracy.

Accommodation is listed by county and we have made the choice of where you stay easier by including a map, a brief description of the area and an illustration of each property.

There is simply no doubt about it, **The Great British Bed & Breakfast** aims to be excellent value for money, and if you haven't tried it yet - we think you'll enjoy it.

Spring sees the launch of our national glossy magazine, Home from Home. If you would like a closer look at some of the houses in **The Great British Bed & Breakfast** you'll enjoy reading **Home from Home**. Together with many general interest articles, each issue will feature some of the fascinating properties listed here.

LONDON

The capital city of the United Kingdom was a Roman settlement in the first century AD. The medieval city developed around the first St. Paul's Cathedral, founded in the seventh century. Later William the Conqueror, recognising the strategic importance of London, chose this site to build his White Tower, the hub of the Tower of London. Over the following centuries the city guilds, now known as the Livery Companies, prospered and their successive elected leaders have become the Lord Mayors of London. Hit by the Black Death in 1348 and the Plague in 1665, four fifths of the city was then consumed by the Great Fire in 1666, cleansing the city of the pestilence and its appalling medieval slums, and making way for a period of planned building, much of it designed by Sir Christopher Wren. Wren rebuilt St. Paul's and a large number of city churches. During the Second World War much of central and suburban London was destroyed, leading to another period of rebuilding.

Most of London's very famous attractions are to be found in the West End, with Trafalgar Square and Nelson's Column at its centre. Here is the National Gallery, the church of St. Martin-in-the-Fields and the impressive Admiralty Arch leading into The Mall, that splendid avenue which leads to Buckingham Palace, the chief residence of the Queen. St. James's Park, arguably the most attractive of the royal parks, borders The Mall on one side and Birdcage Walk on the other. Birdcage Walk leads to Parliament Square, the hub of Westminster,

dominated by St. Stephen's Tower, housing Big Ben. The Houses of Parliament, one of the Capital's most photographed buildings, is a magnificent example of Gothic Revival architecture. Across the Square is Westminster Abbey where William I was crowned on Christmas Day 1066, and the site of every subsequent coronation. The Abbey contains memorials to many of the nation's most honoured dead. The other great city cathedral, St. Paul's, is the burial place of Nelson, Wellington and Sir Christopher Wren, the great architect of London whose epitaph 'If you seek his memorial, look about you' is singularly apt.

London is a great city of pageantry and ceremonial. Each day there is the Changing of the Guard at Buckingham Palace, Mounting the Guard at Horse Guards in Whitehall, and The Ceremony of the Keys at the Tower of London each evening at 9.53pm. Add to this the yearly and casual events such as the Lord Mayor's Show and the Gun Salutes, and there is scarcely an hour without some 'happening' somewhere. Most of the West End department stores are in Oxford Street or Regent Street; St. James' Street has its specialist shops, while Charing Cross Road is the place for books...Harrod's is in Knightsbridge, and Fortnum and Mason's in Piccadilly. There are numerous street markets: Brick Lane, Camden Lock, Portobello Road.....The list is virtually endless, but the Capital is extremely well served with helpful Information Centres, so no visitor should be short of advice on where to go and what to see.....and the best way of all to see the sights is still from the top of a London double-decker bus!

Beautiful B&B in London

Anita Harrison and Rosemary Richardson specialise in arranging good quality Bed and Breakfast accommodation in London homes. All have their individual style and offer exceptional value for money - a very affordable alternative to hotels.

Most of the accommodation is located in the leafy west London areas of Chiswick, Hammersmith, Ealing and Parsons Green, convenient to shops and restaurants and public transport for the central sights. In these areas the average cost for a twin or double sharing bathroom is £24 per person per night: £29 with private bathroom, including breakfast. The listings begin with a small selection of homes in more central areas where prices are higher.

The accommodation has been chosen with great care, with hosts who take pleasure in welcoming guests to their homes. The guest rooms are comfortable and attractively decorated, with the emphasis on cleanliness and warmth. Tea and coffee making facilities are provided and a generous breakfast is included in the tariff. Parking is available at most of the addresses.

How to reserve your London B&B

It is recommended that you telephone Anita or Rosemary to discuss your requirements. To secure your reservation, a deposit of £6 per person per night is required, to be paid by Visa or Mastercard. The balance is settled with your hosts during your stay, but we must point out that hosts are not able to accept credit cards. You will receive an official confirmation of arrangments.

LONDON HOME-TO-HOME
19 Mount Park Crescent, London W5 2RN
Tel and Fax: 0181 566 7976
Email: londonhh@btinternet.com

Home 99/A (Nanette & Stylie) Just off Kensington High Street (Central London)   A315, A3220

A beautifully preserved Victorian town house which is tastefully decorated and incorporates all modern facilities for guest's comfort, whilst retaining the authentic features of the period. TV's, hair dryers and hospitality trays are available in all rooms. Vivacious hosts offer high quality accommodation, serving breakfast in the elegant family dining room. A welcoming atmosphere and friendly service is assured.

London Home-to-Home
Tel/Fax: 0181 566 7976

B&B from £44pp, Rooms: 4 en-suite double/twin, Non smoking, Nearest underground: Earls Court - 10 minutes, Buses to sights, A1 Airbus stops nearby at Earls Court

---

Home 99/B (Peter & Cristina) Camden Town area (Central London)   Nearest Road A1, A4201

Stay in an elegant townhouse in fashionable Camden, close to Regent's Park! The owner architect has created three lovely guest rooms, two of them sharing a bathroom between them. Breakfast is served in a modern kitchen-diner, which is airy and beautiful. Trendy Camden Market nearby! Prefers non smokers. Parking: meters

London Home-to-Home
Tel/Fax: 0181 566 7976

B&B from £35, Rooms: 1 double with private shower room, 1 double/twin sharing bathroom, No smoking, Nearest underground: Camden Town, on Northern line, 5 minutes, Buses to sights

---

Home 99/C (Ann & James) Islington area (Central London)   Nearest Road A1, A1200

Comfortable, modern town-house situated in Canonbury Square, in fashionable Islington. One twin room overlooking a pretty public garden, and a smaller double room with washbasin, sharing a guest bathroom between them. Trendy, vibrant area, just ten minutes from the centre of London. Numerous excellent restaurants nearby. Buses and tubes to the theatre district and all places of interest. Will not accept smokers. Parking for one car available.

London Home-to-Home
Tel/Fax: 0181 566 7976

B&B from £35, Rooms: 1 double, 1 twin, sharing guest bathroom Nearest underground: Highbury & Islington on Victoria line - 6 minutes Buses to all parts

---

Home 99/D (Sue & Rodger) Camden Town area (Central London)   Nearest Road A1

Guests are made most welcome in the modern home of an architect and his wife. They designed the house themselves in the 1970's, with much use of glass. Two guest rooms available: an unusual double-bedded room where the bed is sunk into a low platform, and a single room. Both rooms share a guest bathroom. Breakfast is served in the open-plan dining-area, which overlooks a courtyard garden, or, in summer, in the courtyard itself. Family pets are a macaw and a cat. Smokers not accepted.

London Home-to-Home
Tel/Fax: 0181 566 7976

B&B from £35ppn, Single £52, Rooms: 1 double, 1 single, sharing guest bathroom. Nearest underground station: Camden Town, on Northern line, 8 mins walk, Many bus services.

Home 99/E (Marilyn & Alan) Swiss Cottage (Central London)   Nearest Road A41

A modern townhouse situated off the Finchley Road. Accommodation comprises a double/triple room with TV and en-suite bathroom and shower, a double/triple, twin and dble/single, sharing a guest bathroom. Additional toilet and washbasin available also. Geared for visitors and offering a comfortable sitting area with TV, payphone, fax and word processing facilities. Between Hampstead Heath and Regents Park; 200 yds from Swiss Cottage underground. 6 minutes journey on the Jubilee Line to Baker Street for Madam Tussauds and 10 minutes to Bond Street in the heart of Oxford Street shops.

London Home-to-Home
Tel/Fax: 0181 566 7976

B&B from £28pp, Rooms: 4 comfortable guest rooms, Nearest underground: Swiss Cottage - 3 minutes, Bus services to sights, A2 Airbus at Baker Street

Home 99/F (Julianna & Harry) Putney area   Nearest Road A219/205

Comfortable double room available in this beautifully restored Victorian home, with some unusual architectural features. Private bathroom. Generous Continental breakfast served in the family kitchen/diner which overlooks the garden and river. Excellent restaurants and shopping centre nearby. No pets. Non-smokers, who will not accept smokers.

London Home-to-Home
Tel/Fax: 0181 566 7976

B&B from £29pp, Rooms: 1 double room with private bathroom Nearest Underground station: Putney Bridge, 6-8 mins walk

Home 99/G (Dolores & Bert) Parsons Green area   Nearest Road A308, A3217

Whether staying for 2 nights or a week you can be sure of a warm welcome with these cheerful and generous hosts. They offer a double room with queen sized bed, TV and hot drinks tray. Shower and wash basin are en-suite. The atmosphere is friendly and informal. A popular choice! Some of London's trendiest restaurants in the area.

London Home-to-Home
Tel/Fax: 0181 566 7976

B&B from £29pp, Rooms: 1 en-suite double Nearest underground: Parsons Green - 10 minutes, Buses for Chelsea, Knightsbridge and Central sights

Home 99/H (Moira & Frank) Parsons Green area   Nearest Road A217, A308

Self contained apartment for 2-4 guests on first floor of a family home. Comprises a twin bedroom with private bathroom, dining/living room with TV and comfortable sofa bed, additional bathroom and fully equipped kitchen. Lounge overlooks a pretty park. Frank & Moira are gracious and welcoming hosts who live on the ground floor in their elegant suite. Ideal for longer stays as guests can be totally self catering. However, hosts are delighted to provide breakfast food if guests prefer not to shop. A popular area for quality interior design/furniture and antiques. Excellent restaurants.

London Home-to-Home
Tel/Fax: 0181 566 7976

Self contained apartment from £33 per person, Nearest underground: Parsons Green - 10 minutes, Buses to various parts of London

Home 99/I (Anthea & Mark) Parsons Green **Nearest Road A308, A3217**

Beautiful guest room with private shower bathroom adjacent in the modern custom-built apartment of this welcoming hostess. Twin beds which can zip together as King-size double. Light and airy, luxury standard. Hurlingham Club adjacent. Delightful walks along the Thames within a stone's throw! Non-smokers only, please. Parking is easy, but chargeable during the day.

London Home-to-Home
Tel/Fax: 0181 566 7976

B&B from £35pn, Rooms: 1 twin or double room with private bathroom Nearest underground: Putney Bridge on District line, 3 mins' walk. Numerous buses along the Kings Rd

---

Home 99/J (Marjory & Christopher) Hammersmith/Chiswick area **Nearest Road A4, A315**

Wonderfully close to the tube, this family home offers a very beautiful and spacious twin guest room with wash basin, TV and hospitality tray. The room overlooks a tranquil garden. Private bathroom is adjacent. Christopher, a linguist, and Marjory, a teacher, are anxious to make their guests' stay as pleasant as possible. Enjoy an evening stroll along a lovely stretch of the river Thames, passing picturesque pubs and lovely gardens! Good restaurants and shops nearby.

London Home-to-Home
Tel/Fax: 0181 566 7976

B&B from £29pp, Rooms: 1 twin with private bathroom adjacent, Nearest underground: Stamford Brook - 1 minute, Buses to Trafalgar Square and Kew Gardens, Non smoking

---

Home 99/K (Peter & Catriona) Hammersmith/Chiswick area **Nearest Road A4, A315**

Situated in the heart of historic Brackenbury Village and near delightful Ravenscourt Park. Hosts offer 2 double and a single guest room in their pretty Victorian house, restored by Peter, who is an architect. A comfortable base with an informal atmosphere. Imaginative breakfasts. Trendy restaurants and pubs within an easy walk.

London Home-to-Home
Tel/Fax: 0181 566 7976

B&B from £24pp, Rooms: 2 double, 1 twin/single, 2 guest bathrooms, Nearest underground: Ravenscourt Park - 8 minutes, Hammersmith 15 minutes

---

Home 99/L (Sonia & Family) Hammersmith area **Nearest Road A4**

Cosy loft room with own bathroom and twin beds is offered in this stylish Edwardian home. Quiet street in a thriving cosmopolitan area. Walk along the Thames, past the famous Riverside Cafe to the local tube and buses. Non smokers only, please.

London Home-to-Home
Tel/Fax: 0181 566 7976

B&B from £32pn, 1 double, room en-suite Nearest underground station: Hammersmith, on District, Piccadilly & Metropolitan lines, 10 mins

Home 99/M (Peter & Valerie) Chiswick area   Nearest Road A315, B409

Stay in villagey, unspoiled Chiswick, where writers and actors live! On the Bedford Park Garden Conservation Estate, this 1880's Norman Shaw home is just 3 minutes walk from the tube station, interesting boutiques and eating places. Valerie and Peter offer 3 guest rooms; a double and a twin (which can be triples) with guest bathroom, plus a beautiful double with queen-size bed and private bathroom. Sitting room for guests. A fine home, beautifully furnished by the owner who is a retired architect.

London Home-to-Home
Tel/Fax: 0181 566 7976

B&B from £24pp, Rooms: 1 double with bathroom, 1 double, 1 twin/triple, Nearest underground: Turnham Green - 3 minutes, Easy access to Heathrow, Buses to Central London

Home 99/N (Janice & Jeremy) Acton Town area   Nearest Road A4, M4, A406

Superb accommodation is offered in this home of grace and quality where the hosts delight in providing for guests' every comfort. Beautiful lounge available for guests. The mock-Tudor home is surrounded by beautiful gardens and is located on a lovely estate with a large park of historic interest close by. Kew Gardens and fascinating pubs along the river's edge within a 30 minute walk. Choose between a twin with en-suite bathroom, and a spacious and lovely double room with wash basin and private bathroom close by.

London Home-to-Home
Tel/Fax: 0181 566 7976

B&B from £29pp, Rooms: 1 double or 1 twin (with private facilities), Nearest underground: Acton Town - 10 minutes, Ideal for Heathrow arrivals.

Home 99/O (Ann & Peter) Turnham Green area   Nearest Road A315, B409

One large guest room is offered on the top floor of this welcoming family home. King-size bed plus a single and child's bed provide family accommodation with private bathroom. TV and hot drinks in the room. Breakfast is served in a delightful kitchen/dining room, overlooking a lovely town garden. Non-smokers preferred. Very easy parking.

London Home-to-Home
Tel/Fax: 0181 566 7976

B&B from £29 per night, Rooms: 1 double/family room with private bathroom, Nearest underground: Turnham Green (District line) 10 mins

Home 99/P (John & Jane) Ealing area   Nearest Road M4, A40, A406

A lovely family home of great character offering 1 twin room with private bathroom adjacent, overlooking landscaped patio and gardens. The home, built in the mid 1880's, has been tastefully furnished. Breakfast is served in the family kitchen/breakfast room which leads onto the garden. Hosts take every care to ensure their guests' comfort. Five minutes walk to a modern shopping mall and several first class restaurants. Open parkland nearby.

London Home-to-Home
Tel/Fax: 0181 566 7976

B&B from £29pp, Rooms: 1 twin with private bathroom adjacent, Nearest underground: Ealing Broadway - 7 mins, Ealing Common - 8 mins

Home 99/Q (Anne & Richard) Ealing area   **Nearest Road A406, M4**

Cheerful, welcoming hostess, an actress, offers a lovely, spacious loft room with king-size bed and en-suite shower bathroom. Lovely outlook. Choice of self-catering or traditional breakfasts. Also, one double room (four-poster bed), sharing a bathroom with hosts.

London Home-to-Home   **B&B from £24-£29 pn, Rooms: 2 double, Nearest underground: South**
Tel/Fax: 0181 566 7976   **Ealing, on Piccadilly line, 10 mins' walk**

Home 99/R (Catherine & Janek) Ealing area   **Nearest Road A40, A406**

Polish host and his welcoming Scottish wife offer a suite of a double and a single room with guest bathroom on the second floor of their modern town house. Secluded estate. Guests are happy to return again and again, as the hostess's relaxed welcome encourages them to feel at home. Shops, malls and numerous restaurants and pubs lie 10 minutes walk away, at Ealing Broadway, the attractive local centre. Non smokers.

London Home-to-Home   **B&B from £24pp, Rooms: 1 double, 1 single, share guest bathroom,**
Tel/Fax: 0181 566 7976   **Nearest underground: Ealing Broadway - 10 minutes, British Rail to**
                                 Paddington

Home 99/S (Muriel & Neville) Ealing area   **Nearest Road M4, A406**

This gracious hostess offers 3 single rooms in a home of beauty and charm, decorated with a traditional English quality. A tranquil setting. Muriel, who is piano teacher and keen gardener, does not accept smokers and is not available in August. At nearby Ealing Common tube station, with its choice of tube lines, is a comprehensive range of shops and restaurants. Easy commuting from Heathrow or Central London.

London Home-to-Home   **B&B from £30pn, Rooms: 3 single rooms sharing bathroom, Nearest**
Tel/Fax: 0181 566 7976   **underground: Ealing Common - 3 minutes, Non smoking**

Home 99/T (Rosemary & Ian) Ealing area   **Nearest Road M4, A406**

Bed and Breakfast with a difference! Australian hosts offer a superb self-contained loft room in their beautiful home. Overlooking gardens and a pond. Double bed, en-suite shower bathroom, kitchenette with microwave, dining/sitting area with TV. Linen provided, also breakfast food. A warm and friendly welcome in a lovely home!

London Home-to-Home   **B&B from £29pp, Rooms: 1 double with en-suite shower bathroom, Non**
Tel/Fax: 0181 566 7976   **smoking, Nearest underground: South Ealing - 10 minutes, Buses to**
                                 Kew and Richmond

Home 99/U (Wendy & Michael) Ealing area · Nearest Road M4, A406

Beautiful newly converted loft room, which has incorporated many windows, to give a delightful feel to the large room. En-suite bathroom, with good shower over the bath. Double bed and single bed. Family with 3 children, who all sleep on the floor below. 1 cat. Prefers non-smokers, Very easy parking. Ideal for Heathrow arrivals.

London Home-to-Home
Tel/Fax: 0181 566 7976

B&B from £29pn, Rooms: 1 triple, double or twin room with en-suite bathroom, Nearest underground: South Ealing on Piccadilly line, 5 mins

Home 99/V (Margaret & Colin) Ealing area · Nearest Road M4, A40, A406

A good natured and adaptable Australian and her English husband offer a pleasant double room with washbasin and option of private bathroom in their comfortable family home. Non smokers. Easy access to Heathrow.

London Home-to-Home
Tel/Fax: 0181 566 7976

B&B from £24pp, Rooms: 1 double with washbasin, Nearest underground: North Ealing - 2 minutes

Home 99/W (Maria & Damien) Ealing Common area · Nearest Road M4, A406

Accommodation designed for a comfortable stay! Warm and friendly hosts offer a large loft room, providing triple accommodation with en-suite shower bathroom. Breakfast served in the conservatory overlooking the garden. Situated in a quiet, tree-lined street, a short stroll from shops, restaurants and two underground stations. Very handy for guests arriving from Heathrow. Maria speaks French. No pets. Free parking on street. Another triple room occasionally available also.

London Home-to-Home
Tel/Fax: 0181 566 7976

B&B from £29pp, Rooms: 2 triples with en-suite bathrooms Nearest underground: Ealing Common - 10 minutes

Home 99/X (Rita & Geoff) Ealing Common area · Nearest Road A406, A/M4

These welcoming hosts offer a large, self-contained guest room on the top floor of their home. The rooms is thoughtfully planned, and comprises a sleeping area with double bed, and a sitting/dining area with facilities for self-catering. Generous supply of breakfast food provided. Short or longer term rates available. Private bathroom.

London Home-to-Home
Tel/Fax: 0181 566 7976

B&B from £26pp, Rooms: 1 double, self-catering, private bathroom, Nearest underground: Ealing Common - 5 mins, Unlimited parking.

Home 99/Y (Marian & Daniel) Ealing area   **Nearest Road A406, A40**

In their comfortable Edwardian semi-detached home, Marian and Daniel offer a convenient base. The guest rooms comprise a double with private bathroom adjacent, plus a twin room with small shower bathroom en-suite. Situated on a quiet tree lined street just 5 minutes walk to parade of shops and 2 tube stations. Easy parking. Ideal accommodation for families.

London Home-to-Home
Tel/Fax: 0181 566 7976

B&B from £29pp, Rooms: 1 double, sharing bathroom, 1 twin with en-suite shower bathroom, Nearest underground: North Ealing - 4 mins, West Acton - 7 mins

---

Home 99/Z (Diana & Louis) Ealing area   **Nearest Road A40, A406**

Relaxed, friendly hosts offer a loft conversion comprising a spacious and airy twin/triple room with private shower bathroom en-suite and an additional twin room. TV and hospitality tray. Modern three storey home, conveniently situated for 2 underground lines.

London Home-to-Home
Tel/Fax: 0181 566 7976

B&B from £29pp, Rooms: 1 twin/triple with en-suite facilities, plus 1 twin sharing bathroom, Nearest underground: West Acton - 7 minutes, North Ealing - 7 minutes

---

Also see
SURREY
on page 346

BATH, BRISTOL & NORTH EAST SOMERSET

The small county of Bath, Bristol & North East Somerset was formed in 1974 from the city and county of Bristol, part of South Gloucestershire and part of North Somerset. The Lower River Avon, which used to give the county its name, rises in the Cotswolds and flows south to Bradford-on-Avon, turns northwest to Bath and Bristol, and joins the Bristol Channel at Avonmouth after passing through the spectacular Clifton Gorge. The county is relatively flat with the exception of the Mendips, the limestone mass which stretches some thirty miles from the valley of the Frome virtually to the Bristol Channel and contains many dramatic caves. The views from the Mendips over Sedgemoor and to the Somerset Quantocks are quite breathtaking. This is a county of delights, catering for simply every taste, be it quiet walking, exploring fascinating old villages, wandering over open heath or enjoying traditional seaside pleasures.

At the centre and dominating the county lies Bristol, an ideal holiday venue. At one time the major port on the west coast, its prosperity was based upon trade with the colonies in sugar, tobacco and slaves, until the swift development during the late 1700s of Liverpool. Bristol took a dreadful battering during the Second World War, but there is much of the old Bristol to see

and enjoy. The Cathedral, originally the church of the twelfth century abbey can boast one of the finest Norman interiors in Britain. Not to be missed is the large altarpiece commissioned in 1755 from William Hogarth for the Church of St. Mary Redcliffe, displayed in the Norman church of St. Nicholas - now a museum of ecclesiastical art. The famous Bristol Nails stand outside the Corn Exchange, four small bronze pillars set in the pavement, where city merchants completed their deals by paying 'on the nail'. The Theatre Royal, home since 1943 of the Bristol Old Vic, is the oldest theatre in the country in regular use. This is a fascinating city, packed with interest, and Cabot Tower, the curious architectural folly, provides a wonderful view over its rooftops. The main seafaring activities are now mainly concentrated in Avonmouth, but Bristol dockland still retains its boating atmosphere, with a July regatta and its wealth of sailing dinghies, not forgetting its fine Industrial Museum.

Elegant Clifton is blessed with superb honey-coloured stone squares, crescents and terraces as well as that marvel of Victorian engineering, the Clifton Suspension Bridge; when it was built it was the longest and highest span ever attempted

Splendid as it is, Brunel had also planned for it to have supporting piers in the Egyptian style but he unfortunately died before his plans could be carried out. To the east of Bristol lies Bath, surely one of Britain's most magnificent cities. Although a spa since Roman times, its popularity blossomed during the Regency period. The Romans called the town Aquae Sulis - the waters of Sul (a local Celtic deity) and they built their baths connected with a temple. The delights of these hot springs became fashionable under the critical eye of that archetypal English dandy Beau Nash. Bath can lay claim to the best Roman ruins in England, as well as being the country's most perfect example of eighteenth century architecture. Built in the local golden coloured limestone against a setting of superbly proportioned and planned streets are fine individual features...The Royal Crescent and Lansdown Crescent, the lovely Pulteney Bridge with its Palladian houses by Robert Adam, and of course the spectacular Circus. Like Bristol, Bath is full of interesting places.....the oldest house in Bath, Sally Lunn's house is still baking Sally Lunns to a secret recipe, the Pump Room, Roman Baths, the Abbey, the Bath Industrial Heritage Centre, the Museum of Costume, and at Claverton Manor, the American Museum. Visitors could be excused for spending all their holiday in Bath....but that would be a shame, the county has even more to offer. Weston-super-Mare, built by

the Victorians around an old fishing village, has developed into one of the largest and most popular seaside resorts on the west coast with glorious sands, piers and all one would expect from a first class modern resort. North along the coast is Clevedon which once boasted the finest Victorian pier in England. Built around a small rocky bay with trees coming down to the water's edge, the town has interesting literary connections. Coleridge spent his honeymoon here and Thackeray wrote much of Vanity Fair when staying at Clevedon Court. The house, built about 1320 is one of the few surviving manor houses of this period. Chipping Sodbury, its prefix Chipping being the Old English word for market, is a lovely mixture of Georgian brick houses and golden Cotswold stone cottages, and nearby is magnificent Dodington House, built by James Wyatt for Christopher Codrington at the end of the eighteenth century. An ancestor of the owner was standard bearer to Henry V at Agincourt. The grounds laid out by Capability Brown contain two lakes joined by a picturesque Gothic cascade.

Bath, Bristol & North East Somerset is a compact county of only five hundred and seventeen square miles but within its boundaries is everything to tempt the most discriminating holidaymaker.

BATH, BRISTOL & NORTH EAST SOMERSET

Places to Visit

Royal Crescent, *Bath* ~ built from 1767-1774, the elegant arc of houses was the masterpiece of John Wood the Younger.

Roman Baths, *Bath* ~ the Romans built this world famous bathing complex in the first century, yet the Great Bath was not discovered until the 1870's.

Bath Abbey, *Bath* ~ in 973 AD, Edgar was crowned the first king of England here. In the late 1490's the present abbey was begun with its fan vaulting and monuments.

Clevedon Court

American Museum in Britain, Claverton ~ an 1820 manor house decorated in various Amercan styles with examples of Shaker furniture, quilts, Native American art and a replica of George Washington's Mount Vernon garden of 1785.

Dyrham Park, *near Bath & Bristol* ~ a beautiful William and Mary house now belonging to the National Trust, it was built 1691-1710 and has changed little over the years with fine panelled rooms, Dutch paintings and furniture.

Clifton Suspension Bridge, *Bristol* ~ opened in 1864, it was designed by Isambard Kingdom Brunel. The bridge spans the Avon Gorge at 702 feet (214m) long with the river some 245 feet (74.7m) below.

Bristol Cathedral, *Bristol* ~ a 'hall church' which took an exceptionally long time to build, the choir was built between 1298 and 1330, the transepts and tower were finished in 1515 but it was 350 years later when Victorian architect GE Street built the nave.

City Museum and Art Gallery, *Bristol* ~housing many different collections including Roman tableware, dinosaur fossils and the largest collection of Chinese glass outside China. There is also a collection of European paintings including works of Renoir and Bellini.

Clevedon Court, *Clevedon* ~ a 14th century manor house with 13th century hall, 12th century tower and garden with rare trees. Thackeray wrote most of 'Vanity Fair' here.

Chew Magna ~ a pretty red sandstone village, with many of its buildings and church dating from the Middle Ages, when wool brought prosperity to the village. The High Street features small stone cottages along with fine 18th century mansions.

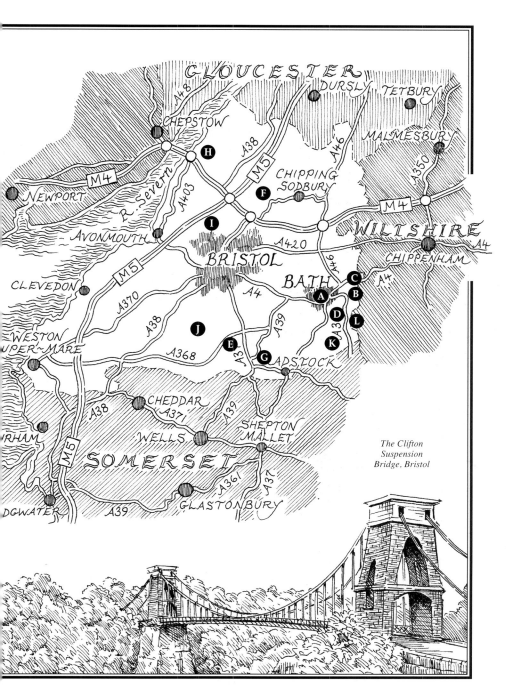

The Clifton
Suspension
Bridge, Bristol

47 Sydney Buildings, Bath BA2 6DB   **Nearest Road A4, A36**

Sydney Buildings 47 is conveniently situated 5 minutes walk along the canal tow-path from the city centre. This beautiful decorated Georgian family home offers the following accommodation, all rooms with TV, tea/coffee facilities, as well as a magnificent city views. The elegant spa city home to Jane Austen is famed for its shopping, restaurant and sites, Roman Bath, the Royal Crescent and the Abbey. Also the city is surrounded by many places to visit Longleat House and Safari Park, American Museum, Cheltenham Spa and the Cotswolds. Mrs Johnson will be only to happy to give her guests any help.

Mrs Johnson
Tel/Fax: 01225 463033

B&B from £24.50-£27.50pp, Rooms 1 single, 1 twin, 1 double en-suite, No smoking or pets, Children welcome, Open all year except Christmas & New Year, Map Ref A

9 Bathwick Hill, Bath BA2 6EW   **On Bathwick Hill**

Listed Georgian family home in much desirable part of Bath. Two twin bedrooms with baths. Full breakfast. Tea/coffee making facilities in bedrooms. Use of drawing room with TV, conservatory and large walled garden. Fine views over Bath. Short walk to the city centre. Frequent bus services. Free car parking outside property. No license for alcohol. This is a private home with peaceful friendly atmosphere. Directions: half a mile up Bathwick Hill pass Cleveland walk on left almost immediately No.9 is on the right.

Mrs Elspeth Bowman
Tel: 01225 460812

B&B from £24pp, Rooms 2 twin with private bathrooms, No smoking, Children over 12, No pets, Open all year except Christmas, Map Ref A

Badminton Villa, 10 Upper Oldfield Park, Bath BA2 3JZ   **Nearest Road A367**

A large Victorian family house located in a tree lined residential road on the southern slopes of Bath, with magnificent city views, yet only a 10 minute walk to the city centre. Sue and John Burton have established a quality bed and breakfast guest house with an international reputation. All rooms have first class en-suite facilities and are equipped with colour TV, hair dryer and tea/coffee making facilities. Lounge and gardens overlook city. A no smoking house. Car park. ETB Highly Commended, RAC Highly Acclaimed.

Sue & John Burton
Tel: 01225 426347
Fax: 01225 420393

B&B from £28pp, Rooms 1 twin, 3 double, all en-suite, No smoking, Children over 8, No pets, Open all year except Christmas & New Year, Map Ref A

Oldfields House Hotel, 102 Wells Road, Bath BA2 3AL   **Nearest Road A367 (Exeter Road)**

Oldfields is an elegant Victorian house built of the honey coloured stone for which Bath is famous. Superbly positioned just 10 minutes walk from the city centre with gardens and panoramic views it has a private car park for guests use. Rooms are beautifully furnished with antiques, Laura Ashley and Liberty fabrics and warm decor. The rooms are en-suite with direct dial telephone, CTV, hair dryers and hospitality tray. Choose between a traditional English a la carte breakfast or a lighter continental from the extensive buffet. Oldfields is the perfect base from which to tour the area.

Berkeley & Moira Gaunt
Tel: 01225 317984
Fax: 01225 444471

B&B from £27.50pp, Rooms 8 double, 6 twin, all rooms have private shower/wc, Open all year except Christmas & January, Map Ref A

see PHOTO opposite

*left, **Oldfields House Hotel,** Bath - see above for details*

Wentworth House, 106 Bloomfield Road, Bath BA2 2 AP Nearest Road A367

A highly recommended up-market bed and breakfast hotel built in 1887, standing in secluded gardens with stunning views of the valley. Situated in quiet area with free car park. Abbey and Roman baths are within walking distance. High standard of comfort. Small lounge/bar and outdoor pool. Horse riding and golf nearby. The tastefully decorated en-suite bedrooms - most with antique beds, offer colour TV, direct dial telephone, hair dryers and tea/coffee making facilities. Breakfast is a choice of full English and you can help yourself to the buffet bar. EMail: wentworthhouse@dial.pipex.com

see PHOTO opposite

Mr & Mrs Kitching
Tel: 01225 339193
Fax: 01225 310460

B&B from £25-£45pp, Rooms 5 twin, 12 double, 1 family, all en-suite, Restricted smoking, Children over 5, Pets by arrangement, Open all year except Christmas & New Year, Map Ref A

Leighton House, 139 Wells Road, Bath BA2 3AL Nearest Road A367

Marilyn and Colin Humphrey extend a friendly welcome to you at their delightful elegant Victorian home set in beautiful gardens, offering views over the city. With ample private parking, they are only 10 minutes walk from the city centre. The rooms offer every comfort. All have king, queen or twin beds and are tastefully decorated and furnished with en-suite facilities (bath, shower, wc and washbasin), direct dial telephone, hair dryer, TV, radio and beverage making facilities. Superb breakfasts served to suit all tastes. Special breaks available. EMail: leighton-house@which.net

see PHOTO on page 22

Marilyn & Colin Humphrey
Tel: 01225 314769
Fax: 01225 443079

B&B from £31pp, Rooms 4 double, 3 twin, 1 family, all rooms have full en-suite facilities, No smoking, Open all year, Map Ref A

Highways House, 143 Wells Road, Bath BA2 3AL Nearest Road A367

A warm and friendly welcome awaits you from the resident proprietors David and Davina James at this delightful and well appointed Victorian house. Guests who stay at Highways House will find a very relaxed and homely atmosphere. All bedrooms have private bath/shower rooms, TV and tea/coffee making facilities. A twin bedded is on the ground floor. The large and very comfortable lounge and breakfast room are also on the ground floor. A full English breakfast. Only 10 minutes walk into Bath city centre. Car park. AA QQQQ Selected, RAC Highly Acclaimed.

see PHOTO on page 23

David & Davina James
Tel: 01225 421238
Fax: 01225 481169

B&B from £28pp, Rooms 1 single with private bathroom, 3 twin, 3 double, all en-suite, No smoking, Children over 5, No pets, Open all year except Christmas, Map Ref A

Bloomfield House, 146 Bloomfield Road, Bath BA2 2AS Nearest Road A367

A ten minute walk from the city, Bloomfield House has been sympathetically restored retaining most of the original features of the period, but providing every modern luxury. You will find the rooms hung with velvet or hand woven silk curtains, half tester or 4-poster beds and graced with antique furniture. The bedrooms are en-suite. The bathrooms are mahogany panelled with polished brass fittings. Breakfast is served with style and friendliness against an open fire and candlelit background.

Bridget & Malcolm Cox
Tel: 01225 420105
Fax: 01225 481958

B&B from £35pp, Rooms 1 single, 1 twin, 6 double, all en-suite, No smoking or pets, Children over 12, Open all year, Map Ref A

*left, **Wentworth House**, Bath - see details above*

Leighton House, Bath
- please details on page 21

right, **Highways House,** *Bath - please see page 21 for details*

Cranleigh, 159 Newbridge Hill, Bath BA1 3PX Nearest Road A431

Away from traffic and noise but just minutes from the heart of Bath. Cranleigh has lovely views, private parking and secluded sunny gardens. Guest bedrooms are all en-suite and exceptionally spacious. Imaginative breakfasts include fresh fruit salad and scrambled eggs with smoked salmon. The Webbers are a mine of information, always happy to help with routes, maps and suggestions. Ground floor bedrooms available. A no smoking house. 'Short Break' reductions off season. AA QQQQ. Recommended by the 'Which' Good Bed & Breakfast Guide. EMail: Cranleigh@btinternet.com

see PHOTO opposite

Christine & Arthur Webber
Tel: 01225 310197
Fax: 01225 423143

B&B from £30pp. Rooms 2 twin, 2 double, 1 family, all en-suite, No smoking, Children from 5 years, No pets, Open all year, Map Ref A

Oakleigh House, 19 Upper Oldfield Park, Bath BA2 3JX 10 minutes walk to city centre

Oakleigh House is situated in a peaceful location 10 minutes from the centre of Bath. Victorian elegance is combined with present day comforts and all bedrooms are en-suite and benefit from tea/coffee making facilities, colour TV, clock radio, hair dryer and tasteful furnishings. There is a car park for guests. A good base for touring Glastonbury, Stonehenge, Bristol, Wells, Salisbury and the Cotswolds.

David & Jenny King
Tel: 01225 315698
Fax: 01225 448223

B&B from £29pp, Rooms 3 double, 1 twin, all en-suite, Open all year, Map Ref A

Holly Lodge, 8 Upper Oldfield Park, Bath BA2 3JZ Nearest Road A367

This charming Victorian town house commands panoramic views of the city and is delightfully furnished with individually designed bedrooms, some with 4 posters and superb bathrooms. Elegant and stylish, it is owned and operated with meticulous attention to details by George Hall. Superb breakfasts are enjoyed in the appealing breakfast room with the yellow and green decor and white wicker chairs. Furnished with antiques, this immaculate establishment, winner of an 'England for Excellence' award makes a pleasant base for touring Bath and the Cotswolds.

George Hall
Tel: 01225 424042
Fax: 01225 481138

B&B from £37.50pp, Rooms 1 single, 2 twin, 4 double, all en-suite, No smoking, Children welcome, No pets, Open all year, Map Ref A

Paradise House, 88 Holloway, Bath BA2 4PX Nearest Road A367

Paradise House is a Georgian (1735) Grade II listed building situated in a quiet cul-de-sac only 5 minutes walk from Bath city centre. Its half acre gardens at the rear command magnificent panoramic views over the entire city and surrounding hills. The comfortable bedrooms, all of which are en-suite, and equipped with tea/coffee making facilities and TV. A full English breakfast is served. Full details of all Bath's famous restaurants are available, including menus, maps and booking advice. The perfect touring base for Bath and the Cotswolds. EMail: paradise@apsleyhouse.easynet.co.uk http://www.s-h-systems.co.uk/hotels/paradise.html

see PHOTO on page 26

David & Annie Lanz
Tel: 01225 317723
Fax: 01225 482005

B&B from £32.50pp, Rooms 3 twin, 4 double, 1 family, all en-suite, Children welcome, No pets, Open all year except Christmas, Map Ref A

---

left, **Cranleigh,** *Bath - see details above*

Cheriton House, Bath - see details on page 29

left, **Paradise House,** *Bath - see details on page 25*

Haydon House, 9 Bloomfield Park, Bath BA2 2BY   **Nearest Road A367**

A true oasis of tranquillity, this secluded, elegantly furnished Edwardian town house is situated in a quiet residential area with easy parking, not far from the city centre. Every conceivable comfort is offered in the 5 tastefully decorated en-suite bedrooms including TV and a generous hospitality tray. Guests can enjoy a welcoming cup of tea in the beautifully appointed antique filled sitting room, with sunshine filtering through the vine clad pergola, and innovative breakfasts are stylishly served to a background of gentle classical music. ETB Deluxe Grading.

Gordon & Magdalene
Ashman-Marr
Tel: 01225 444919/427351

B&B from £32.50pp, Rooms 1 twin, 3 double, 1 family, all en-suite, No smoking, No pets, Children welcome by arrangement, Open all year, Map Ref A

Cheriton House, 9 Upper Oldfield Park, Bath BA2 3JX   **10 minutes walk to city centre**

Dating from the 1880's Cheriton House is located on Bath's southern slopes. Situated in a quiet street with splendid views, yet within easy walking distance of the city. The house has been carefully restored and redecorated and all rooms are attractively furnished. In the dining room a choice of breakfast is offered and in the sitting room there is a plentiful supply of books and brochures to help plan you day. Iris & John will be pleased to advise guests where to eat, visit and what to see. EMail: cheriton@.which.net

Iris & John
Tel: 01225 429862
Fax: 01225 428403

B&B from £30pp, Rooms 6 double, 3 twin, all en-suite, family room available on request, Open all year including Christmas, Map Ref A

see PHOTO on page 27

Apsley House Hotel, Newbridge Hill, Bath BA1 3PT   **Nearest Road A431**

David and Anne Lanz warmly welcome guests into their elegant Georgian house. Beautifully proportioned reception rooms overlook the pretty gardens. Sumptuous decor, antiques and oil paintings create a gracious but relaxed atmosphere. Bedrooms are en-suite, individually furnished and decorated and offer TV, direct dial telephones, hot drinks and hair dryers. Breakfast is a delight with full English and house specialities. Licensed bar. Local information available. Just over 1 mile west of centre. Car park. AA 5Q, ETB Highly Commended. EMail: apsleyhouse@easynet.co.uk http://www.gratton.co.uk/apsley

David & Annie Lanz
Tel: 01225 336966
Fax: 01225 425462

B&B from £32.50pp, Rooms 3 twin, 5 double, 2 garden rooms, 1 family, all en-suite, Restricted smoking, Children over 5, No pets, Open all year except Christmas, Map Ref A

see PHOTO opposite

Brompton House, St John's Road, Bath BA2 6PT   **Nearest Road A46**

Built as a rectory 1777 Brompton House is a charming country style Georgian residence set in beautiful secluded gardens with its own car park. Excellent location only 6-7 minutes level walk from Bath's main attractions. The comfortable en-suite bedrooms are all fully equipped and tastefully furnished. The attractive residents sitting room is furnished with antiques and delicious choice of full English, Continental or Wholefood Breakfasts are served in the elegant dining room. A strictly no smoking house. EMail: bromptonhouse@btinternet.com

David, Sue, Belinda & Tim Selby
Tel: 01225 420972
Fax: 01225 420505

B&B from £30pp, Rooms 2 single, 7 twin, 7 double, 2 family, No smoking, Minimum age 10, No pets, Open all year except Christmas & New Year, Map Ref A

see PHOTO on page 30

left, Apsley House Hotel, Bath - see details above

The Bath Tasburgh Hotel, Warminster Road, Bath BA2 6SH   Nearest Road M4, A36

see PHOTO on page 31

Built in 1890, this lovely Victorian mansion provides ideal country comfort in a city setting. The hotel sits in seven acres of beautiful gardens overlooking the Avon Valley, with the adjacent canal towpath providing idyllic walks into Bath. The 12 en-suite bedrooms (including 4-poster and family rooms) are tastefully furnished, offering all the amenities and comfort of its 2 star rating and more. Elegant drawing room, dining room and stunning conservatory/terrace. Parking, licensed, evening meals, Every effort is made to ensure a memorable stay. ETB Highly Commended. AA 2 Star. RAC 2 Star.

David & Susan Keeling
Tel: 01225 425096
Fax: 01225 463842

B&B from £32.50-£42.50pp, Dinner from £18.50-£20, Rooms 1 single, 1 twin, 4 four-poster, 3 family, 3 double, all en-suite, No smoking or pets, Well behaved children welcome, Open all year, Map Ref A

Gainsborough Hotel, Weston Lane, Bath BA1 4AB   Nearest Road A4

see PHOTO opposite

A large country house hotel in own attractive grounds near botanical gardens, municipal golf course and centre. Both spacious and very comfortable we provide a relaxing and informal atmosphere for our guests stay. The Abbey, Roman baths and pump rooms are all within walking distance via the park. All 17 bedrooms are en-suite with colour and satellite TV, tea/coffee making facilities, direct dial telephones and hair dryers. The hotel has a friendly bar, 2 sun terraces, large private car park and warm welcome.

Anna Ford
Tel: 01225 311380
Fax: 01225 447411

B&B from £28pp, Rooms 2 single, 12 twin/double, 3 family, all en-suite, Open all year, Map Ref A

Pickford House, Bath Road, Beckington, Bath BA3 6SJ   Nearest Road A36

Pickford House is an elegant Regency style house built in honey coloured Bath stone, It stands on top of the hill overlooking the village of Beckington and surrounding countryside. Some bedrooms are en-suite and all have tea/coffee making facilities and TV; all are very comfortable and tastefully decorated. Angela is a talented and enthusiastic cook and offers an excellent 'pot luck' meal, or on request an extensive menu for celebrations. The house is licensed with a large and varied wine list. In summer, visitors may be offered an 'off-the-beaten-track' pre dinner drive.

Ken & Angela Pritchard
Tel: 01373 8303292
Fax: 01373 830329

B&B from £15pp, Dinner from £12, Rooms 1 twin, 1 double, family, some en-suite, Restricted smoking, Children welcome, Pets by prior arrangement, Open all year, Map Ref A

Green Lane House, Hinton Charterhouse, Bath BA3 6BL   Nearest Road A36, B3110

see PHOTO on page 34

Five miles south of Bath in undulating countryside on the borders of Somerset and Wiltshire lies the charming conservation village of Hinton Charterhouse. Green Lane House, originally 3 terraced 18th century stone cottages, has been tastefully renovated and attractively furnished. Traditional features such as exposed beams and open log fireplaces combine with modern comforts introduced throughout the 4 distinctively decorated guest bedrooms, homely resident's lounge and breakfast room. Conveniently located within the village are 2 inns with restaurants.

Christopher & Juliet Davies
Tel: 01225 723631
Fax: 01225 723773

B&B from £20pp, Rooms 2 double, 1 en-suite, 2 twin, 1 en-suite, No smoking, Children over 8, Open all year, Map Ref D

Gainsborough Hotel, *Bath*
- see opposite for details

Grove Lodge, 11 Lambridge, London Road, Bath BA1 6BJ   Nearest Road A4, A46

Grove Lodge is an elegant Georgian house built in 1788 and set in lovely gardens with views onto the wooded hills surrounding the city. Roy and Rosalie Burridge welcome you to their comfortable home which offers 6 excellent large rooms. Each has colour TV and tea/coffee making facilities are available. Continental or 4 course English breakfasts are offered and summer afternoon tea under the apple tree is not to be missed. Bath is an excellent centre for many beautiful and historic locations including the Cotswolds, Stonehenge, Wells and Glastonbury.

Roy & Rosalie Burridge
Tel: 01225 310860
Fax: 01225 429630

B&B from £23pp, Rooms 1 single, 1 twin, 3 double, 1 family, No smoking, Open all year, Map Ref A

Villa Magdala Hotel, Henrietta Road, Bath BA2 6LX   5 mins walk to city centre

A delightful Victorian town house hotel set in its own grounds, the Villa Magdala enjoys a peaceful location overlooking Henrietta Park only a few minutes level walk from the Roman baths and Abbey. All 17 spacious rooms have private bathroom en-suite, telephone, television and tea/coffee making facilities. The hotel has its own private car park and is an ideal base for exploring Bath and the surrounding countryside. EMail: villa@btinternet.com http://www.btinternet.com/~villa

Mrs Alison Williams
Tel: 01225 466329
Fax: 01225 483207

B&B from £35pp, Rooms 5 twin, 12 double, all rooms are en-suite. 4 poster, triples and family rooms available. Open all year, Map Ref A

Eagle House, Church Street, Bathford BA1 7RS   Nearest Road A4, A363

Eagle House is a fine Georgian mansion in 1.5 acres of garden in the lovely, peaceful village of Bathford, 3 miles from Heritage city of Bath. The house is elegant with a large drawing room with an open fire which is lit on chilly evenings. All bedrooms are en-suite and have TV and tea/coffee making facilities; they are spacious and some can accommodate parents with up to 3 children. (Children accompanying parents come free). A very warm welcome from resident owners, John & Rosamund Napier, and the atmosphere here is relaxed and informal. EMail: JONAP@PSIONWORLD.NET

see PHOTO on page 36

John & Rosamund Napier
Tel: 01225 859946
Fax: 01225 859430

B&B from £24pp, Rooms 1 single, 2 twin, 4 double, 1 family, all en-suite, Children welcome, Pets welcome, Open early January - late December, Map Ref C

Bath Lodge Hotel, Norton St Philip, Bath BA3 6NH   Nearest Road A36

Bath Lodge was built in 1806 as the Gate Lodge to Farleigh Castle and Manor. Our AA QQQQQ rating assures you high quality accommodation and service. Many of the rooms retain the castellated features of the building and a huge open fire ensures a warmer welcome in the winter months. Situated seven miles south of Bath and set in five acres of garden and woodland with ample parking. We are an excellent base for visiting such local attractions as Longleat, Stourhead Wells, Glastonbury, Stonehenge and Avebury. EMail: walker@bathlodge.demon.co.uk

Graham & Nicola Walker
Tel: 01225 723040
Fax: 01225 723737

B&B from £27.50pp, Dinner available Friday-Saturday from £23.50, Rooms 1 single, 1 twin, 5 double, 1 family, all en-suite, Restricted smoking, Children over 10, Open all year, Map Ref L

*left, **Green Lane House**, Hinton Charterhouse - see details on page 32*

Irondale House, 67 High Street, Rode, Bath BA3 6PB   Nearest Road A36

A very warm welcome in our 18th century family house, set in lovely walled garden with wonderful views. Open fires, pretty bedrooms with hair dryers and colour TV. Ideal for sightseeing Bath, Wells, Longleat and many other places of interest. An excellent full English breakfast to set you on your way. Jayne and Oliver have a lot of local knowledge and are willing to help you plan your route. AA QQQQQ Premier Selected.

Jayne & Oliver Holder
Tel/Fax: 01373 830730

B&B from £27pp, Rooms 1 twin, 2 double, 1 family, most en-suite, Restricted smoking, Children, No pets, Open all year except Christmas & New Year, Map Ref B

Church House, Wellow, Bath BA2 8QS   Nearest Road A367, A36

Wellow is an ideal base from which to visit Bath and its surroundings, and provides a welcoming retreat at the end of a hard day's sightseeing. The village is just four miles from Bath, in beautiful countryside. Church House, a Georgian wool-merchant's house, offers a twin or double room with private bathroom, and your own sitting room with television. Delicious food is available within walking distance at our local pub. Coffee/tea making facilities provided if required.

Mrs Claire Veysey
Tel: 01225 834853
Fax: 01225 445208

B&B from £22pp, Rooms 1 twin, 1 double, with private bathroom, No smoking, Children welcome, Pets by arrangement, Open all year except Christmas & New Year, Map Ref K

The Manor House, Wellow, Bath BA2 8QQ   Nearest Road A367

The 17th century stone manor house is set in the heart of an attractive farming village six miles from the Georgian city of Bath. Welcome to a comfortable family home with large bedroom which have televisions and tea/coffee trays. The traditional breakfast includes home baked bread. Cream teas are served in the courtyard and garden at weekends in the summer. The village pub serves meals. Wellow is within easy reach of Wells, Glastonbury and Cheddar and stately homes of Longleat, Stourhead and Dyrham.

Sarah Danny
Tel/Fax: 01225 832027

B&B from £20pp, Rooms 1 single, 1 twin, 1 double, most en-suite, No smoking, Children welcome, No pets, Open all year except Christmas & New Year, Map Ref K

Overbrook, Stowey Bottom, Bishop Sutton, Bristol BS39 5TN   Nearest Road A368

Overbrook is a charming house, tastefully furnished with a lovely garden by a brook. Situated in a quiet and peaceful lane with a little ford by the gate. It offers one twin bedded en-suite room and one double room with private shower and wc. Each has TV, clock radio, iron etc. A comfortable sunny sitting room with French windows leading in to the garden for guests use. Bath, Wells, Bristol and Cheddar Gorge within easy reach and superb trout fishing on Chew Valley Lake only 5 minutes away.

Mrs Ruth Shellard
Tel: 01275 332648
Fax: 01179 352052

B&B from £18pp, Rooms 1 single, 1 twin en-suite, 1 double private shower & wc, No smoking, Children welcome, No pets, Open all year except Christmas & New Year, Map Ref E

left, Eagle House, Bathford - see details on page 35

Box Hedge Farm, Coalpit Heath, Bristol BS36 2UW   **Nearest Road Westerleigh Road**

Box Hedge Farm is set in 200 acres of beautiful rural countryside. Local to M4/M5, central for Bristol and Bath. An ideal stopping point for the south west and Wales. We offer a warm family atmosphere with traditional farmhouse cooking. The large spacious bedrooms, one with a four poster, have colour TV and tea/coffee making facilities.

Mrs Marilyn Collins
Tel: 01454 250786

B&B from £17.50 single, £30 double, Dinner from £7.50, Rooms 1 single, 2 double, 1 family, Restricted smoking, Open all year, Map Ref F

Home Farm, Farrington Gurney, Bristol BS39 6UB   **Nearest Road A37, A39, A362**

Our beautifully refurbished 17th century farmhouse and 230 acre working mixed farm is set on the Northern edge of the Mendips. We offer a friendly welcome and delicious breakfast. There is a four poster bedroom and all rooms are en-suite with full facilities. We have a guest lounge with woodburner and a lovely garden. You can watch the cows being milked from a viewing gallery. We are ideally situated for Bath, Wells, Cheddar, Clarks Village, Longleat, Wookey, Stourhead. There is a golf course adjacent.

see PHOTO opposite

Tish & Andy Jeffery
Tel: 01761 452287
Fax: 01761 452287

B&B from £20pp, Rooms 1 double, 1 family, both en-suite, No smoking or pets, Children welcome, Open February - November, Map Ref G

The Old Bakery, The Street, Olveston, Bristol BS35 4DR   **Nearest Road A38, M4, M5**

The Old Bakery is a delightful cottage situated in the centre of Olveston village 12 miles north of Bristol. This lovely 200 year old cottage provides comfortable accommodation in two twin bedded rooms and two single rooms all with TV and tea/coffee making facilities. A lounge over looking a very pretty walled garden is also available for guests, where breakfast is served. Parking is available. Easy access to Bath, Cheltenham, Cotswolds and Cardiff.

Christine Healey
Tel: 01454 616437

B&B from £23pp, Rooms 2 single, 2 twin, Restricted smoking, Children & well behaved pets welcome, Open all year, Map Ref H

Downs Edge, Saville Road, Stoke Bishop, Bristol BS9 1JD   **Nearest Road A4018**

Downs Edge is set in magnificent gardens on the very edge of Bristol's famous Downs, an open park of some 450 acres, and close to the spectacular Avon Gorge and it's breathtaking views. All rooms have televisions and hospitality trays with homemade biscuits. A residents lounge is available and there is generous car parking in the grounds. This uniquely peaceful location is convenient for the city centre, Clifton, the Universities, the many historic locations and places of interest in the city and the Cotswolds.

Mrs Philippa Tasker
Tel/Fax: 0117 9683264

B&B from £26pp, Rooms 2 single, 1 twin, 1 double, most en-suite, No smoking, Children welcome, No pets, Open all year except Christmas & New Year, Map Ref I

left, **Home Farm,** *Farrington Gurney - see details above*

Spring Farm, Regil, nr Winford, Bristol BS40 8BB   Nearest Road A38

Set in a pretty country garden. Spring Farm is a cosy Georgian farmhouse with views across the country side to the Mendips. Guests have a private sitting/breakfast room with an open fire in winter, and two double bedrooms with private and en-suite bathrooms. Regil is a quiet farming village in the foothills of the Mendips with villages and fishing, lakes close by. The beautiful cities of Bath and Wells are within easy reach by car.

Roger & Judy Gallannaugh   **B&B from £20pp, Rooms 2 en-suite double, No smoking, Children &**
Tel: 01275 472735   **pets welcome, Open all year except Christmas & New Year, Map Ref J**

"I think our room's at the back"
BELLE & BERTIE IN YORK

40

Our England is a garden, and such gardens are not made
By singing: 'Oh, how beautiful!' and sitting in the shade.

THE GLORY OF THE GARDEN
RUDYARD KIPLING 1865-1936

41

BEDFORDSHIRE, BERKSHIRE, BUCKINGHAMSHIRE & HERTFORDSHIRE

To see everything these lovely counties have to offer is an impossible task, to savour a taste is all the holiday maker can hope for - little wonder then that they return again and again. These are the Home Counties where seemingly every village has its own fascinating history. Being at the very heart of England and presumably considered safe from attack from 'outsiders' there are consequently few medieval castles, but examples of superb domestic architecture abound. This area has been populated since the very morning of time. The Ridgeway, that black and lonely path across the Berkshire Downs was a vital trade route during the Bronze Age. The Icknield Way, a prehistoric track, follows the high ground southwest from the Wash through East Anglia and the Chilterns to the Berkshire Downs, while the Roman Road Watling Street, running northwest from London, derives its name from the Anglo-Saxon word for St. Albans, which was the first place of importance on the journey from London.

The four counties are simply stippled with centres of interest - the list seems endless. Bedford, a town already well established in Anglo-Saxon times, is renowned for its association with John Bunyan, the author of Pilgrim's Progress who was imprisoned in Bedford gaol for his Nonconformist beliefs. Buckingham was established by Alfred the Great as a county town as far back as 888AD

and remained such until the town was destroyed by fire in 1725 and the county government transferred to Aylesbury - renowned for its fine old inns, its links with the Parliamentary cause during the Civil War...and ducks. A statue of John Hampden, the Buckinghamshire MP who opposed Charles I, stands in the Market Square. Aylesbury of course, gave its name to the Vale which is one of England's richest dairy-farming regions. To the east is St. Albans, Two thousand years ago the largest Roman town in Britain known as Verulamium. It was here that the Roman soldier Alban was executed for sheltering a Christian priest and was later canonised to become Britain's first Christian martyr. In the eighth century the Saxons built an abbey on the site of St. Alban's shrine only to have it replaced by the Norman abbey in 1077. Only the abbey church remained following the Dissolution and is now the Cathedral Church of St. Alban, in length five hundred and fifty feet and one of the longest cathedrals in Britain. There is a wealth of interest in St. Albans...the area in front of the abbey's great gate was a medieval meeting place and the focus of rioting during the Peasants' Revolt of 1381, and the place in 1556 where a Protestant baker was burned at the stake as a heretic. In more pleasant vein, the Royal National Rose Society at Chiswell Green nearby, boasts over thirty thousand bushes...which are a glorious sight in July.

To the south is Windsor, dominated by its castle, the largest in Europe and of course one of the residences of the Royal Family. The castle is hugely popular, attracting large crowds during the holiday season, but in addition to the castle there is the Great Park. This is all that is now left of the royal hunting forest that once stretched across southern Berkshire, but still comprises an impressive four thousand, eight hundred acres, and includes the three mile long Long Walk, a tree-lined avenue leading from the castle to the large artificial lake, Virginia Water. There is also a fascinating Royal and Empire Exhibition in Windsor railway station which is well worth a visit, and over the river is Eton with its college. The college chapel, a fine example of fifteenth century perpendicular architecture, resembles King's College Chapel at Cambridge - and if the holiday visitor can possibly find the time, there are wonderful boat trips down the Thames. Just six miles southwest of Windsor is the village of Ascot where in 1711 Queen Anne established the Royal Ascot race meeting as a social as well as a sporting event. Newbury is an interesting old town and can boast the first factory to operate in England, when in the fifteenth century over a thousand wool weavers were employed by John Winchcombe - known as Jack of Newbury.

clustered round the village green. At one end of the main street of half-timbered cottages, is Milton's Cottage. It was here that the blind poet took refuge in 1665 to avoid the Great Plague raging in London, and it was here that he finished Paradise Lost and started Paradise Regained. First editions of his great works are on display here. In the Chess Valley is the intriguing nineteenth century village of Chenies, built for the estate workers of the medieval manor of the Dukes of Bedford.

If the towns and villages of this lovely area don't occupy the whole of the holiday maker's time there is interest enough in the glorious countryside, and who can resist the appeal of the great houses...Woburn Abbey, the home of the Dukes of Bedford, Hatfield House, seized from the Bishops of Ely by Henry VIII at the Dissolution...and then there is Chequers, the country home of British Prime Ministers, an Elizabethan mansion in the Chilterns near Princes Risborough, given to the nation by Lord Lee of Fareham.

There can really be no recommended centre for exploring this area, select where you will, and you will be surrounded with interest and spectacle that will fill your holiday with delight.

Could there I wonder be a more charming place than Chalfont St. Giles with its picturesque cottages and church

BEDFORDSHIRE, BERKSHIRE, BUCKINGHAMSHIRE & HERTFORDSHIRE

Places to Visit

Woburn Abbey, *Bedfordshire* ~ the abbey was built in the middle of the 18th century on the foundations of a large 12th century monastery. It now has a three hundred and fifty acre safari park and deer park.

Whipsnade Wild Animal Park, *Bedfordshire* ~ this was one of the first zoos to reduce the use of cages. It is Europe's largest conservation park with over six hundred acres containing more than three thousand species. It also has an adventure playground and sea lion display.

Luton Hoo, *Bedfordshire* ~ it was originally built in 1767, but in 1903 Sir Julius Wernher had it rebuilt in a French classical style, by the same architects as the Ritz Hotel. It is still the home of the Wernher family and includes paintings by Hoppner, Titian and Sargent.

Dunstable Priory

Windsor Castle, *Berkshire* ~ the oldest continuously inhabited royal residence in Britain, the castle was orginally built from wood by William the Conqueror in 1070. In 1170, Henry II rebuilt it in stone and in the years to follow various additions have been made.

Stowe, *Buckinghamshire* ~ the gardens were originally laid out in 1680 and in the following hundred years they were enlarged and transformed with monuments, Greek and Gothic temples, statues, bridges, lakes and trees. Many designers and architects including Sir John Vanburgh, James Gibbs and Capability Brown have contributed to the gardens.

Hughenden Manor, *Buckinghamshire* ~ Bejamin Disraeli, Prime Minister from 1874 - 1880, lived here for 33 years until his death. The Georgian villa is still furnished as it was in his day.

Knebworth House, *Hertfordshire* ~ a Tudor mansion and Jacobean banqueting hall, with a 19th century Gothic exterior by Lord Lytton, the statesman and novelist.

Hatfield House, *Hertfordshire* ~ built between 1607 and 1611 for statesman Robert Cecil, it is still owned by his descendants. The palace was partly demolished in 1607 so that the new house could be built. Queen Elizabeth I spent much of her childhood here and she held her first Council of State here when she was crowned in 1558.

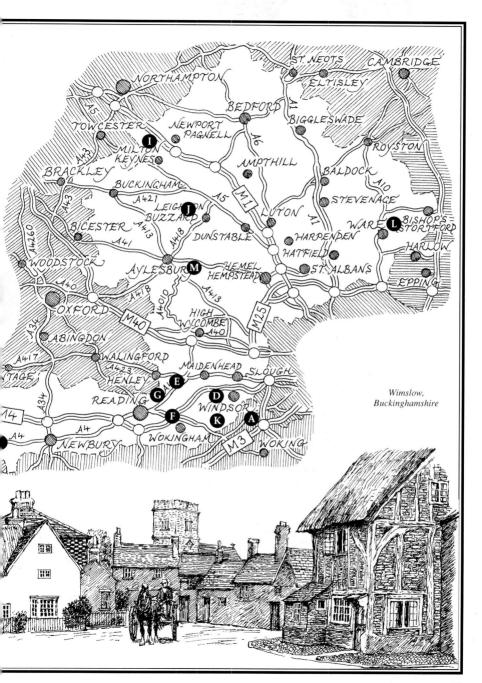

ST. NEOTS
CAMBRIDGE
NORTHAMPTON
ELTISLEY
BEDFORD
BIGGLESWADE
TOWCESTER
NEWPORT PAGNELL
ROYSTON
I
MILTON KEYNES
AMPTHILL
BALDOCK
BRACKLEY
BUCKINGHAM
A421
LEIGHTON BUZZARD
J
STEVENAGE
LUTON
BICESTER
A413
A418
DUNSTABLE
WARE
L
BISHOP'S STORTFORD
HARPENDEN
WOODSTOCK
A41
HATFIELD
HARLOW
AYLESBURY
M
HEMEL HEMPSTEAD
ST. ALBANS
EPPING
OXFORD
M40
HIGH WYCOMBE
A40
M25
ABINGDON
WALINGFORD
A417
A423
MAIDENHEAD
SLOUGH
HENLEY
E
READING
G
D
WINDSOR
F
K
A
NEWBURY
WOKINGHAM
M3
WOKING

*Wimslow,
Buckinghamshire*

Ascot Corner, Wells Lane, Ascot, Berkshire SL5 7DY   **Nearest Road A329 (London Road)**

Ascot Corner provides deluxe accommodation minutes from the famous race-course. All rooms are en-suite with TV, hair dryer, clock radio, mini fridge stocked with complimentary beer, wine, soft drinks and tea/coffee making facilities. Delicious extensive continental breakfast includes homemade muesli, fresh baking, cheese and cold meats. There are great local pubs and restaurants and London is 50 minutes train journey from Ascot main-line station. Heathrow is 30 minutes drive and the M25, M4, M3, are just ten minutes away.

Susan Powell
Tel: 01344 627722
Fax: 01344 873965

B&B from £35pp, Dinner from £25 incl: wine, Rooms 1 twin, 2 double, all en-suite/private facilities, No smoking or pets, Children over 12, Open April - February, Map Ref K

Ennis Lodge Guest House, Winkfield Road, Ascot, Berkshire SL5 7EX   **Nearest Road A330, A329**

Ennis Lodge is situated in the centre of Ascot within easy reach of mainline station, Waterloo 45 mins; M3, M4/M25 close by; Heathrow Airport 25 mins; Windsor Castle 10 mins; Ascot Racecourse 2 mins. Just a short drive to all major international golf courses. Ennis Lodge offers first class accommodation for the tourist and businessman alike. All rooms have en-suite/private facilities and colour TV, trouser press, hair dryer, radio alarm, tea/coffee facilities and more. Price includes full English breakfast. Off street parking is available. 10 minutes from Legoland theme park. German spoken.

John & Siegi Miles
Tel: 01344 621009
Fax: 01344 621009

B&B/Rooms 1 single from £38.50pn, 4 twin from £48.50pn, 2 family from £55-£65, all with private or en-suite facilities, Restricted smoking, Children welcome, No pets, Open all year, Map Ref A

Marshgate Cottage Hotel, Marsh Lane, Hungerford, Berkshire RG17 0QX   **Nearest Road M4, A338**

Marshgate Cottage is tucked away at the end of a quiet country lane just half a mile from Hungerford and four miles from the M4. Guest rooms are in a traditionally designed addition to the original canalside 17th century thatched cottage. All rooms have en-suite shower and toilet, TV, phone and tea/coffee making facilities. Guests lounge and bar. Car park. The town has an abundance of antique and speciality shops, canal trips, pubs and restaurants. Ideal base for touring southern England. Superb walking area.

see PHOTO opposite

Mike Walker
Tel: 01488 682307
Fax: 01488 685475

B&B from £24.25pp, Rooms 1 single, 2 twin, 3 double, 2 family, all en-suite, Restricted smoking, Children & pets welcome, Open all year, Map Ref B

Lodge Down, Lambourn, Hungerford, Berkshire RG17 7BJ   **Nearest Road M4 Jct14**

Lodge Down is a country house within luxury accommodation with en-suite bathroom, set in lovely grounds. Excellent and varied dinning in surrounding villages. Easy access to M4 at junctions 14 and 15. One or less for Heathrow, Row 60 miles, Bath 43 miles, Oxford 26 miles. Our location provides a central base for excursions to the Cotswolds and Stonehenge etc. We have achieved the English Tourist Board and AA 4Q Selected grade.

Sally Cook
Tel: 01672 540304
Fax: 01672 540304

B&B from £22.50pp, 1 twin, 1 double, 1 family, all en-suite, Restricted smoking, Children over 10, No pets, Open all year, Map Ref C

*left, **Marshgate Cottage Hotel,** Hungerford - see details above*

Fishers Farm, Shefford Woodlands, Hungerford, Berkshire RG17 7AB Nearest Road M4, J14

Charming period farmhouse with all modern comforts on a working sheep and arable farm. Surrounded by a large garden and farmland in a peaceful and secluded location yet only 1 mile from junction 14 of M4. An ideal base for exploring the beautiful downland countryside and villages; also within easy reach of Bath, Oxford, Salisbury, Stonehenge, Windsor and Winchester. Heathrow is less than 1 hour away and Gatwick about 1.5 hours. Heated indoor pool available all year.Excellent cooking using home grown produce. EMail: fishersf@globalnet.co.uk

Henry & Mary Wilson
Tel: 01488 648466
Fax: 01488 648706

B&B from £25pp, Dinner from £18, Rooms 1 twin en-suite, 1 double en-suite, 1 family private bathroom, Restricted smoking, Children welcome, Pets by arrangement, Open all year, Map Ref B

Burchett's Place Country House, Burchett's Green, Maidenhead, Berkshire SL6 6QZ Nearest Road A4

Burchett's Place is set in private grounds offering peace and tranquillity in picturesque unspoilt countryside. The house offers an enchanting combination of country house elegance with a warm homely atmosphere, perfect for relaxation. An ideal base for exploring beautiful Berkshire countryside. Close to Marlow, Henley, Windsor and conveniently situated (20 mins) from Heathrow and less than 1 hour from London. Bedrooms are spacious and delightfully furnished with beautiful antique furniture. The main drawing room has a magnificent open fire. Full English breakfast is served.

Hillier Family
Tel: 01628 825023
Fax: 01628 826672

B&B from £27.50, Rooms 1 single, 1 twin, 1 double, 1 family, all en-suite, No smoking, Children welcome, Pets by arrangement, Open all year, Map Ref D

Woodpecker Cottage, Warren Row, Near Maidenhead, Berkshire RG10 8QS Nearest Road A4

A tranquil woodland retreat away from crowds and traffic yet within half an hour of Heathrow, Windsor, Henley and Oxford. Set in a delightful garden of about 1 acre and surrounded by woods where deer abound. The ground floor comprises en-suite double room with its own entrance, en-suite single, and a twin room with private bathroom. All have tea/coffee and TV. There is a cosy sitting room with wood burning stove in winter. A full English breakfast includes homemade bread and jam made from fruit grown in the garden. Local pubs and restaurants within easy reach. EMail: power@woodpecker.co.uk

see PHOTO opposite

Michael & Joanna Power
Tel: 01628 822772
Fax: 01628 822125

B&B from £20pp, Rooms 1 twin with private bathroom, 1 en-suite single, 1 en-suite double, No smoking, Children over 8, Open all year, Map Ref E

Lyndrick Guest House, The Avenue, North Ascot, Berkshire SL5 7ND Nearest Road A30, M3, M4

Lyndrick offers good quality accommodation at less than hotel prices and is just 25 minutes from Heathrow. A warm welcome awaits guests and pride is taken in customer service.Full English breakfast is served in a pleasant conservatory and for early departees a continental breakfast can be supplied. London Waterloo is 40 minutes away on British Rail. Wentworth and surrounding golf courses are 10 minutes away. There is easy access to M3, M4 and M25. Bracknell and Windsor are 10 minutes and Reading 25 minutes. Ascot Racecourse is an easy walk. EMail: lyndrick.house@virgin.net http://homepage.virgin.net/lyndrick.house/index.htm

Sue & Graham Chapman
Tel: 01344 883520
Fax: 01344 891243

B&B from £25pp, Rooms 4 double/twin, 1 single, We take Visa and Mastercard, Open all year, Map Ref F

*left, **Woodpecker Cottage**, near Maidenhead - see details above*

The Hermitage, 63 London Road, Twyford, Berkshire RG10 9EJ   Nearest Road A4, M4

In the heart of the village the Hermitage is a charming combination of Georgian and early Victorian architecture. From here you can explore the Thames Valley and visit Oxford, Henley and Windsor. The railway station is 5 minutes walk away, London 40 minutes and Heathrow 30 minutes by car. There are 5 bedrooms, 3 en-suite, including 2 in the stables. All rooms have TV and tea/coffee making facilities. Guests take breakfast in the elegant dining room overlooking the walled garden. Private car park.

Carel & Colin Barker
Tel: 0118 9340004
Fax: 0118 9340004

B&B from £22.50pp, Rooms 3 twin, 2 double, some en-suite, No smoking, children or pets, Open all year except Christmas & New Year, Map Ref G

Windy Brow, 204 Victoria Road, Wargrave, Berkshire RG10 8AJ   Nearest Road A4

Windy Brow is a large Victorian family home on the edge of this Thameside village. Heather Carver has done B&B for 10 years. All rooms are comfortable and traditionally furnished. Breakfast cooked in the Aga is served in the conservatory overlooking the garden and fields in the summer. Good food pubs and riverside restaurant within walking distance. All rooms have CTV, tea/coffee making facilities and hair dryer. Off road parking. Windsor 10 miles, Heathrow 1/2 hour, M$ 5 miles, Henley 3 miles. One downstairs en-suite room.

Heather & Michael Carver
Tel: 01189 403336

B&B from £22.50-£27.50pp, Rooms 1 single, 2 twin/double, 1 family, some en-suite, No smoking, Children over 8, Pets by arrangement, Open all year except Christmas & Boxing Day, Map Ref E

Chantry Farm, Pindon End, Hanscope, Milton Keynes, Buckinghamshire MK19 7HL   Nearest Road A508

Chantry Farm, built 1650, is a delightful farmhouse on a working farm; overlooking private tout lake and surrounded by glorious countryside. 3 attractively furnished guest rooms, each with colour TV and tea/coffee making facilities (1 en-suite). Guests may enjoy the swimming pool, table tennis and croquet lawn, or relax in the cosy sitting room with inglenook fireplace. Only 15 minutes from Milton Keynes. London 50 minutes by train. Close to Woburn Abbey, Althorpe, Stoke Brueme waterways museum.

Chuff Adams
Tel/Fax: 01908 510269

B&B from £20pp, Rooms 2 twin (1 en-suite), 1 double, Restricted smoking & pets, Children welcome, Open all year except Christmas & New Year, Map Ref I

Spinney Lodge Farm, Forest Road, Hanslope, Milton Keynes, Buckinghamshire MK19 7DE   M1, J15, A508

Spinney Lodge is an arable beef and sheep farm. The lovely Victorian farmhouse with its large gardens has en-suite bedrooms with colour TV and tea/coffee making facilities. Evening meals by arrangement. Many historic houses and gardens to explore, and close to Woburn, Silverstone Stow, 12 minutes to Northampton, 15 minutes to Milton Keynes, 8 minutes to M1, Junction 15.

Mrs Christina Payne
Tel: 01908 510267

B&B from £18pp, Dinner by arrangement, Rooms 1 twin, 1 double, all en-suite, No smoking, Children over 12, No pets, Open all year except Christmas & New Year, Map Ref I

Richmond Lodge, Mursley, Milton Keynes, Buckinghamshire MK17 0LE　　　Nearest Road A421

A country house set in three acres of gardens and orchard with a grass tennis court. Well situated for Woburn and Waddesdon Manor and other National Trust properties. Ideal access for central Milton Keynes and east train journey to London (35 minutes) Leighton Buzzard to Euston. A warm comfortable house with a friendly welcome. Bedrooms are comfortable and have tea/coffee making facilities and TV. A non smoking home. Nearby activities include horse riding, golf and fishing.

Christine & Peter Abbey　　　**B&B from £21pp, Dinner from £12.50 by arrangement, Rooms 2 twin, 1**
Tel: 01296 720275　　　**double, 1 en-suite, No smoking, Open all year, Map Ref J**

Broadway Farm, Berkhamsted, Hertfordshire HP4 2RR　　　Nearest Road A4251

A warm welcome is guaranteed at Broadway, a working arable farm with own fishing lake. 3 comfortable en-suite rooms in converted buildings adjacent to farmhouse. Tea/coffee making facilities, colour TV, central heating, everything for the leisure or business guest - the relaxation of farm life in an attractive rural setting. Yet easy access to London, airports, motorways and mainline rail services. So many places to visit, wherever your interests lie, walking, museums, historic houses, spectacular gardens, planes, canal boats and trains. EMail: a.knowles@broadway.nildram.co.uk

David & Alison Knowles　　　**B&B from £20pp, Rooms 2 twin, 1 double, all en-suite, No smoking,**
Tel/Fax: 01442 866541　　　**Children welcome, No pets, Open all year except Christmas & New Year,**
　　　Map Ref J

Timber Hall, Cold Christmas, Ware, Hertfordshire SG12 7SN　　　Nearest Road A10

Timber Hall is a warm, welcoming house of great character in a quiet location in the Rib Valley and about half way between London and Cambridge. There are colour TV's and tea/coffee making facilities in all the bedrooms, and there is a large drawing room. There is a fine garden and good walks from the house. The varied eating places in the locality include an excellent pub restaurant at the end of the country lane to the house.

Mr & Mrs Shand　　　**B&B from £22pp, Rooms 2/3 single, 1/2 twin, 1 double, some with**
Tel: 01920 466086　　　**private bathroom, No smoking, Children over 8, Pets by arrangement,**
Fax: 01920 462739　　　**Open all year except Christmas & New Year, Map Ref K**

Please mention
THE GREAT BRITISH
BED & BREAKFAST
when booking your accommodation

CAMBRIDGESHIRE & NORTHAMPTONSHIRE

There is a remarkable choice of venues in this area for the holiday-maker. In few other parts of the country would one find so much variation of scenery. In the south of Cambridgeshire are the gently rolling hills and chalk downs, beechwoods and lofty elms. This is a place rich in manor houses, churches and quaint villages, a place defended by the Anglo-Saxons who built their massive earthworks, Fleam Dyke, Devil's Dyke and Bran Ditch to keep out their covetous neighbours. In the north is the treeless bleak and lonely Fen with its wide vistas, strong winds...but fabulous sunsets.

Northamptonshire, the county of 'spires and squires', of wonderful churches and fine country houses, sits on its bed of glorious Cotswold limestone, which forms the Northamptonshire Uplands. This gently undulating country rises to about seven hundred feet above sea level in places.

The cities in this lovely area are naturally enough irresistible attractions. Cambridge, the home of arguably the greatest and certainly one of the oldest universities is a city of seemingly endless pleasures. It is a bustling market town and at the same time a place of cloistered peace. There are thirty colleges distributed over the city, many extremely old and each with a fascinating history. The town developed round the Anglo-Saxon bridge over the river, and William the Conqueror built his castle on the hill in 1068. The heart of the city is probably King's Parade, with grand old houses lining one side and King's College the other. Here too is glorious King's College Chapel begun in 1446 by Henry VI, the founder of the college. The delights of Cambridge are many but the city is also the centre for excellent excursions...to Anglesey Abbey, a National Trust property with impressive grounds... Wimpole Hall, also National Trust, a fantastic Georgian hall with restored Victorian stables and a large park containing rare breeds of domestic animals. Not to be missed is the spectacular Duxford Air Museum, a part of London's Imperial War Museum which houses Europe's largest collection of military aircraft.

Ely, an island in the fens until in the seventeenth century, when the fens were drained, in fact takes its name from the old Saxon word Elig, which means 'eel island'. The small town is dwarfed by its magnificent cathedral. The west front and tower are Norman but in 1250 the east end was rebuilt in Purbeck marble to superb effect. The fine octagonal lantern based upon eight oak pillars is the work of Alan of Walsingham. To the south of Ely is Wicken Fen, the oldest nature reserve in Britain and a heaven for birdwatchers.

Peterborough until 1965 was administered as a separate county - the Soke of Peterborough, and flourished from the nineteenth century as a prosperous industrial town. Little remains of the old Peterborough but the cathedral is a gem. The Norman nave has an impressive early thirteenth century painted roof contemporary with its equally impressive west front.

Northampton on the River Nene was described by Daniel Defoe as 'the handsomest and best built town in all this part of England' the reason very probably being that the town was destroyed by a great fire in 1675, and was rebuilt to a spacious and inspired plan. Northampton possesses one of only four round Norman churches in England, based upon the Crusader's reports of the Holy Sepulchre in Jerusalem. St.

Matthew's church can boast some quite remarkable modern art, commissioned in the 1940s by its vicar, including a Madonna and Child by Henry Moore and a Crucifixion by Graham Sutherland. Not surprisingly for a town at the centre of the shoe industry, the town's museum contains the largest collection of boots and shoes in the world!

Huntingdon is an interesting town lying on the north bank of the Great Ouse and linked to Godmanchester by a fourteenth century bridge. The town is closely associated with the Cromwell family. Oliver Cromwell was born in Huntingdon in 1599, his great grandfather had a manor here and Oliver's grandfather even entertained Queen Elizabeth I here in 1564. Oliver attended the grammar school converted from the old Hospital of St. John the Baptist in 1565, as did the young Samuel Pepys some years later. Near Huntingdon is that other St. Ives once called Slepe, but renamed strangely enough when the remains of a Persian Bishop, St. Ivo, were miraculously discovered in a field near the village.

There is now and has been great industrial achievement in this area - it was, after all at the Cavendish Laboratory in Cambridge that Rutherford split the atom - but within a few short miles of its industrial centres are wonderful areas of typically English countryside.

CAMBRIDGESHIRE & NORTHAMPTONSHIRE

Places to Visit

Fitzwilliam Museum, *Cambridge* ~ one of England's oldest museums with many antiquities, ceramics, illuminated manuscripts and paintings by Monet, Renoir, Picasso and Constable.

Kings College Chapel, *Cambridge* ~ built between 1446 and 1516, it is one of the most important examples of late medieval English architecture. The Chapel is 88 metres long, 12 metres wide and 29 metres high as instructed by Henry VI.

Ely Cathedral, *Cambridgeshire* ~ the cathedral took 268 years to complete, from when it was started in 1068. It dominates the small market town of Ely and the surrounding fens.

Anglesey Abbey, *Cambridgeshire* ~ the original abbey was built in 1135 but the only the crypt survived the Dissolution and was later incorporated into a manor house with furniture from various periods and a rare seascape by Gainsborough.

Imperial War Museum, *Duxford* ~ Duxford was a Spitfire base during the Battle of Britian now it houses over 120 historic aircraft, midget submarines, military vehicles and a collection of civil aircraft including the prototype Concorde 001. In the summer, major air displays are held.

Wicken Fen, *near Soham* ~ over 750 acres of undrained fenland owned by the National Trust, showing how East Anglia would have been before the 17th century.

Rockingham Castle, *near Market Harborough, Northamptonshire* ~ a Norman gateway and walls surrounding a mostly Elizabethan house with extensive gardens. Pictures and Rockingham china are also on display.

Holdenby House, *near Northampton* ~ with Elizabethan garden, original arched entrance, terraces, ponds and falconry and rare breeds centre.

Lamport Hall, *near Northampton* ~ a 17th and 18th century house with a programme of concerts and special events. The house also includes paintings, furniture and china.

Rushton Triangular Lodge, *near Kettering* ~ built by Sir Thomas Tresham in 1593. Everything about the building is triangular with three sides, three floors and trefoil windows.

Delapre Abbey, *Northampton* ~ orginally built as a Cluniac nunnery in 1145, most of its existing building dates from its rebuilding for the Tate family after the Dissolution of Monasteries.

Watermill, Duddington, near Northmapton

Kelmarsh Hall, *Northampton* ~ designed by James Gibbs, it was built in the 1720's and is one of two only surviving houses by this architect. The south lodge gates were designed in the late 18th century but were only made in the 1960's when the original plans where discovered.

*The 15th century
Bridge and Chapel,
St Ives*

THE WASH

DONINGTON

LINCOLN

HOLBEACH

LONG SUTTON

SPALDING

KING'S LYNN

A17

A1101

WISBECH

A47

OAKHAM

STAMFORD

A16

A15

A1

A47

DOWNHAM MARKET

A1122

LEICESTER

UPPINGHAM

A6003

F

CORBY

A43

PETERBOROUGH

A47

MARCH

GUYHIRN

A1139

A16

A6

HUSBANDS BOSWORTH

MARKET HARBOROUGH

H

A1

SAWTRY

CHATTERIS

LITTLEPORT

A14

A227

ROTHWELL

A508

A6

KETTERING

THRAPSTON

A605

A14

HUNTINGDON

A141

A142

ELY

B

A

SOHAM

C

RUGBY

A43

A14

A1

ST. IVES

A14

NEWMARKET

A10

NORTHAMPTON

A45

BEDS

ST. NEOTS

A14

A428

G

BEDFORD

ELTISLEY

D

CAMBRIDGE

OWCESTER

I

A43

NEWPORT PAGNELL

M1

A6

BIGGLESWADE

HAVERHILL

A10

BRACKLEY

A5

MILTON KEYNES

A6

E

ROYSTON

SAFFRON WALDEN

BUCKINGHAM

M11

ESSEX

*Clipston,
Northamptonshire*

Cathedral House, 17 St Mary's Street, Ely, Cambridgeshire CB7 4ER   **Nearest Road A10**

Cathedral House is in the centre of Ely within the shadow of its famous cathedral known as 'the ship of the Fens' and within 2 minutes walk of Cromwell's House, the museums, shops and restaurants. A Grade II listed house retaining many of its original features, accommodation comprises 1 twin en-suite, a family suite and a luxurious double en-suite. All have TV and tea/coffee and overlook the walled tranquil garden. A choice of full English or continental breakfast is served at a farmhouse table by an open fire (lit when cold). Ely is an ideal base to tour East Anglia, Cambridge and Newmarket closeby. EMail: farndale@cambs.net Website: http://www.ely.org.uk./farn/htm

see PHOTO opposite

Jenny & Robin Farndale
Tel/Fax: 01353 662124

B&B from £25pp, Rooms 1 twin, 1 double, 1 family, all en-suite, No smoking, No pets, Open mid January - mid December, Map Ref A

Hill House Farm, 9 Main Street, Coveney, Ely, Cambridgeshire CB6 2DJ   **Nearest Road A10, A142**

A warm welcome awaits you at this spacious Victorian farmhouse, situated in the quiet village of Coveney, 3 miles west of the historic cathedral city of Ely. With open views of the surrounding countryside. Easy access to Cambridge, Newmarket and Huntingdon. Ideally places for touring Cambridgeshire, Norfolk and Suffolk. Wicken Fen and Welney Wildfowl Refuge are nearby. Bedrooms are tastefully furnished and decorated, have central heating, TV, clock radio and tea/coffee making facilities, (1 on the ground floor). A comfortable lounge and garden available for guests' use. ETB 2 Crowns Highly Commended.

Mrs Hilary Nix
Tel: 01353 778369

B&B from £20pp, Rooms 1 twin, 2 double, all en-suite, No smoking, Children over 12, No pets, Open all year except Christmas, Map Ref B

Queensberry, 196 Carter Street, Fordham, Ely, Cambridgeshire CB7 5JU   **Nearest Road A14**

A warm welcome at this very English home, a Georgian house set peacefully in large gardens on edge of the village. 'Queensberry' is the ideal base from which to tour East Anglia; visit the university city of Cambridge; historical cathedral of Ely 'the ship of the Fens', the famous market town of Bury St Edmunds and Newmarket, the horse racing centre of the world. First village off A14 on Newmarket to Ely A142 road. Good restaurant within walking distance. Ample safe parking within the grounds.

see PHOTO on page 58

Jan & Malcolm Roper
Tel: 01638 720916
Fax: 01638 720233

B&B from £20-£25pp, Dinner by arrangement, Rooms 1 single, 1 twin, 1 double, 1 en-suite, No smoking, Children welcome, Pets by arrangement, Open all year except Christmas, Map Ref C

Purlins, 12 High Street, Little Shelford, Cambridgeshire CB2 5ES   **Nearest Road M11, A10**

An individually designed country house set in two acres of fields and woodland, in a quiet pretty village on the Cam, four miles south of Cambridge. An ideal centre for visiting colleges, cathedrals, country houses, the Imperial War Museum and bird watching. The comfortable en-suite bedrooms (two ground floor) all have colour TV, radio and tea/coffee making facilities; a conservatory serves as the guests sitting room and breakfast is provided to suit most tastes. Restaurants are nearby. On drive parking for three cars.

Olga & David Hindley
Tel/Fax: 01223 842643

B&B from £22pp, Rooms 1 twin, 2 double, all en-suite, No smoking, Children over 8, No pets, Open February - mid December, Map Ref D

*left, **Cathedral House**, Ely - see details above*

Chiswick House, Meldreth, Royston, Cambridgeshire SG8 6LZ Nearest Road A10

see PHOTO on page 59

Chiswick House, 8 miles south of Cambridge, is an original timber framed building dating from the late 1400's. Over the years it has been altered and extended but it remains fundamentally as it was built 500 years ago. Old beams, polished oak and flowers in every room combined with a warm welcome provide an atmosphere to relax in comfort. The royal crest of King James I is to be found above the fireplace in the drawing room. It is believed that the house was used by King James as a hunting lodge. The Jacobean panelling in the dining room dates from that period.

Mrs Bernice Elbourn
Tel: 01763 260242

B&B from £21pp, Rooms 2 twin, 4 double, all en-suite, No smoking, Open all year, Map Ref E

The Old Vicarage, Laxton, nr Corby, Northamptonshire NN17 3AT Nearest Road A43

The Old Vicarage (1805) designed by Repton on borders Rutland, Northants and Lincs. Close to Stamford (Burghley House), Rutland Water, Althorp, Oundle, many stately homes. Walks woods opposite. Large garden with outdoor pool, croquet, bikes plus our Herbal Beauty-care Centre (Martha Hill). (Products for use in bedrooms). We have collection animals, books, games, videos, magazines etc. Refreshment on arrival. Tea/coffee, TV/Information Pack in lavishly decorated bedrooms. Iron, phone etc on request. Rooms not en-suite but private bathroom/washroom toilet. Breakfast free-range, times flexible.

Mrs Sue Hill-Brookes
Tel: 01780 450248
Fax: 01780 450398

B&B from £16.50-£17.50pp, Rooms 1 single adjoining a double, 1 twin, 2 double, 1 family, Children & pets welcome, Open all year, Map Ref F

Threeways House, Everdon, Daventry, Northamptonshire NN11 6BL Nearest Road M1, M40, A5, A45

Threeways is a character stone house with delightful gardens, on the Green of charming peaceful, conservation village. The guest rooms are separated from the family house by a large terrace. Come and indulge yourself! The very comfortably furnished bedrooms all have charming views, TV's en-suite bathrooms, tea/coffee trays and central heating. We are proud of our delicious breakfasts which we serve in an elegant dining room. There are many nearby attractions to visit and idyllic local walks to enjoy. ETB 3 Crowns Highly Commended.

Elizabeth Barwood
Tel: 01327 361631 or 0374 428242
Fax: 01327 361359

B&B from £22.50pp, Rooms 1 single, 1 twin, 1 double, 1 family, all en-suite, Restricted smoking, Children welcome, Pets restricted, Open all year, Map Ref G

The Maltings, Aldwincle, Oundle, Northamptonshire NN14 3EP Nearest Road A605, A14, A1

see PHOTO opposite

A lovely 16th century house and former agricultural maltings and granary. The main accommodation is in the granary which has been converted to 2 bedrooms, 2 bathrooms and sitting room. The remainder of the accommodation is in the beamed house which has inglenook fireplaces. There is a very peaceful atmosphere, a lovely garden with unusual plants which is occasionally open under the National Garden Scheme. Many places of interest and activities nearby. Visa and Mastercard accepted.

Margaret & Nigel Faulkner
Tel: 01832 720233
Fax: 01832 720326

B&B from £24.50pp, Rooms 3 en-suite twin, No smoking, Children over 10, No pets indoors, Open all year, Map Ref H

*right, **The Maltings,** Aldwincle - see details above*

Rose Cottage, Plumpton Road Woodend, Towcester, Northamptonshire NN12 8RZ   M1, M40, A5, A43

Rose Cottage is situated on the edge of the village overlooking open countryside. Each guest room is attractively furnished, TV's, tea/coffee tray and central heating. Hospitality, comfort and tranquillity at its very best. Traditional Aga cooking, home grown vegetables and our own free range eggs. Near to Althorp House, Sulgrave Manor, National Trust Canons Ashby and Stowe Gardens. ETB 3 Crowns Highly Commended.

Mrs Ann Davey-Turner
Tel: 01327 860968 or 0589 129988
Fax: 01327 860004

B&B from £22.50pp, Dinner from £16, Rooms 1 single, 1 twin en-suite, 1 double, Children over 7, Dogs at our discretion, Open all year, Map Ref I

"Do you think this is a haunted house?"
BELLE & BERTIE IN YORK

If with me you'd fondly stray
Over the hills and far away.

The Beggar's Opera (1728) act 1, sc 13, air 16
John Gay 1685-1732

CHESHIRE, MERSEYSIDE & GREATER MANCHESTER

To regard this area as the industrial centre of the northwest and dismiss it out of hand as a holiday venue would be extremely short sighted, as even the great commercial and industrial centres of Liverpool and Manchester have their 'other' side, and an extremely fascinating side it is. Manchester, the commercial centre for the Lancashire cotton industry, built impressive monuments to its prosperity. The enormous Gothic Town Hall designed by Alfred Waterhouse possesses a quite remarkable marble interior. In Deansgate, the flamboyant facade of Rylands Library expresses Mancunian pride in their success, as indeed does the Free Trade Hall, the Athenaeum and the Theatre Royal. Modern Manchester can offer the impressive G-Mex exhibition centre; the wonderful Museum of Science and Industry; and for television enthusiasts the Granada Studios offer a tour, which includes the set of the TV soap 'Coronation Street'; also there is the new MetroLink, the light rail tram system which crosses the city. The growth of the cotton industry saw Bolton (now a part of Greater Manchester) prosper, and here is a remarkable black and white half-timbered fifteenth century mansion known fancifully as Hall-i'-th'-Wood. Samuel Crompton, who was born in

Bolton and lived in the mansion for a time is said to have invented his spinning mule here. The spinning mule, together with Hargreave's spinning jenny and Arkwright's water frame are to be seen in the Tonge Moor Textile Museum. Not to be outdone by its sister city, Liverpool, once England's second greatest port, is revamping many of the fine buildings that witnessed its proud maritime past. The Albert Dock, built in 1846, has been renovated to include shops, cafes and an offshoot of the London Tate Gallery and also 'The Beatles Story' a sight and sound experience of the music of the 1960s. The city provides a long list of modern galleries and museums, including an impressive Maritime museum tracing the history of the port. For the football enthusiast, Liverpool Football Club Visitors' Centre, Anfield Road, offers a fascinating display of trophies and memorabilia. Then there is the intriguing Planetarium as well as the traditional Walker Art Gallery, one of the country's finest provincial galleries.

The two Liverpool cathedrals, each masterpieces in their own right, face each other across the city. The Anglican cathedral is a twentieth century Gothic structure designed by Sir Giles Gilbert Scott. The Roman Catholic cathedral designed by Sir Frederick Gibberd has in its modernist lantern tower some stained glass by John Piper and Patrick Reyntiens.

On the curve of the River Dee lies Chester, founded by the Romans during the first century AD as the main base for their legions in the northwest. The Roman name for the town was Deva, however Chester comes from the Latin term Castra Devana meaning 'camp on the Dee'. Chester can claim to be the only city in the country having a complete circuit of Medieval wall. During the Middle Ages the city was an extremely prosperous port, that is until the River Dee silted up. The red sandstone cathedral, restored during the nineteenth century, was originally the church of a Benedictine abbey and became a cathedral in 1541; the Medieval Mystery Plays have been revived and are performed outside the cathedral. The compact city is renowned for its picturesque central streets, a mixture of Tudor half-timbered buildings, Georgian red brick houses and nineteenth century 'fake' black and white buildings. Chester's pride is its wonderful old Rows, an upper tier of shops above those on street level forming a continuous covered shopping arcade. An elaborate wrought-iron clock presented to the city in 1897 to commemorate the Diamond Jubilee of Queen Victoria stands over the east gate of the city. Chester race meeting held since the sixteenth century on the Roodee, a meadow by the

river is the oldest meeting in England.

These three cities dominate this area, but there is a wealth of glorious scenery to explore a short drive from these centres, the lovely Cheshire Plain and the Delamere Forest north of Tarporley which comprises four hundred acres of dense woodland, including Hatch Mere and Oak Mere. The spectacular ruin of Beeston Castle perched on the summit of Peckforton Hills gives view of no less than eight counties, while from rugged Helsby Hill are superb views across Helsby Marsh to the Mersey. Knutsford is an attractive town of old black and white houses, said to have acquired its name from King Canute who it seems forded the local stream. Mrs. Gaskell by the way, used Knutsford as the model for 'Cranford' in her novel of that name. Two miles away is magnificent Tatton Park, fifty-four acres of formal gardens laid out in the eighteenth century by Humphrey Repton. The Hall is one of the National Trust's most visited properties.

If it's seaside that appeals, then Wallasey on the Wirral peninsular has wonderful sands, promenade, and all the amenities of a modern resort within a very short distance of the bright lights of Liverpool. The Wirral was once a great royal forest and game reserve...and also the haunt of footpads. The salt-marsh and tidal flats of the upper Dee estuary is now a great attraction for bird-watchers, the whole area being a wintering ground for waders and wildfowl.

CHESHIRE, MERSEYSIDE & GREATER MANCHESTER

Places to Visit

Quarry Bank Mill, *Styal, Cheshire* ~ one of the very first factories to use water to power its textile machines. Founded in 1784, it has now been fully restored as a working museum with England's largest working waterwheel, measuring over 24feet high and weighing over 50 tons.

Liverpool Cathedral, *Liverpool* ~ the world's largest Anglican cathedral, it was completed in 1978 after 76 years of building work. Made from red sandstone, it was designed by Sir Giles Gilbert Scott and the foundation stone was laid by Edward VII in 1904.

Croxeth Hall and Country Park, *near Liverpool* ~ a historic mansion set in 500 acres of parkland. The rooms have been recreated and furnished in Edwardian style. Other attractions include a Victorian walled garden, rare breeds of farm animals, miniature railway and adventure playground.

Speke Hall, *near Liverpool* ~ a half timbered manor house, parts date from 1490 with courtyard, dry moat and impressive Great Hall. There is also a 16th century priest hole, William Morris wallpaper and Mortlake tapestries.

Tatton Park, *Knutsford* ~ a Georgian house on a country estate with tree lined drive, Japanese gardens, orangery, sailing centre and adventure playground. The Old Hall has rooms showing various periods from the Middle Ages to the 1950's.

Albert Dock, *Liverpool* ~ Grade I listed warehouses, they have been restored to include television studios, museums, galleries, shops, restaurants and business premises.

Museum of Science and Industry, *Manchester* ~ part of the Castlefield Urban Heritage Park, the museum looks at Manchester's industrial past with collections of steam engines, displays of the Liverpool and Manchester Railway and the Electric Gallery about the history of domestic power. Across the road in the Air and Space Gallery, there are hot air balloons and space suits.

Granada Studio Tours, *Manchester* ~ at Granada Studios visit various television shows including the set of Coronation Street, Britain's longest running soap opera.

Dunham Massey Hall, *near Altrincham* ~ a country house set in parkland. 30 rooms in the house are on show with 18th century furniture and silverware. The National Trust have restored the gardens, which include an 18th century orangery and a well house which was used to supply the house with fresh water.

Jodrell Bank, *near Knutsford* ~ an award winning Science Centre standing at the foot of the Lovell telescope, one of the world's largest fully steerable radio telescopes. There are exhibitions on astronomy, satellites and space, as well as a 35 acre arboretum with over 2000 species of plants.

A Liver Bird atop the Royal Liver Building

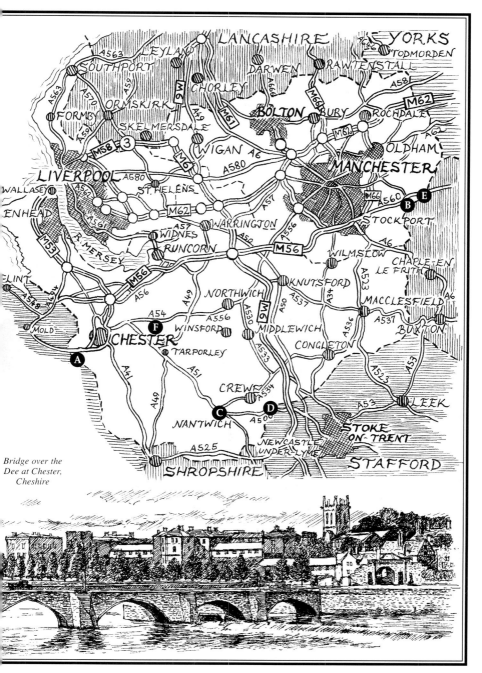

Bridge over the
Dee at Chester,
Cheshire

The Mount, Lesters Lane, Higher Kinnerton, Cheshire CH4 9BQ   **Nearest Road A55**

Victorian country house on the Chester/North Wales border set in an extensive 3 acre garden with tennis court, croquet lawn and large vegetable garden. Spacious bedrooms all with own bathrooms, TV and tea/coffee making facilities. Drawing room and conservatory for guests' use. An ideal place to relax and explore the North Wales coast and Cheshire. 45 minutes to Liverpool and Manchester. 1 hour to Anglesey, Bodnant Gardens, Port Sunlight, historic Chester, Erdigg, Offas Dyke and Llangollen. Excellent pubs in village, half a mile away.

see PHOTO opposite

Jonathan & Rachel Major
Tel: 01244 660275
Fax: 01244 660275

B&B from £20pp, Dinner £16 (bring own wine), Rooms 1 twin en-suite, 1 twin with private bathroom, , 1 double en-suite, No smoking, Children over 12, Open all year, Map Ref A

Needhams Farm, Uplands Road, Werneth Low, Gee Cross, Hyde, Cheshire SK14 3AQ   **Nearest Road A560**

500 year old farmhouse, surrounded by scenic views. Residential licence. Views from all rooms. Log fires in winter. warm welcome. Plenty of car parking. Needhams Farm is a working farm with cattle and sheep. Meals are served from 7pm to 9pm each evening. Special meals for children. Ideally situated for Manchester and surrounding areas including Manchester Airport. Nearest Station is Romiley.

Mrs C Walsh
Tel: 0161 368 4610
Fax: 0161 367 9106

B&B from £18-£20pp, Evening meals £7, Rooms 4 double, 1 family, 1 twin, 1 single, 6 en-suite, Open all year, Map Ref B

Stoke Grange Farm, Chester Road, Nantwich, Cheshire CW5 6BT   **Nearest Road M6, A51**

Attractive farmhouse in a picturesque canalside location. Hearty breakfast, vegetarians catered for. Individually styled en-suite rooms with colour TV. Four poster bedroom with balcony surveying Cheshire countryside also watch canal boats cruising the Shropshire Union. Relax in garden with lawns down to the canal. Pets corner and peacocks. First class service at B&B and self catering accommodation. Past Cheshire's Tourist Development Award winners. Chester 20 mins, Crewe 10 mins. Near to Stapeley Water Gardens, Beeston and Cholmondeley castles, Jodrell Bank, Tatton Park and Chester Zoo. RAC Highly Acclaimed. 2 Crowns, Highly Commended, North West Tourist Board.

Mrs Georgina West
Tel/Fax: 01270 625525

B&B from £20pp, Rooms 1 twin, 2 double, 1 family, Restricted smoking, Children welcome, No pets, Open all year, Map Ref C

Lea Farm, Wrinehill Road, Wybunbury, Nantwich, Cheshire CW5 7NS   **Nearest Road A500**

Charming farmhouse set in landscaped gardens where peacocks roam on a dairy farm. Ample car parking. In beautiful rolling countryside. Spacious bedrooms. Luxury lounge. Pool, snooker and fishing available. From Nantwich take A51 turning left at Stapeley Water Gardens. End of road turn right for village of Wybunbury, turn left down Wrinehill road by church. 1 mile from village.

Mrs Jean Callwood
Tel: 01270 841429

B&B from £16.50pp (children half price if sharing with parents), Dinner from £10, Rooms 1 double, 1 family, 1 twin, 2 en-suite, Open all year, Map Ref D

*left, **The Mount**, Higher Kinnerton - see details above*

Shire Cottage Farmhouse, Benches Lane, Marple Bridge, Stockport, Cheshire SK6 5RY Nearest Road A626

Real Home from home accommodation in peaceful location. Magnificent views over Etherow Country Park and wooded valleys. All rooms have central heating, TV, tea/coffee making facilities and shaver points. Some rooms are en-suite. Situated on the edge of the Peak District yet only 10 miles from airport and 15 miles from Manchester city centre. Many places of interest nearby; country homes, Derwent Dams, Quarry Bank Mill, Chatsworth House & Farm, Granada studio tours, Grand Metro Exhibition Centre, Jodrell Bank etc. Early breakfasts can be catered for. Car parking.

Mrs Monica Sidebottom
Tel: 01457 866536

B&B from £19pp, Rooms 1 single, 1 twin, 1 double, 1 family, most en-suite, also self catering cottage, Children welcome, Dogs by arrangement, Open all year, Map Ref E

Roughlow Farm, Chapel Lane, Willington, Tarporley, Cheshire CW6 0PG   **Nearest Road M6, A54**

A delightful 18th century converted farmhouse in quiet situation with wonderful views to Shropshire and Wales. Attractive garden with cobbled courtyard and tennis court. Elegantly furnished to a high standard with en-suite facilities to 3 twin/.double bedrooms. Roughlow Farm is well situated for easy access to Manchester, Chester, Wales, Liverpool and M6. From M6 (J19) take the A556 towards Chester. A54 Kelsall bypass turn left after passing Morreys Nurseries on right hand side, then left again at the pub in Waste Lane, continue bearing right at the next junction. (150 yds on left). ETB Highly Commended.

Mrs P F Sutcliffe
Tel/Fax: 01829 751199

B&B from £25pp, Dinner from £17.50, (min 4 persons), Rooms 3 twin or double, all en-suite, 1 with own sitting room, Children over 6, No smoking, Open all year Christmas & New Year, Map Ref F

"I should take your carriage ride first, it gets quite busy later"
BELLE & BERTIE IN YORK

Where'er you walk, cool gales shall fan the glade,
Trees, where you sit, shall crowd into a shade.

PASTORALS (1709) 'SUMMER' 1.73
ALEXANDER POPE 1688-1744

CORNWALL

You are seldom more than half an hour's drive from the coast in Cornwall - and what a coast! Granite cliffs withstanding the onslaught of white-crested Atlantic rollers, jagged rocks and treacherous reefs, romantic little fishing villages, wide unspoilt beaches and hidden coves, golden sands and sub-tropical flowers and a coastline that changes with amazing rapidity. This is without doubt a summer playground, with each village and town finely tuned to holiday pleasures. It is hard to believe that before the opening of the Saltash railway bridge in 1859, the River Tamar virtually isolated Cornwall from the rest of the country. Despite its holiday population there are still lonely places - Bodmin Moor, bleak, windswept and scattered with granite Tors, at its highest point, Brown Willy, gives spectacular views across its barren waste. There are some fascinating ancient relics here, Hurlers Stone Circle and the Bronze Age burial chambers of Trethevy Quoit. Launceston, which once guarded the main route from Devon into Cornwall is perched on a hill with the remains of its Norman castle and quaint twisting streets. Just off the A30 is Jamaica Inn, the setting for Daphne du Maurier's novel of smugglers, tales of which abound hereabouts. There are tales too of King Arthur and his knights. Tintagel claims to be King Arthur's Camelot, and the magnificently sited castle ruins on the impregnable headland with its steep-stepped approach certainly thrill the

imagination, but the castle, built for the Earl of Cornwall in 1145, post-dates Arthur.

The tourist may find it hard to believe that up until the end of the nineteenth century Cornwall led the world in the production of tin and copper, but the hinterland is peppered with old workings, and many of today's resorts owe their development to the trade in tin, copper and lead. But it is to the coast that the holidaymakers flock. Bude, at one time notorious for shipwrecks, has a wonderful beach and is now a major surfing centre, while Padstow down the coast, though lacking a beach, can offer a glorious labyrinth of quaint streets and ancient houses - including Raleigh Court where Sir Walter Raleigh stayed when Warden of Cornwall. Newquay, the gem of this part of the coast has all the trappings of a first class resort including swimming, surfing, excellent beaches and a picturesque harbour...a far cry from its early days as a pilchard port. Further down the coast the views from St. Agnes Beacon are superb.

St. Ives needs little introduction, being a magnet to holiday makers and artists alike. Originally a fishing village of course, now what fishing is done is done by the holiday makers. The hotch-potch of cottages that line the narrow twisting streets make it a photographer's paradise. The sculptress Barbara Hepworth settled in St. Ives, as indeed did a number of twentieth century artists; her studio is now a museum. A branch of London's Tate Gallery features the St. Ives school of artists in a magnificent new gallery here. Sennen, the westernmost village in England is the spot, so it is told, where King Arthur routed the Danes - against a backdrop of some of the most spectacular scenery in Cornwall. Penzance, a fine holiday centre with its Georgian houses, marks a change in climate from the harsh and rugged Atlantic coast to the lush, mild sheltered bays to the east.

St. Michael's Mount, a Benedictine church which became a fortress following the Dissolution, can be reached at low tide along a causeway across the sands. Lying some twenty-eight miles southwest of Land's End are the Scillies, a group of one hundred and forty or so rocky islands, although only five are inhabited. The extremely mild climate brought about by the Gulf Stream enables the Scillies to provide out of season flowers for the mainland markets. One of the Scilly Isles Tresco, is renowned for its magnificent gardens constructed around the ruins of a Benedictine Abbey by Augustus Smith and his family. Here is a graveyard of shipping wrecked on the treacherous granite reef, and the site of the first lighthouse constructed in

1858 on Bishop Rock, four miles southwest of St. Agnes. The so-called Cornish Riviera stretches from The Lizard to Looe, and Riviera is certainly no misnomer. The exceptionally mild climate brings holidaymakers in droves to the golden sands, sub-tropical flowers and sparkling blue seas. Truro, the 'capital' of this glorious area boasts a cathedral with three spires. This is a coastline of charming and picturesque fishing villages. St. Mawes dominated by its castle is a fashionable yachting resort. Mevagissey is a highly popular resort of narrow streets, there is breathtaking scenery and lovely beaches at Polstreath and Portmellon, Polperro is charming with its limewashed houses clustered round its small harbour, while Fowey is renowned for its regatta, and home of Sir Arthur Quiller-Couch, who described Fowey as 'the town loved at first sight'.

Cornwall is rich in literary associations and little wonder with so much to inspire. Dame Agatha Christie was born in Torquay. Lord Tennyson called the town, 'the loveliest sea village in England'. Dylan Thomas honeymooned at Mousehole and called it 'really the loveliest village in England'. Thomas Hardy was fascinated by Tintagel. John Betjeman loved Cornwall, as did Virginia Woolf and Winston Graham, author of the Poldark books. But surely there could be no better recommendation for this quite remarkable county than that of Daphne du Maurier, who had no fewer than three Cornish homes.

Places to Visit

Cotehele, *St Dominick, near Saltash* ~ set on the River Tamar in woodland, the medieval house was built between 1485 and 1539. It has an open hall, kitchen, chapel and many private parlours and chambers. Outside are colourful terraced gardens and a valley garden with mediaeval dovecote. Cotehele Mill has been restored to working order with workshops. There are many woodland walks throughout the estate.

Glendurgan Gardens, *near Falmouth* ~ set in a wooded valley, a sub-tropical garden with many rare and exotic plants. Other attractions are the recently restored 1833 laurel maze and the Giants Stride, a pole with ropes to swing from. The garden runs down to a beach and the tiny village of Durgan.

Pencarrow House & Gardens, *Bodmin* ~ an 18th century mansion set in woodlands and gardens. The house has a fine collection of paintings, china and furniture.

St Michaels Mount, *near Penzance* ~ approached by a causeway at low tide, this spectacular castle and church on top of a rocky island dates from the 14th century. The castle has an armoury, Gothic drawing room and magnificent views towards Lands End.

Trelissick, *near Truro* ~ set in three hundred and seventy acres of parkland by the River Fal. Ornamental gardens with camellias, hydrangeas, magnolias and rhododendron. Art and craft gallery. The park has many walks and has views to the sea and Falmouth.

Trenice, *near Newquay* ~ built in 1571, this secluded Elizabethan manor house has an early gabled facade. Inside are fireplaces, plaster ceilings, oak and walnut furniture and a collection of clocks. The garden has many different types of unusual plants and an orchard with many old varieties of fruit trees.

Polperro Harbour

CORNWALL

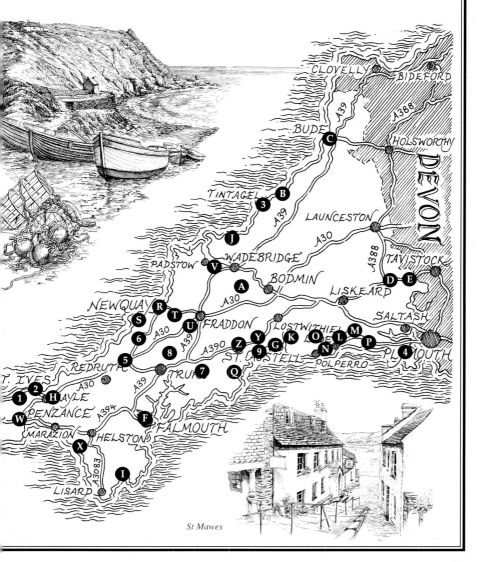

CLOVELLY
BIDEFORD
A39
A388
BUDE
C
HOLSWORTHY
DEVON
TINTAGEL
B
3
A39
LAUNCESTON
J
A30
A388
TAVISTOCK
PADSTOW
WADEBRIDGE
V
D
E
BODMIN
A
LISKEARD
NEWQUAY
R
T
A30
SALTASH
S
FRADDON
U
LOSTWITHIEL
6
A30
A39
Z
Y
G
K
O
L
M
8
A390
9
N
P
5
ST. OSTELL
PLYMOUTH
4
REDRUTH
7
Q
POLPERRO
T. IVES
TRURO
A30
1
2
HAYLE
A39
PENZANCE
A394
W
F
MARAZION
FALMOUTH
X
HELSTON
A3083
I
LISARD

St Mawes

Tregolls Farm, St. Wenn, Bodmin, Cornwall PL30 5PG   Nearest Road A30

Set in a picturesque valley. Tregolls is a family farm of 107 acres, the main farming enterprise being cattle and sheep. At the Grade II Listed farmhouse, traditional farmhouse fare is served in the guests dining room, and the guests lounge with TV/video is always available. The bedrooms each have vanity units and tea/coffee facilities. The fishing village of Padstow, National Trust Lanhydrock House, Lost Gardens of Heligan and Saints Way footpath are all within easy access. W.C.T.B 1 Crown Commended.

Marilyn Hawkey
Tel: 01208 812154

B&B from £14.50pp, Dinner from £8, Rooms 1 single, 1 twin, 2 double, 1 en-suite, No smoking or pets, Children welcome, Open all year except Christmas & New Year, Map Ref A

Tregawne, Withiel, Bodmin, Cornwall PL30 5NR   Nearest Road A30

18th Century, antique furnishing, TV, coffee/tea etc in rooms, use of Drawing Room. Parking, swimming pool, walking, canel trail 10 minutes, fishing and canel, Fowey, Tamar riding, croquet. David is member of St. Enodoc Golf Club and takes guests to play there. Many gardens and National Trust Houses to visit. Equidistant from both North & South Cornwall coasts, 20 minutes from rock with surfing, water skiing, deep sea fishing, cliffs walks etc. Seafood restaurant in Padstow 20 minutes.

David Jackson & Lady Linlithgow
Tel: 01208 831552
Fax: 01208 832122

B&B from £25-£35pp, Dinner from £12.50, Rooms 1 twin, 2 double, all en-suite, Restricted smoking, Children & pets welcome, Open all year, Map Ref A

Bottreaux House Hotel & Restaurant, Boscastle, Cornwall PL35 0BG   Nearest Road B3266

Bottreaux House stands in the old conservation area of this unspoilt beautiful harbour village. Our 3 Crown Highly Commended rating offers superb accommodation for the discerning traveller. The restaurant offers a highly regarded comprehensive menu at affordable prices, and the warm relaxed atmosphere, together with the candlelit tables make this a place for romantics and lovers. The walking in the area is wonderful and we offer free use of mountain bikes. http: //www.chycor.co.uk/bottreaux Please phone for your free video of the Hotel and surrounding area.

Hazel & Graham Mee
Tel: 01840 250231
Fax: 01840 250170

B&B from £15-£20pp, Dinner from £12, Rooms 2 twin, 4 double, 1 family, all en-suite, Restricted smoking, Children over 9, Pets by arrangement, Open all year, Map Ref B

Orchard Lodge, Gunpool Lane, Boscastle, Cornwall PL35 0AT   Nearest Road A39

Orchard Lodge, set in its own attractive gardens, is a large delightful base for a relaxing holiday. Offering 6 very pleasant guest rooms decorated and furnished to a high standard and all with modern facilities. A delicious full English or continental breakfast is served in the pretty dining room with pine furnishings and which overlooks the garden. Ample car parking. An ideal base for touring Cornwall. Overlooks the Jordan Valley. A warm and friendly welcome awaits you.

Bill & Eileen Purslow
Tel: 01840 250418

B&B from £20pp, Rooms 1 twin, 2 double, all en-suite, No smoking, No children, No pets, Open March - December, Closed Christmas & open New Year, Map Ref B

*right, **Cliff Hotel**, Bude - see details on page 78*

see PHOTO on page 77

Cliff Hotel, Maer Down Road, Crooklets Beach, Bude, Cornwall EX23 8NG   **Nearest Road A39**

The Cliff Hotel has a wonderful location being 200 yards from Crooklets Beach and next to the National Trust cliff walk, 'an area of outstanding beauty'. Our facilities are first class with indoor swimming pool, gym, all weather bowling green and tennis, all within 5 acres of lawns and with a wild flower meadow. We feel our greatest attribute though is the home cooked fresh food and informal ambience.

Brian & Lin Sibley
Tel/Fax: 01288 353110

B&B from £25pp, Dinner available, Rooms 2 single, 2 twin, 4 double, 7 family, all en-suite, Children & pets welcome, Open April - end September, Map Ref C

Dozmary, Tors View Close, Tavistock Road, Callington, Cornwall PL17 7DY   **Nearest Road A388, A390**

Dozmary is a deceptively spacious dormer bungalow situated in a quiet cul-de-sac just a few minutes walk from the town centre. Ideal location for exploring south Devon, Cornwall, many National Trust properties and English Heritage monuments. Excellent views of Dartmoor, Bodmin Moor and the Tamar Valley from nearby Kit Hill Country Park. All rooms are en-suite and have colour TV, radio clock alarm, tea/coffee, central heating and hair dryer. ETB 1 Crown Commended. A reduction of £1 per person per night for 4 nights or more consecutive stay.

Thelma & Henry Wills
Tel: 01579 383677

B&B from £16pp, Rooms 1 twin, 1 double, 1 family, all en-suite, No smoking, No pets, Open all year except New Year, Map Ref D

Tamar Valley B&B, Lower Kelly, Calstock, Cornwall PL18 9RX   **Nearest Road A390**

Pat and Bill welcome you to share the tranquillity of their comfortable riverside home and garden. Rooms and residents lounge south facing each have a balcony where you can watch salmon leap and the activities of wildfowl. A short walk brings you to the National Trust Cothele House and gardens. St Mellion golf club, Dartmoor and the coast are within easy reach. Bus and train services to Plymouth and ares from our picturesque village. Evening meals by reservation. Open all year.

Pat & Bill Parnell
Tel: 01822 832380

B&B from £20.50pp, Dinner from £12, Rooms 2 twin, 2 double, 1 family, most en-suite, Restricted smoking, Children welcome, Pets by arrangement, Open all year, Map Ref E

Dolvean Hotel, 50 Melvill Road, Falmouth, Cornwall TR11 4DQ   **Nearest Road A39**

Enjoy early morning tea watching the sun rise over Falmouth Bay. Linger over English breakfast in our elegant dining room. Browse through the local guides in the parlour, and discover our historic Castles, exotic gardens, hidden coves or quaint fishing villages. And let us, and Cornwall, do the rest! The Dolvean has old fashioned standards of care, courtesy, and service, together with all the modern amenities expected by today's traveller. Private car park. Credit cards accepted. AA 4Q's Selected. http://www.cornwall-online.co.uk/dolvean

Paul & Carol Crocker
Tel: 01326 313658
Fax: 01326 313995

B&B from £22pp, Rooms 2 single, 4 twin, 5 double, 1 family, all en-suite, No smoking or pets, Children over 5, Open all year except Christmas & New Year, Map R

Trevanion Guest House, 70 Lostwithiel Street, Fowey, Cornwall PL23 1BQ　　　Nearest Road A390, B3269

A warm and friendly welcome awaits you at this comfortable and spacious 16th century Merchants House situated in the historic town of Fowey in the heart of Daphne Du Maurier country. An ideal base from which to walk the coastal path, visit the Lost Gardens of Heligan and National Trust houses and gardens, or explore the Cornish Riviera. All bedrooms are well furnished and have colour TV and tea/coffee making facilities. Large family room, most en-suite rooms. Non smoking. Car parking.

Jill & Bob Bullock
Tel: 01726 832602

B&B from £16pp, Rooms 2 single, 1 twin, 2 double, 1 family, most en-suite, No smoking, Children over 4, No pets, Open March - November, Map Ref G

Treglisson, Hayle, Cornwall TR27 5JT　　　Nearest Road A30

Situated in the quiet Cornish countryside, Treglisson, a listed 18th century former mine captain's home, offers pretty en-suite rooms with comfortable beds, colour TV, tea/coffee making facilities, hair dryers and fresh flowers. Start the day with a swim in the indoor heated pool before tucking into a hearty breakfast which is served in the elegant dining room or conservatory. St Michael's Mount, St Ives, Lands End and many more places are within easy reach of Treglisson.

Mrs C Runnalls
Tel: 01736 753141
Fax: 01736 753141

B&B from £21pp, Rooms 2 double, 2 family, 1 twin, Open all December - October, Map Ref H

Mellan House, Coverack, Helston, Cornwall TR12 6TH　　　Nearest Road B3294

Mellan House stands in a large garden and is 5 minutes from a safe sandy beach. Fishing, boating and windsurfing are available and a golf course is 6 miles away at Mullion. Coverack is a beautiful small fishing village in an area or outstanding natural beauty. Bedrooms have sea views and garden views and tea/coffee making facilities, and there is a comfortable lounge with colour television available for guests' use.

Mrs Muriel Fairhurst
Tel: 01326 280482

B&B from £18pp, Rooms 2 double, 1 single, No smoking, Pets by arrangement, Open all year except Christmas, Map Ref I

Pennant Farmhouse, St. Veep, Lerryn, Cornwall PL22 0PB　　　Between Lerryn and Fowey

A large secluded 17th century country house, providing accommodation which is both comfortable and elegant. Spacious attractively decorated bedrooms with tea/coffee making facilities. Guest have the freedom of the large gardens in a quiet setting with stunning views over surrounding unspoilt countryside. An area of outstanding natural beauty with many footpaths, beaches and abundant wildlife. The riverside village of Lerryn and the harbour town of Fowey are nearby where pub/restaurant facilities may be found. Please ring for a brochure.

Judith Campbell-Taylor
Tel: 01208 873540

B&B from £18pp, Rooms 1 twin, 1 double, No smoking, Children over 12, Pets restricted to grounds, Open all year except Christmas & New Year, Map Ref K

Fieldhead Hotel, Portuan Road, Looe, Cornwall PL13 2DR

Turn of the century large country house by the sea with spectacular sea views. Set in beautiful terraced gardens with patios and swimming pool. All rooms en-suite, TV, tea/coffee making facilities, tastefully decorated and most with far-reaching sea views. The comfortable lounge, with huge bay windows and candlelit restaurant, serving fresh local produce and seafood, have views across Looe Bay. On site car parking and just an easy stroll along the waterside to the quaint town of Looe with its cobbled streets and pretty cottages.

Gill & Barrie Pipkin
Tel: 01503 262689
Fax: 01503 264114

B&B from £35pp, Dinner from £16.95, Rooms 3 twin, 9 double, 2 family, all en-suite, Children & pets welcome, Open all year except Christmas, Map Ref L

Penvith Barns, St Martin by Looe, Cornwall PL13 1NZ   **Nearest Road A387**

Bed & Breakfast with a difference in Grade II Listed 16th century converted barns exc en-suite facilities. Situated in acres of glorious countryside, close to coastal paths. Enjoy your breakfast in our galleried dining room. Penvith is ideally places for touring Cornwall and Devon. The historic port of Looe is just three miles away. EMail:: anne@penvith.demon.co.uk

Anne & Martin McQueen
Tel: 01503 240772
Fax: 01503 240772

B&B from £22pp, Rooms 1 twin, 2 double, all en-suite, No smoking, children or pets, Open all year, Map Ref M

Allhays Country House, Talland Bay, Looe, Cornwall PL13 2JB   **Nearest Road A387**

Set in extensive gardens just a few minutes walk from the sea. Allhays stands on a gently sloping hillside overlooking the beautiful Talland Bay. The emphasis is on comfort and the house is fully centrally heated and also has a log fire blazing in the lounge during colder weather. Most bedrooms have breathtaking views and are en-suite; all have tea/coffee making facilities, TV and telephone. Food is of a high standard and a new menu appears each day. Vegetarian and special diets can be catered for. An interesting selection of reasonably priced wines will complete your meal.

see PHOTO opposite

Brian & Lynda Spring
Tel: 01503 272434
Fax: 01503 272929

B&B from £29pp, Dinner £16.50, Restricted smoking, Children over 10, Pets welcome, Open all year except Christmas, Map Ref N

Harescombe Lodge, Watergate, Looe, Cornwall PL13 2NE   **Nearest Road A387**

Harescombe Lodge overlooks the upper reaches of the West Looe River, in the idyllic and peaceful wooded valley of Watergate. Set in its own gardens, with a swiftly moving stream, waterfalls and stone bridges, the Lodge was originally built in 1760. Now fully restored and modernised, it offers high standards of comfort with all bedrooms individually furnished, each with its own en-suite shower or bathroom and tea/coffee making facilities. All rooms have views of the river or stream.

Tel: 01503 263158

B&B from £18pp, Rooms 2 double, 1 twin, all en-suite, non-smoking, Open all year, Map Ref O

*left, **Allhays Country House,** Looe - see details above*

see PHOTO opposite

Coombe Farm, Widegates, Looe, Cornwall PL13 1QN   Nearest Road B3253

Relax in a lovely country house in a wonderful setting with superb views down a wooded valley to the sea. Enjoy delicious food, candlelit dining, log fires, a heated outdoor pool and warm, friendly hospitality. Nearby golf, fishing, tennis, horse riding, glorious walks, beaches and National Trust houses and gardens. RAC Small Hotel of the Year, South West England 1996, ETB 3 Crowns Highly Commended, AA QQQQQ Premier Selected. Credit cards Mastercard, Visa, Amex, Diners, Switch, Delta.

Alex & Sally Low
Tel: 01503 240223
Fax: 01503 240895

B&B from £28pp, Dinner from £16, Rooms 3 twin, 3 double, 4 family, all en-suite, No smoking, Children over 5, Open March - November, Map Ref P

Woodlands Guest House, Trewollock, Gorran Haven, Mevagissey, Cornwall PL26 6NS Nearest Road B3273

Woodlands, standing in an acre of south facing gardens with two spring-fed ponds, has magnificent sea views across open fields. Adjacent footpath links with Cornish coastal path (half mile). This family-run guest house offers Bed and Breakfast accommodation with tea/coffee facilities, TV's, most rooms are en-suite; ample parking. Packed lunches available to order. Impromptu barbecues - weather permitting. Close to Lost Gardens of Heligan and Charlestown. Ideal base for visiting the historic sites, gardens, animal sanctuaries and theme parks throughout all of Cornwall.

Dianne Harrison
Tel: 01726 843821

B&B from £20-£25pp, Rooms 2 twin, 2 double, 1 family, some en-suite, No smoking or pets, Children welcome, Open all year except Christmas & New Year, Map Ref Q

Mevagissey House, Vicarage Hill, Mevagissey, Cornwall PL26 6SZ   Nearest Road B3273

Mevagissey House, built as a vicarage in 1847, is superbly situated above the village with panoramic views over the valley and sea beyond. Each room is comfortably decorated and most have en-suite facilities. Tea/coffee makers and colour TV are provided in all rooms. A full English breakfast is served each morning. Licensed bar. The Lost Gardens of Heligan are 2 miles away and several National Trust properties and lovely beaches are nearby.

John & Gill Westmacott
Tel: 01726 842427
Fax: 01726 844327

B&B from £19pp, Rooms 1 twin, 2 double, 2 family, Restricted smoking, Children over 7, No pets, Open March - October, Map Ref Q

Trenance Lodge Hotel & Restaurant, 83 Trenance Road, Newquay, Cornwall TR7 2HW Nearest Road A3075

An attractive lodge standing in its own grounds overlooking Lakes and Gardens of Trenance Valley, leading to the Gannel Estuary. The restaurant has a reputation for serving the finest fresh local products in elegant surroundings. Adjoining the restaurant is a spacious relaxing bar lounge. There are five comfortable en-suite bedrooms with colour TV, radio, tea/coffee facilities. Outdoor swimming pool and terrace gardens. An excellent base for touring this beautiful and historic region and a warm welcome assured.

Mac & Jennie MacKenzie
Tel: 01637 876702
Fax: 01637 878772

B&B from £25pp, Dinner from £15, Rooms 1 twin, 4 double, all en-suite, Restricted smoking, No children or pets, Open all year, Map Ref R

*right, **Coombe Farm**, Looe - see details above*

Tregenna House, West Pentire Road, Crantock, Newquay, Cornwall TR8 5RZ   Nearest Road A3075

Tregenna House is situated in the picturesque coastal village of Crantock with it's splendid sandy beach and through which runs the coastal path. An ideal centre for touring Cornwall with nearby facilities for coarse and sea fishing, riding, surfing and golf. Ample parking. Guests are made to feel 'at home' beside log fires in winter or around the heated swimming pool in summer. Bedrooms are centrally heated and have tea/coffee making facilities and TV, most are en-suite. A warm welcome is provided with good home cooking and friendly atmosphere.

Sue & David Wrigley
Tel: 01637 830222
Fax: 01637 831267

B&B from £16-£17.50pp, Dinner from £9, Rooms 1 single, 1 twin, 1 double, 3 family, most en-suite, Restricted smoking, Children welcome, Pets by arrangement, Open all year, Christmas by arrangement, Map Ref S

Manuels Farm, Quintrell Downs, Newquay, Cornwall TR8 4NY   Nearest Road A392

A delightful 17th century farmhouse, surrounded by charming gardens and set in a sheltered valley, just two miles from Newquay's magnificent beaches. There is a country atmosphere in the stylish bedrooms, which have brass beds, window seats overlooking the garden and which are enhanced by antique and pine furniture. There is a lounge and a fascinating dining room with huge inglenook fireplace and an antique dining table around which guest gather for substantial farmhouse breakfasts. Jean provides local maps and books and can recommend places to visit.

Mrs Jean Wilson
Tel:/Fax: 01637 873577

B&B from £18.50pp, Rooms 1 single, 2 double, 1 family, most en-suite, No smoking, Children welcome, Pets by arrangement, Open all year except Christmas & New Year, Map Ref T

Degembris Farmhouse, St Newlyn East, Newquay, Cornwall TR8 5HY   Nearest Road A3058

The original manor house of Degembris was built in the 16th century and is now used as a barn. The present day house surrounded by attractive gardens, was built a mere two hundred years ago, and its slate hung exterior blends well with the rolling countryside over which many of the rooms have extensive views. Each bedroom is tastefully decorated and well equipped. Hearty breakfasts and traditional evening meals are served in the cosy dining room. Take a stroll along the farm trail wandering through woodlands and fields of corn.

Kathy Woodley
Tel: 01872 510555
Fax: 01872 510230

B&B from £20-£22pp, Dinner from £12, Rooms 1 single, 1 twin en-suite, 1 double, 2 family en-suite, No smoking, Children welcome, No pets, Open all year except Christmas, Map Ref U

The Old Mill Country House, Little Petherick, Padstow, Cornwall PL27 7QT   Nearest Road A389

The Old Mill Country House is a 16th century Grade II listed cornmill complete with waterwheel. Set in its own streamside gardens at the head of Little Petherick Creek just 2 miles from Padstow and in a designated area of outstanding natural beauty. The Old Mill is furnished throughout with antiques and collections of genuine artifacts to complement the exposed beams, original fireplaces and slate floors. This ensures that The Old Mill's original character and charm is retained.

Michael & Pat Walker
Tel: 01841 540388

B&B from £26.75, Rooms 2 twin, 5 double, all en-suite, Children over 14, Open early March - end October, Map Ref V

---

*right, **Ednovean House**, near Penzance - see details on page 86*

Cornwall

Woodstock House, 29 Morrab Road, Penzance, Cornwall TR18 4EZ   Nearest Road A30

Woodstock is a Victorian guest house situated in central Penzance just off the sea front and ideal for the Isles of Scilly ferry and heliport, and also the railway and bus stations. All rooms have TV, radio, hand basins and tea/coffee and many rooms have en-suite shower and toilet. A full English breakfast is served in the dining room and special diets can be catered for. To find us drive into the town past the railway station and along seafront. Turn right into Morrab Road as you approach the Queen's Hotel, 'Woodstock' is 200m on the right. ETB 2 Crowns Commended, RAC Accredited, AA QQQ. EMail: WoodstocP@aol.com

Cherry & John Hopkins
Tel: 01736 369049
Fax: 01736 369049

B&B from £15pp, Visa/Mastercard/Amex/JCB, Rooms 2 single, 3 twin, 3 double, 1 with 4-poster bed, 1 family, many en-suite, Children welcome, Open all year, Map Ref W

Con Amore Guest House, 38 Morrab Road, Penzance, Cornwall TR18 4EX   Nearest Road A30

Highly recommended and family run, we are ideally situated for just relaxing or for touring the Lands End Peninsula. We are situated opposite sub-tropical gardens and only 100 yards from the promenade and panoramic views over Mounts Bay and St Michaels Mount. All rooms have full central heating, colour TV and tea/coffee making facilities. All rooms are tastefully decorated with their own character. We offer a varied menu with all tastes catered for. There is a reduction for children sharing. ETB 2 Crowns Commended. EMail: KRich30327@aol.com Web Site: http://www.conamore.com

Carol & Keith Richards
Tel/Fax: 01736 363423

B&B from £11pp, Rooms 1 single, 2 twin, 3 double, 2 family, most en-suite, Children & pets welcome, Open all year, Map Ref W

Ednovean House, Perranuthnoe, Penzance, Cornwall TR20 9LZ   Nearest Road A394, A30

see PHOTO on page 85

Beautifully situated family run 160 year old Victorian house offering delightful, comfortable rooms, most having en-suite facilities and panoramic sea views. Situated in 1 acre of gardens and overlooking St Michael's Mount and Mount's Bay. It has one of the finest views in Cornwall. Relax in a comfortable lounge, library or informal bar and enjoy fine food and wines in the candlelit dining room. Car park. Ideal for coastal walks and exploring from the Lizard to Lands End. ETB 3 Crowns, AA Recommended QQQ.

Clive & Jacqueline Whittington
Tel: 01736 711071

B&B from £23pp, Dinner from £15, Rooms 5 double, 2 twin, 2 single, most en-suite, Pets by arrangement, Open all year except Christmas, Map Ref X

Long Cross Hotel & Victorian Gardens, Trelights, Port Isaac, Cornwall PL29 3TF   Nearest Road B3314

One of Cornwalls most unusual hotels, a character Victorian country house with a unique garden and its own free house tavern. The Long Cross has 12 en-suite rooms all with TV's and tea/coffee facilities, some ground floor rooms, some sea views. The hotel retains many of the original Victorian features and the Victorian gardens are open to the public. The free house Tavern is a popular drinking and dining spot with an extensive menu and a famous beer garden. Ideal spot for walkers, near surfing beaches.

Mr & Mrs Crawford
Tel: 01208 880243

B&B 3 nights from £50pp, Dinner available, Rooms 4 twin, 8 double, 3 family, all en-suite/private facilities, Children & pets welcome, Open all year except Christmas, Map Ref J

*right, **Anchorage House**, near St Austell - see details on page 88*

The Wheal Lodge, 91 Sea Road, Carlyon Bay, St Austell, Cornwall PL25 3SH   Nearest Road A38

The Wheal Lodge has a superb position just above the sea in an area of outstanding beauty. The hotel, which adjoins the coastal path and is opposite the golf course, is a lovely character residence with an old fashioned homely atmosphere. There is an attractive resident's lounge and spacious dining room with licensed bar. Bedrooms have en-suite facilities and courtesy trays, 5 bedrooms on the ground floor. Breakfast is either continental or full English. Delicious Cornish food is served. Ample safe parking within the grounds. RAC Highly Acclaimed, AA QQQQ. Runner up in the AA Landlady of 1998 Award.

Jeanne & Don Martin
Tel: 01726 815543
Fax: 01726 815543

B&B from £30pp, Rooms 1 single, 2 treble or twin, 2 double, 1 family, all en-suite, Restricted smoking, Children over 8, Open all year except Christmas, Map Ref 9

Anchorage House Guest Lodge, Nettles Corner, Tregrehan, St Austell, Cornwall PL25 3RH   A390

Every attention has been paid to the smallest detail in this impressive antique-filled house. The beautifully furnished en-suite rooms are supremely comfortable with king and super-king size beds, satellite television and many thoughtful touches throughout. The superb breakfast is taken in the elegant conservatory overlooking the private mature garden and pool. Steven and Jane combine wonderful hospitality and pleasing informality for a stay to remember as the bulging album of thank you letters shows. Perfect for visiting historic treasures, gardens and Heligan.

Jane & Steven Epperson
Tel: 01726 814071

B&B from £27-£32pp, Dinner by arrangement £22.50, Rooms 3 double, all en-suite, No smoking, children or pets, Open all year, Map Ref Y

Hembal Manor, Hembal Lane, Trewoon, St Austell, Cornwall PL25 5TD   Nearest Road A3058

Hembal Manor is a Grade II 16th century dwelling set in 6 acres of tranquil gardens. In 1569 Hembal was mentioned in the 'Feet of Fines'. Within the walled garden is a rare twin seater loo, reputed to be around 400 years old, well worth a visit! Tastefully decorated and furnished with period furniture to the highest standard. Bedrooms have TV, tea/coffee making facilities and central heating. A traditional or continental breakfast is served. A licensed bar to relax in after spending the day exploring the many places of interest. Easy access to the Lost Gardens of Heligan. ETB Highly Commended.

Sue & Mike Higgs
Tel: 01726 72144
Fax: 01726 72144

B&B from £25pp, Special rates available, Rooms 2 double, 1 twin, all en-suite, No smoking, Children over 12, No pets, Open all year except Christmas & New Year, Map Ref Z

The Old Vicarage Hotel, Parc-an-Creet, St Ives, Cornwall TR26 2ET   Nearest Road B3306

The Old Vicarage, secluded in wooded grounds in quiet residential area, is a lovingly restored Victorian rectory retaining the period ambience, but with every modern convenience, including full central heating. Lounge with extensive library and TV, well stocked Victorian bar with piano. Large choice of breakfast menu, including vegetarian, served in the elegant blue and gold dining room. Eight bedrooms, most en-suite, all with colour TV and tea/coffee facilities. Victorian conservatory massed with plants. Large garden with putting green, badminton, swing and car park.

Jack & Irene Sykes
Tel/Fax: 01736 796124

B&B from £19pp, Rooms 1 twin, 4 double, 3 family, most en-suite, Restricted smoking, Children & pets welcome, Open Easter - October, Map Ref 1

see PHOTO on page 87

*right, **The Old Rectory**, near Torpoint - see details on page 90*

The Grey Mullet, 2 Bunkers Hill, St. Ives, Cornwall TR26 1LJ　　　　Nearest Road A3074

The Grey Mullet is an 18th century Grade II Listed building centrally situated in the old fishing and artists' quarter of St. Ives. The house is full of interest and character with oak beams and granite walls hung with paintings and old photographs and offers a warm welcome in homely surroundings. The comfortable en-suite bedrooms some with 4 poster beds have TV and tea/coffee making facilities and there is a sitting room with an open fire. Ideal position to enjoy the harbour, beaches, many restaurants and the Tate Gallery.

Moira & Wally Batty
Tel: 01736 796635
Fax: 01736 796635

B&B from £21pp, Rooms 1 single, 1 twin, 5 double, most en-suite, Restricted smoking, Children over 12, No pets, Open all year except Christmas & New Year, Map Ref 2

The Old Borough House, Bossiney Road, Bossiney, Tintagel, Cornwall PL34 0AY　Nearest Road A39, B3263

The Old Borough House is a charming 17th century guest house in a prestige position in an area of outstanding natural beauty. All rooms are comfortably furnished and have tea/coffee making facilities and most have en-suite facilities. Guests have access to sitting room, TV and bedrooms at all times. Dinner a superb 3 course meal at 7pm. Coast path from Boscastle to Tintagel is probably finest in Britain. No matter what time of year, there are seabirds, and sometimes seals to be seen.

John & Christina Rayner
Tel: 01840 770475

B&B from £18pp, Dinner from £12, Rooms 1 twin, 4 double, 1 family, most en-suite, Restricted smoking, Children over 4, No pets, Open all year except Christmas & New year, Map Ref 3

The Old Rectory, St. John-in-Cornwall, nr Torpoint, Cornwall PL11 3AW　　　　Nearest Road A374

see PHOTO on page 89

Regency grade II listed country house with subtropical garden and millpond located by tidal creek. Set in a quiet valley of this 'forgotten corner of Cornwall' adjoining Woodland Trust land. This home, full of interest, allow guests time to reflect, to enjoy its understated elegance with its beautifully appointed and romantic bedrooms. A warm welcome, imaginative breakfasts and relaxing drawing room await our guests. Coastal Path walks, beaches, moors, golf, sailing and National Trust properties are close by. 4 miles from chain ferry.

Clive & Button Poole
Tel: 01752 822275
Fax: 01752 823322

B&B from £20-£25pp, Dinner by arrangement from £15, Light supper from £8.50, Rooms 1 twin/double, 2 double, all en-suite, No smoking, Children welcome, Pets by arrangement, Open all year, Map Ref 4

Rock Cottage, Blackwater, Truro, Cornwall TR4 8EU　　　　Nearest Road A30

Our 18th century beamed cottage was formerly the village schoolmasters home. A haven for non smokers, we offer comfortable, attractive en-suite rooms with central heating, colour TV, radio and beverage tray. Charming stone walled guest lounge always available. Breakfast is served in our cosy dining room with its antique Cornish range. Dinner by arrangement from A'la Carte menu. Situated in countryside village location 6 miles from Truro, 3 miles from the ocean. Parking and delightful gardens. ETB 3 Crowns Highly Commended. AA 4Q Selected, RAC Acclaimed. VISA, Switch, Mastercard accepted.

Mrs Shirley Wakeling
Tel: 01872 560252

B&B from £24pp, Dinner by arrangement, Rooms 1 twin, 2 double, all en-suite, No smoking, children or pets, Open all year except Christmas & New Year, Map Ref 5

Ventongimps Mill Barn, Ventongimps, Callestick, Truro, Cornwall TR4 9LH   **Nearest Road A3075**

Ventongimps Mill Barn is a tastefully converted mill barn of traditional Cornish slate and stone, situated in a quiet hamlet, nestling in a sheltered valley. A steam runs through extensive gardens and lake on our estate of some 7 acres of fields and woods. Local coastal paths, offer breathtaking views and the cathedral city of Truro is some 6 miles away. Evening meals served in our licensed bar with Portuguese cooking is a speciality. All rooms are en-suite and have TV. The coastal village of Perranporth with some 5 miles of sandy beaches is 2 miles distant.

Mr & Mrs Gibson
Tel: 01872 573275

B&B from £16pp, Dinner from £10.50, Rooms 1 single, 1 twin, 2 double, 4 family, all en-suite, Restricted smoking, Children welcome, Pets by arrangement, Open all year, Map Ref 6

Tregony House, 15 Fore Street, Tregony, Truro, Cornwall TR2 5RN   **Nearest Road A3078, B3287**

Tregony House is a Grade II Listed building on the main street of the thriving Roseland village of Tregony. All bedrooms individually furnished some with en-suite bathrooms, all with clock radios and beverage trays. Enjoy your freshly prepared meals using local produce wherever possible in our low beamed 17th century dining room with licensed bar. Relax in guests lounge with information on many National Trust Properties and Gardens - Heligan and Trelissick within easy reach. Large walled garden with off road parking.

Cathy & Andy Webb
Tel: 01872 530671
Fax: 01872 530671

B&B from £19pp, Dinner from £11.50, Rooms 1 single, 2 twin, 2 double, some en-suite, No smoking or pets, Children over 7, Open February - November, Map Ref 7

Manor Cottage, Tresillian, Truro, Cornwall TR2 4BN   **Nearest Road A39**

Manor Cottage is a pretty Regency period house situated in Tresillian, 5 minutes drive from Truro. Tastefully decorated bedrooms have TV's, courtesy trays and central heating. Our licensed restaurant is open Thursday, Friday and Saturday evenings, serving fresh local produce and homemade bread. Several of Cornwall's renowned gardens and National Trust houses, lovely walks, golf, fishing, tennis and fine beaches are nearby. Breakfast is expertly cooked by the chef proprietor and served in our lovely conservatory. Member of the Food Inn Cornwall Association. AA QQQ.

Carlton & Gillian
Tel: 01872 520212

B&B from £18pp, Dinner from £19.50, Rooms 1 single, 1 twin, 2 double, 1 family, Restricted smoking, Children welcome, No pets, Open all year except Christmas, Map Ref 8

Please mention
THE GREAT BRITISH
BED & BREAKFAST
when booking your accommodation

CUMBRIA

The dirt and grime of the Industrial Revolution at home, combined with revolution and the Napoleonic wars abroad, launched the Lake District into the limelight that it has been unable to avoid ever since. The Lake poets and artists eulogized, and the visitors came and went - and returned in ever increasing numbers - and little wonder. Cumbria, formed in 1974 from the ancient counties of Westmorland, Cumberland and the northern part of Lancashire, is of an ideal scale for the holiday maker. The characters of these three areas differ considerably, and the whole is a delight and offers the visitor an amazingly varied mixture of pleasures, all within a relatively small locality. Despite its many attractions and the fact that Cumbria's popularity draws droves of holiday makers, there are still the quiet open spaces, the tranquil villages and lonely fells that so entranced Wordsworth.

The major attractions of this wonderful area are the mountains, four of them over three thousand feet, include Scafell, the highest peak in England; and the lakes, of which there are sixteen, ranging from Windermere the largest at ten and a half miles in length, to Brotherswater only about half a mile long. Each mountain and lake has its own distinctive character and charm. Between the mountains are the spectacular passes, Kirkstone, Hardknott and Wrynose. Negotiating them is an experience not to be missed, although preferably not in high season, and the resultant views are stunning. There are climbs in these mountains to tax the expert, but there is also plenty of scope for the amateur, scrambling over the fells to their heart's content. It is of course vital to note the advice given on correct clothing and weather conditions - the weather here can change swiftly and dramatically. The lakes vary in character considerably, from the sombre Wastwater to bright and breezy Windermere, central to the main holiday

activities. Windermere in summer is alive with pleasure craft of all shapes and sizes, water skiers and of course the lake steamers which ply between Lakeside, Bowness and Ambleside. Bowness, with its landing stage crowded with rowing boats, shingle shore and swans has all the brash sparkle of a lively seaside resort, while Ambleside at the northern end of the lake with its quaint old Bridge House is a fine centre for walking. Stockghyll Force is only a mile away and the 'Struggle', no misnomer, leads to the Kirkstone Pass and the glories of Ullswater. Martindale in the valley to the south of Ullswater is reached along an alarmingly twisting road and must be one of the loveliest parts of the district, a few miles from the holiday traffic and yet wild and deserted. By Gowbarrow Park is Aira Force, a picturesque waterfall close by the hill from which Wordsworth saw his 'host of golden daffodils'.

The spirit of William Wordsworth pervades this district and there are few places he has not written lovingly about, and with good reason. Grasmere is of course the mecca for Wordsworth enthusiasts. Here in the little churchyard are the graves of the poet and his family, simple plain stones under the trees. William, his wife and sister Dorothy lived at Dove Cottage, just outside the village, where they entertained the literary giants of the day including Charles Lamb, Samuel Taylor Coleridge and Sir Walter Scott. Keswick, to the north, is a perfect centre for holiday walking. Situated on the edge of Derwentwater, the widest of the lakes, it is ideally placed for exploring glorious Borrowdale. Close by is the charming hamlet of Watendlath, the setting for Hugh Walpole's novel 'Judith Paris'. Here too is Ashness Bridge, one of the most photographed subjects in the Lake District. A close contender for this honour must be Friar's Crag, the headland on the eastern shore of Derwentwater, and declared by John Ruskin to be one of Europe's finest scenic viewpoints. Castlehead, half a mile from Keswick, gives wonderful views across Derwentwater and Bassenthwaite Lake. It was around Bassenthwaite that John Peel, the subject of the English folk song, 'D'ye ken John Peel' hunted. He is buried in Caldbeck churchyard.

Hawkshead has Wordsworth connections, being the village in which he lodged when attending its tiny grammar school. Beatrix Potter lived and farmed in the district and her house, Hill Top Farm at Sawrey attracts huge numbers of visitors each year. Above Hawkshead is Tarn Hows, one of the prettiest sights and giving superb views of the Langdale Pikes, Fairfield, Helvellyn and Red Screes. It was on nearby Coniston Water in 1967 that Donald Campbell was killed attempting a new world water speed record. John Ruskin, who lived at Brantwood on the eastern shore of the lake is buried in Coniston churchyard.

There are four 'gateways' to this quite extraordinary district - Kendal in the south, the 'auld grey town' of limestone houses, home of Henry Vlll's sixth wife Catherine Parr; Appleby in the east, the ancient county town of Westmorland, renowned for its June horse fair and gypsy gathering; Cockermouth to the west, birthplace of Wordsworth, and Carlisle in the north, a fine cathedral city rich in the history of the border troubles.

The Cumbrian coastline suffers from the proximity of its glamorous neighbour over the mountains and its industrial degeneration...a great pity as there is glorious scenery here, wonderful sands and fascinating villages. The major towns are shaking off their old image and there is a vibrant spirit of rejuvenation.

As if this district was not sufficiently endowed, it stands sandwiched between the Yorkshire Dales National Park to the south and the Northumberland National Park to the north - whichever way the holiday makers choose to go they cannot be disappointed.

Places to Visit

Brantwood, *Coniston* ~ the former home of John Ruskin, a 19th century art critic, writer and philosopher. His paintings and memorabilia can still be seen.

Dalemain, *near Penrith* ~ a Georgian facade with a medieval and Elizabethan structure behind. Rooms open to the public include a Chinese drawing room with hand painted wallpaper, a drawing room with 17th century panelling. In the outbuildings there are several small museums and the gardens have a shrub rose collection.

Dove Cottage, *Grasmere* ~ this is the home of William Wordsworth, where he spent most of his creative years. There is a museum in the barn with many of Wordsworth's artefacts.

Grizedale Forest Park ~ created by the Forestry Commission, it provides the visitor with plenty to do, there is a visitor centre which tells the story of the forest and information on walks and wildlife. There are also many nature trails on which roe and red deer and red squirrels can be seen.

Hardknott Pass, *Eskdale* ~ this is a gruelling mountain road with many steep gradients and bends; at the summit are the Roman remains of Hardknott Fort and a spectacular view of the valley below.

Hill Top, *Near Sawrey, Ambleside* ~ Beatrix Potter bought this little 17th century cottage in 1905, and it is where she wrote many of the Peter Rabbit books. She left the cottage to the National Trust in 1944 with instructions that the rooms should be kept unchanged.

Levens Hall, *near Kendal* ~ an Elizabethan mansion, built around a 13th century fortified tower. The famous topiary gardens were designed in 1694 by French horticulturist Guillaume Beaumont. The topiary trees are shaped into cones, spirals and pryamids and some are over six metres high.

Rydal Mount, *Rydal* ~ the Wordsworths moved here from Dove Cottage in 1813 and lived here until 1850. The gardens have a summerhouse where the poet often sat.

Talkin Tarn, *near Carlisle* ~ a sixty five acre lake in the Talkin Tarn Country Park. The lake has sandy bays and is ideal for boating and swimming and there are also many nature trails through woodland.

Ullswater, *near Penrith* ~ one of the Lake District's most beautiful lakes, stretching from the gentle farmland of Penrith to the dramatic hills and crags at the southern end. In summer, two restored Victorian steamers regularly sail between Pooley Bridge and Glenridding.

Wast Water ~ a mysterious black lake, it is edged on its eastern side by walls of scree over six hundred metres high. The eighty metre lake is England's deepest and whatever the weather it looks black. Boating on the lake is not allowed for conservation reasons but fishing is allowed with permits from the National Trust camp site.

Levens Hall

CUMBRIA

Bridge House,
Ambleside

Grey Friar Lodge Country Guest House, Clappersgate, Ambleside, Cumbria LA22 9NE Nearest Road A593

A warm personal welcome is extended to you by the Sutton family at their traditional Lakeland stone country house. An ideal countryside setting between Ambleside and the Langdales is enhanced by wonderful views and an established reputation for hospitality, comfort and imaginative home cooking. An RAC "Small hotel of the Year', AA Premier selected QQQQQ, ETB 3 Crown Highly Commended. Recommended by other leading hotel guides. Fully illustrated brochure on request. EMail: gflodge@aol.com England's Small Hotel of the Year 1997 - AA

Sheila & Tony Sutton
Tel: 015394 33158
Fax: 015394 33158

B&B from £23pp, Dinner available, Rooms 2 en-suite twin, 6 en suite double, Restricted smoking, Children over 12, No Pets, Open March - October, Map Ref A

2 Swiss Villas, Vicarage Road, Ambleside, Cumbria LA22 9EA Nearest Road A591

A small Victorian terrace house set just off the main road in the centre of Ambleside, near the church, in a slightly elevated position overlooking Wansfell. There is immediate access to the cinema and shops and the wide variety of restaurants and cafes in the town. There are three double bedrooms (one with twin beds) recently refurbished in the traditional style. Each room has central heating, tea making facilities and colour TV. A full English or vegetarian breakfast available. We are open all year round and you are sure of a friendly welcome and good home cooking. For Self Catering see page 493.

Mr D Sowerbutts
Tel: 015394 32691

B&B from £18pp, Rooms 1 twin, 2 double, Open all year, Map Ref B

Borwick Lodge, Outgate, Hawkshead, Ambleside, Cumbria LA22 0PU Nearest Road B5286

A leafy driveway entices you to the most enchantingly situated house in the Lake District, a very special 17th century country lodge with magnificent panoramic Lake and mountain views. Quietly secluded in beautiful gardens. Ideally placed in the heart of the Lakes and close to Hawkshead village with its good choice of restaurants and inns. Beautiful en-suite bedrooms include two king size four poster rooms. Rosemary and Colin welcome you to their Award Winning Lodge in this most beautiful corner of England.

Rosemary & Colin Haskell
Tel: 015394 36332
Fax: 015394 36332

B&B from £20pp, Rooms 1 twin, 4 double, 1 family, all en-suite, No smoking or pets, Children over 8, Open all year, Map Ref C

Riverside Lodge, Rothay Road, near Rothay Bridge, Ambleside, Cumbria LA22 0EH Nearest Road A593

A Georgian country house of immense charm and character offering superior 'B&B' accommodation in an idyllic riverside setting. All bedrooms have en-suite bathrooms and views of the river. Situated approximately 500 yards from the centre of Ambleside, midway between the centre and the head of Lake Windermere.

Alan & Gillian Rhone
Tel: 015394 34208

B&B from £23pp winter, £30pp summer, Rooms 1 twin, 3 double, 1 family, all en-suite, Restricted smoking, Open all year except Christmas, Map Ref B

*right, **The Fairfield**, Bowness-on-Windermere - see details on page 98*

Cumbria

Castlemont, Aspatria, Cumbria CA5 2JU   Situated on A596

Castlemont is a large Victorian family residence in some 2 acres of gardens with unrestricted views of the northern Lakeland Fells and Solway Firth. Built of Lazonby stone, Castlemont combines the best of old world gracious living with benefits of modern facilities Start your day with a traditional English breakfast or a selected oak smoked kipper, perhaps a poached egg with haddock or ham? Loads of toast, butter and marmalade with pots of tea or coffee, all made on the ever willing Aga cooker. Major credit cards accepted.

David & Eleanor Lines
Tel: 016973 20205

B&B from £17pp, Dinner by arrangement, Rooms 1 en-suite double, 1 twin, 1 family, No smoking, Children welcome, Open all year except Christmas & New Year, Map Ref D

The Fairfield, Brantfell Road, Bowness-on-Windermere, Cumbria LA23 3AE   Nearest Road A591

see PHOTO on page 97

Fairfield is a small friendly, family run, 200 year old Lakeland hotel found in a peaceful garden setting. 200 metres from Bowness village, 400 metres from the shores of Lake Windermere and at the end of the Dales Way (81 mile walk from Ilkley to Bowness). The Beatrix Potter exhibition is within easy walking distance. The well appointed and tastefully furnished bedrooms all have colour TV, hair dryer, a welcome tray and private shower/bathroom. Breakfasts are a speciality. Leisure facilities available. On site car parking. Genuine hospitality and warm welcome. EMail: ray+barb@the-fairfield.co.uk

Ray & Barbara Hood
Tel: 015394 46565
Fax: 015394 46565

B&B from £23pp, Rooms 1 single, 1 twin, 5 double, 2 family, all en-suite, No smoking, Children welcome, No pets, Open all year except December & January, Map Ref E

Lowfell, Ferney Green, Bowness-on-Windermere, Cumbria LA23 3ES   Nearest Road A591

see PHOTO opposite

This lovely lakeland house has been our home for almost ten years and we hope that you will be as happy and comfortable here as we are. Ideally situated in one and a half acres of sunny secluded garden, Lowfell is only five minutes walk to lake Windermere, Bowness village and open fells. Lots of restaurants, good shopping and a wealth of activities from sailing to ballooning nearby. The house is beautifully decorated and pretty bedrooms have TV, en-suite facilities and tea/coffee and biscuits. Splendid breakfasts and a warm welcome await you!

Louise Broughton
Tel: 015394 45612
Fax: 015394 48411

B&B from £25pp, Rooms 2 twin, 2 double, 1 family, all en-suite, No smoking or pets, Children welcome, Open all year except Christmas & New Year, Map Ref E

Parson Wyke Country House, Glebe Road, Bowness-on-Windermere, Cumbria LA23 3GZ   A592

Jean & David Cockburn would like to offer you a very warm welcome to their home, the former Rectory to St Martin's Church. Dating from 15th century, it is the oldest inhabited house in the area, being listed Grade II. Situated in 2 acres over looking the lake at Parson Wyke, it is approached by a private drive off Glebe Road, and affords a quiet haven only a short stroll from the hustle and bustle of Bowness. Rooms are tastefully appointed with many period furnishings and en-suite facilities. All are equipped with colour TV. Private access to lake.

Jean & David Cockburn
Tel: 015394 42837

B&B from £27-£37pp, Rooms 1 twin, 1 double, 1 family, all en-suite, Restricted smoking, Children welcome, No pets, Open all year except Christmas & New Year, Map Ref E

*right, **Lowfell**, Bowness-on-Windermere - see details above*

Courtyard Cottages, Warren Bank, Station Road, Brampton, Cumbria CA8 1EX — Nearest Road A69

You won't be staying in someone else's home but in one of our superb double bedded en-suite bedrooms in the courtyard of a Victorian mansion, providing total luxury, independence and privacy. Your day begins with breakfast served in your room allowing you to enjoy the personal service and attention to detail that you will only find at Courtyard Cottages. Explore Hadrians Wall, the Lakes and Scottish Borders or just use us as a stop over and be pampered as you travel North or South.

Janet Hempstead
Tel: 016977 41818

B&B from £25pp, Rooms 2 en-suite double, No smoking, children or pets, Open all year except Christmas & New Year, Map Ref F

Swaledale Watch, Whelpo, Caldbeck, Wigton, Cumbria CA7 8HQ — Nearest Road on B5299

Swaledale Watch is a busy sheep farm just outside the picturesque village Caldbeck, situated within the Lake District National Park. Enjoy great comfort, excellent food, a warm welcome and peaceful unspoilt surroundings. Central for touring, walking or discovering the rolling Northern fells. All rooms have private facilities, are tastefully decorated, have colour TV, radio, tea-tray, clean fluffy towels daily and books for every interest in the lounges. Walk into Caldbeck via the Howk, a wooded limestone gorge, guaranteed to be memorable. Your happiness is our priority.

Arnold & Nan Savage
Tel: 016974 78409
Fax: 016974 78409

B&B from £17pp, Dinner from £11, Rooms 2 double, 2 family/twin, 1 double/twin, all private facilities, No smoking or pets, Children welcome, Open all year except Christmas Eve, Day & Boxing Day, Map Ref G

Bessiestown Farm Country Guest House, Catlowdy, Longtown, Carlisle, CA6 5QP — Nearest Rd A7, B6318

see PHOTO opposite

AA, RAC & ETB Highly Commended. One of the nicest farm guest houses offering many of the delights of a small country hotel combined with the relaxed atmosphere of a comfortable family home. Peaceful and quiet. Delightfully decorated public rooms and warm pretty en-suite bedrooms with colour TV, radio and hostess tray. Delicious traditional home cooking using fresh produce when possible. Residential drinks licence. Touring base. Stop off for England, Scotland and N. Ireland. The indoor heated swimming pool is open mid May to mid September. Family accommodation is in comfortable courtyard cottages. Winner Cumbria for Excellence Bed & Breakfast 1998.

Jack & Margaret Sisson
Tel: 01228 577219/577019
Fax: 01228 577219

B&B from £22.50pp, Dinner from £11, Rooms 2 double 1 family, 1 twin, also 3 courtyard cottages, No smoking, Open all year, Map Ref H

Lightwood Farmhouse Country Guest House, Cartmel Fell, Cumbria LA11 6NP — Nearest Road A592

Lightwood is a charming 17th century farmhouse retaining original oak beams and staircase. Standing in 2 acres of lovely gardens with unspoilt views of the countryside. 2 1/2 miles from the southern end of Lake Windermere. Excellent fell walking area. All rooms are en-suite, tastefully decorated and furnished with central heating, tea/coffee making facilities and some with colour TV. Cosy lounge with log fire and colour TV. We serve a good high standard of home cooking with seasonal home grown produce. ETB 3 Crown Commended. RAC listed.

Evelyn Cervetti
Tel: 015395 31454

B&B from £23pp, Dinner from £13, Rooms 2 twin, 3 double, 1 family, all en-suite, Restricted smoking, Children welcome, No pets, Open February - November, New Year B&B only, Map Ref I

Bessietown Farm Country Guest House, *Catlowdy - see details opposite*

Lakeside, Bassenthwaite Lake, Cockermouth, Cumbria CA13 9YD Nearest Road A66

An elegant family run Lakeland house offering friendly and relaxing hospitality, having oak floors and panelled entrance hall. Superb views across Bassenthwaite Lake to Skiddaw and surrounding fells. Keswick is only a short drive away, also the peaceful western fells and lakes of Buttermere and Crummock Water. The tastefully furnished bedrooms are all en-suite and have TV, radio alarm, hair dryer and tea/coffee making facilities. A pleasant lounge in which to relax and delicious home cooking with a 4-course evening meal plus coffee and mints and wine if required.

Mr Steven Semple
Tel: 017687 76358

B&B from £20pp, Dinner from £12.50, Rooms 1 single, 2 en-suite twin, 5 en-suite double, No smoking, Children welcome, No pets, Open January - November, Map Ref J

Toddell Cottage, Brandlingill, nr Cockermouth, Cumbria CA13 0RB Nearest Road A5086

Toddell Cottage is a beautiful 300 year old listed Cumbrian longhouse situated within the National Park at Brandlingill. Close to the Lakes of Loweswater, Bassenthwaite and Buttermere. We pride ourselves on our hospitality and ability to make our guests feel at home. The breakfast table overflows with lots of different ideas and dinner is a 3 course treat with vegetarian alternatives and can be enjoyed with wine from our specially selected list. Oak beams, log fires, stunning views, absolute tranquillity. Welcomes don't come any warmer!

Janet & Mike Wright
Tel: 01900 828696
Fax: 01900 828696

B&B from £18.50pp, Dinner from £13.50, Rooms 1 single, 1 double, 1 family, 2 en-suite, No smoking or pets, Children over 5, Open all year, Map Ref K

New House Farm, Lorton, nr Cockermouth, Cumbria CA13 9UU Nearest Road B5289

This is the 'real lakes' with all the peace and beauty of the fells, valleys and lakes but without the crowds. This 17th century Grade II listed farmhouse offers very comfortable accommodation. Bedrooms are all en-suite with many little extras. There are two residents lounges, both with open fires and a cosy dining room where delicious five course evening meals are served and hearty breakfasts enjoyed in the morning. Fabulous views from every window. AA 5Q Premier Selected. 1994 Which? Cumbrian Hotel of the Year.

Hazel Hatch
Tel: 01900 85404
Fax: 01900 85404

B&B from £35pp, Dinner from £20, Rooms 1 twin, 2 double, all en-suite, No smoking, Children over 12, Pets by prior arrangement, Open all year, Map Ref L

Greenacres Country Guest House, Lindale, Grange-over-Sands, LA11 6LP Nearest Road A590

A friendly and relaxed atmosphere is assured at our lovely 19th century cottage at the foot of the beautiful Winster Valley in the National Park village of Lindale, 2 miles from Grange-over-Sands and 6 miles from the southern shores of Lake Windermere. 2 golf courses nearby. Our luxury bedrooms all have full en-suite facilities, TV, hair dryer, tea and coffee, and many thoughtful extras. Lovely conservatory and cosy lounge with log fire for the cold winter nights. Excellent home cooking. Licenced. ETB 3 Crowns Highly Commended. No smoking. Diets catered for.

Barbara & Ray Pettit
Tel: 015395 34578
Fax: 015395 34578

B&B from £24pp, Dinner from £12.50, Rooms 1 single, 1 twin, 2 double, 1 family, all en-suite, No smoking, Children welcome, No Pets, Open all year except Christmas & New Year, Map Ref M

Ryelands, Grasmere, Cumbria LA22 9SU Nearest Road A591

Ryelands, a delightful Victorian country house in 3 acres of peaceful and pleasant gardens on the edge of one of the most beautiful villages in Lakeland. Your friendly, helpful hosts have lovingly restored their home to create elegant, spacious and comfortable rooms for discerning guests, the perfect retreat from which to enjoy the Lake District. You can walk from the house into the beautiful countryside, relax as you row round the Lake or make a pilgrimage to Wordsworth's Homes. Exclusively for non smokers. Brochure available.

Lyn & John Kirkbride
Tel: 015394 35076
Fax: 015394 35076

B&B from £30pp, Rooms 3 double, all en-suite, No smoking or pets, Children over 10, Open March - October, Map Ref N

Woodland Crag, How Head Lane, Grasmere, Cumbria LA22 9SG Nearest Road A591

A warm welcome and an informal atmosphere are found in this delightful house, situated on the edge of Grasmere, near Dove Cottage. Secluded but with easy access to all facilities. The accommodation has five tastefully decorated bedrooms, all with individual character and wonderful views of the lake, fells or gardens. Ideal for walking and centrally placed for the motorist. Enclosed parking. Tea/coffee making facilities. Guest lounge. TV in bedrooms. Totally non smoking.

John & Ann Taylor
Tel: 015394 35351

B&B from £25pp, Rooms, 2 single, 1 twin, 2 double, most en-suite, No smoking, Children over 12, No pets, Open all year, Map Ref N

Burrow Hall, Plantation Bridge, near Kendal, Cumbria LA8 9JR Nearest Road A591

Although built in 1648, this delightful guest house offers modern day comforts. It is situated amidst open countryside, mid-way between Kendal and Windermere on the A591, yet only 10 miles from junction 36 on the M6. All 4 en-suite bedrooms which centrally heated, have colour TV, tea/coffee making facilities, radio alarm and hair dryer and are all tastefully decorated. There is a well furnished guests lounge. ETB 2 Crowns Highly Commended, AA QQQQ. A warm and friendly welcome is assured.

Maureen & Jack Craig
Tel: 01539 821711

B&B from £20pp, Rooms 3 double, 1 twin, No pets, No smoking, Open all year, Map Ref P

Low Plain Farmhouse, Brigsteer, nr Kendal, Cumbria LA8 8AX Nearest Road A5074

Low Plain is a charming guesthouse full of character, set completely on its own in the heart of rural countryside yet only half a mile from the picturesque hamlet of Brigsteer and just 3 miles from the bustling market town of Kendal. The farmhouse has recently undergone refurbishment providing 2 double bedrooms and one twin all with en-suite shower rooms, colour TV's and tea and coffee making facilities. For your evening meal, there are several country pubs and eating houses, all within a stone's throw.

Mrs Jean MacBeth
Tel: 015395 68464

B&B from £22.50pp, Rooms 1 twin, 2 double, all en-suite, Restricted smoking, Children welcome, No pets, Open Easter - October, Map Ref O

Cumbria

Garnett House Farm, Burneside, Kendal, Cumbria LA9 5SF **Nearest Road A591**

Garnett House Farm is an AA QQQ RAC acclaimed 15th century farmhouse on a large dairy and sheep farm, just 1/2 mile from the A591 Kendal to Windermere road. All bedrooms have colour TV, radio, tea/coffee making facilities, and most are en-suite. The guests' lounge has 4ft thick walls and 16th century oak panelling. Old beams and an old oak spice cupboard in the dining room where you are served at separate tables. Good parking, close to village and public transport. Lovely views and many country walks from the farm. 6 miles to Windermere.

Mrs Sylvia Beaty
Tel: 01539 724542

B&B from £16pp, Dinner from £9, 3 night breaks during Nov - March from £48, Rooms 5 double and family, no pets, Open all year except Christmas, Map Ref P

Higher House Farm, Oxenholme Lane, Natland, Kendal, Cumbria LA9 7QH **Nearest Road M6 J36, A65**

Higher House Farm is a 17th century beamed farmhouse situated in the tranquil village of Natland. 1 Mile south of Kendal. Ideal for visiting the Lake District, Yorkshire Dales. 6 miles from M6/J36, 9 miles from Windermere. Easy access Oxenholme mainline station (5 minutes by taxi). We welcome you to our comfortable Bed and Breakfast. Central heated, all rooms en-suite, colour TV, tea/coffee facilities in each bedroom. Delightful four poster. Delicious full English breakfast and the luxury of log fires in winter. 3 Crowns Highly Commended, 4 Q's AA Selected. Top Twenty Landlady of the Year AA.

Mrs Val Sunter
Tel: 015395 61177
Fax: 015395 61520

B&B from £22.50-£25pp, Dinner from £8.50, Rooms 1 twin, 2 double, all en-suite, No smoking or pets, Children over 12, Open all year except Christmas, Map Ref Q

The Glen, Oxenholme, Kendal, Cumbria LA9 7RF **Nearest Road Junct 36 M6, A65**

The Glen is a small family run guest house situated in its own grounds in a quiet location on the outskirts of Kendal with ample parking. It is in an idyllic position, affording easy access to the Lake District and Yorkshire Dales, but just a 5 minute walk from Oxenholme main line station and within easy reach of the M6. All rooms are en-suite with colour TV, tea making facilities and central heating. Attractive decor, fabrics and furnishing. Cumbria Tourist Board 2 Crowns Commended.

Christine Green
Tel: 01539 726386

B&B from £20pp, Dinner from £11, Rooms 2 double, 1 family, all en-suite, No smoking or pets, Children over 12, Open January - November, Map Ref R

Tranthwaite Hall, Underbarrow, near Kendal, Cumbria LA8 8HG **Nearest Road M6, A6**

This magnificent farmhouse dates from the 11 century. Beautiful oak beams, doors and rare antique black iron fire range. Tastefully modernised with full central heating. Pretty en-suite bedrooms with tea/coffee making facilities, hair dryer and radio. Attractive decor, fabrics and furnishings. This dairy sheep farm has an idyllic setting in a small picturesque village between Kendal and Windermere up an unspoilt country lane where wild flowers, deer and other wildlife can be seen. Many good country pubs and inns nearby. Cumbria Tourist Board Highly Commended.

Mrs D M Swindlehurst
Tel: 015395 68285

B&B from £20pp, Rooms 2 double, 1 twin, 1 family room, all en-suite, No smoking, Open all year, Map Ref Y

104

*right, **Dale Head Hall**, near Keswick - see details on page 106*

Thornleigh, 23 Bank Street, Keswick, Cumbria CA12 5JZ Nearest Road A591

Thornleigh is a traditional Lakeland stone building situated in the town of Keswick. The attractive, en-suite bedrooms have TV and tea/coffee making facilities and are situated at the rear of the building and generally free from the sound of traffic. All the rooms have magnificent views over the mountains and fells, thus making Thornleigh an idyllic base for walking or touring the Northern Lakes. The charming hosts, Ron and Pauline, offer a warm welcome, advice on enjoying the many aspects of the surrounding area and delicious full English breakfast for all guests, old and new.

Ron & Pauline Graham
Tel: 017687 72863

B&B from £21pp, Rooms 6 double, all en-suite, Restricted smoking, not suitable for children, No pets, Open all year, Map Ref S

Willow Cottage, Bassenthwaite, nr Keswick, Cumbria CA12 4QP Nearest Road A591

We welcome guests to our tastefully converted barn where we have retained many original features, combined with stencilling, antique pine and patchwork quilts this gives a comfortable country atmosphere. Our bedrooms have teatrays, radio and are en-suite. We are no smoking and have no TV, but guests enjoy our books, music and games as they relax by the wood stove or in the cottage garden. Breakfast includes fruit, yoghurt, real bread, our own free range eggs. Country lanes beautiful with wild flowers, duck roam nearby.

Chris & Roy Beaty
Tel: 017687 76440

B&B from £20pp, Rooms 1 twin, 1 double, both en-suite, No smoking, children or pets, Open all year except Christmas week, Map Ref T

Dale Head Hall, Lakeside Hotel, Lake Thirlmere, near Keswick, Cumbria CA12 4TN Nearest Road A591

see PHOTO on page 105

Alone on the shores of the Lake Thirlmere, in acres of mature gardens and woodlands, stands this historic Elizabethan Hall. Now lovingly restored by the resident owners, into one of Lakeland's finest country house hotels. Dale Head Hall offers you a warm welcome, elegant accommodation (including a 4-poster) and award winning cuisine. Just north of Wordsworth's , Grasmere and the heart of the Lake District, Dale Head Hall is an idyllic starting point for exploring this most beautiful corner of England.

Alan & Shirley Lowe
Tel: 017687 72478
Fax: 017687 71070

B&B from £35pp, Dinner £27.50, Rooms 2 twin, 6 double, 1 family, all en-suite, Restricted smoking, Children welcome, No pets, Open all year except New Year, Map Ref Z

Scales Farm Country Guest House, Scales, Threlkeld, Keswick, Cumbria CA12 4SY Nearest Road A66

see PHOTO opposite

Chris and Caroline welcome you to stay at Scales farm, a 17th century farmhouse which has been beautifully renovated and converted. The farm is set on the lower slopes of Blencathra, just 10 minutes by car from Keswick and has wonderful open views to the south. All bedrooms are en-suite (2 ground floor) and have tea/coffee facilities, fridge and TV. The guests' beamed sitting room has a woodburning stove and a full choice breakfast is served in the attractively decorated dining room. Ample parking space and pretty gardens. ETB 2 Crowns Highly Commended. EMail: scalesfarm@scalesfarm.demon.co.uk

Chris & Caroline Briggs
Tel/Fax: 017687 79660

B&B from £24pp, Rooms 2 twin, 3 double, 1 family/double, all en-suite, No smoking, Dogs welcome by arrangement, Open all year except Christmas, Map Ref U

*right, **Scales Farm Country Guest House,** near Keswick - see details above*

Cumbria

The Ravensworth Hotel, 29 Station St, Keswick-on-Derwentwater, Cumbria CA12 5HH Nearest Road A591

Ideally situated near the town centre and all it's amenities the lake and lower fells are just a short walk away. Tastefully furnished en-suite bedrooms have beverage tray, and colour television. Start your day with our hearty breakfast, enjoy the lakes by day and then while away the evening in the Herdwick Bar or relax in the spacious lounge. Personally run for twelve years we now rank among the top small hotels in Keswick. RAC Highly Acclaimed. AA Premier Selected. ETB Three Crowns Highly Commended.

John & Linda Lowrey
Tel: 017687 72476

B&B from £16pp, Rooms 1 twin, 6 double, 1 family, all en-suite, No smoking, Children over 6 years, No pets, Open February - November, Map Ref S

Greystones, Ambleside Road, Keswick-on-Derwentwater, Cumbria CA12 4DP   Nearest Road A66

Greystones is a traditional stone built Lakeland House, Situated in a quiet location, overlooking the grounds of Saint John's Church and with excellent views of the surrounding fells. Keswick town centre is a few minutes walk away as is Lake Derwentwater and the open fells. The spacious, individually designed bedrooms each have their own private facilities, television, radio and hot drinks tray. We have a private car park. Greystones is Two Crown Highly Commended by the Tourist Board, AA QQQQ Selected and RAC Highly Acclaimed.

Janet & Robert Jones
Tel: 017687 73108

B&B from £23.50pp, Rooms 5 double, 2 twin, 1 single, No smoking, No pets, Minimum age 10, Open January - November, Map Ref S

Hipping Hall, Cowan Bridge, Kirkby Lonsdale, Cumbria LA6 2JJ   Nearest Road A65

see PHOTO opposite

16th century country house set in 3 acres of walled gardens on the Cumbria-Yorkshire borders, 2.5 miles East of pretty Kirkby Lonsdale, so an ideal base for touring both Lakes and Dales. Bedrooms are comfortably furnished (mostly antiques) with en-suite bathrooms, colour TV, radio, direct dial phones, tea/coffee making facilities. Guests can help themselves to drinks from a sideboard in the conservatory before dining together very informally at one table in the Great Hall. All dishes are freshly prepared by Jos, accompanied by three wines (optional) selected by Ian. 81/2 miles from M6 Junction 36.

Ian & Jocelyn Bryant
Tel: 015242 71187
Fax: 015242 72452

B&B from £42pp, Dinner £24, Rooms 2 twin, 5 double, all en-suite, No Smoking in bedrooms or dining room, Children over 12 years, Pets welcome, Open March - November, Map Ref V

The Old Rectory, Crosby Garrett, Kirkby Stephen, Cumbria CA17 4PW   Nearest Road A685

Little has changed at the Old Rectory since successive rectors etched their names in the glass window panes in the eighteenth century. This historic Grade II* Listed home is set in a secluded rural village. Relax in front of a log fire enjoy superb AGA cooking after a day walking or exploring Eden, Lakes or Dales two of the three bedrooms are en-suite and all are individually decorated and furnished with antiques. Peace, quiet and a real sense of history are guaranteed.

Anne McCrickard
Tel: 017683 72074

B&B from £20-£23pp, Dinner from £12.00, Rooms 1 twin, 2 double, No smoking, Children welcome, Pets by arrangement, Open all year except Christmas & New Year, Map Ref W

---

*right, **Hipping Hall**, near Kirkby Lonsdale - see details above*

Low Lane House, Newbiggin on Lune, Kirkby Stephen, Cumbria CA17 4NB Nearest Road A685

Low Lane House is a typical 17th century Westmorland farmhouse with a number of interesting features of historical interest. At the same time it has modern facilities to make for a comfortable stay. Guests have their own dining room and sitting room with colour TV. Bedrooms have radios, tea/coffee making facilities and electric blankets. Home grown vegetables and eggs from our own hens are offered whenever possible. We have a residents licence to refresh tired walkers or jaded motorists. M6 6 miles. AA Listed, QQQ Recommended.

Janet & Graham Paxman
Tel: 015396 23269

B&B from £18pp, Dinner from £12, Rooms 1 single, 1 twin, 1 double, No smoking or pets, Children over 8, Open April - October, Map Ref X

Hornby Hall, Brougham, Penrith, Cumbria CA10 2AR Nearest Road M6/A66

Hornby Hall was built about 1550 and is situated in tranquil countryside 1 mile off the A66, 3 miles south east of Penrith. It is a Grade II listed Building with many interesting features, full of antique furniture. All the bedrooms face south overlooking the garden. Guests have their own sitting room with log fire. The 16th century hall, now used as a dining room, has the original sandstone floor. Dinner must be booked in advance. Dry fly fishing on the River Eamont available. Ample car parking.

Mrs Ros Sanders
Tel/Fax: 01768 891114

B&B from £26pp, Dinner from £12, Rooms 1 single, 4 twin, 2 double, 1 family, some en-suite, Restricted smoking. Children welcome, Pets by arrangement, Open all year except Christmas & New Year, Map Ref 1

Near Howe Farm Hotel, Mungrisdale, Penrith, Cumbria CA11 0SH Nearest Road A66

A Cumbrian family home which is situated amidst 300 acres of moorland. 5 of the 7 bedrooms have private facilities and all have tea/coffee making facilities. Meals are served in the comfortable dining room and great care is taken to produce good home cooking with every meal freshly prepared. Comfortable residents lounge with colour TV, games room, smaller lounge with well stocked bar and for the cooler evenings an open log fire. The surrounding area can provide many activities and past-times including golf, fishing, pony trekking, boating and walking. Commended 3 Crowns.

Mrs Christine Weightman
Tel: 017687 79678
Fax: 017687 79678

B&B from £17pp, Dinner from £10, Rooms 3 double, 3 family, 1 twin, Also cottages to let sleep up to 7, Open March to November, Map Ref 2

The Old Vicarage, Mungrisdale, Penrith, Cumbria CA11 0XR Nearest Road A66

The Old Vicarage is a spacious late Victorian house of extreme charm and character with full central heating. It is situated in the unspoilt lakeland village of Mungrisdale which nestles at the foot of Souter Fell and Bowscale Fell. A pub and restaurant are near by, also walks to suit everyone from gentle strolls to energetic climbs and an abundance of wild flowers, birds and animals. Bedrooms are equipped with tea/coffee making facilities. There is a pleasant lounge with TV where guests may relax.

Gordon & Pauline Bambrough
Tel: 017687 79274

B&B from £20pp, Rooms 1 single, 1 twin, 1 double, 1 family, No smoking or pets, Children welcome, Open all year except Christmas, Map Ref 2

---

right, **Orrest Head House,** *Windermere - see details on page 112*

Rockside, Ambleside Road, Windermere, Cumbria LA23 1QA   Nearest Road A591

Rockside offers superb accommodation, and is situated 150 yards from Windermere village, train and bus station. All rooms have colour TV, tea/coffee making facilities, clock radios, telephone and hair dryer, most are en-suite. Large car park. RAC Acclaimed. ETB 2 Crowns. Help given to plan walks, car routes and activities. Choice of hearty English breakfasts.

Neville & Mavis Fowles
Tel: 015394 45343
Fax: 015394 45343

B&B from £17.50pp, Rooms,1 single, 2 twin, 4 double, 4 family, most en-suite, Restricted smoking, Children welcome, No pets. Open all year except Christmas, Map Ref 3

Haisthorpe House, Holly Road, Windermere, Cumbria LA23 2AF   Nearest Road A591

Set in a secluded area of Windermere yet only a few minutes walk from the village centre. Haisthorpe is the perfect location to explore this historic area. Convenient for the train/coach station where we offer complimentary transport by prior arrangement, we also have private car parking. All bedrooms are furnished and decorated to a high standard and offer colour TV with satellite channel, hospitality trays and hair dryers. Bed & Breakfast from £17 to £22pppn. ETB 2 Crown Highly Commended.

Mick & Angela Brown
Tel: 015394 43445
Fax: 015394 43445

B&B from £17-£22pp, Rooms 1 single, 1 twin, 4 double, 1 family, all en-suite, Restricted smoking, Children welcome, No pets, Open all year except Christmas, Map Ref 3

Orrest Head House, Kendal Road, Windermere, Cumbria LA23 1JG   Nearest Road A591

see PHOTO on page 111

Orrest Head House, Windermere, is a charming country house dating back to the 16th century. All bedrooms are en-suite and have colour TV, and tea/coffee making facilities. It is set in 3 acres of garden and woodland and has distant views to mountains and lake. Close to the station and village with very homely atmosphere.

Mrs Brenda Butterworth
Tel: 015394 44315

B&B from £22, Rooms 3 double, 2 twin, all en-suite, Rooms 3 double, 2 twin, Minimum age 6, No smoking, Open all year except Christmas Day, Map Ref 3

Fir Trees, Lake Road, Windermere, Cumbria LA23 2EQ   Nearest Road A591

see PHOTO opposite

Ideally situated midway between Windermere and Bowness villages, Fir Trees offers luxurious bed and breakfast in a Victorian guest house of considerable charm. Antiques and beautiful prints abound in the public areas, while the bedrooms, all having private bath/shower rooms, are immaculately furnished and decorated. Breakfasts are simply scrumptious and the hospitality warm and friendly. Indicative of quality and value for money, Fir Trees has been given a "highly commended" award by the English Tourist Board and is enthusiastically recommended by leading guides.

Mr & Mrs I Fishman
Tel: 015394 42272
Fax: 015394 42272

B&B from £22-£28pp, Rooms 2 twin, 4 double, 2 family, all en-suite, Children welcome, Non smoking, Open all year, Map Ref 3

*right, **Fir Trees**, Windermere - see details above*

Rosemount, Lake Road, Windermere, Cumbria LA23 2EQ   Nearest Road A591

Rosemount is a quality family run guest house offering warm hospitality and value for money. It is ideally situated midway between the charming villages of Windermere and Bowness-on-Windermere within easy walking distance of both. The tastefully furnished and comfortable bedrooms all have private facilities. Delicious breakfasts prepared from superb quality local produce. Ample car parking. NON SMOKING EMail: rosemt3739@aol.com

Steve & Helen Thomas
Tel: 015394 43739   B&B from £19.50 - £27pp, Rooms 4 double, 2 single, 1 twin, 1 family,
Fax: 015394 48978   Children welcome, No smoking, Open February - December, Map Ref 3

St John's Lodge, Lake Road, Windermere, Cumbria LA23 2EQ   Nearest Road A5704

A private licensed guest house situated midway between Windermere and the Lakes. Close to all amenities. All fourteen bedrooms have en-suite/private facilities, colour TV, tea/coffee making facilities. There is a comfortable resident's lounge and a beamed dining room where you can enjoy a fabulous four course dinner (optional) complemented by a good selection of wines. The resident chef/proprietor changes the dinner menu daily with a choice of four main courses including a fish and vegetarian dish. Nearby private leisure facilities available for guests. Parking available.

Barry & Sue Watts
Tel: 015394 43078   B&B from £18.50pp, Dinner 11.50, Rooms 9 double, 3 family, 1 twin, 1
                                  single, Minimum age 3, Open from February - November, Map Ref 3

Oldfield House, Oldfield Road, Windermere, Cumbria LA23 2BY   Nearest Road M6, A6, A591

Oldfield House has a friendly informal atmosphere within a traditionally built lakeland residence. Ideally situated close to Windermere village, yet off the busy main road and also convenient to explore the Lake District. All rooms are en-suite, have colour TV, telephone and tea/coffee making facilities, two have 4-poster beds. The guest house is centrally heated throughout with a comfortable lounge. There are drying facilities and a private car park. Guests have free use of Parklands Country Club which includes a swimming pool and sports facilities. EMail: oldfield.house@virgin.net

Bob & Maureen Theobald
Tel: 015394 88445   B&B from £20-£34.50pp, Rooms 2 single, 2 twin, 3 double, 1 family, all
Fax: 015394 43250   en-suite, No smoking, Children welcome, No pets, Open February -
                                  December, Map Ref 3

Kirkwood Guest House, Prince's Road, Windermere, Cumbria LA23 2DD   Nearest Road A591

Kirkwood is a large Victorian stone house situated on a quiet corner between Windermere and Bowness ideally situated for exploring the Lake District. All rooms are en-suite with colour TV, tea/coffee making facilities. Some rooms have 4-poster beds, ideal for honeymoons, anniversary, or just a special treat. There is a comfortable lounge in which to relax and for breakfast an extensive menu is offered including vegetarian and special diets (with prior notice). Help with planning walks and drives or choosing a mini bus tour is all part of the personal service.

Carol & Neil Cox
Tel: 015394 43907   B&B from £21pp, Rooms 3 twin, 3 double, 4 family, all en-suite,
Fax: 015394 43907   Restricted smoking, Children Welcome, Pets by arrangement, Open all
                                  year, Map Ref 3

The Chestnuts, Princes Road, Windermere, Cumbria LA23 2EF   **Nearest Road A591**

The Chestnuts offers a delightful home from home and a distinctly high standard of comfort and service. The house is a century old, enjoying both lovely gardens and private parking. There is a choice of five elegantly furnished bedrooms each adorned in striking pine, with sumptuous king sized four posters and standard king sized beds all with either en-suite showers, baths or ever luxurious corner baths, there will be a room here to suit you. All our guests have free use of nearby Parklands Leisure Club.

Peter & Chris Reed
Tel: 015394 46999
Fax: 015394 46999

B&B from £25pp, Rooms 5 double, all en-suite, No smoking, Children & pets welcome, Open all year, Map Ref 3

Braemount House Hotel, Sunny Bank Road, Windermere, Cumbria LA23 2EN   **Nearest Road A591**

Braemount House was built in 1879 and still retains much of its Victorian charm and character. Relax in pretty gardens with complimentary tea and cake for afternoon arrivals. We offer individually designed and comprehensively equipped bedrooms including a beautiful 4 poster suite. Start the day with our superb breakfast menu which includes scrambled egg with smoked salmon (an ever popular choice!) Alternatively take continental breakfast in your room. A quiet location only 5 minutes walk from both Windermere and Bowness. Private parking. A warm welcome awaits. AA 3Q. ETB 3 Crowns Highly Commended.

Janine & Duncan Hatfield
Tel: 015394 45967
Fax: 015394 45967

B&B from £23pp, Rooms 1 twin, 2 double, 1 family, 1 four poster, all en-suite, Exclusively non smoking, Children welcome, Pets welcome, Open all year, Map Ref 3

"I was doing that a year or two back, you know"
BELLE & BERTIE IN YORK

115

DERBYSHIRE & STAFFORDSHIRE

Important as these two midland counties were and still are industrially, they can also boast some of England's most picturesque countryside. The Peak District, designated in 1951 a National Park, was Britain's first National Park, covering an area of five hundred and forty two square miles, reaching as far north as the high ground between the industrial areas of Manchester and Sheffield. This is an exhilarating rolling landscape of rugged and wooded dales. Castleton, the nub of the Peak's caving district is superbly sited at the western entrance to the Hope Valley, with Peveril Castle towering over the village. Peak Cavern with its impressive entrance on the edge of Castleton is the largest cave in England. There are five caverns in all open to the public, one of them, Speedwell Cavern features an underground boat trip. Mam Tor, known as Shivering Mountain because of its frequent land-slips is a 1,700 ft. ridge topped by an Iron Age fort. This is magnificent walking, climbing and pot-holing country. Buxton is the undoubted capital of the district, an elegant Victorian Spa town. Its spacious terraces, particularly the beautiful Palladian Crescent by John Carr were built in direct imitation of those in Bath. The town is renowned for its music festival held since 1979 in late July/early August. At Matlock Bath in the Derwent Gorge, another former spa town, there are superb views and a cable car to the Heights of Abraham. The impressive National Tramway Museum is nearby at Crich. This wonderful scenery provides a fitting background to two of the country's most magnificent stately homes. Chatsworth House, landscaped by Capability Brown and Joseph Paxton for the Dukes of Devonshire, has in its grounds the famous Cascade and the Emperor Fountain. The house itself contains a breathtaking collection of furniture and art. Haddon Hall, the famous manor house, is in fact a twentieth century restoration. The oldest parts of the hall date from the thirteenth century with a fourteenth century banqueting hall and a remarkable chapel with fifteenth century murals. The fine oak and walnut panelled long gallery is early seventeenth century. Ashbourne, surrounded by lofty hills, is an attractive market town with Henmore Brook, a tributary of the Dove running through it.

Being on the fringe of the Peak District National Park it is an ideal centre for holiday makers wishing to explore this area. To the southwest is Derby, a modern city - created such by Queen Elizabeth in 1977 - but with a history stretching back to Roman times. Derby was the furthest point south reached by Bonnie Prince Charlie before his retreat in 1745 to his eventual defeat at Culloden. The city is renowned for Royal Crown Derby porcelain and in more recent days the manufacture of Rolls-Royce cars.

Much of the Peak District National Park lies in Staffordshire, and a couple of miles west of Biddulph on the lonely moors is a strange rock formation known as The Old Man of Mow. An eighteenth century folly was built on the summit, Mow Cop Castle, giving glorious views over the Cheshire Plains. At Biddulph Grange are rare shrubs planted amongst follies in an exotic Victorian garden. Stoke-on-Trent, the capital of North Staffordshire is in fact an amalgamation of six towns - Tunstall, Burslem, Hanley, Longton and Stoke, the 'five towns' made famous in the novels of Arnold Bennett, together with Fenton. Arnold Bennett was born near Hanley in 1867. Here in the 'Potteries' is created the wonderful fine pottery and porcelain of Wedgwood, Minton, Copeland and Spode. For lovers of exquisite ceramics there is the Gladstone Pottery Museum, the Minton Museum, the Sir Henry Doulton Gallery, the Wedgwood Visitor Centre as well as the Etruria Industrial Museum and the City Museum and Art Gallery. For the more energetic and in lighter vein, just fifteen miles east is Alton Towers, the ruined home of the 15th Earl of Shrewsbury surrounded by probably Britain's most famous theme park. The lofty two hundred foot steeple of Cheadle's Roman Catholic church dominates this countryside, the church was designed by Pugin, one of the architects of the Houses of Parliament. Cheadle has some lovely half-timbered Elizabethan houses and is ideally situated for exploring the wooded Churnet Valley and the

two hundred and fifty acres of moorland and marsh of the Hawksmoor Nature Reserve.

The Black Country is not a name one readily associates with holiday pleasures but on its very doorstep is Cannock Chase, thirty thousand acres of wild parkland, originally an oak forest and a royal hunting ground since the days of the kings of Mercia. Through the years the woodland has been largely cleared to provide fuel for industry, leaving a heathland plateau. Nevertheless there are still fallow deer and some red deer left. Castle Ring, at eight hundred feet, gives superb views across the Chase. Stafford, on the River Stow, is an ancient town retaining some fine half-timbered houses. It was the birthplace of Izaak Walton the author of 'The Compleat Angler' and a perfect centre for visiting Cannock Chase. Abbots Bromley, renowned for its famous Tudor Horn Dance commemorating the granting of hunting rights to the folk of Needwood Forest, was the home of the Bagot family for four hundred years until they moved in the fifteenth century to nearby Blithfield Hall.

No visitor should leave this lovely area without visiting Lichfield. The beautiful cathedral with its three sandstone spires known as the 'Ladies of the Vale' was built in the thirteenth century. The Lady Chapel houses some magnificent sixteenth century stained glass from the Cistercian abbey of Herkenrode in Belgium. The city's most famous association is with Samuel Johnson whose statue faces that of his biographer James Boswell across Market Square. When Boswell rather disparagingly referred to Lichfield as a sleepy little place that seemed rather work-shy, Dr. Johnson retorted, 'it's a city of philosophers - we work with our heads!

The monuments to hard work are everywhere to be seen in these two counties, so too are sights to gladden the hearts of the most discerning visitors.

DERBYSHIRE &

Places to Visit

Arbow Low, *Derbyshire* ~ known as "the Stonehenge of the North', this stone circle dates from around 2000 BC and consists of forty six stones surrounded by a ditch.

Calke Abbey, *Derbyshire* ~ set in seven hundred and fifty acres of parkland with ponds and oak woods. The current house was built in 1701-1703 for Sir John Harpur, it has a stunning 18th century staircase. Attractive grounds with an 18th century orangery.

Chatsworth House & Gardens, *Derbyshire* ~ one of Britain's most impressive stately homes. Between 1687 and 1707 the old Tudor mansion was replaced with the Baroque palace. Capability Brown landscaped the gardens in the 1760's.

Kedleston Hall, *Derbyshire* ~ built between 1759 and 1765, the rooms feature many paintings. The park includes several original Adam buildings, a bridge, fishing pavillion and fine lakes with cascades.

Alton Towers, *Staffordshire* ~ the English equivalent to Disneyland with over one hundred rides of varying degrees. Entertainment for all ages, along with landscaped

gardens by Capability Brown.

Cannock Chase, *Staffordshire* ~ over twenty thousand acres of heath and woodland. Once a Norman hunting ground, it still has fallow and red deer and has been designated an Area of Outstanding Natural Beauty.

Shugborough Estate, *near Stafford* ~ a magnificient nine hundred acre estate of the Earls of Lichfield. The Park Farm, designed by Wyatt in 1805 houses a rare breeds centre and a working corn mill. There is also an eighteen acre garden with neo-classical monuments by James Stuart.

Wedgwood Visitor Centre, *near Stoke on Trent* ~ with displays of the works by Josiah Wedgwood from 1750 onwards. The skills of the potters are demonstrated and there is an opportunity to buy various pieces.

Haddon Hall, Derbyshire

STAFFORDSHIRE

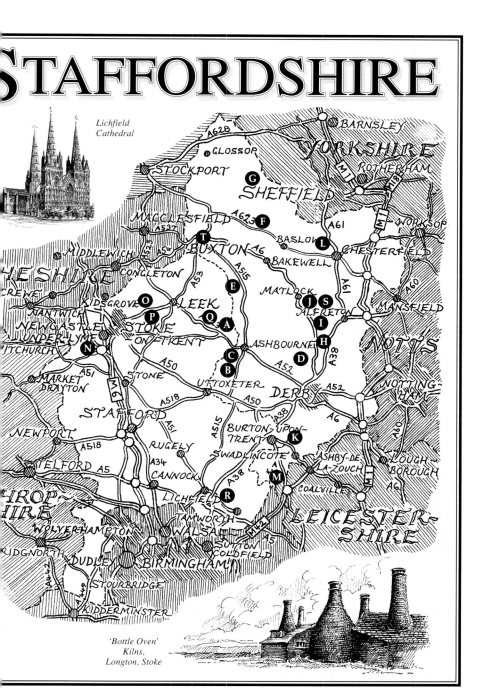

Lichfield
Cathedral

'Bottle Oven'
Kilns,
Longton, Stoke

Bodencote, Lynam Road, Wingfield Park, nr Alfreton, Derbyshire DE55 7LS   Nearest Road M1 jct 28, A38

Bodencote, which is approached via automated gates and a sweeping drive, is a welcoming Victorian country house, in peaceful surroundings, with wonderful views. Discerning guests will appreciate the high standards of food and comfort. For something-special, one room has a traditional half-tester bed, dress room and bathroom with luxurious Victorian bath, plus a complimentary bottle of wine! All rooms have TV, tea and coffee. Excellent breakfast, cooked on the Aga. Only 10 minutes from M1 - ideal for touring area or business. ETB Highly Commended.

see PHOTO opposite

Alan & Joan Bullock
Tel: 01773 853071
Mobile: 0402 377494

B&B from £20pp, Rooms 1 twin, 1 double, 1 en-suite double, No smoking or pets, Children over 10, Open mid January - end November, Map Ref V

The Old Rectory, Blore, near Ashbourne, Derbyshire DE6 2BS   Nearest Road A52, A523

On the Staffordshire/Derbyshire border, in the scenic Peak District National Park, is the tiny, tranquil hamlet of Blore, with magnificent views of Dovedale and the Manifold Valley, four miles from the old market town of Ashbourne. Nearby are many stately homes including Chatsworth, Haddon, Hardwick, Kedleston and Calke Abbey. Stuart and Geraldine Worthington, both well travelled, entertain with style and flair in their attractive stone built house with its gracious drawing room. Dinner is by candlelight with your hosts, in a formal house party atmosphere. Licensed.

see PHOTO on page 122

Mr & Mrs Stuart Worthington
Tel: 01335 350287
Fax: 01335 350287

B&B from £39pp, Dinner from £22, Rooms 2 en-suite double, 1 twin with private facilities, All with TV and tea/coffee making facilities, No children, No pets, Open all year except Christmas, Map Ref A

Beeches Farmhouse, Waldley, Doveridge, nr Ashbourne, Derbyshire DE6 5LR   Nearest Road A50

Relax and unwind in our rural retreat after exploring the Derbyshire Dales or the thrills of Alton Towers. Dine in our Award Winning 18th century licensed farmhouse restaurant on fresh English food and homemade desserts. Guests are invited to meet the Shetland pony, pigs, dogs, rabbits and kittens, whilst enjoying the freedom of the gardens, fields and the beautiful countryside. For the largest of families or the businessman, whether working, exploring or simply relaxing, Beeches offers a refreshing and memorable experience.

Barbara & Paul Tunnicliffe
Tel: 01889 590288
Fax: 01889 590559

B&B from £28-£42pp, Dinner from £13.50, Rooms 1 twin, 2 double, 7 family, all en-suite, Restricted smoking, Children welcome, Guide dogs welcome, Open all year except Christmas, Map Ref B

Rose Cottage, Snelston, Ashbourne, Derbyshire DE6 2DL   Nearest Road A515

A mid-Victorian house in 6 acres, Rose Cottage is a family house in quiet unspoilt beautiful and peaceful countryside. Bedrooms have panoramic views over Dove Valley towards the Weaver Hills, (George Eliot's Adam Bede Country). Ideal for visiting Dales, walking, country houses (Calke, Chatsworth, Haddon Hall, Hardwick, Kedleston, Sudbury)Potteries, Alton Tower (9 miles). TV, tea/hot drinks facilities in rooms. No evening meals but good country pubs nearby. Non-smokers please. Ample car parking.

Cynthia Moore
Tel/Fax: 01335 324230
Fax: 01335 324230

B&B from £22.50pp, Rooms 1 single, 1 twin, 1 double, all en-suite/private, No smoking or pets, Children over 12, Open all year except Christmas & New Year, Map Ref C

*left, **Bodencote**, near Alfreton - see details above*

Park View Farm, *near Ashbourne - see details on page 124*

left, ***The Old Rectory,*** *near Ashbourne - see details on page 121*

Stanshope Hall, Stanshope, near Ashbourne, Derbyshire DE6 2AD   Nearest Road A515

Stanshope Hall, dating from the 16th century, stands on the brow of a hill between the Manifold and Dovedale in the Peak District. The hall faces south across rolling landscape. Lovingly restored and retaining many of its original features. All bedrooms are en-suite with direct dial phone and tea/coffee making facilities. There is a guests' drawing room with piano and record player and local information table. Centrally heated throughout. Home cooked dinners with garden and local produce and a residents licence. Extensive breakfast menu. Brochure available.

Naomi Chambers & Nick Lourie
Tel: 01335 310278
Fax: 01335 310470

B&B from £25pp, Dinner £18, Rooms 1 twin with en-suite facilities, 2 en-suite double, Restricted smoking, Open all year except Christmas, Map Ref A

Park View Farm, Weston Underwood, Ashbourne, Derbyshire DE6 4PA   Nearest Road A38

see PHOTO on page 123

Enjoy country house hospitality in our elegant farmhouse set in large gardens with lovely views overlooking the National Trust's magnificent Kedleston Park, hence the farm's name. Double en-suite rooms with romantic antique four poster beds and drinks facilities. Guests own sitting room. Delicious breakfasts served in the delightful dining room. Country pubs and restaurants close by. English Tourist Board 2 Crown Highly Commended. AA QQQQQ Premier Selected.

Michael & Linda Adams
Tel: 01335 360352
Fax: 01335 360352

B&B from £25pp, Rooms 3 double, all en-suite, No smoking or pets, Children over 6, Open all year except Christmas, Map Ref D

Grosvenor House Hotel, 1 Broad Walk, Buxton, Derbyshire SK17 6JE   Nearest Road A6

Privately run, licensed hotel in quiet centre of historical spa town enjoying spectacular views overlooking 23 acres of gardens and Opera House. Bedrooms, both standard and deluxe are tastefully decorated, en-suite and non-smoking with colour TV, radio/alarm and hospitality tray. Our charming lounge and dining room offer a home-from-home atmosphere with panoramic views. Excellent hearty breakfast. Wide choice of restaurants and pubs within short walking distance. Scenic countryside, Chatsworth and Haddon Hall nearby. ETB 3 Crown Commended, AA 4Q's Selected and 'Which' Recommended.

Graham & Anne Fairbairn
Tel: 01298 72439

B&B from £25pp, Rooms 1 twin, 5 double, 2 family, all en-suite, Restricted smoking, children from 8, Guide dogs only, Open all year, Map Ref C

Biggin Hall, Biggin-by-Hartington, Buxton, Derbyshire SK17 0DH   Nearest Road A515

see PHOTO opposite

Beautifully restored, this stone built house dating from the 17th century, set 1,000 feet up in the Peak District National park, is delightful in every way. Antiques, a log fire, a 4 poster bed give this home a wealth of charm. The food is outstanding with the owners priding themselves on the use of only the freshest and best produce available. The home baked bread is excellent! Perfect in every way. Easy access to the Spa town of Buxton, Chatsworth House, Haddon Hall, etc. Beautiful uncrowded footpaths from the grounds.

Mr J M Moffett
Tel: 01298 84451

B&B from £24.50pp, Dinner from £14.50, Rooms and Apartments, Minimum age 12, Open all year, Map Ref E

*right, **Biggin Hall**, near Buxton - see details above*

Delf View House, Church Street, Eyam, Derbyshire S32 5QH　　　　**Nearest Road A623**

Tranquil and relaxing accommodation in an elegant Georgian country house in historic Eyam, centrally located in the magnificent Peak National Park. Antique furniture, original paintings and books provide a wonderful ambience in the three spacious bedrooms as well as in the guests' drawing room where complimentary tea is served on arrival. Superb breakfasts in the 17th century beamed dining room are a splendid start for walking or for visiting stately Chatsworth, Haddon, Hardwick and Eyam Hall. Hospitality trays and television in all bedrooms. Private parking. EMail: lewis@delfview.demon.co.uk

David & Meirlys Lewis
Tel: 01433 631533
Fax: 01433 631972

B&B from £25pp, Rooms 1 twin, 2 double, all en-suite, No smoking, children or pets, Open all year, Map Ref F

Underleigh Country Guest House, Edale Road, Hope, Hope Valley S33 6RF　　**A6187 (formally A625)**

This immacutaley maintained house situated quietly on hillside, all rooms have been lovingly refurbished. Each room is en-suite and has colour television, tea/coffee facilities, hair dryers etc. and resident Teddy bear. All have wonderful countryside or garden views. New for this year is a lovely suite for the discerning guest. Renowned for house party dinners from owner/chef, Anton. Situated ideally for visiting the beautiful area either on foot or by car, also Chatsworth, Haddon and Eyam Halls are within half an hour drive. EMail: Underleigh.House@btinternet.com

Mr & Mrs A.C. Singleton
Tel: 01433 621372
Fax: 01433 621324

B&B from £32pp, Dinner from £17.50, Rooms 2 twin, 4 double, 1 suite, all en-suite, No smoking or pets, Children over 12, Open all year, Map Ref G

Mount Tabor House, Bowns Hill, Crich, Matlock, Derbyshire DE4 5DG　　**Nearest Road A6**

Once a chapel, Mount Tabor has been fully restored, creating light and space throughout. The en-suite bedrooms are well furnished with hospitality tray, colour TV/video. One has an extra long king size bed, the other is either a twin or king size double with a spacious bathroom. Freshly prepared meals using local and organic produce are taken overlooking the verdant Amber valley. Mount Tabor specialises in vegetarian and vegan cooking. Central heating throughout. Chatsworth, Hardwick and Kedleston houses nearby as are National Tramway, Royal Crown Derby and Wingfield Manor.

Mrs Whitehead
Tel: 01773 857008
Mobile: 0468 438890

B&B from £25pp, Dinner from £14.50, Rooms 1 twin, 1 double, 1 family, all en-suite/private, No smoking or pets, Children welcome, Open all year except Christmas & New Year, Map Ref H

Littlemoor Wood Farm, Littlemoor Lane, Riber, near Matlock, Derbyshire DE4 5JS　　**Nearest Road A615**

This peaceful and informal farmhouse lies at the edge of the Derbyshire Dales and the Peak Park. Set among 20 acres of meadows with wonderful open views it is the perfect place to unwind. Rooms are attractive and comfortable with TV and tea/coffee trays. We provide hearty breakfasts including home-produced bacon and sausages, and cater for vegetarian and special diets. Many stately homes including Chatsworth House and other popular places of interest are nearby. Ashbourne, Bakewell and M1 Junction 28 all within 20 minutes. EMail: Groommatlock@compuserve.com

Simon & Gilly Groom
Tel/Fax: 01629 534302

B&B from £20pp, Dinner from £11.50, Rooms 1 double/twin, 1 double both with private facilities, 1 single/twin, No smoking, Children over 8, Open all year except Christmas & New Year, Map Ref I

Lane End House, Green Lane, Tansley, near Matlock, Derbyshire DE4 5FJ   **Nearest Road A615**

A non-smoking Georgian farmhouse (c 1730) which, since 1990, has been lovingly brought by Marion and David Smith, to its present standard of exceptionally comfortable and attractive accommodation. The house is set in delightful gardens, with waterfalls, a fish pond, surrounded by countryside and overlooking Riber Castle. Quietness personified! 4 bedrooms including downstairs, all en-suite/private facilities with private guests' sitting room. Dogs welcome. Chatsworth, Haddon, Hardwick, Calke and Kedleston await, with walking in Dovedale, Tissington and High Peak Trails. AA Selected 4Q Award.

Marion & David Smith
Tel: 01629 583981
Fax: 01629 583981

B&B from £23pp, Rooms 1 twin, 3 double, all en-suite/private facilities, No smoking, Children & pets welcome, Open all year except Christmas & New Year, Map Ref J

Bower Lodge, Well Lane, Repton, Derbyshire DE65 6EY   **Nearest Road Repton High Street**

Beautifully furnished Victorian house in quiet location near village centre. The comfortable bedrooms are equipped with tea/coffee making facilities and TV. There is a pleasant lounge where guests may relax. Ideally suited for visiting Chatsworth House, Kedleston Hall, Calke Abbey, Alton Towers, Donington Park Race Track, Melbourne Hall and Sudbury Hall. East Midlands Airport and Birmingham Airport are within easy reach as is The National Exhibition Centre. The premises are licensed.

Elizabeth & Peter Plant
Tel: 01283 702245
Fax: 01283 704361

B&B from £25pp, Dinner £17.50, Rooms 1 single, 2 twin/double private facilities, 1 en-suite double, Children welcome, Open all year except Christmas, New Year & Easter, Map Ref K

Springwood House, Cowley Lane, Holmesfield, Sheffield, Derbyshire S18 7SD   **Nearest Road M1**

Situated in 5 acres with beautiful open views of the surrounding countryside in a peaceful location. On the edge of the Peak District National Park, yet within easy reach of Sheffield, Chesterfield - the M1. Golf, horse riding, trout fishing and walking are easily accessible. A wide variety of local hostelries serve excellent food. Springwood is furnished to a high standard. A warm welcome awaits each guest.

Mrs Avril Turner
Tel: 0114 289 0253
Fax: 0114 289 1365

B&B from £22.50pp, Rooms 1 twin en-suite, 1 double with private facilities, Restricted smoking, Children welcome, Pets by arrangement, Open all year except Christmas & New Year, Map Ref L

The Old Hall, Netherseal, near Swadlincote, Derbyshire DE12 8DF   **Nearest Road A444/M42 Jct 11**

The Old Hall is a Grade II* listed house dating from 1640 with an additional Edwardian wing. Originally a monastery, the house retains its unique character and original features whilst benefiting from all modern conveniences. The house is situated in 18 acres of beautiful mature gardens, woodland and open fields. Bedrooms are quiet, comfortable, spacious and attractively furnished. All have en-suite/private bathroom, colour TV and tea/coffee making facilities. There is a lake for fishing and a croquet lawn. There are a variety of pubs and restaurants locally.

Mrs Clemency Wilkins
Tel: 01283 760258
Fax & Ans: 01283 762991

B&B from £25pp, Dinner (3 Course £15), Rooms 1 single, 1 twin, 1 double, No smoking, No children, No pets, Open all year except Christmas & New Year, Map Ref M

Butterton House, Park Road, Butterton, Newcastle-under-Lyme, Staffordshire ST5 4DZ   M6 Jct 15

One and a half miles from junction 15 on M6 and on road to Wales. Visit pottery factory shops, Alton Tower, Chester, Peak District, Newcastle market town, Audlem locks, etc. Easy access to a lot of tourist areas. Georgian/Victorian house is pretty countryside. Large comfortable rooms, garden, tennis court and croquet lawn. As you leave exit 15 it is first right, 3 times then first house on right.

Sarah Jealouse
Tel: 01782 619085

B&B from £20pp, Dinner from £10-£15, Rooms 2 twin, 2 double, 1 family, all en-suite, No smoking or pets, Children welcome, Open all year except Christmas & New Year, Map Ref N

The Hollies, Clay Lake, Endon, Stoke-on-Trent, Staffordshire ST9 9DD   Nearest Road B5051, A53

A warm welcome awaits you in this Victorian house which has been sympathetically developed to its present comfortable standard. Situated in a quiet country setting in Endon and within easy reach of The Potteries, Staffordshire Moorlands and Alton Towers. Bedrooms are spacious, comfortable and have central heating, shaver points, colour TV and tea/coffee making facilities. The lounge and dining room overlook a secluded garden. There is a choice of breakfast and home made preserves. Private parking.

Mrs Anne Hodgson
Tel: 01782 503252

B&B from £18pp, Rooms 5 en-suite, double, twin or family, No smoking, Open all year Map Ref O

The Old Vicarage, Leek Road, Endon, Stoke-on-Trent, Staffordshire ST9 9BH   Nearest Road A53

A traditional Victorian/Edwardian former vicarage, in a quiet setting, with good sized rooms. The comfortable bedrooms have TV, tea/coffee making facilities, wash basin and hair dryer. Guests have their own sitting room which overlooks the front garden. Breakfast is served at a large single table and there is a varied menu. Nearby is the Plough Inn which serves good luncheons and evening meals. Places of interest to visit include The Potteries, Alton Towers, Peak Park and Staffordshire Moorlands.

Mrs I Grey
Tel: 01782 503686

B&B from £17.50pp, Rooms 2 twin, 1 double, No smoking, Open all year, Map Ref O

Micklea Farm, Longsden, near Leek, Stoke-on-Trent, Staffordshire ST9 9QA   Nearest Road A53

A lovely 18th century cottage set in pleasant gardens complete with swing for children. Micklea Farm is ideally situated for visits to Alton Tower, the Peak District and the Potteries. The food is excellent, much of which is home grown garden produce. There is a cosy sitting room with an open fire and the house is traditionally furnished and decorated. Whether relaxing or sightseeing this is an ideal base and a warm welcome is guaranteed.

Mrs Barbara White
Tel: 01538 385006
Fax: 01538 382882

B&B from £17pp, Dinner from £12, Rooms 2 single, 2 twin/double, No smoking, No pets, Open all year except Christmas, Map Ref P

Leehouse Farm, Leek Road, Waterhouses, Stoke-on-Trent, Staffordshire ST10 3HW   **Nearest Road A523**

Josie and Jim welcome you to their lovely Georgian farmhouse, providing excellent accommodation in the centre of a village in the Peak Park. Ideally situated for cycling, walking or touring the beautiful valleys of the Manifold Dove and Churret. Convenient for visiting Stately Homes, Alton Towers and the potteries. The business traveller will find it well situated on the A523. Midway between Derby, Manchester. Our spacious bedrooms are centrally heated with TV and tea/coffee making facilities. Private parking and secure parking for bicycles.

Josie & Jim Little
Tel: 01538 308439

B&B from £20pp, Rooms 1 twin, 2 double, all en-suite, Restricted smoking, Children over 8, Pets by prior arrangement, Open all year except Christmas Day, Map Ref Q

Oak Tree Farm, Hints Road, Hopwas, Tamworth, Staffordshire B78 3AA   **Nearest Road M42**

A country farmhouse with river frontage. Recently renovated to luxurious standards. Large, warm and welcoming bedrooms, all en-suite, with all comforts provided - sofas, courtesy tray, trouser press, hair dryer, iron, mineral water, etc. Set in the pretty village of Hopwas, between the River Tame and the fazely canal, Oak Tree Farm offers tranquil surroundings, but is very convenient for Tamworth, Lichfield, NEC and the Airport.

Sue Purkis
Tel: 01827 56807
Fax: 01827 56807

B&B from £30pp, Rooms 2 twin, 3 double, 2 family, all en-suite/private facilities, No smoking or Children, Pets by arrangement, Open all year, Map Ref U

"York sure is a nice little town!"
BELLE & BERTIE IN YORK

DEVON

Devon has many faces and its great variety of scenery and indeed climate makes it an ideal holiday county. The rugged northern coast, boasting England's highest cliffs, is a spectacular display of dark grey rocks moulded by the crashing beakers whipped up by Atlantic gales. In contrast the southern coast, the so-called Devon Riviera, is noted for its extremely mild climate, its lush vegetation and its sweep of golden sands. Between the two lies the stark desolate beauty of Dartmoor, a large part of which is designated National Park. There are so many diverse attractions in this glorious county that holiday makers are spoilt for choice no matter where they might be.

Bideford, once the most important port in North Devon (the great Elizabethan seafarer Sir Richard Grenville secured the town's first charter from Queen Elizabeth I) is now a busy holiday town with steep narrow streets and a quite spectacular bridge over the River Torridge. Nearby is Westward Ho, named after the novel by Charles Kingsley, while adjacent is Appledore where the River Torridge meets the Taw, a delightful picturesque seaside village. Clovelly to the west needs little introduction, being one of the most photographed villages in the country, and further westward at Hartland Quay is some of the most dramatic coastal scenery with rock strata contorted into fantastic shapes, leading south to Welcome, a pretty village and home of the Rev. R.S.Walker who in the late nineteenth century wrote 'The Song of the Western Men'. Barnstaple was an important port for the wool trade until the River Taw silted up. Still a prosperous market town it has some lovely old houses and an impressive Long Bridge. Ilfracombe, which developed around an ancient fishing port during the nineteenth century, is the largest resort on the North Devon coast. Its beach of shingle with its many caves is overlooked by the town rising steeply in terraces. This lovely holiday centre is close to Exmoor with its two hudred and sixty five square miles of National Park. Great Torrington from its high vantage point above the River Torridge gives spectacular views over the countryside.

There is no denying that Dartmoor is a bleak place...this great expanse of windswept moor, the highest part of England south of the Pennines, is daunting with its granite outcrops known as Tors, its Bronze Age hut circles and its strange burial mounds, but it is wonderful walking, and of course riding country. Close by is a fascinating abandoned Medieval village and another viewpoint, Hound Tor. Widecombe-in-the-Moor is renowned for its large granite fourteenth century church known as 'the Cathedral of the Moor' and of course for 'Widecombe Fair' which is held each September....made famous by the folk song 'Uncle Tom Cobleigh'. The northern terminus of the delightful Dart Valley Railway is at Buckfastleigh. Benedictine monks took thirty years to build Buckfast Abbey a mile to the north of the village. Completed in 1938, the monks sell their tonic wine and honey in theirshop. Tavistock, the western capital of the moor, developed as a town around the tenth century Benedictine abbey. Crowndale Farm, a mile from Tavistock was the birthplace of Sir Francis Drake. Dawlish down to Brixham is regarded as the Devon Riviera. Here are bright blue seas, palm trees and resorts which attract visitors by the thousand and naturally such popularity ensures all the most modern amenities.

Here is yachting and sailing to match any Mediterranean resort. Torquay is the largest and most famous of the Devon seaside resorts, ideally sited overlooking Tor Bay. Its extremely mild climate makes Torquay an all the year round resort. There is a lot to see in and around the town, including twelfth century Torre Abbey and the famous Kent's Cavern, one of the oldest known human dwellings in the country. Nearby Paignton, somewhat overshadowed by its big sister, is nevertheless a popular resort with a zoo, shingle and sand beaches and glorious views from Roundham Head, It was south at Brixham in 1688 that William of Orange landed. Dawlish is an elegant, part Regency, part Victorian town much like its neighbour Teignmouth. Both have lovely gardens and are excellent holiday centres.

Despite its horrendous destruction in one of the World War II Baedeker raids, Exeter retains many interesting features. The Cathedral miraculously escaped the bombing almost unscathed and is a treasure house of Gothic detail, its nave being the longest span of Gothic vaulting in the world. The magnificent west front is covered with carved figures and the intricate detailed carving is continued inside on the remarkable misericordes. The Guildhall in the High Street, its floor resting on granite columns, is claimed to be the oldest municipal building in England. Exeter is an excellent base for touring this corner of Devon. The city has a modern University and all the amenities you would expect to find, but like all the Devon resorts, just a few miles away are secluded villages, quiet lanes and the glories of the Devon countryside.

Places to Visit

Arlington Court, *near Barnstaple* ~ a house covered in lots of lichens and mosses because of the pure air around it. The house contains many collections and the gardens have several walks throughout the grounds.

Burgh Island ~ a short walk across the sands at low tide from Bigbury-on-Sea takes you back to the 1920's and 30's. It was here Archibald Nettlefold built the luxury art deco style Burgh Island Hotel in 1929. The hotel was a famous retreat for Agatha Christie, Noel Coward and the Duke of Windsor.

Castle Drogo, *Drewsteignton* ~ situated on a Dartmoor Crag with views into the wooded gorge of the River Teign, it was the last castle to be built in Britain. It combines 20th century conveniences with a medieval atmosphere. Visitors may play croquet on the large circular lawn.

Coleton Fishacre Garden, *near Dartmouth* ~ a twenty acre garden developed by Lady Dorothy D'Oyly Carte. The garden contains a large collection of tender and exotic plants.

Killerton, *near Exeter* ~ a hillside garden surrounded by parkland and woods. The house was built in 1778 and includes a music room where visitors may play the piano or organ. There is a collection of Paulise de Bush costumes from the 18th century to the present day which are displayed in a series of period rooms.

Lundy Island ~ an unspoilt island with rocky headlands and amazing animal and bird life. Cars are not permitted on the island. so there is a steep walk to the village from the landing beach. In the village there is a church, tavern and castle.

Lydford Gorge, *near Okehampton* ~ best known for the spectacular White Lady Waterfall which falls through the rocks and trees to the river below. A walk through the gorge takes you to the Devil's Cauldron, a whirlpool where the river rushes through a series of potholes.

Morwellham Quay, *near Gunnislake* ~ a neglected and overgrown industrial site until 1970, it has now been restored into a thriving industrial museum. The museum is brought to life by characters in costume who give various demonstrations, or you can ride a tramway deep into a copper mine.

Meavg,
Devon

DEVON

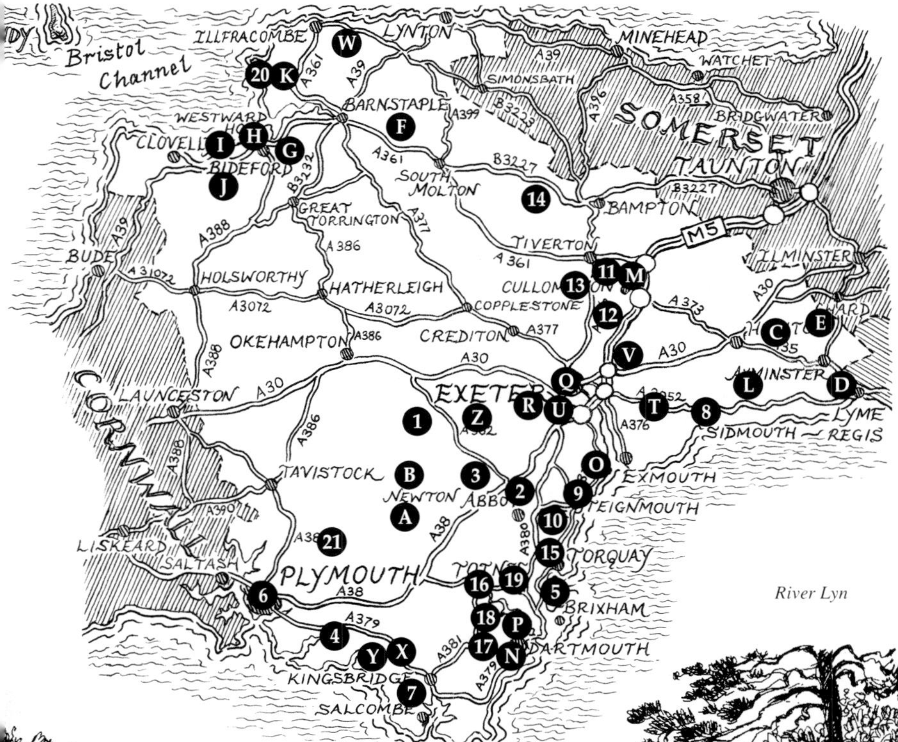

Bristol Channel

ILLFRACOMBE   LYNTON   MINEHEAD
W   SIMONSBATH   WATCHET

20 K   BARNSTAPLE
WESTWARD   F
CLOVELLY   I H
BIDEFORD   G
J   SOUTH MOLTON
GREAT TORRINGTON   14
BUDE   TIVERTON
HOLSWORTHY   CULLOMPTON   13 11 M
HATHERLEIGH   COPPLESTONE   12
OKEHAMPTON   CREDITON   V
LAUNCESTON   EXETER   Q   L   D
1   Z   R U   T 8   LYME REGIS
TAVISTOCK   B   3   O   SIDMOUTH
A   2   9   EXMOUTH
LISKEARD   21   10   TEIGNMOUTH
SALTASH   15   TORQUAY
PLYMOUTH   16 19   5
4   18   BRIXHAM
Y X   17 N   DARTMOUTH
KINGSBRIDGE   7
SALCOMBE

SOMERSET
TAUNTON
BRIDGWATER
BAMPTON
ILLMINSTER
AXMINSTER

River Lyn

Wellpritton Farm, Holne, Ashburton, Devon TQ13 7RX   **Nearest Road A38**

Relax in a lovely Dartmoor farmhouse with lovely views set in the heart of the countryside, yet only 3 miles from A38 Express way, half an hour to Exeter/Plymouth/Torbay. Mouth watering food and Devonshire cream every day as featured in the West country Good Food Guide 1999. Most rooms en-suite. Tea/coffee facilities. Central heating. Original character residents lounge with woodburner. Outdoor swimming pool, garden. Pet goats, lambs, horses, dogs and chickens. Most country pursuits nearby. ETB 2 Crowns Highly Recommended. AA QQQQ Selected.

Mrs Susan Gifford
Tel: 01364 631273

B&B from £19pp, Dinner from £9, Half Board £190 weekly, Rooms 2 twin, 2 double, most en-suite, Restricted smoking, Open all year, Map Ref A

New Cott Farm, Poundsgate, near Ashburton, Devon TQ13 7PD   **Nearest Road A38/B3357**

A friendly welcome, beautiful views, pleasing accommodation awaits you at New Cott Farm. A working farm in Dartmoor National Park. Relax in our conservatory after you have enjoyed the freedom and tranquillity of open moorland and Dart Valley or the many attractions of Devon. Lots of lovely homemade food. Tea/coffee and hot chocolate in your en-suite bedrooms. Ideal for lessable guests. TB category 3. B&B. Dinner by prior arrangement. Telephone for a brochure. ETB 3 Crowns Commended. AA QQQQ.

Mrs Margaret Phipps
Tel/Fax: 01364 631421

B&B from £18.50pp, Dinner from £11, Rooms 1 twin,2 double, 1 family, No smoking, Children from 5, No pets, Open all year except Christmas, Map Ref B

Ham Farmhouse, Ham, Dalwood, Axminster, Devon EX13 7HL   **Nearest Road A30, A303, A35**

Always a warm welcome at Ham Farmhouse our 17th century thatched home. Ten minutes from A30, A303, A35 in area of outstanding beauty. We offer pretty twin-bedded rooms overlooking tranquil walled garden. Tea/coffee facilities, radio, TV, part en-suite, large comfortable bathroom. Traditional breakfast using fresh local ingredients served in dining room or Continental, in your room, if you wish. Evening meals by prior arrangement. Children over 12 welcome. Picturesque walking area. Coast 15 minutes. Good local pubs serving excellent food. No smoking please. Prices from £18pppn.

Mrs Susan Turpin
Tel/Fax: 01404 831697
Mobile: 0370 958530

B&B from £18pp, Dinner from £12, Rooms 2 twin, 1 en-suite, No smoking, Children over 12, Pets by arrangement, Open all year except Christmas & New Year, Map Ref C

The Manor House, Combpyne, near Lyme Regis, Axminster, Devon EX13 6SX   **Nearest Road A3052**

The Manor house was once a nunnery and has a history dating to before the 13th century. Set in spectacular 3 acre grounds and gardens, it offers an ideal centre for exploring beautiful East Devon. One mile from the sea, the tiny village of Combpyne is perfect for those who enjoy peace and country relaxation. Lyme Regis, 5 miles, was the setting for filming Jane Austin's 'Persuasion' and the 'French Lieutenants Woman'. Good pubs and restaurants locally. We look forward to welcoming you. Prebooking only December, January and February. Minimum of 2 nights stay.

see PHOTO opposite

Nicky & Donald Campbell
Tel: 01297 445084
Fax: 01297 445084

B&B from £24pp, Rooms 1 twin, 2 double, all en-suite or private bathroom, Children welcome, Open all year except Christmas & New Year, Map Ref D

left, ***The Manor House,*** *near Lyme Regis- see details above*

Devon

Goodmans House, Furley, Membury, nr Axminster, Devon EX13 7TW   Nearest Road A30, A303

Converted stone cottages/cottages suites each with kitchen/dining and TV lounge areas, tea/coffee facilities etc. Glorious landscaped setting of 9 acres surrounding restored Georgian House. Peaceful tranquil country location, approached only by Devon Lanes. 14th century arched dining room with inglenooks is the setting for fabulous, imaginative fresh cuisine. Dine by candlelight after complimentary aperitif. Close to Dorset/Somerset and east Devon coasts, Forge Abbey, Knights Hayes, Hestercombe gardens, Parnham House, Cricket St Thomas Wildlife park.

Robert & Patricia Spencer
Tel: 01404 881690

B&B from £27pp, Dinner from £19.50, Rooms 4 twin, 6 double, 2 family, all en-suite/private facilities, Restricted smoking, Children welcome, Well behaved dogs welcome, Open mid February - mid November, Map Ref E

Huxtable Farm, West Buckland, Barnstaple, Devon EX32 0SR   Nearest Road A361

Enjoy a memorable candelit dinner of farm/local produce with complimentary homemade wine in this wonderful mediaeval Devon longhouse (dating back to 1520) with original oak panelling, beams and bread ovens. This secluded sheep farm with abundant wildlife and panoramic views is ideally situated on the Tarka Trail for exploring Exmoor National Park and North Devon's dramatic coastline. Tennis court, sauna, fitness and games room. Log fires in winter. 'Which' Recommended. ETB 3 Crowns Commended.

Jackie & Antony Payne
Tel: 01598 760254
Fax: 01598 760254

B&B from £24pp, Dinner £15, Rooms 1 twin, 3 double, 2 family, all en-suite/private, Restricted smoking, Children welcome, No pets, Open February - November, Map Ref F

The Pines at Eastleigh, Bideford, Devon EX39 4PA   Nearest Road A386

A warm and friendly welcome awaits you at The Pine at Eastleigh. Relax and enjoy the Grade II listed Georgian former farmhouse, set in 7 rural acres high above Bideford. Freshly cooked traditional English food, featuring local produce is complemented by an imaginative wine list. Ground floor rooms overlook the quiet courtyard. Colour TV, welcome tray, hair dryers, central heating, telephones are standard. Large selection of books and maps to borrow. Licenced. Log fires in winter. Mastercard/VISA. ETB 3 Crowns Highly Commended. EMail: barry@barpines.demon.co.uk

Barry & Jenny Jones
Tel: 01271 860561
Fax: 01271 861248

B&B from £29pp, Dinner from £14, Rooms 1 single, 1 twin, 4 double, all en-suite, cots available, No smoking, Children & pets welcome, Open all April - October, Map Ref G

Lower Winsford, Abbotsham Road, Bideford, Devon EX39 3QP   Nearest Road A39

Visitors are welcome at Lower Winsford, to share our comfortable family home. Enjoy the relaxing atmosphere with caring attention at all times. Explore the beautiful countryside around here with many coastal walks. Dartmoor and Exmoor are easily accessible. Unique Clovelly is close by. Rosemoor gardens are always worth a visit. Come and see for yourself.

Mrs Margaret Ogle
Tel: 01237 475083
Fax: 01237 425802

B&B from £19pp, Rooms 1 double en-suite, 1 twin with private bathroom, No smoking, Open Easter - September, Map Ref H

right, **Lower Waytown,** *near Clovelly- see details on page 138*

Lower Waytown, Horns Cross, near Clovelly, Bideford, Devon EX39 5DN   Nearest Road A39

see PHOTO on page 137

This beautifully converted barn and roundhouse has been transformed into a delightful, spacious home offering superb accommodation. Tastefully furnished with antiques the unique round, beamed guest's sitting room adjoins the attractive dining room where delicious breakfasts are served. Bedrooms are en-suite and equipped for every comfort. Relax in extensive grounds with ponds, waterfowl and black swans. Situated in unspoilt countryside with spectacular coastal scenery, pretty coves and coastal footpaths nearby, picturesque Clovelly lies 5 miles westward. AA QQQQQ, Premier Selected.

Chris & Caroline May
Tel/Fax: 01237 451787

B&B from £23.50pp, Rooms 1 twin, 2 double, all en-suite, No smoking, Children over 12 years, No pets, Open all year except Christmas & New Year, Map Ref I

The Old Rectory, Rectory Lane, Parkham, Bideford, North Devon EX39 5PL   Nearest Road A39

Charming, delightfully furnished country house, log fires, unique ambience, superb cuisine, 3 en-suite/private facility bedrooms very prettily decorated and furnished with every comfort in mind. Licensed. Dine and enjoy good wine with your excellent evening meal which using fresh local produce is cooked by Jean to the highest of standards, Listed in guide to Good Food in the West country. Set in a sleepy village surrounded by an area of outstanding natural beauty it is ideally situated for the coast, Clovelly, Exmoor and RHS Rosemoor.

Jean & Jack Langton
Tel: 01237 451443

B&B from £37.50pp, Dinner £23, Rooms 3 double, 2 en-suite, 1 private facility, No smoking or pets, Children over 12, Open February - November, Map Ref J

Denham Farm & Country House, North Buckland, Braunton, Devon EX33 1HY   Nearest Road A361

see PHOTO opposite

Off the beaten track this 1700's farmhouse is situated in the centre of a totally unspoilt hamlet only 2 1/2 miles from the superb coastline and sandy beaches of Putsborough and Woolacombe. Allen-suite rooms are warmly inviting. The delicious home cooking is definitely tempting. Close by are many attractions including market towns, and Exmoor. Denham has its own games room and play area. RAC Acclaimed, AA QQQ, ETB 3 Crowns Commended. Short break special offers and self catering available.

Mrs Jean Barnes
Tel: 01271 890297
Fax: 01271 890297

B&B from £25pp, Dinner from £12, Rooms 6 double, 2 family, 2 twin, Restricted smoking, Open all year except Christmas, Map Ref K

The Pantiles, Thorn Cottage, Northleigh, nr Colyton, Devon EX13 6BN   Nearest Road A35, A3052

The Pantiles is a garden cottage in the wooded grounds of Thorn Cottage, itself, where breakfast is served to guests. Accommodation and furnishings are of a high standard and consist of a double bedroom, bathroom, dining/lounge area with colour television and gallery kitchen, central heating and double glazing. It has a private entrance, parking and carport, a patio with barbecue and furniture. Northleigh has peace and tranquillity, yet is fifteen minutes from the beaches and coastal resorts of Seaton, Beer, Branscombe and Sidmouth, and the south west coastal path. A rural retreat near the sea.

Anthony & Peggy Govey
Tel: 01404 871553

B&B from £20pp, Rooms 1 twin, 1 double, both en-suite, No smoking, children or pets, Open February - November, Map Ref L

*right, **Denham Farm & Country House,** near Braunton- see details above*

Rullands, Rull Lane, Cullompton, Devon EX15 1NQ   Nearest Road M5 (Junction 28)

A comfortable 16th century house set amidst beautiful, peaceful, rolling countryside and yet only a few minutes from M5 and historic Tiverton and the market town of Cullompton. Within easy reach of all country pursuits - golf, shooting, fishing, riding, etc. Hard tennis court in grounds. There is an elegant dining room where delicious home cooked meals are served and an interesting wine list is available. All bedrooms are en-suite, have colour TV and courtesy trays.

Georgina Charteris
Tel: 01884 33356
Fax: 01884 35890

B&B from £25pp, Dinner from £15, Rooms 2 double, 1 twin, 2 single, restricted smoking, Open all year Map Ref M

Ford House, 44 Victoria Road, Dartmouth, Devon TA6 9DX   Nearest Road A3122

Ford House is a listed Regency House with three comfortable en-suite bedrooms with king or queen size double beds or twin beds, fridges, telephones, colour TVs, radio clock alarms, tea/coffee. Breakfast is served 8.30am to 12 noon. The traditional full English using free range eggs and dry cured bacon, kippers, smoked haddock, scrambled eggs and orange juice freshly squeezed. We have private parking and are within easy walking distance of the centre of Dartmouth.

Richard & Jayne Turner
Tel/Fax: 01803 834047

B&B from £27.50pp, Dinner from £25.00, Rooms 2 twin, 2 double, all en-suite, Children welcome, Pets welcome, Open March - October, Map Ref N

Broome Court, Broomhill, Dartmouth, Devon TQ6 0LD   Nearest Road A3122

see PHOTO opposite

Broome Court is tucked into a south facing hill, overlooking 3 copses and surrounded by green, undulating south Devon countryside rich in wildlife. The old farm buildings surround a paved courtyard abounding with flowers and shrubs and in the old farmhouse kitchen - the sort of hearty breakfast dreams are made of. No noise or smell of traffic at Broomhill - nor the hub-hub of everyday life - but the peace and tranquillity of the rolling Devon countryside awaiting you.

Tom Boughton & Jan Bird
Tel: 01803 834275
Fax: 01803 833260

B&B from £30pp, Rooms 1 twin, 2 double, all en-suite, also family unit, Restricted smoking, Children over 12 welcome, Pets by arrangement, Open all year, Map Ref N

West Hatch Hotel, 34 West Cliff, Dawlish, Devon EX7 9DN   Nearest Road A379

West Hatch is your guarantee of a warm welcome and a relaxed stay in our small friendly hotel. A detached house of character with stained glass windows, antiques and oak panelled staircase. We're centrally situated, overlooking the sea. All bedrooms are well equipped, en-suite and are on ground and first floor. Luxurious four poster room, bar and separate lounge, invigorating spa bath and private parking. Choose from extensive English or continental menu. Awarded AA 4Q's, RAC Highly Acclaimed and ETB 2 Crowns Highly commended. Major credit cards accepted.

Pat & Dave Badcock
Tel: 01626 864211/862948
Fax: 01626 864211

B&B from £22pp, Rooms 1 twin, 7 double, 2 family, all en-suite, Restricted smoking, Children welcome, No pets, Open all year except Christmas & New Year, Map Ref O

right, **Broome Court,** *near Dartmouth- see details above*

The White House, Manor Street, Dittisham, Devon TQ6 0EX   **Nearest Road A3122/A38**

An 18th century traditional stone built house in this picturesque village overlooking the beautiful River Dart. Friendly atmosphere. Full English breakfast. Guest sitting room. Terrace. Parking. Only a few hundred yards from the River, both village pubs, shops and church. Lovely walks, sailing, fishing, golf, swimming, steam trains and the coast nearby. Easy access to lovely Totnes and the Port of Dartmouth. Plenty of good places to eat a short drive away. Peace and quiet. Dartmoor is also easily reached for riding, driving and walking.

Hugh & Jill Treseder
Tel/Fax: 01803 722355

B&B from £25pp, Rooms 1 twin, 2 doubles, all en-suite or private facilities, No smoking, Children welcome, No pets, Open all year, Map Ref P

Raffles, 11 Blackall Road, Exeter, Devon EX4 4HD   **Nearest Road Exeter Central**

Imagine a large Victorian town house, furnished with antiques, tastefully decorated, a delightful walled garden yet minutes from the town centre, then come to Raffles the home of Richard and Sue. Our aim is to offer high quality accommodation with friendly personal service. All our rooms are en-suite with tea/coffee making facilities, colour television and central heating. Lock up garages are also available upon request. Three Crowns Commended ETB, selected by the Which? Guide. EMail: Raffleshtl@btinternet.com

Sue & Richard Hyde
Tel: 01392 270200
Fax: 01392 270200

B&B from £23pp, Dinner from £14, Rooms 2 single, 1 twin, 2 double, 2 family, all en-suite, Pets by arrangement, Open all year, Map Ref Q

Horse Engine House, Lowton Farm, Bridford, near Exeter, Devon EX6 7EN   **Nrst Road M5, B3212, B3193**

Lowton Farm is peacefully located at the end of a no through road with direct access to footpaths and nature reserve. It has a secluded garden, rustling stream and pond with ducks. Guests are welcomed into our family home, formerly a horse-engine house, the original wheel and oak beam remains intact in our lounge/dining room. Open log fires and central heating. Brass bed in double room, with tea trays in both rooms. English breakfast served with our free range eggs and homemade jams.

Ron & Gina Joslin
Tel: 01647 252209

B&B from £13.50pp, Dinner by arrangement from £8.50, Rooms 1 twin, 1 double, No smoking, Children welcome, No pets, Open all year Map Ref R

Holbrook Farm, Clyst Honiton, Exeter, Devon EX5 2HR   **Nearest Road A3052**

Enjoy the warm the welcome, spectacular views and peaceful surrounding of our dairy farm. Spacious en-suite rooms furnished to a high standard. All with colour TV and hot drinks facilities, off road parking. Excellent local eating places. Situated just off the A3052 Sidmouth Road at Clyst St. Mary 2 1/2 miles Junction 30 (M5). The cathedral city of Exeter is only a short drive away as are the coast and moors making this an ideal base for any holiday. AA QQQQ Selected. Ground floor room available.

Heather Glanvill
Tel: 01392 367000

B&B from £19pp, Rooms 1 twin, 1 double, 1 family, all en-suite, No smoking, Children welcome, No pets, Open all year, Map Ref S

Wood Barton, Farringdon, Exeter, Devon EX5 2HY   Nearest Road A3052

Wood Barton is a 17th century farmhouse in quiet countryside, yet only 3 miles from the M5 junction 30. An excellent traditional English breakfast is served cooked on an Aga. Spacious en-suite bedrooms with central heating, hospitality trays, colour TV's and radios. Within 6 miles are the city of Exeter, sandy beaches, National Trust houses and golf course. Good local eating places. Easy access.

Mrs Jackie Bolt
Tel: 01395 233407
Fax: 01395 227 226

B&B from £20pp, Rooms 1 twin, 1 double, 1 family, all en-suite, No smoking, Children welcome, No pets, Open all year except Christmas & New Year, Map Ref T

Drakes Farm House, Drakes Farm, Ide, near Exeter, Devon EX2 9RQ   Nearest Road A30/M5

Drakes farm House is a listed old oak beamed house with full central heating set in a large garden in the centre of quiet village, with a listed public house and one of the longest road fords in the country. Situated just 2 miles from M5 and cathedral city of Exeter. Convenient for coast and moors. Two restaurants within 5 minutes easy walking distance. Separate TV lounge for guests. Laundry facilities. Tea/coffee, TV, in all rooms. Ample off street private parking.

Mrs Nova Easterbrook
Tel: 01392 256814 & 495564
Fax: 01392 256814

B&B from £16 - £20pp, Rooms 1 twin en-suite, 2 double, 1 en-suite, 1 family en suite, No smoking, Children welcome, No pets, Open all year, Map Ref U

Down House, Woodhayes Lane, Whimple, Exeter, Devon EX5 2QR   Nearest Road M5, A30

Edwardian elegance with 20th century comfort. Down House is a peaceful and secluded country house set in 6 acres of garden, paddocks and orchard. There are splendid views across Whimple Village to cider country, the Tiverton Hills and on a clear day Dartmoor. Easy access from the A30 and M5. Exeter, Honiton and Sidmouth all within 9 miles. The spacious and tastefully appointed rooms have colour TV, tea/coffee, hair dryer and trouser press. There is a large comfortable south facing guest lounge. Garden games: Croquet, 18 hole putting, Boules, Quoits, Skittles and Badminton. AA 4Q's, ETB Highly Commended.

Mike & Joanne Sanders
Tel: 01404 822860

B&B from £18-£23pp, Rooms 1 single, 2 twin, 2 double, 1 family, all en-suite, No smoking, Children welcome, Pets by arrangement, Open all year, Map Ref V

Sloley Farm, Castle Hill, Berrynarbor, nr Ilfracombe, North Devon EX34 9SX   Nearest Road A399

The 17th century farmhouse has 3 bedrooms, 1 suitable for disabled, and is surrounded by farmland. Set in 3 acres the peaceful gardens contain many unusual plants and birds, an orchard and meadow complete with friendly animals. Sloleys overlooks the picturesque village of Berrynarbor and the magnificent Sterridge Valley. The area offers something for everyone:- garden, golf, beaches, watersports and is within easy reach of the North Devon coastal path and Exmoor National Park. Delicious home - cooked meals are available with produce straight from the garden.

Jill & Brian Mountain
Tel/Fax: 01271 883032

B&B from £18-£25pp, Dinner from £12-£14 by prior arrangement, vegetarian meals a speciality, Rooms 1 twin, 2 double, all en-suite, No smoking, children or pets, Open all year, Map Ref W

Court Barton, Aveton Gifford, Kingsbridge, Devon TQ7 4LE   **Nearest Road A379**

Court Barton is a 16th century Grade II listed manor house. The farm dates from before Domesday times and is now a small mixed farm. There is a cosy lounge with lots of holiday reading. Many of the pleasant bedrooms are en-suite and all have colour TV. Central heating throughout with log fires in colder weather. English breakfast, or special diets can be catered for by arrangement. Walking, bird watching, sailing, swimming, golf, tennis and horse riding all close by. EMail: jill@courtbarton.avel.co.uk

see PHOTO opposite

Jill Balkwill
Tel: 01548 550312
Fax: 01548 550312

B&B from £20pp, Rooms 2 double, 2 family, 2 twin, 1 single, most are en-suite, Open all year except Christmas, Map Ref X

Lower Stadbury, Aveton Gifford, Kingsbridge, South Devon TQ7 4PD   **Nearest Road A379**

Lower Stadbury, tucked away in an Area Of Outstanding Natural Beauty between Salcombe and Modbury, is a mellow listed manor house with an informal atmosphere and friendly dogs and cats. An ideal base for exploring the South Hams, its land borders the Avon Estuary Walk joining the South West Coastal Path at Bantham. Relax in the house and gardens with the prospect of a delicious supper if required - most dietary needs can be met. Courtesy trays provided, a laundry and drying service are offered.

Lesley Dawson & Ann Kinning
Tel/Fax: 01548 852159

B&B from £18pp, Dinner from £10, Rooms 1 twin - en-suite, 1 twin - shower, sep wc, 1 double en-suite, Restricted smoking, Children over 14, Pets by prior arrangement, Open all year, Map Ref Y

Helliers Farm, Ashford, Aveton Gifford, Kingsbridge, Devon TQ7 4ND   **Nearest Road A379**

Helliers Farm is a small working sheep farm on a hillside, set in the heart of Devon's unspoilt countryside, 1 mile from the village of Aveton Gifford, 4 miles from Kingsbridge and 15 from Plymouth. Recently modernised, the farmhouse offers spacious accommodation, traditional dining room, comfortable lounge with TV. Adjoining the paved courtyard, spring water feeds a water pond and down the hill there is an extensive fish pool.

Mrs C Lancaster
Tel: 01548 550689
Fax: 01548 550689

B&B from £20pp, Rooms 1 single, 2 double, 1 twin, 1 family, No smoking, Open all year except Christmas, Map Ref X

Wooston Farm, Moretonhampstead, Devon TQ13 8QA   **Nearest Road A30, B3212**

Wooston, once part of the manor house estate owned by Lord Hambleton, is situated high above Teign Valley in the Dartmoor National Park. Views over open moorland and plenty of walks, golf, fishing and riding nearby. The farmhouse is surrounded by delightful and well managed garden of half an acre. There are 3 warm and pleasant bedrooms, 2 en-suite, 1 with 4 poster, 1 with private bathroom with every facility included. Excellent breakfasts are served to start your day. ETB 2 Crown Highly Commended. AA 4Q Selected.

see PHOTO on page 146

Mary Cuming
Tel/Fax: 01647 440367

B&B from £19pp, Rooms 1 twin, 2 double, all en-suite, No smoking, Children over 8 years, No pets, Open all year except Christmas, Map Ref Z

*left, **Court Barton**, Aveton Gifford - see details above*

Great Sloncombe Farm, Moretonhampstead, Devon TQ13 8QF

Nearest Road A382

Share the magic of Dartmoor all year round while staying in our lovely 13th century farmhouse full of interesting historical features. A working dairy farm set amongst peaceful meadows and woodland abundant in wild flowers and animals including badgers, foxes, deer and buzzards. A welcoming and informal place to relax and explore the moors and Devon countryside. Comfortable, en-suite rooms, central heating, TV's and coffee/tea making. Delicious Devonshire suppers and breakfasts with new baked bread. ETB 3 Crowns Highly Commended. AA 4Q Selected.

Trudie, Robert & Helen Merchant
Tel/Fax: 01647 440595

B&B from £21pp, Dinner from £12, Rooms 2 double, 1 twin, Minimum age 8, No smoking, Open all year, Map Ref Z

Gate House, North Bovey, near Moretonhampstead, Devon TQ13 8RB

Nearest Road A30, A38

Gate House, in the Dartmoor National Park is a 15th century thatched home in a medieval village amidst breathtaking scenery. Rooms are charmingly furnished offering classical country style elegance with all modern facilities. Most rooms have beamed ceilings and there is a massive granite fireplace with bread oven and log fires in the sitting room. There is a large secluded garden with swimming pool and spectacular views. There are many opportunities for bird watching, walks on Dartmoor and the coast, or visiting National Trust properties.

John & Sheila Williams
Tel/Fax: 01647 440479

B&B from £25pp, Dinner £16, Rooms 1 twin, 2 double, all en suite, No smoking, Children over 15 years, Pets by arrangement, Open all year, Map Ref 1

see PHOTO on page 148

The Thatched Cottage, 9 Crossley Moor Road, Kingsteignton, Newton Abbot, TQ12 3LE

Nearest Road A380

The Thatched Cottage Restaurant a Grade II listed 16th century thatched longhouse of great character. A licenced restaurant with cosy cocktail bar featuring a large open fireplace. Serving only fresh food prepared to the highest standards at value for money prices. All rooms have central heating, colour TV and Tea/coffee making facilities and are well furnished and decorated.

Klaus & Janice Wiemeyer
Tel: 01626 365650

B&B from £20pp, Dinner a la carte or £12 Table D'hote menu, Rooms 1 single, 2 double/twin, 1 family suite (2 rooms), all en suite, No smoking, Open all year, Map Ref 2

see PHOTO on page 149

Sampsons Farm, Preston, Newton Abbot, Devon TQ12 3PP

Nearest Roads A38, A380, B3195, B3193

Thatched 14th century longhouse with oak beams, panelling and inglenook fireplaces. Sampsons is a Grade II listed building, low beams, creaky floors and hidden away in the hamlet of Preston with lovely walks along River Teign. Always a warm welcome and a cheerful atmosphere. All rooms have tea/coffee and colour TV. The restaurant has an excellent reputation with only the finest produce being used. House speciality $1/_2$ duckling, homemade sweets. Licenced bar and cellar with wines from around the world. Stable barn conversion 3 luxury en-suite rooms, one with bath. Four Poster beds.

Nigel Bell
Tel: 01626 354913
Fax: 01626 354913

B&B from £18.50 - £30pp, Dinner from£14 .50 - £25, Rooms 5 double en-suite, 3 double en-suite, Cottage with 2 bedrooms, (doubles) Open all year, Map Ref 3

*left, **Wooston Farm**, Moretonhampstead - see details on page 145*

Gate House, *North Bovey - see details on page 147*

right, **The Thatched Cottage,** *Kingsteignton - see details on page 147*

see PHOTO opposite

Crown Yealm, Newton Ferrers, South Devon PL8 1AW — Nearest Road B3186, A379

Crown Yealm enjoys a favoured location overlooking part of the River Yealm Estuary. Just one and a half miles from the countries longest footpath, the 620 miles South West Way. Newton Ferrers and Noss Mayo twin waterside villages, jewel of the South Hams, between Dartmoor and the South Devon Coast. A short creek side stroll finds three Inns, Bistro and Yacht Club for meals. Our large bedrooms with comfortable beds and usual facilities overlook the garden to the waters edge. Good breakfasts, Off road parking. Also 3 bedrooms apartment available.

Mrs Jill Johnson
Tel/Fax: 01752 872365

B&B from £19.50pp, Rooms 1 twin, 1 double with private shower, 1 family, Restricted smoking, Children welcome, Pets by arrangement, Open all year, Map Ref 4

Elberry Farm, Broadsands, Paignton, Devon TQ46HJ — Nearest Road A3022

Elberry Farm is a working farm with beef, poultry and arable production. The farmhouse is between 2 beaches both within a 2 minute walk. Broadsands being a safe bathing beach has been awarded the European Blue Flag 1994. As an alternative there is a 9 hole pitch and putt golf course opposite; and a short drive away is the zoo, town centre and the National park. The comfortable bedrooms all have tea/coffee making facilities. Guests are welcome to relax in the lounge; stroll around the secluded garden. Baby sitting available by arrangement.

Mrs Mandy Tooze
Tel: 01803 842939

B&B from £13pp, Dinner from £6, Rooms 1 twin, 2 double/family, 1 en-suite double, Restricted smoking, Pets by arrangement, Open January - November, Map Ref 5

Netton Farmhouse, Noss Mayo, near Plymouth, Devon PL8 1HB — Nearest Road A379

The hamlet of Netton is located about 1/2 mile from the beautiful Yealm Estuary and picturesque village of Noss Mayo. The stunning views of the South Devon Coastal path are but a few minutes walk from the house. We offer 3 beautiful bedrooms with en-suite or private facilities - one room is located on the ground floor - a separate guest lounge/breakfast room is also offered. Within the grounds we have use of a heated indoor swimming pool, tennis court and 'fun' croquet lawn. Homemade museli, preserves and freshly baked bread complement the traditional farmhouse fayre. ETB Highly Commended.

Mrs Lesley-Ann Brunning
Tel: 01752 873080
Fax: 01752 873107

B&B from £23pp, Dinner from £15, Rooms 1 twin, 2 double, all en-suite, No smoking, Children, Pets by arrangement, Open all year except Christmas, Map Ref 6

The Yeomans House, Collaton, Salcombe, South Devon TQ7 3DJ — Nearest Road A381

A fine 1680 stone and thatched farmhouse, The Yeoman's House is set at the head of it's own lush 19 acre valley of meadows orchards and springs; a peaceful and stunning location at the end of a country lane. The Salcombe Estuary is one mile by footpath and Malborough village pubs are 3/4 of a mile. Breakfast on Salcombe smokies, home baked bread, ham and potatoes Farls. Dinner by candlelight, in winter a cosy log fire; in summer a walk by the stream through a flower filled valley.

Barry & Michelle Sames
Tel: 01548 560084
Fax: 01548 560084

B&B from £25-£37.50pp, Dinner from £17.50, Rooms 1 twin, 2 double, 1 family, all en-suite, No smoking or pets, Children by prior arrangement, Open all year except Christmas & New Year, Map Ref 7

right, **Crown Yealm,** *Newton Ferrers - see details above*

Devon

Cheriton Guest House, Vicarage Road, Sidmouth, Devon EX10 8UQ Nearest Road A3052

Cheriton Guest House is a large town house which backs on to the River Sid, with the 'Byes' parkland beyond. There are private parking spaces at the rear. The half mile walk to the sea front, via the town centre, is all on level ground. Cheriton is notorious for its fine cooking and varied menus. There is a comfortable lounge with colour TV. Beautiful secluded rear garden for the exclusive use of guests. All bedrooms have central heating, colour TV and tea/coffee making facilities and all rooms are en-suite.

Diana & John Lee
Tel: 01395 513810

B&B from £20pp, Dinner from £9, Rooms 3 single, 5 double/twin, 2 family, all en-suite, restricted smoking, Children welcome, Pets by arrangement, Open all year, Map Ref 8

Thomas Luny House, Teign Street, Teignmouth, Devon TQ14 8EG Nearest Road A381

Thomas Luny House, the home of Alison & John Allan and their family was built by the marine artist Thomas Luny, tucked away in a conservation area. The house, surrounded by a beautiful secluded walled garden, is tastefully furnished with antiques and has 4 themed en-suite bedrooms, two with views of the River Teign. Each bedroom has remote controlled TV and direct dial telephone. There is ample car parking in the front courtyard. Teignmouth is an excellent centre for exploring South Devon and Dartmoor.

Alison & John Allan
Tel: 01626 772976

B&B from £25pp, Rooms 2 twin, 2 double, Children from 12, No pets, Open February - December, Map Ref 9

Virginia Cottage, Brook Lane, Shaldon, Teignmouth, Devon TQ14 0HL Nearest Road B3199

Virginia Cottage is a Grade II listed 17th century house set within a peaceful, partly walled, garden offering a delightful and relaxing place to stay. The pretty bedrooms with en-suite.private facilities, and tea/coffee makers, overlook the gardens and there is an attractive sitting room with large inglenook fireplace. A short walk to the coastal village of where good pubs and restaurants are to be found. This is an ideal location for walking or exploring the Dartmoor National Park, Cathedral city of Exeter and delights of Devon. Car parking in grounds.

Jennifer & Michael Britton
Tel: 01626 872634
Fax: 01626 872634

B&B from £24pp, Rooms 2 twin, 1 double, all en-suite, No smoking, Minimum age 12, No Pets, Open March - December, Map Ref 10

Fonthill, Torquay Road, Shaldon, Teignmouth, Devon TQ14 0AX Nearest Road A379

see PHOTO opposite

Fonthill is peacefully situated in its own beautiful grounds of 25 acres, close to the pretty coastal village of Shaldon. The 3 delightful bedrooms have views of the gardens and the River Teign, and the village pubs and restaurants are within easy walking distance. There is a hard tennis court and the coastal path to Torquay is nearby. Dartmoor National Park is within easy reach, also Plymouth, Exeter and several fine National Trust properties. Fonthill has been a Highly Commended establishment for many years.

Mrs Jennifer Graeme
Tel: 01626 872344
Fax: 01626 872344

B&B from £25pp, Rooms 3 twin with private or en-suite bathroom, No smoking, No pets, Open March - November, Map Ref 10

152

*right, **Fonthill**, Shaldon - see details above*

Devon

Poole Farm, Ash Thomas, Tiverton, Devon EX16 4NS   Nearest Road A361, M5

Poole Farm is an attractive old farmhouse, which has recently been renovated. It is set in 18 acres of pasture with pretty garden and lovely views. Bedrooms are en-suite with colour television and tea/coffee making facilities. It is in a quiet hamlet but only 15 minutes from the M5 and Tiverton Parkway railway station. An ideal touring centre for Dartmoor, Exmoor and the coast, there are several National Trust properties nearby and places of interest as well as many gardens.

Mrs Jenny Shaw
Tel: 01884 820201

B&B £24pp, Dinner from £15 by prior arrangement, Rooms 1 twin, 1 double, both en-suite, No smoking, Children welcome, Pets by arrangement, Open all year, Map Ref 11

Bickleigh Cottage Hotel, Bickleigh, near Tiverton, Devon EX16 8RJ   Nearest Road A396

see PHOTO opposite

Situated on the bank of the River Exe near Bickleigh bridge, a landmark famous for its scenic beauty, Bickleigh Cottage Country Hotel has been privately owned by the Cochrane family since 1933. The original cottage was built circa 1640 with additions in the 1970's. All bedrooms are en-suite and have tea/coffee making facilities. The location of Bickleigh makes it a perfect centre for touring Devon. Exeter with its cathedral, Tiverton Castle, Knightshayes Court and Killerton House are all nearby.

R S H & P M Cochrane
Tel: 01884 855230

B&B from £23.50, Dinner £11.40, Rooms 1 single, 3 twin, 4 double, all en-suite, Restricted smoking, Minimum age 14, Open April to October, Map Ref 12

Little Holwell, Collipriest, Tiverton, Devon EX16 4PT   Nearest Road M5, A361, A396

see PHOTO on page 156

Little Holwell is a traditional Devon Longhouse believed to be 13th century with beamed ceilings, spiral staircase and an inglenook fireplace. The house is centrally heated, with log fires in the winter. You are assured of a warm welcome with refreshing cup of tea. An optional evening meal is available, cooked on our traditional Aga using the best local produce. from the garden you can enjoy pleasant views over the surrounding countryside, or set off on one of the many interesting walks in the area. Ideal touring centre.

Mrs Ruth Hill-King
Tel/Fax: 01884 257590

B&B from £16pp, Dinner from £9, Rooms 2 double, 1 family, most en-suite, No smoking or pets, Open all Year except Christmas, Map Ref 13

Newhouse Farm, Oakford, Tiverton, Devon EX16 9JE   Nearest Road A396/B3227

see PHOTO on page 157

Enjoy a real taste of country living on our sheep farm on the edge of Exmoor. The farmhouse, built in 1600 is down a stone lane and has pretty bedrooms with en-suite, colour TV and tea/coffee trays. There's a beamed dining room, lounge with inglenook and a quiet garden for relaxing. We serve traditional breakfasts with home made bread and preserves; also delicious four course dinners if you wish. We're ideal for visiting National Trust houses, gardens and touring coast and moors. Recommended by Which? B& B Guide, AA 4Q Selected.

Anne Boldry
Tel: 01398 351347

B&B from £18pp, Dinner from £11, Rooms 1 twin, 2 Double, all en-suite, Restricted smoking, Children from 10, No pets, Open March - December, Map Ref 14

*right, **Bickleigh Cottage Hotel**, near Tiverton - see details above*

Kingston House, 75 Avenue Road, Torquay, Devon TQ2 5LL   **Nearest Road A3022**

Everyone is assured of our West Country welcome, not optional but guaranteed, with Brian & Anita. Combine Victorian elegance with modern amenities, ensuring a relaxing visit. Tastefully decorated en-suite bedrooms with tea/coffee and TV. Comfortable guests lounge and extensive breakfast menu. RAC "Highly Acclaimed" award in recognition of high standards and facilities. AA QQQQ "Selected" award for quality, constantly providing high levels of service and comfort. Level walk seafront, harbour/town via beautiful Torre Abbey Gardens, English Riviera Centre. Private parking.

Brian & Anita Sexon
Tel: 01803 212760

B&B from £16.50pp, Rooms 2 single, 1 twin, 2 double, 1 family, all en-suite, Children over 8, No pets, Open all year except Christmas and New Year, Map Ref 15

The Old Forge at Totnes, Seymour Place, Totnes, Devon TQ9 5AY   **Nearest Road A381, A384, A38**

Find a warm welcome in relaxing surroundings all year round in this 600 year old stone building with cobbled drive and coach arch leading into the walled garden. It is a rural haven, 4 minutes from Totnes town centre and riverside. Luxurious and cosy cottage style rooms are all en-suite with CTV, radio-alarm, hair dryer and beverage tray. Licensed. Parking. Huge breakfast menu, (traditional, vegetarian, continental and special diets). Conservatory lounge with whirlpool spa. Golf breaks. AA Selected Award. ETB Highly Commended. Working blacksmith's forge. As featured on BBC TV's holiday programme.

see PHOTO opposite

Mrs Jeannie Allnutt
Tel: 01803 862174
Fax: 01803 865385

B&B from £26pp en-suite dble/£40 single, Rooms 1 sgle, 2 twin, 2 dble, 5 family, all en-suite, ground floor rooms available, No smoking indoors, Children Welcome, Pets only in cars. Open all year, Map Ref 16

Wadstray House, Wadstray, Blackawton, nr Dartmouth, Totnes, Devon TQ9 7DE   **Nearest Road A3112**

Wadstray House - A Georgian country house with beautiful peaceful gardens and views across rolling fields to the sea. Situated in the centre of the South Hams, three miles from Dartmouth; River trips and sailing on the River Dart, Sandy beaches at Blackpool Sands and Slapton. A short drive is Dartmoor vast and rugged with wild ponies and many interesting walks. Dartmouth Golf and Country Club is only 200 yards away. Arrangements can be made for daily/week membership including sauna, swimming and gym facilities.

Mrs Merilyn Smith
Tel: 01803 712539
Fax: 01803 712539

B&B from £30pp, Rooms 2 twin, 1 double, all en-suite, No smoking, Children over 10, Pets welcome if they sleep in car overnight, Open all year except Christmas & Boxing Day, Map Ref 17

Tailrace, Crowdy Mill, Harbertonford, Totnes, Devon TQ9 7HU   **Nearest Road A381**

This working watermill lies in a sunny valley on the banks of the River Harbourne. The 18th century stone and slate buildings form a picturesque group, sheltered by the surrounding hills. The secluded garden provide a peaceful and relaxing retreat. Totnes is within 3 miles. Moors and spectacular South Devon Coast. All within easy reach. All the warm and comfortable bedrooms are en-suite and have TV and tea/coffee facilities. The house is very well furnished and all the produce is local, fresh and extremely well cooked. EMail: abarnes@aol.com

Don & Ann Barnes
Tel/Fax: 01803 732340

B&B from £18.50pp, Dinner from £15.50, Rooms 2 twin, 3 double, 1 family, all en-suite, No smoking, Children over 8, Pets by arrangement, Open all year except Christmas & New Year, Map Ref 18

---

*right, **The Old Forge at Totnes,** Totnes - see details above*

The Red Slipper, Stoke Gabriel, Totnes, Devon TQ9 6RU   Nearest Road A385

A small, friendly, licensed establishment appointed to a high standard, located in the centre of a picturesque and peaceful village on the River Dart. The attractive, en-suite, bedrooms (mainly on the ground floor), have remote control colour television, clock.radio, hair dryer, tea/coffee making facilities, and sweets. A sheltered courtyard garden is available all day. Dinner available on request. From Thursday -Saturday an A' la Carte menu is also served, using fresh produce. Traditional Sunday lunches also served. Parking Available. AA 4Q's.

Clive & Pam Wigfall
Tel: 01803 782315
Fax: 01803 782315

B&B from £27.50pp, Dinner from £12.50, Rooms 3 twin, 1 double, 1 family, all en-suite, Restricted smoking, Children welcome, Pets by arrangement, Open March - end December, Map Ref 19

Sandunes, Beach Road, Woolacombe, Devon EX34 7BT   Nearest Road A361

Sandunes is a very pleasant, most comfortable, modern, non smoking guest house. All rooms are en-suite with tea/coffee trays and most rooms have television. There is also a guest television lounge, garden and sun patio with stunning views out to sea. Ample car parking facilities are available. This is an ideal base for touring or for enjoying our "Blue Flag" award beach. Ilfracombe, Lynton, Lynmouth and Exmoor are within easy reach also the gardens of Marwood and Rosemoor. Regret no children or pets.

Jean & Charles Boorman
Tel: 01271 870661

B&B from £18pp, Dinner £10, Rooms 1 single, 1 twin, 5 double, all en-suite, No smoking, No children, No pets, Open March - October, Map Ref 20

Burrator House, Sheepstor, Yelverton, Devon PL20 6FF   Nearest Road A386

From the welcoming cup of tea you will feel at home, secluded in Burrator's peaceful and tranquil setting , ready to admire the magnificent of the Tor, the moorland stream, the trout lake, enjoy the tastefully furnished reception rooms, the comfort of your bedroom, the excellence of your breakfast. Relax with a gentle stroll around our 27 acres or explore the wilds of Dartmoor, visit many nearby National Trust properties, discover Tavistock and Plymouth. There is much variety throughout the year, much to do and see.

John & Liz Flint
Tel/Fax: 01822 855669

B&B from £50pp, Dinner by prior arrangement from £15.00, Rooms 1 single, 1 twin, 3 double, most en-suite/private facilities, No smoking, Children over 8, Pets welcome, Open all year except Christmas & New Year, Map Ref 21

Please mention
THE GREAT BRITISH
BED & BREAKFAST
when booking your accommodation

Give me the clear blue sky over my head, and the green turf beneath my feet,
a winding road before me, and a three hours' march to dinner
- and then to thinking!
It is hard if I cannot start some game on these lone heaths..

TABLE TALK VOL. 2 (1822) 'ON GOING A JOURNEY'
WILLIAM HAZLITT 1778-1830

DORSET

The many lovers of the novels of Thomas Hardy know that his fictional county of Wessex is in fact Dorset, and there are few parts of Dorset he doesn't include under a pseudonym in his novels. Dorset is a perfect holiday venue as its scenery varies so considerably, and being such a small county - only fifty miles from east to west and twenty-five from north to south, the visitor is able to move conveniently from one attraction to another. Not only does the county offer delightful rural scenery, it also boasts a fascinating coastline and in the east of the county there is wonderful walking country, wild heath-land and lonely hills. In direct contrast is the valley of the Stour, Shaftsbury is a fine centre for exploring this valley and the Blackmoor Vale. Hardy calls the town by its ancient name 'Shaston' in his novels. Built seven hundred feet above the Blackmoor Vale, the town developed around a nunnery endowed by King Alfred the Great.

The picturesque cobbled Gold Hill with its eighteenth century stepped houses is one of the most photographed subjects in a county of glorious sights. Dorchester is the administrative centre of Dorset, and a market town of great antiquity and charm, today little changed I fancy from Thomas Hardy's 'Casterbridge'. Hardy's birthplace at nearby Bockhampton affords a view of the heathland which so inspired him.

Overlooking Chesil Beach and the Isle of Portland is the Hardy Monument -

commemorating another Thomas Hardy, Nelson's flag-captain at the Battle of Trafalgar. North-east of Dorchester is Tolpuddle, the village made famous by six farm labourers who formed their own trade union in 1834 and are known as the Tolpuddle Martyrs, as for their efforts they were sentenced to seven years transportation to Australia. Maiden Castle, south-west of Dorchester is the most impressive Iron Age fort in Britain, believed to have been occupied first around 2,000 BC.

For anyone who is interested in fossils, the coast of Dorset is renowned. Lyme Regis in a National Nature Reserve is a lovely resort much enjoyed by Jane Austen and its Regency houses are much the same as they were in her day. The winding sea wall known as the Cobb is of Medieval origin and was made famous through the film of John Fowles' novel The French Lieutenant's Woman. At Weymouth, whose popularity was ensured when George III took to sea-bathing, are elegant houses in Classical style reflecting the taste of those who flocked to emulate their monarch. But long before these times the town was a notable port appreciated by Romans, Saxons and Normans before eventually Henry VIII developed it as his naval base. The harbour is protected by the Isle of Portland, a plateau of rock connected to the mainland by a shingle causeway, which is in turn a part of the ten miles of Chesil Beach. The enclosed lagoon, known as Fleet, is a haven for birds. Poole, one of the largest shallow-water anchorages in the country, was developed as a major port in the thirteenth century and was the haunt of pirates and smugglers. The town is a marvellous holiday centre with fine sandy beaches and wonderful historical buildings. In the middle of the bay is Brownsea Island, the birthplace of the Boy Scout movement and a Nature Reserve owned by the National Trust. Across the bay is impressive Corfe Castle, its ruined Norman keep towering over the quaint village of grey stone houses. It was here in 978AD that King Edward the Martyr was murdered. North of Poole stands Wimborne Minster, home for some years of Thomas Hardy, who wrote in one of his poems of the twin-towered chequered Minster Church of St. Cuthberga. To the north is Cranborne, an attractive village with a grand main street lined with brick and timber houses. Here the Chase Court controlled the hunting rights in Cranborne Chase, a royal forest and now an area of beautiful rolling, wooded countryside. The highest village in Dorset is Ashmore, surrounded by fine beech and sycamore trees. From its lofty perch there are magnificent views over Cranborne Chase and across the Solent to the Isle of Wight. Sherborne is a perfect base for exploring west Dorset, and is rich in historical associations. Sir Walter Raleigh lived in Sherborne Old Castle for fifteen years. Its Medieval abbey church was built in the eighth century as a cathedral, and is constructed of golden Ham Hill stone. The famous Sherborne School was rebuilt in 1550 replacing a cathedral school reputedly attended by King Alfred the Great. To the south, and cut into the turf of the chalk hillside is the monstrous one hundred and eighty feet tall naked figure of the Cerne Abbas Giant. Probably 1500 years old, it is believed to be associated with pagan fertility rites.

Whether it is fossils, ancient monuments, impressive manor houses, seaside pleasures, lazy days in wonderful countryside or the sampling of Dorset's Blue Vinny cheese, there is more than enough in this glorious county to keep the holiday maker occupied and anxious to return for more.

Places to Visit

Abbotsbury Swannery, *Abbotsbury* ~ a unique colony of swans established by monks in the 14th century.

Brownsea Island, *Poole* ~ a five hundred acre nature reserve with deer, red squirrel and water fowl. It was used in 1907 by Baden Powell to launch the Boy Scout movement; today it is owned by the National Trust.

Chesil Beach, *Dorset* ~ a strange phenomenon, it is made up of a seventeen mile bank of peebles up to thirty five feet high and up to two hundred yards wide enclosing the Fleet Lagoon. The stones are naturally graded by the currents.

Compton Acres, *Dorset* ~ over nine acres of beautiful gardens with views over Poole Harbour and the Purbeck Hills. Italian and Japanese gardens have been reproduced in detail and there are water gardens and woodland walks.

Corfe Castle, *Wareham* ~ the ruins of a one thousand year old castle dominating the Isle of Purbeck. The ruins have many mediaeval defensive features and with some of the best early Gothic architecture in England.

Guildhall Museum, *Poole* ~ an insight into the civic and social life of Poole during the 18th and 19th centuries, displayed in a Georgian market house.

Kingston Lacey, *Dorset* ~ a 17th century mansion restored with ornate interiors. The Spanish Room in gilded leather with a guilded ceiling from a Venetian palace. It also houses an amazing art collection with work by Van Dyck, Rubens, Lely, Lawerence and Jan Brueghel the Elder and a collection of Eygptian artefacts.

Maiden Castle, *near Dorchester* ~ this is a not castle but is the finest earthworks in Britain. Built in the 1st century BC, it was fortified with ramparts and complex entrances. In 43 AD, the Romans slaughtered its inhabitants and today all its structures have gone but its series of concentric rings covering one hundred and fifteen acres are still impressive.

Wimborne Minster, *Dorset* ~ founded in 705 AD and rebuilt in 1120, the Minster Church of St Cuthburga dominates this small market town. On the outside of the Minster is a colourful Quarter Jack figure which strikes the church bell every fifteen minutes.

Milton Abbas

164

DORSET

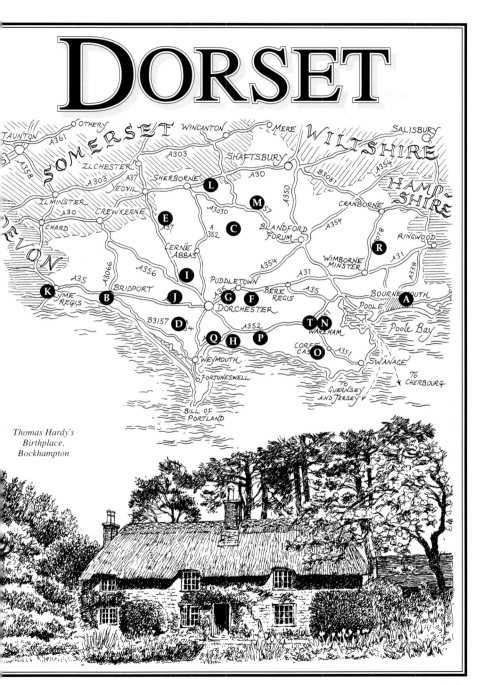

Thomas Hardy's Birthplace, Bockhampton

Dorset

Gervis Court Hotel, 38 Gervis Road, Bournemouth, Dorset BH1 3DH Nearest Road A338

see PHOTO opposite

Gervis Court Hotel is a Victorian house of character set in its own grounds nestling amongst the pine trees. It is a pleasant surprise to find the beautiful sandy beach, conference centre, shops and theatres only a few minutes walk away. We have ample parking, some ground floor bedrooms all with bathrooms, TV and Tea/coffee facilities. Gervis Court Hotel is in an ideal spot for exploring the delights of Bournemouth, New Forest and the unspoilt Dorset countryside and coastline. http://www.gerviscourthotel.co.uk

Alan & Jackie Edwards
Tel: 01202 556871
Fax: 01202 556871

B&B from £18pp, Rooms 1 single, 2 twin, 6 double, 3 family, all en suite, No smoking, Children welcome, No pets, Open all year, Map Ref A

Britmead House, West Bay Road, Bridport, Dorset DT6 4EG Nearest Road A35

A recently refurbished, licenced hotel with a reputation for friendliness and high standards. Pleasantly located a short walk from West Bay Harbour, Chesil Beach and the Dorset Coastal Path. Bedrooms are well equipped with many extras. The south west facing lounge and dining room overlook the garden beyond which is open countryside. Private car parking. Food is renowned for its excellence using local fish and fresh produce when possible. Swimming, golf, fossil hunting, seafishing, walking all nearby. AA 4QQQQ Selected, RAC Acclaimed, ETB 3 Crown Highly Commended.

Ann & Dan Walker
Tel: 01308 422941
Fax: 01308 422516

B&B from £21-30pp, Dinner £14, Rooms 4 double, 3 twin, all en-suite, 1 room is on the ground floor, Minimum age 5, Restricted smoking, Pets by arrangement, Open all year, Map Ref B

Rew Cottage, Buckland Newton, Dorchester, Dorset DT2 7DN Nearest Road B3143

A warm welcome awaits you in a peaceful cottage in the heart of Hardy's Dorset. Surrounded by a pretty garden and green farmland with lovely views on all sides. Ideal centre for walking or touring and within easy reach of Sherborne, Dorchester and the sea. Bedrooms are comfortably furnished and have tea/coffee making facilities and TV. Numerous attractive pubs with in easy reach for evening meals.

Annette & Rupert McCarthy
Tel: 01300 345467
Fax: 01300 345467

B&B from £20pp, Rooms 1 single, 1 twin, 1 double, Restricted smoking, Children & pets by arrangement, Open Mid January - Mid December, Map Ref C

The Old Post Office, Martinstown, Dorchester, Dorset DT2 9LF Nearest Road B3159

Situated in the Winterbourne Valley, The old Post Office, is a stone and slate Georgian cottage used as the village post office until 1950. It is part of a row of cottages that are all listed buildings. Winterbourne St Martin (Martinstown) is in the heart of Hardy country, 2 miles from the Neolithic Hill Fort of Maiden Castle, Hardy's monument and the town of Dorchester. The coast and beach are 5 miles away and it is an ideal walking and touring base. The bedrooms all have washbasins, tea/coffee making facilities, and some have TV.

Mrs Jane Rootham
Tel: 01305 889254

B&B from £15 - £20pp, Dinner from £10, Rooms 2 twin, 1 double, Children welcome, Pets by arrangement, Open all year, Map ref D

right, **Gervis Court Hotel**, *Bournemouth - see details above*

Dorset

see PHOTO opposite

Brambles, Woolcombe, Melbury Bubb, near Dorchester, Dorset DT2 9LF   Nearest Road A37

A delightful thatched cottage set in peaceful countryside near historic towns of Dorchester and Sherborne, and a short drive to the coast. Beautifully appointed and well equipped, it offers every comfort, and a friendly welcome. The pretty bedrooms always have fresh flowers, also colour TV and Tea/coffee making facilities. There is a wide choice of breakfast, including traditional, continental, vegetarian or fruit platter. There are many places of interest to visit and walks to explore. Parking within grounds. Special rates for longer stays.

Anita & Andre Millorit
Tel: 01935 83672
Fax: 01935 83003

B&B from £20pp, Rooms 2 single, 1 twin en-suite, 1 double en-suite, No smoking, Children welcome, No pets, Open all year except Christmas & New Year, Map Ref E

Vartees House, Moreton, Dorchester, Dorset DT2 8BE   Nearest Road B3390, off A35

A peaceful, secluded, country house built by Hermann Lea, a friend of Thomas Hardy, set in 3 acres of picturesque woodland gardens which attract wildlife. Accommodation throughout is spacious and comfortable. Tea/coffee making facilities in all rooms. TV lounge. Situated near the pretty village of Moreton with its renowned church containing engraved windows by Laurence Whistler and the burial place of Lawrence of Arabia. Coast 4 miles. Station 1/4 mile. Excellent local pubs. A delightful base for a peaceful and relaxing holiday.

Mrs D M Haggett
Tel: 01305 852704

B&B from £18pp, Rooms 2 double, 1 twin, Children - minimum age 10, Pets by arrangement, Open all year, Map Ref F

Muston Manor, Piddlehinton, Dorchester, Dorset DT2 7SY   Nearest Road B3143

Originally built in 1609 by the Churchill family, it remained in their ownership until bought by the present owners in 1975. Situated in the peaceful Piddle Valley with its many good pubs, the house is set in five acres, surrounded by farmland. Large comfortable, well furnished rooms with tea/coffee making facilities and central heating. Heated swimming pool in season.

Mr & Mrs O B N Paine
Tel: 01305 848242

B&B from £19pp, Rooms 2 double, 1 en suite, No smoking, Children welcome over 10, Pets by arrangement, Open March - October, Map Ref G

The Creek, Ringstead, Dorchester, Dorset DT2 8NG   Nearest Road A353

Ringstead is situated on the Heritage Coastal path approximately 7 miles from both Weymouth and Dorchester. It is within east reach of many important National Trust properties and is ideally situated for artists, bird watchers, walkers and watersport enthusiasts. The house has a large garden overlooking the seashore and surrounded by farmland. There is full central heating and showers in all bedrooms and a spacious sitting room and comfortable dining room. Gourmet evening meals available by arrangement. A heated swimming pool during summer months.

Mrs Fisher
Tel: 01305 852251

B&B from £18.50pp, Dinner from £10.50, Rooms 2 double, Minimum age 8, No smoking, No pets, Open all year, Map Ref H

*right, **Brambles**, near Dorchester - see details above*

Lamperts Farmhouse, 11 Dorchester Road, Sydling St. Nicholas, Dorchester, Dorset DT2 9NU   A37

Four hundred year old thatched listed farmhouse nestling in the peaceful village of Sydling St. Nicholas. Set in own ground with car parking. Prettily decorated en-suite bedrooms with Laura Ashley soft furnishings, Victorian brass beds and antique pine furniture. Guests own sitting room with log fire and colour TV. Calm sheltered gardens situated in Dorsets beautiful countryside. Ideal for walking or touring. Map, guide books and video of area provided.

Mrs R. Bown
Tel: 01300 341 790

B&B from £20pp, Dinner from £15, Rooms 1 twin, 1 double, both en-suite, Open all year, Map Ref I

Lamperts Cottage, Sydling St. Nicholas, near Cerne Abbas, Dorchester, Dorset DT2 9NU   Nearest Rd A37

see PHOTO opposite

16th century thatched listed cottage with stream running in front. Situated in a peaceful village in the beautiful Sydling Valley. Bedrooms are prettily decorated with dormer windows. Breakfast is served in the dining room which has an Inglenook fireplace, bread oven and beams. Central heating and tea/coffee makers. West Dorset is an ideal touring centre with beaches. The countryside is excellent for walking with footpaths over chalk hills and through hidden valleys. Guidebooks and maps available.

Nicky Willis
Tel: 01300 341659
Fax: 01300 341699

B&B from £20pp, Rooms 1 double, 1 twin, 1 family, Open all year including Christmas, Map Ref I

Lower Lewell Farmhouse, West Stafford, Dorchester, Dorset DT2 8AP   Nearest Road A35, A352

A 17th century farmhouse authentically improved and situated among a patchwork of fields in rolling Dorset countryside. Reputed to be Talbothays Dairy from Thomas Hardy's 'Tess of the D'Urbervilles'. Built in Portland stone under a red tiled roof with a Victorian brick and slate extension, this is a homely farmhouse with beams, log fires and plenty of space. hearty breakfasts from the farmhouse kitchen are served at separate tables in the dining room with inglenook fireplace. There are good local pubs offering snacks and restaurant meals.

Mrs Marian Tomblin
Tel: 01305 267169

B&B from £19pp, Rooms 1 twin, 1 double, 1 family all with tea/coffee making facilities, TV lounge, Open all year, Map Ref G

Churchview Guest House, Winterbourne Abbas, Dorchester, Dorset DT2 9LS   Nearest Road A35

see PHOTO on page 172

Our 17th century Guest House noted for warm, friendly hospitality, traditional breakfasts and delicious evening meals, makes an ideal base for exploring beautiful West Dorset. Our character bedrooms are comfortable, well appointed and include televisions and hospitality trays. Meals taken in our period dining room feature local produce, cream and cheeses. Relaxation is provided by two attractive lounges and licenced bar. Your hosts will give every assistance with local information on attractions, walks and touring to ensure you of a memorable stay. ETB 3 Crown Commended. AA QQQ

Michael & Jane Deller
Tel: 01305 889296

B&B from £21pp, Dinner from £13, Rooms 1 single, 3 twin, 4 double, 1 family, most en-suite, Pets welcome, No smoking, Open all year, Map Ref J

*right, **Lamperts Cottage,** near Cerne Abbas - see details above*

Rashwood Lodge, Clappentail Lane, Lyme Regis, Dorset DT7 3LZ   Nearest Road A3052

Rashwood Lodge is an unusual octagonal house located on the Western hillside with views over Lyme Bay. Just a short walk away is the coastal footpath and Ware Cliff famed for its part in "The French Lieutenants Woman". The bedrooms have their own private facilities. There is an additional twin room for extra family members. The rooms have colour TV and tea/coffee making facilities and benefit from their south facing aspect overlooking a large and colourful garden set in peaceful surroundings. Golf course 1 mile away.

Mrs Diana Lake
Tel: 01297 445700

B&B from £20pp, Rooms 1 twin, 2 double, most en-suite, No smoking, Children from 5, Pets by arrangement, Open February - November, Map Ref K

Willow Cottage, Ware Lane, Lyme Regis, Dorset DT7 3EL   Nearest Road A3052

Willow Cottage enjoys tranquillity and unrivalled views over National Trust pastureland and coastline. Within 200 yards is the South West Coastal Path and the Cobb, Lyme's harbour is a short cliff top walk away. The cottage annexe offers privacy to a party of up to three guests. Both bedrooms command splendid seaviews and the double bedded room with colour TV, opens onto a sun balcony. Tea/coffee making facilities in private breakfast room.

Geoffrey & Elizabeth Griffin
Tel: 01297 443199

B&B from £23pp, Rooms 1 single, 1 double en-suite, Minimum age 8, Pets by prior arrangement, Open March - November otherwise by special arrangement, Map Ref K

Amherst Lodge, Uplyme, Lyme Regis, Dorset DT7 3XH   Nearest Road A35

A small country estate with a casual atmosphere where traditional elegance and comfort border on luxury. Huge gardens, walks and coarse/fly fishing are within the 140 acre grounds, whilst the coast, good pubs and picturesque villages are nearby. Wake up to the bird song and finish the day slumped in front of the enormous fireplace in the ancient oak panelled lounge. Gourmet meals (selected nights only) and a bar with 30 single malt whiskies. http://www.AmherstLodge.com

Andrew & Katie Bryceson
Tel: 01297 442773
Fax: 01297 442625

B&B from £25pp, Dinner from £15-£24, Rooms 2 twin, 2 double, all en-suite, Restricted smoking, No children or pets, Open all year, Map Ref K

The Old Vicarage, Sherborne Road, Milborne Port, Sherborne, Dorset DT9 5AT   Nearest Road A30

Situated at the edge of a charming village overlooking open country at the far side of the Sherborne Castle estate. The entire town of Sherborne has that 'olde world' feel and is well worth a visit, so are the many houses and gardens in the area. It's ideal for hiking, cycling (bikes for hire), golf and walking. The Old Vicarage is spacious and elegantly furnished with antiques. On Friday and Saturday evenings the former owners of a highly acclaimed London restaurant serve delicious food - ask for sample menu . On other nights you can eat in an excellent pub restaurant, 200 yards from the Old Vicarage.

Jorgen Kunatha& Anthony Ma
Tel: 01963 251117
Fax: 01963 251515

B&B from £25pp, Dinner from £18.50, Rooms 1 single, 2 twin, 3 double, 1 family, all en-suite, Restricted smoking, Children over 5, Pets restricted, Open February - December, Map Ref L

*left, **Churchview Guest House**, Winterbourne Abbas - see details on page 170*

Stourcastle Lodge, Gough's Close, Sturminster Newton, Dorset DT10 1BU   **Nearest Road B3092**

Built in 1732 this residence offers very high standards and quality throughout. The bedrooms have impressive Victorian bedsteads, stencilled borders, antique furniture and modern well equipped bathrooms some with whirlpool baths. Peacefully situated down a lane yet moments from the town centre of fields and riverside walks. Oak beams, log fires and view of the lovely garden from every room. Jill is a gold medalist chef so with dishes like baked poussin with creamy curry sauce followed by boozy bread and butter pudding this is an excellent place to both stay and eat.

Ken & Jill Hookham-Bassett
Tel: 01258 472320
Fax: 01258 473381

B&B from £27.50-£35pp, Dinner from £17, Rooms 1 twin, 4 double, all en suite, all have tea/coffee making facilities, Restricted smoking, Open all year, Map Ref M

Fiddleford Millhouse, Fiddleford, Sturminster Newton, Dorset DT10 2BX   **Nearest Road A357**

A peaceful magical Grade I listed farm/manor house of great architectural interest with lovely garden running down to the river Stour in totally secluded quiet location. Beautifully furnished and decorated home. 3 large bedrooms one with half tester bed and 16th century moulded plaster ceiling and own bathroom, one large bedroom with king size 4 poster and one very pretty double bedroom. Central heating, TV and tea/coffee in all bedrooms. Pub in easy walking distance. Ideally situated for beautiful walks.

Jennifer & Anthony Ingleton
Tel: 01258 472786

B&B from £20pp, Rooms 3 double, 1 en-suite, No smoking, Children over 12 years, Pets by arrangement, Open all year, Map Ref M

Gold Court House, St John's Hill, Wareham, Dorset BH20 4LZ   **Nearest Road A351**

Gold Court House is a fine Georgian house with walled garden on a small square on the south side of Wareham, the gateway to the Isle of Purbeck. The three double or twin bedrooms, each with private bathrooms, are light and airy and pleasantly furnished, with all facilities at hand. We are ideally situated for exploring Dorset, 'the Thomas Hardy country' or the magnificent coastline. For a weekend break, touring or on business, there is a wide choice for the active or restful holiday, much of historic interest and a wealth of sporting opportunities.

Anthea & Michael Hipwell
Tel: 01929 553320
Fax: 01929 553320

B&B from £22.50pp, Dinner from £10-£12 (November - March), Rooms 3 twin/double, all private facilities, Restricted smoking, Children over 10, No pets, Open all year except Christmas & New Year, Map Ref T

Old Granary, The Quay, Wareham, Dorset BH20 4LP   **Nearest Road A351**

This 250 year old former grain store nestles beside the River Frome and the Quay in this interesting town. On the restaurant menu fresh grilled sea bass is a popular choice. The bedrooms are beamed on the three upper floors and have bathrooms. Scenic water colours by local artist cover the walls. The restaurant, with swagged curtains and riverside bar make, a delightful setting to enjoy drinks and cream teas with food served all day. Staff are friendly and efficient. Mooring, boat hire and trips arranged locally.

Mr & Mrs D Sturton
Tel: 01929 552010
Fax: 01929 552482

B&B from £20pp, Dinner from £17.50, Rooms 3 double, 2 twin, 1 private bathroom, 4 en-suite, all have tea/coffee making facilities, No smoking, Open all year, Map Ref N

Bradle Farm, Church Knowle, nr Corfe Castle, Wareham, Dorset BH20 5NU   Nearest Road A351

Bradle Farm lies in a valley three miles west of Corfe Castle, surrounded by the Purbeck Hills in an area of outstanding natural beauty. We farm 550 acres at Bradle with our land extending to the highest point in Purbeck right down to the sea at Kimmeridge. Our accommodation is very spacious and is traditionally furnished to a high standard. We have two double rooms with en-suite showers and a twin-bedded room with private bathroom. All rooms have colour TV's, clock radios and tea/coffee facilities.

Mrs Gillian Hole
Tel: 01929 480712
Fax: 01929 481144

B&B from £20pp, Rooms 1 twin, 2 double, all en-suite, Restricted smoking, Children welcome, No pets, Open all year except Christmas, Map Ref O

Long Coppice, Bindon Lane, East Stoke, Wareham, Dorset BH20 6AS   Nearest Road A352

Long Coppice is situated in a peaceful country lane 11/2 miles from the A352 at Wool and is ideal for those who wish to get away from it all and relax in rural surroundings. We have 8 acres of our own gardens, woodlands and meadows. Guest accommodation is separate and the rooms are spacious and comfortably furnished, the family room has its own garden where guests can relax and is ideal for young children. Centrally situated for local attractions, Lulworth Cove is 4 miles away as well as many good pubs nearby for evening meals.

Sarah Lowman
Tel: 01929 463123

B&B from £19pp, Rooms 1 twin, 1 family, both en-suite, No smoking, Children, Welcome, Pets by arrangement, Open all year except Christmas, Map Ref P

Dingle Dell, Osmington, Weymouth, Dorset DT3 6EW   Nearest Road A353

Dingle Dell lies down a quiet lane at the edge of this charming village, a mile from the coast. Set back among old apple trees in its own lovely garden, with roses covering the mellow stone walls, it provides a peaceful spot to relax, and a pleasant base from which to explore the many local attractions. Large, attractive rooms overlook gardens and countryside, providing comfort, colour TV and tea/coffee facilities. Generous English breakfasts, or special diets by request. A warm personal welcome guaranteed. ETB listed Highly Commended.

Joyce & Bill Norman
Tel/Fax: 01305 832378

B&B from £19.50pp, Rooms 1 twin, 1 double en-suite, No smoking, children or pets, Open March - October, Map Ref Q

Rookery Nook, Chapel Lane, Osmington, Weymouth, Dorset DT3 6ET   Nearest Road A353

Take a well earned break in our modern home, situated in the picturesque conservation village of Osmington. Just four miles from Weymouth. Surrounded by beautiful Hardy countryside. Close to NT houses and gardens. Your pretty twin en-suite bedroom has colour TV, radio and tea/coffee making facilities. Relax in our attractive secluded garden and conservatory. Guide books and maps to borrow. Carol offers a generous cooked vegetarian breakfast with free range eggs and home made preserves. Special diets with notice. Short walk to pub. Parking. Brochure available.

Carol Sutton
Tel: 01305 835933

B&B £20pp, Rooms 1 en-suite twin, No smoking, children or pets, Open April - October, Map Ref Q

The Beehive, Church Lane, Osmington, Weymouth, Dorset DT3 6EL   Nearest Road A353

The quaint village of Osmington with its enchanting array of pretty stone and thatched cottages like 'The Beehive' is probably one of Dorset's best kept secrets. This is an area of great natural beauty with scenic coastal and inland walks. Mary is a most convivial host having led an interesting life working in Africa for some years. She can provide light suppers of imaginative soups with local cheese, bread & fruit. In winter Dorset dinners are offered using local recipes of tipsy rabbit or long piddle lamb followed by Tyneham pears or buttered oranges, served around the cosy kitchen table.

Mary Kempe
Tel: 01305 834095

B&B from £17pp, Light suppers from £5, Dinner from £10, Rooms 1 twin/double, 1 double en-suite, 1 single, all with tea/coffee makers, No smoking, Min age 6, Pets by request, Open February - December, Map Ref Q

Thornhill, Holt, Wimborne, Dorset BH21 7DJ   Nearest Road A31

see PHOTO opposite

You are sure of a warm welcome in this charming thatched family home which is set in peaceful, rural surroundings. There is a large garden and hard tennis court which guests may use. The house is situated 3 1/2 miles from Wimbourne, near the centre of a village, but well away from the road and the location is ideal for exploring the coast, New Forest and Salisbury area. There are plenty of local pubs offering good food.

John & Sarah Turnbull
Tel: 01202 889434

B&B from £20pp, Rooms 1 single, 1 twin, 1 double, No smoking, No children, No pets, Open all year including Christmas & New year, Map Ref R

Bertie "Which gate was that please?" Driver "High Petersgate, Sir"
BELLE & BERTIE IN YORK

*right, **Thornhill**, near Wimborne - see details above*

ESSEX

Few counties in Britain can match Essex for varied scenery. Epping Forest fringing London, now covering something in the region of five and a half thousand acres is all that is left of an enormous sixty thousand acre royal hunting ground. Here is glorious heath, forest and rolling countryside ideal for rambling. In stark contrast the southern coastline is highly industrialised but contains Southend, London's own seaside resort, boasting seven miles of uninterrupted seafront, and the world's longest pier along which a railway runs. It has changed considerably since the Prince Regent sent his Princess Caroline here. Georgian elegance has given way to the brash seaside resort offering all the fun of the fair. Southend is the day-tripper's delight, and if it's bright lights and loud music and mud you're after, then Southend is the place for you. But to the north from Shoeburyness up to the Blackwater Estuary is a wild, lonely windswept expanse of land. This is the place of wildfowlers and marsh farmers. This great area was reclaimed from the sea during the seventeenth century by Dutch engineers, resulting in many miles of dyke and walls, outside of which the remote islands, creeks and waterways are enjoyed by small boat sailors. Further north, the glorious water meadows are dominated by Colchester, the capital city before the Roman invasion, standing on a ridge above the River Colne. Colchester was in fact the earliest Roman town in Britain. The great Norman keep, built on the ruins of the Roman temple of Claudius is the largest in Europe. Colchester owed its later prosperity to the cloth trade, being a centre of the Flemish weavers who settled here in the sixteenth and seventeenth centuries. It is claimed that Old King Cole of the nursery rhyme gave the town its name. Colchester is a perfect holiday centre with its one hundred and eighty acres of public parks and gardens. To the south are the Layers...Layer-de-la-Haye offering superb views over the 1200 acre Abberton reservoir, haunt in season of innumerable wildfowl, Layer Breton and Layer Marney having some fine old houses. To the south of Colchester is the lovely valley of the Stour leading to Manningtree, famous for its swans and sailing barges. Jutting out to sea south of the busy port of Harwich is the Naze with its tower built to warn mariners of the treacherous West Rocks. Walton on the Naze offers safe bathing and excellent fishing while the salt marshes behind the town are a paradise for bird-watchers. Further along the coast is Clacton-on-Sea, a Victorian seaside resort with fine tree-lined streets, attractive gardens and a sandy beach. Chelmsford, the county town of Essex, was once an agricultural centre with a livestock market dating back to 1200 AD, but with the construction of the Chelmer and Blackwater Navigation in 1797, and the development of the railway in 1843, the town swiftly grew as an industrial centre. It is nevertheless an excellent holiday venue. Nearby Danbury gives glorious views across sweeping gorse common and over the Blackwater Estuary.

Danbury's six hundred year old church and timber-framed Griffin Inn are well worth a visit, as is Danbury Place set in a large park. Ingatestone to the south is a fascinating village possessing some grand Georgian brick and mock-Tudor houses. Ingatestone Hall was built in 1540 for the Tudor Secretary of State, Sir William Petre. The Elizabethan composer William Byrd was a frequent visitor to the Hall. To the east of Chelmsford is Maldon, the site of 'The Battle of Maeldune' celebrated in the tenth century epic poem, where in 991 AD the Anglo-Danish army of Brythnoth was routed by Viking invaders. The estuary of the Blackwater is packed with pleasure boats and barges. The rolling countryside north to Saffron Walden has a liberal scattering of lovely villages. The east is pleasantly wooded, the west to the borders of Cambridgeshire windswept low chalk hills. The ancient woolen town of Saffron Walden is one of the most attractive in the county. From the Middle Ages until the eighteenth century this was the centre of the saffron crocus industry reflected in its name. Nearby is spectacular Audley End, originally the Benedictine Abbey of Walden given to Lord Audley by Henry VIII following the Dissolution. In 1603 the Earl of Suffolk laid the foundations there of one of the largest Jacobean houses in England. Although now only a fraction of its original size, it is a wonderful sight in its Capability Brown landscaped park. To the south are the quaint villages known collectively as The Rodings. Immortalised in the paintings of George Morland and the writings of Anthony Trollope, these villages are a delight that no visitor to Essex should miss.

ESSEX

Places to Visit

Audley End House, *Saffron Walden* ~ when it was built in 1614, this was the largest house in England. A Jacobean mansion with original hall and many fine plaster ceilings. The gardens the 18th century park, which has many temples and monuments.

Coggeshall Grange Barn, *near Colchester* ~ the oldest surviving timber framed barn in Europe, it was originally part of a monastery. It was restored in the 1980's and houses a small collection of farm carts and wagons.

Colchester Castle, *Colchester* ~ built by the Normans on the site of a Roman temple. Only the keep remains and is now a museum housing some of the country's best archaeological collections.

Dedham Church, *Dedham* ~ this tall church tower appears in many of landscape painter John Constable's pictures including the 'View on the Stour near Dedham' painted in 1822.

Finchingfield

Epping Forest ~ over six thousand acres of forest, in the past it was a favourite hunting ground of kings; now it is popular with walkers. A variety of wildlife live in the forest and its open land and lakes, including deer.

Layer Tarney Tower, *near Tiptree* ~ an eight storey Tudor gatehouse built in the 16th century, it was

supposed to be part of a mansion which never got built. The Tower offers panoramic views over the Essex countryside.

Mistley Towers, *near Manningtree* ~ Richard Rigby, Paymaster General, poured his money into a spa at Mistley, and employed Robert Adam to deisgn a church, but it was discovered that he had embezzled money and work stopped. Today a green waterside with maltings buildings, Georgian facades and swans are the only reminder of what it was. The twin towers of a demolished Mistley church have been kept as a landmark.

St Osyth's Priory, *St Osyth* ~ a former Augustinian Abbey, it still has a 13th century chapel and various other buildings dating from the 13th to the 18th century. The gatehouse contains many works of art including ceramics and Chinese jade.

St Peter's-on-the-Wall, *Bradwell-on-Sea* ~ a simple stone building standing isolated on the shore. It was built in 654 from the remains of a Roman fort by St Cedd, who used it as his cathedral. It was restored in the 1920's after being used as a shed since the 17th century.

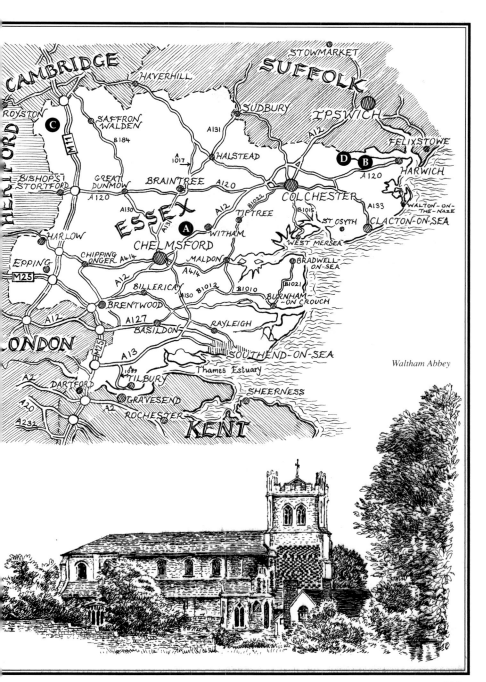

CAMBRIDGE

SUFFOLK

STOWMARKET

HAVERHILL

SUDBURY

IPSWICH

FELIXSTOWE

ROYSTON

C

SAFFRON WALDEN

B184

A131

A1017

HALSTEAD

D **B**

HARWICH

A120

HERTFORD

BISHOP'S STORTFORD

A120

GREAT DUNMOW

BRAINTREE

A120

COLCHESTER

A133

WALTON-ON-THE-NAZE

A130

A12

ESSEX

A131

TIPTREE

B1022

B1015

ST OSYTH

CLACTON-ON-SEA

HARLOW

A

WITHAM

WEST MERSEA

CHELMSFORD

EPPING

CHIPPING ONGAR

A414

MALDON

BRADWELL-ON-SEA

M25

A12

BILLERICAY

A414

B1012

B1010

B1021

BURNHAM-ON-CROUCH

A130

BRENTWOOD

A127

RAYLEIGH

LONDON

M25

BASILDON

A13

SOUTHEND-ON-SEA

A2

DARTFORD

A1089

TILBURY

Thames Estuary

Waltham Abbey

A20

A2

GRAVESEND

ROCHESTER

SHEERNESS

A232

KENT

181

The Wick, Terling Hall Road, Hatfield, Peverel, nr Chelmsford, Essex CM3 2EZ   **Nearest Road A12**

The Wick is a Grade II listed 16th century farmhouse in a pleasant rural setting with a large garden, duck pond and stream. The drawing room is nicely furnished as is the pretty dining room. Bedrooms are pleasantly decorated and have tea/coffee making facilities. Delicious home cooked evening meals are available on request. Well situated for London, Suffolk and East Coast ports.

see PHOTO opposite

Mrs Linda Tritton
Tel: 01245 380705
Mobile: 0976 246082

B&B from £21pp, Dinner from £12, Rooms 2 twin, Minimum age 10, Open all year , Map Ref A

Aldhams, Bromley Road, Lawford, Manningtree, Essex CO11 2NE   **Nearest Road A120, A137**

Aldhams offers a peaceful stay for guests who enjoy countryside and lovely garden. A rose garden gives colour all summer and in the spring the drive is yellow with daffodils. Tea is offered in the afternoon and a wide choice is available for breakfast. There are many excellent places to eat nearby, and for those wishing to explore, Constable country and Beth Chatto's garden are only a few minutes drive. Ideal too for the Port of Harwich, walking, bird watching and sailing. A popular base for a break all year round.

Mr & Mrs C McEwen
Tel/Fax: 01206 393210

B&B from £20pp, Rooms 1 twin, 2 double, en-suite available, No smoking, Children welcome, No pets, Open all year except Christmas & New Year, Map Ref D

Dairy House Farm, Bradfield Road, Wix, near Manningtree, Essex CO11 2SR   **Nearest Road A120**

We love welcoming visitors to our spacious farmhouse set in 700 arable acres. Peace and beautifully furnished en-suite accommodation are offered with tea and homemade cakes on arrival. The guests' lounge and bedrooms have drinks trays and colour TV. There is a large garden for relaxation and a games room for the energetic. Suffolk villages, Constable country, Beth Chatto's garden, seaside towns and historic Colchester are all within easy reach as are the ports of Harwich and Felixstowe. AA "QQQQ". English Tourist Board Highly Commended.

Bridget & Alan Whitworth
Tel: 01255 870332
Fax: 01255 870186

B&B from £18pp, Rooms 1 single, 1 twin, 1 double, all private/en-suite, Restricted smoking, Children from 11, No Pets, Open all year except Christmas and New Year, Map Ref B

Duddenhoe End Farm, Duddenhoe End, near Saffron Walden, Essex CB11 4UU   **Nearest Rd B1039, B1383**

Duddenhoe End Farm is a 17th century house with beams and inglenook fireplaces. There are 3 delightful bedrooms all with en-suite or private bathroom and tea/coffee making facilities and TV. A warm welcome is assured. Excellent restaurant and pubs within 3 miles for dinner. Ideally situated for Cambridge, Audley End House, Saffron Walden, Newmarket, Duxford Air Museum, Wimpole Hall. London 1 hour away by train. A no smoking house.

Mrs Peggy Foster
Tel: 01763 838258

B&B from £20pp, Rooms 1 twin, 2 double, all en-suite, No smoking, Minimum age 10, No pets, Open all year. Map Ref C

*left, **The Wick**, near Chelmsford - see details above*

GLOUCESTERSHIRE

There is so much choice in this fair county. If the Vale of Gloucester, the Forest of Dean, the Vale of Berkeley and the Cotswolds are not enough, then there are the cities of Gloucester, Cheltenham and Cirencester together with a clutch of some of the most attractive villages in England to explore.

The honey-yellow stone towns and villages of the Cotswolds have enchanted visitors for generations. The range of gently rolling limestone hills intersected by small deep valleys stretching north-east from Bath provides the glorious stone which adds so much to the picturesque charm of the region, a region rich since Medieval times from the wool of Cotswold sheep. This is a perfect holiday county, with its meandering roads and quaint villages. Stow-on-the-Wold, its ancient houses clustered round a large market square, was once a busy wool centre which held one of the largest livestock markets in Britain. Northleach to the south, also in the past an important centre of the wool trade, retains much of its Medieval past in its narrow winding streets, including some fascinating Tudor houses and a magnificent fifteenth century woolmerchants' church. Cirencester is a wonderful centre for touring the whole area. Named Corinium by the Romans, three great Roman highways originate here, Akeman Street, Foss Way and Ermine Street. The three thousand acre Cirencester Park in the grounds of Lord Bathurst's stately home is at the far end of Cecily Hill, one of Cirencester's finest streets. At nearby Bibury, described by William Morris as the most beautiful village

in England, are some delightful former weaver's cottages, and in Arlington Mill is the impressive Cotswold Museum. North Cerney, Nailsworth, Bisley and Tetbury each have their own particular charm and features. Two miles west of Tetbury at Beverstone are the ruins of the castle which in 1051 sheltered King Harold. At Sapperton on the River Frome just west of Cirencester are lovely views over Golden Valley. North is Cheltenham, an elegant Regency Spa - a market town until the discovery of mineral springs in 1718, and patronised by George III under whose approval the handsome terraces and tree-lined avenues were developed. The house in which the composer Gustav Holst was born is now a museum. Cheltenham has two festivals, the Music Festival in June or July and the Festival of Literature held in the Autumn.

Gloucester on the River Severn is the administrative centre of the county and was the Roman settlement of Glevum, an important fort established to defend the river crossing west into Wales. It is renowned for its magnificent cathedral which houses a stained glass window endowed in 1352 to commemorate the victory at Crecy, and the superb fan vaulting of the cloisters which is the earliest in the country. Gloucester is one of the locations of The Three Choirs Festival.

At the head of the Vale of Gloucester stands the ancient town of Tewkesbury. Steeped in history, it was here in 1471 that Edward IV confirmed his claim to the throne. The town has some splendid timbered black and white houses and old inns, but Tewkesbury's pride is the abbey church of St. Mary the Virgin, saved by the people of the town from destruction at the Dissolution. They collected £453 in 1539 to buy the church from Henry VIII. The high altar is a thirteen and a half feet long slab of Purbeck marble consecrated in 1239. Amongst Tewkesbury's many interesting inns is the Royal Hop Pole Inn mentioned in the Pickwick Papers. South of Gloucester is Stroud at the junction of five valleys, and famous for its West of England cloth. Below the town is Minchinhampton Common, a National Trust property of six hundred acres giving wonderful views over the Golden Valley and the Stroudwater Hills. To the north is the interestingly named Paradise, where Charles I stayed while laying siege to Gloucester. So delightful did he find the spot that he named it Paradise. The birdwatcher's paradise is Slimbridge, the Wildfowl Trust founded by the artist Peter Scott, boasting the world's largest and most varied collection of wildfowl. For the nature lover the Forest of Dean is an irresistible attraction. St. Briavels situated above the River Wye is the ideal walking centre. Its medieval castle used by early English Kings when they came to hunt in the forest, gives glorious views across twenty seven thousand acres.

The Valley of Berkeley, thousands of acres of low-lying land on the eastern bank of the Severn criss-crossed by lanes with hump-backed bridges over gently flowing waterways, is dominated by Berkeley Castle, in the dungeons of which Edward II was murdered in 1327. No visitor to this lovely town should leave without seeing the fine east window of the parish church, a memorial to Edward Jenner who was born in Bereley and who invented vaccination.

GLOUCESTERSHIRE

Places to Visit

Berkeley Castle, *Berkeley* ~ a compact fortress with circular Norman keep and inner bailey. It has been the home of the Berkeley family for eight hundred and fifty years. King Edward II was murdered in the dungeon in the keep. Magnificent collections of paintings, tapestries and carvings are on display and outside there is a deer park and terraced gardens.

Cirencester Park, *Cirencester* ~ it was laid out in 1714 by the 1st Earl of Bathurst with the assistance of poet Alexander Pope. The mansion is surrounded by a yew hedge, which is supposedly the tallest in the world.

Gloucester Cathedral, *Gloucester* ~ built in the 14th century. The ceiling has fan vaulting and the east windows commemorate the Battle of Crecy.

Hidcote Manor Garden, *near Chipping Campden* ~ a ten acre arts and crafts garden on a hilltop created by horticulturist Major Lawerence Johnstone. Consisting of a series of small gardens separated by walls and hedges.

Painswick, *Gloucestershire* ~ a picturesque Cotswold village with a collection of old stone cottages. The churchyard has ninety nine yew trees, trimmed into giant lollipops and tunnels.

Pitville Pump Room, *Cheltenham* ~ built 1825 to 1830, the domed Pump Room is modelled on the Greek Temple of Ilissos in Athens. The salty alkaline water can still be tasted and Cheltenham's Gallery of Fashion can be visited.

Slimbridge Wildfowl and Wetlands Trust, *Slimbridge* ~ founded in 1946 by naturalist Sir Peter Scott, its the world's largest collection of wildfowl with over one hundred and eighty different types of ducks, geese and swans. The Tropical House has a pink flamingo colony and other exotic varieties of bird.

Sudeley Castle, *near Winchcombe* ~ set in the Cotswolds and originally built in the 15th century, it became ruins after the Civil War and was rebuilt in the 19th century. Sudeley was favoured by Tudor royalty and became the home of Katherine Parr, the only of Henry VIII's wives to outlive him.

Chipping Camden

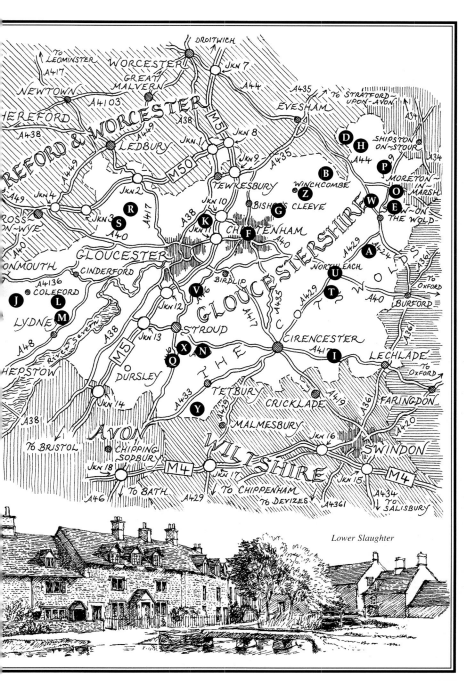

To LEOMINSTER
A417
NEWTOWN
HEREFORD
A438
A49
ROSS-ON-WYE
A40
MONMOUTH
A4136
COLEFORD
LYDNE
A48
CHEPSTOW
A38

DROITWICH
WORCESTER
GREAT MALVERN
A4103
LEDBURY
JKN 7
A44
EVESHAM
A435
To STRATFORD-UPON-AVON
A34
M5
A38
A449
M50
JKN 8
JKN 1
JKN 9
A435
TEWKESBURY
WINCHCOMBE
BISHOP'S CLEEVE
CHELTENHAM

JKN 2
JKN 3
A417
JKN 10
A38
A40
JKN 11
GLOUCESTER
CINDERFORD
BIRDLIP

SHIPSTON-ON-STOUR
A44
A34
MORETON-IN-MARSH
STOW-ON-THE-WOLD

D H
P
B
Z
G
F
R
S
W O E
V
A
U
T

A429
A424
A361
To OXFORD
A40
BURFORD
NORTHLEACH

JKN 12
STROUD
M5
JKN 13
DURSLEY
A38
A417
A4173
CIRENCESTER
A419
LECHLADE
To OXFORD
A361
FARINGDON
A419
A36
A420
CRICKLADE
MALMESBURY
JKN 16
SWINDON
M4

J
L
M
X
Q N
Y
I

GLOUCESTERSHIRE
THE
AVON
WILTSHIRE
JKN 14
CHIPPING SODBURY
JKN 18
M4
JKN 17
JKN 15
M4
To BRISTOL
A38
A46
To BATH
A429
To CHIPPENHAM
To DEVIZES
A4361
A434
To SALISBURY

Lower Slaughter

187

Coombe House, Rissington Road, Bourton-on-the-Water, GL54 2DT Nearest Road A429, A424

Coombe House is a quiet, non-smoking haven. Ideal for guests who appreciate high levels of cleanliness and gentle elegance. Serene small drawing room. Pretty, thoughtfully equipped en-suite bedrooms. Talking to plants encouraged, in a garden created by your Hosts, planted with the interesting and unusual. A great central base for exploration of the Cotswolds, Hidcote, Kiftsgate, Blenheim/Oxford, Sudeley and Warwick Castle. London 75 miles. Liquor Licence. Visa/MC/Amex.

Graham & Diana Ellis
Tel: 01451 821966
Fax: 01451 810477

B&B from £31pp, Rooms 2 twin, 5 double, family on request, all en-suite, No smoking, No pets, Open all year except Christmas Eve and Day & New Year's Eve, Map Ref A

Upper Farm, Clapton on the Hill, Bourton-on-the-Water, Gloucestershire GL54 2LG Nearest Road A429

see PHOTO opposite

A working family farm of 140 acres in a peaceful undiscovered Cotswold village 2 miles from the famous Bourton-on-the-Water. The listed 17th century farmhouse has been tastefully restored and offers a warm and friendly welcome with exceptional accommodation and hearty farmhouse fayre. The heated bedrooms are of individual character some are en-suite with TV and one is ground floor. From its hill position Upper Farm enjoys panoramic views of the surrounding countryside and being centrally located makes it an ideal base for touring, walking or merely relaxing.

Helen Adams
Tel: 01451 820453
Fax: 01451 810185

B&B from £17.50pp, ETB 2 Crown Highly Commended, Rooms 3 double, 1 family, 1 twin, some en-suite, No smoking, Minimum age 5, Open March - November, Map Ref A

Lansdowne Villa Guest House, Lansdowne, Bourton-on-the-Water, Glos GL54 2AT Nearest Road A429

Situated at a quiet end of this lovely village and within easy reach of the many attractions of the beautiful Cotswolds. Tony and Marie-Anne Baker extend a warm welcome to their guests and invite them to enjoy the relaxed atmosphere of their tastefully modernised home, bedrooms have been well equipped and comfortably furnished with coordinated fabrics, there is a cosy lounge for guests a choice is offered from the table evening menu. A wide range of beers, wines and spirits are also available. EMail: lansdowne@star.co.uk http://www.star.co.uk/lansdowne/

Tony & Marie-Anne Baker
Tel: 01451 820673
Fax: 01451 822099

B&B from £22.50pp, Dinner from £12.95, Rooms 2 single, 1 twin, 8 double, 1 family, all en-suite, Restricted smoking, Children welcome, No Pets, Open February - December, Map Ref A

Ashwood House, Snowshill, Broadway, Worcestershire WR12 7JU Nearest Road A44

Enjoying spectacular views Ashwood House stands in a unique position at the head of the Snowshill valley. Jon and Sue Collett enjoy welcoming guests to this beautiful rural setting on the outskirts of the picturesque Cotswold village of Snowshill. The spacious double en-suite room is comfortably furnished and has television, radio, refrigerator and tea facilities. There is a separate staircase enabling guests to come and go as they please. Restaurants abound in nearby Broadway or the Snowshill Arms offers good bar meals and local ales.

Jon & Sue Collett
Tel: 01386 853678

B&B from £25pp, Rooms 1 en-suite double, No smoking or pets, Children welcome, Open all year except Christmas Day, Map Ref B

---

*right, **Upper Farm,** near Bourton-on-the-Water - see details above*

The Old Rectory, *near Broadway - see details opposite*

The Old Rectory, Church Street, Willersey, Broadway, Gloucestershire WR12 7PN   Nearest Road A44

The Cotswold stone 17th century Rectory is quietly tucked away opposite the Church. With hills behind and a dry stone wall surrounding the delightful garden, this is an idyllic spot. Superb breakfasts in an elegant dining room, log fires in the winter. Many places for eating close by. Specialist paint finishes used to great effect in the en-suite bedrooms. 4 poster beds, TV and all facilities. Crabtree and Evelyn toiletries. No smoking. Special Winter rates. Supper trays by prior arrangement. Car Parking. Good base for walking and touring. For self catering see page: 503. EMail: beauvoisin@btinternet.com

see PHOTO opposite

Chris & Liz Beauvoisin
Tel: 01386 853729
Fax: 01386 858061

B&B from £32.50 - £47.50pp, Rooms 1 twin, 5 double, 2 family, 6 ensuite, 2 private, No smoking, Children over 8, Guide dogs only, Open all year except Christmas, Map Ref D

College House, Chapel Street, Broadwell, Gloucestershire GL56 0TW   Nearest Road A429

College House is a 17th century house located in a quiet and enchanting Cotswold village. It has delightful accommodation with luxurious bedrooms and bathrooms two of which are en-suite. Exposed beams, shutters, flagstone floors and mullioned windows abound. Sitting room with large stone fireplace for exclusive guest use. Breakfast and, if desired, 3 course dinners are served in the beamed dining room. The popular villages of Bourton-on-the-Water and Chipping Camden are close by and Cheltenham, Oxford and Stratford are easily accessible.

Sybil Gisby
Tel: 01451 832351

B&B from £25, Dinner from £17.50, Minimum age 16, No Pets, Open all year except Christmas, Map Ref E

Parkview, 4 Pittville Crescent, Cheltenham, Gloucestershire GL52 2QZ   Nearest Road M5, A435

We offer accommodation in a fine regency house in Cheltenham's nicest area. The bedrooms are large and airy with views onto Pittville Park and have tea/coffee and television. We are inspected by the RAC, Which? books and the Tourist Board who give One Crown Commended. Cheltenham is venue for racing and festivals of music and literature while proving a fine base for touring the area. The Cotswold villages stand in the surrounding hills. Gloucester is nearby while Stratford is only an hour away.

Sandra Sparrey
Tel: 01242 575567

B&B from £17.50pp, Rooms 1 single, 2 twin, 2 family, Restricted smoking, Children & pets welcome, Open all year, Map Ref F

Clarence Court Hotel, Clarence Square, Cheltenham, Gloucestershire GL50 4JR   M5, J9 & J10

This privately owned B&B Hotel was once the townhouse of the Duke of Wellington. He came to Cheltenham to take the waters in-between fighting all those battles against Napoleon! The house overlooks gardens in a peaceful, tree lined regency square yet is only a short stroll from the amenities and shops of Cheltenham. It is an ideal touring centre for the Cotswolds with its numerous stately homes and gardens. There is a lovely lounge, ample free parking, a licensed bar, and TV and tea/coffee making facilities in all the individually decorated rooms. Delicious bar meals also available.

Brian & Susan Howe
Tel: 01242 580411
Fax: 01242 224609

B&B from £25 - £33.50pp, Rooms 6 single, 9 twin/double, 3 family, all en-suite, Children welcome, Pets by arrangement, Open all year, Map Ref F

Lypiatt House Hotel, Lypiatt Road, Cheltenham, Gloucestershire GL50 2QW   Nearest Road A40

Lypiatt House is a charming Victorian house set in its own grounds with private parking. There is an elegant drawing room leading into a delightful conservatory with an 'honesty' bar. All bedrooms are en-suite with TV, complimentary tea and coffee and direct dial telephone. The emphasis is on comfort and relaxation combined with personal and friendly service. An excellent breakfast is served in the pretty dining room with lovely stencilled walls. Situated in Monpellier it is within five minutes walk of numerous and varied restaurants.

see PHOTO opposite

Jane & Michael Medforth
Tel: 01242 224994
Fax: 01242 224996

B&B from £30pp, Rooms 2 single, 3 twin, 5 double, all en-suite, Restricted smoking, Children welcome, No pets, Open all year, Map Ref F

Cleeve Hill Hotel, Cleeve Hill, Cheltenham, Gloucestershire GL52 3PR   Nearest Road B4632

This award winning No Smoking hotel offers the ultimate in Bed & Breakfast. Positioned near the summit of Cleeve Hill, the bedrooms offer some of the most spectacular views in the Cotswolds. All bedrooms are elegantly furnished to the highest standards with en-suite bathrooms, TV with movie channel, direct dial telephone, hair dryers and hospitality tray. The generous breakfasts have been described as the best ever, excellent pub and restaurants abound in the area. ETB Deluxe, AA Premier Selected, Which Hotel Guide, County Hotel of the year 95. Good Hotel Guide.

see PHOTO on page 194

John & Marian Entstone
Tel: 01242 672052
Fax: 01242 679969

B&B from £32.50pp, Rooms 1 single, 2 twin, 5 double, 1 family, all en-suite, No smoking, Children from 8, No pets, Open all year except Christmas & New Year, Map Ref G

The Pond House, Lower Fields, Weston Rd, nr Chipping Camden, WR11 5QA   Nearest Road B4035

Superb country home, peaceful position in farmland, without passing traffic. Friendly, relaxed atmosphere with high standard of comfort and service. Wonderful breakfasts in our conservatory with panoramic views of the Cotswold Hills. The perfect base to explore many famous gardens, historical sites, castles, 3 miles from Broadway, Chipping Camden, Near to Stratford-upon-Avon, Cheltenham and Evesham. All bedrooms are en-suite, with colour TV, radio, hair dryer and tea/coffee facilities. Ample parking. AA 5Q Premier Selected, ETB 2 Crown Highly Commended. Phone for a detailed brochure.

Anne & Ray Payne
Tel/Fax: 01386 831687

B&B from £22-£28pp, Rooms 2 twin, 1 ground floor, 2 double, all en-suite, No smoking, Children over 5, No pets, Open all year, Map Ref H

The Masons Arms, Meysey Hampton, Cirencester, Gloucestershire GL7 5JT   Nearest Road A417

Set beside the village green this Cotswold 17th century coaching inn provides you with modern amenities and comfort in a beautiful rural setting. Individually decorated en-suite rooms have tea/coffee making facilities and colour TV; some with beams and open stonework. They offer an ideal base to explore the Cotswolds and surrounding countryside. The traditional bar, with log fires and cosy pews, is also an ideal haven for residents and local customers alike with a warm welcome assured. Home-made fayre and wines available daily in the bar and separate restaurant.

Andrew & Jane O'Dell
Tel: 01285 850164
Fax: 01285 850164

B&B from £32pp, Dinner from £5, Rooms 1 twin, 6 double, 1 family, all en-suite, Children welcome, Dogs by arrangement, Open all year, Map Ref I

*left, **Lypiatt House Hotel**, Cheltenham - see details above*

Cleeve Hill Hotel,
Cheltenham
see details on page 193

Tudor Farmhouse Hotel & Restaurant, Clearwell, near Coleford, Glos GL16 8JS   **Nearest Road A466**

Set in a gentle valley between the Forest of Dean and the Wye Valley, this peaceful and welcoming old farmhouse has stood since the 13th century and features oak beams and original wall panelling. The bedrooms are tastefully furnished in traditional style, some have 4 poster beds and all have colour TV, tea/coffee facilities, central heating and en-suite bath or shower and wc. In the lounge is an inglenook fireplace. The dining room has open stonework, oak beams and is the ideal way to enjoy the imaginative freshly prepared cuisine. AA Restaurant Red Rosette, ETB 3 Crown Highly Commended. Freephone: 0800 7835935 EMail: reservations@tudorfarmhse.u-net.com

Colin & Linda Gray
Tel: 01594 833046
Fax: 01594 837093

B&B from £29pp, Dinner from £18.95, Rooms 7 double, 4 family, 2 twin, all en-suite, Open all year, Map Ref J

see PHOTO on page 196

Frogfurlong Cottage, Frogfurlong Lane, Down Hatherley, Gloucestershire GL2 9QE   **Nearest Road A38**

Frogfurlong Cottage is situated on the green belt area within the triangle formed by Gloucester, Cheltenham and Tewksbury. Originally 2 cottages, built in 1812 but recently modernised and extended. It stands on its own, back from the road and surrounded by fields. There is an indoor heated swimming pool which guests may use mornings and evenings. The accommodation, which is totally self contained, consists of a double bedded room equipped with tea/coffee tray, TV, luxury bathroom and jacuzzi. Garden and ample parking. A real 'get away on our own' break.

Clive & Anna Rooke
Tel: 01452 730430

B&B from £18pp, Dinner from £10.50 by arrangement, Rooms 1 en-suite double, No smoking, No Pets, No children, Open all year except Christmas, Map Ref K

Edale House, Folly Road, Parkend, near Lydney, Royal Forest of Dean GL15 4JF Nearest Road A48, B4234

Edale House is a fine Georgian residence facing the cricket green in the village of Parkend at the heart of the Royal Forest of Dean. Once the home of local GP, Bill Tandy, author of " A Doctor in the Forest". The house has been tastefully restored to provide comfortable en-suite accommodation with every facility including tea/coffee equipment, TV, and hair dryer, etc. Enjoy delicious, imaginative cuisine prepared by your Hosts and served in the attractive dining room. Within easy reach of Wye Valley. Riding, cycling, canoeing, walking, etc., are all close to hand. EMail: edale@lineone.net

Christine & Alan Parkes
Tel: 01594 562835
Fax: 01594 564488

B&B from £21.50pp, Dinner from £17.50, Rooms 1 twin, 4 double, all en-suite, Children and pets by arrangement, Open all year, Map Ref L

Upper Viney Farmhouse, Viney Hill, Lydney, Gloucestershire GL15 4LT   **Nearest Road A48**

This lovely stone built Grade II Listed farmhouse has feature oak spiral staircase and inglenook fireplaces. Many of the artifacts found during renovation work to the house are on show and visitors are welcome to see Malcolm's Mini Museum of Horticulture and farm implements. Originally a two bedroomed house extensions were made during the 1700's and again in 1960's. Situated just off A48 and overlooking the village of Blakeney. Upper Viney is acclaimed for delicious breakfasts. Character bedrooms with hospitality trays, television and hair dryers.

Malcolm & Mary Litten
Tel: 01594 516672

B&B from £20pp, Rooms 1 twin, 1 double, 1 family, all en-suite, No smoking, Children & pets by prior arrangement, Open March - November, Map Ref M

Hunters Lodge, Dr. Browns Road, Minchinhampton, Gloucestershire GL6 9BT   Nearest Road A419, A46

Hunters Lodge is a beautiful furnished old Cotswold Stone house situated 650ft up in South Cotswolds on the edge of 600 acres of National Trust land - Minchinhampton Common. Spacious bedrooms, en-suite/private bathrooms, colour TV, tea/coffee making facilities. Separate guest lounge leads into a delightful conservatory and large garden. Ideal centre for walking and touring the lovely Cotswold towns. Selection of local menus, maps and brochures, and help available to plan your daily itinerary. Non-smokers only, children over 10. ETB Highly Commended 2 Crowns.

Margaret & Peter Helm
Tel: 01453 883588
Fax: 01453 731449

B&B from £20-£23pp, Rooms 1 twin, 2 double/twin, all en-suite/private, No smoking or pets, Children over 10, Open all year except Christmas, Map Ref N

Townend Cottage, High Street, Moreton-in-Marsh, Gloucestershire GL56 0AD   Nearest Road A429

A warm welcome awaits you in our 17th century cottage and coach house in the heart of the Cotswolds. Each room is unique with TV and tea/coffee. We welcome all families to the comfort of our family home. Why not relax in our superb garden after a day touring the lovely Cotswold country. We have a separate guest lounge plus TV. A full English breakfast is part of the holiday treat. We are near Stratford, Cheltenham, Bath and Oxford and we can meet you at the local station.

Chris & Jenny Gant
Tel: 01608 650846

B&B from £38 per room, Rooms 1 twin, 2 double, 1 family, all with private bathroom or en-suite, Restricted smoking, Children welcome, No pets, Open all year except Christmas and New Year, Map Ref O

Treetops Guest House, London Road, Moreton-in-Marsh, Gloucestershire GL56 0HE   Nearest Road A44

A beautiful family home offering traditional Bed & Breakfast. 6 attractive bedrooms all with en-suite facilities and 2 of which are on the ground floor and thus suitable for disabled persons or wheelchair users. All rooms are comfortably furnished with either sofas or armchairs, TV, radio, hair dryer and tea/coffee facilities. A guests sun lounge and delightful secluded gardens to relax in. Cots and high chair available. Ideally situated for exploring the Cotswolds. A warm and homely atmosphere awaits you here.

Elizabeth & Brian Dean
Tel/Fax: 01608 651036

B&B from £21pp, Rooms 2 twin, 3 double, 1 family, all en-suite, No smoking, Children & pets welcome, Open all year except Christmas, Map Ref O

Newlands Farmhouse, Aston Magna, Moreton-in-Marsh, Gloucestershire GL56 9QQ   Nearest Road A429

If you would like to stay 'off the beaten track' this 16th century Tudor House offers a high standard of accommodation. The house sympathetically restored is attractive having beams, stone floors and furnished with antiques. Bedrooms are large and comfortable having their own vanitory units, tea/coffee facilities and central heating. Every where are fresh flowers and pot plats. Guests have their own lounge with television. Nearby are lovely gardens, Hidcote, Kiftsgate plus many more. Centrally situated for touring Stratford, Broadway, The Slaughters, Campden and Bilbury.

Mr & Mrs Hessel
Tel: 01608 650964

B&B from £18.50pp, Rooms 1 twin, 1 double, 1 en-suite, No smoking, children or pets, Open February - November, Map Ref P

left, **Tudor Farmhouse Hotel & Restaurant,** *near Coleford - see details on page 195*

The Vicarage, Nailsworth, Gloucestershire GL6 0BS   Nearest Road A46 - Avening Road

The Vicarage is a large family house, built in 1874. All bedrooms are spacious, warm and comfortable, well furnished, ad have tea/coffee making facilities. The house is set in two acres of mature garden, and is an excellent base for walks and exploring the Cotswolds. The town centre is two minutes walk with several good restaurant and nearby pubs with excellent food.

Mrs P Strong
Tel: 01453 832181

B&B from £20pp, Rooms 2 single, 1 twin, No smoking, Pets welcome, Open all year except Christmas, Map Ref Q

Old Court Hotel, Church Street, Newent, Gloucestershire GL18 1AB   Nearest Road M50

Once the family home of the Lord of the Manor this magnificent house is set in a delightful one acre walled garden. Thoughtful modernisation has ensured many period features remain creating a relaxing and elegant atmosphere. The Georgian panelled dining room offers superb cuisine, resulting in an enviable reputation for both quality and imagination. All bedrooms are individually styled with private facilities, tea/coffee, direct dial telephone, radio and colour TV. The 4-poster bedroom is particularly spacious and is perfect for special occasions. Snooker Room. Falconry course and wine producing area. ETB 3 Crowns.

Ron & Sue Wood
Tel: 01531 820522

B&B from £22.50pp, Dinner £13.75, Rooms 1 family, 1 4-poster, 2 double, 2 twin, all en-suite, Open all year, Map Ref R

Orchard House, Aston Ingham Road, Kilcot, near Newent, Glos GL18 1NP   Nearest Road M50, B4222

see PHOTO opposite

Orchard House is a delightful Tudor style country house completely surrounded by 5 acres of peaceful gardens. A beautifully appointed home with a relaxed and friendly atmosphere, every modern comfort and delicious food. A very high standard of accommodation, including a Regency style dining room, luxurious double and en-suite bedrooms, original oak beams, TV lounge, a conservatory, fountain courtyard and croquet lawn. Residential licence. Bargain breaks for 2 or more days D,B&B.

Anne Thompson
Tel: 01989 720417
Fax: 01989 720770

B&B from £26.50pp, Dinner £19.50, Minimum age 12, No pets, No smoking, Open all year, Map Ref S

Northfield, Cirencester Road, Northleach, Gloucestershire GL54 3JL   Nearest Road A429, A40

Detached family house in the country close to all services in the small market town of Northleach with its magnificent church, musical and countryside museums - sure to please. Excellent centre for visiting lovely Cotswold villages. Easily reached by car are Cheltenham, Oxford, Cirencester, Stratford, Burford Wildlife Park, local golf course, fishing, Cotswold walks and horse riding. All rooms are en-suite, with central heating, TV, and tea/coffee trays, log fire in lounge. Large gardens to relax in or to enjoy a selection of freshly prepared evening meals. Brochure. 3 Crowns Highly Commended.

Pauline Loving
Tel: 01451 860427

B&B from £22pp, Dinner from £7, Rooms 1 twin, 1 double, 1 family, all en-suite, No smoking, Children welcome, No pets, Open all year except Christmas & New Year, Map Ref T

*right, **Orchard House,** near Newent - see details above*

Cotteswold House, Market Place, Northleach, Gloucestershire GL54 3EG   Nearest Road A40, A429

Relax in our 400 year old Cotswold stone wealthy wool merchants home with beamed ceilings, original panelling and Tudor archway. We have a luxury private suite and two en-suite double or twin rooms - all spacious, elegant and well equipped. Enjoy traditional English food and a friendly welcome. Find us in the centre of this ancient market town of Northleach in the centre of the Cotswolds - an ideal touring base. AA QQQQ Selected. ETB 3 Crowns Commended.

Elaine & Graham Whent
Tel/Fax: 01451 860493

B&B from £22.50pp, Dinner from £14.95, Rooms 1 private double suite, 1 double, 1 twin both en-suite. No smoking, children or pets, Open all year except Christmas and New Year, Map Ref U

Market House, The Square, Northleach, Gloucestershire GL54 3EJ   Nearest Road A429, A40

A 400 year old Cotswold stone house of 'olde worlde' charm yet with modern facilities. This enchanting and pretty Grade II listed house features an inglenook fireplace and many exposed beams. The very comfortable, well appointed and centrally heated, bedrooms (1 en-suite), all have wash hand basins, tea/coffee makers, and touring guides. Northleach is a tiny, tiny town with a wonderful selection of restaurants and inns. A delicious English breakfast completes your stay. Packed lunches on request. Ideal base for touring locally and Stratford, Bath, Oxford and Woodstock. Which recommended.

Theresa & Mike Eastman
Tel: 01451 860557

B&B from £19pp, Rooms 1 double en-suite, 1 twin/double, 2 single, No smoking, No pets, Minimum age 12, Open all year, Map Ref U

Prospect Cottage, West End, Northleach, Gloucestershire GL54 3HG   Nearest Road A429, A40

Prospect Cottage is a listed, traditional Cotswold stone house built in the XVIIth Century. It is situated in the old wool town of Northleach, and retains many original features including exposed beams and stone walls. A high level of comfort is provided: tea/coffee facilities and TV in guest rooms; a guest sitting room with log fire, TV and hi-fi. Evening meals by arrangement. Menu features both traditional and more exotic dishes. Homemade preserves a specialty. Ideal Cotswold touring base; Burford, Moreton, Stow, Bourton, The Slaughters, Cirencester and Cheltenham within 12 miles.

Mrs Margaret Hogan
Tel: 01451 860875

B&B from £27.50pp, Dinner from £12.50-£15, Rooms 1 twin, 1 double, both en-suite, No smoking, Children over 10, Pets welcome, Open mid January - mid December, Map Ref U

Painswick Mill, Kingsmill Lane, Painswick, Gloucestershire GL6 6SA   Nearest Road A46

A beautiful Grade II listed Cotswold stone mill house dating from 1634 is set in 4 acres of lawn and trees traversed by 2 streams featuring a water garden. The property has rare old fireplaces, beamed ceilings and oak panelling. Two of the bedrooms are beamed and have tea/coffee making facilities with TV. A lounge, garden and hard tennis court available for guests. Painswick, Queen of the Cotswold is a good base for touring and walking. Superb local pubs and restaurant serve delicious meals.

Mrs J M Wells
Tel: 01452 812245

B&B from £25pp, Rooms 1 twin with private bathroom, 2 double en-suite, Restricted smoking, Children over 10 years, No pets, Open all year except Christmas, Map Ref V

Hope Cottage, near Stroud - see details on page 203

The Limes, Evesham Road, Stow-on-the-Wold, Gloucestershire GL54 1EJ   **Nearest Road A424**

The Limes is a large Victorian, family house, established as bed and breakfast accommodation for over 20 years. Pleasantly situated over-looking fields and the attractive garden with ornamental pool. The comfortable bedrooms are spacious and are equipped with radio/alarms, tea/coffee making facilities and Satellite TV. A short walk of about 4 minutes to the town centre. Car parking available. Choice of breakfast including vegetarian catered for. Many guests, from home and abroad, return each year. Recommended by the AA and RAC.

Helen & Graham Keyte
Tel: 01451 830034/831056

B&B from £17.50pp, Rooms 4 en-suite double - £20pp, 1 family, 1 twin, Children welcome, Pets by arrangement, Open all year except Christmas, Map Ref W

Woodlands, Upper Swell, near Stow-on-the-Wold, Gloucestershire GL54 1EW   **Nearest Road B4077**

Luxurious small guest house in 1/4 acre of gardens. In quaint Cotswold village with breathtaking views over lake and hills. All bedrooms are deluxe en suites with colour TV and tea/coffee facilities. There is a lounge for guests where light snacks are served. Ample car parking is available. We are situated in the village of Upper Swell just 1 mile from the tourist town of Stow-on-the-Wold. ETB 2 Crown Commended, AA 4Q's Selected.

Brian & Kathryn Sykes
Tel: 01451 832346

B&B from £26pp, Rooms 1 single, 3 double, 1 twin, all en-suite, Children & Pets welcome, Open all year, Map Ref W

Hope Cottage, Box, nr Stroud, Gloucestershire GL6 9HD   **Nearest Road A46, A419**

For peace and tranquillity, this charming undiscovered village of Box 10 miles from Cirencester is unrivalled. Hope Cottage is in an area of outstanding natural beauty and enjoys glorious Cotswold views. Here, you can savour the charm of this delightful country house, set in 3 acres with landscaped gardens and an outdoor heated pool for guests use in the summer. Comfortable en-suite rooms, all with colour TV and hospitality tray. Sumptuous traditional English breakfasts. Excellent local restaurants and pubs. Strategic base for walking and touring.

see PHOTO on page 201

Sheila & Garth Brunsdon
Tel: 01453 832076

B&B from £20pp, Rooms 1 twin, 2 double, all en-suite, Children welcome, No smoking or pets. Open January - November, Map Ref X

Tavern House, Willesley, near Tetbury, Gloucestershire GL8 8QU   **Nearest Road A433**

Delightfully situated 17th century former Cotswold coaching inn, only 1 mile from Westonbirt Arboretum. Superb luxury bed & breakfast. All rooms en-suite with direct dial phone, colour TV, tea maker, hair dryer, trouser press, etc. Guests lounge. Charming secluded walled garden. Ample parking. Convenient for visiting Bath, Bristol, Gloucester, Cheltenham, Bourton-on-the-Water, Castle Combe. AA, RAC, ETB Highly Commended. English Tourist Board Silver award winner for excellence. Bed & Breakfast of the year 1993. Colour brochure with pleasure. EMail:Tavern House Hotel@uk business.com

see PHOTO opposite

Janet & Tim Tremellen
Tel: 01666 880444
Fax: 01666 880254

B&B from £29.50pp, Rooms 1 twin, 3 double, all en-suite, Restricted smoking, Minimum age 10, No pets, Open all year, special rates for Christmas and New Year, Map Ref Y

*left, **Tavern House**, near Tetbury - see details above*

Gower House, 16 North Street, Winchcombe, Gloucestershire GL54 5LH   Nearest Road B4632

Gower House, a 17th century town house, is situated close to the centre of Winchcombe, a small picturesque country town on the 'Cotswold Way', and is an ideal base for exploring the Cotswolds. Ramblers, cyclists and motorists are all equally welcome and there is ample parking to the rear. The three comfortable bedrooms all have colour TV, radio, tea/coffee making facilities, washbasins, full central heating and are served by 2 bathrooms each with shower and bath. In addition a TV lounge and a large garden are available for guests' use.

Sally & Mick Simmonds   **B&B from £18pp, Rooms 2 twin, 1 double, Restricted smoking, No pets,**
Tel: 01242 602616   **Open all year except Christmas, Map Ref Z**

Almsbury Farm, Vineyard Street, Winchcombe, Gloucestershire GL54 5LP   Nearest Road B4632

This 400 year old Grade II listed Cotswold stone house offers a high standard of comfortable accommodation and a very warm welcome. Set in lovely countryside on the edge of the village. Almsbury Farm offers the best of both worlds. Leave your car and explore the Cotswold Way and local walks and visit Sudeley Castle on foot or travel to Stratford, Broadway, Cotswold villages or Oxford which are all within easy reach.

Annie Hitch   **B&B from £22pp, Rooms 2 double, 1 family, all en-suite, Restricted**
Tel: 01242 602403   **smoking, Children over 10 years, Pets by arrangement, Open all year,**
                                              Christmas by arrangement, Map Ref Z

"Thank you Bess, that was lovely"
BELLE & BERTIE IN YORK

I come from haunts of coot and hern,
I make a sudden sally
And sparkle out among the fern,
To bicker down a valley.

THE BROOK
ALFRED, LORD TENNYSON 1809-92

HAMPSHIRE
& the ISLE of WIGHT

From north to south this lovely county unrolls to reveal a staggering variety of holiday pleasures. Probably the most diverse of the counties of southern England, the chalk North Downs and the sandy heathland of the north-east change into a charming landscape of wooded wold cut by streams and scattered with delightful villages. The most attractive scenery is probably around Selborne in the east and the woodlands of the New Forest in the west. Selborne is the birthplace of Gilbert White, the pioneer of natural history who in 1789 published The Natural History and Antiquities of Selborne, one of the finest records of the English countryside written.

The north of the county is cut by the Roman Road known as Portway which ran from the Roman camp of Calleva Atrebatum at Silchester to Salisbury. Andover is well placed for visiting this section of Hampshire - the Andover Downs, the valley of the River Anton, Hurstbourne Tarrant on the Bourne Rivulet in the pretty valley of Uphusband, and Wherwell, an ancient and attractive village of thatched cottages giving magnificent views across the Test valley. Further north is Highclere Castle, the seat of the Earls of Carnarvon, and on the summit of nearby Beacon Hill is the grave of the Fifth Earl, who in 1922 opened a tomb to

reveal the spectacular treasures of Tutankhamen. In the extreme east of the county is Farnborough, the home of the Royal Aircraft Establishment and the impressive Air Show held every other year in the first week of September. Close by is Aldershot, the 'home of the British Army'. The Heroes Shrine in Manor Park is dedicated to the dead of World War II.

Filtered clear by the chalk downs is the River Test, one of England's finest trout rivers. To travel the length of this river is a delight, as the valley contains some picturesque villages. It was near the source of the river at Steventon that Jane Austen was born in 1775, and lived for the first twenty three years of her life. At Longstock, a village of fascinating old houses, the Danes had a shipyard where their longships were serviced. And speaking of fascinating old houses, the three Wallop villages, Over, Middle and Nether are renowned for their thatched cottages and fine churches. Romsey's development followed that of its abbey founded by the son of

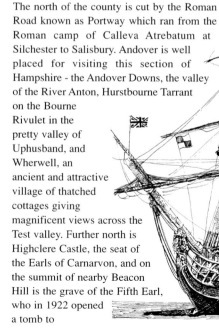

Alfred the Great. Regrettably all that now remains is the Norman abbey church, which incidentally contains the remarkable Ramsey Psalter, a fifteenth century illuminated manuscript. Broadlands House, a mile from the town, was the home of Lord Palmerston whose statue stands in Romsey Market Place. The house later became the home of the Mountbatten family.

At the centre of Hampshire lies Winchester, a major religious and commercial centre in medieval times, and the capital city of Saxon England. The city is rich in every period of architecture after the thirteenth century. Its cathedral, the longest medieval cathedral in Europe, is a magnet to visitors, and contains monuments to Jane Austen and Isaak Walton, the 'Compleat Angler' who lived for some time in the cathedral close. During the Middle Ages St. Swithin's Shrine here was an important centre for pilgrims from Europe on their way to Becket's Shrine at Canterbury. The Tourist Information Centre is housed in the impressive Gothic revival guildhall built in 1871. Near the west gate is the Great Hall containing "King Arthur's Round Table' - interesting, but unfortunately a medieval fake! A statue of King Alfred, King of Wessex, stands in Broadway. Winchester College, founded in 1382 by Bishop William of Wykeham, is one of the country's leading and oldest public schools and was very probably used as a model for Eton College. The great natural amphitheatre just three miles from Winchester at Cheesefoot Head was used by General Eisenhower when he addressed the allied troops before the D-Day landings in 1944. There is a great deal to attract the visitor around the city - Avington House for instance, where Nell Gwynne lived when Charles II was in Winchester, Twyford,

where Alexander Pope spent his school years and Crawley, immortalised by Thackeray in his novel 'Vanity Fair'.

The New Forest, a royal hunting ground established in 1079 for the Norman kings, strangely enough in so populated an area, still retains its remoteness. It is a splendid place for walking, picnics and camping. Near Minstead is the Rufus Stone, marking the supposed spot where William II was killed by an arrow fired by Walter Tyrrell, while hunting in 1100. Beaulieu Abbey, built by King John, destroyed by Henry VIII and rebuilt in part in 1872 as Palace House, is the home of Lord Montagu, whose National Motor Museum holds the finest collection of its kind. To the south is Buckler's Hard, which in the eighteenth centuy employed no fewer than four thousand men building the ships for Nelson's navy, of oak from the New Forest.

The Isle of Wight is extremely popular with the holidaymaker, having a scenic beauty all of its own. The walks over Tennyson Downs from Freshwater Bay provide memorable views of The Needles. Godshill, Mottistone, Shorwell, Sandown and Calbourne offer the visitor special delight. At Carisbrooke, the old capital of the Island, there is the great Norman Castle in which Charles I was imprisoned, while Osborne House, designed by Prince Albert and Thomas Cubitt, was a great favourite of Queen Victoria. Newport, capital of this busy holiday island, is of course the ideal centre for the visitor who has the difficult if pleasant task of choosing priorities. There are picturesque villages in profusion, breathtaking coastal walks, seaside towns with golden sands and excellent bathing, and for the sailor, Cowes, which is the home of the Royal Yacht Squadron.

HAMPSHIRE
& the ISLE of WIGHT

Places to Visit

Carisbrooke Castle, *Isle of Wight* ~ a mediaeval castle which for centuries was the home of the island's governor. Donkeys still raise water from the well in the middle courtyard.

Hillier Gardens and Arboretum, *Ampfield* ~ founded by Sir Harold Hillier, the famous nurseryman, in 1953. 166 acres of gardens with over 42,000 plants and trees.

Historic Dockyard, *Portsmouth* ~ now partly opened to the public, it houses a collection of historic ships including the hull of the Mary Rose, Henry VIII's flagship which sank on its maiden voyage to fight the French in 1545. HMS Victory, the English flagship on which Nelson was killed at Trafalgar, has now been fully restored; also on display is HMS Warrior, the 1860 ironclad warship.

The New Forest, *Hampshire* ~ 145 square miles of heath and woodland. William the Conqueror's 'new' forest, despite its name, is one of the few primeval oak woods in England.

Osborne House, *Isle of Wight* ~ overlooking Osborne Bay and the Solent, Queen Victoria and her husband Prince Albert built this house in 1855 as a seaside retreat for their family. The house is based on an Italian villa with terraced gardens. It is still furnished very much as it was when they left it. When Queen Victoria used to swim in her own private beach, she was carried into the water by a wheeled bathing machine which is still on show today.

Shanklin Old Village,
Isle of Wight

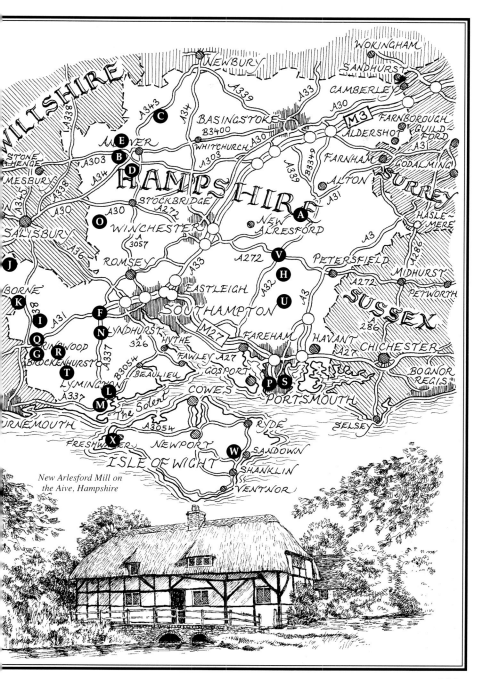

WOKINGHAM
WILTSHIRE
NEWBURY
SANDHURST
CAMBERLEY
A339
A33
A30
A343
A34
FARNBOROUGH
M3
BASINGSTOKE
ALDERSHOT
GUILD-
FORD
B3400
A338
C
WHITCHURCH
A30
A31
ANDOVER
E
B
WHITCHURCH
FARNHAM
GODALMING
STONE
HENGE
A303
A303
B3349
A339
A31
SURREY
A34
D
HAMPSHIRE
ALTON
MESBURY
A338
A31
HASLE-
MERE
A345
A30
STOCKBRIDGE
A272
NEW
ALRESFORD
A
SALISBURY
O
WINCHESTER
A3057
A3
A36
A272
PETERSFIELD
MIDHURST
ROMSEY
A33
A272
V
PETWORTH
J
H
A32
A3
A272
SUSSEX
BORNE
EASTLEIGH
U
A286
K
SOUTHAMPTON
I
F
A31
M27
FAREHAM
HAVANT
CHICHESTER
Q
N
LYNDHURST
HYTHE
A27
A286
G
R
RINGWOOD
A326
FAWLEY
A27
GOSPORT
BOGNOR
REGIS
A337
BROCKENHURST
B3054
BEAULIEU
T
LYMINGTON
COWES
P
S
L
The Solent
PORTSMOUTH
A337
M
RNEMOUTH
A3054
RYDE
SELSEY
X
FRESHWATER
NEWPORT
W
SANDOWN
ISLE OF WIGHT
SHANKLIN
VENTNOR

*New Arlesford Mill on
the Aive, Hampshire*

Thickets, Swelling Hill, Ropley, Alresford, Hampshire SO24 0DA Nearest Road A31

This spacious country house surrounded by a two acre garden has fine views across the Hampshire countryside. There are two comfortable twin bedded rooms with private bath or shower room. Tea/coffee making facilities available. Guests sitting room with TV. Full English breakfast. Local attractions are Jane Austen's House ten minutes by car. Winchester with its fine cathedral twenty minutes away. Salisbury, Chichester and The New Forest within easy reach. Heathrow Airport one hour.

David & Sue Lloyd-Evans
Tel: 01962 772467

B&B from £20pp, Rooms 2 twin, both with private facilities, Restricted smoking, Children from 10, No pets, Open all year except Christmas and New Year, Map Ref A

Broadwater, Amport, near Andover, Hampshire SP11 8AY Nearest Road A303

A 17th century listed thatched cottage with old oak beams, offering quiet and cosy accommodation in a relaxed and friendly atmosphere, set in a secluded cottage garden, in a peaceful village near Stonehenge. Within minutes of the A303 and having easy access to airports and ferries. A private sitting room with traditional fireplace and colour TV. ETB 2 Crown Highly Commended, AA QQQ. Also flat sleeps 2/3, B&B or self catering. Credit cards taken. EMail: carolyn@dmac.co.uk

Mrs Carolyn Mallam
Tel: 01264 772240
Fax: 01264 772240

B&B from £22.50, Rooms 2 en-suite twin, Restricted smoking, Children welcome, No pets, Open all year, Map Ref B

Frenches Lodge, Little London, Andover, Hampshire SP11 6JG Nearest Road A343, A303

Frenches Lodge is a Grade II listed 300 year old thatched farm house with old oak beams and open fire, offering quiet accommodation in a friendly atmosphere. It is reached by driving through the village and woods. It has a secluded garden with country walks into the surrounding woods. Breakfast times are flexible and served in the sunny conservatory overlooking the garden. It is within half an hour of Winchester, Cathedrals, Salisbury and Newbury Racecourse. Golf courses are close by. Dinner is served by arrangement. Car park.

Charles & Gilly Radford
Tel: 01264 365358

B&B from £22pp, Dinner from £15, Rooms 1 single, 1 twin, 1 double, adjacent facilities, Children welcome, Pets by arrangement, Open all year except Christmas & New Year, Map Ref C

May Cottage, Thruxton, nr Andover, Hampshire SP11 8LZ Nearest Road A303

see PHOTO opposite

May Cottage dates back to 1740 and is situated in the heart of this picturesque and tranquil village with post office and old inn. A most comfortably furnished home all with en-suite/private bathrooms, colour TV, tea trays, 1 on ground floor. Guests own sitting/dining room. An ideal base for visiting ancient cities, stately homes and gardens yet within easy reach of ports and airports, parking facilities. Hosts can be contacted on mobile 0468 242166. ETB 2 Crowns Highly Commended. AA 4Q's Selected, Ashley Courtney Highly Recommended.

Tom & Fiona Biddolph
Tel: 01264 771241
Fax: 01264 771770

B&B from £25pp, Dinner from £15, Rooms 1 single, 2 twin, 1 double, most en-suite, No smoking or pets, Children over 6, Open all year except Christmas, Map Ref E

*right, **May Cottage**, near Andover - see details above*

Malt Cottage, Upper Clatford, Andover, Hampshire SP11 7QL   Nearest Road A303

Walk around the beautiful garden with chalk stream and lakes, or sit by the fire in beamed sitting room. Malt Cottage, an ideal stop from London/Heathrow to the West country, set in a picturesque village with thatched cottages. 3 attractive bedrooms with private or en-suite facilities. This is an central position for exploring Stonehenge, Salisbury and Winchester or within an hour Bath, Oxford, and Portsmouth. A warm welcome in a delightful home. Local fishing, airport collection and summer barbecues. EMail: maltcottage.accommodation@virgin.net http://freespace.virgin.net/maltcottage.accommodation

Patricia & Richard Mason
Tel: 01264 323469
Fax: 01264 334100

B&B from £20pp, Rooms 1 twin, 2 double, all en-suite/private, Restricted smoking, Children welcome, No pets, Open all year except Christmas & New Year, Map Ref D

Walnut Cottage, Old Romsey Road, Cadnam, Hampshire SO40 2NP   Nearest Road M27, A31

Walnut Cottage is a Victorian Foresters Cottage on the edge of the New Forest and set in an attractive garden with an old well and a river. Here Eric and Charlotte make you most welcome, all the bedrooms have en-suite facilities, TV and tea making facilities, and one bedroom is downstairs with a door onto the garden. In old Romsey Road are two renowned local pubs for an evening meal. Many places are easily accessible from Cadnam such as Southampton, Beaulieu, Salisbury and Winchester.

Eric & Charlotte Osgood
Tel: 01703 812275
Fax: 01703 812275

B&B from £21.50pp, Rooms 2 twin, 1 double, all en-suite, No smoking, Children over 14, No pets, Open all year except Christmas week, Map Ref F

Tothill House, Black Lane, off Forest Road, Burley, Christchurch, Hampshire BH23 8DZ Nearest Road A35

Tothill House is in an idyllic woodland setting on the southern fringe of the New Forest adjoining Poors Common, an area designated for outstanding natural beauty and noted for its flora and fauna All bedrooms are en-suite, have colour TV, and tea/coffee making facilities. A wide variety of local sporting and recreational activities available with fine sailing waters on the Solent, bathing beaches and excellent selection of golf courses. Private fishing lakes nearby. AA QQQQ Selected.

Mrs Wendy Buckley
Tel: 01425 674414
Fax: 01425 672235

B&B from £25pp, Rooms 2 double, 1 twin, all en-suite, Minimum age 15, No pets, No smoking, Open all year except Christmas & New Year, Map Ref G

Drayton Cottage, East Meon, Hampshire GU32 1PW   Nearest Road A32, A272

Drayton Cottage is an immaculately maintained 200 years old flint and chalk country cottage, with superb views surrounded by pasture land. Antiques and oak beams in the guest lounge and breakfast room, and a conservatory overlooking the attractive garden, provide a luxurious yet cosy atmosphere in which to relax. Bedrooms have TV, tea/coffee facilities and excellent beds. Parking is easy and guests have their own entrance and stairs. Portsmouth, Chichester, Winchester, Selbourne and Petworth are all within easy reach. ETB Highly Commended.

Mrs Joan Rockett
Tel: 01730 823472

B&B from £20pp, Rooms 1 twin/double en-suite, 1 double with private shower room, Restricted smoking, No children or pets, Open all year except Christmas, Map Ref H

A Green Patch, Furzehill, Fordingbridge, Hampshire SP6 2PS Nearest Road A338

Elegant house in beautiful setting of eight acres. Direct access onto New Forest. Wonderful views. All rooms spacious, colour TV, tea and coffee making facilities. Wide choice of breakfast served in lovely oak panelled dining room or on terrace. Huge conservatory and garden for guests to use at any time. Easy reach Bournemouth, Southampton, Salisbury, Winchester, Portsmouth. Plenty of things to see and do. Good eating places nearby. Proprietor loves her job and will give you a good welcome.

Meg Mulcahy
Tel: 01425 652387
Fax: 01425 656594

B&B from £21-£25pp, Rooms 1 twin, 1 double, 1 family, 1 en-suite, 2 private, No smoking or pets, Children welcome, Open all year, Map Ref I

Hendley House, Rockbourne, Fordingbridge, Hampshire SP6 3NA Nearest Road A338, A354

Overlooking water meadows a beautiful, south facing, 16th Century house elegantly decorated with a wealth of beams in a relaxed family atmosphere. So much to visit in Hampshire, Wiltshire and Dorset. Walking and cycling in New Forest, surrounding countryside and south coast. Returning to relax by log fires in winter or swimming pool in spacious garden in summers, then walk through the picturesque village for excellent food in charming thatched pub. Riding, fishing, golf and racing nearby. Discounts for 3 nights or more.

Mrs Pat Ratcliffe
Tel: 01725 518303
Fax: 01725 518546

B&B from £25pp, Rooms 1 twin with en-suite shower, 1 double with private bathroom, Minimum age 10, No pets, Open February - end November, Map Ref J

Cottage Crest, Woodgreen, Fordingbridge, Hampshire SP6 2AX Nearest Road A338

Cottage Crest is situated in a delightful spot on the edge of the New Forest, set in its own 41/2 acres of garden surrounded by ancient and ornamental forest with superb views of the River Avon in the Valley. The en-suite bedrooms are spacious, decorated to very high standard and have TV and tea/coffee making facilities. A short walk takes one into the village with it's local pub which serves excellent meals, Within easy reach of the coast and Isle of Wight. It is the ideal place to either relax, in the peaceful surroundings, or visit the many interesting places in the area.

Mrs Lupita Cadman
Tel: 01725 512009

B&B from £20pp, Rooms 1 twin, 2 double, all en-suite, Children welcome, No pets, Open all year except Christmas, Map Ref K

Albany House, 3 Highfield, Lymington, Hampshire SO41 9GB Nearest Road A337

Built about 1830, this elegant Regency residence has large, well proportioned rooms with quality furnishings and sumptuous bathrooms, Situated in a quiet position overlooking a green yet only moments from Lymington's thriving shopping centre with interesting boutiques, narrow cobbled streets and ancient Saturday market. A ferry to the Isle of Wight operates all year. A comfortable lounge with books and log fire. An excellent dinner is served in the elegant dining room. bedrooms have tea/coffee making facilities, TV and are en-suite.

Mrs Wendy Gallagher
Tel: 01590 671900

B&B from £26pp, Dinner from £12.50, Rooms 1 twin, 1 double, 1 family, all en-suite, Open all year except Christmas. Map Ref L

Jevington, 47 Waterford Lane, Lymington, Hampshire SO41　　　　　**Nearest Road A337**

Comfortable family home situated in a quiet lane midway between High Street/Marinas. Ideal base for New Forest, Solent coastline walks. 10 minutes drive to Isle of Wight ferry, 10 minutes walk to ancient market town. Good selection of pubs and restaurants. Tea/coffee making facilities, TV, off street parking. Children welcome. No smoking. Places of interest to visit include Beaulieu, Winchester, Stonehenge, Portsmouth, Bournemouth and Southampton. Bike hire, riding, sailing and nature walks in the New Forest can all be arranged.

Ian & June Carruthers
Tel: 01590 672148

B&B from £18pp, Rooms 1 twin, 1 double, 1 family, all en-suite, No smoking, Children and pets welcome, Open all year, Map Ref L

St Mary's Lodge, Captains Row, Lymington, Hampshire SO41 9RR　　　　　**Nearest Road M27**

An elegant Georgian interior designed house situated in the old area of Lymington close to the town quay. Quaint with fishing boats and visiting yachts. Boutiques, shops, pubs and first class restaurants minutes away. Well known Saturday antiques market. Two marinas and ferry to the Isle of Wight. Wonderful walks in the New Forest and Beaulieu. Convivial hosts providing a memorable stay.

Mrs P A Thomson
Tel: 01590 678576

B&B from £25pp, Rooms 2 double, 1 twin, 2 single, Minimum age 8, No smoking, Pets by arrangement, Open all year, Map Ref L

Efford Cottage, Everton, Lymington, Hampshire SO41 0JD　　　　　**Nearest Road A337**

Our friendly, Award Winning Guest House is a spacious Georgian cottage, with an acre of garden. All rooms are shower en-suite with beverage facilities, colour TV, heated towel rail, hair dryer, electric blanket, trouser press and mini fridge. A four course, multi-choice breakfast with homemade bread and preserves, by qualified chef, using homegrown produce. As excellent centre for exploring both the New Forest and the South Coast with sports facilities, fishing, bird watching and horse riding in the near vicinity. Guest lounge. Private parking. AA 5Q's. EMail: effcottage@aol.com

Patricia Ellis
Tel: 01590 642315
Fax: 01590 641030/642315

B&B from £22pp, Dinner from £30, Rooms 1 twin, 3 double, 1 family, all en-suite, Restricted smoking, Children over 14, Dogs welcome, Open all year, Map Ref M

The Penny Farthing Hotel, Romsey Road, Lyndhurst, Hampshire SO43 7AA　　　　　**Nearest Road A337**

see PHOTO opposite

Ideally situated in Lyndhurst village centre, The Penny Farthing Hotel, offers smart en-suite rooms with remote control colour TV and tea/coffee making facilities. We also have a residents lounge with bar and a large private car park to the rear. The Hotel was completely refurbished in 1993 and all rooms named after bicycles. We have bicycles to hire and secure lock up store if you would like to bring your own. Lyndhurst village has a good selection of pubs, restaurants, cafes, shops and the New Forest Visitor Centre and Museum.

Tel: 01703 284422
Fax: 01703 284488

B&B from £22.50pp, Rooms 1 single 2 twin, 6 double, 2 family, Restricted smoking, Children welcome, Pets by arrangement, Open all year except Christmas, Map Ref N

*right, **The Penny Farthing Hotel**, Lyndhurst - see details above*

Yew Tree Farm, Bashley Common Road, New Milton, Hampshire BH25 5SH   Nearest Road A35

Two lovely spacious bed sitting rooms marvelously comfortable, with double or twin beds and both with own bathroom, in a traditional, cosy, thatched farm house on the edge of the New Forest. Extensive breakfast (taken in bedroom), homemade dinners (if ordered in advance), using top quality produce. Private entrance and ample parking. Very easily located. Turn off the A35 between Lyndhurst and Christchurch onto the B3058. Yew Tree Farm is a small holding with 9 acres of grassland and is home to a charming home bred cow named Holly.

Mrs Daphne Matthews
Tel/Fax: 01425 611041

B&B from £27.50 - £35pp, Dinner £18.50 - £27.50pp (A la Carte), Rooms 1 twin with private bathroom, 1 en-suite double, No smoking, No Children, Pets if kept in car, Open all year except Xmas & New Year, Map Ref O

Fortitiude Cottage, 51 Broad Street, Old Portsmouth, Hampshire PO1 2JD   Southern End of A3

A charming unusual town house overlooking the quayside in the heart of Old Portsmouth. Built on the site of a 16th century cottage destroyed during the 2nd war and named after an 18th century warship. The immaculately maintained bedrooms and bathrooms are decorated in delicate pastel shades and needlepoint pictures and flowers abound. Breakfast is served on pine tables in a beamed room with views over the water. Carol has won 'Britain in Bloom' awards for her window boxes and hanging baskets; and 'Heartbeat' for healthy food choices. Most major credit cards accepted.

Mrs C A Harbeck
Tel: 01705 823748
Fax: 01705 823748

B&B from £22pp, Rooms 3 rooms all en-suite with tea/coffee making facilities, No smoking, No children, Open all year, Map Ref P

The Nest, 10 Middle Lane off School Lane, Ringwood, Hampshire BH24 1LE   Nearest Road A31, B3347

A lovely Victorian family house. Situated in a quiet residential lane within 5 minutes walk of Ringwood town centre, an ancient market town with many restaurants and inns. Ample parking. Beautifully decorated, very clean and well maintained. Breakfast times are flexible and served in the delightful sunny conservatory overlooking the gardens. Pretty colour co-ordinated 'Laura Ashley' style bedrooms with pine furnishings. Local activities include fishing, golf, riding and forest walks. An excellent base to explore the new Forest. 30 mins drive Bournemouth, Salisbury & Southampton. AA QQQQ's Selected. Highly recommended. Friendly helpful service.

Mrs Yvonne Nixon
Tel/Fax: 01425 476724
Mobile: 0589 854505

B&B from £17pp, Rooms 2 double, 1 twin, 1 single, No smoking, Open all year, Map Ref Q

Holmans, Bisterne Close, Burley, Ringwood, Hampshire BH24 4AZ   Nearest Road A31, A35

Holmans is a charming country house in the heart of the New Forest, set in four acres with stabling available for guests' own horses. Superb walking, horse riding and carriage driving with golf course nearby. A warm friendly welcome is assured. All bedrooms are en-suite and tastefully furnished with tea/coffee making facilities, radio and hair dryer. Colour TV in guests lounge with adjoining orangery and log fires in winter.

Robin & Mary Ford
Tel/Fax: 01425 402307

B&B from £22pp, Rooms 1 twin, 2 double, all en-suite, No smoking, Children welcome, Open all year except Christmas, Map Ref R

Burbush Farm, Pound Lane, Burley, nr Ringwood, Hampshire BH24 4EF   Nearest Road A31, A35

Burbush Farm nestles in twelve acres of peace and tranquillity in the heart of the New Forest. Delicious Aga cooked breakfast, award winning 'New Forest' sausages, farm eggs, homemade marmalade, served on fine Spode china. Comfortable guest lounge with log fire. All bedrooms are beautifully furnished with en-suite, coffee/tea making facilities, colour TV. Ideal touring location. Walking, riding, (stables/paddocks available for guests' horses) cycle hire, sailing, golf - a naturalist delight. Unlimited parking, enchanting gardens leading directly onto forest.

David & Carole Hayles
Tel: 01425 403238
Fax: 01425 403238

B&B from £22pp, Rooms 1 twin, 2 double, 1 family, all en-suite/private facilities, No smoking, Children welcome, Pets restricted, Open all year except Christmas & New Year, Map Ref R

Plantation Cottage, Mockbeggar, near Ringwood, Hampshire BH24 3NL   Nearest Road A338

A charming 200 year old Grade II listed cottage set in three acres in the beautiful new Forest between Ringwood and Fording bridge. Mockbeggar is a peaceful hamlet where wild ponies graze by the roadside, and is also within easy reach of Bournemouth, Poole and Salisbury. There are many excellent pubs and restaurants in the area, which is ideal for walking, cycling and riding at stables close by. Guest lounge and garden available all day. Holiday cottage also available. All rooms en-suite. Sorry no smoking and no children. ETB Two Crowns Highly Commended.

Jane Yates
Tel: 01425 477443
Fax: 01425 477443

B&B from £25, Rooms 1 twin, 1 double, all en-suite, No smoking, children or pets, Open all year, Map Ref Q

Glencoe Guest House, 64 Whitwell Road, Southsea, Hampshire PO4 0QS   Nearest Road M27, M275

Glencoe is a Victorian town house ideally situated in a quiet residential road yet convenient to all amenities. Only 2 minutes from the sea front and a short drive to the Continental Ferry Port. Places of historic interest are within walking distance, also the Hovercraft which will get you to the Isle of Wight in 10 minutes. Glencoe offers high standards of comfort with attractive rooms. For added comfort bedrooms are all equipped with tea/coffee making facilities and TV.

Mrs June Gwilliam
Tel/Fax: 01705 737413

B&B from £17.50pp, Rooms 2 single, 2 twin, 2 double, 1 family, most en-suite, Restricted smoking, Children welcome, No pets, Open all year, Map Ref S

Yew Tree House, High Street, Broughton, Stockbridge, Hampshire SO20 8AA   Nearest Road A30

This delightful Grade II listed early Georgian house is set in the heart of the peaceful award-winning village of Broughton. It is furnished with many antiques, guests may use the sitting room and their bedrooms are a good size with comfortably firm beds. The beautiful walled garden always provides flowers for every room. Many guests comment upon the special atmosphere of this home and the exceptional warm welcome they receive. The place to stay awhile and visit Winchester, Salisbury and Jane Austen country.

Philip & Janet Mutton
Tel: 01794 301227

B&B from £22pp, Rooms 1 single, 1 twin, 1 double, all private/en-suite, No smoking, Children Welcome, No pets, Open all year, Map Ref T

Forest Gate, Hambledon Road, Denmead, Waterlooville, Hampshire PO7 6EX   Nearest Road B2150

This is a fine Grade II Georgian residence, built around 1790, and is situated on the outskirts of the village overlooking farmland. Set in approximately 2 acres of garden with lawns, rose beds, pond and tennis court. The elegant drawing and dining rooms have mahogany floors with French doors opening onto a paved garden terrace. The comfortable bedrooms are en-suite have tea/coffee making facilities and TV. Nestling in the South Downs, Denmead is on the Wayfarers Way, a scenic 70 mile walk from Emsworth to Newbury. Dinner is available by arrangement.

Torfrida & David Cox
Tel: 01705 255901

B&B from £18pp, Dinner from £10, Rooms 2 twin (en-suite), No smoking, Minimum age 10, Open all year except Christmas & New Year, Map Ref U

Home Paddocks, West Meon, Hampshire GU32 1NA   Nearest Road A32, A272

Home Paddocks is the much cherished home of the Ward family. It is on the outskirts of West Meon set in a large garden with tennis court and croquet lawn. Parts of the house date back to the 1560s and there is a Victorian conservatory. The comfortable bedrooms with garden views, have private facilities. Our guests have the exclusive use of the drawing room and dining room. Ideally situated for Winchester, Southampton, the New Forest and many places along the South Coast. There is a good selection of pubs, restaurants, golf courses and gardens to visit in the area. EMail: Homepaddocks@compuserve.com.uk

Mr & Mrs Ward
Tel: 01730 829241
Fax: 01730 829577

B&B from £22pp, Dinner from £14, Rooms 2 en-suite twin, Restricted smoking, Minimum age 7, Pets by arrangement, Open all year except Christmas, New Year and Easter, Map Ref V

The Grange Country House, Alverstone, near Sandown, Isle of Wight   Nearest Road A3055, A3056

The Grange is in the centre of the hamlet of Alverstone. Built in 1877 this was the Island home of Lord Alverstone. Peaceful garden of 3/4 acre surround the house. An excellent English breakfast is served in the dining room. There is a comfortable lounge with open log fire. The en-suite bedrooms with tea/coffee making facilities, are bright and airy with views overlooking the rolling Downs. The Grange is situated for all aspects of the Island and is ideal for walking, the E Yar nature walk and Nunwell trail pass through the village. EMail: grange_alverstone@compuserve.com

Geraldine & David Watling
Tel: 01983 403729
Fax: 01983 403729

B&B from £20pp, Rooms 1 single, 2 twin, 3 double, 1 family, all en-suite, Children welcome, No pets, No smoking, Open February - November, Map Ref W

Strang Hall, Uplands, Totland Bay, Isle of Wight PO39 0DZ   Nearest Road B3322

Strang Hall is an Edwardian family home decorated in the arts and craft style with splendid views over the Downs and Solent, set peacefully in the hills above Totland Bay. The large garden leads onto a short walk to the beach. Yarmouth and Freshwater are within 2 miles with golf, tennis etc. The West Wight is famous for its good country walks.

Vera F. Mc Mullan
Tel/Fax: 01983 753189

B&B from £22.50pp, Dinner from £12, Rooms 1 single, 1 twin, 1 double, 1 family, some en-suite, Restricted smoking, Children welcome, No pets, Open all year except Christmas & new year, Map Ref X

Great things are done when men and mountains meet
This is not done by jostling in the street.

MS NOTE-BOOK P. 43
WILLIAM BLAKE 1757-1827

HEREFORDSHIRE
& WORCESTERSHIRE

The glorious Malvern Hills stand between the low plains of Herefordshire and the Worcestershire Vale of Evesham. Used extensively by ancient man as defensive positions, the well preserved hill forts of the Hereforshire Beacon and the Worcestershire Beacon remain witness to their prowess as military builders. Today, these lovely hills offer the holidaymaker wonderful walking country and superb views ranging from the Welsh Marches in the west to the Cotswolds in the east. The Malverns inspired much of the music of Sir Edward Elgar who until his death in 1934 directed his own music at the Three Choirs Festival - the major music festival which takes place in August each year rotating between Worcester, Hereford and Gloucester cathedrals. Not only do Herefordshire and Worcestershire offer the visitor two quite remarkable 'capital' cities, they offer also some of the most spectacular river scenery in the country.

Hereford, once the Saxon capital of West Mercia, is delightfully situated by the River Wye in an area renowned for its cattle and its cider making. A perfect centre for touring, the city has some excellent medieval architecture, but its pride and joy is undoubtedly its sandstone cathedral begun in 1107, with its impressive library of over 1400 chained books, the largest of its kind in the world, and its priceless thirteenth century map of the world, the famous Mappa Mundi. Also of interest is the plaque marking the birthplace of Nell Gwynne in nearby Gwynne Street. A short distance away at Abbey Dore are the remains of a huge Cistercian abbey, while to the east is Kilpeck, whose fine Norman church is lavishly carved with mythical beasts. West from Hereford is an excellent Black-and-White Village Trail, taking the visitor through Weobley, Pembridge whose six hundred year old fortified church tower was used by villagers as a defence against Welsh raiders, Eardisland with its fourteenth century Staick House and lovely Lyonshall.

The River Wye, famous for its salmon, enters a spectacular wooded sandstone gorge as it nears its end. It's hard to visualise this beautiful place at one time being a centre of industry, but during the fifteenth and sixteenth centuries these woodlands supplied charcoal for a flourishing iron-smelting industry - in fact brass was actually invented here in 1568. Symonds Yat, a popular visitors attraction, overlooks the meander of the Wye. Ross-on-Wye is the main tourist centre of the district with its Georgian houses and arcaded market house. To the north is Ledbury with another impressive market house built in the sixteenth century, half-timbered and standing on pillars of chestnut. The Feathers Inn is one of the finest examples of seventeenth century half-timbering in Britain. John Masefield, a former Poet Laureate, was born here and the town was a favourite of the Brownings and Wordsworth - and little wonder, the place is picturesque in the extreme. Malvern Wells and Great Malvern, sheltering under the Malvern Hills, were brought to prominence in the eighteenth century when a Dr. Wall advertised the medicinal efficacy of its spa water.

Leominster is wonderfully situated at the junction of Pinsley Brook and the River Lugg, amongst cider-apple orchards and hopfields, although its prosperity is based upon its fine-spun wool from local sheep, which long ago were exported to establish the great Australian and South American flocks. Like Herefordshire, Worcestershire is blessed with lovely rivers and none more attractive than the Teme which, when the river is in flood can flow a rich red from the underlying red sandstone. The countryside here is lush, the banks of the River Teme bordered by hop fields, orchards and market gardens. A mile from where the Teme and the Severn join stands glorious Worcester, the administrative centre of Worcester and Hereford, dominated by its eleventh century cathedral. Worcester became an Anglo-Saxon town after becoming a diocese in 680AD. Wool was the source of the city's medieval wealth, but since 1751 the manufacture of Worcester porcelain has become its best known activity. The city is rich in ancient and interesting houses. The Guildhall, designed in 1722 by a pupil of Sir Christopher Wren, incorporates a carving of the head of Oliver Cromwell nailed by the ears over the doorway. Worcester was an important centre during the Civil War, and Charles II's headquarters during the Battle of Worcester were the Commandery, founded in 1085 as a hospital by St. Wulstan. The cathedral houses the tomb of King John who died in 1216. Above the tomb is the oldest royal effigy in England. The County Cricket Club founded in 1865 must have one of the finest locations in the country.

And could there be a finer sight than the Vale of Evesham in Spring when the fruit trees are in blossom. Evesham, the centre of this fruit growing area, is an elegant town built around a now-ruined Benedictine abbey, whose one hundred and ten feet high Bell Tower stands in the centre of the town. The obelisk on Green Hill is in memory of Simon de Montfort, the father of the House of Commons who died in battle in 1265. On the edge of the Vale of Evesham under the Cotswold Hills stands arguably the prettiest of the many lovely villages hereabouts, Broadway, a riot of colourful cottage gardens and honey-coloured stone.

The southern area of the county is undeniably lovely, but despite its proximity to the industries of Birminham there is fine walking country in the hills of Clent and Lickey.

HEREFORDSHIRE
& WORCESTERSHIRE

Places to Visit

Berrington Hall, *near Leominster, Herefordshire* ~ an elegant, compact house designed by Henry Holland and built between 1778 and 1783 for the Rt. Hon. Thomas Harley. The Digby Collection of French Regency furniture is on display. The gardens contain many exotic and interesting plants.

Goodrich Castle, *Goodrich, Herefordshire* ~ situated five miles south of Ross-on-Wye, this 12th century red sandstone fort sits on the top of a rock high above the river.

Hereford Cathedral, *Hereford* ~ a small Norman cathedral with pink sandstone columns lining the nave. The central tower was built around 1325, the building underwent an extensive restoration after the 14th century west tower collapsed in 1786. The cathedral houses the Mappa Mundi, a map of the world drawn in 1290 by clergyman Richard of Haldingham and a chained library with over 1400 books.

Hanbury Hall, *Droitwich, Worcestershire* ~ set in 400 acres of parkland, it has been the Vernon family home for over 3 centuries and was remodelled in 1701. Showrooms are open to the public; they include paintings by Sir James Thornhill and Dutch flower paintings and there is also a collection of fine porcelain.

Lower Brockhampton, *Bringsty, Worcestershire* ~ a late 14th century moated manor house with a detached half timbered 15th century gatehouse and there are also ruins of a 12th century chapel in the grounds.

Worcester Cathedral, *Worcester* ~ the tower collapsed in 1175 then it suffered a terrible fire in 1203 before the present structure was started in the 13th century. The nave and central tower were completed in the 1370's. In 1874, Sir George Gilbert Scott designed the High Gothic choir with 14th century carved misericordes. Henry VIII's brother is buried in the chantry chapel.

The Wye at Symonds Yat

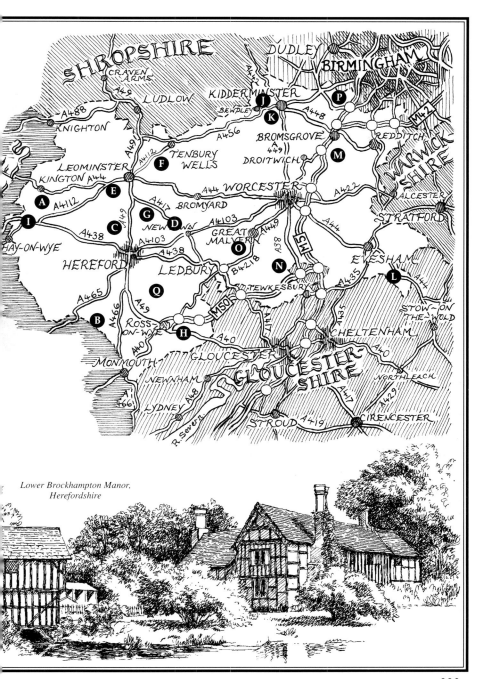

SHROPSHIRE
DUDLEY
BIRMINGHAM
CRAVEN ARMS
A49
LUDLOW
KIDDERMINSTER
BEWDLEY
M42
A448
A488
KNIGHTON
A456
BROMSGROVE
REDDITCH
A449
WARWICKSHIRE
A4112
TENBURY WELLS
DROITWICH
A422
ALCESTER
LEOMINSTER
KINGTON A44
A44 WORCESTER
STRATFORD
A4112
A4103 BROMYARD
A44
NEW
OWN
A4103
A438
GREAT MALVERN
A449
A38
M5
EVESHAM
A4103
B4218
HEREFORD
A438
LEDBURY
A435
TEWKESBURY
STOW-ON-THE-WOLD
A465
M50
A466
A49
ROSS-ON-WYE
A40
CHELTENHAM
A40
MONMOUTH
NEWNHAM
GLOUCESTER
GLOUCESTERSHIRE
NORTHLEACH
A466
LYDNEY
A48
R.Severn
A417
A429
CIRENCESTER
STROUD
A419

Lower Brockhampton Manor,
Herefordshire

223

The Bowens Country House, Fownhope, Hereford HR1 4PS   **Nearest Road B4224**

Peacefully situated opposite the church on the edge of the village on the B4224 in the Wye Valley AONB, midway between Hereford and Ross-on-Wye. Ideal for touring, walking, and exploring the Welsh Borders, Malverns, Cotswolds, Brecon Beacons and the countryside of Herefordshire. Tastefully restored 17th century country house set in 2 acres of gardens. Well appointed bedrooms, with TV, telephone, central heating and tea/coffee. Oak beamed lounge with inglenook fireplace. Superb home-cooked meals, including vegetarian dishes, using local/home produce. ETB 3 Crowns Highly Commended.

Mrs Carol Hart
Tel: 01432 860430
Fax: 01432 860430

B&B from £25pp, Dinner available D'Hote £12, Rooms 1 single, 6 twin/double, 3 family, all en-suite, Children welcome, Pets by arrangement, Open all year, Map Ref Q

Bollingham House, Eardisley, Herefordshire HR5 3LE   **Nearest Road A4111**

Quite breathtaking. This Georgian gentleman's residence overlooks one of the finest views in England. Gracious rooms with log fires, spacious bedrooms, fresh cut flowers and an interesting English garden to wander around. These extensive gardens include terracing, ponds and a walled garden with a special rose walk, and just outside the dining room window is a Victorian chapel. Conveniently situated for the Welsh Marches, Offa's Dyke, the well known book town, Hay-on-Wye and golf at the famous Kington Golf Club.

John & Stephanie Grant
Tel: 01544 327326
Fax: 01544 327880

B&B from £23pp, Dinner from £12, Rooms 1 single, 1 twin, 2 double, all with private facilities, Restricted smoking, Children welcome, Pets by arrangement, Open all year except Christmas & New Year, Map Ref A

The Old Rectory, Garway, Herefordshire HR2 8RH   **Nearest Road A466, B4521**

Our home has a very welcoming atmosphere, smell of log fires, a grandfather clock, arrangements of flowers and Aga cooking make you feel at home. The Blue room has a double four poster, the Pink room has twin beds. They both have TV, tea/coffee making facilities and hand basins. They share a bathroom, plus separate loos and shower room. Private sitting room. Acre of peaceful garden, wonderful views to Black Mountains and Brecon Beacons. Hereford 15 miles, Ross 11, Monmouth 8. ETB Highly Commended.

Caroline Ailesbury
Tel: 01600 750363
Fax: 01600 750364

B&B from £20pp, Dinner from £16, Rooms 1 twin, 1 double, No smoking, Children over 8 years, No pets, Open all year, Map Ref B

Appletree Cottage, Mansell Lacy, Hereford, Herefordshire HR4 7HH   **Nearest Road A480**

Appletree Cottage was originally one cottage and then a cider house and eventually 2 converted farm cottages. One cottage was built in 1450 and the more modern on around the late 16th century. The house is fully centrally heated. There is an open plan sitting room with wood burning stove and dining room. English country breakfasts are served. We are surrounded by many places of interest.

see PHOTO opposite

Mrs Monica Barker
Tel: 01981 590688

B&B from £15pp, Rooms 1 single/double, 2 twin, 1 en-suite, All rooms have tea/coffee making facilities, No smoking, Open all Year, Map Ref C

*right, **Appletree Cottage**, near Hereford - see details above*

Upper Court, Ullingswick, Hereford, Herefordshire HR1 3JQ   Nearest Road A417, A465

Upper Court is peaceful, historic and rambling, friendly and warmed by central heating and log fires. Surrounded by a large garden and orchard, easy walks to two excellent pubs and panoramic views of the countryside. Cathedrals, castles, stately homes, beautiful gardens, black and white villages, hills, all nearby.

Susan Dalton
Tel: 01432 820295
Fax: 01432 820174

B&B from £20pp, Dinner from £18, Rooms 1/2 twin, 1/2 double, No smoking, Children & pets welcome, Open all year, Map Ref D

Highfield, Newtown, Irvington Road, Leominster, Herefordshire HR6 8QD   Nearest Road A44

Highfield stands in a large garden with unspoilt views of open farmland and distant mountains and enjoys a pleasant rural situation just 11/2 miles from the old market town of Leominster. The house was built around the turn of the century and accommodation is elegant, comfortable and friendly being well proportioned and attractively decorated. Meals are carefully prepared from good fresh ingredients and delightfully served in the charming dining room. All gastronomic needs and desires are catered for and a modest wine list is available. Groups and house parties welcome. ETB 2 Crowns Commended.

Catherine & Marguerite Fothergill
Tel: 01568 613216

B&B from £18.50pp, Dinner from £12.50 by arrangement, Rooms 1 double, 2 twin en-suite/private facilities, Open all year, Map Ref E

Woonton Court Farm, Leysters, Leominster, Herefordshire HR6 0HL   Nearest Road A49, A4112

Welcome to our Tudor farmhouse. Enjoy the atmosphere of oak beams and wood-burning stove in our guest lounge/dining room. Bedrooms en-suite/private facilities, central heating, TV and tea/coffee making facilities. Farm produce. Freedom to walk on our mixed family farm. Excellent centre to explore ancient market towns of Ludlow, Leominster, Hereford, Malvern and the Welsh Border. Local walk, gardens, castles, festivals and National Trust properties. Antique and Bric-A-Brac shops, plus many attractions for children.

Elizabeth Thomas
Tel/Fax: 01568 750232

B&B from £18pp, Dinner by arrangement from £8.50, Rooms 1 twin, 2 double, all en-suite, Restricted smoking & pets, Children welcome, Open all year except Christmas, Map Ref F

Fives Ashes House, Middleton on the Hill, Leominster, Herefordshire HR6 0HX   Nearest Road A49, B4112

Lovely secluded country house set in 10 acres of gardens and grounds. Offering peace and quiet being 2 miles from main A49 between Ludlow and Leominster. Several lovely gardens, craft centre and two National Trust properties with acres of Trust and Forestry Commission land to ramble over close by. Several good eating inns are only 2/3 miles away. The accommodation, which is en-suite, has been tastefully decorated and furnished to a high standard with colour TV and tea/coffee. A large inglenook fireplace graces the guests lounge with individual tables in a spacious dining hall. Drying facilities available. Packed lunches. Even stabling/grazing for your horse. AA QQQQ Selected. Brochure.

Lindsay Christian
Tel/Fax: 01568 750334

B&B from £22pp, Dinner by arrangement from £12.50, Rooms 1 double, 1 twin, both en-suite, Non smoking, Open all year, Map Ref F

---

*right, **Rudhall Farm**, Ross on Wye - see details on page 228*

The Vauld Farm, The Vauld, Marden, Herefordshire HR1 3HA   Nearest Road A49

The perfect accommodation for relaxing and discovering the delights of Herefordshire. The Vauld Farm is a 16th century Elizabethan manor with spacious en-suite bedrooms including four poster. All have private lounge areas with TV and tea/coffee facilities overlooking duck pond and open countryside. Breakfast and optional evening meals are served in the dining room which has a large open fire, massive oak beams overhead and flagstone floor. Guests are welcome to bring their own wine etc. Quiet location with ample parking. Hereford 8 miles.

Mrs Jean Bengry
Tel: 01568 797898

B&B from £22.50pp, Dinner from £16.50, Rooms 1 twin, 2 double, 1 family, all en-suite, Restricted smoking, Children over 12, No pets, Open all year, Map Ref G

Rudhall Farm, Ross-on-Wye, Herefordshire HR9 7TL   Nearest Road B4221

see PHOTO on page 227

Set in rolling countryside with millstream and lake, yet central for exploring the picturesque Wye Valley and beyond. Elegant early-georgian farmhouse offering accommodation of character and charm with that touch of luxury, bedrooms having co-ordinated fabrics and every 20th century facility. Friendly hospitality where guests' comfort is of prime importance. AGA cooked breakfasts (diets catered for). Welcoming tea tray on arrival served either in the sitting room or terraced garden. Excellent eating houses nearby. Non smokers preferred. Also self catering Mill cottage for 4 nearby.

Mrs Heather Gammond
Tel: 01989 780240
Mobile: 0585 871379

B&B from £20pp, Rooms 2 double, guests bathroom, No smoking No pets, Open all year except Christmas and New Year, Map Ref H

Winforton Court, Winforton, Herefordshire HR3 6EA   Nearest Road A438

see PHOTO opposite

Winforton Court - circa 1500 - offers a warm welcome and hospitality at its best. Set in the beautiful Wye Valley the historic Manor House has 2 double rooms with en-suite, one with 4 poster, also the newly opened De Mortimer suite with king size oak 4 poster and luxury bathroom. Hearty breakfasts - vegetarian available - served in former court room, drawing room with log fires, small library and gardens. Antiques, old china collections and samplers. Explore Hay-on-Wye, Black Mountains, Brecon Beacons and Golden Valley. Fishing available. Also self-catering cottage. AA QQQQ Selected.

Mrs Jackie Kingdon
Tel/Fax: 01544 328498

B&B from £23.50pp, Rooms 3 double, all with en-suite, tea/coffee making facilities & Hair dryers, Restricted smoking, Pets by arrangement, Open all year except Christmas, Map Ref I

Lightmarsh Farm, Crundalls Lane, Bewdley, Worcestershire DY12 1NE   Nearest Road B4190

Lightmarsh Farm is a small pasture farm which lies a little over 1 mile north of the picturesque and historic settlement of Bewdley. The 18th century farmhouse enjoys an elevated position with fine views southwards towards Worcester. Inside there is a cosy lounge with inglenook fireplace where a log fire burns on chilly evenings and the bedrooms which enjoy delightful views, have tea/coffee making facilities. The pleasant garden offers an opportunity to relax and watch the wildlife. ETB Highly Commended 2 Crowns.

Mrs P A Grainger
Tel: 01299 404027

B&B from £20pp, Rooms 1 double, 1 twin, both with private facilities, Minimum age 10, Restricted smoking, Open all year except Christmas, Map Ref J

Winforton Court, *Winforton - see details on opposite page*

Tarn, Long Bank, Bewdley, Worcestershire DY12 2QT   Nearest Road A456

Attractive country house with library. Set in 17 acres of gardens and fields with spectacular views, in a tranquil area by an ancient coppice. All bedrooms have basins and there are 2 bathrooms and a shower room. Excellent breakfasts with home baked rolls, served in the elegant dining room. Conveniently situated for Worcestershire Way Walk (guests can be collected), Wyre Forest, River Severn (fishing), Midland Safari Park, Severn Valley Steam Railway, gardens, stately homes, golf. 2 miles west of Georgian Bewdley on A456. Ample Parking.

Mrs Topsy Beves
Tel: 01299 402243

B&B from £18pp, Rooms 2 single, 2 twin, No smoking, Children welcome, No pets, Open February - end November, Map Ref K

Leasow House, Laverton Meadow, Broadway, Worcestershire WR12 7NQ   Nearest Road A44

Leasow House is a Cotswold stone farmhouse dating back to the early 1500's sympathetically renovated to offer guests all the comforts of the 20th century. All bedrooms are individually decorated have en-suite facilities, hospitality tray, colour TV and direct dial telephones. In a converted barn we have created a ground floor room with disabled guests in mind giving full wheelchair access. We are superbly located for touring the Cotswolds, Stratford upon Avon, Warwick and Sudeley Castles. Wonderful country walks and Hidcote Manor garden. EMail: 100653.3225@compuserve.com

Barbara & Gordon Meeking
Tel: 01386 584526
Fax: 01386 584596

B&B from £27.50pp, Rooms 3 twin, 3 double, 1 family, all en-suite/private facilities, No smoking, Children welcome, Pets restricted, Open all year, Map Ref L

Grimley Farm, Grimley Lane, Finstall, nr Bromsgrove, Worcestershire B60 3AF   Nearest Road A38, A448

Grimley Farm is a tasteful converted coach house. Approximately 200 years old, set in 30 acres of pasture land. It is very peaceful, yet within easy access of many historic places and the M5 junction 4 and 5, M42, Birmingham, NEC, Airport, Stratford and Cotswolds. All bedrooms are centrally heated with private bathroom, colour TV and tea/coffee making facilities. A warm welcome is assured.

Mrs S Harfield
Tel: 01527 874883

B&B from £22.50, Rooms 1 single, 1 twin, 1 double, all en-suite, Restricted smoking, Pets allowed in stables only, Open all year, Map Ref M

Old Parsonage Farm, Hanley Castle, Worcestershire WR8 0BU   Nearest Road M5, M50

see PHOTO opposite

Old Parsonage Farm is a fine mellow brick 18th century country residence. The location is superb enjoying beautiful views of the Malvern Hills and surrounding countryside. The house is beautifully decorated with attention to detail thanks to Ann Addison's natural flair for interior design. Besides this she is an accomplished cook producing imaginative dishes of a high standard. To complement this, husband Tony, is a wine expert. There are over 100 wines in stock. All in all a very impressive house.

Mrs Ann Addison
Tel: 01684 310124

B&B from £21, Dinner £15.90, Rooms 2 double/twin, 1 family, Restricted smoking, Minimum age 12, Open January to December, Map Ref N

*right, **Old Parsonage Farm**, Hanley Castle - see details above*

Wyche Keep, 22 Wyche Road, Malvern, Worcestershire WR14 4EG　　　　Nearest Road B4218

Wyche Keep is a unique arts and crafts castle style house, perched high on the Malvern Hills, built by the family of Sir Stanley Baldwin, Prime Minister to enjoy the spectacular 60 mile views, having a long history of elegant entertaining. Three large luxury double suites, including 4 poster. Traditional English cooking is a speciality and guests can savour memorable four course candlelit dinners, served in a 'house party' atmosphere in front of a log fire. Fully licenced. Magical setting with private parking. AA/RAC/ETB Highly Acclaimed.

see PHOTO opposite

Mr & Mrs Williams
Tel: 01684 567018
Fax: 01684 892304

B&B from £25-£30pp, Dinner from £18pp, Rooms 2 twin, 1 double, all en-suite, No smoking, Children over 13 years, No pets, Open all year, Map Ref O

St Elisabeth's Cottage, Woodman Lane, Clent, Stourbridge, Worcestershire DY9 9PX　　　Nearest Road A491

Beautiful country cottage in tranquil setting with 6 acres of landscaped garden plus outdoor heated swimming pool. Lovely country walks. Accommodation includes TV in all rooms plus coffee and tea making facilities. Residents' lounge available. Plenty of pubs and restaurants nearby. Easy access to M5, M6, M42 and M40. 25 minutes from NEC and Birmingham Airport. Destinations within easy reach: Symphony Hall and Convention Centre in Birmingham, Black Country Museum, Dudley, Stourbridge Crystal Factories, Severn Valley Railway.

Mrs Sheila Blankstone
Tel: 01562 883883

B&B from £24, Rooms 1 twin, 2 double, all en-suite, No smoking, Pets welcome, Open all year, Map Ref P

"Thank you so much, miss"
BELLE & BERTIE IN YORK

KENT

'Kent, sir - everybody knows Kent - apples, cherries, hops and women,' so declared Mr. Jingle in Dickens' Pickwick Papers and Dickens knew Kent well. G.K. Chesterton even described Dickens' life as 'moving like a Canterbury pilgrimage along the great roads of Kent'. And what a joy this lovely county is, with its rolling downs - the North Downs passing through the full length of Kent and ending in the magnificent white cliffs of Dover. Between the North and the South Downs lies the Weald, once a vast forest. The High Weald is a highly fertile area, the Low Weald much heavier and colder. Although the estates here are small, the great houses are impressive. Between The Weald and the sea lie the flat, windswept Romney Marshes. Left by the receding sea, this drained and fertile farmland is grazed by Romney sheep. At the foot of the escarpment marking the ancient Saxon shore line is the Royal Military Canal built as a defence during the Napoleonic Wars. The canal runs through the charming town of Hythe, one of the Cinque Ports. The Romney, Hythe and Dymchurch narrow gauge railway runs between Hythe and Dungeness, by the massive nuclear power station at the tip of Denge Marsh. There is good bathing at Dymchurch, an old smuggling port. At Saltwood, just north of Hythe, are the ruins of the Norman castle in which the four knights stayed before the murder of Thomas Becket.

Kent has more than its fair share of magnificent houses. Penshurst Place is an outstanding example of fourteenth century domestic architecture owned by the Sidney family, descendants of Sir Philip Sidney, the Elizabethan poet. Close-by Hever Castle, the birthplace of Anne Boleyn, Henry VIII's second wife, has wonderful gardens including a yew maze and yew topiary. Imposing as this moated manor house beside the River Eden is, it owes much of its charm to twentieth century adaptations by William Waldorf Astor. Knowle can claim to be England's largest house, having no fewer than three hundred and sixty five rooms. Formerly an archbishop's palace, like so many great houses of the period it became the property of Henry VIII. Set like a jewel amongst these stately homes is Royal Tunbridge Wells, an elegant old spa town greatly favoured by Beau Nash who considered it a rival to Regency Bath. This is an ideal base for visiting the glories of The Weald. It was Lord North who discovered the medicinal springs here which brought the town its royal patronage. The Pantiles, bordered by a collonade of eighteenth and nineteenth century houses and shops with Italianate columns, are a delight. Nearby is Ashdown Forest, the landscape of A.A. Milne's Winnie the Pooh stories. Here too is Chartwell, the country home of Sir Winston Churchill.

234

Maidstone, standing on the Rivers Medway and Len in the centre of the 'Garden of England' and at the foot of the North Downs, is a perfect centre for exploring the lovely valley of the Medway which for centuries played a major role in the history of Kent. Of course, road and rail transport has reduced the commercial importance of the river, but today it is a glorious path through orchards and hop gardens and it offers excellent fishing and boating.

The countryside is charming, but no visitor should leave the area without seeing Leeds Castle to the east of Maidstone, and also Sissinghurst Gardens, the wonderful 1930s creation of Harold Nicholson and Vita Sackville-West.

Canterbury on the River Stour is of course the centre of the Anglican church and seat of the Archbishop of Canterbury. The city was an important settlement in Roman times and became the capital of Ethelbert, king of Kent. It was his conversion to Christianity by St. Augustine here that established the importance of Canterbury. With the murder of Archbishop Thomas Becket in 1174, the town became a place of pilgrimage, prompting the building of a number of charitable hospitals for their accommodation. The Poor Priest's Hospital is now a fine city heritage museum. Canterbury suffered devastating bombing in a Baedeker raid in 1942 in which most of the medieval city centre was destroyed. Fortunately the cathedral was spared. What remains from the bombing is well worth seeing. The cathedral, built in Caen limestone with Bell Harry, its central tower, is a gem. The cathedral houses a magnificent collection of twelfth and thirteenth century stained glass and the tomb of the Black Prince. A stone marking the spot upon which Becket was murdered is in the fifteenth century Great Cloister.

East from Canterbury is fascinating scenery, thatched cottages and lovely timbered houses leading to Sandwich, another of the Cinque Ports although the sea is now a couple of miles away. There are many reminders in the medieval centre of this charming town of the Flemish weavers who in the sixteenth century flocked into Kent.

And pleasurable as the beautiful interior of Kent is, it also offers the holidaymaker a fine coastline. Margate is Kent's Blackpool with superb sands, while Whitstable, Ramsgate, Herne Bay and Broadstairs provide between them all the delights of the seaside. The Channel towns - Dover, Folkestone, Deal and Hythe, have a charm of their own, superb walks, picturesque harbours and an endless and fascinating passing show of ships.

Places to Visit

Canterbury Cathedral, *Canterbury* ~ the spiritual home of the Church of England, it contains mediaeval stained glass and some 12th century wall paintings.

Chartwell, *near Hever* ~ the home of Winston Churchill from 1922 to 1964. It remains furnished as it was when he lived there. To relax he would rebuild parts of the house, and some of his paintings are on display.

Dover Castle, *Dover* ~ dates back to 1066, much of the castle seen today is 12th century. A second elaborate set of fortifications built as a defence against Napoleon consists of a network of tunnels. The castle was used during World War II by Vice Admiral Bertram Ramsey to organise the evacuation of three hundred and thirty thousand troops from Dunkirk.

Hever Castle, *Edenbridge* ~ a small, moated castle, it was the home of Anne Boleyn, the wife Henry VIII executed for adultery. In 1903 it was bought by William Waldorf Astor, who restored the castle and built a Neo-Tudor village alongside to accommodate guests and servants. The gatehouse and moat were built in 1270 and still remain.

Ightham Moat, *near Sevenoaks* ~ a moated manor house in a wooded valley with lovely gardens and walks. The house underwent a massive restoration by the National Trust and includes an exhibition explaining the work involved.

Knole, *near Sevenoaks* ~ built in the late 15th century, this immense Tudor mansion was built on the foundations of an older house. The house is set in a thousand acre park and gardens and contains valuable collections of paintings and of 17th century furniture including a state bed made for James II.

Leeds Castle, *Maidstone* ~ surrounded by a lake, it is often considered to be one of the most beautiful castles in England. It was begun in the 12th century and has been continuously inhabited. Henry VIII visited the castle often and it contains a life size bust of him from the 16th century. The gardens were designed by Capability Brown and have a maze.

Sissinghurst Castle Garden, *near Cranbrook* ~ created by Vita Sackville-West and her husband SIr Harold Nicholson, their gardens between the surviving parts of an Elizabethan mansion. The gardens include an orchard, spring garden, white garden and herb garden.

South Foreland Lighthouse, *St Margaret's at Cliffe* ~ built in 1843 it has views to France. It was used by Marconi for the first radio communications as an aid to navigation in 1898. You can climb the spiral stairs to the balcony around the light.

Dover
Castle

KENT

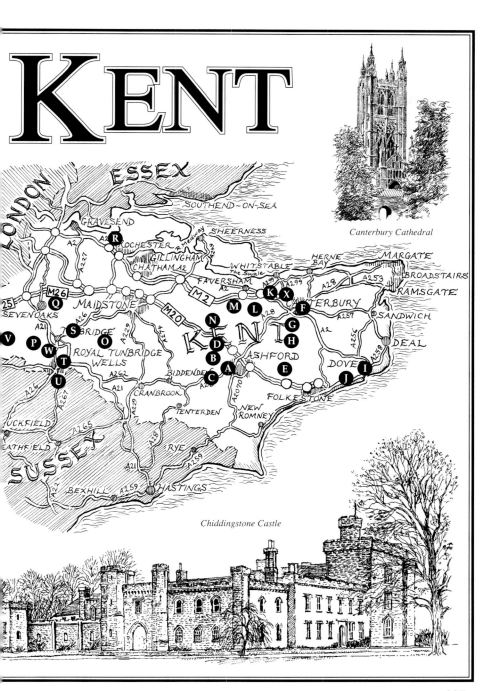

Canterbury Cathedral

Chiddingstone Castle

Kent

The Coach House, Oakmead Farm, Bethersden, near Ashford, Kent TN26 3DU

The Coach House with old world Charm is set amidst "Darling Buds of May" country one mile from Bethersden Village, being well served with country pubs for the evening meals and within reach of many tourist attractions. Guests are warmly welcomed with an informal atmosphere. Your host's speciality is breakfast of your choice cooked with fresh local produce. Secluded courtyard parking and garden. Dutch spoken. TV and tea/coffee making facilities. Easy reach Eurotunnel, Ferry ports, Leeds Castle and Canterbury.

Bernard & Else Broad
Tel: 01233 820583

B&B from £17.50pp, Rooms 1 twin, 1 double, with private bathroom, 1 family, all en-suite, Restricted smoking, Children Welcome, No pets, Open March - October, Map Ref A

Goldwell Manor, Great Chart, Ashford, Kent TN23 3BY   Nearest Road M20 (Junction 9)

A peaceful secluded historic 11th century manor mentioned in the Doomsday Book (1066) as 'Godsel'. Surrounded by farmland with 10 mile views over the Weald. Antiques, oak beams galore and 13 foot fireplaces provide comfortable relaxed atmosphere. Easy for sea, gardens, castles, Canterbury, London, Paris and Brussels. Golf, walks, riding shooting, flying and ballooning also nearby.

Mr & Mrs P Wynn Green
Tel/Fax: 01233 631495

B&B from £23-£28pp, Dinner arranged, Rooms 1 single, 1 double, 1 twin/family, short and long stay reductions. Open all year except Christmas and New Year, Map Ref B

Lion House, Church Hill, High Halden, Ashford, Kent TN26 3LS   Nearest Road A28

see PHOTO opposite

Situated on the village green with pub, village shop, historic church; Lion House is a listed Queen Anne farmhouse set in a large mature garden. Caroline and Gerald offer a friendly welcome, comfortable centrally heated accommodation with en-suite bath & shower, TV tea/coffee making facilities and trouser press, etc. Private dining room and patio garden. Within easy reach Sissinghurst and Leeds castles, Canterbury, channel tunnel and ports. Early departures and late arrivals catered for. Supper or dinner by arrangement.

Gerald & Caroline Mullins
Tel: 01233 850446
Fax: 01233 850446

B&B from £20pp, Dinner incl wine from £5/£15 by arrangement, Rooms 1 single, 1 twin, 1 family, all en-suite, Restricted smoking, Children welcome, Open all year except Christmas, Map Ref C

Elvey Farm Country Hotel, Pluckley, Ashford, Kent TN27 0SU   Nearest Road M20/A20

Stay in the 15th century Yeoman Barn, Oast House, or Elvey Stables. All traditional oak beamed Kentish farm buildings converted to give comfortable, charming accommodation in the heart of "The Garden of England". Very secluded and peaceful with beautiful views, yet near the channel ports, tunnel, Canterbury, and the castles, country houses, and gardens of Kent and Sussex. Large car park and garden, licenced dining room, lounge. All rooms have colour TV and hospitality facilities.

Mr & Mrs Harris
Tel: 01233 840442
Fax: 01233 840726

B&B from £27.75, Dinner available, Rooms 2 twin, 2 double, 5 family, all en-suite, Children welcome, Pets restricted, Open all year, Map Ref D

*right, **Lion House,** near Ashford - see details above*

Kent

Bulltown Farmhouse, Bulltown Lane, West Brabourne, Ashford, Kent TN25 5NB Nearest Road M20

Bulltown Farmhouse is a period restored 15th Century large timber framed medieval farmhouse. It is set in over 1 acre of attractive cottage gardens and surrounded by quiet, unspoilt, North Downs Kent farmland. The Channel Tunnel is only 10 minutes away with Canterbury and the channel port 10 and 15 miles respectively. There are several excellent country inns nearby serving food. All rooms are large, period furnished and have unspoilt outlooks.

Lilly Wilton
Tel: 01233 813505 or
01227 709818

B&B from £20pp, Rooms 1 twin, 1 double, 1 family, all en-suite, No smoking, Children welcome, No pets, Open all year, Map Ref E

Zan Stel Lodge, 140 Old Dover Road, Canterbury, Kent CT1 3NX Nearest Road B2068, A2

see PHOTO opposite

Gracious Edwardian House offering high standards of cleanliness and service. The individually styled bedrooms include colour TV with tea/coffee making facilities. Hair dryer and ironing facilities also available. The elegant dining room overlooks a pretty cottage garden including fishponds. Ten minute walk to city centre, thirty minute drive to Channel Tunnel and Ferry ports. Private car park. Recommended by the Which? Good Bed & Breakfast Guide. ETB 2 Crown Highly Commended.

Zandra & Ron Stedman
Tel: 01227 453654

B&B from £22pp, Rooms 1 twin, 2 double, 1 family, 2 rooms en-suite, No smoking, Open all year, Map Ref F

Oriel Lodge, 3 Queens Avenue, Canterbury, Kent CT2 8AY Nearest Road A2

In a tree-lined residential avenue, five minutes' walk from the city centre and restaurants, Oriel Lodge is an attractive Edwardian detached house, retaining a warm and restful period character. The six well-furnished bedrooms have clean up-to-date facilities. Afternoon tea is served in the garden or lounge, with a log fire in winter. There is private parking for six cars. ETB 2 crowns Highly Commended, AA QQQ, RAC Acclaimed.

Keith & Anthea Rishworth
Tel/Fax: 01227 462845

B&B from £20pp, Rooms 1 single, 1 twin, 3 double, 1 family, some en-suite, Restricted smoking, Children from 6, No pets, Open all year, Map Ref F

Clare Ellen Guest House, 9 Victoria Road, Canterbury, Kent CT1 3SG Nearest Road A28

A warm welcome and bed and breakfast in style. Large quiet elegant rooms with colour TV, clock/radio, hair dryer and tea/coffee. Ironing centre with trouser press for guests' convenience. Full English breakfast, Vegetarians and special diets catered for, on request. Cosy residents lounge. Numerous restaurants/pubs close by. 6 minutes walk to city centre, cathedral, Marlow Theatre and Canterbury bus station. 4 minutes' walk to Canterbury East railway station. Close proximity to cricket ground and University. Private car park and garage available. 2 Crown Highly Commended. EMail: loraine.williams@virgin.net

Mrs Loraine Williams
Tel: 01227 760205
Fax: 01227 784482

B&B from £22-£26pp, Rooms 1 single, 2 twin, 2 double, 1 family, all en-suite, Restricted smoking, Children welcome, No pets, Open all year, Map Ref F

*right, **Zan Stel Lodge**, Canterbury - see details above*

Iffin Farmhouse, Iffin Lane, Canterbury, Kent CT4 7BE　　　　　**Nearest Road A2, M2**

see PHOTO opposite

A warm welcome awaits you at this old 18th century farmhouse, renovated to a high standard in the mid 50's. Offering luxury en-suite bedrooms with TV and tea/coffee trays and set in 10 acres of gardens, orchards and paddocks in a quiet rural setting only 6 minutes drive to the centre of historic Canterbury. In an ideal position for touring Kent and East Sussex, and the following are only a short drive away: Chilham, Dover, Leeds and Hever castles; Chartwell, Penshurst Place, Sissington Gardens and many more. Also within easy reach of channel ports and tunnel.

Rosemary & Colin Stevens
Tel: 01227 462776
Fax: 01227 462776

B&B from £23.50pp, Rooms 1 twin, 2 double, 2 family, all en suite, No smoking, Minimum age 5, No pets, Open all year except Christmas and New Year, Map Ref G

---

1 Dryden Close, Pilgrims Way, Canterbury, Kent CT1 1XW　　　　　**Nearest Road A2**

Situated between the cricket ground and golf course on the 16 cycle route, we are a quietly located family home offering non-smoking throughout. TV, tea/coffee tray. Central heating. Grade 3 Disability. Excellent full English breakfast. Special diets catered for by prior arrangement. Free street parking. Cycle lock up. Full use of lounge-diner and garden. Whether your interests are golf, cycling, swimming, riding, fishing, walking, sightseeing, theatre or business book early to avoid disappointment. ETB Commended.

Elaine & Tony Oliver
Tel/Fax: 01227 764799

B&B from £18pp, Rooms 2 single, 2 double, 1 en-suite, 3 shower, No smoking, Children from 14, No pets, Open from March - December, Map Ref F

Stour Valley House, Pilgrims Lane, Chilham, nr Canterbury, Kent　　　　　**Nearest Road A28**

Beautifully decorated B&B with magnificent views over looking the "Stour Valley" between the picturesque villages of Chilham & Chartham. Chilham Village 2 mins. Canterbury 6 mins, Dover 30 mins, M2 to London - 15 mins. Ideal for the south east of England. Bedrooms en-suite with views, colour TV, radio alarms, tea/coffee and easy chairs. A hearty breakfast, fulfilling any large appetite! Weekly and daily stays welcome. Homemade evening meals available. An ideal setting for an ideal bed & breakfast to relax and unwind. Scheduled to open Spring 1999. Former owner of Maynard Cottage Guest House, Canterbury.

Fiona Ely
Tel: 01227 738991
Mobile: 0468 074177

B&B from £21pp, Dinner available by prior arrangement from £14, Rooms 1 twin, 2 double, all en-suite/private facilities, No smoking or pets, Children welcome, Open all year, Map Ref F

Upper Ansdore, Duckpit Lane, Petham, Canterbury, Kent CT4 5QB　　　　　**Nearest Road B2068, A2**

Medieval farmhouse in a very quiet secluded valley, with beautiful views. Once the home of the Lord Mayor of London, it overlooks a Kent nature reserve. Take a short break or a longer stay, and sample over 600 years of history. Breakfast served in the oak beamed dining room with Tudor inglenook fireplace and furnished with antiques. Canterbury 15 minutes, Dover 30 minutes, AA QQQ Listed. SAE please for a colour brochure.

Roger & Susan Linch
Tel/Fax: 01227 700672

B&B from £20pp, Rooms 1 twin, 3 double, 1 family, all en-suite, No smoking, Open all year except Christmas, Map Ref H

Iffin Farmhouse,
Canterbury
- see details
opposite

Kent

Castle House, 10 Castle Hill Road, Dover, Kent CT16 1QW   Nearest Road A2/M2 and A20/M20

Ideally situated just below Dover Castle, close to Town Centre, Ferries, Hoverport and Cruise Liner Terminal, and 10 mins from the Channel Tunnel, this non-smoking establishment offers good food, comfortable accommodation and genuine hospitality from Rodney & Elizabeth. All rooms have shower and W.C., colour television, hospitality trays and alarm clock, and a hearty breakfast is assured to see you on your way. ETB 3 Crowns Commended. AA QQQ. EMail: Dimechr@aol.com

Rodney & Elizabeth Dimech
Tel: 01304 201656
Fax: 01304 210197

B&B from £18pp, Rooms 4 double, 1 twin, 1 single, No smoking, Open all year, Map Ref I

Rose Hill Farm, Mill Lane, West Houghton, Dover, Kent CT15 7BD   Nearest Road M20, A20

A sympathetically restored 17th century farmhouse in peaceful, unspoilt countryside, 10 minutes' drive from Dover and Channel Tunnel. 1.5 acres of beautiful gardens, croquet lawn, swimming pool - a joy for garden lovers and an excellent centre for touring, walking, sailing, golf and visiting the numerous castles, historic houses and gardens of Kent. Comfortable en-suite bedrooms with colour TV, tea/coffee making facilities. Two fully equipped luxury cottages with wood burning stoves for longer, self catering stays.

Diana & Roger Brooks
Tel: 01304 240609

B&B from £21pp, Rooms 1 twin, 1 double, Restricted smoking, Children welcome, No pets, Open all year except Christmas and Boxing Day, Map Ref J

Tenterden House, 209 The Street, Boughton, Faversham, Kent ME13 9BL   Nearest Road M2, A2

The renovated gardener's cottage of this listed Tudor house, provides two bedrooms (one double, one twin) with guests own shower and toilet. Situated in the village of Boughton, close to Canterbury, the ferry ports and Euro Tunnel, it makes an ideal touring base for day trips to France and for touring rural, historic and coastal Kent. Off-road parking is provided. Both rooms have tea/coffee facilities and TV. Full English breakfast is served in the main house, and excellent pub food is within easy walking distance.

Prudence & Peter Latham
Tel: 01227 751593

B&B from £20pp, Rooms 1 twin, 1 double, Children welcome, No pets, Open all year except Christmas, Map Ref K

Leaveland Court, Leaveland, Faversham, Kent ME13 0NP   Nearest Road A251, M2

15th Century Leaveland Court is an enchanting timber framed farmhouse with adjoining granary and stables. In a quiet rural setting the house nestles between 13th century Leaveland Church and woodlands and retains its true character as the heart of a 300 acre working downland farm. Offering a high standard of accommodation and cuisine, a warm welcome is always assured. All bedrooms are en-suite and have tea/coffee making facilities. Guests are invited to use the heated outdoor swimming pool set in secluded and attractive gardens.

see PHOTO opposite

Mrs Corrine Scutt
Tel: 01233 740596
Fax: 01233 740015

B&B from £22.50pp, Rooms 1 twin, 2 double, all en-suite, No smoking, Children welcome, Pets restricted, Open February - November, Map Ref L

*left, **Leaveland Court**, near Faversham - see details above*

The Granary, Plumford Lane, Ospringe, Faversham, Kent ME13 0DS   Nearest Road A2, M2

Set deep in apple orchard country, The Granary - recently part of a working farm has been tastefully and beautifully converted to provide an interesting and spacious home. All rooms are delightfully furnished to a very high standard, whilst retaining a certain rustic charm. The guests' lounge with balcony, overlooks countryside. Well situated for local pubs specialising in excellent food. Ideal for touring Kent. Alan and Annette assure you of a warm welcome.
EMail: THE GRANARY@COMPUSERVE.COM
http//ourworld.compuserve.com/homepages/thegranary

Alan & Annette Brightman
Tel/Fax: 01795 538416
Mobile: 0410 199177

B&B from £22pp, Rooms 1 twin 1 double, 1 family, all en-suite, No smoking, Children under 1 or over 12, No pets, Open all year except Christmas & New Year, Map Ref M

Frith Farm House, Otterden, Faversham, Kent ME13 0DD   Nearest Road A20, A2

Frith Farm is situated on the North Downs in an area of outstanding natural beauty. The house, an elegant Georgian building, is reached by a sweeping drive and surrounded by well looked after lawns and gardens. The interior is decorated with flair and great individuality using fine fabrics and antiques. A delightful and relaxing place to stay. One bedroom has 4 poster and all have en-suite shower, tea/coffee making facilities, and TV. Horse riding, golf, Pilgrims and North Downs Way are all nearby. A warm welcome is assured.
EMail: markham@frith.force9.co.uk

Markham & Susan Chesterfield
Tel: 01795 890701
Fax: 01795 890009

B&B from £25pp, Dinner £19.50, Rooms 1 twin 2 double, all en-suite, No smoking, Minimum age 10, Open all year, Map Ref N

Merzie Meadows, Hunton Road, Marden, nr Maidstone, Kent TN12 9SL   Nearest Road A229, B2079

Merzie Meadows is a country home individually designed with water fowl and horse paddocks. Tranquil surroundings central to many historical interest including Leeds, Sissinghurst Castle and London. Traditional elegance with modern comforts the spacious rooms are decorated to a high standard and include a guest wing with sitting room, study and terrace the rooms overlook landscaped gardens with swimming pool all designed for conservation. ETB Highly Commended, Recommended by Which? Good Bed & Breakfast.

Pamela & Rodney Mumford
Tel: 01622 820500

B&B from £22pp, Rooms 2 double, both en-suite, No smoking, Children over 5 years, No pets, Open mid January - mid December, Map Ref O

Swale Cottage, Poundsbridge Lane, Penshurst, Kent TN11 8AH   Nearest Road A26, B2176

see PHOTO opposite

Swale Cottage, listed Grade II*, is a large converted Kentish barn of architectural merit. In a unique and tranquil setting, it overlooks a medieval manor house, gardens and glorious countryside. Furnished with antiques and decorated throughout in English country style decor. There are three spacious and luxurious bedrooms including a romantic 4 poster. Colour TV. Memorable breakfasts. Nearby is 14th century Penhurst Place with its Tudor garden. Within 10 minutes drive of Hever, Chartwell, Chiddingstone NT and Tunbridge Wells. ETB Highly Commended. AA Premier Selected (5Q's) and prestigious awards.

Mrs Cynthia Dakin
Tel: 01892 870738

B&B from £30 - £35pp, Midweek winter breaks, Rooms 1 twin, 2 double, en-suite, No smoking, Children over 10 years, Open all year, Map Ref P

right, **Swale Cottage,** *Penhurst - see details above*

Jordans, Sheet Hill, Plaxtol, Sevenoaks, Kent TN15 0PU

Nearest Road A227

An exquisite picture postcard 15th century Tudor house situated in the picturesque village of Plaxtol among orchards and parkland. Jordans, awarded a historic building of Kent plaque, has an enchanting English cottage garden with winding paths, rambler roses and espalier trees. Inside there are oak beams, inglenook fireplaces, leaded windows and beautifully furnished with antiques and paintings many by Mrs Lindsay, who is also a Blue Badge Guide and can help in planning your tour. Jordans is close to Ightham Mote, Hever, Chartwell, Penshurst Knole, Leeds Castle and Great Camp Garden and Great Comp Garden.

see PHOTO opposite

Mrs Jo Lindsay N.N.D., A.T.D.
Tel: 01732 810379

B&B from £30pp, Rooms 2 double/single, 2 en-suite, No smoking, Open mid January - mid December, Map Ref Q

Gardeners Cottage, Puckle Hill, Shorne, Kent DA12 3LB

Nearest Road A2, M2

Delightfully situated in five acres with a bluebell wood, an ancient lime tree, lovely gardens and a croquet lawn. All rooms are en-suite with refreshments, colour TV and radio alarms with beautiful views from all windows. The dining room where delicious breakfasts are served is oak beamed and has a fine dresser. Ideally situated for touring Kent. London is approximately 45 minutes and Canterbury half an hour. The cathedral city of Rochester and Charles Dickens' Gads Hill Place are close by.

Mrs Valerie Peters
Tel/Fax: 01474 823269

B&B from £25pp, Dinner from £12.50, Rooms 1 single, 1 twin, 1 double, all en-suite/private facilities, No smoking, Children welcome, No pets, Open all year, Map Ref R

Leavers Oast, Stanford Lane, Hadlow, Tonbridge, Kent TN11 0JN

Nearest Road A26

A warm welcome awaits you at Leavers Oast. An excellent base for touring the many historic buildings including Leeds and Hever Castles, Chartwell and Sissinghurst. Built circa 1880, Anne and Denis have modernised the accommodation and created a very attractive garden. They have many interests including antiques, art and travel. Two bedrooms are in roundels, the other in the barn. All are spacious and comfortably furnished with TV and coffee/tea making facilities. There are many good places to eat or by prior arrangement excellent evening meals are available.

Anne & Denis Turner
Tel/Fax: 01732 850924

B&B from £27pp, Dinner £17.50 (guests bring own wine), Rooms 1 twin, 2 double. 1 en-suite, No smoking, Children from 12, No pets, Open all year, Map Ref S

Blundeston, Eden Road, Tunbridge Wells, Kent TN1 1TS

Nearest Road A21

Blundeston is a beautifully decorated period home situated in the centre of old Tunbridge Wells within easy walking distance of the Pantiles, shops and mainline station to London. Mrs Day is an interior designer and her flair is apparent throughout. The comfortable bedrooms with their own en-suite and private facilities have courtesy trays and televisions. This is a very convenient base from which to visit a large number of the English gardens, castles and country homes. There is ample parking.

see PHOTO on page 250

Mrs Gillian Day
Tel: 01892 513030
Fax: 01892 517682

B&B from £22.50pp, Rooms 1 twin/double en-suite, 1 twin/double private bathroom, No smoking or pets, Children over 8, Open all year except Christmas & New Year, Map Ref T

*left, **Jordans**, near Sevenoaks - see details above*

The Old Parsonage, Church Lane, Frant, Tunbridge Wells, Kent TN3 9DX   **Nearest Road A267**

The Old Parsonage is a magnificent Georgian house in a quiet, pretty village providing superior accommodation:luxurious en-suite bedrooms including two 4 posters, antique-furnished reception rooms and a spacious sunny conservatory, where guests may relax in armchair comfort with afternoon tea, overlooking the ballustraded terrace and secluded walled garden. For evening meals the village pub restaurants are 2 mins walk away. Short drive to many historic houses and gardens. SEETB award winner 'Bed & Breakfast of the Year', AA Premier selected. ETB Deluxe.

Mrs Mary Dakin
Tel: 01892 750773
Fax: 01892 750773

B&B from £32pp, Rooms 1 twin, 2 double, all en-suite, restricted smoking, Pets by arrangement, open all year, Map Ref U

Danehurst House, 41 Lower Green Road, Rusthall, Tunbridge Wells, Kent TN4 8TW   **Nearest Road A264**

Danehurst is a charming gabled house standing in a lovely village setting in the heart of Kent. Our tastefully furnished bedrooms afford you excellent accommodation - breakfast is served in our delightful Victorian conservatory. We are licensed, guests can enjoy a relaxing drink in our drawing room. We would be delighted to welcome you to our home. We like to feel that once you are in our care you can relax and enjoy everything we and the area have to offer. Private parking is available.

Angela & Michael Godbold
Tel: 01892 527739
Fax: 01892 514804

B&B from £25pp, Rooms 2 twin, 2 double, all en suite, 1 small twin/double with private bathroom, No smoking, Children over 8 years, No pets, Open all year, Map Ref V

Number Ten, Modest Corner, Southborough, Tunbridge Wells, Kent TN4 0LS   **Nearest Road A26, A21**

Situated in a lovely quiet hamlet with beautiful views and walking facilities from the doorstep. Stone throw away from Royal Tunbridge Wells and Tonbridge railway station, where the trains frequently take you into London within the hour. Tea/coffee and TV in all rooms. Excellent showers in bathrooms. A unique welcoming and homely atmosphere and so tranquil that only the birds wake you in the morning. Full English breakfast served. (In garden, weather permitting). Dutch, German and a little French spoken.

Anneke Leemhuis
Tel: 01892 522450

B&B from £20pp, Dinner from £10, Rooms 2 twin, 1 en-suite double, Restricted smoking, Children & pets welcome, Open all year, Map Ref W

Windyridge Guest House, Wraik Hill, Whitstable, Kent CT5 3BY   **Nearest Road M2, A299**

Directions for Windyridge Guest House: on leaving M2 - A299 Ramsgate, First roundabout, 3rd exit Canterbury - A290. Next roundabout 2nd exit, Wraik Hill

Elisabeth Dyke
Tel: 01227 263506
Fax: 01227 771191

B&B from £25pp, Rooms 3 single, 1 twin, 3 double, 1 family, all en-suite, Children & pets welcome, Open all year, Map Ref X

251

*left, **Blundeston,** Tunbridge Wells - see details on page 249*

LANCASHIRE

It was the soft water, moist climate and swiftly running streams, together with an abundance of coal and iron-ore that laid in Lancashire the foundations of the Industrial Revolution, and unfortunately its reputation as a holiday venue has suffered ever since. This is a shame, as within a short distance of the great industrial cities of this area is scenery which can compare with some of the best in the country - the Trough of Bowland with its exhilarating views across the lovely Fylde and the Wyre valley, and the Rivers Lune, Ribble and Hodder, their valleys scattered with lovely villages. There is no doubt that the great cities dominate this area, but because their populations have demanded local resorts, there is also a coastline blessed with some of the finest seaside resorts in Britain, their attractions honed through the years to international prominence. Blackpool, surely the Queen of seaside resorts, offers over seven miles of sandy beaches, a massive amusement park and pleasure beach, and every conceivable form of entertainment - plus the tower, a 518ft imitation of the Eiffel Tower, and the best known seaside landmark in Britain, as well as the spectacular Illuminations which considerably extend the resort's season. Blackpool has its brash side, but behind its garish facade there is a resort of delightful parks, wooded gardens and also a Zoo. The town is ideally situated to explore the Fylde, Lytham St. Anne's with its bracing promenade and windmill, and of course the Royal Lytham St. Anne's championship golf course; Morecambe, Blackpool's sister resort; Heysham, and Lancaster at the head of the Lune estuary, the ancient county town with the imposing castle of John of Gaunt, father of Henry IV. The city with its fine Georgian houses was once a busy port handling a bigger tonnage than Liverpool. Lancaster possesses two impressive monuments - the imposing castle housing the Shire Hall of 1796 in which assizes are held; and the Ashton Memorial - sometimes known as the "Taj Mahal of the North', built by Lord Ashton in 1909 as a memorial to his wife.

Southport, a seaside resort renowned for its beautiful Lord Street, a shaded tree-lined boulevard of fine shops, is the annual venue of the international Southport Flower Show, as well as being the home of the famous Royal Birkdale golf course. Five miles east of the town is the Martin Mere Wildfowl Sanctuary.

Preston, at the head of the estuary of the River Ribble and of strategic importance since Roman times, became rich from the weaving of wool during the Middle Ages only to switch to cotton in 1786. It was Sir Richard Arkwright, a Preston man, who in the middle of the eighteenth century invented the spinning frame that revolutionised the textile industry. Another Preston man to make his mark was a certain Joseph Livesay, who founded the Temperance Movement. The Preston Temperance Advocate' was England's first newspaper for abstainers. The town's prosperity during the Industrial Revolution is reflected in some fine architecture. The Harris Museum and Art Gallery opened in 1893 is a magnificent Classical building containing an outstanding collection of paintings. Well sited to visit the Fylde, the

Trough of Bowland and the west coast seaside resorts, this pleasant town was in 1648 at the very centre of a battle which saw Cromwell's army rout twenty thousand Scottish supporters of Charles I.

Until the early eighteenth century Lake Martinmere covered a large area of land around Ormskirk. It was the Scarisbrick family who were largely responsible for draining this land, the produce from the resulting rich farming land established Ormskirk as an important market town. Scarisbrick Hall, rebuilt in the nineteenth century in the Neo Gothic style is three miles north-west of the town. Rufford Old Hall a short distance away is a quite magnificent half-timbered medieval mansion not to be missed. Nor indeed should one miss the wonderful views over the Lancashire Plain from Parbold Beacon. It is hard to believe today that the delightful country roads around the pretty village of Wrightington Bar were once the haunt of footpads and highwaymen.

There are some fascinating cotton towns in the east of the county - Clitheroe beneath its Norman keep is a pleasant market town close to Pendle Hill from which are superb views over the Forest of Bowland. The hill is forever associated with witches, ten of whom were hanged in Lancaster. However it was on Pendle Hill that George Fox had a vision which inspired him to form the Society of Friends (Quakers). It was at Hoghton Tower near Blackburn that James I jokingly dubbed a loin of Lancashire beef 'Sir Loin', and at Chorley where the founder of the Tate Gallery was born is Astley Hall, a wonderful Elizabethan mansion. Healey Nab close by, at 682 feet gives wonderful views across the moors and valleys of Anglezarke and White Coppice. Turton Bottoms with its twelfth century Turton Tower is a grand centre for walking this area - the Hall i' th' Wood nearby is an impressive half-timbered manor house built in 1483 and one time home of Samuel Crompton. Between these towns immortalized by such painters as L.S. Lowry is much unspoilt countryside, expanses of moor and forest scattered with ancient manor houses, Tudor farmhouses and old stone churches.

LANCASHIRE

Places to Visit

Blackpool Tower, *Blackpool* ~ it was built in 1894, and is a five hundred and nineteen feet tall replica of the Eiffel Tower in Paris. It rises out of a large building containing a world famous circus and the Tower Ballroom with its Wurlitzer organ. A lift can be taken to the top of the tower to enjoy the views of the town and along the coastline.

Gawthorpe Hall, *near Burnley* ~ built between 1600 and 1605, it was restored in the 1850's by Sir Charles Barry. Gawthorpe was the home of the Shuttleworth family; it now houses Rachel Kay-Shuttleworth's textile collections and a collection of paintings on loan from the National Portrait Gallery.

Leighton Hall, *Carnforth* ~ the estate dates back to the 13th century but most of the present building is 19th century including its Neo-Gothic facade. There is a large collection of birds of prey and in the afternoon there is an air show by eagles and falcons.

Martin Mere Wildlife and Wetlands Trust Centre, *near Ormskirk* ~ established in 1976, it has birds from all over the world which can be observed from hides overlooking the floodwaters. Up to one tenth of the world's population of pink-footed geese arrive here in winter. They can also be viewed from the hides or from the comfort of the heated Raines Observatory.

Lancaster Castle, *Lancaster* ~ a Norman castle which was expanded in the 14th and 16th centuries. Since the 18th century the castle has housed the county courts and prison. The famous Pendle witches, who were convicted and hanged in 1612, were held here while awaiting their trial. The Shire Hall is decorated with six hundred heraldic shields.

Morecambe Bay ~ the best way to explore Morecambe Bay is by train from Ulverston to Arnside. The train travels over a series of low viaducts across the tidal flats where many wading birds feed and breed. Hampsfield Fell and Humphrey Head Point give the best views of the bay. The bay can walked across but is very dangerous as there are strong currents, quicksands and a speedy incoming tide. Walks are available with an official guide taking three hours and subject to the weather.

Rufford Old Hall, *near Ormskirk* ~ built in 1530, it became the Hesketh family home for the next two hundred and fifty years. It houses collections of 16th and 17th century oak furniture, arms, armour and tapestries.

Leighton Hall

254

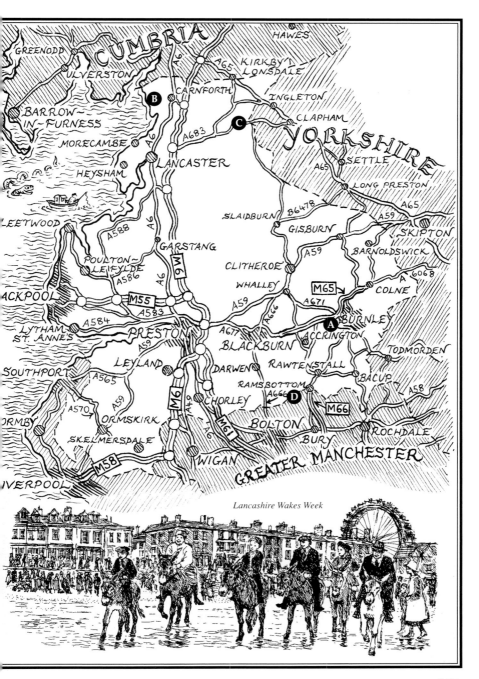

Lancashire Wakes Week

Eaves Barn Farm, Hapton, Burnley, Lancashire BB12 7LP   Nearest Road A679, M65

Eaves Barn is a working farm with a spacious cottage attached to the main house offering luxurious facilities. The elegant guests lounge has a log open fire and is traditionally furnished including antiques. Individually designed bedrooms with colour TV, en-suite facilities. A full English breakfast is served in the Victorian style conservatory. "Best Bed & Breakfast" in Lancashire 1992. Situated within easy reach of the Ribble Valley and Fylde Coast, Lake District, Yorkshire Dales and the Lancashire hills. Burnley, Blackburn, Preston and Manchester Airport can be reached using the motorway network.

Mrs M Butler
Tel: 01282 771591
Fax: 01282 771591

B&B from £22.50pp, Dinner from £12, Rooms 1 single, 1 twin, 1 double, all en-suite, Children welcome over 12, No pets, Open all year except Christmas, Map Ref A

The Limes Village Guest House, 23 Stankelt Road, Silverdale, near Carnforth, Lancs LA5 0TF   A6, M6

The Limes, a charming Victorian house set in beautiful landscaped gardens, has been tastefully refurbished. The spacious bedrooms, decorated with flair, have private bathrooms, TV, easy chairs, and tea and coffee tray. The owners serve delicious food, with an incredibly wide breakfast choice and optional five course candlelit dinner. Silverdale, an area of outstanding natural beauty, with a wealth of coastal and wooded footpaths, is in close proximity to the Lake District, and Yorkshire Dales and an ideal stopover between England and Scotland. Secure parking.

see PHOTO opposite

Noel & Andree Livesey
Tel: 01524 701454
Fax: 01524 701454

B&B from £19, Dinner £13.50, Rooms 1 twin, 1 double, 1 family, all with private bathrooms, No smoking, No pets, Open all year, Map Ref B

Stonegate House, Main Street, Low Bentham, via Lancaster LA2 7DS   Nearest Road A683

House dates from 1609 with Victorian Tower. En-suite rooms with romantic 4-poster beds and beverage tray, plus, TV. residents lounge. Large off road car park. Dovecot Room has kingsize 4-poster bed, private balcony, three piece suite, TV. Large private bathroom with shower and hot air bubble bath. Stonegate House; the ideal base from which to explore the Yorkshire Dales, Lake District, The Forest and Trough of Bowland, plus, the west coast seaside resorts.

Anne Wardlow
Tel: 015242 61362

B&B from £20pp, Dinner from £14.95 by arrangement, Rooms 1 twin, 2 double all en-suite, Restricted smoking, Children welcome from 5 years, Small dogs only, Open all year, Map Ref C

Knotts Cottage, Bury Road, Edgworth, Turton, Lancashire BL7 0BY   Nearest Road A676

Built in 1635 this picturesque former farmhouse is set in two acres of gardens overlooking rolling countryside. A rural location but centrally situated for easy access to the motorway network, and 10 minutes from Bury or Bolton and 30 minutes from Manchester Airport. The two double bedrooms, both en-suite are south facing, beautifully furnished and decorated, have colour TV's, tea/coffee making facilities. There is a guest sitting room and breakfast is served in the Imari dining room. Guests are invited to use the games room, with its full size snooker table and mini gym. There is also ample secure parking. ETB Deluxe.

Mrs Tolhurst
Tel: 01204 852062

B&B from £25pp, Dinner by arrangement, Rooms 2 double, all en-suite, Restricted smoking, No children, No pets, Open all year except Christmas and New Year, Map Ref D

*left, **The Limes Village Guest House,** near Carnforth - see details above*

LEICESTERSHIRE, NOTTINGHAMSHIRE & RUTLAND

Leicestershire in the west part of the industrial East Midlands is endowed with large country estates and lovely rolling countryside. Leicester, on the River Soar, was an important Roman settlement where the great Roman road, the Fosse Way crossed the river. Simon de Montfort, who led the revolt against his brother-in-law Henry III and set the pattern for future parliamentary government, was a great benefactor of the city. The fine fifteenth century Guildhall was the scene of a great banquet to celebrate the defeat of the Spanish Armada. A branch of the Grand Union Canal joins Leicester and Market Harborough, a delightful town rich in Georgian architecture and the centre of fox hunting country. The canal passes in a wide loop through Foxton, where a series of locks lifts the water level by seventy five feet. Built in the early nineteenth century for the busy canal-borne trade, the town is now a centre for pleasure craft. Lutterworth, once a busy coaching town, was the parish of John Wycliffe the great reformer, who preached against the abuses of papal politics and promoted the first translation of the Bible into the common tongue. The wolds around Melton Mowbray present magnificent walking country. Much of the land is planted with small coverts for the breeding of foxes with the Quorn, Cottesmore and Belvoir hunting this area. The kennels of the Belvoir, one of the oldest of the hunts are at Belvoir (pronounced 'Beever') Castle, the massive nineteenth century Gothic Revival mansion of the Dukes of Rutland, built on the site of a Norman castle which dated back to the eleventh century. Ashby Castle was chosen by Sir Walter Scott as the setting for Ivanhoe's tournament. The castle has had a turbulent history; in the seventeenth century Royalist forces were besieged there for more than a year by Cromwell's troops. Ashby-de-la-Zouch, its name taken from the La Zouch family from Brittany, can boast a wide variety of interesting architecture. The houses in the Classical style date from the nineteenth century when the town developed as a Spa. This is an area of great appeal, from the open heath of Charnwood Forest with its glorious views from Bardon Hill and Beacon Hill, to the pleasures of Bradgate Park.

Nottinghamshire to many is simply the county of Robin Hood and Sherwood Forest, and indeed the county was once virtually covered with forest. Sherwood Forest, stretching for more than twenty miles north of Nottingham, is now considerably smaller and less wild than it once was. It is more a region of glades and open tracts, but nevertheless some fine great oaks still stand, most of the oak long since gone for the building of castles, abbeys and churches. One section however which survives more or less unaltered is the Sherwood Forest Country Park, which contains an old tree known as the Major Oak, now supported on crutches. Traditionally said to be the oak under which Robin Hood held his camp, the tree must be at least five hundred years old. Nottingham, an ancient city on the River Trent, is a fine centre for exploring the surrounding countryside and is in itself of great interest. Occupied in the ninth century by the Danes, its Norman castle on a high outcrop of rock was dismantled during the Commonwealth, the mansion which replaced it was then burnt down during the riots of 1831 leading to the Reform Act. The ruins, restored in 1870 became the town Museum and Art Gallery. The rock on which the castle stands is riddled with passages and caves. At the foot of the rock is the famous inn, 'Ye Olde Trip to Jerusalem' established in 1189, and said to be the oldest Inn in England. The old Market Square, the town centre since Norman times, was until 1928 the site of the Goose Fair held each October. The fair now held a mile away is no longer the traditional livestock market, but a huge fun-fair.

North of Nottingham is Southwell whose lovely Minster is well worth visiting. Its Chapter House boasts some of the finest medieval stone carving to be seen. The Leaves of Southwell are a celebration of the foliage of Sherwood Forest in stone. The Saracen's Head, the oldest inn in the town, is where Charles I surrendered to the Scots in 1646. Newstead Abbey in the west was built by Henry II as an atonement for the murder of Archbishop Thomas Becket, and after the Dissolution the abbey became the home of the Byron family. Lord Byron's body was brought from Greece for burial at Hucknall. It was however D.H. Lawrence who was the true Nottinghamshire man; his early novels, poems and stories are set in the mining and farming area around Eastwood. He described the area as, 'an extremely beautiful countryside, just between the red sandstone and the oak trees of Nottingham, and the cold limestone, the ash trees, the stone fences of Derbyshire'.

LEICESTERSHIRE, NOTTINGHAMSHIRE & RUTLAND

Places to Visit

Belvoir Castle, Leicestershire ~ although it looks more like a fairy tale medieval castle, Belvoir Castle is 19th century, but there has been a castle on the site since the 11th century. Inside are many lavishly decorated rooms with works by Poussin, Reynolds and Holbein.

Burrough Hill, *near Burrough on the Hill, Leicestershire* ~ an Iron Age hill fort, with high earthen ramparts making it an important fort in its time. It was in use from the Bronze Age until the last years of the Roman occupation.

Castle Donington, *Leicestershire* ~ the village is well known for its race track and the Donington Collection, the largest collection of single seater racing cars in the world including those driven by Ayrton Senna, Stirling Moss and Juan Fangio. There is also a reconstructed 1920's garage and the Speedway Hall of Fame.

Rutland Water, *Leicestershire* ~ created in the 1970's, it is one of the largest man-made lakes in Europe. On the banks of the lake is 18th century Normanton Church which is now a museum.

Clumber Park

Welland Viaduct, *Leicestershire* ~ built in 1876-8, its arches carry the Midland Railway Line across the Welland Valley for three quarters of a mile.

Holme Pierrepont Hall, *Nottinghamshire* ~ a 16th century Hall containing period furnishings and the ceiling of one of the bedrooms has been taken down to show how the roof was constructed.

Nottingham Castle, *Nottingham* ~ stands on a rock with many underground passages. Today, only the 13th century gatehouse, sections of the medieval wall and moat remain. It houses a museum with information on the city's history and collections of ceramics, glass, silver and alabaster carvings.

Sherwood Forest Visitor Centre, *near Edwinstone, Nottinghamshire* ~ set in four hundred and fifty acres of ancient oak woodland. The Visitor Centre has an exhibition on the forest and the story behind Robin Hood, who supposedly lived there.

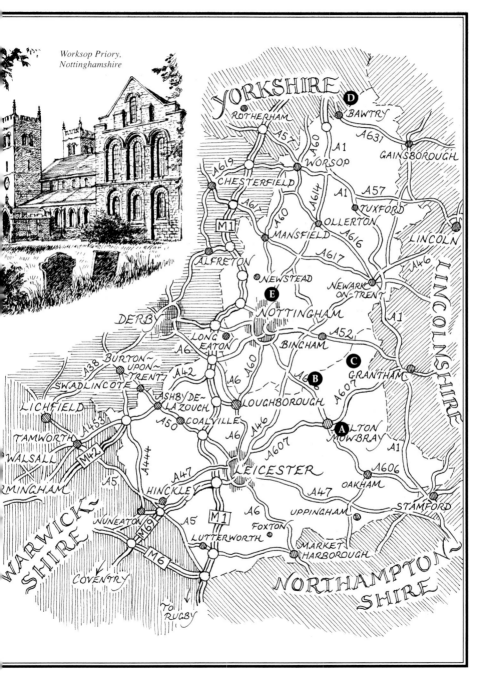

*Worksop Priory,
Nottinghamshire*

YORKSHIRE

ROTHERHAM

BAWTRY **D**

A57

A60

A619

A1

A631

GAINSBOROUGH

WORSOP

CHESTERFIELD

A617

A614

A1

A57

A60

TUXFORD

A61

OLLERTON

LINCOLN

M1

MANSFIELD

A616

A46

ALFRETON

A617

NEWSTEAD

NEWARK
ON-TRENT

E

NOTTINGHAM

A1

LINCOLNSHIRE

DERBY

LONG
EATON

A52

BINGHAM

A6

LICHFIELD

A38

BURTON-
UPON-
TRENT

A42

A60

A6

GRANTHAM **C**

A607

B

SWADLINCOTE

ASHBY DE-
LA ZOUCH

LOUGHBOROUGH

A50

COALVILLE

A46

MELTON
MOWBRAY **A**

A6

A607

A1

TAMWORTH

A453

A444

A606

WALSALL

M42

A5

A47

LEICESTER

OAKHAM

STAMFORD

BIRMINGHAM

HINCKLEY

A47

A6

UPPINGHAM

NUNEATON

A5

M1

FOXTON

WARWICK-
SHIRE

M69

LUTTERWORTH

MARKET
HARBOROUGH

M6

COVENTRY

NORTHAMPTON
SHIRE

TO
RUGBY

261

Leicestershire, Nottinghamshire & Rutland

Hillside House, 27 Melton Road, Burton Lazars, Melton Mowbray, Leicestershire LE14 2UR   A606

Charming converted comfortable old farm buildings with superb views over rolling countryside. Accommodation comprises 3 double rooms, 2 en-suite. 1 with private facilities. Centrally heated throughout. All rooms have colour TV, radio alarm, hair dryer and tea/coffee making facilities. Pleasant garden. Situated within easy reach of Burghley House, Belvoir Castle, Stamford and Rutland Water - or just enjoy the villages and countryside.

Mrs Sue Goodwin
Tel: 01664 566312
Fax: 01664 501819

B&B from £17pp, Rooms 1 twin en-suite, 1 twin private facilities, 1 double en-suite, Minimum age 10, Open all year except Christmas, Map Ref A

The Grange, New Road, Burton Lazars, Melton Mowbray, Leicestershire LE14 2UU   Nearest Road A606

This beautiful country house surrounds you with elegance, comfort and friendly care. Outstanding views and lovely formal garden of 2 ¹/₂ acres. Formerly a hunting lodge now provides attractive accommodation. Each bedroom is en-suite with telephone, TV and tea/coffee making facilities. The drawing room is furnished with antiques and has an open log burning fire. Dinner is served in a spacious dining room. Pam Holden presents a Cordon Bleu 3 course meal (by prior arrangement only). Only 1¹/₂ miles to Melton Mowbray and close to Rutland Water and Belvoir Castle.

Pam & Ralph Holden
Tel: 01664 60775
Fax: 01664 60775

B&B from £22.25pp, Dinner from £15, Rooms 1 single, 1 twin, 1 double, 1 family, all en-suite, Children welcome, No pets, Restricted smoking, Open all year, Map Ref A

Sulney Fields, Colonel's Lane, Upper Broughton, Melton Mowbray, Leicestershire LE14 3BD   A606

Situated in a quiet position on the edge of the village with magnificent views over the Vale of Belvoir. The accommodation is spacious. Most rooms having private bathrooms, TV's - all having tea/coffee making facilities. Midway between M1 and A1. There is easy access to Nottingham or Leicester. Evening meals are available at the pub within walking distance or two others just one mile away. Warwick, Stratford, the Peak District, Cambridge, York and many Stately Houses are within two hours drive.

Hilary Dowson
Tel: 01664 822204
Fax: 01664 823976

B&B from £17.50pp, Rooms 1 single, 2 twin, 2 double, 2 en-suite, Restricted smoking, Children & pets welcome, Open all year except Christmas & New Year, Map Ref B

Peacock Farm Guest House & Feathers Restaurant, Redmile, Leicestershire NG13 0GQ   Nearest Road A52

Peacock Farm is a 280 year old farmhouse tastefully modernised and surrounded by open farmland. Most rooms have an unbroken view of the village and Belvoir Castle. All bedrooms are en-suite have TV, and tea/coffee making facilities. After 21 years in pursuit of excellence we feel the service we offer is ideal for business people and holiday makers alike. Redmile is surrounded by stately homes, parks and market towns. Local attractions include swimming pool, croquet, riding, golf, fishing, cycling, walking country and much more. Art and Craft Centre.

Miss Nicky Need
Tel: 01949 842475
Fax: 01949 843127

B&B double £49, single £35, terms for children and long stay, Dinner £14.50, 1 single, 2 twin, 4 double, 3 family, all en-suite, Restricted smoking, Children welcome, Pets by arrangement, Open all Year, Map Ref C

The Old George Dragon, Scrooby, near Bawtry, Doncaster, Nottinghamshire DN10 6AU   A638, A1M

A warm welcome awaits you at this 18th century cottage. Situated in the picturesque and historic village of Scrooby. Internationally known for it's links with the Pilgrim Fathers and within easy reach of Robin Hood country. Accommodation is tastefully furnished retaining many original features and offers 2 double rooms and 1 twin room all with en-suite/private facilities, colour TV, tea/coffee making facilities. 2 miles from A1M. The Old George Dragon is not a pub.

John & Georgina Smithers   **B&B from £20pp, Rooms 1 twin, 2 double, all en-suite, Open all year,**
Tel: 01302 711840   **Map Ref D**

Greenwood Lodge City Guesthouse, Third Avenue, Sherwood Rise, Nottingham NG7 6JH   A60 Mansfield Rd

Greenwood Lodge City Guest House is less than a mile from the centre of Nottingham. Just off the A60 Mansfield Road, situated in a quiet area and is the home of Sheila and Michael Spratt who offer superior accommodation, all en-suite with hospitality tray, trouser press, TV, hair dryer and fine four poster. Magnificent conservatory dining room in elegant gardens. Ample off-street parking. English Tourist Board Three Crowns Highly Commended. Within short distance of Newstead Abbey, Chatsworth House, Sherwood Forest, Belvoir Castle.

Michael & Sheila Spratt   **B&B from £25pp, Dinner from £12.95, Rooms 1 single, 1 twin, 4 double,**
Tel: 0115 9621206   **all en-suite, Restricted smoking, Children welcome, Pets by**
Fax: 0115 9621206   **arrangement, Open all year, Map Ref E**

"And some of those, please"
BELLE & BERTIE IN YORK

LINCOLNSHIRE

The glorious and ancient city of Lincoln, strategically situated at the junction of the two great Roman highways, Fosse Way and Ermine Street, was the headquarters of the Roman Ninth Legion, and by the time of the Norman Conquest was one of the largest settlements in the country. The cathedral, mainly built during the thirteenth and fourteenth centuries, was to replace a Norman structure destroyed by an earthquake of all things. The cathedral was begun just four years after the adjacent Norman castle, built in 1068 by William the Conqueror. The huge central tower contains the five and a half ton bell - Great Tom of Lincoln. The magnificent Angel Choir was built during the later thirteenth century to contain the shrine of St. Hugh. No visitor should miss seeing the cheeky Lincoln Imp, a stonemason's joke carved between the arches. The prosperity of early Lincoln was based upon wool and the city had a rich and influential Jewish community. The Jew's House in The Strait dates from around 1170 and is one of the oldest houses in Britain still in use. Lord Tennyson, Poet Laureate and lover of Lincolnshire, whose statue stands outside the cathedral, was born at Somersby rectory. His favourite poem 'Maud', of 'come into the garden' fame is traditionally linked to the gardens of Harrington Hall in the Lincolnshire Wolds. Lincoln Cathedral was described by Ruskin as being 'out and out the most precious piece of architecture in the British Isles'. Lincoln dominates the Plain of Lincolnshire renowned during World War II for its airfields... Scampton being the home base of six hundred and seventeen Squadron, the 'Dambusters'. Grantham, south of Lincoln is a fine old coaching town. The George Inn dating from the eighteenth century is described by Charles Dickens in Nicholas Nickleby. A statue of Sir Isaac Newton stands before the Guildhall. Newton, who formulated the Theory of Gravity lived at nearby Woolsthorpe and attended Grantham's fifteenth century King's School. The chalk uplands of the Lincolnshire Wolds is wonderful walking country. Louth is the ideal holiday centre and contains some fine Georgian houses. The church of St. James built in 1506 has an impressive spire built of Ancaster stone. Old Bolingbroke is a lovely Wolds village, the birthplace of Henry IV, and just three and a half miles away near Winceby is the site of one of the major battles of the Civil War. Boston, the capital of Lincolnshire's Fenland was a major port during the Middle Ages. The great tower of the fourteenth century church of St. Botolph, at 288 feet is a landmark for miles around- in fact from the top a third of the county can be seen. Known as the Boston Stump, the church has impressive misericordes dated 1390. It was from Boston that the main group of Pilgrim Fathers embarked in 1608 to eventually reach the New World. Boston in Massachusetts is so named because many of the leading settlers came from the area around Lincolnshire's Boston. Over the centuries the marsh has been drained section by section to provide rich agricultural land. The marshes, once the domain of Hereward the Wake, now supply tulips to the markets of London. Spalding is the main bulb-growing area. Every May it holds a Flower Parade which must be one of the most spectacular free shows in England.

Over three million tulips are used to decorate the procession of floats. No visitor should leave this county without visiting Stamford with its glorious buildings. Its number of medieval churches includes St. Martin's, with its alabaster monument to Lord Burghley, and St. Mary's, with its gold-star-embellished fifteenth century chapel of the 'golden choir'. Burghley House, the palatial mansion with its Capability Brown landscaped park was built for William Cecil, chief minister to Elizabeth I, and is a veritable treasure house of art and superb furniture.

Here in Lincolnshire is so much to attract the holidaymaker, wonderful architecture, fascinating history, bright and breezy seaside resorts, sailing, fishing, splendid expanses of sand dunes and salt marsh and glorious open skies.

LINCOLNSHIRE

Places to Visit

Belton House, *Grantham* ~ Edward VIII often stayed here during his reign and two hundred and fifty years earlier William III also stayed here. The house contains many Old Masters and outside the gardens are formal with an orangery.

Boston Parish Church, *Boston* ~ a huge church with a distinctive octagonal tower, locally known as 'The Boston Stump'. It can be seen for miles across the surrounding fens.

Burghley House, *near Stamford* ~ an impressive late Elizabethan mansion, built between 1565 and 1585 it is surrounded by parkland landscaped by Capability Brown. It houses a collection of 17th century Italian paintings, as well as furniture and porcelain.

Doddington Hall, *near Lincoln* ~ set in formal gardens, it was built for Thomas Taylor in the late 16th century by the architect of Longleat, Robert Smythson. The Hall has a Georgian interior but the outside has hardly changed at all.

Lincoln Cathedral, *Lincoln* ~ the third largest mediaeval cathedral in the country, after St. Paul's and York Minster. It was built in the 11th century but has had many additions and alterations since. The Library contains four copies of the Magna Carta.

Old Hall, *Gainsborough* ~ parts date back to 1484 when Richard III stayed here. In later years, the Hickmans built a new house and the Old Hall was put to a variety of uses including an inn, theatre and Congregational chapel. In 1952 it was saved for posterity and is now one of Britain's best preserved manor houses.

Stamford Museum, *Stamford* ~ covers the history of the town. The most popular exhibit is a waxwork of the country's fattest man, Daniel Lambert; he weighed fifty three stone and died at Stamford Races in 1809.

St Edith's, *Coates-by-Stow* ~ a small church whose interior has been barely touched since the Middle Ages. It also has a Norman font, Elizabethan brasses, early pews and 15th century rood screen.

Woolsthorpe Manor, *Woolsthorpe-by-Colsterworth* ~ Sir Isaac Newton grew up in this 17th century house. His study has prints of other famous scientists of his day, it also has an upright desk reflecting the 17th century fashion for writing while standing up.

On the Lincolnshire Wolds

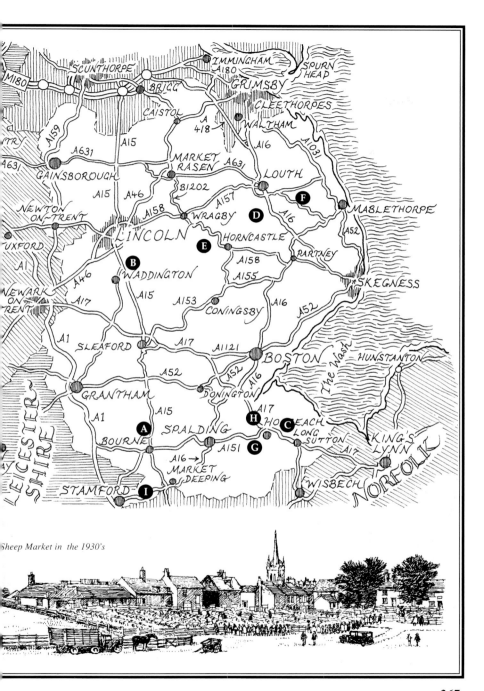

Sheep Market in the 1930's

267

Lincolnshire

Cawthorpe Hall, Bourne, Lincolnshire PE10 0AB   Nearest Road A15

Cawthorpe Hall specialises in space and tranquillity. All ages are welcome to this large eighteenth century residence home to Englands' only rose distillery. Accommodation is en-suite and our ground floor room is suitable for those with difficulties. Full English breakfast included. Visitors are encouraged to wander around the gardens and rose fields. Exceptionally located for exploring Lincolnshire, Cambridge, Burghly House, Stamford and other historic gardens and houses. The beautiful countryside is ideal for outdoor pursuits especially golf, rambling and visiting the excellent choice of pubs.

Chantal Armstrong
Tel: 01778 423830
Fax: 01778 426620

B&B from £25pp, Rooms 1 single, 2 twin, 1 double, 1 family, most en-suite, Restricted smoking, Children & pets welcome, Open January - November, Map Ref A

The Manor House, Bracebridge Heath, Lincoln LN4 2HW   Nearest Road A15

The Manor House is a charming late 18th century stone-built house set in an attractive walled garden. All rooms are spacious and comfortable with en-suite or private facilities and tea/coffee making facilities. Great care is paid to every detail in this beautiful home where the atmosphere is relaxed and you are assured of an individual welcome. ETB 2 Crown Highly Commended.

Jill & Michael Scoley
Tel: 01522 520825
Fax: 01522 542418

B&B from £22pp, Rooms 2 twin, 1 double, No smoking, Minimum age 10, No pets, Open mid January - mid December, Map Ref B

Cackle Hill House, Cackle Hill Lane, Holbeach, Lincolnshire PE12 8BS   Nearest Road A17

A warm friendly welcome awaits you at our comfortable home set in a rural position. All rooms are tastefully furnished, have en-suite/private facilities and hospitality trays. There is an attractive guests lounge with colour TV. We are ideally situated for many attractions in Lincolnshire, Norfolk and Cambridgeshire. ETB 2 Crowns, Highly Commended.

Mrs Maureen Biggadike
Tel: 01406 426721
Fax: 01406 424659

B&B from £20pp, Rooms 2 twin, 1 double, 2 en-suite, 1 private facilities, No smoking, Pets by arrangement, Open all year except Christmas & New Year, Map Ref C

The Old Rectory, Fulletby, near Horncastle, Lincolnshire LN9 6JX   Nearest Road A153

see PHOTO opposite

Experience our lovely country house nestling in the beautiful Lincolnshire Wolds, an area of outstanding natural beauty. Undiscovered, rural tranquillity awaits you, yet we are near to historic Lincoln and the coast. Enjoy walks, cycling, fishing, golf, bird watching, antiques, gardens or just relaxing! We offer Aga home cooking, fresh flowers, 4 acres of gardens, wonderful views and a warm welcome - with superior B&B en-suite, lovingly furnished, accommodation. Our guests often return having discovered this 'real gem'. We look forward to meeting you for a truly relaxing, memorable stay.

Michael & Jill Swan
Tel: 01507 533533
Fax: 01507 533533

B&B from £20pp, Dinner £15 (4 course) by prior booking, Rooms 2 twin en-suite, 3 double, 2 en-suite, No smoking, Dogs by arrangement, Open all year except Christmas & New Year, Map Ref D

The Old Rectory, *near Horncastle - see details on opposite page*

Greenfield Farm, Mill Lane/Cow Lane, Minting, near Horncastle, Lincs LN9 5RX **Nearest Road A158**

Judy & Hugh welcome you to stay at their comfortable farmhouse set in a quiet location yet centrally placed for all the major Lincolnshire attractions. Play tennis, relax by the large pond or enjoy the forest walks that border the farm. Guests have their own sitting room with colour television and wood burning stove, modern en-suite shower rooms with heated towel rails and tea/coffee making facilities. Ample parking. Excellent pub with traditional country cooking, 1 mile. ETB 2 Crowns Highly Commended , AA Selected QQQQ, All private facilities.

Judy & Hugh Bankes Price
Tel/Fax: 01507 578457
Mobile: 0468 368829

B&B from £20pp, Rooms 2 double, 1 twin, all private facilities, No smoking, Children over 10, No pets, Open mid January - mid December, Map Ref E

Gordon House, Legbourne, Louth, Lincolnshire LN11 8LH **Nearest Road A157**

A warm welcome awaits you at Gordon House, an elegant country house on the fringe of the Lincolnshire Wolds. There are many lovely country walks from the doorstep which encompass the beauty of this unspoilt area of Lincolnshire. The comfort of our guests is our primary concern. Both guest rooms are individually decorated to a high standard, have tea/coffee making facilities, washbasins and colour TV. The 'Gordon House Breakfast' which includes local sausage and Lincolnshire plum bread must be tried. The large rear garden is available for guests to relax in.

see PHOTO opposite

Keith & Elizabeth Norman
Tel: 01507 607568

B&B from £18pp, Dinner from £9, Rooms 2 double, No smoking, Children welcome, Pets by arrangement, Open all year. Map Ref F

Guy Wells Farm, Eastgate, Whaplode, Spalding, Lincolnshire PE12 6TZ **Nearest Road A 151**

Anne and Richard welcome you to their "listed" Queen Anne farmhouse set in a peaceful country garden, close to the famous Fenland churches, the Wash with its marshes and nature reserves as well as Sandringham, Boston, Peterborough and Stamford. Guy Wells is their home offering good food, spacious accommodation, with full central heating, three double bedrooms, two en-suite, radios, tea and coffee making facilities plus guests' own bathroom, sitting room, colour TV, woodburning stove, old beams as well as guests' dining room with separate tables.

Anne & Richard Thompson
Tel/Fax: 01406 422239

B&B from £20pp, Dinner by arrangement from £10-£12.50, Rooms 1 twin, 2 double, all en-suite, No smoking, Children over 10, Open all year except Christmas, Map Ref G

Pipwell Manor, Saracens Head, Holbeach, Spalding, Lincolnshire PE12 8AL **Nearest Road A17**

This Georgian house was built around 1740 and is a Grade II listed building. It has been tastefully restored and redecorated in the appropriate style and retains many of its original features. All 4 bedrooms are attractive and well furnished and have tea/coffee making facilities. Parking is available and guests are welcomed with home made cakes and tea. Pipwell Manor stands amid gardens and paddocks in a small village just off the A17 in the Lincolnshire Fens. A lovely place to stay. AA Selected QQQQ, 'Which' Good B&B Guide, 'Country Living' Highly Recommended. ETB 2 Crowns Highly Commended.

Mrs Lesley Honnor
Tel/Fax: 01406 423119

B&B from £20pp, Rooms 2 double, 1 twin, 1 single, all with en-suite or private facilities, No smoking or pets, Open all year except Christmas & New Year, Map Ref H

---

*left, **Gordon House,** near Louth - see details above*

The Mill, Mill Lane, Tallington, Stamford, Lincolnshire PE9 4RR   **Nearest Road A16**

Recently renovated to provide en-suite accommodation of the highest standard without losing any of the atmosphere of bygone years. Many original features are intact including the mill working situated in the dining room. Also available a unique room in barn conversion attached to the mill and by the mill pond. All rooms have a river view. The historic town of Stamford is only four miles away, whilst the Cathedral city of Peterborough is 10 miles. Non smoking. Tea and coffee facilities. Car park.

see PHOTO opposite

Sue & John Olver
Tel: 01780 740815
Fax: 01780 740280

B&B from £22.50pp, Dinner from £13, Rooms 2 twin, 3 double, 1 family, all en-suite, No smoking, Children & pets welcome, Open all year, Map Ref I

""Whoops! Look out - they're off!"
BELLE & BERTIE IN YORK

*left, **The Mill,** near Stamford - see details above*

NORFOLK

Little wonder that in this county of deep blue skies, crystal clear visibility and singularly low rainfall, there was established probably the greatest School of English landscape painters, the Norwich School. Add to this, wonderful heathland and marsh, water meadows, ancient manor houses and picturesque thatched cottages, and you have in Norfolk an area of irresistible appeal to the holiday maker.

The Norfolk Broads National Park is a magnet which attracts birdwatchers and boat enthusiasts of every level of proficiency. The Broads, to the east of Norwich, contain the slow-moving rivers of Yare, Waveney and Bure which all meander languidly between the shallow expanses of water which are in fact the flooded sites of ancient peat workings, eventually converging on Breydon Water before joining the coast at Great Yarmouth. The Broads are best appreciated from a boat, and there are numerous boatyards where boats can be hired, particularly at Wroxham and Hoveton, but there is fine walking too around Horsey where the pumping mill is open to the public. Why the Norfolk Broads should be such an attraction to crime writers I simply can't tell, but for some reason the lakes, pools and rivers of the Broads have provided inspiration to dozens of crime writers, including Wilkie Collins, P.D. James, Dorothy L. Sayers and C.P. Snow.

The north Norfolk coast is a wide and wonderful holiday area with Europe's largest expanse of saltmarshes, fine sandy beaches and of course quite dramatic skyscapes. Cromer, famed for its crabs, is the centre of this area and with its neighbour Sheringham are fine holiday resorts retaining much of their old fishing-village character. Picturesque Cley, with its grand windmill boasts some fine flint houses, as does nearby Blakeney, a busy yachting centre, Wells-next-the-Sea, now certainly not next-the-sea is famous for its sprats and whelks. Inland at Little Walsingham is the Shrine of Our Lady of Walsingham, a centre for pilgrimage for over nine hundred years for both Roman Catholics and Anglicans. Hunstanton, the largest of the north western resorts, is unique amongst East Anglian seaside towns in that it faces west, its heavily eroded cliffs formed of multicoloured layers of rock.

The slightly Continental atmosphere of King's Lynn may well be due to its ancient membership of the fourteenth century Hanseatic League. The town's prosperity is revealed in the grand seventeenth and eighteenth century houses, chief among them being the fine Customs House. The two market places each contain a guildhall. The Saturday Market boasts the fifteenth century Guildhall of the Holy Trinity with a chequerboard facade of flint and stone and the Tuesday Market, St. George's Guildhall - the largest medieval guildhall in England. It was a charter of 1537 that gave Lynn its regal prefix. Sandringham, the large estate and country home built for the Prince of Wales, later to become King Edward VII, is to the north of King's Lynn.

Norwich has been a regional centre of importance since Anglo-Saxon times and its fascinating medieval city centre is rich in fine old streets - Elm Hill, Bridewell Alley and Colegate - and outstanding churches, St. Peter Mancroft and St. Peter Hungate being two not to be missed. The cathedral is of course the jewel of the city, its glorious fifteenth century spire, at three hundred and fifteen feet, is second in England only to Salisbury. The Norman cloister is the largest in the country.

Norwich possesses some quite outstanding museums; the Castle Museum shows a magnificent collection of paintings by the Norwich School, also a remarkable collection of tea-pots; the Sainsbury Centre for Visual Arts, part of the University of East Anglia campus, houses a superb collection of modern sculpture and paintings, displayed in a gallery designed by Norman Foster.

Great Yarmouth, at the mouth of Breydon Water, Norfolk's east coast port and busy holiday resort, was badly bombed during the war, but much of the old town has been restored including the narrow streets of fisherman's houses known as the Rows. Five miles of promenade, golden beaches and a spectacular pleasure beach make it one of Britain's major seaside resorts. Scattered over this county are some extremely fine houses - Houghton Hall, an elegant Palladian mansion, once the seat of Sir Robert Walpole, the first English Prime Minister; Holkham Hall, another Palladian house built for Thomas Coke, the eighteenth century agricultural pioneer; Blickling Hall, a grand seventeenth century house with lavish Jacobean plasterwork belonging to the National Trust; and Felbrigg, another seventeenth century National Trust property with Georgian furniture. The list is long, but so too is the list of pleasures facing the holidaymaker in this glorious county.

NORFOLK

Places to Visit

Blicking Hall, *Aylsham* ~ with symmetrical Jacobean front was where Anne Boleyn, Henry VIII's second wife, spent her childhood. Very little of the original house survives and most of the present building dates from 1628 when it was the home of James I's Chief Justice Sir Henry Hobart. The house features reliefs of Anne Boleyn and her daughter, Elizabeth I, a huge tapestry and paintings by Gainsborough.

Bure Valley Railway, *Aylsham to Wroxham* ~ a narrow gauge railway running diesel and steam trains across Broadland between Aylsham and Wroxham with three stops at Coltishall, Brampton and Buxton.

Burgh Castle ~ a well preserved Roman fort that formed part of the so-called Saxon Shore. It is in a secluded setting, close to the junction of the Rivers Waveney and Yare.

Norwich Cathedral, *Norwich* ~ founded in 1096 by Bishop Losinga who had the white stone shipped in from Normandy in France. The thin cathedral spire was added in the 15th century making it the second tallest in Britain. In the nave, Norman pillars support the 15th century vaulted roof with stone bosses.

Oxburgh Hall, *near Kings Lynn* ~ built in 1482 on an island in the Fens by Sir Edmund Bedingfeld, the surrounding land has been drained but the house is has a mediaeval moat. The rooms and their contents range from Tudor to Georgian and Victorian times and feature a Mary Queen of Scots embroidery and a tapestry map of Oxfordshire and Berkshire.

Sandringham House ~ a large 18th century house, which has been in royal hands since 1862 when it was bought by the Prince of Wales, later Edward VII, who refurbished it. The Royal Family spend every Christmas at Sandringham House.

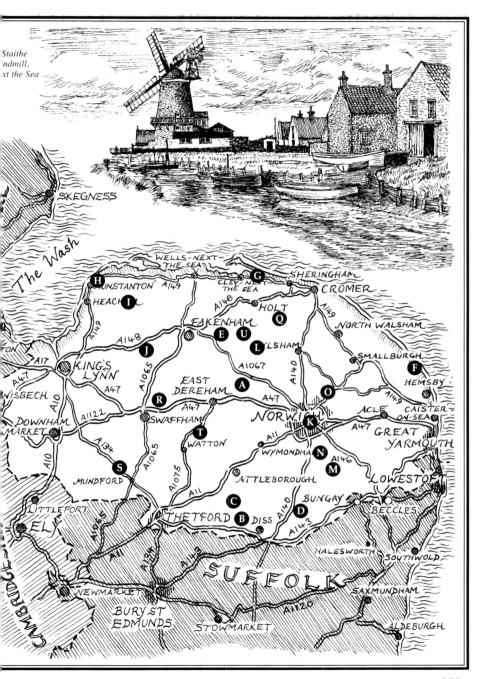

Staithe
'ndmill,
xt the Sea

SKEGNESS

The Wash

WELLS-NEXT-THE-SEA

SHERINGHAM

H HUNSTANTON A149 **G** CLEY-NEXT-THE-SEA CROMER

HEACHAM **I** A148 HOLT A149 NORTH WALSHAM

FAKENHAM **Q**

A148 **E** **U** YLSHAM

A1065 **J** A1067 SMALLBURGH

A47 A140 **F** HEMSBY

WISBECH A10 EAST DEREHAM **A** **O** CAISTER-ON-SEA

KING'S LYNN A1122 A47 ACLE

DOWNHAM MARKET **R** A47 **K** GREAT YARMOUTH

SWAFFHAM NORWICH A47

A134 A1065 **T** WATTON A11 WYMONDHAM **N** A146 LOWESTOFT

S MUNDFORD A1075 ATTLEBOROUGH **M** BECCLES

A11 **C** A140 BUNGAY

LITTLEPORT THETFORD **B** DISS **D** A143

EL HALESWORTH SOUTHWOLD

CAMBRIDGE SUFFOLK SAXMUNDHAM

NEWMARKET A120

BURY ST EDMUNDS STOWMARKET ALDEBURGH

277

Bartles Lodge, Church Street, Elsing, Dereham, Norfolk NR20 3EA   **Nearest Road A47, A1067**

If you would like a peaceful, tranquil stay in the heart of Norfolk's most beautiful countryside, yet only a short drive to some of England's finest beaches, then Bartles Lodge could be the place for you. All rooms are tastefully decorated in country style, and have full en-suite facilities etc. Overlooking 12 acres of landscaped meadows with its own private fishing lakes. Although the lodge is fully licenced the local village inn is nearby. Why not telephone David or Annie so that we can tell you about our lovely home.

David & Annie Bartlett
Tel: 01362 637177

B&B from £22.50pp, Rooms 3 double, 1 family, 3 twin, Minimum age 10, Open all year, Map Ref A

Lodge Farm, Algar Road, Bressingham, Diss, Norfolk IP22 2BQ   **Nearest Road A1066**

Traditional B&B accommodation in our rambling Grade II sixteenth century farmhouse set in large and old-fashioned gardens surrounded by peaceful countryside and woodlands. The bedrooms are cottagey in style with separate sitting room, dining room and bathroom for the use of guests. Tea/coffee making facilities available. Bressingham Gardens and Steam Museum are close and there is a good choice of local pubs for evening meals.

Mr & Mrs Bateson
Tel: 01379 687629

B&B from £17pp, Rooms 1 double, 1 family, Children over 6, Pets restricted, Open all year except Christmas, Map Ref B

Strenneth, Airfield Road, Fersfield, Diss, Norfolk IP22 2BP   **Nearest Road A1066**

Strenneth is a family run business, situated in unspoiled countryside just 10 minutes drive from the market town of Diss and Bressingham Gardens. The 17th century building has exposed beams, and has been fully renovated with a single storey courtyard wing with off road parking and plenty of walks nearby. The seven bedrooms, including a Four Poster are tastefully arranged with period furniture. All have colour TV, hospitality trays, central heating and en-suite facilities. The main house is smoke free and the guest lounge has a log fire on cold winter evenings. There is an extensive breakfast menu using local produce. EMail: ken@mainline.co.uk

Ken & Brenda Webb
Tel: 01379 688182
Fax: 01379 688260

B&B from £22.50pp, Rooms 1 single, 2 twin, 4 double, all en-suite, Restricted smoking, Children and Pets welcome, Open all year, Map Ref C

The Old Bakery, Church Walk, Pulham Market, Diss, Norfolk IP21 4SJ   **Nearest Road A140**

see PHOTO opposite

Welcome to a superb combination of a licenced listed 16th century oak-beamed house with excellent cooking from your host, a Master Chef. We stand by the village green in an award winning conservation village. All rooms are spacious and en-suite and have hospitality tray and colour TV. Log fires in winter, sunny walled garden in summer. Visit Norfolk and Suffolk with their NT coasts, Historic Buildings, splendid gardens, windmills and thatched churches. Convenient for Bressingham, the Broads and Norwich yet only 1 1/2 hours from London. ETB Highly Commended.

Martin & Jean Croft
Tel: 01379 676492
Fax: 01379 676492

B&B from £23pp, Dinner from £15, Rooms 2 twin, 1 double, all en-suite, No smoking, No pets, Open all year except Christmas & New Year, Map Ref D

The Old Bakery,
Puilham Market
- see details
opposite

Manor Farm House, Stibbard Road, Fulmodeston, nr Fakenham, Norfolk NR21 0LX   Nearest Road A1067

Manor Farm House is a period farmhouse set in 500 acres of peaceful arable farmland. The 1 acre of garden has croquet set out in summer. All bedrooms have tea/coffee making facilities and colour TV. Sandringham House, Blickling Hall and Felbrigg Hall are within 1/2 hour drive; and the coast at Blakeney is 20 minutes; both Norwich and Kings Lynn can be reached in 35 minutes. An evening meal is available by arrangement and special diets catered for. ETB 1 Crown Commended. Parking Available. Visa & Mastercard accepted.

Anne Savage
Tel: 01328 829353
Fax: 01328 829741

B&B from £20pp, Dinner from £13.50 by arrangement, Rooms 1 twin, 2 double, minimum age 7, No pets, No smoking, Open all year, Map Ref E

Tower Cottage, Black Street, Winterton-on-Sea, Gt Yarmouth, Norfolk NR29 4AP   Black Street

A charming, flint cottage, with many original features in a pretty village. Attractive bedrooms (2 on ground floor) have beverage trays, colour TV and wash hand basins, (one double is en-suite with its own sitting room, in a converted barn). Generous breakfasts including homemade preserves are served amongst the grapevines in the conservatory in summer. A beautiful, unspoilt sandy beach and traditional village pub are a few minutes walk away. Norfolk broads 2 miles, Norwich 19 miles. 'Which' entry since 1994.

Alan & Muriel Webster
Tel: 01493 394053

B&B from £17pp, Rooms 1 twin, 2 double, 1 double is en-suite, Restricted smoking, Minimum age 8, Dogs in barn accom only, Open all year except Christmas & New Year, Map Ref F

Rosedale Farm Guesthouse, Holt Road, Weybourne, Holt, Norfolk NR25 7ST   A149 Coast Road

Ideally set for getting away, "Rosedale" a traditional flint and brick farmhouse is situated within it's own walled gardens on the Norfolk coastline, equidistant from Cley-Next-The-Sea and Cromer. Whether sightseeing or rambling no one will be short of places to visit with Sheringham Park and Kelling Heath on the doorstep and the "Shire Horse Centre", Felbrigg and "Thursford Museum" all nearby. Excellent cuisine awaits you at "Rosedale" and a good rest is assured with large comfortable bedrooms and residents own sitting room. Licensed. Cycle hire available.

Charles & Pauline Lacoste
Tel: 01263 588778

B&B from £22.50pp, Dinner from £10.50-£14, Rooms 1 twin, 2 double, 1 family, all en-suite, Restricted smoking, Children welcome, Pets restricted, Open all year except Christmas & New Year, Map Ref G

Fieldsend, Homefields Road, Hunstanton, Norfolk PE36 5HL   Nearest Road A149

Come and stay at Fieldsend and enjoy the comfort of a large Edwardian carrstone house, close to the Town Centre and the sea with Panoramic views over the Wash. Guests have a choice of 3 rooms, 2 en-suite and one with a private bathroom, all individually decorated by the owner who specialises in rag rolling, making the drapes and pelmets as well as upholstery and collecting coloured glass. One bedroom has a four poster! Delicious breakfasts are served by a Cordon Bleu cook. Parking in grounds.

Sheila & John Tweedy-Smith
Tel: 01485 532593
Fax: 01485 532593

B&B from £22.50pp, Rooms 1 twin, 1 double, 1 family, all en-suite/ private facilities, Children welcome, No pets, Open all year, Map Ref H

North Farmhouse, Station Road, Docking, Kings Lynn, Norfolk PE31 8LS   Nearest Road A149

North Farmhouse is an attractive typical Norfolk Flint and Brick building standing in an acre. It is at least 300 years old and has accommodation for four people. We have one twin bedroom and one double bedroom both with their own facilities. We are excellently situated for anyone wishing to visit the North Norfolk area Sandringham. We are fairly central for Kings Lynn, Wells, Fakenham and Hunstanton. The area is superb for walking, bird watching, cycling, golf and beaches.

Helen & Roger Roberts
Tel: 01485 51493

B&B from £18-£22pp, Rooms 1 twin, 1 double, all en-suite, No smoking, Children welcome, Open February - November, Map Ref I

Lower Farm, Harpley, Kings Lynn, Norfolk PE31 6TU   Nearest Road A148

Lower Farm is set in delightful countryside, off the beaten track. It is south east of Sandringham, 1 1/2 miles from Peddars Way, and 20 minutes from the coast. There is an excellent pub in the village. Stabling available for horses. Lovely garden and trees. The comfortable and spacious bedrooms are well equipped and include TV, tea/coffee making facilities and fridge. Parking available.

Mrs Amanda Case
Tel: 01485 520240

B&B from £18pp, £5 extra for supplement for single occupancy, Rooms 1 twin with private bathroom, 2 double with en-suite bathroom, Pets by arrangement, Children by arrangement, Restricted smoking, Open all year except Xmas week, Map Ref J

Kingsley Lodge, 3 Kingsley Road, Norwich, Norfolk NR1 3RB   Nearest Road A11, A140

Quiet, friendly, Edwardian house in Norwich city centre. Situated less than 10 minutes walk to the Market Place, castle, shops, restaurants and other places of interest in this historic city. All rooms have en-suite bathroom, colour TV and tea/coffee making facilities. Guests are issued with keys to enable easy access. A full English breakfast is cooked to order - in summer this can be taken in the conservatory. Permits provided for parking in the street. Kingsley Lodge is graded 2 crowns commended by the English Tourist Board. Self Catering also available.

Sally Clarke
Tel: 01603 615819
Fax: 01603 615819

B&B from £19pp, Rooms 1 single, 1 twin, 1 double (all en-suite), No smoking, No children, No pets, Open February - December, Map Ref K

EdMar Lodge, 64 Earlham Road, Norwich, Norfolk NR2 3DF   Nearest Road A11

A welcoming smile, friendly service and every comfort are all provided at Edmar Lodge, situated only 10 minutes walk from the city centre and with 2 car parks. Ideal for exploring Norwich and the Norfolk countryside. Advice is readily given on walks in the city with its attractions from modern shops to fascinating museums, together with tour planning in and around the county. 4 bedrooms with every amenity, including tea/coffee and TV. EMail: edmar@dial.pipex.com

Eddie & Margaret Lovatt
Tel: 01603 615599
Fax: 01603 495599

B&B from £18pp, Rooms 1 single, 1 double, 1 twin, 1 family, en-suite available, Children welcome, No pets, Open all year, Map Ref K

The Old Laundry, Heydon Hall, Norwich, Norfolk NR11 6RE   **Nearest Road B1149**

You are guaranteed a warm welcome to The Old Laundry, an annexe to the Elizabethan Heydon Hall. The accommodation has recently been renovated to a very high standard and the pretty bedrooms include tea/coffee making facilities. There is a large dining/sitting room with woodburner, colour TV and telephone. Stabling available for horses. Guests are served a delicious full English or Continental breakfast using local and home produced ingredients as available. Ideally situated for exploring the North Norfolk Coast, the Broads and Norwich.

Mrs Bulwer Long
Tel: 01263 587343
Fax: 01263 587805

B&B from £25pp, Rooms 2 double/twin, both with private bathroom (one en-suite), No smoking or pets, Children by arrangement, Open all year except Christmas, Map Ref L

Waterfield Cottage, High Green, Brooke, Norwich, Norfolk NR15 1JE   **Nearest Road B1332**

Waterfield Cottage, is an attractive 400 year old thatched cottage, set in an acre of delightful gardens and surrounded by a moat. It is situated on the edge of a conservation village amongst fields and woodlands. The accommodation is very comfortable, bedrooms have tea/coffee making facilities, and TV. A delightful lounge is available for guests to relax in. The fine cathedral city of Norwich is only 15 minutes away by car, and the Norfolk Broads and coasts of Norfolk and Suffolk are within easy reach.

Mrs Rosemary Price
Tel: 01508 550312

B&B from £20pp, Dinner £12, Rooms 1 double, 1 twin, 1 bed/sitting room en-suite, Restricted smoking, Minimum age 5, Open all year except Christmas week, Map Ref M

Greenacres Farmhouse, Woodgreen, Long Stratton, Norwich, Norfolk NR15 2RR   **Nearest Road A140**

A period 17th century farmhouse on a 30 acre common with ponds and wildlife, only 10 miles from Norwich. All en-suite bedrooms (2 double/1 twin) are tastefully furnished to complement the oak beams and period furniture, with tea/coffee facilities and TV. The beamed sitting room with inglenook fireplaces invites you to relax. A sunny dining room encourages you to enjoy a leisurely breakfast. Snooker table and all-weather tennis court. Enjoy the peace and tranquillity of this charming home.

Joanna Douglas
Tel: 01508 530261

B&B from £18pp, Dinner available from £12, Rooms 1 twin, 2 double, all en-suite, Children & pets welcome, Open all year, Map Ref N

Brooksbank, 1 Lower Street, Salhouse, Norwich, Norfolk NR13 6RW   **Nearest Road Salhouse Road**

see PHOTO opposite

Brooksbank House is next door to a quiet public house, where meals are obtainable, centred in the broadland village of Salhouse. TV lounge for guests use only. Extensive breakfast menu. 2 double on first floor and 1 twin bedded ground floor en-suite rooms. Satellite colour TV, hospitality trays in all rooms. Ample car parking at rear. Outside heated swimming pool in summer only. Salhouse is situated 2 miles from Wroxham and 6 miles from Norwich. Also adjoining self catering cottage with TV. Please telephone for brochure.

Phil & Ray Coe
Tel: 01603 720420

B&B from £18pp, Rooms 1 twin, 2 double, all en-suite, No smoking, Children welcome, No pets, Open all year, Map Ref O

right, **Brooksbank,** *Salhouse - see details above*

Westwood Barn, Crabgate Lane South, Wood Dalling, Norwich, Norfolk NR11 6SW   Nearest Road B1149

Outstanding accommodation all on ground floor level. All rooms have en-suite bathroom with TV and tea/coffee making facilities. Magnificent guest sitting room with original beams and an enormous inglenook fireplace. Beautiful four poster bedded room. ETB Highly Commended. Idyllic rural location for discovering the charms and tranquillity of north Norfolk. Two miles from the picturesque village of Heydon, the location of many films. National Trust properties, Norwich, the coast and Norfolk Broads within a twelve mile radius. Illustrated brochure on request.

Sylvia & Geoffrey Westwood
Tel: 01263 584108

B&B from £22, Dinner £16, Rooms 1 en-suite twin, 2 en-suite double, 1 4-poster, Restricted smoking, Children welcome, No pets, Open all year, B&B only at Christmas, Map Ref Q

Corfield House, Sporle, Swaffham, Norfolk PE32 2EA   **Nearest Road A47**

Corfield House is an attractive brick-built house standing in half an acre of lawned gardens in the peaceful village of Sporle near Swaffham, an ideal centre for touring Norfolk. The comfortable en-suite rooms (one ground floor) have fine views across open fields or the garden, and all have television, clock/radio, tea tray and a fact file on places to visit. There is a separate guest living room. Good home cooking using excellent local produce. Licenced. ETB 3 Crowns Highly Commended. No smoking throughout.

Martin & Linda Hickey
Tel: 01760 723636

B&B from £21.50pp, Dinner £12.50, Rooms 2 twin, 2 double, all en-suite, No smoking, Children welcome, Pets by arrangement, Open March - December, Map Ref R

Old Bottle House, Cranwich, Mundford, Thetford, Norfolk IP26 5JL   **Nearest Road A134**

A warm welcome is assured at The Old Bottle House. This is a 275 year old former coaching inn, which has a lovely garden and rural views set in a wonderful position on the edge of Thetford Forest. The spacious colour co-ordinated bedrooms have tea/coffee making facilities, and colour television. Delicious meals are served in the dining room which has an inglenook fireplace. There is a pleasant lounge where guests may relax after a busy day.

Mrs Marion Ford
Tel: 01842 878012

B&B from £18pp, Dinner from £12, Rooms 2 twin, 1 double/family, No smoking, Minimum age 5, Open all year, Map Ref S

White Hall, Carbrooke, near Watton, Thetford, Norfolk IP25 6SG   **Nearest Road B1108**

White Hall is an elegant listed Georgian house standing in delightful grounds of 3 acres with large natural pond, surrounded by fields and providing a haven of peace and tranquillity. Spacious accommodation, full central heating, log fires on chilly evenings, early morning tea and evening drinks ensure your stay is enjoyable and relaxing. Situated on the edge of Carbrooke village and in the centre of the interesting and attractive area of Breckland, we are ideally situated for the many attractions in both Norfolk and north Suffolk. Good choice of local eating places. ETB 2 Crown Highly Commended.

Mrs S Carr
Tel: 01953 885950
Fax: 01953 884420

B&B from £19pp, Rooms 1 double en-suite, 1 twin and 1 double, Restricted smoking, Open all year, Map Ref T

The Old Rectory, Wood Norton, Norfolk NR20 5AZ   **Nearest Road B1110**

Set in secluded gardens and grounds of 5 acres, in rural north Norfolk. This fascinating house originated in the 17th century with later Victoria additions and is now a delightful family home. Large bedrooms, double with en-suite bathroom and huge canopied brass bedstead. Twin room with private bathroom is similarly attractive. Both rooms have easy chars, colour TV, tea/coffee making facilities. Full English breakfast, optional evening meal in large elegant dining room.This is a strategic location for the coast, 10 miles, the Georgian market town of Holt and Cathedral city of Norwich, 20 miles.

Jo & Giles Winter
Tel: 01362 683785

B&B from £20pp, Dinner from £12.50, Rooms 1 twin, 1 double, Restricted smoking, Children welcome, Pets by arrangement, Open all year except Christmas and New Year, Map Ref U

"Here you are Madame, he hadn't gone far"
BELLE & BERTIE IN YORK

NORTHUMBRIA & COUNTY DURHAM

This great and glorious region contains ,amongst a seemingly never-ending list of places to visit, four hundred square miles of National Park running from Hadrian's Wall in the south to the Cheviots and the Scottish border in the north. The Wall itself is a great attraction and to walk along its length is a wonderful experience, with spectacular views from the ridge of the Great Whin Sill across the Northumberland moors. Northumbria, in the seventh century the most powerful of the Anglo-Saxon kingdoms, now combines the four counties of Cleveland, Durham, Tyne and Wear and Northumberland. Each of the old counties has its own particular qualities, combined they form the ideal holiday venue.

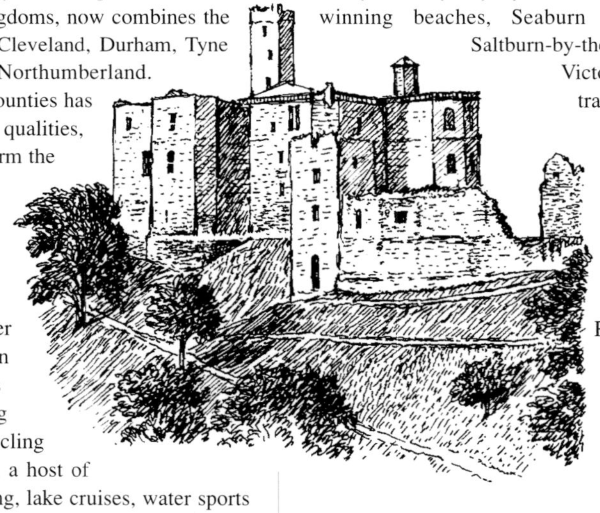

The varied countryside is staggering. Kielder Forest, a vast open expanse of woods and lakes, offering many walking, cycling and riding trails, a host of picnic sites, fishing, lake cruises, water sports on Europe's largest man-made lake, exhibitions, shops and restaurants. For the holiday maker who appreciates nature on a slightly smaller scale there are the glorious woodland gardens of Howick Hall, the Gertrude Jekyll gardens at Lindisfarne Castle, Kirkley Hall College gardens, the quarry gardens of Belsay Hall or the lovely rock-gardens at Cragside House, Wallington Hall

and the National Thyme collection at Hexham Herbs. These are just a few from the long list of delights awaiting the visitor. Add to this list a host of garden centres and the choice is quite astonishing. For the visitor who favours the seaside, this north east coast without doubt offers the finest stretches of sand in the kingdom, not overcrowded resorts, but unspoiled beaches - Alnwick, Marsden with its spectacular cliffs and world famous seabird colony, Whitley Bay, Tynmouth with its award winning beaches, Seaburn and Roker, Saltburn-by-the-Sea with its Victorian inclined tramway and its intriguing Smugglers Heritage Centre and Redcar with its fine sands and RNLI Zetland Lifeboat Museum. This remarkable coastline is also rich in magnificent castles - Bamburgh Castle superbly sited on a basalt crag overlooking its charming village and Alnwick, known as 'The Windsor of the North'. This great fortress is a treasure house of paintings, furniture and Meissen china. And could there be a more emotive castle than Lindisfarne perched on Holy Island. The castle was converted in 1903 into a private house by Edwin Lutyens. The ruined Benedictine Priory here was founded in 635AD by St. Aidan from Iona, and is regarded as the cradle of British Christianity. Close to Holy Island are the Farne Islands, a bird reserve containing no fewer than fifty five thousand breeding birds and also the breeding ground of grey seals. And then there are the cities. Durham, its cathedral 'Half Church of God, half castle 'gainst the Scots', magnificently situated on sandstone cliffs overlooking a loop of the River Wear and the city, is a wonderful jumbled collection of ancient streets. The cathedral, the finest Norman church in Britain, is the resting place for the remains of St. Cuthbert and the Venerable Bede. Newcastle, the capital of Northumbria, is the ideal base from which to explore this area, a major shopping centre and an elegant example of early nineteenth century townscaping. Its six great river bridges include the famous double-decker road and rail bridge built by Robert Stephenson in 1840. There are theatres and superb galleries and museums, including the remarkable 'interactive' Museum of Science and Engineering. Middlesbrough, the administrative centre of Cleveland, developed rapidly from a tiny fishing village, with the extension of Stephenson's Stockton and Darlington railway. At the heart of the

beautiful valley of the Tees, the town is an excellent centre from which to visit the picturesque fishing villages of Staithes, Robin Hood's Bay, Runswick Bay and Whitby. There is much to see in Middlesbrough itself - the Newport Bridge, the largest vertical lift bridge in the country if not the world, the unique Transporter bridge, the Captain Cook Birthplace Museum in Stewart Park and Fairy Dell Park. Between these larger centres are the little gems - Guisborough with its quaint streets and fascinating antique shops; Hartlepool with its remarkable reconstructed eighteenth century North East Seaport together with two of the world's oldest floating warships; South Shields, the centre of Catherine Cookson country; Jarrow where the Venerable Bede wrote the first history of England. Beamish, that quite remarkable North of England Open Air Museum with its recreation of colliers' cottages, its trams, buses and steam engines and Barnard Castle with the wonderful Bowes Museum.

Through the year this region abounds with exhibitions, gatherings, marches, festivals and shows, ranging from the colourful Durham Miners' Gala to the prestigious Teesside International Eisteddfod. Truly this region is alive with interest for the holiday maker the whole year round.

Places to Visit

Beamish Open Air Museum, *County Durham* ~
set in three hundred acres, it recreates northeast life
before World War I. It features a high street, a colliery
village, a disused mine, a school, a chapel and a farm
with guides dressed in period costume.

Bowes Museum, *Barnard Castle* ~ started in 1860 by
local aristocrat John Bowes and his French wife
Josephine. It was always intended as a museum and
it finally opened in 1892, by which time the couple
had died. The museum houses a collection of Spanish
art, clocks, furniture, porcelain, toys and tapestries. It
also features a mechanical silver swan.

Cragside House and Gardens, *near Morpeth* ~ the
former home of William Armstrong, it was the first
house in the world to be lit by hydro electric power
with hydraulics powering both the new lift systems
and telephones which amazed his guests. Today,
hydro electric and hydraulic machinery are housed in
the Ram and Power Houses. The Victorian Garden is
a short walk from the house.

Farne Islands ~ it is home to over seventeen
different species of seabird and large colony of seals.
St Cuthbert died on Inner Farne in 687, where a
chapel was built in his memory in the 14th century
and was later restored in 1845.

Gibside, *near Burnopfield* ~ set in the Derwent
Valley, it is supposed to be
haunted by its previous owners, the Bowes-Lyons.
The chapel contains a rare triple mahogany pulpit.

Kielder Water, *near Hexham* ~ surrounded by
spectacular scenery, it is Europe's largest man-made
lake. Sailing, windsurfing, canoeing, water-
skiing and fishing facilites are all
available at the lake.

Lindisfarne Castle, *Holy Island* ~
built in the 1520's as a defence against
the frequent border raids by the Scots. It
fell into ruins and was bought by Edward
Hudson, the founder of "Country Life'
magazine who commissioned Edwin
Lutyens to restore it as his summer
retreat and Gertrude Jekyll designed
the pretty walled garden.

St Nicholas Cathedral, *Newcastle* ~ one of Britain's
tiniest cathedrals. Inside, there are remnants of the
original Norman church on which the current 14th
and 15th century building is founded. It has a rare
'lantern tower' which is half tower and half spire, of
which there are only three in the country.

Wallington, *near Morpeth* ~ inherited by Sir Walter
Calverley Blackett in 1728, he laid out the gardens
and park and transformed the house. There is a
collection of dolls houses, a 19th century gentleman's
bathroom and a collection of coaches and carriages.

Hadrian's Wall

NORTHUMBRIA & COUNTY DURHAM

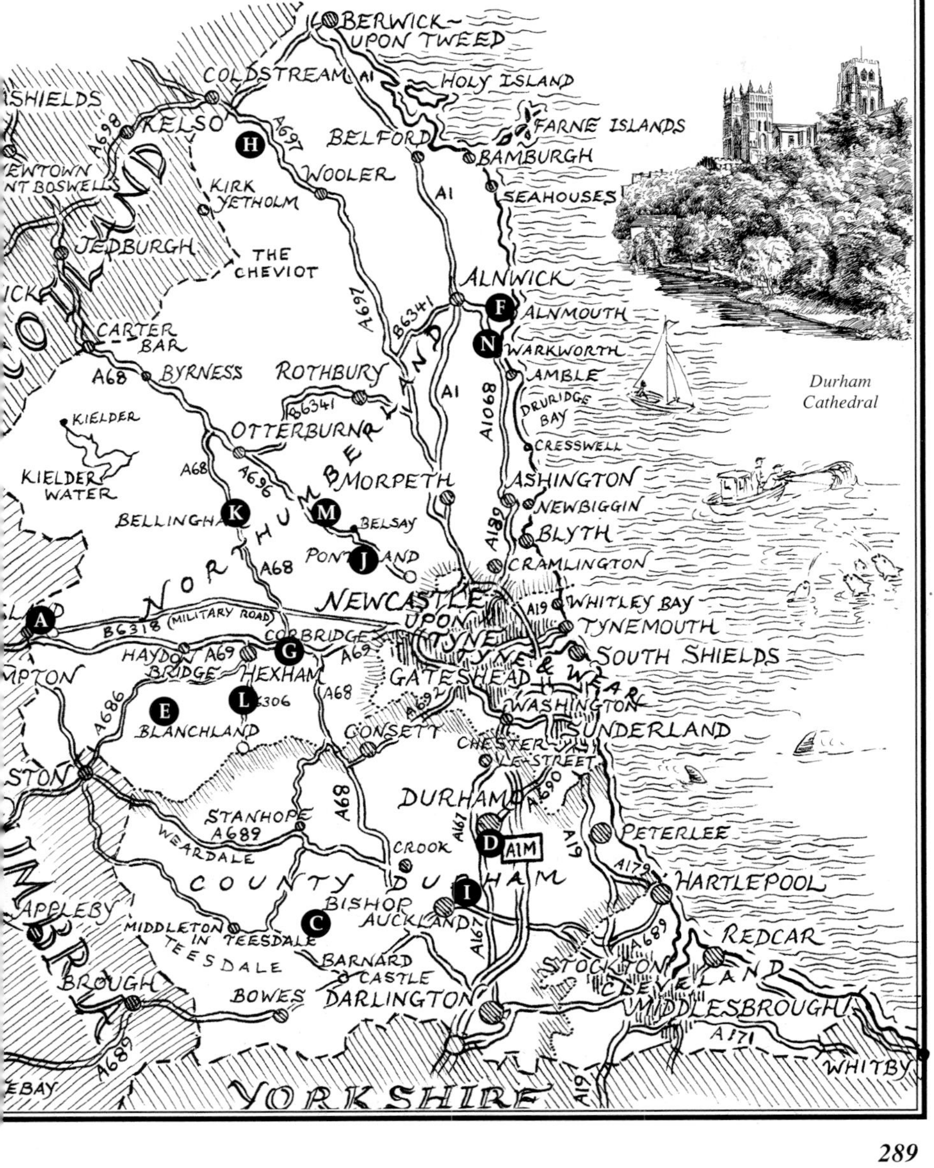

BERWICK-UPON TWEED
COLDSTREAM
A1
HOLY ISLAND
SHIELDS
A698
KELSO
A697
BELFORD
FARNE ISLANDS
H
BAMBURGH
EWTOWN
NT BOSWELLS
KIRK YETHOLM
WOOLER
SEAHOUSES
JEDBURGH
THE CHEVIOT
ALNWICK
F
ALNMOUTH
A697
B6341
CARTER BAR
N
WARKWORTH
A68
BYRNESS
ROTHBURY
A1
AMBLE
A1068
DRURIDGE BAY
KIELDER
B6341
OTTERBURN
CRESSWELL
KIELDER WATER
A68
A696
MORPETH
ASHINGTON
NEWBIGGIN
BELLINGHAM
K
M
BELSAY
A189
BLYTH
PONTELAND
J
CRAMLINGTON
A68
NORTHUMBERLAND
NEWCASTLE UPON TYNE
A19
WHITLEY BAY
A
B6318 (MILITARY ROAD)
TYNEMOUTH
CORBRIDGE
G
HAYDON BRIDGE
A69
HEXHAM
TYNE & WEAR
SOUTH SHIELDS
GATESHEAD
A68
L
B6306
WASHINGTON
A686
E
BLANCHLAND
CONSETT
A692
SUNDERLAND
CHESTER-LE-STREET
STANHOPE
A689
A68
DURHAM
A690
WEARDALE
A167
D
A1M
A19
PETERLEE
CROOK
A179
COUNTY DURHAM
HARTLEPOOL
APPLEBY
I
BISHOP AUCKLAND
C
MIDDLETON IN TEESDALE
REDCAR
A167
A689
TEESDALE
BARNARD CASTLE
STOCKTON
CLEVELAND
BROUGH
BOWES
DARLINGTON
MIDDLESBROUGH
A171
A689
WHITBY
A19
YORKSHIRE

Durham Cathedral

Holmhead Guest House, Thirlwall Castle Farm, Hadrians Wall, Greenhead, via Carlisle CA6 7HY

Enjoy fine food and hospitality with a personal touch, in a smoke free atmosphere. This lovely old farmhouse is built with Hadrians wall stones, near the most spectacular remains. Four cosy bedrooms with shower/wc en-suite. Quality home cooking using fresh produce, guests dine together at candlelit table dinner party style. Speciality list of organically grown/produced wines featuring world award winners. Small cocktail bar and TV books, maps and guides in lounge. Your host was a former Northumbria Tour Guide and is an expert on Hadrians Wall. Special breaks arranged.

see PHOTO opposite

Brian & Pauline Staff
Tel/Fax: 016977 47402

B&B from £24.50pp, Dinner from £16 95, Rooms 2 twin 1 double, 1 family, all en-suite, No smoking, Children welcome, No pets, Open all year except Christmas & New Year, Map Ref A

Cloud High, Eggleston, Barnard Castle, County Durham DL12 0AU   **Nearest Road B6278**

Idyllically situated at 1000' in peaceful, secluded countryside, Cloud High commands magnificent unrivalled views of Teesdale and surrounding dales. At Cloud High the emphasis is on comfort, luxury and relaxation with every amenity in the three lovely en-suite bedrooms (one with balcony) and private lounge. Breakfasts taken in the conservatory overlooking the garden and with a backdrop of the Pennies, are our speciality with a choice of traditional or interesting alternatives. The perfect base for exploring this historical, cultural and scenic area.

Frank & Eileen Bell
Tel/Fax: 01833 650644

B&B from £20-£23.50pp, Rooms 1 twin, 2 double, all en-suite No smoking or pets, Children over 12, Open March - November, Map Ref C

Ash House, 24 The Green, Cornforth, Durham DL17 9JH   **Nearest Road A1M, A167, A688**

Ideally situated on lovely quiet conservation village green in the heart of "The Land of the Prince Bishops". Adjacent A1(m) motorway, 10 minutes Durham city. Ash House is a beautifully appointed Victorian home, lovingly restored. The elegant rooms are spacious and include clock/radio and hair dryer. Traditional carved four poster available. Mature trees surround the property, all bedrooms have open views. Hearty breakfast provided. Private parking. Convenient for Hartlepool Napoleonic Quay and Marina, Metro Centre and Beamish Museum. Well placed between York and Edinburgh.Excellent value.

Delia Slack
Tel: 01740 654654

B&B from £18pp, Rooms 1 twin, 1 double, 1 family, Restricted smoking, Children from 8, Pets welcome, Open all year except Christmas & New Year, Map Ref D

Thornley House, Allendale, Northumberland NE47 9NH   **Nearest Road B6303**

Beautiful country house in spacious and peaceful grounds surrounded by field and woodland. 1 mile out of Allendale. Relaxed comfortable accommodation, 3 roomy light bedrooms, 2 en-suite, 1 with private bathroom next door. All have tea/coffee facilities. 2 lounges, 1 with TV, 1 with Steinway grand piano, ample books, games, Maps, good food and home baking. Bring your own wine. Marvellous walks (guided sometimes available) and bird watching. Hadrian's Wall, Stately homes, Kielder Forest nearby. Vegetarian meals and packed lunches on request. Brochure available.

see PHOTO on page 292

Mrs Finn
Tel: 01434 683255

B&B from £18.50pp, Dinner from £11.00, Rooms 1 twin, 2 double, all en-suite, No smoking, Children over 10 years, Pets by arrangement, Open all year, Map Ref E

291

left, ***Holmhead Guest House,*** *Greenhead - see details above*

Marine House Private Hotel, Alnmouth, Northumberland NE66 2RW   Nearest Road A1

see PHOTO on page 293

Relax in the friendly atmosphere of this 200 year old listed building of considerable charm, on the edge of the Village golf links with panoramic sea views. 10 individually appointed bedrooms, some with tester/crown drapes. All en-suite with colour TV and teas-made. 4-course gourmet candlelit dinners by our resident chef. Cocktail bar, spacious seafront lounge. Children over 7 years and pets welcome. Visit the Farne Islands or Kielder Forest. Discover the Roman Wall. Impressive border fortresses, romantic ruins and elegant stately homes.

Sheila & Gordon Inkster
Tel: 01665 830349

B&B from £25pp, Dinner from £14.00, Rooms 2 twin, 6 double, 2 family, all en-suite, Restricted smoking, Children over 7 years, Pets welcome, Open all year except Christmas & New Year, Map Ref F

Clive House, Appletree Lane, Corbridge, Northumberland NE45 5DN   Nearest Road A68, A69

Originally built in 1840 as part of Corbridge village school, Clive House has been tastefully converted to provide 3 lovely bedrooms, one of which has a four-poster. All are en-suite with tea/coffee making facilities, colour TV, hair dryer and telephone. The village centre with many speciality shops and eating places is a few minutes walk away. At the centre of Hadrian's Wall country, historic Corbridge is an ideal base for exploring Northumberland and a convenient break between York and Edinburgh. ETB 2 Crowns Highly Commended.

Ann Hodgson
Tel: 01434 632617

B&B from £24pp, Rooms 2 double, 1 single, all en-suite, No smoking or children, Open March - November, Map Ref G

The Coach House at Crookham, Cornhill on Tweed, Northumberland TD12 4TD   Nearest Road A697

see PHOTO opposite

Ideally situated for exploring Northumberland's National Trust coastline. The Coach House is one hour's drive on excellent roads from Edinburgh or Newcastle. Built about 1680 the brick and stone buildings around a courtyard have been converted into spacious bedrooms. They are accessible to wheelchair bound guest. The food is fresh and varied reflecting modern ideas on healthy eating with some Mediterranean influence. Where possible, local produce is used. Breakfast satisfies all tastes with fruits, homemade cereals and porridge plus a cooked breakfast using top quality ingredients.

Lynne Anderson
Tel: 01890 820293
Fax: 01890 820284

B&B from £23pp, Dinner £16.50, Rooms 1 single, 5 en-suite twin, 2 en suite double, Restricted smoking, Children & pets welcome, Open Easter - November, Map Ref H

Idsley House, 4 Green Lane, Spennymoor, Durham, Northumberland DL16 6HD   Nearest Road A167, A688

see PHOTO on page 296

Idsley House is a long established guest house run by Joan and David Dartnall. A large detached house in a quiet area just off the A167/A688, 8 minutes from Durham City. All rooms are spacious and furnished to a high standard. Double, twin and family rooms are en-suite and have TV and welcome trays. Breakfast is served in a pleasant conservatory overlooking a mature garden. A large quiet lounge for guests to relax in. Ample safe car parking in walled garden. ETB 2 Crowns Highly Commended. Evening meals by arrangement. Mastercard, Visa, Eurocard and Switch welcome.

Joan & David Dartnall
Tel: 01388 814237

B&B from £22pp, Rooms singles, doubles, twins, & family, most en-suite, Children welcome, Pets by arrangement, Open all year except Christmas, Map Ref I

right, **The Coach House at Crookham,** *Cornhill on Tweed - see details above*

Dalton House, Dalton, near Ponteland, Newcastle-upon-Tyne, Northumberland NE18 0AA   A696

Dalton is a small peaceful village near Hadrian's Wall yet an easy 30 minute drive from Newcastle, Morpeth and the airport. Ideal for exploring the beautiful county of Northumberland and very convenient for business people who prefer to stay out of town. A warm welcome and friendly atmosphere are assured. Bedrooms have tea/coffee making facilities, and guests have a large sitting room with TV and separate dining room. Evening meal by arrangement.

Mrs Trevelyan
Tel: 01661 886225

B&B from £20pp, Dinner by arrangement from £12, Rooms 2 single, 2 twin (with private bathroom), No smoking, Minimum age 12, Open April - October, Map Ref J

Westfield House, Bellingham, Hexham, Northumbria NE48 2DP   Nearest Road B6320

see PHOTO on page 297

Westfield is a truly hospitable home. Built as an elegant, but cosy Victorian gentleman's residence, with nearly an acre of gardens. The 5 bedrooms including 4 en-suite and a 4-poster, are comfortable with more than a touch of luxury. Tea trays in all rooms. Breakfast and dinner are superb, with traditional cooking at its best. Lounge always available. Ideal touring spot with wonderful countryside, Roman wall, castles and NT properties. Safe parking. Licensed. Stay awhile and be spoilt. EMail: westfield.house@virgin.net http://freespace.virgin.net/westfield.house/index.htm

David & June Minchin
Tel: 01434 220340
Fax: 01434 220694

B&B from £25-£28pp, Dinner from £15, Rooms 4 en-suite rooms, 1 family, 2 twin, 1 double, 1 double with private facilities, No smoking, Children welcome, Pets by arrangement, Open all year, Map Ref K

Rye Hill Farm, Slaley, Hexham, Northumbria NE47 0AH   Nearest Road A68, A69, B6306

see PHOTO opposite

Rye Hill Farm offers you the freedom to enjoy the pleasures of Northumberland throughout the year whilst living comfortably in the pleasant family atmosphere of a cosy farmhouse adapted especially to receive holidaymakers. Bedrooms are all en-suite, centrally heated and have large bath towels. A full English breakfast and an optional 3 course evening meal are served in the dining room which has an open log fire and a table licence. Telephone and tourist information in the reception lounge. Guests are invited to use the games room and look around the farm. Credit cards accepted. EMail: enquires@courage.u-net.com

Mrs E A Courage
Tel: 01434 673259
Fax: 01434 673608

B&B from £20pp, Dinner from £12, Rooms 3 double, 2 family, 1 twin, Pets welcome by arrangement, Open all year, Map Ref L

Shieldhall, Wallington, Morpeth, Northumbria NE61 4AQ   Nearest Road A696

Shieldhall has been charmingly and elegantly restored from the original 18th century house, nestling in the rolling landscape and overlooking the National Trust estate of Wallington. The main buildings form a well ordered courtyard onto which each of the guests suites have their own entrances. The bedroom suites are self contained with independent heating, television and tea/coffee making facilities. The oak dining room has an inglenook fireplace and antique furniture. The lounge and library both have French doors which open into the large garden with croquet lawn and herbaceous borders.

Stephen & Celia Gay
Tel: 01830 540387
Fax: 01830 540387

B&B from £19pp, Dinner from £13.50, Rooms 2 twin, 2 double 1 family, all en-suite, No smoking, Minimum age 10, Open March - November, Map Ref M

*right, **Rye Hill Farm**, near Hexham, - see details above*

North Cottage, Birling, Warkworth, Northumbria NE65 0XS   Nearest Road A1068

Dating back to the 17th century, North Cottage has a cosy home from home atmosphere. Substantial full breakfasts are served in the dining room. Afternoon tea served free on arrival or when required. The bedrooms, which are all on the ground floor, are comfortable and well furnished with tea/coffee making facilities, electric blanket, clock radio, colour TV and the beds have either duvet or blankets. The double and twin rooms are en-suite and the single has wash hand basin.

John & Edith Howliston
Tel: 01665 711263

B&B from £20pp (weekly rate from £137), Rooms 2 double, 1 twin, 1 single, most en-suite, No smoking, Open all year except Christmas, Map Ref N

"My dears! Three tickets for my recital tonight, I insist!"
BELLE & BERTIE IN YORK

I fear thee, ancient Mariner!
I fear thy skinny hand!
And thou art long, and lank, and brown,
As is the ribbed sea-sand.

THE RIME OF THE ANCIENT MARINER (1798) PT.4
SAMUEL TAYLOR COLERIDGE 1772-1834

OXFORDSHIRE

The holiday visitor could be excused for believing that the handsome city of Oxford is the sum total of the county's offerings, but they would be quite wrong. There is considerably more than the undoubted glories of this ancient city.

The region is made up of four areas quite different from each other, even to the extent of each area having architecture of its own. The great Oxfordshire plain extends over most of this county. It is the basin of the Thames which is fed by four tributaries, the Windrush, Thame, Cherwell and Evenlode, each bordered by charming and picturesque villages. Down the eastern side of the county is moorland ringed with villages of thatched cottages and bordered by the Oxfordshire Chilterns, an area of beechwoods and chalk. Here the ancient pre-Roman grass track, the Ridgeway, runs to the Vale of the White Horse, named after the prehistoric horse cut into the escarpment of the Berkshire Downs on the Vale's southern border. There are superb views of this monument from Uffington, the village at the heart of the Vale. Uffington Castle, the Iron Age camp, stands on White Horse Hill straddling the old Ridgeway. The fine town of Wantage was the birthplace of Alfred the Great, whose statue stands in the market place. It is claimed that at nearby Faringdon Alfred had a great palace - certainly the town was mentioned in the Domesday Book.

William Morris lived for twenty years at the impressive Elizabethan manor house at Kelmscot. In fact the whole of this lovely area has strong literary associations; Rossetti, Arnold and Pope all lived and worked here. Thomas Hughes, the author of 'Tom Brown's School Days' opens his book with chapters set in Uffington where he was born. Of course these delightful places pale against the Baroque splendours of Blenheim. This sumptuous palace at Woodstock is reckoned to be the finest truly Baroque house in Britain. Built to the design of John Vanbrugh for the 1st. Duke of Marlborough in recognition of his victory at Blenheim, it was also the birthplace of Winston Churchill. The gardens laid out by Henry Wise include the Triumphal Way, the Column of Victory and the superb Italian Gardens.

The Oxfordshire Cotswolds offer the visitor undulating wolds, excellent walking country and the rich honey coloured stone buildings so typical of this region. Chipping Norton, with its superb nineteenth century Tweed Mill, is an ideal centre for touring. Nearby Burford has an impressive church, the second largest in the county, and a distinguished main street lined with shops and inns leading down to an old stone bridge. Witney with its strange gabled seventeenth century Butter Cross is close to Minster Lovell, one of the loveliest villages on the Windrush, with its fascinating fifteenth century manor house steeped in legend. Banbury to the north is an interesting town with a long history dating back to Saxon times. Best known for its cakes and its cross, the latter is in fact a Victorian replacement of the original cross of nursery rhyme fame. Bicester, set in lovely countryside, is a well-known hunting centre with some fine buildings. But at the end of the day, no matter what the attractions of the countryside, all roads do lead to Oxford, the medieval town first mentioned in the tenth century and site of Britain's oldest university. The city grew up at the junction of two rivers, the Thames, known locally as the Isis, and the Cherwell.

The university began in the twelfth century and probably the most famous of its colleges is Christ Church, known as 'the House', which was founded by Cardinal Wolsey. Each college has its own intriguing history, treasures and charm. Alongside the colleges have developed some remarkable public buildings - the Sheldonian Theatre, based on the Theatre of Marcellus in Rome; the Radcliffe Camera and the Bodleian Library, the oldest section of which is Duke Humfrey's library completed in 1488. The seventeenth century Ashmolean Museum now houses the Museum of History and Science. The university church of St. Mary is the church in which Cranmer, Ridley and Latimer were tried for heresy, and later burnt at the stake.

But the university apart, Oxford offers other delights for the visitor. There is boating on the Thames and Cherwell, there is excellent fishing, there are festivals and happenings the year through, there are large swathes of greenery along the rivers with delightful walks....and of course all the other amenities of a modern city.

Places to Visit

Ashmolean Museum, *Oxford* ~ the first purpose - built museum in England, it opened in 1683 and is based on a collection curiosities collected by two John Tradescants, father and son. On their many visits to the Orient and and the Americas they collected stuffed animals and tribal artifacts. There are also paintings on display by Bellini, Raphael, Turner, Rembrandt and Picasso.

Blenheim Palace, *Woodstock* ~ Queen Anne gave the 1st Duke of Marlborough the Manor of Woodstock in 1704 after he defeated the French at the Battle of Blenheim and had this palace built for him. Winston Churchill was born here in 1874. The palace is set in two thousand acres of parkland with lakes and woodlands landscaped by Capability Brown.

Botanic Gardens, *Oxford* ~ founded in 1621, they are Britains oldest botanic gardens with one ancient yew tree surviving from that period. The Earl of Danby paid for the garden to be created and now his statue adorns the gate along with those of Charles I and Charles II. The gardens are well labelled and have a walled garden, herbaceous border and rock garden.

Kelmscott Manor ~ the designer and writer William Morris lived here from 1871 until his death in 1896. The house, a classic Elizabethan building is now home to works of art by members of the Arts and Crafts movement which included William Morris.

The Rollright Stones, *near Great Tew* ~ three Bronze Age monuments, they comprise a stone circle of stones, thirty metres in diameter, known as the Kings Men. There is also a burial chamber called the Whispering Knights and and the solitary King Stone.

The Sheldonian Theatre, *Oxford* ~ completed in 1669, this was the first building Christopher Wren designed. Its classical design is based on the Theatre of Marcellus in Rome, Italy. The spectacular painted ceilings in the theatre illustrate the triumphs of religion, art and science over envy, hatred and malice.

Vale of the White Horse, *Uffington* ~ a lonely valley dominated by a huge chalk horse, which it gets its name from. The horse measures one hundred metres from nose to tail. Some say it was created by Saxon leader Hengist, whose name means stallion in German, and others think it was to do with Alfred the Great, who is thought to have been born nearby.

A corner of Henley on Thames

OXFORDSHIRE

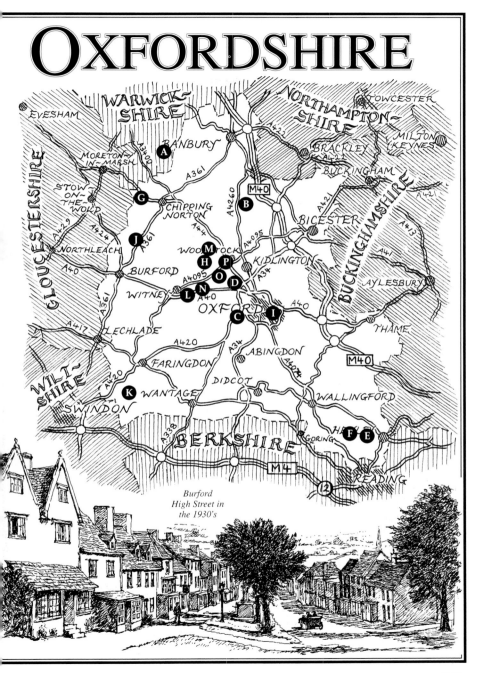

Burford High Street in the 1930's

Mine Hill House, Lower Brailes, near Banbury, Oxfordshire OX5 5BJ   Nearest Road B4035

Mine Hill House, 1733, is situated on top of a hill with stunning views over miles of unspoilt countryside. A Cotswold farmhouse full of wonderful paintings, flagstone floors and open log fire. Hester is a highly trained cook and is delightful to cook dinner on request. It is a superb location to explore the Cotswolds, Stratford, Oxford, Blenheim Palace and the famous gardens of Hidcote and Kiftsgate, all within a 20 mile radius. There is also a golf course at the bottom of Mine Hill.

Hester & Edward Sale
Tel: 01608 685594

B&B from £20pp, Dinner from £20, Rooms 1 twin, 1 double, both en-suite, Restricted smoking & pets, Children welcome, Open all year, Map Ref A

Home Farm House, Middle Aston, Bicester, Oxon OX6 3PX   Nearest Road A4260

Home Farm House is a 17th century former farmhouse which offers a tranquil stay in beautiful countryside. Relax in the lovely garden and enjoy the stunning view. Eat breakfast in the oak beamed dining room with its ancient inglenook fireplace. The large bedrooms are a double en-suite or a twin with private bathroom. Rousham House, Woodstock and Blenheim Palace are nearby. We are 12 miles North of Oxford and within easy reach of the Cotswolds.

Glen & Caroline Parsons
Tel: 01869 340666
Fax: 01869 340666

B&B from £23pp, Rooms 1 twin with private bathroom, 1 en-suite double, No smoking or pets, Children over 12, Open all year except Christmas & New Year, Map Ref B

Tilbury Lodge, 5 Tilbury Lane, Eynsham Road, Botley, Oxfordshire OX2 9NB   M40, A34, B4044

Tilbury Lodge Private Hotel, is situated in a quiet country lane just 2 miles west of the city centre, 1 mile from the railway and 2 miles from Farmoor Reservoir with trout fishing and sailing. All rooms are en-suite with telephone, hair dryer, TV radio and tea/coffee making facilities. The hotel benefits from central heating, double glazing and ground floor bedrooms. There is a guest lounge,jacuzzi, 4 poster and ample parking. An Ideal base for touring the Cotswolds or visiting Blenheim and Stratford upon Avon. AA 'Selected', RAC High Acclaimed.

Eileen & Eddie Trafford
Tel: 01865 862138
Fax: 01865 863700

B&B from £30, Rooms 2 family, 5 twin/double, 2 single, Non smoking, Open all year, Map Ref C

Burleigh Farm, Bladon Road, Cassington, Oxfordshire OX8 1EA   Nearest Road A40, A4095

A listed stone farmhouse in a quiet position. This is a working pedigree Holstein/Friesan dairy farm on the Blenheim Estate. The comfortable bedrooms, have private/en-suite facilities, all have TV, and tea/coffee making facilities. There is a pleasant lounge and garden for guests' use. Situated conveniently for Blenheim Palace, Oxford and the Cotswolds. ETB 2 Crowns Commended, Elizabeth Grundy Recommended.

Mrs Jane Cook
Tel: 01865 881352

B&B from £21pp, Rooms 1 twin, 1 family, both en-suite, No smoking, Pets welcome, Open all year, Map Ref D

Slater's Farm, Peppard Common, Henley on Thames, Oxon RG9 5JL   Nearest Road B481

A warm and friendly home. Slater's Farm is a quietly situated, attractive Georgian country house with an acre of lovely garden including a hard tennis court, which guests are welcome to use. All the bedrooms are attractively furnished for the comfort of our guests. Traditional pubs within a few hundred yards, serve good evening meals. Lovely walks through unspoilt countryside. The Chilterns, Windsor, Oxford, Cotswolds all within easy driving distance. Driving to Heathrow takes under 1 hour. French and German spoken.

Mrs Penny Howden
Tel: 01491 628675
Fax: 01491 628675

B&B from £23pp, Dinner from £16 (on request), Rooms 2 twin, 1 double, 2 private, Restricted smoking, Children welcome, No pets, Open all year except Christmas & New Year, Map Ref E

Shepherds, Shepherds Green, Rotherfield Greys, Henley on Thames, Oxon RG9 4QL   M4, M40

Comfortable, peaceful and welcoming, Shepherds is a delightful part 18th century house which stands in its own gardens on the quiet village green. All bedrooms have either en-suite or private facilities, clock radios, TV and tea/coffee making facilities. Guests have their own splendid drawing room furnished with antiques and have a cosy open fire. Conveniently situated for touring Windsor, Oxford and the Chilterns. Good access to Heathrow.

Mrs Susan Fuford-Dobson
Tel/Fax: 01491 628413

B&B from £21pp, Rooms 2 double, 2 twin, Minimum age 12, Restricted smoking, Open all year except Christmas and New Year, Map Ref F

Kings Head Inn, The Green, Bledington, near Kingham, Oxfordshire OX7 6XQ   Nearest Road B4450

Quintessential Cotswold Inn which enjoys peaceful location beside village green with brook and resident ducks. Retains all olde worlde charm of bygone years, original old beams, inglenook fireplace, pews and settles. Delightful en-suite rooms compliment with full facilities and thoughtful extras. Award winning restaurant offering 'personal' inventive cuisine, includes bar fayre, lunch table d'hote and A la carte evenings. Excellent value and well situated for exploring prime attractions, Blenheim, Stratford on Avon, etc. EMail: kingshead@btinternet.com

Annette & Michael Royce
Tel: 01608 658365
Fax: 01608 658902

B&B from £60 per room per night, Dinner from £10.95, Rooms 2 twin, 10 double, 2 family, all en-suite, Restricted smoking, Children welcome, No pets, Open all year except Christmas Eve & Day, Map Ref G

Wynford House, 79 Main Road, Long Hanborough, Oxon OX8 8JX   Nearest Road A4095, A44

Wynford Guest House is situated in the village of Long Hanborough only 1 mile from Bladon, final resting place of sir Winston Churchill and 3 miles from famous Woodstock and Blenheim palace. There is a warm welcome, excellent food and comfortable accommodation. All bedrooms, one of which is en-suite, have colour TV and tea/coffee making facilities. Conveniently situated for the Cotswolds. The City of Oxford is 12 miles away. Evening meal is available by arrangement and there are several local pubs and restaurants within walking distance.

Mrs C Ellis
Tel: 01993 881402
Fax: 01993 883661

B&B from £19pp, Dinner £10 by arrangement, Rooms 1 family, 1 twin, 1 double, 1 en-suite, No smoking, Pets by arrangement, Open all year, Map Ref H

Green Gables, 326 Abingdon Road, Oxford OX1 4TE

Green Gables is a characterful, detached Edwardian house, secluded from the road by trees and 1 mile from city centre on frequent bus route. Bright, spacious rooms, many en-suite. Ample parking.
EMail: ellis.greengab@pop3.hiway.co.uk

Connie & Charles Ellis
Tel: 01865 725870
Fax: 01865 723115

B&B from £19pp, Rooms 1 single, 2 twin, 4 double, 2 family, No pets, Open all year except Christmas and New Year, Map Ref I

Shipton Grange House, Shipton-under-Wychwood, Oxfordshire OX7 6DG   Nearest Road A361

A unique conversion of a Georgian Coach House and stabling situated in the former grounds of Shipton Court. Secluded in its own walled garden and approached by a gated archway. There are three elegantly furnished guest bedrooms each with an en-suite/private bathroom, colour TV and tea/coffee making facilities. Shipton Grange House is a delightful house and ideal for visiting Blenheim Palace, Oxford, Stratford, Warwick and many beautiful and well known gardens. Excellent restaurants within walking distance.

see PHOTO opposite

Veronica Hill
Tel: 01993 831298
Fax: 01993 832082

B&B from £25pp, Rooms 1 twin, 2 double, all en-suite/private facilities, No smoking, Children from 12, No pets, Open all year except Christmas, Map Ref J

The Craven, Fernham Road, Uffington, Oxon SN7 7RD   Nearest Road A420, M4 jct 14, B4507/8

Roses and clematis cover this pretty 17th century thatched cottage, where breakfast is served around a huge pine table in the farmhouse kitchen, with an old dresser nearby ladened with blue and white china. The beamed bedrooms have lovely views and are all individual. One has a 17th Century 4 poster bed with cabbage rose chinz drapes and, as with all bedrooms, hand-embroidered sheets and pillowslips. In winter there is always a log fire for guests to sit around and sip their tea or wine!

see PHOTO on page 310

Carol Wadsworth
Tel: 01367 820449

B&B from £20-£30pp, Dinner from £15.50, Rooms 1 single, 1 twin, 3 double (2 en-suite), Restricted smoking, Children welcome, Pets restricted, Open all year, Map Ref K

Field View, Wood Green, Witney, Oxfordshire OX8 6DE   Nearest Road A40, A4095

Attractive Cotswold stone house set in 2 acres, situated on picturesque Wood Green, Witney midway between between Oxford University and the Cotswolds. It is an ideal centre centre for touring, yet only 8 minutes walk from the centre of this lively Oxfordshire market town. A peaceful setting and a warm, friendly atmosphere awaits you. Three comfortable, en-suite rooms with colour TV and tea/coffee making facilities. ETB 2 Crowns Highly Commended. EMail: jsimpson@netcomuk.co.uk

Liz & John Simpson
Tel: 01993 705485
Mobile: 0468 614347

B&B from £21pp, Rooms 2 twin, 1 double, all en-suite, No smoking, No children, No pets, Open all year except Christmas and New Year, Map Ref L

*left, **Shipton Grange House**, Shipton under Wychwood - see details above*

Mayfield Cottage, West End, Combe, Witney, Oxon OX8 8NP **Nearest Road A4095**

Welcome to our home, a delightful Cotswold stone cottage with oak beams and Inglenooks, situated in a quiet country lane. Combe, a small unspoilt village is an ideal base for touring the Cotswolds, with Blenheim Palace, Oxford and Stratford within easy driving distance. There are scenic walks and many good pubs and restaurants in the area. What better place to unwind? A twin or double room is available with private bathroom. Bed and Breakfast from £20; 3 night breaks from £55. ETB Listed Highly Commended.

Stan & Rosemary Fox
Tel: 01993 898298

B&B from £20pp, Rooms 1 twin/double, both with private bathroom, No smoking, children or pets, Open March - October, Map Ref M

Wrestler's Mead, 35 Wroslyn Road, Freeland, Witney, Oxford OX8 8HJ **Nearest Road A4095**

Wrestler's Mead is a chalet bungalow with a spacious garden for guests to use if required. The name of the bungalow refers to the wrestling bouts held on ground in the 1700's and not to the antics of your hosts Babs and David, who assure you of a warm welcome. Accommodation consists of a double en-suite and single room at ground floor level and a family room on the first floor. Tea/coffee making facilities, and colour TV are provided in the double and family rooms. The family room also has en-Suite shower, washbasin and toilet. VISA and Mastercard accepted.

Babs & David Taphouse
Tel/Fax: 01993 882003

B&B from £19pp, Rooms 1 single, 1 double, 1 family, Pets by arrangement, Open all year, Map Ref N

Forge Cottage, East End, near North Leigh, Witney, Oxon OX8 6PZ **Nearest Road A4095**

Knock yourself out in our old Cotswold cottage, recover with a delicious English breakfast including homegrown and homemade preserves. Our home is traditionally furnished with firm comfortable beds and there are hot drink facilities and TV in the rooms. Off road parking. Good walking. Home of conservation crazy and cat loving biologist. Take A5095 to Witney from A44 for 4 miles. Then twice right to East End following Roman Villa signs. Forge Cottage is 8 utility poles on the left beyond the telephone box. Non smoking home.

Jill French
Tel: 01993 881120

B&B from £18pp, Rooms 1 single, 2 double or twin, 1 en-suite, No smoking, No children, Pets Welcome, Open February-November, Map Ref H

Manor Farmhouse, Manor Road, Bladon, Woodstock, Oxon OX20 1RU **Nearest Road A4095**

Listed Cotswold stone house (1720) in quiet conservation area of Bladon village, within walking distance of two pubs and one mile from Blenheim Palace and historic Woodstock. Ideal for exploring Oxford and the Cotswold. The large double room featured in a Laura Ashley catalogue. The small twin room is approached by a spiral staircase so is not for the unsprightly. Both rooms have colour TV's and tea/coffee making facilities. They share a shower room, so are ideal for families or 4 people travelling together.

Helen Stevenson
Tel: 01993 812168
Fax: 01993 812168

B&B from £20pp, Rooms 1 twin, 1 double, No smoking, Children welcome, Pets by arrangement, Open all year except Christmas & New Year, Map Ref O

left, **The Craven,** *Uffington - see details on page 309*

Gorselands Farmhouse Auberge, Boddington Lane, Long Hanborough, near Woodstock OX8 6PU A4095

Old Cotswold stone farmhouse with oak beams, flagstone floors and log fires in winter, situated in one acre of grounds and surrounded by idyllic countryside. Full sized billiards table and lawn tennis court for guests' use. En-suite facilities. French style evening meals by arrangement. Table licence. Ideal location for visiting Blenheim Palace, Woodstock, Oxford, Cotswold villages, North Leigh Roman Villa, etc. Lovely walks by the River Windrush. Tourist Board 2 Crowns Commended, RAC listed. Credit cards accepted.

see PHOTO opposite

Mrs B Newcombe-Jones
Tel: 01993 881895
Fax: 01993 882799

B&B from £23pp, Dinner from £12.95, Rooms 1 twin, 3 double, 1 family, all en-suite, No smoking, Pets by arrangement, Open all year, Map Ref H

Old Farmhouse, Station Hill, Long Hanborough, near Woodstock, Oxfordshire OX8 8JZ A4095, A44

We welcome you to our former farmhouse dating from 1670 with many original features and charming bedrooms. Delicious breakfasts with freshly baked bread, marmalade/jams and fresh orange juice which can be enjoyed in our delightful cottage garden on summer mornings. Lovely country walks and good pubs within walking distance. Woodstock & Blenheim Palace 3 miles and Oxford a ten minute train ride. ETB 2 Crowns Highly Commended.

Robert & Vanessa Maundrell
Tel: 01993 882097

B&B from £19.50pp, Rooms 2 double, 1 en-suite, No smoking, Minimum age 12, Open all year except Christmas, Map Ref P

"I keep thinking of 'er sittin in me barrow!"
BELLE & BERTIE IN YORK

SHROPSHIRE

Shropshire is a gem amongst holiday counties. A mere fifty miles long by forty wide, this county of so many faces is more or less cut in two by the River Severn, the longest river in England and Wales. At the centre of the county is a spectacular isolated mass of volcanic rock, the oldest in England, the Wrekin, from which are impressive views across the rich arable plains cut by the Severn. In the west of the county the hills rise gradually to the mountains of Wales, while to the south is the heather-covered plateau of the Long Mynd and the narrow spine of Wenlock Edge. In the north are the lovely Shropshire meres, seven glorious lakes, a magnet to anglers and boat enthusiasts, rich in bird life and a paradise for walkers.

Ellesmere is the obvious centre for exploring this district, a town of handsome Georgian houses and interesting half-timbered buildings. To the west is Oswestry, where remains of Offa's Dyke and Wat's Dyke, built along the border of Anglo-Saxon Mercia to keep out the wild Welsh, tell of the constant friction between English and Welsh in this region. For centuries the two factions battled for Oswestry, until in 1535 by an Act of Union, Henry VIII made the town a part of England. Market Drayton, in the east, well endowed with fine architecture, was the birthplace in 1725 of Robert Clive of India fame. If the wonderful black and white houses of this region excite your interest, then Hodnet is the place to visit. The grand fourteenth century church of St. Luke has a

chained Nuremberg Bible dated 1479.

Telford, sited on the slopes of Wrekin and named after Thomas Telford, the eighteenth to nineteenth century engineer who was County surveyor of Shropshire, is one of the 'new towns', a concept pioneered by the Labour Government after the Second World War. This town combines many sites responsible for the Industrial Revolution. Here, where the Severn rushes through the Iron Bridge Gorge, is the two hundred foot bridge built in 1779 by Abraham Darby - the first use of iron in industrial architecture. Here in 1709, Darby's grandfather discovered how to smelt iron using coke instead of charcoal. Here too in 1804 Richard Trevithick made the first steam engine to run on rails. Bridgnorth is a delight, perched above the River Severn, its high and low towns connected by a cliff railway, as well as by quaint winding lanes and steep paths. The mixture of Half-timbered architecture and red brick is most attractive - as too is Castle Walk, the cliff top esplanade. It is claimed that Ethelward, the grandson of Alfred the Great, lived in a cave here at Bridgnorth, a recluse surrounded by his books. His four rock caves are still to be seen on Hermitage Hill. Not to be missed is the Severn Valley Railway which runs between Bridgnorth and Kidderminster through beautiful countryside.

Ludlow's 'Broad Street' is undoubtedly its most celebrated thoroughfare, lined with Tudor timber-framed buildings and seventeenth and eighteenth century red brick houses. The Feathers must be one of the country's finest examples of seventeenth century half-timbering. Ludlow claimed, and with good cause, to be England's finest country town, owing much to its glorious hilltop setting and spacious town planning. The poet A.E. Housman, who in 1896 wrote 'The Shropshire Lad' is buried in the churchyard of the cathedral-like church of St. Lawrence. Ludlow Castle is a spectacular sight, it was built in the eleventh century to repel Welsh raiders. John Milton saw the first production of his masque 'Comus' performed in the castle in 1634, a tradition continued today when during the Ludlow Festival in June and July, outdoor performances of Shakespeare plays are held in the inner bailey. No visitor to Ludlow should miss seeing Stokesay Castle, a wonderfully preserved thirteenth century fortified manor house. Another place of interest, Clun, in the valley of the River Clun, overlooked by its Norman keep, is one of the most ancient settlements in the country.

Shrewsbury, the administrative centre of Shropshire, has been a place of strategic importance between England and Wales from the fifth century. It holds a natural defensive position within the tight loop of the River Severn, its proud Norman castle having been adapted for modern living by Thomas Telford, it now provides the council chamber. The town owes much of its fine architecture to its prosperous wool trading period. Charles Darwin was born and educated here. Leading out of the town across the river in opposite directions are two wonderful eighteenth century bridges, the Welsh Bridge and the English Bridge. Edith Pargeter, creator of Brother Cadfael under the pen name Ellis Peters, centred her medieval whodunits on the city, in fact there are metal footprints let into Shrewsbury's pavements as clues to the crime sites!

SHROPSHIRE

Places to Visit

Acton Scott Working Farm and Museum, *near Little Stretton* ~ experience farming on Shropshire hills before the days of tractors and combine harvesters. Ploughing and pulling carts is done by Shire horses, and there is also a varied range of demonstrations from this era.

Attingham Park, *Atcham* ~ a Palladian mansion, built in 1782 by Lord Berwick to designs by John Nash. The grounds were landscaped by Humphrey Repton and have deer and views towards the Wrekin.

Dudmaston, *near Bridgnorth* ~ a late 17th century house with collections of modern art and sculpture. The house is surrounded by an extensive lakeside garden with rockery and woodland walks.

Ironbridge, *near Telford* ~ a lace-like iron bridge spanning the River Severn, it was the first iron bridge in the world. It was built in 1777 by the son of Abraham Darby, who first used coke to fire an iron furnace, which led to the start of the Industrial Revolution.

Coalport China Museum, *Ironbridge Gorge* ~ one of the largest porcelain producers in the 19th century. The company still makes porcelain but now at Stoke on Trent. The china shops have been converted into a museum, where visitors can watch demonstrations of the stages of making porcelain.

Jackfield Tile Museum, *Ironbridge Gorge* ~ there were two tile making factories here, they produced a large variety of tiles from the clay mined nearby. The museum has a collection of decorative wall and floor tiles produced from the 1850's to the 1960's.

Ludlow Castle, *Ludlow* ~ the castle, now in ruins, is sited on cliffs high above the River Teme. Built in 1086, it was damaged in the Civil War and abandoned in 1689.

Stokesay Castle, *near Craven Arms* ~ a 13th century fortified manor house with a half timbered construction topping its North Tower, this was built around 1240. It also has a polygon South Tower and an Elizabethan gatehouse.

Stokesay Castle

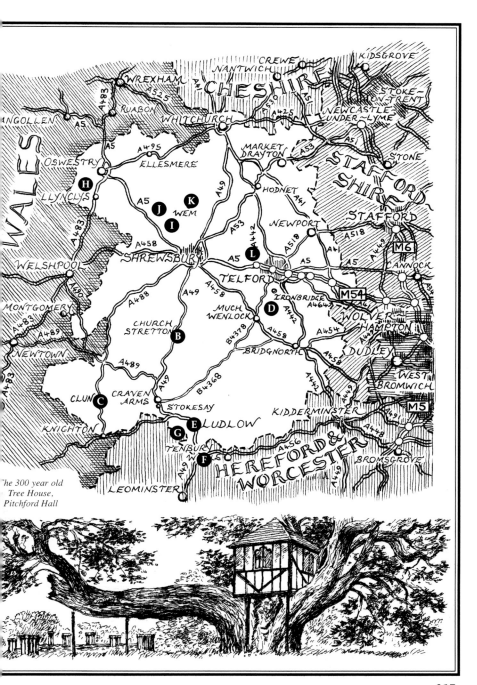

KIDSGROVE

CREWE
NANTWICH

CHESHIRE

STOKE-ON-TRENT

WREXHAM
A525
RUABON
A483
WHITCHURCH

NEWCASTLE-UNDER-LYME

LLANGOLLEN
A5

A5
OSWESTRY

A495
ELLESMERE

MARKET DRAYTON

A53

STAFFORDSHIRE

STONE

STAFFORD

H LLYNCLYS
A483

A5
J **K**
WEM
I

HODNET

A41

NEWPORT

A518

A5
WELSHPOOL

A458
SHREWSBURY

A49
A53
A442
L

A518

M6

MONTGOMERY
A483
A489

A5

TELFORD
IRONBRIDGE
D

A5
A5

CANNOCK
M54

A454

NEWTOWN
A489

A488
A49
A458
MUCH WENLOCK
A442
A464

WOLVERHAMPTON

CHURCH STRETTON
B

B4378
A458
A454
DUDLEY

A483
A489

A49
B4368
BRIDGNORTH
A458

A442
WEST BROMWICH

CLUN **C**
CRAVEN ARMS

A449
M5

KNIGHTON

STOKESAY
E LUDLOW
KIDDERMINSTER

A456
G
TENBURY WELLS
F
A448
BROMSGROVE

A49
HEREFORD & WORCESTER

LEOMINSTER

*The 300 year old
Tree House,
Pitchford Hall*

Belvedere Guest House, Burway Road, Church Stretton, Shropshire SY6 6DP **Nearest Road A49**

Belvedere is a 12 bedroomed Edwardian house standing in its own gardens. All rooms are centrally heated and contain teas-made, clock/radios and hair dryers. We have a drinks licence for your benefit, and evening meals and packed lunches are available on request. There are two guest lounges - one with TV and one with books and games. There is adequate off road parking and Belvedere is ideally situated for both town and hills. Shrewsbury, Ironbridge and Ludlow are a short drive away.

Don & Rita Rogers
Tel/Fax: 01694 722232

B&B from £23pp, Dinner from £10, Rooms 3 single, 4 twin, 3 double, 2 family, most en-suite, Restricted smoking, Children welcome, Open all year except Christmas, Map Ref B

New House Farm, Clun, Shropshire SY7 8NJ **Nearest Road A488, A489**

see PHOTO opposite

Isolated and peaceful 18th century farmhouse set high in Clun Hills near Welsh border - a hill farm which includes an Iron Age Hill Fort. Walks from the doorstep include 'Offa's Dyke', 'Shropshire Way' and 'Kerry Ridgeway'. Accommodation is spacious with scenic views. Tea/coffee facilities, TV and furnished to a high standard. Books and more books to browse in a large country garden. "New House provides a family welcome and a standard of comfort which a grand hotel would find hard to match." - B'ham Evening Post. ETB 2 Crowns Highly Commended. AA QQQQ Selected.

Miriam Ellison
Tel: 01588 638314

B&B from £22.50pp, Rooms 1 family, 1 twin, all with private/en-suite facilities, No smoking, Open Easter - November, Map Ref C

The Severn Trow, Church Road, Jackfield, Ironbridge, Shropshire TF8 7ND **Nearest Road M54, A442**

For centuries, travellers to the area have enjoyed the hospitality and comfort of The Severn Trow, a former ale house, lodgings and brothel, catering for boatmen of the river. Today, more discerning visitors are able to enjoy luxurious four poster beds. Rooms have TV, all have tea/coffee making facilities. Superb English breakfast served, vegetarian or special diets prepared on request. There is accommodation for guests of limited mobility. Lounge with TV. Ample car parking space.

Jim & Pauline Hannigan
Tel: 01952 883551

B&B from £20pp, Rooms 1 twin, 2 double, all en-suite, No smoking, Open January to October, Map Ref D

Number Twenty Eight, Lower Broad Street, Ludlow, Shropshire SY8 1PQ **Nearest Road A49**

A warm welcome awaits you at this Premier Selected guest house which now comprises three period houses in this historic street. Snug sitting rooms, book lined walls and open fires make for a very relaxed atmosphere. Every bedroom is en-suite and furnished individually with much loving care. Ludlow now has a wealth of excellent eating houses, all within walking distance. Riverside and hill walks, castle and lots of antique and book shops to explore in this most lovely Tudor and Georgian market town where Wales meets England and Shropshire meets Herefordshire.

Patricia & Philip Ross
Tel: 01584 876996
Fax: 01584 876860

B&B from £28pp, Rooms 2 twin, 4 double, all en-suite, No smoking, Dogs allowed in the house, Open all year, Map Ref E

*right, **New House Farm**, Clun - see details above*

The Marcle, Brimfield, Ludlow, Shropshire SY8 4NE   Nearest Road A456, A49

Parts of this delightful house date back to the 16th century, in more recent times it has been extensively renovated and tastefully modernised. Separate tables are provided in the traditionally furnished dining room, which has exposed oak beams and wall timbers. Similar features can also be found in the spacious and comfortable lounge with an attractive original inglenook fireplace. The house is set in a large garden is situated in the centre of the village and both the A49 and A456 are a short distance away. Colour TV and tea/coffee in all bedrooms. AA 4Q Selected. ETB 2 Crowns Highly Commended.

Mrs Patricia Jones
Tel/Fax: 01584 711459
Mobile: 07970 591158

B&B from £25pp, Dinner from £19, Rooms 1 twin, 2 double, all en-suite, No smoking, Children from 5, No pets, Open February - November, Map Ref F

The Brakes, Downton, near Ludlow, Shropshire SY8 2LF   Nearest Road A4113, A49

In the heart of beautiful rolling countryside only 5 miles from the historic town of Ludlow, The Brakes offers delightful accommodation with excellent cuisine. A period farmhouse tastefully furnished with central heating throughout, standing in 3 acres of grounds with a beautiful garden. Bedrooms are en-suite with TV and there is a charming lounge with log fire. Excellent walking country including Offa's Dyke and the Long Mynd; also golf, riding, and fishing are available. Steeped in history with many places of interest nearby. ETB 2 Crowns Highly Commended.

Tim & Tricia Turner
Tel: 01584 856485
Fax: 01584 856485

B&B from £25pp, Dinner from £19, Rooms 2 twin, 1 double all en suite, Restricted smoking, Minimum age 13, Pets by arrangement, Licenced, Open all year, Map Ref G

Four Gables, Nantmawr, near Oswestry, Shropshire SY10 9HH   Nearest Road A5

June and Bill offer you a warm and friendly welcome and good home cooked food at their country home, set in a small hamlet on the borders of Wales. The guest lounge overlooks 5 acres of landscaped gardens, which are abundant with wildlife, birds and butterflies. Excellent for bird watchers. The garden and 2 large coarse fishing pools have been featured on BBC Midlands TV. The countryside is unspoilt and near to horse riding and Offa's Dyke footpaths. ETB 2 Crown Highly Commended. Licenced to sell alcohol to our guests.

June & Bill Braddick
Tel: 01691 828708

B&B from £18pp, Dinner from £8.50, Rooms 1 twin, 1 double, 1 single, all en-suite, Children welcome, Open all year, Map Ref H

Mytton Hall, Montford Bridge, Shrewsbury, Shropshire SY4 1EU   Nearest Road A5

An elegant white listed Georgian house built in 1790. There are 3 attractive and tastefully furnished rooms all en-suite and a sitting room with TV and log fire. Full central heating. Lovely gardens adjoining the River Perry. Tennis Court. The welcoming atmosphere of a country house 6 miles North-west of Shrewsbury a good base for touring Wales and in easy reach of Ironbridge and several National Trust Houses. Children over 12.

John & Hermione Bovill
Tel: 01743 850264

B&B from £24pp, Rooms 1 twin, 2 double, all bath en-suite, Restricted smoking, Children over 12, No pets, Open all year, Map Ref I

Brownhill House, Ruyton XI Towns, nr Shrewsbury, Shropshire SY4 1LR   Nearest Road A5, B4397

Home from home without the washing-up! One ground-floor room. Non-stop tea/coffee. Extensive breakfast menu. Dinners provided using home grown and local produce. Ideal for business people - credit cards accepted, fax, email and secretarial services, also modern computers and business software available for guests. 2 acre hillside garden bordering River Perry, in the garden rich corner where England meets Wales. Plants for sale. Easy access - Ironbridge to Snowdonia, Chester to Ludlow. EMail: brownhill@eleventowns.demon.co.uk Website: http://www.eleventowns.demon.co.uk

Roger & Yoland Brown
Tel: 01939 261121
Fax: 01939 260626

B&B from £18.50pp, Dinner from £12, Rooms 1 single, 1 twin, 1 double, all en-suite, Restricted smoking, Children welcome, No pets, Open all year, Map Ref J

Foxleigh House, Foxleigh Drive, Wem, near Shrewsbury, Shropshire SY4 5BP   Nearest Road A49, B5476

Foxleigh House a home of character in the heart of Wem. Relax in the spacious rooms, delightfully furnished in the style of a more leisured age with modern comforts. Foxleigh offers bed and breakfast in a large twin bedded room with private bathroom, and a family suite of 3 rooms (sleeps 5-6) with private bathroom. All rooms have colour TV and tea/coffee. Wem is a small market town and is ideal for Shropshire, Cheshire and Wales. Beautiful gardens and National Trust properties abound and Hawkstone Golf Club and famous park and follies are four miles away. Brochure. ETB 2 Crown Commended, AA 4Q.

Mrs Barbara Barnes
Tel: 01939 233528

B&B from £19, Dinner £11.50 by arrangement, Rooms 1 twin, 1 family suite (sleeps 5-6), both with private bathroom, Minimum age 8, Open all year except Xmas, Map Ref K

Church Farm, Wrockwardine, Wellington, Telford, Shropshire TF6 5DG   Nearest Road M54, A5

Down a Lime Tree Avenue in a peaceful village betwixt Shrewsbury and Telford, lies our superbly situated Georgian farmhouse. Mature gardens with mediaeval stonework, old roses and many unusual plants. Attractive bedrooms with TV's, tea/coffee/chocolate, some en-suite with ground floor available. Enormous inglenook fireplace in spacious guests' lounge. Delicious breakfasts helped by free range hens! Minutes from Ironbridge, Shrewsbury and Telford. 1 mile M54 (J7) and A5. Open all year.

Mrs Jo Savage
Tel: 01952 244917
Fax: 01952 244917

B&B from £20pp, Rooms 2 twin, 3 double, most en-suite, Children over 10, Pets restricted, Open all year, Map Ref L

Please mention
THE GREAT BRITISH BED & BREAKFAST
when booking your accommodation

SOMERSET

Where does the visitor to this holiday county start? Such is the variety of countryside and attractions offered, that I suppose the simple answer is anywhere. Certainly it would be impossible to see and enjoy everything Somerset offers in one stay - little wonder that visitors return again and again. From between Taunton and Bridgwater stretching to the sea are the Quantock Hills, twelve miles of gloriously undulating uplands that so attracted Wordsworth and Coleridge. Not that all the Lakeland poets were equally impressed. Robert Southey was singularly disappointed with the weather when he stayed at Porlock. He must have been very much in the minority however, as this attractive seaside village, the choice of Saxon kings as their base for hunting the Exmoor Forest, is the haunt of artists, has a renowned riding centre and is a popular centre for touring the region. Porlock Weir, a haven for small pleasure craft, has a quaint shingle beach. But beware, Porlock Hill, despite the spectacular views from its summit, is one of the steepest in Britain. Minehead, an ancient harbour and popular resort situated within the wide bay of the Bristol Channel, offers all the attractions of a seaside town and is a perfect base for exploring the surrounding countryside. Dunster close by was once the centre of a prosperous cloth industry, and with its quaint Yarn Market and its picturesque street of medieval houses leading up to its castle, is one of England's most perfect small towns.

The West Somerset Steam Railway, the largest privately run railway in the country, meanders its way from Minehead to Bishops Lydeard, the home of the fascinating National Museum of Fire and Firefighting. In this area the visitor must certainly visit Hestercombe House garden which is near Cheddon Fitzpaine. The garden, designed by Gertrude Jekyll and Sir Edwin Lutyens, is arguably the finest of its kind in the country.

Taunton, the county town of Somerset, lies in the valley of Taunton Deane on the River Tone. In fact the river flows through the centre of the town, providing the opportunity of leisurely narrow-boat trips on the river and on the Taunton and Bridgwater Canal. The town has a very long and interesting history. Founded in the seventh century, it was here that the infamous Judge Jeffreys held his 'Bloody Assizes' resulting in the hanging of hundreds of rebels following the Battle of Sedgemoor in 1685. The town has some noteworthy buildings and the towers of the churches of St. Mary and St. James are particularly splendid. From Taunton, the Blackdowns and Brendons are within easy reach, and are marvellous areas for walking, riding and cycling. The Blackdown area of outstanding natural beauty is rich in attractive villages, walks and picnic sites. The Neroche Forest is only a short distance from the Widcombe Wildlife Park. Outside Wellington, another tourist centre with some fine Georgian buildings, stands the Wellington Memorial, commemorating the Duke's victory at Waterloo. Standing on the highest point of the Blackdown Hills, the monument gives magnificent views across some of the most beautiful landscape in Somerset. To the east, at the foot of the Mendip Hills is the lovely city of Wells. Its cathedral, noted for its wonderful west front, is part of England's largest medieval ecclesiastical precinct. At the moated Bishop's Palace, swans ring a bell near the drawbridge for food. Nearby are the intriguing Wookey Hole caves, a massive underground system hollowed out of the Mendips by the River Axe. Towering over the surrounding countryside is the 520 feet pinnacle of Glastonbury Tor. Glastonbury, probably founded in Celtic times has a strange and fascinating mixture of history and legend. It is claimed that King Arthur is buried in Glastonbury Abbey. Bridgwater, where the ill-fated Duke of Monmouth proclaimed himself king in 1685, is close to Sedgemoor where the last battle fought on English soil took place. South at Burrow Bridge and Burrow Mump are glorious views across the Mendips. Somerton was in Saxon times the capital of Somerset, and is renowned for its fine market place surrounded by handsome old buildings which include the seventeenth century

Town Hall and Hext almshouses. At nearby Huish Episcopi there is a glorious church possessing probably the finest fifteenth century church tower in the country, as well as magnificent glass by Burne-Jones. Cadbury Castle to the east was once thought to be King Arthur's Camelot, certainly Ethelred the Unready established his mint here in Saxon times.

From Taunton the holidaymaker has a bewildering number of attractions within a remarkably small area, being a mere seventy-five minutes by car from the glories of Bath or the delights of the Cheddar Gorge. In the same time you could visit Stourhead or Selworthy, while the pleasures of Exmoor are only an hour away. Incidentally, did you know that John Horner, the steward to the Abbot of Glastonbury, lived at the Elizabethan manor house in the pretty village of Mells. The good Abbot Selwood, hoping to save his abbey from the Dissolution sent the title deeds of the manor to Henry VIII hidden in a pie. John Horner it appears stole the pie...hence the nursery-rhyme 'Little Jack Horner'.

Places to Visit

Barrington Court, *near Ilminster* ~ a garden laid out in a series of 'rooms' with a kitchen garden. The Tudor manor house was restored in the 1920's by the Lyle family.

Cheddar Gorge, *Cheddar* ~ a spectacular ravine cut through the Mendip Hills by fast flowing streams in the Ice Age. The limestone rocks either side rise vertically to a height of four hundred feet. The Gorge has many caves which were once used for storing and maturing Cheddar cheese.

Dunster Castle, *Dunster* ~ for six hundred years, the Luttrell family have moulded the property from a coastal fortress to a secluded country house. The house and medieval ruins are surrounded by sub tropical plants including palm trees and kiwi fruit.

Montacute House, *Montacute* ~ an Elizabethan mansion, built by Sir Edward Phelips between 1558 and 1601. It has the longest Gallery in Britain, where there are portraits on loan from the National Portrait Gallery.

Glastonbury Abbey, *Glastonbury* ~ founded around 700AD, monks encouraged the association between Glastonbury and Avalon, the last resting page of King Arthur and the Holy Grail. The abbey was left in ruins after the Dissolution, yet some relics survive including parts of the Norman Abbey church, the Abbot's Kitchen with its octagonal roof and the abbey barn.

Lytes Cary Manor, *near Somerton* ~ a manor house with a 14th century chapel, 15th century hall and 16th century great chamber.

Tintinhull House Garden, *near Yeovil* ~ the inspiration of Mrs Phyllis Reiss who moved here in 1933. A delightful walled garden separated into sections by clipped hedges.

Wells Cathedral, *Wells* ~ building of the cathedral started in the 1100's, a massive 'scissor arch' was installed in 1338 to support the collapsing tower. The west front features three hundred and sixty five mediaeval statues of kings, knights and saints, many of which are life size.

Wookey Hole, *near Wells* ~ three underground chambers through which the River Axe flows into a lake from the Mendip Hills. Here there is evidence of Iron Age and possibly Stone Age occupation. There is a guided tour of the floodlit caves.

Cheddar Gorge

SOMERSET

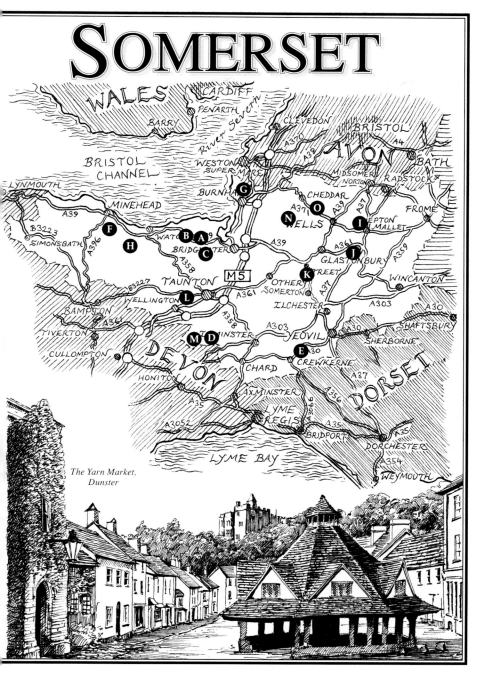

WALES
CARDIFF
PENARTH
BARRY

BRISTOL CHANNEL

River Severn

CLEVEDON
BRISTOL
A4
BATH
M1
A370
A38
AVON
WESTON-SUPER-MARE
MIDSOMER NORTON
RADSTOCK
A39

LYNMOUTH
MINEHEAD
A39
BURNHAM
G
CHEDDAR
A371
A39
A37
FROME
A359

B3223
SIMONSBATH
A396
WATCHET
A39
F
B **A**
H
BRIDGWATER
C
A358
N WELLS
O
I EPTON MALLET
J
A361
GLASTONBURY
WINCANTON

TAUNTON
M5
A39
A361
A358
K STREET
OTHERY
SOMERTON
ILCHESTER
A37
A303
A30
SHAFTSBURY

WELLINGTON
L
B3227
BAMPTON
A361
TIVERTON
CULLOMPTON
M **D** ... MINSTER
A303
YEOVIL
A30
A37
SHERBORNE
SERBORNE

DEVON
CHARD
E 30
CREWKERNE
A37

HONITON
AXMINSTER
A35
A3066
A356
DORSET

LYME REGIS
A3052
A3066
A35
BRIDPORT
DORCHESTER
A35
354
WEYMOUTH

LYME BAY

The Yarn Market,
Dunster

Blackmore Farm, Blackmore Lane, Cannington, Bridgwater, Somerset TA5 2NE　　Nearest Road A39

A unique Grade One Listed, 14th century Manor House retaining many period features including oak beams, stone archways, garderobes. Situated in a rural location with views to the Quantock Hills and within easy reach of Wells, Glastonbury, Exmoor and the West Somerset coast. All bedrooms are en-suite (one with 4-poster bed) with tea/coffee making facilities, TV, hair dryers and many other little extras. Traditional farmhouse breakfast is served around the carved oak table in the great hall. ETB Two Crowns Highly Commended. Facilities for disabled. EMail: Dyerfarm@aol.com

Mrs Ann Dyer
Tel: 01278 653442
Fax: 01278 653427

B&B from £20pp, Rooms 3 double, 1 family, all en-suite, No smoking & pets, Children welcome, Open all year, Map Ref A

Honeymead, Holford, Bridgwater, Somerset TA5 1RZ　　Nearest Road A39

see PHOTO opposite

Honeymead is an 'Arts & Crafts' style house nestling at the foot of the Quantock Hills. Walk in the footsteps of the Wordsworths and Coleridge, through moorland and secluded Combes, on cliff paths with views of the Welsh coast and islands of the Severn sea. Visit places of interest: Dunster Castle and Cleeve Abbey. Very high standards: en-suite, televisions, coffee/tea making facilities. Dinner optional: (vegetarian cuisine a speciality); all meat is free range. Car park, beautiful gardens and guest conservatory. ETB Highly Commended.

Dr Leslie & Mrs Lucille Hoose
Tel: 01278 741668

B&B from £24pp, Dinner from £5-£15, Rooms 1 twin, 1 double both en-suite, No smoking, Children & pets welcome, Open all year except Christmas, Map Ref B

Friarn Cottage, Over Stowey, Bridgwater, Somerset TA5 1HW　　Nearest Road A39

If you seek peace and quiet, comfort, and lovely views, surely this is the place for you; what's more we're on the Quantock hills with direct access to 38 square miles of area of outstanding natural beauty moorland, combes and woodlands. Our Edwardian cottage, in lovely large garden. Own produce and free range hens. Breakfast on the terrace, watch the buzzards and ravens. Dine by candlelight, vegetarians catered for, relax by the fire with TV and local interest videos to hand. Reductions for short break two/three nights.

Penny & Michael Taylor-Young
Tel: 01278 732870
Fax: 01278 732870

B&B £22-£25pp, Dinner by arrangement, Rooms 1 twin en-suite, 1 double private bathroom, No smoking, Children by arrangement, Well behaved dogs welcome, Open all year, Map Ref C

Plainsfield Court, Plainsfield, Over Stowey, Bridgwater, Somerset TA5 1HH　　Nearest Road A39

Ancestral home of Robert Blake, Bridgwater's MP in 1640. Tread the same flagstones in the restored 15th century farmhouse. Magnificent views across the sea to Wales and Somerset levels. Two double bedrooms with private bathroom. TV, tea/coffee facilities. Open log fires. Keel sized timbers in the dining room. The cider press, a detached property, former cider press to Plainsfield Court. Four poster bed, en-suite bathroom, large family room, 3 single beds with own shower and wc. TV's, videos, open log fires and a wealth of beams.

Nicky Thompson
Tel: 01278 671292
Fax: 01278 671292

B&B from £20-£25pp, Dinner from £15, Rooms 1 twin/family, 2 double/four poster, all en-suite/private, Children & pets welcome, Open all year, Map Ref C

Hawthorne House, Bishopswood, Chard, Somerset TA20 3RS   **Nearest Road A303, B3170**

Hawthorne House is situated in the scenic Blackdown Hills just 1 mile off the A303, ideal for overnight stops for Cornwall or the Plymouth Ferries. The coast, Exmoor and at least six National Trust Properties are reached within the hour. Guests have unrestricted access to their rooms, the garden and a comfortable lounge with colour TV. The dining room overlooks the terraces and has panoramic views over the garden down to the wildlife pond and over the surrounding hills. AA QQQ's Recommended. ETB Two Crowns Commended.

Roger & Sarah Newman-Coburn
Tel: 01460 234482

B&B from £19.50pp, Dinner from £10-£12.50, Rooms 1 twin, 2 double, all en-suite, No smoking, Children over 12, Pets welcome, Open all year, Map Ref D

Broadview Gardens, East Crewkerne, Crewkerne, Somerset TA18 7AG   **Nearest Road A30**

Unusual colonial bungalow. En-suite rooms overlooking acre of secluded gardens. Rooms with colour TV, easy chairs, tea facilities, fridge, hair dryer, elect fans, central heating. Carefully furnished with our personal collection of antiques: guest lounge, dining hall. Winners of top quality awards for comfort. Traditional English home cooking. 20 mins from Dorset coast. 30-60 mins from Lyme Regis, Stonehenge, Bath, Exeter, Dartmouth, Wells, Glastonbury, Salisbury, Cheddar. Perfect base for antique enthusiasts and garden lovers. EMail: broadgdn@eurobell.co.uk http://www.broadgdn.eurobell.co.uk

Gillian & Robert Swann
Tel: 01460 73424
Fax: 01460 73424

B&B from £25-£28pp, Dinner from £14, Rooms 1 twin, 2 double, all en-suite, No smoking, Children welcome, Pets by arrangement, Open all year, Map Ref E

The Old Priory, Dunster, Somerset TA24 6RY   **Nearest Road A39**

Small historic mediaeval house within old-fashioned walled gardens in peaceful setting opposite a dovecot and adjoining the church. An interesting home offering combination of highest standards with informal atmosphere. Whole food/farmhouse breakfasts. One double, 4-poster bedroom adjoining bathroom. One twin en-suite bathroom. One ground floor twin adjoining shower. Dunster is overlooked by the National Trust castle and on the edge of Exmoor National Park with its coastal path; moorland walks, superb riding. Several private and National Trust properties open within an hour's drive.

Jane Forshaw
Tel: 01643 821540

B&B from £25pp, Rooms 2 twin, 1 double, all private bathroom, Children over 12, No pets, Open all year except Christmas, Map Ref F

Dollons House, 10 Church Street, Dunster, Somerset TA24 6SH   **Nearest Road A396**

see PHOTO opposite

A Grade II listed building, Dollons House, is an attractive house believed to be much older than its early 19th century facade. The house is situated in the heart of Medieval Dunster, and is probably the prettiest village in the Exmoor National Park. The en-suite bedrooms are individually decorated, and have tea/coffee making facilities and TV. There is a sitting room for guests which leads onto a large verandah overlooking the pleasant garden. Recommended by 'Which', ETB 2 Crown Highly Commended. AA QQQQQ's Premier Selected.

Major & Mrs G H Bradshaw
Tel: 01643 821880
Fax: 01643 822016

B&B from £25pp, Rooms 1 twin, 2 double all en-suite, No smoking, Minimum age 16, No pets, Open all year except Christmas & Boxing Days, Map Ref F

*right, **Dollons House,** Dunster - see details above*

Knoll Lodge, Church Road, East Brent, Somerset TA9 4HZ   Nearest Road M5, A38, A370

Knoll Lodge is a 19th century Somerset house set in an acre of old orchard at the foot of the Brent Knoll in the quiet Sedgemoor village of East Brent. 2.5 miles from the M5 and 3 miles from the coast, it is an ideal centre for visiting Axbridge, Cheddar, Wookey Hole, Wells and Bath. There is ample parking, a guest lounge and conservatory; and all rooms have colour TV, tea/coffee, hairdryer and American patchwork quilts. A Non Smoking house. Highly Recommended for good food.

Jaqui & Tony Collins
Tel: 01278 760294

B&B from £21pp, Dinner from £11, Rooms 1 twin with private bath, 2 double en-suite, No smoking, Children over 12 years, No pets, Open all year except Christmas, Map Ref G

Wood Advent Farm, Roadwater, Exmoor National Park, Somerset TA23 0RR   Nearest Road A39

Wood Advent Farm was built in the early 1800's. It has been farmed by "The Brewers" family since the 1700's. Situated in the Exmoor National Park, this working farm is set in its own picturesque valley, with beautiful rolling hills, grazed by a large flock of sheep and suckler cows. All bedrooms have hospitality trays for your convenience and full central heating. Heated swimming pool, tennis court. The area is famous for Red Deer and Exmoor Ponies.

John & Diana Brewer
Tel: 01984 640920
Fax: 01984 640920

B&B from £40pp, Dinner from £14.00, Rooms 2 twin, 2 double, 1 family, all en-suite/private bathroom, Restricted smoking or pets, Children over 8, Open all year except Christmas, Map Ref H

Park Farm House, Forum Lane, Bowlish, Shepton Mallet, Somerset BA4 5JL   Nearest Road A371

Formerly a working farm, this gracious and comfortably converted 17th century house is situated in a conservation area. Accommodation comprises a twin bedded room (bathroom en-suite) and a suite of double and a twin room with private bathroom. Situated close to the cathedral city of Wells, Cheddar Gorge and Wookey Hole, Clarke's Village at Street, Longleat Fleet Air Arm and Haynes motor museum, Bath, Bristol, Sherborne and Yeovil. Shepton Mallet has good restaurants, pubs and easy access to the Mendip Hills plus many National Trust houses and gardens.

Mr & Mrs J Grattan
Tel: 01749 343673
Fax: 01749 345279

B&B from £17.50pp, Rooms 1 en-suite twin, 1 double & twin with private bathroom, Children welcome, Open all year, Map Ref I

Pennard House, East Pennard, Shepton Mallet, Somerset BA4 6TP   Nearest Road A37

A beautiful Georgian house situated on the last south facing slope of the Mendip Hills, in secluded gardens, surrounded by meadows, woodlands and cider orchards. Grass tennis court and Victorian spring-fed swimming pool. Furnished in antique furniture. Television and tea/coffee making facilities available. The house is ideally situated for visiting Glastonbury, Wells, Bath and the historic houses and gardens of Stourhead, Longleat, Montacute and many others. Nearby golf courses and riding available. Email: m.dearden@ukonline.co.uk

Susie & Martin Dearden
Tel: 01749 860266
Fax: 01749 860266

B&B from £28pp, Dinner from £20, Rooms 1 single, 2 twin (1 en-suite), 1 double, Restricted smoking, Children welcome, No pets, Open all year except Christmas & New Year, Map Ref J

Church Farm Guest House, Compton Dundon, Somerton, Somerset TA11 6PE   **Nearest Road B3151**

Church Farm Guest House is a part thatched farm house reputed to be 400 years old. It enjoys a tranquil setting in a typically English village nestling below St Andrew's Church in the Dundon part of the village about 1 mile off the B3151 so is very peaceful. The Down's of Glastonbury, Wells, Street and Somerton are only a few minutes drive. The rooms are in converted farm building and are all en-suite with television, tea making facilities and central heating. Full fire reg's. Car park.

Brian & Jean Middle
Tel: 01458 272927

B&B from £19.50pp, single£25, Dinner by arrangement, Rooms 1 single, 2 double, 2 family, all en-suite, Restricted smoking, Children over 5 years, No pets, Open January-November, Map Ref K

Huntersmead, Hele, Taunton, Somerset TA4 1AJ   **Nearest Road A38**

Huntersmead is an old farmhouse set in 15 acres of garden and grounds offering a warm welcome in a rural, peaceful and tranquil situation yet within 4 miles of the county town of Taunton and the M5 motorway. The rooms are attractively decorated and furnished with antiques. There are log fires in winter and a large garden. A hearty cooked breakfast is provided and a quality dinner available if booked in advance. An ideal centre for touring the West Country including the Quantock and Blackdown Hills, Exmoor and north and south coasts.

Mrs Bimmy Amor
Tel: 01823 461315

B&B from £20pp, Dinner from£12, Rooms 1 twin, 1 double, Restricted smoking, Children welcome, No pets, Open all year except Christmas, Map Ref L

Pear Tree Cottage, Stapley, Churchstanton, Taunton, Somerset TA3 7QA   **Nearest Road M5, A303, A30**

Charming south facing thatched country cottage, idyllically rurally located near Somerset/Devon border in Area Of Outstanding Natural Beauty. Wildlife abounds. Centrally placed for North/South coasts of Somerset/Devon/Dorset. Exmoor, Dartmoor, Torbay and even Cornwall reachable for day trips. Wealth of National Trust and other famous gardens encircle. Traditional cottage garden with lawns, borders, vegetable raised beds, approx 1 acre leading to 2.5 acre meadow arboretum newly planted. TV's, beverages in all rooms. Stress free paradise found. Email: colvin.parry@virgin.net

Pam Parry
Tel: 01823 601224
Fax: 01823 601224

B&B from £14pp, Dinner from £9-£10, Rooms 1 single, 1 double, 1 family/twin, all en-suite, No smoking, Children welcome, Well behaved smaller pets welcome, Open all year, Map Ref M

Sand House, Sand, Wedmore, Somerset BS28 4XG   **Nearest Road B3151**

A beautiful Grade II listed manor house in a secluded and peaceful setting of 30 acres of gardens, parkland, woodland, courtyards and pasture with wonderful far reaching views of the Somerset Levels. The Georgian conservation village of Wedmore lies ¾ mile to the south offering a good selection of pubs, restaurants and tea rooms. All bedrooms are individually furbished to a high standard with tea/coffee making facilities and TV. Situated conveniently close to Wells. Cheddar Gorge, Wookey Hole, Clarke's village at Street, Glastonbury and Tor, Bath, Bristol and the coast. Sorry no smoking.

Mrs Goodfellow
Tel: 01934 712224
Fax: 01934 712061

B&B from £22.50pp, Rooms 1 twin, 1 double, 1 family, all en-suite/private facilities, No smoking or pets, Children welcome, Open all year except Christmas & New Year, Map Ref N

Box Tree House, Westbury-sub-Mendip, Wells, Somerset BA5 1HA   **Nearest Road A371**

A warm welcome is assured at this delightful converted 17th century farm house, located in the heart of the village next to a local inn where excellent food is served. Accommodation is in 3 comfortable rooms with en-suite and private facilities. There is a charming TV lounge. Generous breakfast with local preserves, croissants and home made muffins. Also work shops for stained glass and picture framing with many unique items for sale. Email: doug@willowsys.demon.co.uk

see PHOTO opposite

Mrs Carolyn White
Tel: 01749 870777

B&B from £20pp, Rooms 2 double, 1 twin, all en-suite, Restricted smoking, Open all year, Map Ref O

Stoneleigh House, Westbury-sub-Mendip, near Wells, Somerset BA5 1HF   **Nearest Road A371**

A delightful 18th century farmhouse with lovely garden and wonderful views across open countryside. Situated on the southern slopes of the Mendip Hills between Wells and Cheddar. Excellent accommodation is offered. En-suite rooms available with TV and tea/coffee making facilities. A guests' lounge for your relaxation. A generous breakfast is served with homemade preserves and free range eggs. Vegetarians catered for. Good pub nearby. Tourist information available. Ideal position for walking or touring holiday. Large car park.

Mrs Wendy Thompson
Tel: 01749 870668
Fax: 01749 870668

B&B from £20pp, Rooms 2 double, 1 twin, 2 en-suite, Minimum age 10, No smoking, Open all year except Christmas, Map Ref O

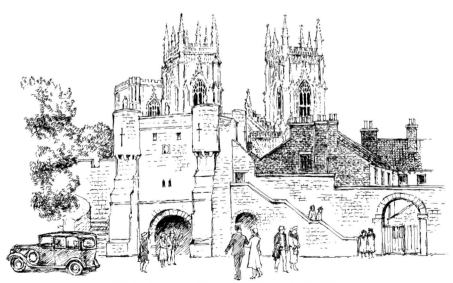

"Walk the walls first, then the cathedral?"
"No, walls, then lunch, then the cathedral"
BELLE & BERTIE IN YORK

SUFFOLK

Breckland, in the north west of the county of Suffolk, is an area of some three hundred square miles which is shared between Suffolk and Norfolk, and in the early days was populated with settlers who found the low-lying land and plentiful supply of water ideal for their simple farming methods. Today, the stability of this Breckland soil is dependant on extensive afforestation. Between Breckland and the crumbling and constantly eroded coastline lies fertile high Suffolk, reliant upon a complicated system of drainage to carry off the winter rains. Suffolk is a perfect holiday venue because there are so many contrasts. From Great Yarmouth down to Felixstowe, the coastline is punctuated with delightful coves and bays offering excellent sailing; Southwold, Orford, Woodbridge and Aldeburgh, particularly so. Southwold, the former home town of George Orwell, is a wonderful centre for exploring coastal Suffolk. After a disastrous fire in 1659, the town was replanned around a series of green areas bordered by quaint flint, brick and colour-washed cottages. Behind the Sole Bay Inn stands the white painted lighthouse, while the grand church in the Perpendicular style boasts an impressive interior. The region surrounding the town is excellent for walking and is a naturalist's paradise. To the south is Aldeburgh. It was here that the Rev. George Crabbe lived. His poem 'The Borough' was adapted by Benjamin Britten for his opera 'Peter Grimes' - an evocation of life on the Suffolk coast. Britten is buried in the churchyard of St. Peter and St. Paul. Visitors mustn't miss seeing his memorial window designed by John Piper. Benjamin Britten was co-founder of the Aldeburgh Music Festival held in June at The Maltings at Snape. The hall was burnt down just two years after its opening, but within a year was restored. At nearby Thorpeness, beside the village's artificial lake, the Meare, is a former corn windmill. Woodbridge, set in the slopes above the River Deben, is an attractive town of small boats and pleasure craft.. On the opposite bank is the site of the Sutton Hoo ship-burial where in 1939 a Saxon ship and its priceless treasure were unearthed.

The River Stour which separates Suffolk and Essex runs through delightful water-meadows and is crossed by picturesque bridges. This is Constable country. John Constable was born in this valley, and his father owned mills at Flatford and Dedham, which became the subjects of the artist's paintings. Probably England's greatest landscape artist, Constable has immortalised this beautiful region. Another great English artist, Thomas Gainsborough - renowned for his elegant portraits, was born at Sudbury where his statue overlooks the market place. The town was to become 'Eatanswill' in Dickens' Pickwick Papers. Two towns dominate the county of Suffolk, Ipswich and Bury St. Edmunds. The latter an ancient town, was a Saxon settlement when the bones of St. Edmund the Martyr were brought to the monastery of Beodricsworth in 910 AD. Edmund was the last king of East Anglia, and was killed by the Danes for refusing to deny Christianity. His shrine became a major centre of pilgrimage during the Middle Ages. Except for its two gateways the abbey is now a ruin, but two fine fifteenth century churches survive, St. James', now the cathedral of the diocese of St. Edmundsbury, and Ipswich. It was at the great altar of the abbey in 1214 that the Barons swore to force King John to honour the Magna Carta. There is a great deal of wonderful seventeenth and eighteenth century architecture in the town. Cupola House and Angel Corner are excellent examples. The lovely rivers Lark and Linnet flow into the city from delightful countryside, at one time almost exclusively hunting land. At nearby Newmarket is the historic centre of English horseracing, and the home of the Jockey Club. It was Charles II who established the sport here, although horses had been raced here since the times of James I. The National Stud was formed at Newmarket in 1967.

Ipswich is the county town and administrative centre of Suffolk, and there has been a settlement here from the Stone Age. King John granted the town its first charter in 1200. Its position as a safe harbour at the head of the estuary of the River Orwell ensured its place as an important port trading Suffolk cloth with the Continent. Ipswich was the birthplace of Cardinal Wolsey, who established a college here in 1536, although it was abandoned when the Cardinal fell from power, and all that now remains is the Wolsey Gateway. The visitor should certainly not miss the Ancient House in Buttermarket built in 1560 and sometimes known as Sparrowe's House. Its exterior is covered in Pargeting, a peculiarly East Anglian form of plaster decoration.

Suffolk has attracted a remarkably large number of writers - E.M.Forster, who wrote 'Billy Budd'; M.R. James, who wrote that vintage ghost story 'Oh, Whistle, and I'll Come To You'; Susan Hill, who wrote 'The Woman in Black' - I wonder why it inspires so many ghost stories!

Places to Visit

Bridge Cottage, *Flatford* ~ a thatched cottage on the banks of the River Stour, upstream from Flatford Mill. It has been restored and contains a display of the actual places that John Constable featured in his paintings.

Euston Hall, *Euston* ~ built in the 1660's by the Earl of Arlington, it overlooks a lake. The house contains a fine art collection including portraits of Charles I and Charles II as well as paintings by Stubbs and Van Dyck.

Framlingham Castle, *Framlingham* ~ built in 1190 by the Earl of Norfolk, today little of the castle survives except for the curtain wall and its turrets.

Ickworth House, *near Bury St Edmunds* ~ an unusual house started in 1795 and based around a large rotunda with two wings. It is set in parkland landscaped by Capability Brown, and in the house is a collection of paintings, includings works by Gainsborough and Tiziano.

Little Hall, *Lavenham* ~ a timber framed house built in the 15th century. Now the headquarters of the Suffolk Preservation Society, it is a good example of life in the 15th century.

Melford Hall, *Long Melford* ~ a turreted Tudor mansion, which has changed little since 1578. It still has its original 18th century drawing room, Regency library and Victorian bedroom.

National Horseracing Museum, *Newmarket* ~ tells the story of the sport and contains many unusual exhibits such as the skeleton of Eclipse, one of the greatest horses, unbeaten in eighteen races in 1769 and 1790. There is also a large collection of sporting art.

Theatre Royal, *Bury St Edmunds* ~ built in 1819 by William Wilkins, it is a rare example of a late Georgian playhouse with pit, boxes and gallery. Throughout the year it presents a programme of professional drama, comedy, dance, music, pantomime and amateur work.

West Stow Counrty Park ~ set in one hundred and twenty five acres of country park is a recreated Anglo Saxon village. The village was built on the site of excavations made between 1965 and 1972 of a settlement dated 420-650 AD. Six buildings have been reconstructed using the same techniques, tools and materials that would have been used in the original village.

The 18th century Postmill on Saxted Green

SUFFOLK

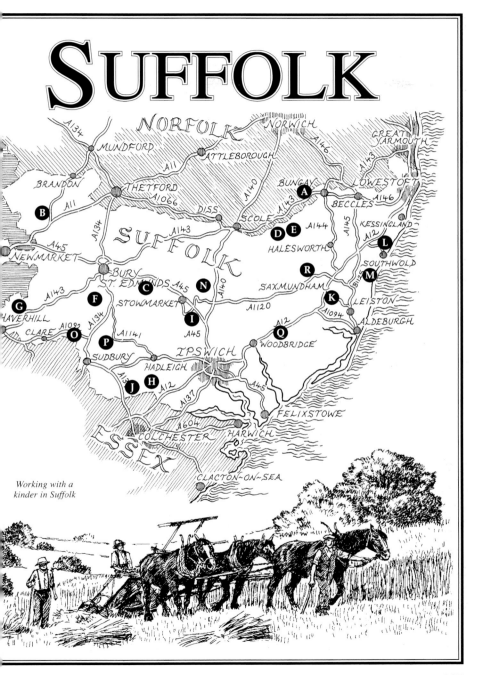

NORFOLK

NORWICH

GREAT YARMOUTH

A134
MUNDFORD

ATTLEBOROUGH

A11

A146

A143

LOWESTOFT

BRANDON

THETFORD
A1066

DISS

SCOLE

BUNGAY

BECCLES

A146

A12

KESSINGLAND

A11

B

A

SUFFOLK

A143

E
D

A144

HALESWORTH

A145

SOUTHWOLD

L

A45

NEWMARKET

A134

BURY
ST. EDMUNDS

A45

C

N

A140

R

SAXMUNDHAM

A1120

M

SOUTHWOLD

A143

F

STOWMARKET

A12

K

LEISTON

A1094

ALDEBURGH

G

HAVERHILL

A1092

A134

O

CLARE

P

A1141

I

A45

Q

WOODBRIDGE

SUDBURY

HADLEIGH

IPSWICH

A12

A45

FELIXSTOWE

J **H**

A12

A137

A604

COLCHESTER

HARWICH

ESSEX

CLACTON-ON-SEA

*Working with a
kinder in Suffolk*

337

Earsham Park Farm, Harleston Road, Earsham, Bungay, Suffolk NR35 2AQ   Nearest Road A143

Escape to the countryside. This family run delightful quiet and friendly farmhouse is set in a superb location overlooking the Waveney Valley. The rooms are spacious and elegantly furnished, but with comfort as a priority. They have extensive facilities from TV's, tea-trays, 4 poster available, easy chairs etc. to embroidered white linen and thick towels. Enjoy the lovely gardens and farm walks. Delicious local food. Many local places to visit Norwich, coast 1/2 hours drive away. AA 4Qs Selected. ETB 2 Crown Highly Commended.

Mrs Bobbie Watchorn
Tel/Fax: 01986 892180

B&B from £20pp, Dinner from £14.50, Rooms 1 twin, 2 double, all en-suite, No smoking, Children welcome, Pets by arrangement, Open all year, Map Ref A

Brambles, Mildenhall Road, Worlington, Bury St Edmunds, Suffolk IP28 8RY   Nearest Road A11

see PHOTO opposite

Set in 3 acres of lovely gardens surrounded by countryside, an ideal base for Cambridge, Bury Saint Edmunds, Ely and Newmarket. Quick access to A11 for excursions into the heart of East Anglia with its many historical houses and gardens, or on to the lovely Norfolk coast. Brambles is a peaceful house with a relaxing atmosphere, where a warm welcome and comfortably furnished rooms combine with Genny's imaginative and creative cooking, for a stay to remember. Licensed.

Genny & Tony Jakobson
Tel: 01638 713121
Fax: 01638 713121

B&B from £25pp, Dinner from £22, Rooms 2 twin, 1 double, all en-suite, No smoking or pets, Children over 8, Open all year except Christmas & New Year, Map Ref B

Manorhouse, The Green, Beyton, nr Bury St. Edmunds, Suffolk IP30 9AF   Nearest Road A14

This 16th century Suffolk longhouse overlooks "The Green", in centre of pretty village, with local hostelries. This is a place to relax and unwind. The 4 en-suite, well-appointed bedrooms all have seating areas, colour TV's, tea-making, radio, hair dryer and access to fridge/freezer and laundry facilities. Oak beams, inglenooks, antiques, large garden. Choice of breakfasts at individual tables, dinner available by arrangement or 'where to eat' list. 4 mile east of Bury St. Edmunds. Which? Good B&B Guide Recommended.

Kay & Mark Dewsbury
Tel: 01359 270960
Fax: 01359 271425

B&B from £22pp, Dinner from £14, Rooms 2 twin, 2 double, all en-suite, No smoking or pets, Children over 6, Open all year except Christmas, Map Ref C

Gables Farm, Earsham Street, Wingfield, Diss, Suffolk IP21 5RH   Nearest Road B1118 or A143

Gables Farm is a 16th Century timbered farmhouse set in moated gardens. Wingfield is a quiet village in the heart of East Anglia, convenient for Norwich, Bury St Edmunds and coast and many places of interest. Ideal for cycling and walking, fishing two miles away. Two double and one twin bedrooms (all en-suite) and having colour TV and hospitality tray Full English breakfast with free range eggs and local produce (where possible). Leaflet on request. EMail: sue.harvey@lineone.net

Michael & Sue Harvey
Tel: 01379 586355
Fax: 01379 586355

B&B from £20pp, Dinner by arrangement from £12.50, Rooms 1 twin, 2 double, all en-suite, No smoking, Children welcome, Restricted pets, Open all year except Christmas & New Year, Map Ref D

Brambles, *near Bury St Edmunds - see details opposite*

Priory House, Priory Road, Fressingfield, Eye, Suffolk IP21 5PH　　　**Nearest Road B1116**

A warm welcome awaits visitors to this lovely 16th century farmhouse, set in an acre of secluded lawns and gardens. The comfortable bedrooms have tea/coffee facilities, and 2 rooms have private bathroom. Centrally heated. The house has a wealth of exposed beams, and is furnished with antique furniture. There is a guests lounge and pleasant dining room. Fressingfield is ideal for a peaceful relaxing holiday and as touring base for Norwich, Bury St Edmunds, the Broads, coasts, historic buildings and gardens. Excellent food available in the village, 8 minutes walk. Colour brochure on request.

Mrs Rosemary Willis
Tel: 01379 586254

B&B from £23.50pp, Rooms 1 twin, 2 double, private bathrooms, Restricted smoking, Children from 10 years, Pets by arrangement, Open all year except Christmas & New Year, Map Ref E

The Hatch, Pilgrims Lane, Cross Green, Hartest, Suffolk IP29 4ED　　　**Nearest Road B1066**

see PHOTO opposite

The Hatch is a gorgeous thatched timber-framed listed 15th century house situated just outside the attractive "High Suffolk" village of Hartest. Surrounded by farmland the house is comfortably furnished with fine fabrics and antiques. Guests have the use of the delightful drawing and sitting rooms, both having wonderful inglenook fireplaces with log fires for cooler evenings. There is a lovely garden for guests to enjoy. Hartest is an ideal centre for visiting West Suffolk, Cambridge and Ely. Many lovely gardens to visit. Great antique hunting area.

Bridget & Robin Oaten
Tel: 01284 830226

B&B from £25pp, Rooms 1 single, 1 twin, 1 double, No smoking, Children over 9, Open all year, Map Ref F

The Old Vicarage, Great Thurlow, Haverhill, Suffolk CB9 7LE　　　**Nearest Road A1307, A143**

Set in mature grounds and woodlands this delightful Old Vicarage has a friendly family atmosphere. Complete peace and comfort are assured with wonderful views of the Suffolk countryside. Open log fires welcome you in winter. Guests are welcome to use the large garden and there is ample parking space. Perfectly situated for Newmarket, Cambridge, Long Melford and Constable Country, the attractively furnished bedrooms have en-suite or private facilities. Tea and coffee trays are provided in all rooms. (No smoking in bedrooms). Evening meals are available with prior notice.

Mrs Jane Sheppard
Tel: 01440 783209

B&B from £24pp, Dinner by arrangement from £15, Rooms 1 single, 1 twin, 1 double, all en-suite, Restricted smoking, Children over 7, Pets by arrangement, Open all year except Christmas, Map Ref G

Sparrows, Shelley, Hadleigh, Ipswich, Suffolk IP7 5RQ　　　**Nearest Road A12, A14**

Sparrows is a 15th century former farmhouse set in 2 acres of garden in unspoilt countryside. Grass tennis court, table tennis and bicycles for use by guests. Beach hut available in the summer by arrangement. Within easy reach of the Suffolk coast, Constable country and many other pretty Suffolk villages. Two golf courses within 3 miles and many first class pubs and restaurants in the immediate vicinity. Dinner provided by Inglenook fireplace in dining hall at 24 hours notice. King size bed, private bathroom/shower, colour TV, tea making facilities, central heating.

Mrs Rachel Thomas
Tel: 01206 337381

B&B from £23pp, Dinner from £15, Rooms 1 double in house, 1 double in annexe, Open all year except Christmas, Map Ref H

right, **The Hatch,** *near Hartest - see details above*

Pipps Ford, Needham Market, Ipswich, Suffolk IP6 8LJ   Nearest Road A14, A140

Fine and beautiful long, low, black and white timbered house parts of which date from 1540. A house with sloping floors, beams, inglenooks, with log fires and historic associations. The cottagey sitting rooms are filled with antique furniture and china collections and have a wonderful atmosphere. Bedrooms are attractive with en-suite bathrooms and have tea/coffee making facilities, radio/clock alarms, and hair dryers. More bedrooms in the Stables.

see PHOTO opposite

Mrs Raewyn Hackett- Jones
Tel: 01449 760208
Fax: 01449 760561

B&B from £22.50-£33.50pp, Dinner from £17.50, Rooms 4 double, 3 twin, Restricted smoking, Pets by arrangement, Open all year except Christmas & New Year, Map Ref I

Hill House, Gravel Hill, Nayland, Suffolk CO6 4JB   Nearest Road A134

Comfortable 16th century timber framed "Hall House" set on edge of "Constable" village in quiet location. Secluded garden with views over the valley. Good base for touring. Easy reach for Lavenham, Dedham and Flatford Mill. Golf course 1 miles. Excellent restaurants and good pub food locally. Easy access to A12. Convenient for Harwich and Felixstowe. Colchester 6 miles. 1 twin, 1 double, 1 family and 1 single room with private bathroom, tea/coffee making facilities, CTV, radio and central heating. Tourist Board - Highly Commended. AA QQQ.

Mrs P Heigham
Tel: 01206 262782

B&B from £20pp, Rooms 1 single, 1 twin, 1 double, all with private bathrooms, No smoking, Children welcome over 10, No pets, Open all year except Christmas & New Year, Map Ref J

Sternfield House, Saxmundham, Suffolk IP17 1RS   Nearest Road A12

An exquisite Queen Anne country house set in delightful parkland and formal gardens of 25 acres. Former royal retreat. Swimming pool and tennis court. Luxurious en-suite facilities offer pampered accommodation to the discerning guest. Close to Aldeburgh (5 miles), Snape Maltings (1 mile), Minesmere and Southwold.

Mrs M Thornton
Tel: 0728 602252
Fax: 0728 604082

B&B from £35pp, Rooms 1 single, 1 twin, 6 double, 1 all en-suite, Minimum age 12, No pets, No smoking, Open all year except Christmas, Map Ref K

Poplar Hall, Frostenden Corner, Frostenden, Southwold, Suffolk NR34 7JA   Nearest Road A12

Peaceful and quiet yet only 31/2 miles from the lovely seaside town of Southwold. Poplar Hall is a 16th century thatched house in 11/2 acre garden. Walks abound in the area, either coastal or country. Walberswick, Dunwich, Aldburgh, Snape are just a short distance. Poplar Hall offers luxury accommodation with TV, tea/coffee making facilities and vanity units in all rooms. Guests library, sitting, dining rooms are a pleasure to be in whilst enjoying our famed breakfast of fresh fruit, local fish, sausage, bacon and home made preserves.

Anna & John Garwood
Tel: 01502 578549

B&B from £17pp, Rooms 1 single, 2 double, cot available, 1 en-suite, No smoking, Children welcome, No pets, Open all year except Christmas, Map Ref L

*left, **Pipps Ford**, Needham Market - see details above*

Suffolk

Ferry House, Walberswick, Southwold, Suffolk IP18 6TH **Nearest Road A12**

Just 200m from the River Blyth and seashore in this picturesque artists village. Ferry House was built to an unusual design for a playwright's summer residence. The fireplace surround in the dining room depicts scenes believed to be from one of his plays. Now this character home offers a warm welcome with stylish, well provided guest accommodation. Snape Maltings, Minsmere Bird Reserve and Regency town of Southwold are within easy reach. Good pubs serving food are well within walking distance.

Mrs C Simpson
Tel/Fax: 01502 723384

B&B from £18pp, Rooms 2 single, 1 double, No smoking, Children from 10, No pets, Open all year except Christmas & New Year, Map Ref M

Cherry Tree Farm, Mendlesham Green, Stowmarket, Suffolk IP14 5RQ **Nearest Road A140**

Cherry Tree Farm is a traditional timber framed farmhouse situated in the heart of rural Suffolk, where guests are welcomed with warm hospitality. Accommodation is in three en-suite bedrooms. The guests lounge has an inglenook fireplace with a woodburning stove for cool evenings. Great care is taken in the preparation of meals which are served around a refectory table, bread is home baked and seasonal vegetables are garden fresh, traditional puddings are a speciality. Licensed, specialising in East Anglian wines.

Martin & Diana Ridsdale
Tel: 01449 766376

B&B from £23pp, Dinner from £16, Rooms 3 en-suite double, Restricted smoking, No Children or pets, Open February - December, Map Ref N

The Red House, Stour Street, Cavendish, Sudbury, Suffolk CO10 8BH **Nearest Road A1092**

Come and be spoilt in lovely sixteenth century home set in delightful garden overlooking the River Stour. Enjoy home-made biscuits and preserves and savour mouth-watering breakfasts. Both comfortably furnished bedrooms with guests' every need considered, adjoin cosy beamed upstairs sitting room with TV, books and games. Self-contained accommodation with low doorways and narrow stairs reflects age and character of house. Off-road parking. Central for beautiful Stour valley villages and Bury St. Edmunds. Excellent eating places nearby. Cambridge, Harwich ferries, one hour.

Maureen & Brian Theaker
Tel/Fax: 01787 280611

B&B from £22pp, Rooms 2 twin, 1 en-suite, 1 private facilities, No smoking or pets, Children welcome, Open all year except Christmas & New Year, Map Ref O

Lavenham Priory, Water Street, Lavenham, Sudbury, Suffolk CO10 9RW **Nearest Road B1071**

Benedictine monks originally owned this "Grade 1 listed" house, Bed chambers feature crown posts, wall paintings and oak floors, with four-poster, lit bateau and polonaise beds. Visitors can relax by inglenook fires in the 13th century hall. Breakfast can be enjoyed in the courtyard herb garden. A relaxed family atmosphere, good humour and a memorable visit are Gilli & Tim's objectives. Lavenham is often described as the finest mediaeval village in England with its historic buildings and streets. Abandon your car for the day.

Tim & Gilli Pitt
Tel: 01787 247404
Fax: 01787 248472

B&B from £35pp, Dinner by arrangement from £22, Rooms 1 twin, 3 double, all en-suite, No smoking or pets, Children over 10, Open all year except Christmas & New Year, Map Ref P

The Old Rectory, Campsea Ashe, Woodbridge, Suffolk IP13 0PU   Nearest Road A12

Peaceful Georgian rectory set in mature gardens. Relaxed and homely atmosphere. Log fires in drawing rooms and dining room. Spacious conservatory. Honesty bar. Fully licensed. All bedrooms en-suite with tea/coffee making facilities. Delicious home cooked food in restaurant. Outside diners welcome. Local home-made bread, variety of home-made marmalade, jam and local honey. Ideally situated for Snape, Woodbridge and coastal areas. Brochure available on request. Children welcome, Television and games in drawing room.

Stewart Bassett
Tel/Fax: 01728 746524

B&B from £27pp, Dinner from £18, Rooms 1 single, 2 twin, 6 double, all en-suite, Restricted smoking, Children and pets welcome, Open all year except Christmas, Map Ref Q

Grange Farm, Dennington, Woodbridge, Suffolk IP13 8BT   Nearest Road A1120

This is charming house with a delightful hostess in a superb spot. The house dates from the 15th century but there has been a farmhouse on the site since the 13th century and the remains of an old moat now form a lake and ponds. There is a lovely garden with tennis court. The beamed guests' dining room and sitting room are very comfortable and beautifully furnished. The bread and marmalade are homemade. Situated on the Stowmarket - Yoxford Road.

Mrs E Hickson
Tel: 01986 798388
Mobile: 0374 182835

B&B from £20pp, Dinner from £10, Rooms 1 double, 3 twin, 1 single, No smoking, Open all year except Christmas, Map Ref R

"It's about 3 ¹/₂ miles, just enough to give us an appetite"
BELLE & BERTIE IN YORK

SURREY

Despite the massive development in commuterdom, this small county with its ever increasing population remains Britain's most wooded county. The glorious North Downs cut through the middle of Surrey, with the low-lying belt of the Thames valley in the north, the fresh heather-covered moorlands of Bagshot Heath, Bisley, Chobham and Pirbright Commons in the west, and the fertile Surrey Weald in the south.

Lacking a coastline, the county is certainly not without its wide stretches of water. Great Pond at Frensham covers over one hundred acres, and is popular for sailing and fishing. The Little Pond, something of a misnomer, is not much smaller than its neighbour. Both are renowned for birdwatching, as many rare species are to be seen here. Virginia Water, an artificial lake one and a half miles long in a lovely wooded setting, is a part of Windsor Great Park. Virginia Water was laid out during the reign of George III by the landscape gardeners Paul and Thomas Sandby. No one should leave the vicinity of Virginia Water without visiting Runnymede, that meadow on the south bank of the River Thames just downstream from Windsor where in 1215 King John signed Magna Carta. The American Bar Association built the Magna Carta Memorial, a domed Classical temple at the foot of Cooper's Hill. Overlooking the memorial on the top of the hill is the Air Forces Memorial, commemorating the 20,456 Allied airmen who died in World War II and have no known grave. The view

from the monument is quite superb, covering seven counties and Windsor Castle. Following the assassination of John F. Kennedy in 1963, an acre of ground here was given to the people of America by the people of Britain as a memorial to their president. At the beautiful village of Shere under the North Downs, and with glorious views across the Weald is the Silent Pool. Legend tells that a country girl was startled by King John while she was bathing and drowned in its dark waters.

Guildford, the county town of Surrey though not the administrative centre, has held on to much of its Georgian character. Many of the Georgian facades cover even older buildings. The fine seventeenth century facade of the Guildhall actually conceals a Tudor building. The Guildhall is famous for amongst other things its clock, which projects over the town's steep High Street. The cathedral, designed by Sir Edward Maufe in a simplified Gothic style, has a red brick exterior and stands on a hilltop north-west of the town. The University of Surrey occupies sites by the cathedral and north of the town. Guildford is a fine holiday centre and is within easy reach of Sutton Place, an Elizabethan mansion and one of the first non-fortified manors in Britain. Losely House, another Elizabethan mansion has panelling from Henry VIII's Nonesuch Palace; Hatchlands has Robert Adams interior decoration and for plant lovers there is Wisley, the gardens of the Royal Horticultural Society, containing many specialist sections laid out for fruit, herbs, hedges and ground cover, and three gardens showing what can be achieved in small areas and one for the elderly or disabled. Nearby is Ripley, a fine old coaching village of quaint half-timbered houses. Godalming is another place with superb half-timbered Tudor buildings. The famous Charterhouse School is on the outskirts of the town, and Winkworth Arboretum is only three miles to the east, 95 acres of rare trees and shrubs, with a lake and spectacular views across the North Downs. North of Guildford is Bagshot Heath, once notorious for its highwaymen. To the North-west is the Royal Military Academy of Sandhurst, while to the south-east is Bisley Camp, which has been since 1890 the headquarters of the National Rifle Association. The most prestigious event at Bisley is the Queen's Prize.

Dorking is sited in some of the finest scenery in Surrey, standing where the Roman Stane Street crosses the ancient Pilgrim's Way. The town is surrounded by hills. Leith Hill at 965 feet is the highest point in south-east England. Twelve counties can be seen from its summit on a clear day. Leith Hill Place was the home of composer Ralph Vaughan Williams. The Burford Bridge Hotel on the River Mole is where Lord Nelson and Lady Hamilton said their final farewell in 1800. Box Hill, named after the ancient box trees which grew here, is one of the most popular viewpoints in southern England...a glorious area for walking and picnics. North is Epsom, well known as a health resort after the discovery in 1618 of mineral springs, which later led to the manufacture of Epsom Salts, but today Epsom is renowned for its racecourse, home to the Oaks and Derby. Racing has been a permanent feature here since 1730. A bridleway extends along the old Roman road to Box Hill. Esher is a pleasant Georgian town surrounded by lovely countryside, including the National Park Claremont Woods with its lake. Close by is Sandown Park Racecourse, opened in 1875. The Whitbread Gold Cup, a steeplechase established here in 1957, was one of the first examples in Britain of the commercial sponsorship of sport.

Surrey has always been a magnet to literary names. To Jane Austen, Box Hill was familiar ground, Sheridan too; Keats immensely enjoyed his visits. E.M. Forster, Lord Tennyson and George Meredith revelled in the peace and tranquillity of this lovely region - little wonder holiday makers follow in their footsteps.

Places to Visit

Claremont Landscape Garden, *Esher* ~ one of the earliest surviving English landscape gardens, carefully restored to its former glory with lake, island with pavillion, grotto and avenues.

Hampton Court, *East Molesey* ~ it was not originally a royal palace, as it was built by Cardinal Wolsey, Henry VIII's most powerful minister, but the display of power and wealth was not to the king's liking, so the Cardinal gave the palace to the king. The palace was remodelled by Christopher Wren for William and Mary. Many of the state rooms are decorated with furniture, paintings and tapestries taken from the Royal Collection.

Hatchlands Park, *near Guildford* ~ built in 1758 for Admiral Boscawen with interors by Robert Adam. It has been extensively restored and now houses the Cobbe collection of keyboard instruments, paintings and furniture. The garden was designed by Gertrude Jekyll.

Kew Gardens, *Richmond* ~ three hundred acres of landscaped gardens devoted to the propagation, study and display of plants.

Polesden Lacey, *near Dorking* ~ a peaceful country estate surrounded by trees. The elegant Regency house was furnished in Edwardian times by the Hon. Mrs Greville. Lovely walled garden with walks through the North Downs.

Oakhurst Cottage, *near Godalming* ~ a small 16th century timber framed cottage. It has been restored and furnished as a simple dwelling with delightful cottage garden.

Runnymede, *Egham* ~ one hundred and eighty eight acres of historic meadows where King John sealed the Magna Carta in 1215. One hundred and ten acres of woodland on Cooper's Hill overlook the meadows. There are also memorials dedicated to the Magna Carta, John F. Kennedy and the Air Forces.

Winkworth Arboretum, *Godalming* ~ planned and planted as a woodland in the 1930's, it covers over one hundred acres and has two lakes and many trees, shrubs and plenty of wildlife including butterflies and moths.

Box Hill from
Ranmore Common,
The South Downs

SURREY

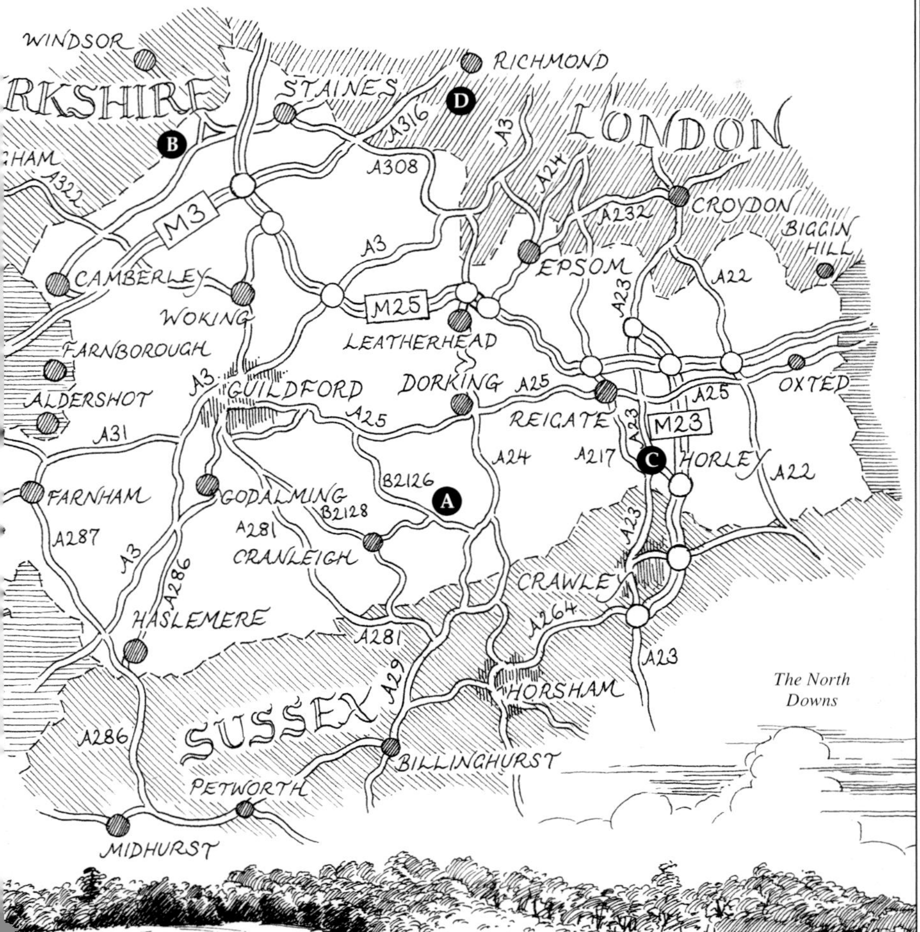

WINDSOR

RICHMOND

RKSHIRE

STAINES

D

LONDON

A316

A308

A3

A24

B

HAM

A322

M3

A232

CROYDON

BIGGIN HILL

CAMBERLEY

A22

WOKING

M25

EPSOM

A23

FARNBOROUGH

LEATHERHEAD

ALDERSHOT

A3

GUILDFORD

DORKING

A25

OXTED

A31

A25

REIGATE

A25

M23

FARNHAM

GODALMING

A24

A217

HORLEY

A22

A287

B2126

A

A23

C

A3

A281

B2128

A286

CRANLEIGH

CRAWLEY

HASLEMERE

A264

A23

A281

HORSHAM

The North Downs

A286

SUSSEX

A29

BILLINGHURST

PETWORTH

MIDHURST

Doughty Cottage, *Richmond- see details opposite*

High Edser, Shere Road, Ewhurst, Cranleigh, Surrey GU6 7PQ   Nearest Road A25

High Edser is an early 16th century farmhouse set in an area of outstanding natural beauty surrounded by its own land. A tennis court is available for guests' use. There is a guests' lounge with television and all rooms have tea/coffee making facilities. Within easy reach of Guildford, Dorking and Horsham. Many National Trust properties and other places of interest are close by. Gatwick and Heathrow are approximately 30 minutes drive. We welcome children and dogs prior arrangement.

Mrs C A Franklin-Adams
Tel: 01483 278214
Fax: 01483 278200

B&B from £22.50pp, Rooms 1 twin, 2 double, Restricted smoking, Children welcome, Pets by arrangement, Open all year except Christmas, Map Ref A

The Old Parsonage, Parsonage Road, Englefield Green, Surrey TW20 0JW   Nearest Road A30

The Old Parsonage is a late Georgian house set in a pretty village on the edge of Windsor Great Park. Guest accommodation is traditionally furnished and overlooks the old fashioned gardens. Bedrooms are equipped with TV and tea/coffee making facilities. All meals are freshly prepared to order and wine is available. Local facilities include a health spa with beauty salon, swimming, golf and horse riding. Conveniently situated for Heathrow (20 minutes), M25, M4, Windsor Ascot, Wisley Gardens and Egham mainline station (Waterloo 25 minutes).

Peter & Sandi Clark
Tel: 01784 436706
Fax: 01784 436706

B&B from £25pp, Dinner from £15, Rooms 1 single, 1 twin, 3 double, 1 family, most en-suite, No smoking or pets, Children welcome, Open all year except Christmas, Map Ref B

The Lawn Guest House, 30 Massetts Road, Horley, Surrey RH6 7DE   Nearest Road A23

The Lawn Guest House is an attractive Victorian house set in pretty gardens just 11/2 miles from Gatwick airport and 2 minutes walk from Horley where there are pubs, restaurants, shops and a main line railway to London. The comfortable bedrooms are all en-suite with colour TV, tea/coffee/chocolate facilities, hair dryers and direct dial phones. A full English breakfast is served and/or a healthy alternative - fruit/yoghurt/muesli etc. For guests comfort this is a totally non smoking home, with plenty of holiday and overnight parking on site.

Carole & Adrian Grinsted
Tel: 01293 775751
Fax: 01293 821803

B&B from £22.50pp, Rooms 4 twin, 1 double, 2 family, all en-suite, No smoking, Children welcome, Pets welcome, Open all year, Map Ref C

Doughty Cottage, 142A Richmond Hill, Richmond, Surrey TW10 6RN   Nearest Road A316, Near to M4

Beautiful house top of Richmond Hill overlooking the Thames, is a very special place to stay. A period house with an Italianate walled garden, choose from the Florentine with hepplewhite style 4 poster or Venetian twin, frescoed ceiling. Both bedrooms lead onto your private patio garden. Romantic Sienna room. Silver-leaf 4 poster views of the river. 5 minutes, historic Richmond. Wealth of shops, cafes, restaurant, theatre an abundance of places to see. Central London 7 miles away, District Line tube station. Heathrow airport 25 minutes by car.

see PHOTO opposite

Denise O'Neill
Tel: 0181 332 9434
Fax: 0181 332 9434

B&B from £36-£48pp, Light Supper from £6.50, Rooms 1 twin, 2 double, all en-suite/private bathroom, No smoking or pets, Children over 12, Open all year except Christmas, Map Ref D

SUSSEX

The South Downs form the backbone of Sussex, sandwiched between the forest ridge composed of St. Leonards Forest, Ashdown Forest and the Sussex Weald, and the narrow coastal strip. Now almost entirely built up, this 'Sussex by the Sea' has long been a magnet to the holiday maker, and with very good reason. The many amenities, historical associations and excellent weather records ensure a regular and loyal clientele. Eastbourne, arguably the Queen of the Sussex coast, has a remarkable natural beauty, and is truly a floral town. Motcombe Gardens, containing the pond which was the town's first reservoir, and through which flows the Bourne which gave the town its name, Hampden Park, Princes Park, and Manor Gardens are a blaze of colour in season. The famous Carpet Gardens on the sea front have charmed visitors for over a hundred years. Eastbourne has been a fashionable seaside resort since the late eighteenth century when the children of George III holidayed here. As you would expect the town offers all the amenities of a first class resort, excellent shops, theatres, restaurants, nightclubs, a magnificent pier and the Grand Parade Bandstand, featuring traditional military and brass bands. Drusillas Zoo Park at Alfriston is a great attraction to adults as well as children.

The South Downs is a designated area of outstanding beauty and part of the Heritage Coast, a region of glorious walks and breathtaking sights. At Beachy Head, a short distance south of Eastbourne, the spectacular chalk cliffs rise to over five hundred feet giving fine views to the distant Royal Sovereign light tower. Between Cuckmere Haven and Beachy Head the South Downs end in seven dramatic chalk cliffs known as the Seven Sisters. At the Seven Sisters Country Park, there are 700 acres of unspoiled countryside, through which flows the River Cuckmere. To the north is the intriguing Long Man of Wilmington, a striking 226 feet high Saxon figure, etched into the chalk hillside overlooking the picturesque village of Wilmington with its Benedictine monastery. To the east of Eastbourne is lovely Pevensey, an historic village of quaint houses dominated by the ruins of Pevensey Castle - the first castle to be built by William the Conqueror on English soil in 1066.

Hastings, like its sister Eastbourne, can boast a pleasant summer climate and a host of seaside attractions. Hastings is an ancient town and part of its particular attraction is its Old Town where, built between the East and West Hills, the Tudor houses are crushed cheek by jowl. A singular delight is charming Sinnock Square between Bourne Street and the High Street, the haunt of artists. Fine Georgian houses with wrought iron balconies border elegant Wellington Square, and another Georgian attraction is Pelham Crescent built by the Earl of Chichester in 1824. Here St. Mary-in-the-Castle is worth a visit - a natural spring which once fed the baptismal font flows through the building. The West Hill Cliff Railway, sliced through a natural cave in the rock leads to the castle at the very heart of Hastings.

This is certainly the area for castles. At nearby Battle, where in fact the Battle of Hastings actually took place, are the ruins of the abbey William the Conqueror vowed he would build here if he was victorious. The high altar marks the spot where Harold is said to have fallen. Only the gatehouse of 1338 and the east range of the abbey are intact, but there is an interesting battlefield trail and audiovisual display detailing the story of the battle. Twelve miles inland from Hastings is the fourteenth century Bodiam Castle, surrounded by a wide moat filled with water lilies, a wonderful medieval fortress in a perfect setting. At Herstmonceux Castle is a fascinating hands-on science centre, but the pride of the castle is the spectacular Elizabethan gardens. The visitor to this area should try not to miss Northiam, a pretty country village with a station on the Kent and East Sussex Railway line - a treat for steam train enthusiasts. Virtually a part of Hastings is St. Leonards-on-Sea, a relatively modern town by comparison. Built in the early nineteenth century by James Burton, it is a charming mixture of styles, elegantly laid out in squares with beautiful gardens. Sir Henry Rider Haggard lived at the top of St. Leonards Gardens in North Lodge.

Of course no visitor to Sussex could miss that other seaside resort, Brighton, the oldest of British seaside resorts. Here the Prince Regent, later to become George IV, initiated the fashion for seaside holidays and bathing and here he built his Royal Pavilion, an oriental extravaganza with one of the most extraordinary interiors in Europe. The Lanes survive from Brighton's humble fishing village days, now a very upmarket warren of antique shops, galleries and pavement cafes. Lewes, north-east of Brighton, is an interesting town with some fine architecture, while Ditchling Beacon gives splendid views across open country.

Sussex's longest river, the Arun, rises in St. Leonards Forest, cutting through the South Downs by Arundel to the sea at Littlehampton. Arundel, a handsome town, is an excellent centre for touring, its main street climbing up to the medieval-Victorian castle home of the Dukes of Norfolk. To the north of the town is a large wildfowl reserve.

Few counties can claim so much to see in so small an area - rich in history, blessed with glorious countryside and a pleasant climate, the visitor can only regret that in a limited stay, so much must be missed out.

Places to Visit

Arundel Castle, *Arundel* ~ a hilltop castle surrounded by castellated walls. The castle was originally built by the Normans, but only the keep remains. It was rebuilt in 1643 and restored in the 19th century.

Bodiam Castle, *Rye* ~ a late 14th century castle surround by a wide moat. It was built as a defence against an anticipated invasion by the French, which attack never came though the castle was damaged in the Civil war. It has been uninhabited ever since; the roof was restored in 1919 by Lord Curzon who gave the castle to the nation.

Brighton Pavillion, Brighton ~ a lavish Oriental palace by John Nash, built for George IV. It was completed in 1822, and the exterior has remained largely unchanged. Queen Victoria sold the Pavillion to the town of Brighton in 1850.

Nymans Garden, *Haywards Heath* ~ thirty acres of rare and beautiful tress, shrubs and plants collected from around the world. The garden features a walled garden with fountain and hidden sunken garden. The ruins of the house overlook the lawns and many woodland walks start from the garden.

Petworth House and Park, *Petworth* ~ set in seven hundred acres of park, landscaped by Capability Brown. There are over three hundred paintings on display including works by Turner, Van Dyck, Gainsborough, Reynolds and Blake. Also on display are collections of ancient and neo classical sculpture, furniture and wood carvings by Grinling Gibbons.

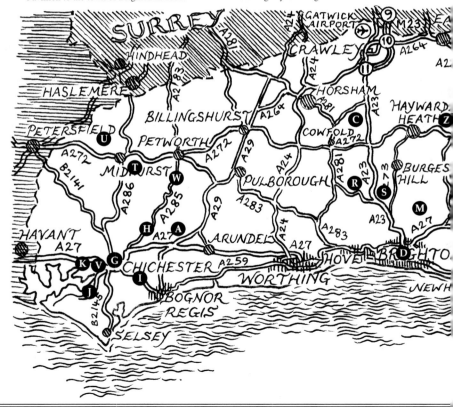

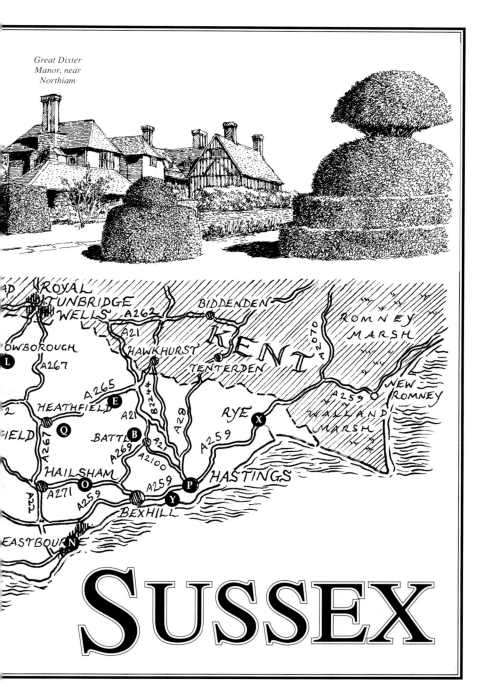

*Great Dixter
Manor, near
Northiam*

SUSSEX

Mill Lane House, Slindon, Arundel, Sussex BN18 0RP — Nearest Road A27, A29

A mainly 17th century house with coach house, a large garden and magnificent views to the coast; situated in a beautiful National Trust village of the South Downs. Direct access to walking on the Downs; super bird watching locally and at nearby reserves. Within easy reach of Arundel Castle; Goodwood; Chichester with Roman Palace, cathedral and festival theatre. Good pubs within easy walking distance. Central heating, log fires. All rooms are en-suite and have television. 2 rooms have wheelchair access. Evening meals by arrangement.

Peter & Sarah Fuente
Tel: 01243 814440

B&B from £20.90pp, (weekly terms), Dinner by arrangement from £10.70, Rooms 1 single, 2 twin, 3 double, 1 family, all en-suite, Children welcome, Pets by arrangement, Open all year, Map Ref A

Fox Hole Farm, Kane Hythe Road, Battle, East Sussex TN33 9QU — Nearest Road A271

Fox Hole Farm is a beautiful and secluded 18th century woodcutters cottage nestling in over 40 acres of its own rolling lush East Sussex land. The farmhouse retains many of its original features and is heavily beamed with a large inglenook fireplace featuring a woodburing stove. It has been carefully converted to offer three traditionally furnished and well appointed double rooms, all with en-suite bathrooms, TV and tea making facilities. Outside a large country garden containing many species of flower, shrubs, trees and natural pond.

Paul & Pauline Collins
Tel: 01424 772053
Fax: 01424 773771

B&B from £24.50pp, Rooms 3 en-suite double, No smoking, Children over 10, Pets restricted, Open all year except Christmas & New Year, Map Ref B

Timbers Edge, Longhouse Lane, off Spronketts Lane, Warninglid, Bolney, Sussex RH17 5TE — A272, A23

Beautiful Sussex country house set in over two acres of formal gardens surrounded by woodlands. Breakfast is served in the spacious conservatory overlooking the pool. Timbers Edge is located within easy reach of Gatwick (15 mins), Brighton (20 mins) and Ardingly (South of England Showground) (20 mins). The beautiful gardens of Nymans and Leonardslee (10 mins), Hickstead Show Jumping Ground (10 mins). All rooms have TV and beverage making facilities. EMail: Gearlam@aol.com

see PHOTO opposite

Sally & Geoffrey Earlam
Tel: 01444 461456

B&B from £25pp, Rooms 2 twin, 2 single, No smoking, Open all year, Map Ref C

Adelaide Hotel, 51 Regency Square, Brighton, Sussex BN1 2FF — Nearest Road A259

A warm welcome, friendly service, comfort and delicious food are the hallmarks of this elegant Grade II listed Regency Town House Hotel, modernised but retaining the charm of yester year. Centrally situated in Brighton's Premier sea-front square with NCP underground car park. There are 12 peaceful en-suite bedrooms, individually designed and furnished with coordinating decor, and equipped with phone, colour TV etc. A beautiful 4-poster bedroom available. Easy access to A23, 30 minutes to Gatwick. Discounts available when staying 2 nights or more.

Ruth & Clive Buxton
Tel: 01273 205286
Fax: 01273 220904

B&B from £32.50pp, Rooms 3 single, 1 twin, 7 double, 1 family, all en-suite, Restricted smoking, Children welcome, No pets, Open all year, Map Ref D

right, **Timbers Edge,** *near Bolney - see details above*

Glydwish Place, Fontridge Lane, Burwash, Sussex TN19 7DG Nearest Road A265

A charming mock Tudor home set on a lovely wooded site with infinite peace and far reaching views. Four attractively furnished rooms with hot/cold. Colour TV's, tea/coffee, two rooms have 7ft sq beds. Also available is a beautiful self contained wing (sleeps four) own terrace with gas barbecue for B&B or self catering. The surrounding countryside is delightful with numerous interesting places to visit including many National Trust Houses/Gardens. Lovely walks, excellent pub/restaurants in surrounding villages. Sauna, Solarium, games room, gymnasium. EMail: dolores@easynet.co.uk

Mrs Dolores Collins
Tel: 01435 882869
Fax: 01435 882749
Mobile: 0860 624197

B&B single room £30, Double rooms £55, Wing B&B £60 2 person, £100 4 persons, Wing s/c £50 2 person, 2 en-suite, 2 private, No smoking, Children over 12, No pets, Open all year, Map Ref E

Holly House, Beaconsfield Road, Chelwood Gate, Sussex RH17 7LF Nearest Road A275

On the edge of Ashdown Forest in a rural village setting stands Holly House a 130 year old forest farmhouse. Now converted to form a comfortable family home which has seen Chelwood Gate change from a hamlet to a pleasant village with Church, 2 pubs and a well stocked village shop. We offer a warm welcome with an inviting lounge, comfortable beds and memorable breakfasts served in the conservatory overlooking the interesting garden. Guests may use the heated swimming pool in summer.

Deirdre & Keith Birchell
Tel: 01825 740484

B&B from £42pp, Dinner from £12-£14, Rooms 1 single, 2 twin, 2 double, some en-suite, Children & pets welcome, Open all year, Map Ref F

The Old Store Guest House, Stane Street, Halnaker, Chichester, Sussex PO18 0QL Nearest Road A285, A27

An impressive 18th century Grade II listed house adjoining the Goodwood Estate. All bedrooms at The Old Store Guest House have en-suite shower rooms, colour TV, tea/coffee facilities, hair dryer and trouser press. A full English breakfast is served in a charming break fast room. Guests lounge and car park. Excellent pub/restaurant within walking distance. Well situated for Goodwood House, Goodwood racecourse and Chichester Festival Theatre. Also close by are Petworth House, Arundel Castle, Fishbourne Roman Palace and at Portsmouth, Nelson's Flag ship The Victory.

Robert Grocott
Tel/Fax: 01243 531977

B&B from £27.50pp, Rooms 1 single, 3 twin, 3 double, all en-suite, Restricted smoking, Pets by prior arrangement, Open all year except Christmas & New Year, Map Ref H

Abelands Barn, Merston, Chichester, Sussex PO20 6DY Nearest Road A259

see PHOTO opposite

A traditional 1850 Sussex Barn converted in to a beautiful, interesting family home. It provides spacious and flexible accommodation, with all facilities. A period, flint outbuilding contains a large, en-suite bedrooms, and the imposing main Barn offers a ground floor 'family' suite of two bedrooms, bathroom and 'snug'. Attractive gardens overlook the lovely South Downs, and a courtyard offers secure, overnight, parking. Abelands Barn is situated two miles from Chichester, with many local attractions including Goodwood, Arundel, the coast and prestigious Festival Theatre. ETB 2 Crowns Highly Commended.

Mike & Gaile Richardson
Tel: 01243 533826
Fax: 01243 555533

B&B from £22.50pp, Rooms 1 twin, 2 double, 1 family, en-suite, Children welcome, No pets, Open all year except Christmas & New Year, Map Ref I

Barn Main House

The Cow Shed

Abelands Barn, *near Chichester - see details opposite*

Chichester Lodge, Oakwood, Chichester, Sussex PO18 9AL   **Nearest Road A27, B2178**

Chichester Lodge is a charming 1840 Gothic Lodge with wonderful interior design and antique furnishings. Lots of flag stone floors, polished wood, beautiful Gothic windows, every attention to detail. Wood burning stove in hall way. There are two acres of very pretty garden with hedges and honeysuckle and hidden corners. The en-suite bedrooms are comfortable with nice decorations and furnishings and all rooms have TV. There is also a garden room with wood burning stove for winter evening. Nearby activities include fishing, golf, theatre and Goodwood.

see PHOTO opposite

Jeanette Dridge
Tel: 01243 786560

B&B from £25pp, Rooms 3 double, 1 single, all en-suite, No smoking, Minimum age 14, Open all year, Map Ref G

Hatpins, Bosham Lane, Old Bosham, Chichester, Sussex PO18 8HG   **Nearest Road A259**

Mary Waller, a former designer of hats and wedding dresses, has combined her talents with a natural flair for decorating to transform her home into delightful bed and breakfast accommodation. Enhancing the decor is the warmth of Mary's hospitality. Bosham is an appealing coastal town and Old Bosham brims with charm and it is fun to wander down to the waterfront and explore the tiny lanes. Also nearby are Portsmouth and the cathedral city of Chichester with its lovely harbour. A few miles inland is Downland Museum a collection of very old cottages and buildings. Honeymoon couples welcome. ETB Listed.

see PHOTO on page 362

Mrs Mary Waller
Tel: 01243 572644
Fax: 01243 572644

B&B from £25-£35pp, Rooms 5 with en-suite/private bathroom, No smoking, Children welcome, No pets, Open all year, Map Ref J

White Barn, Crede Lane, Old Bosham, Chichester, West Sussex PO18 8NX   **Nearest Road A259**

An outstanding unique single storey house with timbered interior and complete wall of glass in the dining area. Memorable dinners and breakfasts served overlooking a red terrace and a colourful garden. Located in the attractive Saxon harbour village of Old Bosham. Accommodation comprises 3 delightful en-suite bedrooms with colour TV, radio and tea/coffee. Relax in the charming sitting room with log fire on chilly evenings. Places of interest to visit include National Trust Houses, Historic naval ships, Roman Palace and Goodwood House. A very warm welcome awaits you. ETB Highly Commended.

Sue & Tony Trotman
Tel: 01243 573113
Fax: 01243 573113

B&B from £28pp, Dinner from £19-£21, Rooms 2 twin, 1 double, all en-suite, No smoking or pets, Children over 10, Open all year except Christmas Eve, Christmas Day & Boxing Day, Map Ref K

Laurel Tree Farmhouse, Boars Head, Crowborough, Sussex TN6 3HD   **Nearest Road A26**

Grade II listed farmhouse with beams and inglenooks. 16th century charm, situated in its own grounds, adjacent to a fruit farm. Off street parking. An area of outstanding natural beauty. Tea/coffee making facilities in both bedrooms. Private guest lounge with TV. Close by are Great Dixter, Sheffield Park, Sissinghurst Garden, Hever Castle, Leeds Castle, Scotney Castle and many more attractions. Ideal for National Trust properties. Local pub for evening meals is within easy walking distance. ETB 2 Crown Highly Commended. A home from home.

see PHOTO on page 363

Carol Carlile
Tel/Fax: 01892 652061

B&B from £20pp, Rooms 2 twin, 1 en-suite, 1 private facilities, No smoking, Children over 10, No pets, Open all year except Christmas & New Year, Map Ref L

---

left, **Chichester Lodge,** *near Chichester - see details above*

Sussex

*above, **Hatpins,** near Chichester - see details on page 361*

*right, **Laurel Tree Farmhouse,** near Crowborough - see details on page 361*

Longcroft House, Beacon Road, Ditchling, Sussex BN6 8UZ   Nearest Road A23, A27, B2112

Longcroft House is situated near the foot of Ditchling Beacon in 2 acres of garden and paddock, between the vineyard and the centre of the village, in easy walking distance of all amenities, and easy access to reach the main roads to Gatwick. Longcroft is a beautiful house built in traditional style and offers a relaxing and comfortable stay in one of three rooms all with private or en-suite facilities and TV. Guests may chose a 4-poster bed. Beautifully decorated throughout, and there is a lounge where guests may relax. Ditchling with its ancient buildings and charm has much to offer visitors.

Robert & Helen Scull
Tel: 01273 842740

B&B from £25pp, Dinner from £22, Supper £15 including wine, Rooms 1 twin, 2 double, 2 en-suite, No smoking, Children by arrangement, Open all year, Map Ref M

Brayscroft Private Hotel, 13 South Cliff Avenue, Eastbourne, Sussex BN20 7AH   Nearest Road A259

Brayscroft is an Edwardian family house typical of the fine architecture which makes Eastbourne one of England's most attractive towns. All rooms have their own facilities and colour TV's and tea/coffee facilities, and the hotel is licensed for residents and their guests. The seafront is minutes away and provides views towards Beachy Head. A seaside holiday wouldn't be complete without a pier, Carpet Gardens, bandstand, deckchairs and ice cream - Eastbourne has them all. For those who enjoy the outdoors, the walks around Beachy Head and the Seven Sisters can accessed from the hotel or a short car journey will take you to some pretty Sussex villages. ETB Highly Commended.

Gerry Crawshaw
Tel: 01323 647005
Fax: 01323 720705

B&B from £23pp, Rooms 1 single, 2 twin, 2 double, all en-suite, Children over 14, Pets by arrangement, No smoking, Open all year, Map Ref N

Cleavers Lyng Country Hotel, Church Road, Herstmonceux, Hailsham, Sussex BN27 1QJ   A271

Photogenic Cleavers Lyng is a small family run hotel adjacent to the west gate of Herstmonceux Castle dating from 1577 with oak beams and inglenook fireplace. Panoramic views. Good home cooking in traditional English style and full English breakfast and lunches served daily. Fully licensed with lounge bar serving fine wines and draught beers. TV lounge. All bedrooms are fully en-suite, centrally heated and have tea/coffee making facilities. Special attraction - badger watch! EMail: scil999@aol.com

see PHOTO opposite

Sally & Douglas Simpson
Tel: 01323 833131
Fax: 01323 833617

B&B from £25pp, Dinner from £12.95, Rooms 4 double, 3 twin, Open all year, Map Ref O

Parkside House, 59 Lower Park Road, Hastings, East Sussex TN34 2LD   Nearest Road A21, A259

High standards of hospitality, comfort and cleanliness are provided at Parkside House where an informal and friendly atmosphere is created in the elegant Victorian non-smoking house. We are situated overlooking the beautiful and extensive Alexandra Park with the town centre and main amenities within 10-15 minutes walk. Luxurious en-suite rooms include colour TV, video recorders, bathrobes, complimentary toiletries, beverage trays etc. Unrestricted parking in quiet road. Open all year.

Brian W. Kent
Tel: 01424 433096
Fax: 01424 421431

B&B from £25pp, Rooms 2 single, 1 twin, 1 double, 1 family, all en-suite, No smoking or pets, Children welcome, Open all year, Map Ref P

---

*right, **Cleavers Lyng Country Hotel,** Herstmonceux - see details above*

Great Crouch's, Rushlake Green, Heathfield, East Sussex TN21 9QD   **Nearest Road B2096**

This Grade II country house is set in the conservation village of Rushlake Green, an area of outstanding natural beauty, in the heart of rural East Sussex. Oak beams, original doors and antiques furnish the house, whilst the bedrooms, both with en-suite or private bathroom, have TV, magazines, fruit, etc. One bedroom in adjacent Sussex barn is a small suite. 15 acres of garden and pasture, an indoor heated swimming pool, plus a warm and friendly welcome, make this a great place to relax and unwind.

see PHOTO opposite

Richard & Ruth Thomas
Tel: 01435 830145

B&B from £27.50pp, Rooms 1 twin, 1 double, both en-suite, No smoking, children or pets, Open all year except Christmas & New Year, Map Ref Q

Yeomans Hall, Blackstone, nr Henfield, West Sussex BN5 9TB   **Nearest Road A23**

Yeomans Hall is a listed 15th century hall house situated in a conservation area in the heart of the farming hamlet of Blackstone, yet close to A23, Brighton and fast trains to London. With comfortable country style furnishings, beams and inglenook fireplaces. Attractive cottage garden. Convenient for National Trust Properties, Hickstead, Ardingly Showground, Glyndebourne and coast. Nearby welcoming pubs and excellent walks including South Downs way. Bedrooms have tea/coffee making facilities and colour TV's. Parking available. Old charm with 20th century comforts.

Alan & Caroline Kerridge
Tel: 01273 494224
Fax: 01273 494224

B&B Double from £23pp, Rooms 1 single, 2 double, all en-suite, No smoking, children or pets, Open all year except Christmas & New Year, Map Ref R

Clayton Wickham Farmhouse, Belmont Lane, Hurstpierpoint, Sussex BN6 9EP   **Nearest Road A23**

A warm welcome awaits you in this beautifully restored 16th century farmhouse with masses of beams and huge inglenook in the drawing room. Set in 3 acres of splendid gardens with tennis court and lovely views. Enviably quiet and secluded, yet conveniently situated for all transport facilities and places of interest. Rooms, including 1 4-poster en-suite have all usual amenities and more, plus room service for early morning tea, etc. The genial hosts serve truly delicious food with a wide breakfast choice. An excellent candlelit dinner, or simpler meal, available on request.

Mike & Susie Skinner
Tel: 01273 845698
Fax: 01273 846546

B&B from £30pp, Rooms 2 twin/double, 1 double four poster en-suite, 1 single, Restricted smoking, Children welcome, Pets by arrangement, Open all year, Map Ref S

Amberfold, Heyshott, Midhurst, West Sussex GU29 0DA   **Nearest Road A286**

Amberfold, situated in the scenic hamlet of Heyshott, dates back to Tudor times. Miles of unspoiled woodland walks start on your doorstep. An ideal hideaway for nature lovers, yet only five minutes drive from historic Midhurst and local attractions of Goodwood, Chichester and coast. Accommodation comprises: private self-contained annexe, with access all day. Double bedroom, shower room, toilet, central heating, TV. In addition, electric kettle, cafetiere, toaster. A fridge, lavishly replenished daily with selection of food, is provided for self-service continental breakfast.

Annabelle & Alexander Costaras
Tel: 01730 812385

B&B from £20pp, Rooms 1 en-suite double, No smoking, children or pets, Open all year, Map Ref T

---

left, **Great Crouch's,** *near Heathfield - see details above*

Redford Cottage, Redford, Midhurst, West Sussex GU29 0QF   Nearest Road A272,A3,A286

A warm welcome in attractive country house dating back to the 16th century in an area of outstanding natural beauty. Comfortable rooms include a self-contained garden suite with own beamed sitting room and en-suite facilities. Rates include full English breakfast and tea/coffee making facilities, television provided in bedrooms and drawing room. Convenient to Midhurst, Petworth, Goodwood, Chichester and South Downs. Excellent walks and National Trust Properties within easy reach. An ideal retreat for a peaceful stay. ETB Two Crowns Highly Recommended. AA Four QQQQ.

Caroline Angela
Tel/Fax: 01428 741242

B&B from £28pp, Rooms 1 twin, 1 double, 1 en-suite, Restricted smoking, Children & pets welcome, Open all year except Christmas & New Year, Map Ref U

Critchfield House, Bosham Lane, Old Bosham, West Sussex PO18 8HE   Nearest Road A259

Critchfield dates from the early 18th century and is in a lovely peaceful location 5 minutes walk from the harbour. There is a large garden and sheltered sun terrace for our guest's use. The house is furnished to a high standard with many antiques. The charming bedrooms all have private facilities. Breakfast is served in the oak beamed dining room and there is an excellent hotel restaurant and 2 pubs within easy walking distance. Easy access to Chichester, Arundel, Portsmouth and the lovely South Downs. ETB Highly Commended - Listed.

Janetta Field
Tel: 01243 572370
Fax: 01243 572370

B&B from £25pp, Rooms 2 twin/double, 1 double, all en-suite, No smoking, Children over 8, Restricted pets, Open March - October, Map Ref V

The Old Railway Station, Petworth, West Sussex GU28 0JF   Nearest Road A285

This unique building was once Petworth Railway Station, now it is perfect place to relax in colonial style splendour. Guests have their own sitting-room and entrance. Roaring log fires in the winter, and in the summer breakfast is served on the old platform. We are licensed, and Champagne Breakfast is available on request. Ideal for Petworth House, Arundel, and for exploring gorgeous local villages and antique shops. Excellent pub, a short walk. Special price winter breaks available. http:// www.old-station.co.uk

see PHOTO opposite

Mary Louise Rapley
Tel: 01798 342346
Fax: 01798 342346

B&B from £29pp, Rooms 2 double, both en-suite, No smoking or pets, Children over 10, Open all year except Christmas & New Year, Map Ref W

Playden Cottage Guesthouse, Military Road, Rye, East Sussex TN31 7NY   Nearest Road A259

On the old Saxon Shore, less than a mile from Rye Town and on what was once a busy fishing harbour, there is now only a pretty cottage with lovely gardens, a pond and an ancient right of way. The sea has long receded and sheltered by its own informal gardens. Playden Cottage looks over the River across sheep-studded Romney Marsh. ETB Highly Commended, AA Premier Selected and Recommended by "Which". It offers comfort, peace, a care for detail - and a very warm welcome.

see PHOTO on page 370

Sheelagh Fox
Tel: 01797 222234

B&B from £25pp, Dinner from £12.00, Rooms 2 twin, 1 double, all en-suite, Restricted smoking, Children over 12 years, No pets, Open all year, Map Ref X

*left, **The Old Railway Station,** Petworth - see details above*

Old Borough Arms, The Strand, Rye, East Sussex TN31 7DB　　　　　**Nearest Road M20**

A three hundred year old former sailors Inn now a family run licensed hotel situated adjacent to the cobbled streets and riverside walks of Rye. A flower decked patio overlooks the bustling Strand full of interesting antique centres. Breakfasts are served in our beamed dining room where a log fire is alight during the winter months. Via the M20 we are 40 minutes away from the Channel Tunnel and ferry ports of Dover and Folkestone and 11/2 hours from central London. EMail: Old.BoroughArms@BTInternet.com

Mrs Cox
Tel/Fax: 01797 222128

B&B from £25pp, Dinner from £8.50, Rooms 2 single, 1 twin, 5 double, 1 family, all en-suite, Restricted smoking, Children welcome, Pets by arrangement, Open all year except Christmas, Map Ref X

Little Orchard House, West Street, Rye, Sussex TN31 7ES　　　　　**Nearest Road A259,A268**

Little Orchard House is centrally situated in peaceful surroundings. Rebuilt in 1745, the house has been lovingly renovated over the years and retains it original fascinating character. All bedrooms are en-suite two with a 4 poster. There are personal antiques, paintings, books and bears throughout the house. There is a peaceful book room and a sitting room with an open fire. The generous breakfast provides as much as can be eaten at a time to suit you. Large walled garden available for guests' use. ETB Highly Commended.

Sara Brinkhurst
Tel: 01797 223831

B&B from £30pp, Rooms 2 double, 1 twin, Minimum age 12, Open all year, Map Ref X

Filsham Farm House, 111 Harley Shute Road, St Leonards on Sea, East Sussex TN38 8BY　　**A21/A27**

see PHOTO on page 371

An historic 17th century listed Sussex farm house, with old beams and a large inglenook fireplace, where a log fire burns at breakfast time in the winter months. The house is within easy reach of the town centre, sea and the surrounding countryside and is furnished with an interesting collection of antiques to provide a high standard of accommodation. All rooms have TV sets and tea/coffee making facilities and there is ample parking space at the rear of the house.

Barbara Yorke
Tel: 01424 433109
Fax: 01424 461061

B&B from £17.50pp, Rooms 1 twin, 2 double, 1 family, most en-suite, Restricted smoking, Pets restricted, Open all year except Christmas & New Year, Map Ref Y

Sliders Farm, Furners Green, Uckfield, Sussex TN22 3RT　　　　　**Nearest Road A275**

see PHOTO opposite

Sliders Farm is quietly situated, surrounded by fields and woodland within walking distance of Sheffield Park Gardens. The Bluebell Railway and Ashdown Forest. Gatwick, Ardingly Showground, Glyndebourne and Brighton are easily accessible. London 45 minutes away. The 30 acres of grounds and gardens contain swimming pool, tennis court and fishing lakes. All bedrooms have TV and tea/coffee making facilities. The guests' lounge and oak panelled dining room both have large inglenook fireplaces. A 400 year old barn contains two self-catering units. Plenty of parking.

Jean & David Salmon
Tel: 01825 790258
Fax: 01825 790258

B&B from £22pp, Dinner by arrangement, Rooms 1 twin, 2 double, all en-suite, Restricted smoking, Children welcome, No pets, Open all year except Christmas, Map Ref Z

*right, **Sliders Farm,** Uckfield - see details above*

WARWICKSHIRE & WEST MIDLANDS

The great forest of Arden once covered a large proportion of the county northwest of the River Avon, which is now the highly industrialised and densely populated Metropolitan county of West Midlands, consisting of seven districts; Birmingham, Coventry, Dudley, Sandwell, Solihull, Walsall and Wolverhampton. South of Coventry, itself a fascinating and ancient city, with its war-ruined medieval cathedral blending with Sir Basil Spence's innovative modern replacement, the visitor is faced with a wonderful selection of stately homes, palaces and manor houses. This is the very heart of England, and the holidaymaker could do worse than to select Warwick, the administrative centre, as the base for touring the delights of the county - and there are many.

It is believed that Ethelfleda, a daughter of Alfred the Great, built the first fortress here in a wood in 915AD, as a defence against the Danes. The great castle of Warwick the Kingmaker, with its two splendid towers, Caesar's Tower and Guy's Tower, dates from the early fourteenth century, and is best seen from Castle Bridge. The sumptuous and opulent interior is of the seventeenth and eighteenth centuries and is filled with treasures collected on the Grand Tour. The gardens are splendid, and include a re-created Victorian rose garden, the formal Peacock Gardens and a wonderful expanse of parkland. Warwick itself, although largely destroyed by a fire in 1694, contains some excellent buildings, particularly around

High Street and Northgate Street. The Lord Leycester Hospital, a spectacular half-timbered building of the fourteenth to fifteenth century was built originally for religious guilds, but since 1571 has been an almshouse. Whatever the attractions of glorious Warwick, only a short distance south-west is Stratford-upon-Avon, the birthplace of William Shakespeare. The town is dedicated to the Bard, and monuments to him and to his family are all around, and conveniently close. Within a small radius is Shakespeare's birthplace; Hall's Croft, the home of his daughter and her husband Dr. John Hall; Anne Hathaway's Cottage (though hardly most people's idea of a cottage) home of William's wife before her marriage; and Mary Arden's House, the home of Shakespeare's mother. The grand Memorial Theatre, the Stratford home of the Royal Shakespeare Company, stands very attractively by the Avon. To the south of Stratford-upon-Avon is Compton Wynyates, a quite remarkable Tudor house, claimed by many to be the most beautiful house in England, and scarcely changed since it was built in 1520. It is said that it was in Charlecote Park, with its fine lime avenue approach, that the young William Shakespeare was caught poaching deer, and that it was his banishment to London which established his career and fortune. Only the gatehouse of the 1550 mansion remains unaltered, the rest being reconstructed in the nineteenth century. Upton House, a delightful William and Mary mansion surrounded by lovely grounds, is in the valley south-west of Edge Hill, at the foot of which the first major battle of the Civil War took place in 1642.

To the east of Warwick is Royal Leamington Spa on the River Leam, whose chalybeate and saline springs made it a fashionable place to take the waters from the late eighteenth century. Queen Victoria designated the town a Royal spa following her visit in 1838. The Royal Pump Room was opened in 1814. The Parade, a magnificent example of Georgian architecture dates from around 1820. Kenilworth Castle, situated on the western edge of the town, built in Norman times, but much altered by Queen Elizabeth I's favourite, the Earl of Leicester, is the venue for events featuring medieval pageantry, music and drama. Now mostly an impressive ruin, the sixteenth century northern gatehouse survives, as well as John of Gaunt's banqueting hall.

Rugby, an important engineering centre since the arrival of the railway in the nineteenth century, is of course renowned for its public school founded in 1567. The school's most famous headmaster was Dr. Thomas Arnold, whose son the poet Matthew Arnold was a scholar at Rugby. Another well known scholar Thomas Hughes, described Dr. Arnold in his novel 'Tom Brown's Schooldays'.

Despite being known as the Black Country, there is a great deal to see and enjoy around the big cities, themselves no cultural backwater. There is Arbury Hall, the Gothic-style mansion with a large landscaped garden; Henley-in-Arden, a fine centre for walking by the River Alne; and Packwood House which has a quite remarkable seventeenth century garden of clipped yew trees depicting the Sermon on the Mount. - the list is seemingly endless. Certainly visitors would be well advised to plan their itinerary most carefully, as there are so many fascinating diversions.

WARWICKSHIRE &
WEST MIDLANDS

Places to Visit

Charlecote Park, *Charlecote* ~ an Elizabethan mansion by Sir Thomas Lucy, set in parkland filled with deer and Jacob sheep. The grounds were landscaped by Capability Brown and the house built in 1558 was altered and enlarged in the 19th century with some buildings remaining unchanged. On display is a collection of ceramics, lacquerware and furniture, much of which was collected by 18th century eccentric William Beckford.

Warwick Castle, *Warwick* ~ the original Norman castle was rebuilt in the 14th century when huge outer walls and towers were added. In the 17th and 18th century, the Greville family transformed it into a country house. In 1978, the owners of Madame Tussaud's bought the castle and set up a selection of wax figures to illustrate the castle's history.

Coventry Cathedral, *Coventry* ~ in 1940 the mediaeval cathedral was hit by German bombing raids. After the war the first totally modern cathedral, designed by Sir Basil Spence, was built alongside the ruins of the bombed building. Sir Jacob Epstein added sculptures of 'St Michael subduing the Devil, and Graham Sutherland did the tapestry 'Christ in Majesty'.

Wightwick Manor, *Wolverhampton* ~ begun in 1887, the house was influenced by William Morris, with many original Morris wallpapers and fabrics. There are also Pre-Raphaelite pictures, Kempe glass and de Morgan ware. The Victorian/ Edwardian garden has yew hedges and topiary, terraces and two pools.

Warwick Castle

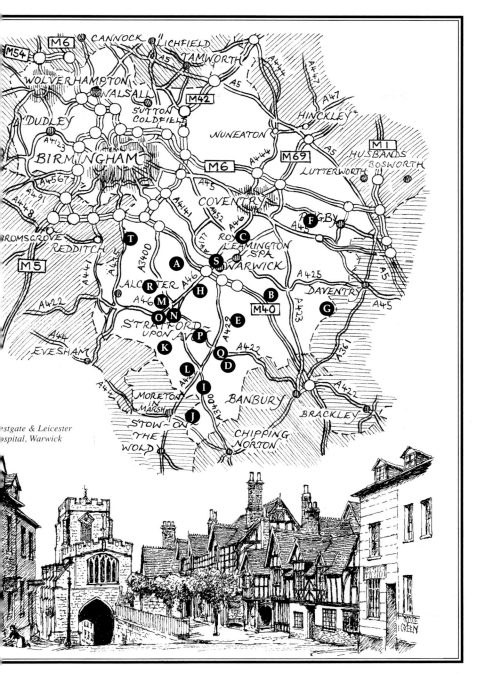

M54 M6 CANNOCK LICHFIELD TAMWORTH
A5
WOLVERHAMPTON WALSALL
DUDLEY SUTTON COLDFIELD M42 NUNEATON HINCKLEY A47
A4123 A5 HUSBANDS BOSWORTH M1
BIRMINGHAM M6 A444 M69 LUTTERWORTH
A4567 A45 COVENTRY
A491 A446 RUGBY F
A448 A4141 A452 A45
BROMSGROVE A4177 ROYAL LEAMINGTON SPA
REDDITCH T A3400 C
M5 A441 A S WARWICK A425 DAVENTRY
A422 ALCESTER A46 H DAVENTRY
A46 M B M40 A45
EVESHAM A44 O N E A423 G
STRATFORD-UPON-AVON P A361
K Q A422
L D A422
A44 I BANBURY A422
MORETON IN MARSH J BRACKLEY
STOW-ON-THE-WOLD CHIPPING NORTON

stgate & Leicester
ospital, Warwick

377

Woodside, Langley Road, Claverdon, Warwickshire CV35 8PJ   **Nearest Road A4189**

Set in 22 acres of conservation woodland and garden. All bedrooms are spacious, furnished cottage style with antiques and period furniture, and have tea/coffee making facilities, TV and radio. Lovely outlook over woodland and garden. Full central heating. large log fire with TV and video in comfortable lounge makes for a relaxed evening after a busy day and after a home cooked dinner served to order. Or visit one of the interesting eating places locally. Doreen and her Burmese mountain dog will give you a warm welcome.

Mrs Doreen Bromilow
Tel: 01926 842446

B&B from £18pp, Dinner from £12.50, Rooms 1 double, 1 single with shower, 2 twin with bathroom, 1 family en-suite, Restricted smoking, Pets by arrangement, Open all year except Christmas, Map Ref A

Crandon House, Avon Dassett, Leamington Spa, Warks CV33 0AA   **Nearest Rd B4100,A423,M40 J12**

Lovely farmhouse set in 20 acres with views over unspoilt countryside. The attractive bedrooms all have private or en-suite facilities, colour TV, tea/coffee and central heating. Guests dining room and 2 comfortable sitting rooms, 1 with colour TV and woodburning stove. Excellent breakfast menu offers traditional farmhouse or a selection of other dishes. Excellent pubs and restaurants nearby. Situated in a peaceful part of Warwickshire within easy reach of Stratford upon Avon, Warwick and Heritage Motor Centre and National Herb Centre. ETB 2 Crowns Highly Commended. Winter breaks.

David Lea & Deborah Lea
Tel: 01295 770652/07775 626458
Fax: 01295 770652

B&B from £19.50-£25pp, Rooms 3 double, 2 en-suite, 2 twin en-suite, Minimum age 10, Restricted smoking, Open all year except Christmas, Map Ref B

Stonehouse Farm, Leicester Lane, Cubbington Heath, Leamington Spa, Warks CV32 6QZ Nearest Rd A445

A delightful, Grade II Queen Anne farmhouse set within Warwickshire's unspoilt countryside, enjoying extensive views from all of its large and comfortable rooms. Only 2 miles from the Regency town of Royal Leamington Spa, 5 miles from Warwick, and 11/2 miles from the Royal Showground at Stoneleigh. The bedrooms are comfortable with tea/coffee making facilities and there is a guests' sitting room with television. Meals are served in the traditional dining room which overlooks mature gardens and orchard.

Mrs Kate Liggins
Tel: 01926 336370

B&B from £18.50pp, Evening meal from £8.50, Rooms 3 twin, 1 en-suite, Restricted smoking, Minimum age 2, Open all year except Christmas & New Year, Map Ref C

Nolands Farm, Oxhill, Warwickshire CV35 0RJ   **Nearest Road A422**

see PHOTO opposite

The farm is situated in a tranquil valley with fields, woods and wildlife. It is a working arable farm and offers the country lover a happy relaxing stay. The bedrooms, all en-suite with TV and hostess trays are mostly on the ground floor in tastefully restored annexed converted stables. There are romantic 4 poster bedrooms with bathroom. There is a licensed bar adjoining the garden conservatory. For the energetic, fly and coarse fishing is available, clay pigeon shooting, cycles for hire and riding nearby. Ample parking. Stratford 8 miles, Warwick 12 miles. Dinner by arrangement. EMail: nolandsfm@compuserve.com

Sue & Robin Hutsby
Tel: 01926 640309
Fax: 01926 641662

B&B from £18pp, Dinner from £16.95, Rooms 6 double, 1 family, 2 twin, all en-suite, Minimum age 7, Open all year, Map Ref D

*right, **Nolands Farm**, Oxhill - see details above*

Docker's Barn Farm, Oxhill Bridle Road, Pillerton Hersey, Warwick CV35 0QB

Docker's Barn is an idyllically situated old barn conversion surrounded by its own land. Handy for Warwick, Stratford, NEC, NAC, Cotswolds and Heritage Motor Centre. M40 J12 is six miles. The attractive, beamed en-suite bedrooms have hospitality trays and CTV, and the 4 poster suite has its own front door. Wildlife abounds and lovely walks lead from the Barn. We keep a few sheep, horses and hens. Service is friendly and attentive. French and Spanish are spoken.

Carolyn Howard
Tel: 01926 640475
Fax: 01926 641747

B&B from £19pp, Rooms 1 twin, 2 double, all en-suite, No smoking, Children over 8, Pets by arrangement, Open all year except Christmas, Map Ref E

Lawford Hill Farm, Lawford Heath Lane, nr Rugby, Warwickshire CV23 9HG　　　Nearest Road A428

We invite you to relax and enjoy our Georgian home set in a picturesque garden. Lawford Hill has much character, it is spacious for those seeking solitude yet sufficiently small and informal for those who wish to enjoy the company of their fellow guests. Our bedrooms, three in the main house and three in our converted stables are charmingly decorated and comfortably furnished. Some en-suite, colour television and all with tea and coffee making facilities. Perfectly placed for touring Stratford, Warwick and the lovely Cotswolds.

Don & Susan Moses
Tel: 01788 542001
Fax: 01788 537880

B&B from £21.50pp, Rooms 1 single, 1 twin, 3 double, 1 family, some en-suite, No smoking, Children & pets welcome, Open all year except Christmas & New Year, Map Ref F

Marston House, Priors Marston, Rugby, Warwickshire CV23 8RP　　　Nearest Road A361

see PHOTO opposite

Marston House is a stylish turn of the century family home furnished with antiques, situated in a conservation village of charm. Excellent base to explore Warwick, Stratford, Blenheim and the Cotswolds. Silverstone and Gaydon Motor Museum are also handy. TV in drawing room (guests lounge). Tea/coffee making facilities on request. Large car park. Tennis court and croquet lawn. One good pub in the village within walking distance. Our postal address is misleading, our location is between Banbury and Leamington Spa. £5 supplement for singles (adults).

Mrs K S Mahon
Tel: 01327 260297
Fax: 01327 262846

B&B from £22pp, Dinner from £18, Rooms 1 single for children, 1 twin with private bathroom, 1 double with private bathroom, No smoking, Children welcome, Pets by arrangement, Open all year, Map Ref G

The Old Rectory, Vicarage Lane, Sherbourne, Warwick CV35 8AB　　　Nearest Road A46,M40 (J15)

A licensed Georgian country house rich in beams, flagstones and inglenooks, perfectly situated between those two tourist honeypots of Warwick and Stratford-upon-Avon. 14 elegantly appointed en-suite rooms, antique brass beds; a romantic French bed and Victorian style bathrooms. The coach house is ideal for families, Spa bath and 4 poster available. Hearty English breakfasts and a la carte licensed restaurant and bar. Walled garden and safe parking in a courtyard, pretty with flower baskets. Telephones in bedrooms. Recommended by all major guides. AA QQQQ. ETB 3 Crowns. Which magazine Selected.

Ian & Dawn Kitchen
Tel: 01926 624562
Fax: 01926 624995

B&B from £26pp, Dinner a la carte, Rooms 4 single, 5 double, 5 twin, all en-suite, Pets by arrangement, Open all year except Christmas, Map Ref H

*right, **Marston House,** Priors Marston - see details above*

Wolford Fields, Shipston on Stour, Warwickshire CV36 5LT Nearest Road A44, A3400

A large Cotswold farmhouse and gardens built by Lord Campendown in 1857 and farmed by the Mawle family since 1901. The 3 comfortable bedrooms share 2 warmly decorated bathrooms which are fitted with power showers. Guests may relax in the pleasant TV lounge where tea, coffee and chocolate making facilities are available. Guests may also stroll in the large garden. Space available for car parking. Conveniently situated for Stratford-upon-Avon and the Cotswolds.

Richard Mawle
Tel: 01608 661301
Mobile: 0958 649306

B&B from £15, Rooms 2 double, 1 twin, No smoking, Open all year, Map Ref I

Lower Farm Barn, Great Wolford, Shipston on Stour, Warks CV36 5NQ Nearest Road A44, A3400

This lovely 100 year old converted barn stands in the small, peaceful Warwickshire village of Great Wolford. The property retains much of its original form including exposed beams and ancient stonework. Now modernised and very comfortable. The beautifully furnished bedrooms have tea/coffee making facilities. A warm welcoming, sitting room with TV is for guests' use. Great Wolford has a lovely old pub, only 5 minutes walk from Lower Farm Barn, where traditional home made food is served. Convenient for Warwick and Stratford upon Avon.

Mrs Rebecca Mawle
Tel: 01608 674435

B&B from £17.50pp, Rooms 1 double, 1 en-suite family, Restricted smoking, Pets by arrangement, Open all year, Map Ref J

Folly Farm Cottage, Ilmington, Shipston on Stour, Warwickshire CV36 4LJ Nearest Road A3400, A429

see PHOTO opposite

Large Cotswold country cottage surrounded by English cottage gardens in delightful village nr Stratford on Avon, Warwick and Cotswold villages. Romantic, luxury B&B, en-suite double or king size 4 poster rooms with TV, video, tea tray. Cottage memorabilia, lamps and flowers give an old world charm. Breakfast may be served in the privacy of your room overlooking cottage gardens. For the really lazy, self catering Honeymoon apartment suite with double whirlpool bath, breakfast hamper provided, true luxury for that special occasion. Brochure available, http://www.follypages.mcmail.com

Malcolm & Sheila Lowe
Tel: 01608 682425
Fax: 01608 682425

B&B from £25-£35pp, Rooms 1 double, 3 four poster's, all en-suite, No smoking, children or pets, Open all year except Christmas & New Year, Map Ref K

Blackwell Grange, Blackwell, Shipston-on-Stour, Warwickshire CV36 4PF Nearest Road A3400/A429

Blackwell Grange is a Grade II listed farmhouse, part of which dates from 1603. It is situated on the edge of a peaceful village with an attractive garden and views of the Ilmington Hills. The spacious bedrooms are all en-suite and have tea/coffee making facilities (one ground floor bedroom suitable for guests with disabilities). A stone flagged dining room with inglenook fireplace and guests drawing room with a log fire in winter and deep sofas to sink into, make it a very relaxing place to stay.

Mrs L Vernon Miller
Tel/Fax: 01608 682 357

B&B from £28pp, Dinner by arrangement, Rooms 1 single, 1 twin, 2 double, all en-suite, Restricted smoking, Children from 12, No pets, Open mid February - December, Map Ref L

*right, **Folly Farm Cottage**, Ilmington - see details above*

Nando's, 18-20 Evesham Place, Stratford-upon-Avon, Warks CV37 6HT　　　Nearest Road A439

A Victorian town house where Pat and Peter Short extend a warm welcome to all their guests. We pride ourselves on our quality of food and high standard of hygiene. Nando's is conveniently located only minutes away from the Royal Shakespeare Theatre. 20 rooms, 17 with en-suite facilities and all with colour TV and tea/coffee making facilities. A residents TV lounge is also available. Nando's makes the perfect base for visiting the many places of interest in the town and surrounding area.

Pat & Peter Short
Tel: 01789 204907
Fax: 01789 204907

B&B from £15pp, Dinner from £8 by request, Rooms 6 single, 4 twin, 6 double, 4 family, most en-suite, Restricted smoking, Children welcome, Pets by arrangement, Open all year Map Ref N

Ravenhurst, 2 Broad Walk, Stratford-upon-Avon, Warks CV37 6HS　　　Junction of B439 and A4390

Victorian town house ideally situated in a quiet part of town, centrally located for places of interest. Five minutes to theatre and town centre and ten minutes walk to railway station. Very popular with theatre goers. Short drive to Cotswold and Warwick Castle. Pleasant bedrooms are all en-suite with tea/coffee making facilities, and colour TV. Four poster bed available. Enjoy a 'Ravenhurst' substantial English breakfast. The Workman family, born and bred Stratfordians, offer a warm welcome and plenty of local knowledge. All major credit cards accepted.

The Workman Family
Tel: 01789 292515

B&B from £19, Rooms 1 twin, 4 double, all en-suite, No smoking, Open all year, Map Ref N

Parkfield Guest House, 3 Broad Walk, Stratford-upon-Avon, CV37 6HS　　　Nearest Road B439

Parkfield is an elegant Victorian house in a quiet road, yet only a few minutes walk to the theatres and town centre. Most rooms are en-suite with TV, clock/radio, hot drinks and central heating. Breakfast is ample with a wide choice including vegetarian, and are served on fine china. Warwick Castle is 7 miles drive away and the Cotswolds are only a short drive. The rail station is 10 minutes walk with connections to London, Warwick and Birmingham. Brochure with pleasure on request. AA QQQ, ETB Commended.

Roger & Joanna Pettitt
Tel/Fax: 01789 293313

B&B from £18pp, Rooms 1 single, 1 twin, 4 double, 1 family, most en-suite, No smoking, Children from 5, No pets, Open all year, Map Ref N

Penshurst Guest House, 34 Evesham Place, Stratford-upon-Avon CV37 6HT　　　Nearest Road A439

You'll get an exceptionally warm welcome from Karen and Yannick at this prettily refurbished, totally non-smoking, Victorian townhouse, situated just 5 minutes walk from the town centre. The bedrooms have been individually decorated and are well equipped with many little extras apart from the usual TV and beverages. Perhaps you'd like a lie-in while on holiday? No problem!! Delicious English or Continental breakfasts are served from 7.00am right up until 10.30am. Home-cooked evening meals by arrangement. Facilities for disabled. Brochure available. ETB Listed Commended.

Mrs Karen Cauvin
Tel: 01789 205259
Fax: 01789 295322

B&B from £15pp, Dinner from £7.50, Rooms 2 single, 2 twin, 2 double, 2 family, some en-suite No smoking, Open all year, Map Ref N

right, **Victoria Spa Lodge,** *Stratford upon Avon - see details on page 386*

Moonraker House, 40 Alcester Road, Stratford-upon-Avon, Warwickshire CV37 9DB   Nearest Road A422

Pretty hanging baskets adorn Moonraker which is situated on the North West side of town and easy 5-10 minutes stroll from town centre. Moonraker is 2 separate buildings offering 19 beautifully decorated en-suite rooms with TV, tea/coffee making facilities. The charming 4-poster rooms also have a garden terrace. Moonraker II has the advantage of a spacious sun lounge an excellent location from which to explore Stratford and its many attractions. EMail: moonraker.spencer@virgin.net

Mauveen & Michael Spencer
Tel: 01789 267115/299346
Fax: 01789 295504

B&B from £23.50pp, Rooms 3 twin, 14 double, 2 family, all en-suite, Restricted smoking, Children over 6, Pets restricted, Open all year, Map Ref O

Victoria Spa Lodge, Bishopton Lane, Stratford-upon-Avon, CV37 9QY   Nearest Road A3400,A46

see PHOTO on page 385

An attractive Victorian building, originally, a Spa opened in 1837. Queen Victoria graciously gave it her name and her coat of arms is built into the gables. Situated in a country setting overlooking Stratford canal. Pleasant walks along the canal tow path to Stratford and other villages. Bruce Bairnsfather (creator of "Old Bill" during the Great War) lived here as also did Sir Barry Jackson founder of the Birmingham Repertory Theatre. Comfortable bedrooms equipped with hostess tray, TV, hair dryer and radio/alarm. Parking. http://www.scoot.co.uk/victoria_spa/ EMail: ptozer@victoriaspalodge.demon.co.uk

Paul & Dreen Tozer
Tel: 01789 267985
Fax: 01789 204728

B&B from £25pp, Rooms 1 twin, 3 double, 3 family, all en-suite, No smoking, Children welcome, No pets, Open all year, Map Ref N

Grove Farm, Ettington, Stratford-upon-Avon, Warwickshire CV37 7NX   Nearest Road A422,A429

Lovely, comfortable old farmhouse dating from the 1790's with a friendly and warm welcome assured. Rooms are furnished with antiques. Log fires and excellent views are some of the delights awaiting you at Grove Farm. This a a 500 acre working farm complete with 2 labrador's and a spaniel. Guests are welcome to meander through the fields and woods. The bedrooms are delightful and have private bathroom facilities. The Cotswold and Stratford upon Avon are within easy travelling distance and the local inns serve delicious food.

Bob & Meg Morton
Tel: 01789 740228

B&B from £19pp, Rooms 1 twin, 2 double, all en-suite, Restricted smoking, Minimum age 12, Pets by arrangement, Open all year except Christmas, Map Ref P

Burton Farm, Bishopton, Stratford-upon-Avon, Warwickshire CV37 0RW   Nearest Road A46

see PHOTO opposite

Burton Farm is a 140 acre working farm. Approx 2 miles from Stratford. The farmhouse and barns date from Tudor time and are steeped in the character for which the area is, world famous. The accommodation, all of which has en-suite facilities; enjoys an environment of colourful gardens and pools which support wildlife and a collection of unusual birds and plants. The friendly atmosphere and quiet retreat will ensure a pleasant stay. Antique furniture enhances the charming home.

Eileen & Tony Crook
Tel: 01789 293338
Fax: 01789 262877

B&B from £22.50pp, Rooms 1 single, 1 twin, 2 double, 1 family, all en-suite, No smoking or pets, Children welcome, Open all year except Christmas & New Year, Map Ref M

*right, **Burton Farm,** near Stratford upon Avon - see details above*

Thornton Manor, Ettington, Stratford-upon-Avon, Warwickshire CV37 7PN   Nearest Road A429

16th century stone manor house overlooking open countryside and woodland on a working farm. Ideal for relaxing, walking and touring. Tea/coffee facilities in bedrooms, and a log fire with a television and piano. Conveniently situated for Stratford-upon-Avon, Cotswolds, Warwick, Banbury and NEC.

Mrs G Hutsby
Tel: 01789 740210

B&B from £18.50pp, Rooms 1 twin, 2 double en-suite or private facilities, Restricted smoking, Minimum age 5, Open March - mid December except Christmas & New Year, Map Ref Q

Pear Tree Cottage, Church Road, Wilmcote, Stratford-upon-Avon, Warwickshire CV37 9UX   A3400

The stone and half timbered house of great character and period charm is quietly situated in its country garden overlooking Mary Arden's house. Three and a half miles from Stratford and seven miles from Warwick. All rooms have individual luxury furnishings and private facilities. There is plenty of parking and pubs to eat at within walking distance. Close to major attractions yet away from the bustle of towns. We offer a cosy and welcoming B&B base for long or short stays, when touring or visiting the NEC.

Margaret & Ted Mander
Tel: 01789 205889
Fax: 01789 262862

B&B from £24pp, Rooms 2 twin, 4 double, 1 family, all en-suite, No smoking or pets, Children over 3, Open all year except Christmas & New Year, Map Ref R

Ardendane Manor, Outhill, Studley, Warwickshire B80 7DT   Nearest Road A4189

Ardendane Manor is a non-smoking house set in 25 acres. Luxury double and twin accommodation with private facilities, central heating, tea/coffee making trays and TV. Situated on the A4189 halfway between Redditch and Henley-in-Arden. Close to NAC, NEC, ICC. Access to motorway network (M42 junction 3).

Michael & Sue Neale
Tel: 01527 852808

B&B from £45 single, £60 double, Rooms 1 twin, 1 double, both en-suite, No smoking, No children, No pets, Open 1 January - 23 December, Map Ref T

Forth House, 44 High Street, Warwick, Warwickshire CV34 4AX   Nearest Road A429

Our rambling Georgian family home within the old town walls of Warwick provides two peaceful guest suites hidden away at the back. One family sized ground floor suite opens onto the garden whilst other overlooks it. Both en-suite with private sitting rooms and dining rooms. TV, fridges, hot and cold drink facilities. Ideally situated for holidays or business. Stratford, Oxford, Birmingham and Cotswold villages within easy reach. Breakfasts, full English or continental at times agreed with our guests. J15 of M40 two miles away.

Mrs Elizabeth Draisey
Tel: 01926 401512
Fax: 01926 490809

B&B from £25pp, Rooms 1 double, 1 family, both en-suite, No smoking, Children & pets welcome, Open all year, Map Ref S

Come live with me, and be my love,
And we will all the pleasures prove,
That valleys, groves, hills and fields,
Woods or steepy mountain yields.

THE PASSIONATE SHEPHERD TO HIS LOVE
CHRISTOPHER MARLOWE 1564-93

WILTSHIRE

The inland county of Wiltshire has been described as a lonely county, dominated by the vast chalk-lands of Salisbury Plain, a region of strange monuments and scattered villages. Salisbury is certainly the jewel in the county's crown, with a cathedral which is the pinnacle of the early English style. It is sited below the Plain where three chalk streams, the Nadder, the upper Avon and the Bourne join. Salisbury is quite unlike many medieval cities, which are usually an unplanned jumble of quaint streets clustering under their cathedral. Old Sarum - medieval Latin for Salisbury - was built on the site of an old Iron Age hill fort, but the thirteenth century builders of its cathedral found the position too windy and waterless, so they transferred to the watermeadows a couple of miles away and planned Salisbury on a grid system around it. Regarded as one of the most beautiful cities in England, the city as well as the surrounding countryside is dominated by its magnificent cathedral, its slender spire rising higher than any other in England. The body of the building was finished in 1258, the spire was added some fifty years later. The octagonal chapter house has a remarkable medieval carved frieze depicting scenes from the books of Genesis and Exodus, and contains the finest of four manuscripts of the Magna Carta. Britain's earliest clock - faceless, as its sole purpose is to strike a bell in the tower - dates from 1386 and is in the north aisle of the nave. The cathedral boasts the largest and finest close in the country, including Malmesbury House built in 1327 and Mompesson House, a fine Queen Anne house with a walled garden and a rare collection of English drinking glasses.

Wilton, a small town close to Salisbury, has long been associated with the manufacture of high quality carpets. The Royal Wilton Carpet Museum opened in 1983 explains the history of carpet making. Nearby is Wilton House, originally a Tudor house built on the site of Wilton Abbey. The house is famous for its elegant 'double cube' room, built to hold a magnificent collection of paintings by Van Dyck. The priceless Wilton Dyptich was here for two centuries before going to the National Gallery. Strangely enough, much of the D-Day planning during World War II took place here.

If the visitors can drag themselves away from the fascination of Salisbury and its surrounding district, a little way to the north is Stonehenge, Britain's most famous prehistoric stone circle, standing on Salisbury Plain. Established around 2,800 BC, with local Sarsen stones and stones from the Preseli Hills of Wales, which were added later, the whole was eventually remodelled during the Bronze Age. Its purpose remains a mystery to this day....its central axis aligns with the sun on Midsummer's Day, so the arrangement may perform a calendar function. Whatever its true function theories abound, even to suggesting that it was built by beings from outer space, from Atlantis, or by King Arthur! The monument attracts vast numbers of visitors at the time of the summer solstice.

To the north of Stonehenge is one of the largest and most important Stone Age monuments in Europe. Constructed before 2000 BC at Avebury, is a ring of over a hundred standing stones of sandstone from the North West Downs, each weighing up to fifty tons. The West Kennet Avenue of stones, now partly restored, stretches two and a half miles south, and ends in a double circle of stones known as the Sanctuary.

Within a short distance of this is Silbury Hill, the largest prehistoric mound in Europe. It has been calculated that it would have taken seven hundred men over ten years to build.

Stourhead is one of England's first Palladian mansions. Built by the successful banker Henry Hoare and completed in 1785, it is most famous for its quite remarkable gardens, probably the finest landscape design of the eighteenth century. Inspired by the Grand Tour, in 1741 Henry Hoare's son, with the architect Henry Flitcroft set about creating an exotic landscape scattered with classical follies - the temple of Apollo and Flora, a grotto, a pantheon - he dammed the River Stour and constructed the famous picturesque curving stone bridge across the newly formed lake. The mansion is filled with many treasures, including carvings by Grinling Gibbons, paintings by Angelica Kauffman and furniture by Chippendale.

Warminster at the head of the lovely Wylye Valley, is a handsome town of eighteenth-century houses and an excellent centre for touring the area. There are fine views from Cley Hill on the ancient Ridgeway. Nearby is Longleat House built for John Thynne in 1580,

the earliest and one of the most attractive Elizabethan mansions, greatly embellished by the fourth Marquess of Bath after his Grand Tour. The mansion looks out over a park made hugely popular by its safari park and many other modern attractions. The grounds, landscaped by Capability Brown include the world's largest maze.

With such attractions the holidaymaker should not lose sight of the pleasures of Georgian Marlborough, the Savernake Forest and the delightful Marlborough Downs; Chippenham, and Malmesbury high above the rivers Avon and Inglebourne; and Castle Combe, one of the most picturesque villages in England.

WILTSHIRE

Places to Visit

Avebury Stone Circle, *Avebury* ~ built around 2500 BC, the stone circle surrounds the village of Avebury and was probably a religious centre. Superstitious villagers smashed many of the stones in the 18th century believing the circle to have been a place of pagan sacrifice.

Dyrham Park, *Chippenham* ~ there has been a deer park here from Saxon times, but the present house dates from the time of William and Mary and much of its contents reflect this period. There is a collection of Delft, and painting by Dutch masters.

Lacock Abbey, *near Chippenham* ~ founded in 1232, it was converted to a country house in the 16th century. At the gates is the Fox Talbot Museum of Photography about early photography.

Longleat House, *Warminster* ~ the house was started in 1540 when John Thynn bought the ruins of a priory on the site. Over the years, its owners have each added their own eccentric touches. The grounds were landscaped by Capability Brown and were turned into a safari park in 1966 where lions, tigers and other wild animals may roam freely.

Silbury Hill, near Beckingham ~ the largest man-made mound in Europe. It was constructed in three stages around 2800 BC. Its purpose is not known as no remains have ever been found in this one hundred and thirty feet high mound.

Stourhead, *near Warminster* ~ the gardens were started in the 1740's by Henry Hoare who inherited the estate and turned it into a work of art. He created a lake surrounded by rare trees and plants, Neo-Classical temples, grottos and bridges. The house dates from 1724 and was reconstructed in 1902 after a fire. It contains Chippendale furniture and an art collection.

The Kennet & Avon Canal near Devizes

392

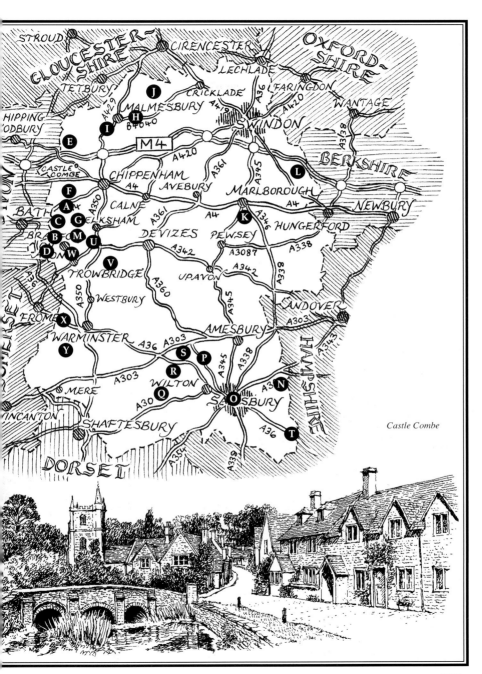

STROUD

GLOUCESTERSHIRE

CIRENCESTER

OXFORDSHIRE

LECHLADE

TETBURY

CRICKLADE

FARINGDON

WANTAGE

J

MALMESBURY

A429

A36

A419

A420

A338

H
B4040

I

SWINDON

E

M4

A420

BERKSHIRE

CASTLE COMBE

CHIPPENHAM

A361

A345

L

MARLBOROUGH

A4

NEWBURY

F

A4

AVEBURY

A350

CALNE

A4

A

C

G

MELKSHAM

A361

K

A346

HUNGERFORD

BATH

DEVIZES

PEWSEY

B

M

U

BRA

D

W

A342

A3087

A338

TROWBRIDGE

A360

UPAVON

A342

A338

V

A345

ANDOVER

WESTBURY

A303

A350

AMESBURY

A303

FROME

X

WARMINSTER

A36

A303

HAMPSHIRE

Y

S

P

A345

A338

A343

R

A3

N

MERE

A303

WILTON

Q

A30

O

SALISBURY

INCANTON

SHAFTESBURY

A354

A36

T

A339

DORSET

Castle Combe

Hillcrest, Bradford Road, Winsley, Bradford on Avon, Wiltshire BA15 2HN   **Nearest Road B3108**

AA QQQQQ Premier Selected. Situated 6 miles from Bath and 2 miles from the pretty town of Bradford on Avon. 'Hillcrest' is surrounded by old Drystone walls with magnificent views across the Avon valley. Both double bedrooms are fully en-suite and have colour TV and tea/coffee making facilities. 'Hillcrest' has a south facing terrace and guests sitting room. Our A la'carte menu offers an excellent choice for breakfast. A quaint 17th century village pub selling excellent food is only 10 minutes walk away. Hillcrest is strictly non-smoking.

Barbara & Rob Litherland
Tel: 01225 868677
Fax: 01225 868655

B&B from £22.50pp, Dinner from £16-£20, Rooms 2 double, both en-suite, No smoking or pets, Children over 7, Open all year except Christmas & New Year, Map Ref B

Fern Cottage, Monkton Farleigh, Bradford-on-Avon, Wiltshire BA15 2QJ   **Nearest Road A363**

Delightful stone cottage dating from 1680, in quiet conservation Village. Oakbeams, open fire, antiques and family heirlooms. Three beautifully appointed bedrooms with private bath/shower, colour TV, tea/coffee facilities. Traditional English breakfast is served at a large attractively arranged table and there is a lovely Conservatory where guests may relax and look out over a well maintained garden. No smoking. Ample parking. Local Inn, 100 yards away, serves excellent fare. Many places of interest within a few minutes drive.

Christopher & Jenny Valentine
Tel: 01225 859412
Fax: 01225 859018

B&B from £25pp, Rooms 3 double, all en-suite, No smoking, Children welcome, No pets, Open all year, Map Ref C

Burghope Manor, Winsley, Bradford-on-Avon, Wiltshire BA15 2LA   **Nearest Road A36**

This historic 13th century family home is set in beautiful countryside on the edge of the village of Winsley, 5 miles from Bath and 1 1/2 miles from Bradford on Avon. Although steeped in history, it is first and foremost a living family home, which has been carefully modernised so that the wealth of historical features may compliment the present day comforts which include full central heating and en-suite bathrooms with bath and shower. Colour TV and tea/coffee making facilities.

see PHOTO opposite

Elizabeth & John Denning
Tel: 01225 723557
Fax: 01225 723113

B&B from £35pp, Rooms 3 twin, 2 double, 2 family, all en-suite, No smoking, Children over 10 years, No pets, Open all year except Christmas & New year, Map Ref D

Manor Farm, Alderton, Chippenham, Wiltshire SN14 6NL   **Nearest Road B4040**

Manor farm is a beautiful 17th century farmhouse. It may be found nestling near the church in picturesque Alderton. Home to the Lippiatt family the house offers warmth and comfort coupled with high standard in a relaxed setting. The lovely bedrooms are spacious and well equipped, with delightful views. The farm is only 4 miles from junction 17 and 18 of the M4. Bath, Malmesbury, Badminton and Castle Combe are all a short drive away. We have a selection of super English country pubs nearby.

Jeffrey & Victoria Lippiatt
Tel/Fax: 01666 840271

B&B from £30pp, Rooms 1 twin, 2 double, all en-suite, Restricted smoking, Children from 6, Pets restricted, Open all year except Christmas and New Year, Map Ref E

*left, **Burghope Manor,** Winsley - see details above*

Wiltshire

Pickwick Lodge Farm, Corsham, Wiltshire SN13 0PS   Nearest Road M4-J17, A4

Enjoy a stay at our beautiful home set in wonderful countryside where you can take a short stroll or longer walk and see rabbits, pheasant and occasional deer, or relax in our garden, yet only 15 minutes drive from bath. Ideally situated to visit Lacock, Castle Combe, Avebury, Stonehenge, many National Trust properties or explore some of the idyllic villages and have lunch or supper at a quaint pub. 2 well appointed and tastefully furnished bedrooms, refreshment trays with home-made biscuits. Start the day with a hearty delicious breakfast using local produce.

Mrs Gill Stafford
Tel: 01249 712207
Fax: 01249 701904

B&B from £18pp, Rooms 1 twin, 2 double, en-suite or private bathroom, No smoking, Children welcome, No pets, Open all year except Christmas and New Year, Map Ref F

Owl House, Kingsdown, nr Box, Corsham, Wiltshire SN13 8BB   Nearest Road A4

Breakfast on the high terrace overlooking the wonderful spectacle of Bath in the distance and the Avon valley. Enjoy the exotic Asian art displayed in Owl House and relax in the spacious en-suite bedrooms. Wander to the local pub for an excellent meal. Admire the splendour of Bath and explore the picturesque local villages. Adjacent to golf course. Lovely walks. Guests frequently comment on great hospitality, excellent breakfasts, and superb views. TV, tea and coffee in all rooms. Unlimited parking. EMail: venus@zetnet.co.uk

Anne Venus
Tel: 01225 743883
Fax: 01225 744450

B&B from £25pp, rooms 1 single, 1 twin, 1 double/family, all en-suite, No smoking or pets, Children welcome, Open all year, Map Ref A

Hatt Farm, Old Jockey, Box, Corsham, Wiltshire SN13 8DJ   Nearest Road A365, B3109

Extremely comfortable Georgian farmhouse in peaceful surroundings, far from the madding crowd. A scrumptious breakfast is served overlooking beautiful views of the rolling Wiltshire countryside. What can be nicer than sitting by a log fire in winter or enjoying the spacious garden in summer? Lovely walks and good golfing nearby. Ideally situated for touring the Cotswolds or visiting the endless delights of the relatively undiscovered county of Wiltshire. All this yet only 15 minutes away is the city of Bath. West Country Tourist Board 2 Crowns Commended.

Carol & Michael Pope
Tel: 01225 742989
Fax: 01225 742779

B&B from £20pp, Rooms 1 en-suite twin, 1 double/family with private bathroom, Restricted smoking, Children welcome, No pets, Open all year except Christmas & New Year, Map Ref G

Heatherly Cottage, Ladbrook Lane, Gastard, near Corsham, Wiltshire SN13 9PE   Nearest Road A4, A350

Delightful 17th century cottage in a quiet country lane with 2 acres and ample parking, overlooking open countryside. The accommodation, with separate entrance, has three well appointed and tastefully furnished bedrooms with colour TV and tea/coffee making facilities. The cottage is located eight miles from the M4 and nine miles from Bath. Ideal for visiting Avebury, Stonehenge, the National Trust village of Lacock and Lacock Abbey, Castle Combe, Bowood House, Corsham and Corsham Court and other historic places of interest. Excellent pubs nearby for evening meals.

Peter & Jenny Daniel
Tel: 01249 701402
Fax: 01249 701412

B&B from £19pp, Rooms 1 twin en-suite, 2 double en-suite, No smoking, Children welcome from 8 years, No pets, Open all year except Christmas and New Year, Map Ref G

*right, **Clench Farmhouse**, near Marlborough - see details on page 398*

Stonehill Farm, Charlton, Malmesbury, Wiltshire SN16 9DY   Nearest Road B4040

STOP! you've found us!!! 15th century Cotswold stone farmhouse on family run dairy farm in lush rolling countryside on the Wiltshire/Gloucestershire border. Three pretty rooms, 1 en-suite all with hospitality trays. Wonderful breakfasts, friendly welcome and pets can come too. Ideal for 1 night or several days. Oxford, Bath, Startford upon Avon, Stonehenge and the delightful Cotswold hills and villages are all within easy reach by car. Hope to see you soon.

Mrs Edwards
Tel/Fax: 01666 823310   B&B from £17.50pp, Rooms 2 double 1 twin, Open all Year, Map Ref H

Manor Farm, Corston, Malmesbury, Wiltshire SN16 0HF   Nearest Road A429

Relax and unwind in this charming award winning 17th century farmhouse on a working dairy arable farm. Six spacious tastefully furnished bedrooms, four en-suite, all with tea/coffee making facilities, radio and TV. A beautiful lounge with inglenook fireplace as well as a secluded garden for guests' use. Meals available in the local pub within walking distance an ideal base for one night or longer stays for exploring the Cotswolds, Bath, Stonehenge, Avebury Lacock and many stately homes. Children over 10 years.

Mrs Ross Eavis
Tel: 01666 822148
Fax: 01666 826565   B&B from £21pp, Rooms 1 single, 1 twin, 3 double, 1 family, some en-suite, No smoking or pets, Children over 10, Open all year except Christmas & New Year, Map Ref I

Flisteridge Cottage, Flisteridge Road, Upper Minety, Malmesbury, Wiltshire SN16 9PS   A429, B4040

Meander through the leafy country lanes where a warm welcome awaits you at Flisteridge Cottage. A truly peaceful retreat set in an acre of garden surrounded by farmland and ancient woodland. The three pretty bedrooms, one with private bathroom, have TV and tea making. Sitting room with TV and log burner in winter. Choice of delicious breakfasts, home made preserves. Excellent food at nearby villages. Ample parking. Ideal touring base. Bath, Cotswolds or just walk in the Cotswold country park. Golf, fishing in vicinity.

Fay Toop-Rose
Tel: 01666 860343   B&B from £18-£22pp, Rooms 1 twin, 2 double (1 en-suite), No smoking, Children over 11, Pets restricted, Open all year, Map Ref J

Clench Farmhouse, Clench, Marlborough, Wiltshire SN8 4NT   Nearest Road A345, A346

see PHOTO on page 397

Attractive 18th century farmhouse in its own grounds with lovely views and surrounded by farmland. There are 3 double bedrooms each with their own bathroom (2 of which are en-suite). The house has a happy and relaxed atmosphere and a warm welcome awaits guests. There is a tennis court, heated pool and croquet lawn for guests use. Delicious dinners are offered by prior arrangement. We also have a 2 bedroom and 2 bathroom self catering cottage. Lovely walks and within easy reach of Avebury, Stonehenge, Oxford, Salisbury and Bath.

Mrs Clarissa Roe
Mobile: 0374 784601
Tel: 01672 810264
Fax: 01672 811458   B&B from £22pp, Dinner from £18, Rooms 1 single, 1 twin, 1 twin/double, 1 double, some en-suite, Children welcome, Pets by arrangement, Open all year, Map Ref K

Marridge Hill, Ramsbury, Marlborough, Wiltshire SN8 2HG   **Nearest Road B4192, M4**

A mainly Victorian family home set in glorious countryside, yet only 1 hour's drive from Heathrow Airport. You will be warmly welcomed into a relaxed, informal atmosphere. 3 comfortable, attractive bedrooms (one with spacious en-suite facilities) and both bathrooms have power showers. Pleasant sitting room and dining room, books galore and an acre of well kept garden. Ideal base for touring this historic area, including Neolithic Avebury, Salisbury, Bath, Oxford and the Cotswolds. Good pubs and restaurants nearby. Car Parking. ETB 2 Crowns Highly Commended. EMail: dando@impedaci.demon.co.uk

Mrs Judy Davies
Tel: 01672 520237
Fax: 01672 520053

B&B from £19pp, Rooms 3 twin, 1 en-suite, No smoking, Minimum age 5, Pets by arrangement, Open all year except Christmas & New Year, Map Ref L

Frying Pan Farm, Broughton Gifford, Melksham, Wiltshire SN12 8LL   **Nearest Road A350, B3107**

Frying Pan Farm is a cosy 17th century farmhouse overlooking meadowland with spacious garden with ample parking. The accommodation is tastefully furnished en-suite rooms with colour TV, tea and coffee making facilities. Guests own lounge with amply stocked book case. We are situated to the east of Bath. Ideal for visiting Lacock, Bradford on Avon, Caen Hill, Flight of canal locks, also many National Trust Properties. Good pub in the village. 1 mile away.

Ralph & Barbara Pullen
Tel: 01225 702343
Fax: 01225 793652

B&B from £19pp, Rooms 1 twin, 1 double, both en-suite, No smoking or pets, Children welcome, Open all year except Christmas & New Year, Map Ref M

The Beadles, Middleton, Middle Winterslow, Wiltshire SP5 1QS   **Nearest Road A30**

Delightful Georgian-style residence in quiet village, 7 miles east of Salisbury. Tastefully decorated. Beautiful drawing room and well equipped en-suite bedrooms. Breakfast and evening meals served in elegant dining room or conservatory. Special diets catered for. Non smoking household. Collection from airports. Briefing on routes to take and what to see. Tours of gardens in Wessex. TV and tea/coffee making facilities in rooms. Car parking on property. Warmth and tranquillity abound in this welcoming home. AA Premier Selected 5Q's. ETB Highly Commended 3 Crowns.

David & Anne Yuille-Baddeley
Tel/Fax: 01980 862922

B&B from £25pp, Dinner from £17.50, Rooms 2 twin, 1 double, all en-suite, No smoking, Children over 4 welcome, No pets, Open all year, Map Ref N

Farthings, 9 Swaynes Close, Salisbury, Wiltshire SP1 3AE   **Nearest Road A30**

Central but very quiet, Farthings is the charming home of Mrs Gill Rodwell. Parking is no problem in this peaceful Close. The comfortable, nicely furnished, bedrooms all have tea/coffee making facilities, and there is a good choice of breakfast. The breakfast room, with its interesting collection of old family photos, opens onto a delightful garden. This is an ideal base for visiting this old Cathedral/market town and the surrounding area.

Mrs Gill Rodwell
Tel/Fax: 01722 330749

B&B from £18pp, Rooms 2 single, 1 twin, 1 double, twin & double rooms are en-suite, No smoking, Open all year, Map Ref O

The Mill House, *near Salisbury - see details opposite*

The Mill House, Berwick St James, near Salisbury, Wiltshire SP3 4TS   Nearest Road A303, A36

Stonehenge 3 miles, Diana welcomes you to the Mill House set in acres of nature reserve abounding in wild flowers and infinite peace. An island paradise with the River Till running through the working mill and beautiful garden. Diana's old fashioned roses long to see you as do the lovely walks; Antiquities and Houses. Built by the miller in 1785, the bedrooms all with tea/coffee making facilities, and TV, command magnificent views. Fishing or swimming in the mill pool and close to golf courses and riding. Attention to healthy and organic food. Sample superb cuisine at Boot Inn, Berwick St James.

see PHOTO opposite

Diana Gifford Mead
Tel: 01722 790331

B&B from £23pp, Rooms 2 single, 2 twin, 4 en-suite double, Minimum age 5, Open all year, Map Ref P

Morris' Farmhouse, Baverstock, near Dinton, Salisbury, Wiltshire SP3 5EL   Nearest Road Hindon Road

100 year old farmhouse with attractive garden set in open countryside. Very peaceful with homely and friendly atmosphere. Plenty of car parking. Small guest sitting room with TV. Breakfast served in south facing conservatory. Tea, coffee and hot chocolate making facilities in each room. Excellent pub 2 minutes walk for evening meals. Local attractions include Wilton House and Wilton carpet factory 4 miles; Salisbury with Cathedral and Museum 7 miles; Old Sarum 9 miles; Stonehenge 12 miles; Stourhead 15 miles; Longleat Safari Park 15 miles.

Martin & Judith Marriott
Tel/Fax: 01722 716874

B&B from £18pp, Rooms 1 twin, 1 double, shared bathroom, No smoking, Children & pets welcome, Open all year except Christmas, Map Ref Q

Wyndham Cottage, St Mary's Road, Dinton, Salisbury, Wiltshire SP3 5HH Nearest Road A303, A36, B3089

Stonehenge lies two beautiful valleys north, an evenings drive of 15 minutes from idyllic thatched 300 year old Wyndham Cottage, an English dream set in a national Trust area. Most sensitively renovated for extreme comfort. The views and walks are exceptional, as are the bluebells, lambs and calves in spring. Ian, a horticulturalist, has created a delightful cottage garden. Rosie is a nurse and will attend to all medical needs! Excellent pubs nearby. Close to Salisbury, Wilton House, Longleat, Stourhead, Bath and many other historical sites. Tea/coffee making facilities and TV.

see PHOTO on page 402

Rosie & Ian Robertson
Tel: 01722 716343

B&B from £23pp, Rooms 2 en-suite double or 1 double, 1 twin, No smoking, Children welcome over 12 years old, No pets, open all year, Map Ref R

Elm Tree Cottage, Chain Hill, Stapleford, Salisbury, Wiltshire SP3 4LH   Nearest Road A36, A303

This 17th century cottage with inglenook is set in a picturesque village. The attractively decorated bedrooms, each with en-suite/private bathrooms, have TV and tea/coffee making facilities. A self-contained unit with kitchenette is suitable for families and longer staying guests. It has use of a garden room. Breakfast is served as required. The flower garden is available for guests to enjoy. Good walking with spectacular views of the countryside. Central to Salisbury, Wilton, Stonehenge, Avebury and Stourhead. Pubs nearby provide excellent. Meals.

Chris & Joe Sykes
Tel: 01722 790507

B&B from £23pp, Rooms 2 double, 1 family, all en-suite, Restricted smoking & pets, Children welcome, Open March - November, Map Ref S

Brickworth Farmhouse, Whiteparish, Salisbury, Wiltshire SP5 2QE   Nearest Road A36

A perfectly situated 18th century listed farmhouse, renovated and furnished to maintain its period charm. Salisbury, Stonehenge, Romsey, the New Forest, Winchester and Bath are all with easy reach and Sue Barry is a registered tourist guide and will assist you to plan ideal excursions. There are excellent local pubs which provide good meals at realistic prices. Home baked bread and fresh farm eggs for your breakfast. A warm welcome awaits you at this family home.

Mrs Sue Barry
Tel: 01794 884663
Fax: 01794 884186

B&B from £20pp, Rooms 1 single, 2 double, 1 family, all en-suite, No smoking, Open all year except Christmas, Map Ref T

Newton Farmhouse, Southampton Road, Whiteparish, Salisbury, Wiltshire SP5 2QL   Nearest Road A36

Historic listed 16th century farmhouse bordering the New Forest and originally part of the Trafalgar Estate. Convenient for Salisbury, Stonehenge, Romsey, Winchester, Portsmouth and Bournemouth. Delightful rooms, all with pretty en-suite, 3 with genuine period 4 poster beds. Beamed dining room with flagstone floor and fireplace with bread oven and collection of Nelson Memorabilia and antiques. Superb breakfast complimented by fresh fruits, homemade breads, preserves and free range eggs. Swimming pool set in extensive grounds. Dinner by arrangement using kitchen garden produce. 2 Star Highly Commended. http://website.lineone.net/~newton.farmhouse.b-b/

see PHOTO on page 404

Suzi Lanham
Tel: 01794 884416

B&B from £17.50pp, Dinner from £16, Rooms 2 twin, 5 double, 1 family, all en-suite, No smoking, Children welcome, Open all year, Map Ref T

Brook House, Semington, Trowbridge, Wiltshire BA14 6JR   Nearest Road A350

This Georgian bath stone house has been in the family for several generations. Its extensive gardens include tennis and croquet lawns and a swimming pool. The property is bordered by a brook and Kennet and Avon canal with cycling towpath to Devizes and Bradford-on-Avon. Bath, Avebury, Longleat, Stonehenge, Glastonbury, Castle Combe and Lacock are all within easy reach. The village has an excellent pub for evening meals. The bedrooms are equipped with facilities to make guests feel at home.

Mr & Mrs M Bruges
Tel: 01380 870232

B&B from £19pp, Rooms 1 twin, 1 en-suite double, 1 family, Restricted smoking, Children & pets welcome, Open January-November, Map Ref U

Spiers Piece Farm, Steeple Ashton, Trowbridge, Wiltshire BA14 6HG   Nearest Road A361

Try our 'home away from home' farmhouse bed and breakfast in the heart of the Wiltshire countryside. Spacious Georgian farmhouse, large garden, great views, peace and tranquillity. Adjacent to an historical, picturesque village. Many tourist attractions including Bath and Stonehenge within easy reach. All rooms have tea/coffee making facilities and washbasins. Guests own luxury bathroom, sitting room/colour TV and dining room. Great breakfasts to last you all day.

Mrs Jill Awdry
Tel: 01380 870266
Fax: 01380 870266

B&B from £16pp, Rooms 2 double, 1 twin, Open February-November, Map Ref V

left, ***Wyndham Cottage,*** *Dinton - see details on page 401*

The Old Manor Hotel, Trowle, Trowbridge, Wiltshire BA14 9BL   Nearest Road A363

Probably 500 years old but changed over the years, the house still has a wealth of beams and past relics. A Grade II listed building standing in 4.5 acres, with lovely gardens, lounge and additional rooms, created from old barns and stables, in keeping with the house. All rooms are en-suite with colour and satellite TV, alarm radio, direct dial telephone, beverage facilities. There is residents only restaurant with a varied menu at reasonable cost. Fully licensed. The restaurant and some rooms are non-smoking with ample parking. EMail: queen.anne.house@dial.pipex.com

Barry & Diane Humphreys
Tel: 01225 777393
Fax: 01225 765443

B&B from £27.50pp, Dinner from £12, Rooms 1 single, 1 twin, 12 double, all en-suite, Restricted smoking, Children welcome, No pets, Open all year except Christmas, Map Ref W

Sturford Mead Farm, Corsley, Warminster, Wiltshire BA12 7QU   Nearest Road A362

Sturford Mead Farm is on the A362 between Frome and Warminster, nestling under the historic monument of Cley Hill (National Trust) and opposite Longleat with its safari park, lake and grounds. Stourhead, Cheddar Gorge, Wookey Hole and the prettiest English village of Castle Combe are close by. The Cathedral cities of Wells and Salisbury are within easy distance as is Bath. A real steam train still runs at the East Somerset Railway. The comfortable bedrooms, all with private facilities, have tea/coffee makers, and TV.

Lynn Corp
Tel/Fax: 01373 832213

B&B from £20pp, Rooms 2 twin, 1 double, all en-suite or private facilities, Restricted smoking, Open all year, Map Ref X

Springfield House, Crockerton, near Warminster, Wiltshire BA12 8AU   Nearest Road A36 A350

Situated in the beautiful Wylye Valley and on the edge of the famous Longleat Estate, this is a charming and welcoming village house dating from the 17th century. Guests enjoy tastefully furnished rooms with lovely garden and woodland views. Grass tennis court. The cities of Salisbury, Wells and Bath are easily reached, with Stonehenge, Stourhead Gardens, Stately homes and castles nearby. There are endless walks through woodland or over Salisbury Plain, 2 golf courses nearby. Excellent village pub and lakeside restaurant just a few minutes walk. ETB 2 Crowns Commended.

Rachel & Colin Singer
Tel: 01985 213696

B&B from £24pp, Dinner from £15, Rooms 2 double, 1 twin, all with private/en-suite facilities, tea/coffee facilities, No smoking, Open all year, Map Ref Y

Please mention
THE GREAT BRITISH
BED & BREAKFAST
when booking your accommodation

405

*left, **Newton Farmhouse**, Whiteparish - see details on page 403*

YORKSHIRE

In so small a space it is impossible to give more than the briefest impression of the pleasures to be experienced in this the largest of the English counties. This is a region of great national parks, of picturesque dales and vast tracts of open moorland. The Pennine chain of hills forms the backbone of the county, along which stretches the Pennine Way, a two hundred and fifty mile footpath, though prospective walkers should realise that in places this is an extremely rugged route. Historically split into North, East and West Ridings, in 1971 it was divided into North Yorkshire and Humberside, and includes the two metropolitan counties of West and South Yorkshire. The industrial parts of West Yorkshire however should certainly not be overlooked by the holiday visitor. There is some spectacular scenery between these towns, the 'Bronte country' around Haworth being only one example.

The Vale of York is a magnet to the holiday maker, dominated by York, itself under the Romans the ancient capital of the region. The city is a treasure house of delights. The city walls complete a three mile circuit of the city, and are the finest of their type in Europe. The magnificent Minster, the largest Gothic cathedral in Britain, is the city's crowning glory, and contains more than half of all the medieval glass surviving in England. There is so much to see in York - the castle, museums, great houses, churches and quaint medieval streets - that a single day's visit could not do it justice. Within easy reach of the city is Castle Howard, one of the most spectacular houses in Britain, and accepted as Vanbrugh's greatest achievement. The great domed mansion overlooks grounds of over a thousand acres, containing Hawksmoor's circular mausoleum and the lovely Temple of the Four Winds. At Hovingham the stone cottages cluster round the village green under the Saxon tower of All Saints' Church, by the yellow limestone eighteenth century Hovingham Hall, while at

nearby Slingsby is the romantic ruin of an eleventh century castle. Kirkham Priory to the south between the Yorkshire Wolds and the Howardian Hills is the ruin of an ancient Augustinian house. From the seventeenth century visitors came to Harrogate to take the waters from 88 separate mineral springs, and the Royal Baths, opened in 1897, grew to be one of the largest hydrotherapy establishments in the world. As the demand for 'the cure' declined, Harrogate developed into a major conference centre. The Northern Horticultural Society have here at Harlow Car Gardens, sixty acres of ornamental, woodland and rock gardens.

Malton, an important market town above the River Derwent is the gateway to the North York Moors and the Vale of Pickering. Two important houses the visitor must not miss in this area are Sledmere House and Elizabethan Burton Agnes Hall. The North York Moors form the barrier between the North-east coastal region and the Vale of York. The Lyke Wake Walk, a very popular track named after an ancient Cleveland Dirge, crosses the Cleveland Hills from Osmotherly, over the moors to Ravenscar, a distance of forty miles.

Helmsley on the southern rim of the moor is a perfect centre for touring. Nearby is Kilburn, renowned for the fine woodcarving of the Thompson family, whose trademark is a carved mouse. The White Horse was cut into the turf above the village in 1857 by the local schoolmaster and his pupils. At Coxwold there is the home of Laurence Sterne, the author of 'Tristram Shandy', and only a short walk away are the lovely ruins of Byland Abbey. A little way further to the north are the majestic ruins of Rievaulx Abbey founded in 1131.

The north-east coast can justly claim superb stretches of sandy beach. Robin Hood's Bay, Runswick Bay and Staithes are picturesque little fishing villages clinging precariously to the cliffs, their narrow cobbled streets a great attraction to artists and holiday makers. Whitby, a once famous whaling centre, is overlooked by the ruins of the abbey of St. Hilda. It was here that Captain Cook's vessel 'Endeavour' was built. The great man was born at Marton, now a part of Middlesbrough, lived at Great Ayton and was apprenticed at Staithes. The ruins of twelfth century Scarborough Castle stand on the headland above the region's most popular seaside resort, a Regency spa and a Victorian favourite. The church of St. Martin-on-the-Hill contains a wealth of pre-Raphaelite work. Anne Bronte died in the town, and is buried in the graveyard of St. Mary's church. South along the coast at Filey, Bridlington and Hornsea are excellent sandy beaches, while at Burton Constable is a grand eighteenth century Hall with 200 acres of parkland. Beverley is dominated by its Minster with its twin western towers. It contains the impressive Percy Tomb, shrine to the Percy family who owned land in the area.

The Yorkshire Dales, each with its own particular character, provide the holiday visitor with a bewildering choice of activities. The National Park is of course a perfect venue for walking, climbing, riding or simply getting away from the stress of life into the wide open spaces. There is quite spectacular scenery: Hardraw Force, the tallest waterfall in England; glorious Aysgarth Falls; the White Scar caverns at Ingleborough and Gaping Gill, a cavern big enough to swallow St. Paul's cathedral; Pen-Y-Ghent, where potholers come to sample the joys of Hell Pot and Hunt Pot. From the top of Pen-Y-Ghent one of the famous Three Peaks, are superb views across to the Lake District. At Malham Cove is some of the finest scenery in the National Park...a huge natural amphitheatre surrounded by a sheer 240 feet cliff, while at Gordale Scar is a winding gorge of crashing waterfalls and cascades. Skipton is a fine old market town, dominated by its handsome castle of the Cliffords, and a perfect centre for exploring the Dales, Bolton Abbey, The Strid and Barden Tower, Grassington and Kilnsey Crag.

From quiet Swaledale down to the busy industry of the north-west, across to the fresh and blustery Hornsea Mere then up to the Cleveland Hills - within these boundaries lies a vast incomparable holiday area, that once sampled leaves a lasting impression.

YORKSHIRE

Places to Visit

Beverley Minster, *Beverley* ~ co-founded in 937 by Athelstan, King of Wessex in place of the church John of Beverley had chosen as his resting place in 721. The nave is the earliest surviving building work dating from the 1300's. On the north side of the altar is the Fridstol or Peace Chair said to date from 924-39. Anyone who sat on it would then be granted thirty days sanctuary.

Buttertubs, *near Thwaite* ~ a series of potholes that streams fall into, these became known as Buttertubs when farmers going to market lowered their butter into the holes to keep it cool.

Castle Howard, *near Malton* ~ Charles, 3rd Earl of Carlisle commissioned Sir John Vanbrugh to design a palace in 1699, the grand designs were put into practice by architect Nicholas Hawksmoor and the main body of the house was completed in 1712. The West Wing was built in 1753-1759. Today, the Howard family still lives here. The Long Gallery has a large number of portraits of the Howard family, including works by Lely, Holbein and Van Dyck. The Great Hall, rising twenty metres to the dome from its floor has columns by SamuelCarpenter and wall paintings by Pellegrini.

National Railway Museum, *York* ~ set in a steam engine maintenance shed, it is the world's largest railway museum. It covers two hundred years of history and visitors can try wheel tapping and shunting in the interactive gallery. On display are uniforms, rolling stock from 1797 onwards and Queen Victoria's carriage from the Royal Train.

Nunnington Hall, *near Helmsley* ~ a 17th century manor house on the banks of the River Rye. It has a panelled hall with a fine carved chinmey piece, fine tapestries, china and the Carlisle Collection of Miniature Rooms. Parliamentarian troops left their sword marks in the window frames.

Rievaulx Abbey, *near Helmsley* ~ founded in 1132, it was the first major monastery in Britain. It is set in the steep wooded valley of the River Rye. The remains of the Norman nave show how the abbey would have looked all those centuries ago.

Yorkshire Sculpture Park, *Wakefield* ~ an open air gallery, set in one hundred and ten acres of parkland. The park includes work by Barbara Hepworth, Sol LeWitt and Mimmo Paladino. Henry Moore, the parks first patron, believed that to appreciate sculpture, sun and daylight were necessary.

King Street.
Robin Hood's Bay

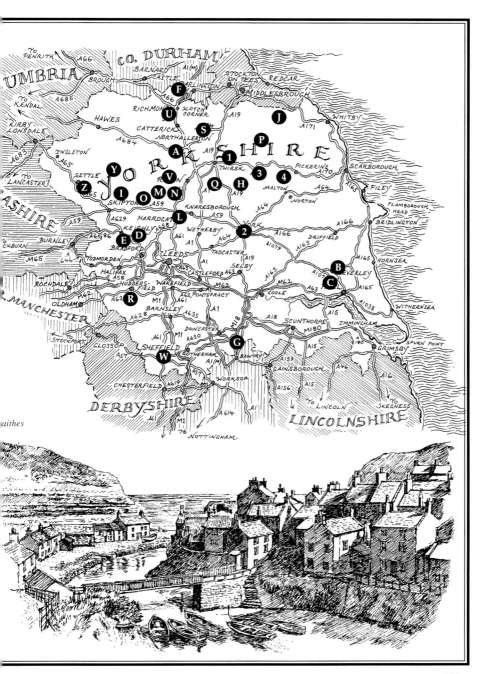

Hyperion House, 88 South End, Bedale, North Yorkshire DL8 2DS   Nearest Roads A684, A1

Hyperion House is large with spacious accommodation and every comfort. Attractively furnished rooms with excellent beds, TV and tea/coffee. Guests' lounge with TV and video with opportunity to view videos on this lovely area and its attractions. We are well situated 10 minutes walk to bar meals and restaurants. Lots of advice from your hosts Sheila and Ron on the Dales, Yorkshire Moors walks, etc. Private car park, guests' entrance with your own key. 3 night bargain breaks please enquire. "Which" Recommended. ETB 2 Crowns Highly Commended.

Sheila & Ron Dean
Tel: 01677 422334
Fax: 01677 422334

B&B from £20pp, Rooms 1 double en-suite, 1 double (private bathroom), 1 twin, 1 single (for use of doubles), No smoking or pets, Children over 12, Open all year except Christmas, New Year & February, Map Ref A

---

1 Woodlands, Beverley, Yorkshire HU17 8BT   Nearest Road A164

A warm welcome awaits you in this interesting Victorian family house in a quiet conservation area within two minutes walk of this charming, historic market town. Delicious home cooking, guests are welcome to bring their own wine. Enjoy breakfast and dinner in library/dining room and relax and watch TV in our comfortable sitting room. The house is full of character, interesting decor, many pictures, books, log fires and a lovely garden. Bedrooms have tea/coffee making facilities. Car parking. A good centre from which to explore York, Lincoln, the coast, the Wolds and the Moors.

Neil & Sarah King
Tel: 01482 862752

B&B from £17.50pp, Dinner from £12, Rooms 1 twin, 2 double, some en-suite, Restricted smoking, Children welcome, Pets by arrangement, Open all year except Christmas & New Year, Map Ref B

Rudstone Walk, South Cave, nr Beverley, East Yorkshire HU15 2AH   Nearest Road B1230, A1034, M62

A unique country house hotel set in its own acres on the edge of the unspoilt Yorkshire Wolds, with views over the Vale of York and Humber Estuary. Luxurious en-suite bed & breakfast accommodation is provided in a courtyard garden development surrounding the 400 year old farmhouse, where delicious home-cooked meals are served. If you prefer, self-catering accommodation is available, sleeping 1-6 people. An ideal location for exploring the historic towns of York and Beverley and the surrounding countryside and the heritage coastline, all within easy reach of us. EMail: admin@rudstone-walk.co.uk

Laura & Charlie Greenwood
Tel: 01430 422230
Fax: 01430 424552

B&B from £27.50pp, Dinner from £16.50, Rooms 6 twin, 7 double, 1 family, all en-suite, Restricted smoking & pets, Children welcome, Open all year, Map Ref C

Five Rise Locks Hotel, Beck Lane, Bingley, West Yorkshire BD16 4DD   Nearest Road A650

Welcome to an hotel of charm and character, where each en-suite bedroom is as individual as you - from the seclusion of the Turret Rooms, the panoramic views from the Studio - each has the same extraordinary peacefulness. Welcome to an interesting selection of home cooking using only the finest fresh ingredients and to a wine list chosen well. Whether you intend to tour the Dales, Haworth, Saltaire, mill shopping, or relax - stroll along the Canal and admire the engineering feat of the Five Rise Locks.

Pat Oxley
Tel: 01274 565296
Fax: 01274 568828

B&B from £27.50-£29.50pp, Dinner from £14, Rooms 1 single, 3 twin, 5-7 double, 2 family, all en-suite, Children & pets welcome, Open all year, Map Ref D

right, **March Cote Farm,** *near Bingley - see details on page 412*

March Cote Farm, Cottingley, Bingley, Yorkshire BD16 1NB   **Nearest Road A650**

see PHOTO on page 411

Friendly atmosphere awaits you in our 17th century farmhouse, fully modernised with central heating and a high standard of furnishings and decor. Character still maintained with original oak beams and mullion windows. Top quality farmhouse cooking, served in guests dining room. Colour TV and tea/coffee making facilities in all rooms. Many places of interest within comfortable travelling distance - Moors, Dales, museums and National Trust properties. Pretty garden. Many repeat bookings. Professional, business and tourist guests all welcome. Plenty of car parking. Also holiday cottage.

George & Jean Warin
Tel: 01274 487433
Fax: 01274 488153

B&B from £20pp, Dinner from £9 by arrangement, All rooms en-suite or private facilities, 2 double, 1 family suite, Restricted smoking, Children welcome, No pets, Open all year except Christmas, Map Ref E

Cliffe Hall, Piercebridge, Darlington, Yorkshire DL2 3SR   **Nearest Road B6275, A1**

A massive Virginia creeper covers this large spacious family house. There are open fires downstairs and full central heating. Bedrooms have a light, airy feel, pale painted walls and gracefully worn furniture. There are lovely walks from the house, fishing and a tennis court. Within easy reach of Durham and York, the Yorkshire Dales and Moors. The house is set in its own peaceful parkland on the Yorkshire bank of the River Tees and has a wonderful friendly atmosphere.

Mrs Wilson
Tel: 01325 374322
Fax: 01325 374947

B&B from £30pp, Dinner from £15, Rooms 1 single, 2 en-suite twin, Restricted smoking, Children welcome, No pets, Open February - November, Map Ref F

Ashcroft Lodge, 1 Warning Tongue Lane, Bessacarr, Doncaster, South Yorkshire DN4 6TB   **A638**

Situated on the A638 5 miles south of the historic Roman town of Doncaster, and 10 minutes from Bawtry and the counties of Lincolnshire and Nottinghamshire. A warm welcome is extended. 3 miles to the Racecourse, Dome, leisure centre and business parks. 2 miles from the proposed International airport! A quarter of a mile from golf and fishing pursuits! The ground floor bedrooms are elegant, well appointed, en-suite. Lovely walled garden with water features. Ample private parking. Excellent restaurant/pub 2 minutes walk.

Mr & Mrs D. Jensen
Tel: 01302 865223

B&B from £25pp, Rooms 1 twin, 2 double, all en-suite/private facilities, Children welcome, Pets restricted, Open all year, Map Ref G

The Old Vicarage, Market Place, Easingwold, Yorkshire YO6 3AL   **Nearest Road A19**

A charming Grade II house standing in pleasant gardens adjacent to the Georgian market square, having the benefit of good and varied places to dine.§ Equi-distant from York, the Yorkshire Moors and Dales which are all within 30 minutes drive. Bedrooms are en-suite and equipped with remote colour TV, radio alarm and beverage tray. Guests may enjoy relaxing in their own sitting room, or perhaps a game of croquet, or just sitting in the secluded gardens surrounding the house. Ample private parking.

Christine & John Kirman
Tel: 01347 821015
Fax: 01347 823465

B&B from £25pp, Rooms 2 twin, 3 double, all en-suite, No smoking, Children welcome, No pets, Open February - November, Map Ref H

Town Head Guest House, 1 Low Lane, Grassington, Yorkshire BD23 5AU   **Nearest Road B6265**

Our friendly guest house stands at the head of the village between the cobbled streets and the Moors. The ideal location for unspoilt walks and for touring the Dales. The comfortable bedrooms are all equipped with H & C, TV and tea/coffee making facilities.

Marian Lister
Tel: 01756 752811

B&B from £22, Rooms 1 twin, 3 double, all en-suite, No smoking, Open all year except Christmas, Map Ref I

Manor House Farm, Ingleby Greenhow, Great Ayton, North Yorkshire TS9 6RB   **Nearest Road A172**

Delightful farmhouse (part 1760) built of Yorkshire stone, set in 164 acres of park and woodlands at the foot of the Cleveland hills in the North York Moors National Park. Environment is tranquil and secluded. Ideal for nature lovers, relaxing, touring and walking. Accommodation is attractive with exposed beams and interior stonework.Atmosphere is warm and welcoming. Guests have separate entrance, lounge and dining room. Fine evening dinners, special diets if required, excellent wines. ETB 2 Crowns Highly Commended, AA QQQQ Selected. Brochure. Credit & debit cards accepted.

Dr & Mrs M Bloom
Tel: 01642 722384

Dinner, Bed & Breakfast from £41pp, Rooms 2 twin, 1 double, all have en-suite/private facilities, No smoking, Children over 12, Open all year except Christmas, Map Ref J

Crescent Lodge, 20 Swan Road, Harrogate, North Yorkshire HG1 2SA   **Nearest Road A61, A1**

Charming Grade II listed family home overlooking Crescent Gardens and close to Valley Gardens and Pump Room. Four well appointed rooms, 2 en-suite, with tea/coffee trays, clock radios and complimentary toiletries. A hair dryer and laundry facilities on request. An elegant and comfortable guests' drawing room with colour TV. Ideally placed for Harrogate town centre as well as for Yorkshire's finest scenery. Limited off street parking.

Julia Humphris
Tel/Fax: 01423 503688

B&B from £24pp, Rooms 1 single, 3 twin, most en-suite, No children, Open all year except Christmas & New Year, Map Ref L

Acacia Lodge, 21 Ripon Road, Harrogate, North Yorkshire HG1 2JL   **Nearest Road A61**

'Highly Commended', warm, lovingly restored family run Victorian hotel with pretty gardens in select central conservation area. Short stroll from Harrogate's fashionable shops, many restaurants and conference/exhibition facilities. Retaining original character with fine furnishings, antiques and paintings. All Bedrooms luxuriously en-suite with every comfort and facility. Award winning breakfasts served in oak furnished dining room. Beautiful lounge with open fire and library of books. Private floodlit parking for all guests. Entirely 'No smoking'. 'Somewhere special'. AA QQQQ Selected. Brochure on request.

Dee & Peter Bateson
Tel: 01423 560752
Fax: 01423 503725

B&B from £27pp, Rooms 2 twin, 2 double, 2 triple, all en-suite. No smoking, Children over 10, No pets, Open all year, Map Ref L

Ashley House Hotel, 36-40 Franklin Road, Harrogate, North Yorkshire HG1 5EE   **Nearest Road A1**

Ron & Linda Thomas offer you a cheery welcome and value for money in quality bedrooms, all en-suite with colour TV and hospitality tray. Sample our generous breakfast before walking into the town centre or Valley Gardens. Drive through the Yorkshire Dales or Moors, visit Fountains Abbey or Harewood House or take the train to Knaresborough, York or Leeds. Try one of over 100 superb whiskies in our cosy bar before enjoying a delicious dinner (home cooked from fresh ingredients).

Ron & Linda Thomas
Tel: 01423 507474
Fax: 01423 560858   **B&B from £30pp, Dinner from £15, Rooms 5 single, 5 twin, 5 double, 2 family, all en-suite, Children & pets welcome, Open all year, Map Ref L**

Daryl House Hotel, 42 Dragon Parade, Harrogate, North Yorkshire HG1 5DA   **Nearest Road A59**

Friendly run home with excellent accommodation. Tea/coffee making facilities and colour TV in all rooms. An attractive lounge and garden for guest enjoyment. Home cooked food and personal attention are all the hallmark of Daryl House. Close to the Conference Centre and railway station. Ideal for visiting Harrogate's famous gardens. Also gateway for visiting the Dales. A very warm welcome awaits all visitors.

Mick & Liz Young
Tel: 01423 502775   **B&B from £17pp, Dinner on request £7.50, Rooms 2 single, 2 twin, 2 family/double, Restricted smoking, Children & pets welcome, Open all year, B&B only at Christmas, Map Ref L**

The Duchy Hotel, 51 Valley Drive, Harrogate, North Yorkshire HG2 0JH   **Nearest Road A61, A1**

This warm and welcoming small hotel offers 10 comfortable en-suite bedrooms each with TV, direct dial telephone and courtesy trays. The hotel is located on Valley Drive overlooking the Valley Gardens, yet only a 5 minute walk from the town centre with its fashionable shops, restaurants and conference facilities. An ideal base for touring the Yorkshire Moors and Dales. Licensed for residents and their guests with an attractive bar and lounge. Noreen and Brian assure their guests of a very pleasant stay in Harrogate.

Noreen & Brian Ellis
Tel: 01423 565818
Fax: 01423 504518   **B&B from £27.50pp, Dinner from £12.50, Rooms 2 single, 2 twin, 4 double, 2 family, all en-suite, Children welcome, No pets, Open all year except Christmas, Map Ref L**

High Winsley Cottage, Burnt Yates, Harrogate, North Yorkshire HG3 3EP   **Nearest Road A61**

A traditional Yorkshire Dales stone cottage situated well off the road in peaceful countryside with lovely views all around and ideally placed for both town and country. A warm welcome, good food and comfortable accommodation are assured. All bedrooms are en-suite, and have tea/coffee making facilities. There are 2 guests' sitting rooms with television, books, magazines, local guides and maps. Great care is taken to provide first class fare and includes home bred beef, fresh fruit and vegetables from the garden, free range eggs and home baked bread.

Clive & Gill King
Tel: 01423 770662   **B&B from £24pp, Dinner is £12.50, Rooms 2 twin, 2 double, all en-suite, Residential license, Restricted smoking, Children over 11, Open March - December, Map Ref M**

---

*right, **Grassfields Country House Hotel**, Pateley Bridge - see details on page 416*

Croft House, Little Croft, Markington, Harrogate, North Yorkshire HG3 3TU Nearest Road A61

Janet welcomes you to her lovely comfortable home in a pleasant village two miles from Fountains Abbey and four miles from Ripon. Busy Harrogate is a 20 minute drive away and the best of Nidderdale close by. The accommodation is comfortably furnished with attention to detail, each room has colour TV, hair dryer, radio alarm and courtesy tray. Car parking. A friendly welcome is always assured.

Janet Anderson
Tel: 01765 677782
Fax: 01765 677782

B&B from £22.50pp, Rooms 1 twin en-suite, 1 double private bathroom, No smoking or pets, Children over 12, Open February - end November, Map Ref N

Woodlands, Bewerley, Pateley Bridge, Harrogate, North Yorkshire HG3 5HS Nearest Road B6265

Beautifully situated late Victorian house with magnificent views over parkland from residents' sitting room. In quiet area with interesting garden but only five minutes walk from small country town of Pateley Bridge, where excellent restaurant and pub meals can be found. Woodlands is warm and welcoming and a very good centre for walking in Nidderdale and touring the other Dales. Private car park, tea/coffee making facilities and TV in residents lounge. Many outstanding beauty spots nearby including Fountains Abbey, Newby Hall, Harewood and Ripley Castle.

John & Pauline Shaw
Tel: 01423 711175

B&B from £20pp, Rooms 1 twin, 1 double, both en-suite, No smoking or children, Pets welcome, Open all year except Christmas & New Year, Map Ref O

Grassfields Country House Hotel, Low Wath Rd, Pateley Bridge, Harrogate, N. Yorkshire HG3 5HL B6265

see PHOTO on page 415

Set in private grounds, Grassfields is a listed Georgian building, quietly reflecting the elegance of the period. Grassfields has been recommended since 1986 as a 'hidden jewel' in 'Staying off the Beaten Track' with wholesome Yorkshire food prepared from local produce and an excellent wine cellar. Only a few miles from Harrogate. Grassfields is situated in beautiful walking country with many walks from the hotel door and an ideal centre for touring the Yorkshire Dales, 'Heartbeat' and 'Herriot' country. AA 2 Star, ETB 3 Crowns Commended.

Barbara Garforth
Tel: 01423 711412

B&B from £25pp, Dinner from £13.95, Rooms 1 single, 2 twin, 3 double, 1 family, all en-suite, Children & pets welcome, Open all year, Map Ref O

Laskill Farm, Hawnby, near Helmsley, Yorkshire YO62 5NB Nearest Road B1257

Charming, warm country farmhouse on 600 acre farm in the north Yorkshire National Park in the heart of James Herriot and Heartbeat country. All rooms are lovingly cared for well equipped. Lovely garden with own lake, peace and tranquillity. Lots of places of historical interest and stately houses nearby. York only 45 minutes away. Generous cuisine of high standard using fresh produce whenever possible. Natural spring water. A walkers paradise.

Mrs S Smith
Tel: 01439 798268

B&B from £24pp, Dinner from £11, Rooms 3 en-suite double, 3 en-suite twin, 1 single, Open all year, Map Ref P

*right, **Laurel Manor Farm**, Brafferton - see details on page 418*

Yorkshire

Laurel Manor Farm, Brafferton, Helperby, Yorkshire YO61 2NZ   **Nearest Road (5 miles) A1, A19**

see PHOTO on page 417

A gracious Georgian residence amid orchards, gardens and 28 acres of pastures which run down to the river Swale. Antiques and family portraits abound, and Sam and Annie Key, from an old Yorkshire family, will take a personal interest in your needs. Within 5 minutes walk are 4 delightful village pubs, all serve excellent meals. York and Harrogate are 20 minutes and Sam has mapped 200 places of tourist interest within easy reach. They keep black sheep, ducks and horses, and boast complete tranquillity! EMail: laurelmf@globalnet.co.uk

Sam & Annie Key
Tel: 01423 360436
Fax: 01423 360437

B&B from £25pp, Dinner from £18, Rooms 1 twin, 2 double en-suite, Restricted smoking, Children welcome, Pets welcome, Open from March - November, (Closed December - February), Map Ref Q

Forest Farm Guest House, Mount Road, Marsden, Huddesfield, West Yorkshire HD7 6NN   **A62**

Forest Farm is situated on the edge of the village of Marsden 1,000ft above sea level overlooking the golf course and moorland. It is over 200 years old, a former weavers cottage constructed in stone. It has been restored keeping many aspects of it's original character. Forest Farm offers evening meals, B&B, packed lunches. TV room. Car parking. We can boast spring water, free range eggs: special diets available with prior arrangement. Come as a guest and leave as a friend!

May & Ted Fussey
Tel/Fax: 01484 842687

B&B from £16pp, Dinner from £7, Rooms 1 twin, 1 double, 1 family, Restricted smoking & pets, Children welcome, Open all year except Christmas & Boxing Day, Map Ref R

Porch House, High Street, Northallerton, North Yorkshire DL7 8EG   **Nearest Road A684**

Porch House was built in 1584 and took its name from the porch that still frames the entrance. Throughout its history Porch House has offered comfort and shelter to travellers including royalty - James (VI of Scotland I of England) and Charles I. All rooms are en-suite, have tea/coffee facilities and TV. Traditional English breakfast/vegetarian. Original fireplaces and beams; walled garden; private parking; central position (opposite church). ETB 2 Crowns Highly Commended. 2nd in 1996 Best B&B White Rose Award. 1997 Best B&B White Rose Award.

Janet Beardow
Tel: 01609 779831
Fax: 01609 778603

B&B from £24pp, Rooms 1 twin, 4 double, 1 family, all en-suite, No smoking, No pets, Open all year, Map Ref S

Millgate House, Richmond, North Yorkshire DL10 4JN   **Nearest Road A1, A66**

Georgian town house, ideally placed for touring with secluded national award winning garden (RHS/Daily Mail 1995). Town centre location yet blissfully peaceful with views beyond the garden over the River Swale and its waterfalls. A very special house with its own enchanting character and atmosphere. Bedrooms overlook the garden. French and Italian spoken. All rooms with full facilities including tea/coffee and colour TV. EMail: oztim@millgatehouse.demon.co.uk

Austin Lynch
Tel: 01748 823571
Fax: 01748 850701

B&B from £27.50pp, Rooms 1 twin, 1 double, both en-suite, Children over 10, No pets, Open all year, Map Ref U

right, St GEORGE'S COURT, near Ripon - see details on page 420

St George's Court, Old Home Farm, Grantley, Ripon, North Yorkshire HG4 3EU   **Nearest Road B6265**

see PHOTO on page 419

Enjoy the friendly welcome and warm hospitality of St George's Court, situated in the beautiful Yorkshire Dales, near Fountains Abbey in 20 acres of peaceful farmland. Our en-suite rooms in renovated farm building, offer comfort and all modern facilities - TV and tea/coffee making facilities whilst retaining character and charm. Delicious breakfasts served in our lovely listed farmhouse, breakfast with a view in a charming conservatory dining room. Lots of parking. Peace and tranquillity is our password.

Mrs Sandra Gordon
Tel: 01765 620618

B&B from £20pp, Rooms 1 twin, 3 double, 1 family, all en-suite, Restricted smoking, Children & pets welcome, Open all year except Christmas,as, Map Ref V

The Briary, 12 Moncrieffe Road, Nether Edge, Sheffield, Yorkshire S7 1HR

Detached Victorian residence of character, within spacious gardens (with squirrels) in mature leafy district, 10 minutes drive from city centre, 15 minutes to Derbyshire Peak District. Imaginative cuisine - excellent choice of breakfast; dinners by arrangement featuring Cordon Bleu, International and British dishes. Refurbished accommodation has been sympathetically restored with antique furniture throughout. The dining room has a solid fuel stove. All bedrooms are en-suite with colour television, hair dryers and tea-making facilities. Credit cards not taken. AA QQQ Recommended.

Mr & Mrs C. H. Clarke
Tel/Fax: 0114 2551951

B&B Single from £28pp, Double from £23pp, Dinner by arrangement from £9-£11, Rooms 1 single, 1 twin, 3 double, 1 family, all en-suite, No smoking or pets, Children over 10, Open all year except Christmas, Map Ref W

Langcliffe Country House, Kettlewell, Skipton, North Yorkshire BD23 5RJ   **Nearest Road B6160**

Yorkshire Dales. 6 pretty en-suite bedrooms, all individually furnished. Conservatory restaurant with panoramic views. Emphasis on freshly prepared imaginative food using local produce. Lounge with log fire in winter. Personally run by resident owners. Ground floor adapted room. Places of interest include Malham Cove and Tarn, Bolton Abbey, Skipton and Aysgarth Falls. Which? Hotel Guide 1998, AA QQQQ Selected, RAC Highly Acclaimed, ETB 4 Crowns Commended. Car park and fully licensed. Special rates November to Easter. Telephone for brochure ad tariff. Ideal walking country.

Mr & Mrs Elliott
Tel: 01756 760243

B&B from £30pp, Dinner from £16, Rooms 2 twin, 2 double, 1 family, all en-suite, Restricted smoking, Children welcome, Pets by arrangement, Open all year, Map Ref Y

The Country House Hotel, Long Preston, Skipton, North Yorkshire BD23 4NJ   **Nearest Road A65**

An elegant Victorian country house situated in its own grounds in the Yorkshire Dales, in the village of Long Preston, 3 miles from Settle. 7 double en-suite rooms with colour TV, tea/coffee facilities. Drawing room with log fire. Extensive Library. Piano. Fine food. Please bring your own wine. Sauna and spa bath provided for relaxation. Delightful house offering a personal service in homely, informal and restful surroundings. Secure car parking. ETB 3 Crowns Highly Commended. Ideal for touring the beautiful countryside and walking, there are many places of interest to visit.

Don & Dorothy Hutton
Tel: 01729 840246

B&B from £28.00pp, Dinner by advance booking £16, Rooms 2 twin, 4 double, 1 family, all rooms en-suite, No smoking, Children from 4, No pets, Open February-mid December, New Year Party, Map Ref Z

right, **Holmwood House Hotel,** *York - see details on page 423*

Thornborough House Farm, South Kilvington, Thirsk, North Yorkshire YO7 2NP   **Nearest Road A19**

Thornborough House Farm is a 200 year old farmhouse which provides first class accommodation and a warm welcome. Guests can enjoy their own sitting and dining room which has an open fire and colour TV, Two of the bedrooms are en-suite and the third has private facilities. All rooms are warm and comfortable and have tea.coffee making facilities, and colour TV. Families are very welcome and a cot and high chair are available. The house lies 11/2 miles north of Thirsk, the town made famous by James Herriot. 2 Crown Commended.

Mrs Tess Williamson
Tel: 01845 522103
Fax: 01845 522103

B&B from £14.50pp, Dinner from £9,50, Rooms 1 double, 1 twin/single, 1 family, open all year, Map Ref 1

Holmwood House Hotel, 114 Holgate Road, York YO2 4BB   **Nearest Road A59**

Holmwood House Hotel was built as two private houses in the 19th century, backing onto one of the prettiest squares in York. The 2 listed buildings have been lovingly restored to retain the ambience of a private home and provide peaceful elegant rooms where the pressures of the day disappear. Bedrooms have their own en-suite facilities with shower, bath or even spa-bath, plus the usual TV, coffee & tea making facilities, direct dial telephone, etc. There is a car park to the rear and we are only 5 minutes walk from the City Walls with railway station and city centre 5-10 minutes walk away. EMail: holmwood.house@dial.pipex.com

Bill Pitts & Rosie Blanksby
Tel: 01904 626183
Fax: 01904 670899

B&B from £27.50pp, Rooms 3 twin, 8 double, family suites, all en-suite, No smoking, Minimum age 8, No pets, Open all year, Map Ref 2

see PHOTO on page 421

Arnot House, 17 Grosvenor Terrace, York YO30 7AG   **Nearest Road A19**

Built in the 1860's, Arnot House stands over looking Bootham Park, five minutes walk from York Minster. The four guest bedrooms are furnished with antiques and paintings, brass or wooden beds, colour TV, alarm clock radio, hair dryer and hospitality tray. There is a guest lounge and car parking. Breakfast includes cereals, fruit juices, fresh fruit salad, English or vegetarian breakfast or even scrambled eggs with smoked salmon! Arnot House is totally non smoking.

Kim & Ann Sluter-Robbins
Tel/Fax: 01904 641966

B&B from £22.50pp, Rooms 1 twin, 3 double, all en-suite, No smoking, Children over 10 years, No pets, Open all year, Map Ref 2

see PHOTO opposite

Barbican House, 20 Barbican Road, York YO10 5AA   **Nearest Road A19**

Friendly northern welcome in this delightful Victorian residence with lots of charm and character. Carefully restored to retain many of its original features. All bedrooms are en-suite and have TV and tea/coffee making facilities. One room is at ground floor level. There is a comfortable guests' lounge and the dining room retains a classic 19th century cooking range where a substantial traditional English breakfast or a vegetarian breakfast is served. Central York is only a 5 minute walk and the Barbican Leisure centre a 100 yards. A private car park is situated at the rear of the hotel. EMail: barbican@thenet.co.uk

Elsie & Len Osterman
Tel: 01904 627617
Fax: 01904 647140

B&B from £20pp, Rooms 1 twin, 5 double, 1 family, all en-suite, No smoking, Open all year, Map Ref 2

see PHOTO on page 424

*left, **Arnot House,** York - see details above*

St George's Hotel, 6 St George's Place, York YO2 2DR **Nearest Road A1036, A64**

A 10 bedroomed Victorian house in a quiet cul-de-sac by York's beautiful racecourse. All the comfortably furnished bedrooms are en-suite and have TV and tea/coffee trays. St George's has quality awards from the Tourist Board, AA and RAC. There is excellent access from the A64 from the south and A19 from the north so it is well placed for Castle Howard, Scarborough, Herriot country, the North Yorkshire Moors and many historic places in York. Just a short walk into the centre of York. All pets very welcome. Private enclosed car parking.

Brian & Kristine Livingstone
Tel: 01904 625056
Fax: 01904 625009

B&B from £22.50pp, Dinner £5.00, Rooms 5 double (2 4-posters), 5 family, all en-suite, Pets welcome, Open all year, Map Ref 2

Alcuin Lodge, 15 Sycamore Place, Bootham, York YO30 7DW **Nearest Road A19**

Alcuin Lodge is a fine old Edwardian House situated in a quiet cul de sac overlooking a bowling green, yet only five minutes walk through the beautiful Museum Gardens to the heart of our historic city. A warm welcome is assured. Within walking distance of York train station. Twin and double en-suite rooms, tea/coffee facilities, central heating. Access to rooms at all times. Ample parking. English Tourist Board Commended. Just telephone for a comfortable and memorable stay.

Susan Taylor
Tel: 01904 632222

B&B from £17pp, Rooms 1 twin, 3 double, 1 family, all en-suite, No smoking or pets, Children over 10, Open all year except Christmas, Map Ref 2

Grange Lodge, 52 Bootham Crescent, Bootham, York YO3 7AH **Nearest Road A19**

The Grange Lodge offers a warm and friendly welcome. Accommodation is in a choice of 7 comfortable and attractively furnished bedrooms, Many with en-suite facilities and all have TV and tea/coffee making facilities. Conveniently located for all of York's attractions and only 10 minutes away from York Minster. An ideal place for touring this most beautiful region.

Jenny Robinson
Tel: 01904 621137

B&B from £16, Dinner from £8, Rooms 3 double, 2 family, 1 twin, 1 single, many en-suite, No pets, Open all year, Map Ref 2

Four Seasons Hotel, 7 St Peters Grove, Bootham, York YO30 6AQ **Nearest Road A19**

A delightful Victorian residence, ideally situated in a peaceful tree lined grove, yet only eight minutes walk from Minster and York's historical attractions. Awarded Highly Commended by the English Tourist Board and offering beautifully appointed en-suite bedrooms, all fully equipped. A cosy residents lounge and bar. Ample private car parking. Delicious four course breakfast. This is an ideal base from which to explore York and surrounding countryside.

see PHOTO on page 426

Steve & Bernice Roe
Tel: 01904 622621
Fax: 01904 620976

B&B from £28pp, Rooms 1 twin en-suite, 2 double en-suite, 2 family en-suite, Non smoking, Children welcome, Open February - December, Map Ref 2

The Hazelwood, 24-25 Portland Street, Gillygate, York YO3 7EH　　　Nearest Road Gillygate

see PHOTO on page 428

Situated in the centre of York only 400 yards from York Minster yet with a private car park and in an extremely quiet location, the Hazelwood comprises two elegant Victorian houses with many original features. In our tastefully decorated dining room, we offer a wide choice of quality breakfast which cater for all tastes including vegetarian. Our beautifully furnished en-suite bedrooms have colour TV, radio alarm, hair dryer and tea/coffee making facilities. Relax in our secluded garden or in our peaceful residents' lounge with its original kitchen range and selection of books and local information where tea and coffee are available.

Ian & Carolyn McNabb
Tel: 01904 626548
Fax: 01904 628032

B&B from £24pp, Rooms 1 single, 4 twin, 7 double, 2 family, all en-suite, No smoking, Open all year, Map Ref 2

Dairy Guest House, 3 Scarcroft Road, York, Yorkshire YO23 1ND　　　Nearest Road A64

Beautifully appointed Victorian town house, that was once the local Dairy! Well equipped cottage styled rooms around a flower-filled courtyard. Some en-suite. One four-poster. Informal atmosphere. Commended by the ETB. Smoke free environment. Offers traditional or vegetarian. B&B from £18pp, Please phone for colour brochure.

Keith Jackman
Tel: 01904 639367

B&B from £18pp, Rooms 1 single, 1 twin, 2 double, 1 family, some en-suite, Children welcome, Pet by arrangement, Open February - mid December, Map Ref 2

Curzon Lodge & Stable Cottages, 23 Tadcaster Road, Dringhouses, York, Yorkshire YO24 1QG　　A64, A1036

see PHOTO on page 429

A charming early 17th century former farmhouse and stables within a city conservation area overlooking racecourse. Once a home of the Terry 'chocolate' family, guests are now invited to share the relaxed atmosphere in 10 comfortably furnished, en-suite rooms, some with 4 poster or brass beds. Country antiques, rugs, prints, books, fresh flowers and complimentary sherry in the cosy sitting room lend traditional ambience. Friendly and informal. Delicious English breakfasts. Parking in grounds. Restaurants 1 minute walk. AA QQQQ 'Selected', RAC, ETB, Which ?, 'Highly Recommended'.

Richard & Wendy Wood
Tel: 01904 703157

B&B from £27.50pp, Rooms 1 single, 3 twin, 5 double, 1 family, all en-suite, No smoking or pets, Children over 7, Open all year except Christmas, Map Ref 2

Shallowdale House, West End, Ampleforth, York YO62 4DY　　　Nearest Road A170

Situated on the southern edge of the North York Moors National Park, all the rooms at Shallowdale House command sublime views of unspoilt English countryside. The bedrooms are stylish and spacious, with tea/coffee making facilities, television and direct-dial telephones. As well as comfort and caring service, there is a strong emphasis on imaginative, freshly cooked food, and the house is licensed. An ideal centre for touring, and visiting the abbeys, castles and stately homes of North Yorkshire. Delightful gardens.

Phillip Gill & Anton Van Der Horst
Tel: 01439 788325
Fax: 01439 788885

B&B from £32.50pp, Dinner from £20, Rooms 2 double/twin, 1 double, all en-suite/private, No smoking or pets, Children over 12, Open all year except Christmas & New Year, Map Ref 3

Orchard House, Marton, nr Sinnington, York, Yorkshire YO62 6RD　　　　Nearest Road A170

Built in 1784, situated four miles west of Pickering and set in a two acre garden bordering the river Seven, Orchard House offers peace and comfort, wonderful food and wine, log fires, low beams and high standards. Marton is an excellent base for exploring the North York Moors and coast with many historic houses and sites in the area. Castle Howard (Brideshead) is just eight miles away while York or Whitby are easily reached within 40 minutes. Heartbeat country, steam trains; a Yorkshire experience. Brochure available.

Alison & Paul Richardson　　　　B&B from £20pp, Dinner from £12.50, Rooms 1 twin, 2 double, all en-
Tel: 01751 432904　　　　suite, No smoking, pets, or children, Open March - October, Map Ref 4

"What a day! Good walking, excellent lunch, time in the bookshop, time in the cathedral - who could ask for more?"

BELLE & BERTIE IN YORK

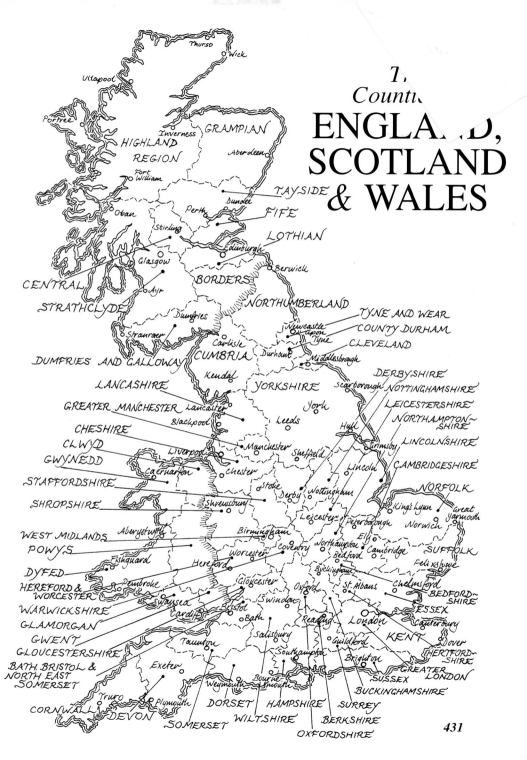

The Countries of
ENGLAND,
SCOTLAND
& WALES

Thurso
Wick
Ullapool
Portree
HIGHLAND
REGION
Inverness
GRAMPIAN
Aberdeen
Fort William
Oban
TAYSIDE
Dundee
Perth
FIFE
Stirling
LOTHIAN
Glasgow
Edinburgh
CENTRAL
Ayr
BORDERS
Berwick
STRATHCLYDE
NORTHUMBERLAND
Dumfries
TYNE AND WEAR
Stranraer
Newcastle upon Tyne
COUNTY DURHAM
Carlisle
Durham
CLEVELAND
DUMFRIES AND GALLOWAY
CUMBRIA
Middlesbrough
DERBYSHIRE
Kendal
Scarborough
NOTTINGHAMSHIRE
LANCASHIRE
YORKSHIRE
LEICESTERSHIRE
GREATER MANCHESTER
Lancaster
York
NORTHAMPTON~
SHIRE
CHESHIRE
Blackpool
Leeds
Hull
LINCOLNSHIRE
CLWYD
Liverpool
Manchester
Grimsby
GWYNEDD
Sheffield
Lincoln
CAMBRIDGESHIRE
Chester
Caernarfon
Stoke
NORFOLK
STAFFORDSHIRE
Derby
Nottingham
SHROPSHIRE
Shrewsbury
King's Lynn
Great Yarmouth
Leicester
Peterborough
Norwich
WEST MIDLANDS
Aberystwyth
Birmingham
POWYS
Worcester
Coventry
Northampton
SUFFOLK
Ely
Fishguard
Hereford
Bedford
Cambridge
Felixstowe
DYFED
Buckingham
Pembroke
HEREFORD &
WORCESTER
Gloucester
Oxford
St. Albans
Chelmsford
BEDFORD~
SHIRE
WARWICKSHIRE
Swansea
Swindon
ESSEX
GLAMORGAN
Cardiff
Bristol
London
Canterbury
GWENT
Bath
Reading
KENT
GLOUCESTERSHIRE
Salisbury
Guildford
Dover
BATH, BRISTOL &
NORTH EAST
SOMERSET
Taunton
Southampton
Brighton
HERTFORD~
SHIRE
Exeter
GREATER
LONDON
CORNWALL
Truro
Plymouth
Weymouth
Bournemouth
SUSSEX
DEVON
DORSET
HAMPSHIRE
SURREY
BUCKINGHAMSHIRE
SOMERSET
WILTSHIRE
BERKSHIRE
OXFORDSHIRE

SCOTLAND

The history of Scotland is rich and complicated, the nation always being divided between the Highlands and the Lowlands. Despite inter-trading, the two factions always kept their distance even their language was different, the Highlanders largely Gaelic speaking, the Lowlanders English speaking.

The Highlanders were mobile cattle farmers, while the Lowlanders were static arable farmers, who firmly established themselves in burghs. The division still remains obvious today. The Lowlands, the land of Sir Walter Scott and Robert Burns, is a land of impressive castles, palaces, medieval burghs and the great cities of Glasgow and Edinburgh. The Highlands, is a region of magnificent mountain scenery, an awesome and majestic coastline, lonely glens and haunting open moors. Scottish history is written

deep in every region. The Jacobite rebellions of the 'Fifteen' and Forty-five' ending in the tragedy of Cullodon, were followed by the systematic destruction of the Highland way of life and the loss of the power of the Clan Chiefs, followed later by the Clearances - the eviction of the traditional highland crofters to make way for lowland sheep farmers.

Against such a background each region has jealously preserved its own particular and very distinctive character, making Scotland the perfect holiday venue. Of course, add to this some of the most spectacular and stimulating scenery in Great Britain and you have attractions that the holiday visitor will find hard to resist.

SCOTLAND

Places to Visit

Castle Fraser, *Inverurie* ~ begun in 1575, it incorporates an earlier building and the work was completed in 1636. The interior was remodelled in 1838 and some of the decoration and furnishings of that period survive.

Drumlanrig Castle, *Thornhill* ~ built from pink sandstone between 1679 and 1691 on the site of a 15th century Douglas stronghold. It contains a collection of treasures and Jacobite relics including Bonnie Prince Charlie's camp kettle, sash and money box. There are paintings by Leonardo da Vinci, Holbein and Rembrandt.

Glencoe & Dalness ~ a historic glen with visitor centre, set in some of the finest climbing and walking country in the Highlands. The Glencoe hills are an important geological site as they demonstrate the phenomenon of a volcano collapsing in on itself during eruptions.

Glamis Castle, *Forfar* ~ it was a royal hunting lodge in the 11th century but underwent extensive reconstruction in the 17th century. It was the childhood home of Queen Elizabeth, the Queen Mother, and her former bedroom can be seen.

Loch Ness Monster Exhibition Centre, *Inverness* ~ first sighted in the 6th century by St Columba, the Loch Ness monster has attracted increasing attention. The exhibition centre provides audio visual information on the loch's most famous resident.

Stirling Castle, *Stirling* ~ the present castle dates from the 15th and 16th centuries, but legend says that King Arthur took the original castle from the Saxons. From 1881 until 1964 the castle was a depot for recruits into the Argyll and Sutherland Highlanders.

Willow Tea Room, *Glasgow* ~ created by Charles Rennie Mackintosh at the turn of the century. Everything was his own design, including the cutlery and chairs.

Kilfinnan Fall,
near Spean Bridge

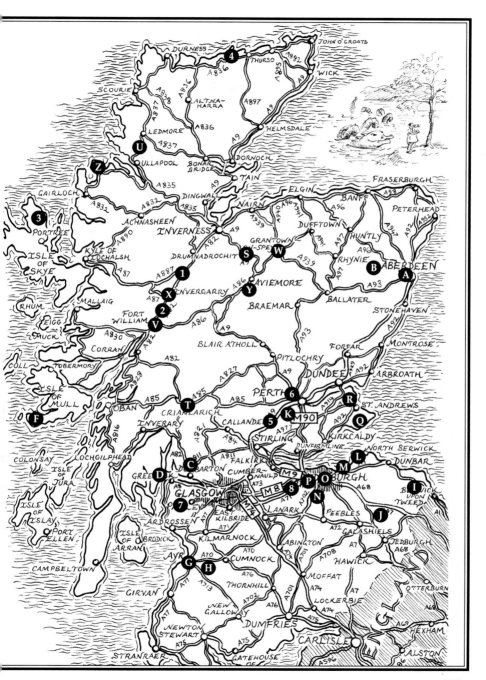

435

ABERDEENSHIRE

Craiglynn Hotel, 36 Fonthill Road, Aberdeen, Grampian AB11 6HJ   **Nearest Road A90**

Built in 1901 of local granite Craiglynn offers modern comforts with Victorian elegance. Situated in a residential area between Union Street and the award winning Duthie Park. Craiglynn is ideally positioned for business or leisure. All bedrooms and the dining room are strictly non smoking. However, there are 2 lounges where smoking is permitted. The bedrooms have colour TV, telephone, welcome tray, central heating and most have en-suite facilities. STB 3 Crowns Highly Commended and a member of 'Taste of Scotland' good food scheme. EMail: CRAIGLYNN@COMPUSERVE.COM http://www.craiglynn.co.uk

Chris & Hazel Mann
Tel: 01224 584050
Fax: 01224 212225

B&B from £29pp, Dinner from £15.95, Rooms 3 single, 1 twin, 3 double, 1 family, Restricted smoking, Children welcome, No pets, Open all year except Christmas, Map Ref A

Backhill of Burnhervie, By Kemnay, Inverurie, Aberdeenshire AB51 5JT

19th Century farmhouse set in 6 acres of garden and woodland, in a peaceful riverside location. A warm welcome, comfortable beds and a cosy sitting room await you. The day begins with a hearty, country breakfast. Home produced breads, preserves, honey and muesli with local eggs and bacon, or choose from a range of specialities. You will then be ready for the Castle and Whisky Trails, golf, fishing or walking the Bennachie Range and discovering the magic of this unique retreat. STB 4 Stars.

Julie Dainty
Tel: 01467 642139
Fax: 01467 642139

B&B from £25pp, Rooms 1 twin en-suite, 1 double with private bathroom, No smoking, Children over 12, No pets, Open April - October, Map Ref B

SEE BELLE & BERTIE IN SCOTLAND NEXT YEAR

ARGYLL & BUTE

Kirkton House, Darleith Road, Cardross, Argyll & Bute G82 5EZ Nearest Road A814

see PHOTO on page 437

An 18/19th century converted farmstead, in a tranquil country setting, commanding panoramic views of the Clyde. Loch Lomond, Glasgow city or Airport and the main West Highland routes are easily accessible. Guest lounge and dining areas have original stone walls. Rooms have full hotel amenities - bath/shower, TV, telephone, tea/coffee tray, desk and hair dryer. Wines, draught beer and spirits available. Dine by oil lamplight! Extensive daily menu for home cooked dinners. Guest comment ' One of the finest places we have stayed'. EMail: Kirktonhouse@compuserve.com

Stewart & Gillian MacDonald
Tel: 01389 841951
Fax: 01389 841868

B&B from £29.75pp, Dinner from £15.10, Rooms 2 twin, 4 family, all en-suite, Restricted smoking, Children welcome, Pets welcome, Open all year except December & January, Map Ref C

Abbot's Brae Hotel, West Bay, Dunoon, Argyllshire PA23 7QJ Nearest Road A815

see PHOTO opposite

Welcoming and friendly country house hotel in secluded 2 acre woodland glen with breathtaking views of the sea and hills.Spacious and tastefully furnished bedrooms, all en-suite with colour TV, radio, direct dial telephone, tea/coffee making facilities and full central heating. Unwind with a drink in the well appointed lounge and dine in the cosy dining room with delicious a la carte menu and select wine list. Residential licence. The perfect base to explore Argyll and the Western Highlands. Only one hour from Glasgow airport.   EMail: enquiry@abbotsbrae.ndirect.co.uk
http://www.abbotsbrae.ndirect.co.uk

Helen & Gavin Dick
Tel: 01369 705021
Fax: 01369 701191

B&B from £25pp, Dinner £15, Rooms 4 double, 2 family, 1 four poster, all en-suite, Open all year, Map Ref D

Red Bay Cottage, Deargphort, Fionnphort, Isle of Mull, Argyllshire PA66 6BP Nearest Road A849

Red Bay Cottage is a modern house built on the shoreline of the south west coast of Mull. John & Eleanor have built up a very good reputation for the quality of food in their adjoining restaurant and guests can eat in the pleasant dining room, overlooking Iona Sound and the white sands of Iona. An ideal base for touring Mull, Iona and the Treshnish Isles. Eleanor is a qualified practising silversmith so why not enjoy a winter break. Send for details of residential silversmithing courses.

John & Eleanor Wagstaff
Tel: 01681 700396

B&B from £16pp, Dinner from £7.50, Rooms 2 twin, 1 double, Pets by arrangement, Open all year, Map Ref F

*right, **Abbot's Brae Hotel**, Dunoon - see details above*

AYRSHIRE

The Crescent, 26 Bellevue Crescent, Ayr KA7 2DR   **Nearest Road B7024**

Built in 1898 at the height of Victorian splendour, The Crescent lies amidst an impressive row of imposing terraced houses. Its location allows guests complete peace and quiet, yet enjoys close proximity and easy access to Ayr's busy shopping centre and seafront. The charming bedrooms have all been individually styled and decorated in a manner befitting the opulence of the Victorian era. Good location for Robert Burns Heritage, Culzean Castle, golfing and horse racing. Glasgow Airport 45 minutes. Prestick Airport 10 minutes.

Caroline & Iain McDonald
Tel: 01292 287329
Fax: 01292 286779

B&B from £23pp, Rooms 2 twin, 2 double, all en-suite, No smoking or pets, Children over 5, Open mid January - mid December, Map Ref G

Low Coylton House, Manse Road, Coylton, Ayrshire KA6 6LE   **Nearest Road A70**

Spacious, very comfortable and quiet country house (Old Manse 1820) set in attractive garden. TV and tea/coffee making facilities in bedrooms, all with private bathroom. Golfers paradise, courses nearby including Ayr, Troon and Turnberry. Ayr 6 miles. Safe, sandy beaches 7 miles. Hill walking 15 miles. Culzean Castle (national Trust). Glasgow 35 miles. Edinburgh 70 miles. Dinner by arrangement. Email: xyi22@dial.pipex.com

Anne & George Hay
Tel: 01292 570615
Fax: 01292 570615

B&B from £23pp, Dinner £15 on request, Rooms 2 twin, 1 double, all with private/en-suite facilities, Children welcome, Open all year except Christmas & New Year, Map Ref H

Please mention
THE GREAT BRITISH BED & BREAKFAST
when booking your accommodation

BORDERS

Fairlaw, Reston, Eyemouth, Berwickshire TD14 5LN **Nearest Road A1**

Fairlaw is an Eighteenth century farmhouse. All original features, set in 5 acres beautiful, secluded gardens and woodland. 45 miles South East Edinburgh; 3 miles from St Abbs; 25 miles from Lindisfarne. We are ideally situated for outdoor pursuits or cultural/historical activities in and around Edinburgh and the Borders. We are well served by local pubs with seafood a speciality in this area. Guests have use of a lovely drawing room; all rooms have tea/coffee making facilities, radios, hair dryers. There is plenty of off street parking.

Mrs Katie Henderson
Tel: 018907 61724

B&B from £20pp, Rooms 2 twin (1 private), 1 double, No smoking, Children & pets welcome, Open April - October, Map Ref I

Whitehill Farm, Nenthorn, Kelso, Roxburghshire TD5 7RZ **Nearest Road A6089**

Whitehill is an early Victorian farmhouse on a mixed farm in a wonderful location with marvellous views of the cheviots. Carefully renovated to provide a comfortable, homely, peaceful atmosphere in which to unwind and relax. A sitting room is available to guests with log fire on cooler evenings. An area of with a wealth of history, Abbeys historic houses, golf, walking, fishing and the coast within easy reach. Edinburgh one hour approx. Four pretty bedrooms one twin en-suite, one twin sharing bathroom with two single rooms.

Mrs Betty Smith
Tel/Fax: 01573 470203

B&B from £22pp, Dinner by arrangement from £14, Rooms 2 single, 2 twin (1 en-suite), Restricted smoking, Children & pets welcome, Open all year except Christmas & New Year, Map Ref J

CLACKMANNANSHIRE

Westbourne, 10 Dollar Road, Tillicoultry, Clackmannanshire FK13 6PA **Nearest Road A91**

A fascinating Victorian mill owner's mansion set within wooded grounds, beneath the Ochil Hills. The atmosphere at Westbourne is warm and friendly with log fires on cool evenings and a croquet lawn. Off the road parking is available. Located amid glorious countryside in central Scotland, with The Trossachs, Loch Lomond, Edinburgh and Glasgow just 1 hour away. Motorway connections are within 15 miles. A wide range of activities are available nearby: sight seeing in historic Stirling, numerous golf courses, fishing and hill walking in Braveheart country! EMail: odellwestbourne@compuserve.com

Jane & Adrian O'Dell
Tel: 01259 750314
Fax: 01259 750642

B&B from £20pp, Rooms 1 twin, 2 double en-suite, 1 family, No smoking, Children welcome, Pets by arrangement, Open all year except Christmas & New Year, Map Ref K

EAST LOTHIAN

Faussetthill House, 20 Main Street, Gullane, Lothian EH31 2DR   Nearest Road A198, A1

see PHOTO below

Very comfortable private Edwardian house providing a high standard of bed and breakfast with TV in guest lounge. Tea/coffee making facilities in bedrooms. Car parking. Situated in a delightful quiet coastal village on A198 road where there is a wide choice of local restaurants, many golf courses within easy reach, 4 in village including Muirfield. Nearby is Aberlady Nature Reserve. Edinburgh 30 minutes by car. Scottish Tourist Board 4 Stars. Also QQQQ Selected by AA. Non smoking.

George & Dorothy Nisbet
Tel/Fax: 01620 842396

B&B from £22pp, Rooms 2 twin, 1 en-suite, 2 double, 1 en-suite, No smoking, Children over 12, No pets, Open March - December, Map Ref L

Delta House, 16 Carberry Road, Inveresk, Musselburgh, East Lothian EH21 7TN   Nearest Road A1, A720

A beautiful Victorian stone built house situated in a quiet conservation village 7 miles east of central Edinburgh, overlooking fields and close to a lovely river walks and seaside with harbour. Buses from door to city, near sports centre with swimming pool and within easy reach of several golf courses. Spacious accommodation with central heating, colour TV and tea/coffee making facilities. Two large bathrooms adjacent. Full cooked breakfast included. Parking in a quiet side road or within the large walled garden by arrangement.

Judith & Harper Cuthbert
Tel: 0131 6652107

B&B from £18-£25pp, Rooms 3 double (1 en-suite), 1 family, No smoking or pets, Children welcome, Open all year except Christmas & New Year, Map Ref M

EDINBURGH

Craig Cottage, 5 New Pentland, By Loanhead, Midlothian EH20 9NT **Nearest Road A701**

A warm welcome awaits you from the hosts and their assorted pets. We are 100 yards off the A701 and within half a mile of Edinburgh bypass which facilitates travel to all parts of Scotland. For golf, riding and sightseeing. There is a good bus service to city centre. Hot drinks are served on request and bedrooms have TV, there is ample off street parking. A variety of breakfasts will suit all tastes. There are several good restaurants nearby.

Mrs Ciupik
Tel: 0131 440 0405

B&B from £15pp, Rooms 1 twin, 1 double, No smoking, Children over 6, Pets by arrangement, Open February - October, Map Ref N

---

60 Braid Road, Edinburgh EH10 6AL **Nearest Road A702**

No.60 Braid Road is a comfortable Victorian family house conveniently located for the centre of Edinburgh and all its attractions. Both the bedrooms are situated at the back of the house overlooking the garden and have tea and coffee making facilities and a hair dryer. There is free on-street parking outside the house and an excellent bus service from just around the corner to Princes Street. You will get a warm welcome here and all the help you need with your visit to Edinburgh. Email: Fass@dial.pipex.com

Iola & Michael Fass
Tel: 0131 446 9356
Fax: 0131 447 7367

B&B from £26pp, Rooms 1 twin, 1 double, both private facilities, No smoking or pets, Children welcome, Open all year except Christmas & New Year, Map Ref O

---

16 Lynedoch Place, Edinburgh EH3 7PY **Nearest Road A1**

Lynedoch Place is unusual example of a complete Georgian Town House, designed and built in 1821 by the famous Edinburgh Architect, James Milne. It is located two minutes walk from Princes Street, Edinburgh's main shopping area. The house has been beautifully restored and decorated by the owners, Andrew and Susie Hamilton. Their objective is to make their guests feel comfortable and at home. Breakfast is a veritable feast of fresh fruit salad, cereal, hot croissant and the full cooked Great British Breakfast - not to be missed!

Susie & Andrew Hamilton
Tel: 0131 2255507
Fax: 0131 2264185

B&B from £35pp, Rooms 1 single, 1 twin, 1 double, all en-suite, Open all year except Christmas, Map Ref O

Rowan Guest House, 13 Glenorchy Terrace, Edinburgh EH9 2DQ **Nearest Road A701, A7**

Elegant 19th century Victorian home in quiet leafy conservation area with free parking and only 10 minute bus ride to the centre. The castle, Royal Mile, Holyrood Palace, University, theatres, restaurants and other amenities are easily reached. Rooms are charmingly decorated and have TV, tea/coffee and biscuits. A hearty Scottish breakfast is served including porridge and freshly baked scones. Alan and Angela will make every effort to ensure an enjoyable stay. 10% reduction on production of this book. (Excluding August and New year).

Alan & Angela Vidler
Tel: 0131 667 2463
Fax: 0131 667 2463

B&B from £21pp, Rooms 2 single, 3 twin, 3 double, 1 family, some en-suite, Restricted smoking & pets, Children welcome, Open all year except Christmas, Map Ref O

Ben Cruachan, 17 McDonald Road, Edinburgh EH7 4LX   Nearest Road A1

A most friendly welcome awaits you at our centrally located high standard accommodation within walking distance of the Castle the Royal Mile, Holyrood Palace and Princes Street one of Britain's most picturesque shopping venues. Many varied restaurants within 5 minute walk. Our en-suite rooms are tastefully decorated, have TV, central heating and tea/coffee making facilities. Excellent breakfast served. Unrestricted street parking. Non smoking. STB 3 Star Commended.

Nan & Eden Stark
Tel: 0131 556 3709

B&B from £25pp, Rooms 1 twin, 1 double,1 family, all en-suite, No smoking or pets, Children over 10, Open April - November, Map Ref O

Ailsa Craig Hotel, 24 Royal Terrace, Edinburgh EH7 5AH   Nearest Road A1, A74

Georgian house situated in Edinburgh's famous Royal Terrace. The hotel is within walking distance to Princes Street, Holyrood Palace, Royal Mile and many other attractions. Waverly Train Station, St. Andrew's bus station short walk away. Edinburgh Airport approximately 7 miles away has regular bus services. A warm welcome friendly atmosphere, comfortable rooms are ensured at the hotel, tastefully decorated 17 bedrooms offer colour TV, tea/coffee making facilities, hair dryers, telephones, centrally heated. 15 with en-suite, spacious rooms for family sharing available throughout the year.

Cathie Hamilton
Tel: 0131 5566055/1022
Fax: 0131 556 6055

B&B from £25pp, Rooms 4 single, 4 twin, 4 family, 5 double, most en-suite, Children welcome, Pets restricted, Open all year, Map Ref O

The Lodge Hotel, 6 Hampton Terrace, West Coates, Edinburgh EH12 5JD   Nearest Road A8

The Lodge Hotel is an elegant family run hotel situated 1 mile from city centre and all major tourist attractions. All our en-suite rooms are beautifully furnished throughout, each with many personal touches for our guests comfort. Relax in the cosy cocktail bar or lounge after a day exploring Scotlands capital. Our choice of menu offers well prepared dishes with a good selection of wines. Car parking is available with a good bus service from outside the hotel. STB 4 Stars.

George & Linda Jarron
Tel: 0131 3373682
Fax: 0131 3131700

B&B from £29-£40pp, Dinner from £14.50, Rooms 1 single, 2 twin, 6 double, all en-suite, Restricted smoking, Children welcome, No pets, Open all year except 7th-28th December, Map Ref P

---

27 Heriot Row, Edinburgh, Lothian EH3 6EN   Nearest Road Heriot Row

Built in 1804, 27 Heriot Row is in Edinburgh's premier residential street and although only 4 street away from Princes Street and the world famous Edinburgh castle, your stay here will not only be luxurious but it will also be quiet and relaxing. Each room is furnished to the highest deluxe standard with en-suite bath and shower facilities, direct dial telephone, hair dryer, TV and tea/coffee making facilities. Your hosts will be delighted to help plan your sightseeing. French,German and Spanish are spoken. Scottish Tourist Board 3 Crowns Deluxe.EMail: t.a@cableinet.co.uk

Andrea & Gene Targett Adams
Tel: 0131 225 9474
Fax: 0131 220 1699

B&B from £45pp, Rooms 1 single, 1 twin, 1 double, all en-suite, No smoking, Children welcome, Map Ref O

Ellesmere House, *Edinburgh - see details on page 446*

Ellesmere House, 11 Glengyle Terrace, Edinburgh, Lothian EH3 9LN   Nearest Road A702

see PHOTO on page 445

Attractive and comfortable house centrally located in a residential area and facing south over a park. The castle, Royal Mile (Edinburgh's old historic town) and Princes Street (one of Britain's best shopping venues) are all within very easy reach. Close to International Conference Centre. Rooms are spacious, individually decorated and well equipped with TV, heating and tea/coffee making facilities. All rooms are en-suite and a 4 poster bed is available. There are many varied restaurants and pubs locally. Scottish Tourist Board award 2 Crowns Highly Recommended, AA QQQQ Selected.

Celia & Tommy Leishman
Tel: 0131 229 4823
Fax: 0131 229 5285

B&B from £25pp, Rooms 1 single, 2 twin, 2 double, 1 family, all en-suite, Children over 10, Open all year, Map Ref O

Hopetoun Guest House, 15 Mayfield Road, Edinburgh, Lothian EH9 2NG   Nearest Road City Bypass

Hopetoun is a small, friendly, family run guest house close to Edinburgh university. 1.5 miles south of Princes Street, with an excellent bus service into city. Very comfortable accommodation is offered in a completely smoke free environment. Having only 3 guest bedrooms, and now offering private facilities, the owner prides herself in ensuring personal attention to all guests in a friendly, informal atmosphere. All rooms have central heating, wash basins, colour TV and tea/coffee. Parking is available. Which? - Good B&B Guide. AA QQ. STB 2 Crowns Commended. Access/Visa. Email: hopetoun@aol.com

Rhoda Mitchell
Tel: 0131 667 7691
Fax: 0131 466 1691

B&B from £20-£30pp, Rooms 1 twin, 1 double, 1 family, 2 en-suite, No smoking, Children welcome, No pets, Open all year except Christmas, Map Ref O

International Guest House, 37 Mayfield Gardens, Edinburgh, Lothian EH9 2BX   Nearest Road A701

Attractive stone built Victorian house situated one and a half miles south of Princes Street on the main A701. Private parking. Luxury bedrooms with en-suite facilities, colour television, telephone and tea/coffee makers. Magnificent views across the extinct volcano of Arthur's Seat. Full Scottish breakfast served on the finest bone china. International has received many accolades for its quality and level of hospitality. A 19th century setting with 21st century facilities. 'In Britain' magazine has rated the International as their 'find' in all Edinburgh.

Mrs Niven
Tel: 0131 667 2511
Fax: 0131 667 1112

B&B from £19.35pp, Rooms 3 single, 1 twin, 2 double, 3 family, all en-suite, Restricted smoking, Children welcome, No pets, Open all year, Map Ref O

Avenue Hotel, 4 Murrayfield Avenue, Edinburgh, Midlothian EH12 6AX   Nearest Road A8

Located in a quiet tree lined avenue the hotel is an imposing Victorian villa, situated west of and only minutes from the city centre. Ideal for both the business traveller and the tourist, with easy access to the motorway links to both the north and west of Scotland. All nine individually designed rooms are en-suite with TV, direct dial telephone, hair dryer and tea/coffee making facilities. Ample free parking. Full Scottish breakfast included.

Adrian & Jackie Hayes
Tel: 0131 346 7270
Fax: 0131 337 9733

B&B from £20pp, Rooms 2 single, 2 twin, 3 double, 2 family, 2 en-suite, Children & pets welcome, Open all year except Christmas, Map Ref O

*right, **The Town House**, Edinburgh - see details on page 448*

Scotland - Edinburgh

Barony House, 4 Queen's Crescent, Edinburgh, Lothian EH9 2AZ   **Nearest Road Dalkeith Road**

Comfortable Victorian house. Just 15 minutes from city centre. En-suite rooms with colour TV, direct dial telephone, hair dryers, tea/coffee making facilities, ironing boards available on request. Barony House is famous for its full Scottish buffet style breakfast, and the friendly helpful staff managed by Susie Berkengoff. Scottish evenings and dinner at local restaurants can be arranged. Susie will also cater for special dietary requirements. Car parking. A memorable stay.

Susie Berkengoff
Tel: 0131 667 5806

B&B from £18pp, Evening meals available, Rooms 2 single, 2 en-suite twin, 2 en-suite double, 3 family, 1 en-suite, No smoking, Children welcome, No pets, Open all year except Christmas, Map Ref O

The Town House, 65 Gilmore Place, Edinburgh, Lothian EH3 9NU   **Nearest Road A702, A1**

see PHOTO on page 447

Attractive privately owned Victorian town house, located in the city centre. Theatres and restaurants are only minutes walk away. The Town House has been fully restored and tastefully decorated, retaining many original architectural features. Our bedrooms are tastefully furnished and individually decorated, all have en-suite bath or shower and wc, central heating, radio alarm, colour TV, hair dryer and tea/coffee tray. Our parking is situated at the rear of the house. Scottish Tourist Board 2 Crowns Highly Commended, AA QQQQ Selected, Les Routiers. Totally non smoking.

Susan Virtue
Tel: 0131 229 1985

B&B from £25-£35pp, Rooms 1 single,1 twin, 3 double, all en-suite, No smoking, Children over 10,No pets, Open all year except Christmas, Map Ref O

above, **The Hermitage Guest House,** *Anstruther - see details opposite*

FIFE

The Hermitage Guest House, Ladywalk, Anstruther, Fife KY10 3EX Nearest Road A917

Part of The Hermitage existed in 1588 when exhausted sailors from the ill fated Spanish Armada were helped ashore and shown mercy and kindness by 'Anster folk'. Today, The Hermitage carries on that tradition, offering the stranger friendship and relaxation in a beautifully restored 'home from home'. The house faces south with superb views across the River Forth. Our 'secret garden' is a joy. The area is a golfers mecca, with St Andrew's only 10 miles away. STB 4 Stars, AA QQQQQ Premier Selected. STB Welcome Host.

see PHOTO opposite

Margaret McDonald &
Eric Hammond
Tel: 01333 310909

B&B from £20pp, Rooms 2 suites each comprising 2 double bedrooms, bathroom & lounge, Non smoking, Licensed, Children welcome, No pets, Open all year except Christmas, Map Ref Q

Todhall House, Dairsie, By Cupar, Fife KY15 4RQ Nearest Road A91

Todhall is a Georgian style country house set in attractive gardens overlooking the superb vistas of the Eden Valley, 7 miles from St Andrews. You will experience quality accommodation in this warm friendly home. The Kingdom of Fife - rich in history, offers a wide variety of pursuits. Golf on some of Scotland's finest courses. Explore the university town of St Andrews, East Neuk, fishing villages and National Trust properties. There are quality restaurants and good pub food nearby. STB Highly Commended. AA QQQQQ Premier Selected. STB - Scotland's best. Come!

John & Gill Donald
Tel: 01334 656344
Fax: 01334 656344

B&B from £23-£30pp, Dinner from £16, Rooms 1 twin, 2 double, all en-suite, No smoking, Children over 12, No pets, Open mid March - October, Map Ref R

Please mention
THE GREAT BRITISH
BED & BREAKFAST
when booking your accommodation

Feith Mhor Country House, Station Road, Carr-bridge, Inverness-shire PH23 3AP   **Nearest Road B9153**

The peaceful secluded setting of Feith Mhor, 1.5 miles from the village, enables you to relax and enjoy the beauty of the Highlands. This lovely late 19th century house, set in 1.5 acres of attractive garden, offers a warm welcome and traditional comfort. The pleasantly furnished bedrooms are all en-suite with colour TV, radio and tea/coffee making facilities. We offer a varied breakfast menu, and home made preserves, with fruit from the gardens. This is a wonderful area for birdwatchers, tourists, walkers, fishing and golf. STB 2 Stars, AA QQQ, Recommended by 'Which?'.

Penny & Peter Rawson
Tel: 01479 841621

B&B from £25pp, Rooms 3 twin, 3 double, all en-suite, Restricted smoking, Minimum age 10, Pets by arrangement, Open all year, Map Ref S

Allt-Chaorain House, Crianlarich, Perthshire FK20 8RU   **Nearest Road A82**

Allt-Chaorain Country House affords guests the amenities, comfort and atmosphere of their own home. The lounge has a log fire burning throughout the year, a trust bar and adjoining sun room which offers one of the most picturesque views of the Highlands, with Ben More dominating the landscape. We are a Taste of Scotland member and proud of our reputation for home cooked food which is made from fresh local produce. An honesty bar and a comprehensive wine list is available for those guests who enjoy a relaxing drink.

Roger McDonald
Tel: 01838 300283
Fax: 01838 300238

B&B from £35 -£39pp, Dinner from £15, Rooms 4 en-suite twin, 4 en-suite double, No smoking, Children over 7, Pets welcome, Open 20th March - 30th October, Map Ref T

Birchbank Holiday Lodge, Knockan, Elphin, Sutherland IV27 4HH   **Nearest Road A835**

Conveniently located on the boundary of Inverpolly National Nature Reserve, 14 miles north of Ullapool. Birchbank Holiday Lodge offers comfortable licensed accommodation with purpose built modern facilities, including sauna suite and drying room, and a friendly family atmosphere - the ideal base for exploring the unspoiled lochs, glens and mountains of north west Sutherland. Organised hill walking and glen rambling excursions by arrangement, boat and bank fishing for wild brown trout also available on well known local lochs. All with professional guidance and expert local knowledge.

Tom & Ray Strang
Tel/Fax: 01854 666215

B&B from £20pp, Dinner from £14, Rooms 1 single, 4 twin/double, most en-suite, Restricted smoking, Children & pets welcome, Open May - October, Map Ref U

Ashburn House, 2 Ashburn Lane, Fort William, PH33 6RQ   **Nearest Road A82**

Overlooking Loch Linnhe. Ashburne is a most relaxing B&B. The Highland owners pay every attention to detail but do not impose on your privacy, even separate tables in the Victorian Corniced breakfast room. The house has achieved all the highest accolades, AA 5Q, RAC Highly Acclaimed, STB De-luxe. All rooms are en-suite, central heating, TV. Free off road parking. Full fire certificate. An excellent centre to tour the magical Highlands and Skye. Discount for week booking. Colour brochure. Web site http://www.ark.uk.com/bb/ashburnhouse/ashburnhouse.htm

Alexandra Henderson
Tel/Fax: 01397 706000

B&B from £30-£35pp, Rooms 3 single, 1 twin, 3 double, all en-suite, No smoking or pets, Children welcome, Open February - November, Map Ref V

The Grange, Grange Road, Fort William, PH33 6JF   **Nearest Road A82**

Set in three quarters of an acre overlooking the Loch. This is a luxurious town house recently refurbished. The Grange has large rooms all with Loch views. Guests are made welcome with tea on arrival and looked after, nothing seems too much trouble. Awarded Best B&B in Scotland by the STB in 1996 and Best B&B Scotland by the AA Association in 1997. The Grange really offers excellent accommodation, close to local amenities and walking distance from local seafood restaurants makes this a good base for touring the West Highlands.

Joan & John Campbell
Tel: 01397 705516   **B&B from £37-£47pp, Rooms 4 double, No smoking or pets, Children**
Fax: 01397 701595   **over 12, Open Easter - November, Map Ref V**

Ardconnel House, Woodlands Terrace, Grantown on Spey, Moray PH26 4JU   **Nearest Road A95**

Built in 1890, during the Victorian era of elegance, Ardconnel House stands in its own spacious grounds overlooking a glorious pine forest, Lochan and Cromdale Hills. Six bedrooms are en-suite, with quality beds, colour TV, hair dryer and welcome tray, and are charmingly decorated. A superb 4-poster bedroom. Excellent home cooking is complemented by a well-selected, modestly priced wine list. Taste of Scotland selected member. AA 5Q Premier Selected. Non smoking throughout.

Michel & Barbara Bouchard   **B&B from £25pp, Dinner from £18, Rooms 1 single, 1 twin, 2 double, 2**
Tel: 01479 872104   **family, all en-suite, No smoking or pets, Children over 10, Open Easter**
Fax: 01479 872104   **- October, Map Ref W**

Craigard House, Invergarry, Inverness-shire PH35 4HG   **Nearest Road A82**

Set in the breathtaking splendour of the Highlands, Craigard, a large country house on the western outskirts of the village of Invergarry is the perfect base for a relaxing and varied holiday. Each of the well furnished bedrooms has a washbasin and tea/coffee making facilities. Guests can enjoy a quiet drink in the relaxed atmosphere of the residents' lounge and on cooler evenings pull up to a roaring log fire. TV in all bedrooms. The magnificent scenery surrounding Craigard makes it an ideal point for touring.

Mr R L Withers   **B&B from £18pp, Dinner £15, Rooms 2 double en-suite, 1 single en-**
Tel: 01890 501258   **suite, 3 double, 1 twin with wash hand basin, Non smoking, No children,**
                            No pets, Open all year, Map Ref X

March House, Feshiebridge, Kincraig, Inverness-shire PH21 1NG   **Nearest Road A9**

Secluded in beautiful Glenfeshie surrounded by forest trails, river and mountain walks, on the edge of the Cairngorm Nature Reserve. Relaxing, friendly and informal atmosphere with a spacious pine conservatory overlooking the mountains and Glen, with plants, books, maps and a large log fire. Meals are specially prepared with local ingredients, free range eggs and homegrown herbs. Imaginative yet simple, tasting distinctly fresh. Comfortable, individually decorated bedrooms have en-suite bath/showers with many extras. They also enjoy great views. Brochures available ask for Caroline.

Caroline Hayes   **B&B from £20pp, Dinner from £16, Rooms 2 twin, 2 double, 2 family, 5**
Tel: 01540 651388   **en-suite, 1 private, Restricted smoking, Children & pets welcome, Open**
Fax: 01540 651388   **December - October, Map Ref Y**

Balcraggan House, Feshiebridge, by Kincraig, Inverness-shire PH21 1NG   **Nearest Road A9, B970**

Balcraggan House is situated at Inshriach Forest where pine marten, buzzard, osprey, roe deer and red squirrel abound, with a badger sett nearby. Miles of cycle routes and walks straight from the front door or use your car to explore the magnificent Highlands. All rooms are tastefully and traditionally furnished with log, peat fires in drawing room and dining room.

Helen Gillies
Tel: 01540 651488

B&B from £25pp, Dinner from £15, Rooms 1 twin, 1 double, both en-suite with baths, No smoking, No pets, Children over 10, Open all year, Map Ref Y

The Sheiling, Achgarve, Laide, Rosshire IV22 2NS   **Nearest Road A832**

The Sheiling is a modern bungalow situated on the Gruinard Peninsula near Gruinard Bay on the west coast of Scotland. Set amongst beautiful hills with distant views of the high mountains of An Teallach. You can explore the outstanding scenery and walk the fine shell beaches whilst watching seals possibly otters and a myriad of sea birds. Rooms are furnished to a high standard offering typical Scottish hospitality, TV and tea/coffee facilities. Within easy reach of Gairloch, Ullapool, AN Teallch mountains, Inverewe Gardens and Beinn Eighe Nature Reserve.

Annabell MacIver
Tel: 01445 731487

B&B from £21pp, Rooms 1 twin, 1 double, both en-suite, No smoking, Children over 14, No pets, Open March - October, Map Ref Z

Foyers Bay House, Lower Foyers, Loch Ness, Inverness-shire   **Nearest Road A82, A9**

In its own magnificent grounds of wooded pine slopes abundant rhododendrons and apple orchard with fabulous view of Loch Ness, nestles the splendid Victorian villa of Foyers Bay House. The grounds are set amid beautiful forest, nature trails and adjoin the famous Falls of Foyers. The villa is tastefully and luxuriously refurbished. Rooms have telephone, TV and en-suite bath or shower room, tea/coffee making facilities, fresh fruit and bath/shower gel, compliments of your hosts Otto & Carol Panciroli. The guest house is not licensed but guests are welcome to bring their own wine.

Mr & Mrs O E Panciroli
Tel: 01456 486624
Fax: 01456 486337

B&B from £19.50pp, Dinner from £10.50, Rooms 3 double, 2 twin, Open all year, Map Ref 1

Invergloy House, Spean Bridge, Inverness-shire PH34 4DY   **Nearest Road A82**

see PHOTO opposite

Invergloy House welcomes non smokers. This is a converted coach house and stables set in 50 acres of attractive wooded grounds. Guests have their own large sitting room with magnificent views over Loch Lochy and mountains. All rooms are tastefully and traditionally furnished. Bedrooms have en-suite facilities. The house lies 5.5 miles north of Spean Bridge on the main road to Inverness overlooking Loch Lochy where free fishing is available from a private shingle beach, reached by footpath. Rowing boats for hire. Hard tennis court. SAE for details.

Mrs M H Cairns
Tel: 01397 712681

B&B from £21pp, Rooms 3 twin, en-suite facilities, Children over 8, No smoking, Open all year, Map Ref 2

Glenview Inn & Restaurant, Culnacnoc, Staffin, Isle of Skye IV51 9JH   **Nearest Road A855**

A charming inn nestling between mountains and sea and ideally situated for exploring the magnificent scenery of North Skye. We have pretty country style bedrooms with private facilities and tea/coffee making trays and our cosy lounge has television and open peat fire. Our restaurant, fully licensed, is much acclaimed and offers the best of fresh Skye seafood, as well as traditional, ethnic and vegetarian specialities. Members of Taste of Scotland and STB 3 Crowns Commended.

Paul & Cathie Booth
Tel: 01470 562248
Fax: 01470 562211

B&B from £25pp, Dinner from £12.95, Rooms 1 twin, 3 double, 1 family, all en-suite, Restricted smoking, Children welcome, Pets welcome, Open March - October, Map Ref 3

Catalina Guest House, Aultivullin, Strathy Point, Sutherland KW14 7RY   **Nearest Road A836**

Out on a headland along the remote far north coastline with only two people per square kilometre! The Atlantic Ocean on three sides. Totally non smoking. We take only two guests with their own private suite complete with its own lounge, dining room and shower room. Treat it as your own home, stay in all day if you wish, books, television, tea/coffee, delicious home cooked meals served at any time. Excellent walking area. Which? Book Good Bed & Breakfast Guide, AA QQQQ Selected, STB 3 Crowns Highly Commended.

Peter & Jane Salisbury
Tel: 01641 541279
Fax: 01641 541314

B&B from £18pp, Dinner £10, Rooms 1 en-suite twin, No smoking, children or pets, Open all year except Christmas, Map Ref 4

above, **Invergloy House,** *Spean Bridge - see details opposite*

PERTHSHIRE & KINROSS

Dunearn House, High Street, Auchterarder, Perthshire PH3 1DB   **Nearest Road A9**

"The Perthshire Experience" Hidden behind the High Street you will find a Victorian country house hotel. Quiet and peaceful, sympathetically restored throughout with spectacular views and a wide variety of outdoor pursuits. Gleneagles and many other stunning golf courses are on the doorstep. All rooms en-suite with colour TV, hair dryer, telephone and courtesy tray. Fully licensed with restaurant, cosy lounge, bar. We are well used to caring for your needs and able to provide a relaxing environment for you to unwind in.

Bob & Maureen Cox
Tel: 01764 664774
Fax: 01764 663242

B&B from £35pp, Supper from £7, Rooms 2 single, 1 twin, 3 double, 1 family, en-suite, Non smoking bedrooms, Children welcome, No pets, Open all year, Map Ref 5

Kinniard Guest House, 5 Marshall Place, Perth, Perthshire PH2 8AH   **Nearest Road M90, A85**

Would you like to relax in comfort? Then the warm friendly atmosphere at Kinnaird is just the place. We aim for high standards and traditional home comforts and cater for individual needs. Beautifully situated overlooking a leafy park to the south and our charming town centre is within easy walking distance. Buses and trains also within easy reach. An ideal base from which to explore this beautiful region and its many historical attractions.

John & Tricia Stiell
Tel: 01738 628021
Fax: 01738 444056

B&B from £22pp, Dinner from £10, Rooms 3 twin, 4 double, all en-suite, No smoking, Children over 12, No pets, Open all year except Christmas & New Year, Map Ref 6

RENFREWSHIRE

East Lochhead, Largs Road, Lochwinnoch, Renfrewshire PA12 4DX   **Nearest Road A760**

Janet Anderson guarantees you a warm welcome at East Lochhead where you will find every home comfort. The one hundred year old farmhouse has spectacular views over Barr Loch and the Renfrewshire hills. You can wander around the landscaped gardens or explore the Paisley/Irvine cycle track which passes close to the house. Janet is an enthusiastic cook and would be delighted to prepare you an evening meal with prior notice. Both rooms are beautifully furnished and have colour TV and tea/coffee making facilities. STB 4 Stars. EMail: winnoch@aol.com

Janet Anderson
Tel/Fax: 01505 842610

B&B from £30pp, Dinner from £18, Rooms 1 twin, 1 double, both en-suite, Restricted smoking, Children welcome, Pets by arrangement, Open all year, Map Ref 7

*right, **Whitecroft**, East Calder - see details on page 456*

PERTHSHIRE & KINROSS

Whitecroft, East Calder, Livingston, West Lothian EH53 0ET   **Nearest Road A71**

see PHOTO on page 455

Douglas and Lorna extend a warm Scottish welcome with all bedrooms on ground level. The bedrooms are all en-suite and furnished to the highest stand. Each bedroom has a remote control colour TV and tea/coffee making facilities. Whitecroft is surround by farmland yet only 10 miles from Edinburgh city centre. Safe private parking. A full hearty Scottish breakfast is served using local produce, even whisky marmalade. There are restaurants in the area providing evening meals. STB 3 Stars, AA QQQQ Selected. Email: LornaScot@aol.com

Douglas & Lorna Scott
Tel: 01506 882494
Fax: 01506 882598

B&B from £22pp, Rooms 1 twin, 2 double, all en-suite, No smoking, Children over 12, No pets, Open all year, Map Ref 8

Please mention

THE GREAT BRITISH
BED & BREAKFAST

when booking your accommodation

If Winter comes, can Spring be far behind?

'ODE THE THE WEST WIND' (1819) L.69
PERCY BYSSHE SHELLEY 1792-1822

WALES

Tourism is now Wales' largest industry, and little wonder, Wales has such a lot to offer, and so much that is peculierly Welsh. The wonderful lilting Welsh language is the first language of many in the north and west of the country, in fact roughly one in five of its inhabitants are Welsh speaking. The Welsh are famously musical, and this is expressed in festivals and events all over the country, culminating in the colourful Llangollen International Musical Eisteddfod, where singers and dancers from all over the world gather; and Wales' most important cultural festival, the Royal National Eisteddfod which dates back to 1176. Needless to say Wales possesses some superb theatres and concert halls including the very fine St. David's Hall, Cardiff. Wales is very much an 'outdoor' country, and has a fine reputation as a sporting nation. The three National Parks offer all the walking and climbing visitors could wish for. The Snowdon National Park, rugged and rocky; the Brecon Beacons National Park, presenting the walker with a much more open and rolling landscape; and one of Europe's classic coastal walks which follows the Pembrokeshire Coast National Park coast path a distance of one hundred and ninety miles around the western shore of Wales. For the slightly less energetic and for families, there are the delights of forest walks in the Coed-y-Brenin Forest and around lovely Betws-y-Coed.

But surely the glory of Wales must be in its magnificent medieval castles, well over a hundred in number, and varying considerably in style and size. The superb fortress of Caernarfon, reputed to be the birthplace of the Emperor Constantine, has the Eagle Tower, one of the largest built in the Middle Ages. Here in 1284 Edward I presented his son to the Welsh people as Prince of Wales. HRH Prince Charles was similarly invested in 1969. The grand Beaumaris Castle, which was never attacked; Harlech Castle built by Edward I, at Owen Glendower's wife and family were captured by Henry V; and glorious Conwy Castle, guards the Conwy estuary.

As well as the spectacular mountains and waterfalls, historic castles and houses, the rugged coasts, the music and song, the wide spaces and open skies, there are also some grand traditional seaside resorts - Llandudno, Colwyn Bay, Prestatyn and Rhyl, Aberystwyth, Aberdovey and Porthcawl .and then there are the delights of Clough Williams-Ellis's Portmeirion.

WALES

Places to Visit

Cardiff Castle, *Cardiff* ~ it began as a Roman fort whose remains are separated from later work by red stone. The keep was built in the 12th century and in 1867 William Burges created an ornate mansion. The Banqueting Hall shows the castle's history with murals and a castellated fireplace.

Llechwedd Slate Mines, *Blaenau Ffestiniog* ~ opened to visitors in the early 1970's, a tramway takes passengers into the caverns. On the Deep Mine tour, visitors go down Britain's steepest passenger incline railway to the underground chambers. Also, there are demonstrations of slate splitting and reconstructed quarrymen's cottages, showing the cramped living conditions of workers.

Pentre Ifan, *between Fishguard and Cardigan* ~ a Neolithic chambered long barrow on the northern slopes of the Preseli Hills. The capstone is thought to weigh over seventeen tons and is balanced on three pointed uprights.

Pen y Fan, *Brecon Beacons* ~ at over two thousand and nine hundred feet high this is the highest point in South Wales. Its flat summit was once a Bronze Age burial ground and can be reached by footpaths from Storey Arms.

Powis Castle, *Welshpool* ~ it began life in the 13th century as a fortress, to control the border with England. The dining room is decorated with 17th century panelling and family portraits. The gardens were created between 1688 and 1722 and are the only gardens of this period in Britain to keep their original form.

St David's Cathedral, *St Davids* ~ set in Britain's smallest city, St David, the patron saint of Wales founded a monastic settlement here in 550, but the cathedral was built in the 12th century and the nearby Bishops Palace was added in the 13th century. Inside is St David's Shrine; the original was stolen in 1089 and the present shrine of 1275 was stripped of jewels in the Dissolution.

Strata Florida Abbey, *near Pontrhydfendigiad* ~ Prince Rhys ap Gruffydd founded a community of Cistercian monks here in 1184 and they looked after large sheep ranches over the surrounding Cambrian Mountains. All that remains of their abbey is a western doorway, some foundations laid out in the grass and some medieval floor tiles.

Saint David's Cathedral

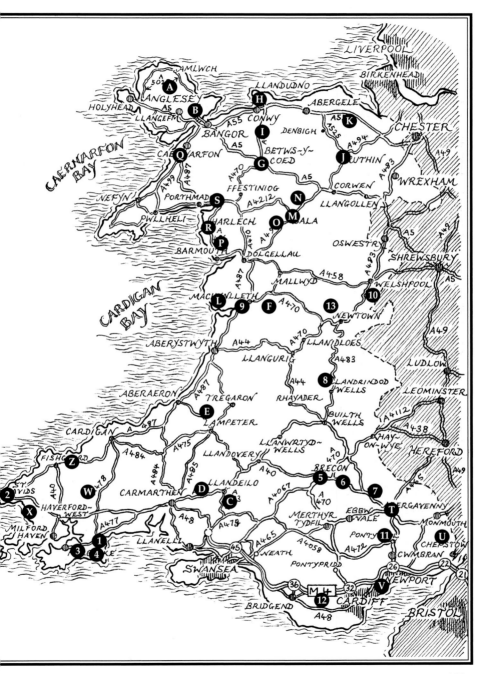

461

ANGLESEY

Drws y Coed Farm, Llannerch y Medd, Isle of Anglesey LL71 8AD   **Nearest Road A5, A5025**

With wonderful panoramic views of Snowdonia and unspoilt countryside, enjoy peace and tranquillity at this beautifully appointed farmhouse on a 550 acre working beef, sheep and arable farm. It's centrally situated to explore Anglesey. Tastefully decorated and furnished en-suite bedrooms with all facilities. Excellent meals served in cosy dining room. Inviting spacious lounge with log fire. Full central heating. Games room. Historical farmstead with lovely private walks. Warm welcome assured from Tom and Jane. WTB 2 Crowns Deluxe Graded. 25 minutes to Holyhead for Irish Sea crossings.

Mrs Jane Bown
Tel: 01248 470473

B&B from £21.50-£23.50pp, Rooms 1 twin, 1 double, 1 family, all en-suite, No smoking, Children welcome, No pets, Open all year except Christmas, Map Ref A

Bwthyn, Brynafon, Menai Bridge, Isle of Anglesey LL59 5HA   **Nearest Road A545**

Warm, welcoming, non smoking B&B, 1 minute from beautiful Menai Strait and bowling green. Bwthyn ('dear little house' in Welsh), a former Victorian quarryman's cottage, offers comfort, character and hospitality. 2 en-suite rooms with power shower (1 also with bath), TV, tea/coffee and complemented by scrumptious real home cooking. 2 miles rail/coaches, 40 mins Holyhead Ferry. Limited private parking. Special over 45's break - 3 nights dinner, bed & breakfast £79pp. WTB 2 Crown Highly Commended. Editors Top 20 UK B&B's, WHICH Recommended Guide 1999. Come as guests - leave as friends.

Rosemary Abas
Tel: 01248 713119
Fax: 01248 713119

B&B from £15pp, 4 course dinner £12.50 by arrangement, Rooms 2 double en-suite, No smoking, No children or pets, Open all year except Christmas, Map Ref B

*above, **The Glynhir Estate**, Llandybie - see details on page 463*

CARMARTHENSHIRE

The Glynhir Estate, Glynhir Mansion, Llandybie, Carms SA18 2TD   **Nearest Road A483**

Unique 18th century estate of character, situated in the foothills of the Black Mountain. A quiet, relaxing location, surrounded by the beautiful Welsh countryside. A magnificent 30' waterfall on grounds. Stroll through our farmyard to meet pot-bellied pigs, pea-cocks, ducks and horses. There is a myriad of things to do and places to see in the locality ranging from golfing (a quarter mile walk), fishing and riding to bird watching and rambling. Excellent home-cooked food using the freshest local and home-grown produce, special diets catered for with advance warning.

see PHOTO opposite

Katy Jenkins
Tel: 01269 850438
Fax: 01269 851275

B&B from £23pp, Dinner from £15.00, Rooms 1 single, 1 twin, 2 double (both en-suite), 1 family, Restricted smoking, Children welcome, No pets, Open April - November, Map Ref C

Plas Alltyferin, Pontargothi, Nantgaredig, Carmarthenshire SA32 7PF   **Nearest Road A40**

A classic Georgian country house lying in the hills above the beautiful Towy Valley, overlooking a Norman hillfort, the River Cothi - famous for salmon and sea trout, and its own private cricket pitch. There are two spacious twin bedrooms, each with private bathroom and stunning views, for guests who are welcomed as friends of the family. Antique furniture. Log fires. Excellent local pubs and restaurants. Marvellous touring country for castles, beaches and Welsh speaking Wales. Total peace but under 4 hours from London.

see PHOTO below

Charlotte & Gerard Dent
Tel/Fax: 01267 290662

B&B from £20pp, Rooms 2 twin, both en-suite, Children over 12, Pets welcome, Open all year except Christmas & New Year, Map Ref D

above, **Plas Alltyferin,** *Pontargothi - see details above*

CEREDIGION

Dremmdu Fawr Farm, Creuddyn Bridge, Lampeter, Ceredigion SA48 8BL   Nearest Road A482

Ann, Dilwyn and their family extend a warm welcome (croeso cynnes) to their Edwardian farmhouse on 163 acre working farm. Bedrooms have en-suite facilities, central heating throughout, equipped with hair dryer, hospitality tray and colour TV. Guests lounge and dining room. Candle light dinners and open fires. Former winner of 'All Wales Top Cook' award. Conveniently located off A482 between Lampeter and Aberaeron - Georgian coastal town. WTB 3 Crowns Highly Commended. WTB Farmhouse award. Welcome host. Credit and debit cards accepted. Attractive scenery and Cambrian mountains.

Dilwyn & Ann Jones
Tel: 01570 470394

B&B from £20pp, Dinner from £12.50, Rooms 1 twin, 1 double, both en-suite, No smoking, Children welcome, Pets by arrangement, Open all Year, Map Ref E

Yr Hen Felin (The Old Mill), Abercegir, Machynlleth SY20 8NR   Nearest Road A489

see PHOTO below

Relax at our stone watermill, built in 1820 on the peaceful banks of the River Gwydol, where you can listen to the sound of the river from your bedroom window. The walking and scenery are some of the finest in Wales and the coast with its fine sandy beaches can be reached in 20 minutes. Heavily beamed throughout with original pine floors and antique furniture. All our bedrooms are en-suite and there is a large guests sitting room with TV. Private parking. Brochure available. AA QQQQ Selected. WTB 3 Stars.

Jill & Barry Stevens
Tel: 01650 511868

B&B from £20pp, Rooms 2 twin, 1 double, all en-suite, No smoking, Children over 12, No pets, Open all year except Christmas & New Year, Map Ref F

*above, **Yr Hen Felin**, Abercegir - see details above*

CONWY

Royal Oak Farm Cottage, Betws-y-Coed LL24 0AH Nearest Road A5

An attractive old stone farm cottage and buildings set in a sunny courtyard on the banks of the beautiful River Llugwy. The cottage is quiet and secluded but three minutes walk from the village centre and railway station. Betws-y-Coed is a walkers paradise with its rivers, lakes and tumbling streams amid forested hills and rugged mountains. Salmon and trout fishing, golf, walking, climbing, riding, shops, motor and railway museums are all available locally.

Mrs Kathleen Houghton
Tel: 01690 710760

B&B from £17pp, Rooms 1 twin with private facilities, 2 double en-suite, No smoking, Open all year except Christmas, Map Ref G

Fron Heulog Country House, Betws-y-Coed LL24 0BL Nearest Road A5, A470

see PHOTO on page 465

'The Country House in the Village', Fron Heulog offers the warm welcome for which Wales is famous. This stone built house of Victorian charm has an excellent standard of comfort and modern amenities. The atmosphere is friendly and the home cooking delicious. Turn off the busy A5 road over picturesque Pont-y-Pair Bridge (B5106), immediately turn left between shop and river. Fron Heulog is up ahead 150 metres from bridge in quiet peaceful wooded riverside scenery with private parking. Recommended by "Which?" WTB 3 Crowns Highly Commended. Guest House award.

Jean & Peter Whittingham
Tel: 01690 710736
Fax: 01690 710736

B&B from £20-£26pp, Longer holidays; lower prices, Rooms 2 double, 1 twin, all en-suite, Independent Children over 12, No smoking, No pets, Open all year, Map Ref G

Tan Dinas, Coed Cynhelier Road, Betws-y-Coed LL24 0BL Nearest Road A5, A470

see PHOTO opposite

A Victorian country house, offering peace, seclusion and a wonderful view, surrounded by woodland. Start with a delicious breakfast and finish your day with a candlelit dinner in our elegant dining room. Relax in the comfortable lounge or retire with a video or book to an attractive individually furnished bedroom which is appointed for your comfort. Forest walks from the house. Ideal touring centre for Snowdonia. Ample parking. We welcome you to Tan Dinas. 3 Crowns Highly Commended.

Ann Howard
Tel: 01690 710635
Fax: 01690 710815

B&B from £18-£25pp, Dinner from £13, Rooms 1 single, 2 twin, 3 double, 2 family, most en-suite, No smoking or pets, Children welcome, Open all year, Map Ref G

Henllys Hotel, The Old Courthouse, Old Church Road, Betws-y-Coed, Conwy LL24 0AL Nearest Road A5

Unique converted Victorian Magistrates Court in peaceful landscaped riverside gardens. No smoking throughout, No pets, Children welcome. Spotless en-suite rooms, all facilities. Galleried dining room, superb food with vegetarian option. Cosy fireside bar. Panoramic view of Conwy River and valley. Warm welcome. Centre for walking, climbing, mountain bikes, etc. Nine hole golf course next door. 3 minutes from town and Railhead. Quiet secluded spot yet adjacent to village amenities. Private car park, security lit. Ground floor rooms. You could not choose a more picturesque setting.

Ray & Barbara Valadini
Tel/Fax: 01690 710534

B&B from £30pp, Dinner from £15.95, Rooms 1 single, 4 twin, 4 double, 1 family, all en-suite/private bathroom, No smoking or pets, Children welcome, Open February - November, Map Ref G

*right, **Tan Dinas**, Betws-y-Coed - see details above*

White Lodge Hotel, Central Promenade, Llandudno LL30 1AT   Nearest Road A470, B5115

White Lodge Hotel is in an excellent position on the promenade and has retained the character of the Victorian period. A well kept hotel with a friendly and relaxing atmosphere. The en-suite bedrooms are all spacious and individually decorated, with tea/coffee making facilities and colour TV. Breakfast and dinner are served in the pleasant dining room. Guests may relax in the lounge, enjoy a drink in the licensed bar and have use of the nearby swimming pool. There is a private car park. Well situated for Llandudno's many attractions.

Eileen & Peter Rigby
Tel: 01492 877713

B&B from £24pp, Dinner from £9, Rooms 4 twin, 6 double, 2 family, all en-suite, Children over 5, Open March - November, Map Ref H

Firs Cottage, Maenan, Llanrwst LL26 0YR   Nearest Road A470

see PHOTO below

Our 17th century Welsh cottage is a comfortable family home on the A470 with a beautiful garden and patio where guests may relax and plan visits to all the many local attractions. Bodnant Gardens, Conwy Castle, Llandudno and Snowdon are all within easy reach - as are many excellent places for a pleasant evening meal. We offer 3 well furnished cottage bedrooms and a full cooked Welsh breakfast with homemade bread, jams and marmalades.

Mary & Jack Marrow
Tel: 01492 660244

B&B from £15.50pppn, Rooms 2 twin or double, 1 double, Restricted smoking, Well behaved pets by arrangement, Open all year except Christmas, Map Ref I

above, **Firs Cottage,** *Maenan - see details above*

DENBIGHSHIRE

The Castle Hotel, St Peter's Square, Ruthin, Denbighshire LL15 1AA   **Nearest Road A494**

see PHOTO *on page 469*

Mediaeval town centre family run hotel dating from fifteenth century situated in he beautiful vale of Clwyd. All rooms en-suite, TV, Sky, tea/coffee facilities.Four poster bed available. A'la carte restaurant fully licensed bar offering informal meals. Beer garden. Private car park. Ideal base for visiting or walking in the surrounding countryside, Snowdonia National Park, famous castles, Welsh coastline and Roman city of Chester. A warm Welsh welcome awaits you in this friendly hotel. You may even meet some friendly spirits!

Roy & Janet Hughes
Tel: 01824 702479
Fax: 01824 703488

B&B from £21pp, Dinner from £5-£14, Rooms 3 single, 5 twin, 5 double, 3 family, all en-suite, Children & pets welcome, Open all year, Map Ref J

The Old Barn, Esgairlygain, Llangynhafal, Ruthin, Denbighshire LL15 1RT   **Nearest Road B5429**

Sleep in the haylofts; breakfast in the Shippon where the cows used to be milked. Our stone barn has been sensitively converted for guests keeping the low sloping ceilings, beams etc. Lovely views over vale of Clwyd with spectacular sunsets. Especially suited to two couples travelling together. Direct access to Clwydian hills, Offa's Dyke and mountain bike tracks. Horse riding nearby. Central for Llangollen, Chester, Snowdonia, Castles and coast with a wealth of National Trust properties. Refreshments on arrival and warm welcome assured.

Mrs I Henderson
Tel: 01824 704047
Fax: 01824 704047

B&B from £17.50pp, Rooms 1 double, 1 family, all e-suite, Restricted smoking, Children & pets welcome, Open March - October, Map Ref J

Bach-Y-Graig, Tremeirchion, St. Asaph, Denbighshire LL17 0UH   **Nearest Road A55, A525, A541**

see PHOTO *opposite*

16th Century farmhouse nestling at the foot of the Clwydian range with undisturbed views of the surrounding countryside. Walk a 40 acre mediaeval woodland trail on the farm where the Royal Prince once hunted and enjoy the wealth of rare plants and flowers. All rooms are en-suite/private with tea/coffee, radio/alarms and colour TV's. A large inglenook in the oak beamed lounge with log fires (during the colder part of season). Full central heating. Ideal base for Chester, Coastal resorts and Snowdonia many castles in the immediate area.

Anwen Roberts
Tel: 01745 730627
Fax: 01745 730627

B&B from £21pp, Rooms 1 twin, 1 double, 1 family, all en-suite, No smoking, Children welcome, Open all year except Christmas & New Year, Map Ref K

right, **Bach-Y-Graig,** *Tremeirchion - see details above*

GWYNEDD

Preswylfa, Aberdovey, Gwynedd LL35 0LE   **Nearest Road A489**

Three Crowns Highly Commended. Preswylfa is an attractive Edwardian family home with breathtaking sea views, secluded in a large mature garden. Only 3 minutes walk from the beach and village. The en-suite luxury bedrooms have central heating, TV and tea/coffee making facilities. The period lounge has a grand piano and leads into a large sunny dining-room, with double doors into the garden. Ample car parking. Evening meals by arrangements. Friendly, unpretentious and relaxing. Telephone for brochure.

Marion & Jim Billingham
Tel: 01654 767239
Fax: 01654 767983

B&B from £22pp, Dinner from £16, Rooms 1 twin, 2 double, all en-suite, Restricted smoking, Children over 5, Pets Restricted, Open April - October, Map Ref L

Melin Meloch, Bala, Gwynedd LL23 7DP   **On the B4401**

see PHOTO opposite

This picturesque former watermill close to Bala stands in 2 acres of beautiful water scaped gardens, a delight for garden lovers. Pretty en-suite rooms some with own front doors in Granary and Millers Cottage, TV and hot drinks tray. The spectacular galleried interior of the mill is furnished with antiques and paintings. Here home cooked meals with fresh produce are served in a friendly relaxed atmosphere. 2 minutes drive to Bala lake and town, excellent for touring. Ample easy parking. Peaceful location. Highly Commended, WTB 2 Crowns. Please phone for special low prices on early and late season weeks.

Richard & Beryl Fullard
Tel: 01678 520101

B&B from £20pp, Dinner from £12.50, Rooms 2 single, 2 twin, 2 double, 1 family, most en-suite, No smoking, Children welcome, Pets by arrangement, Open March - November, Map Ref M

Cwm Hwylfod, Cefnddwysarn, Bala, Gwynedd LL23 7LN   **Nearest Road A494**

Set in the hills near Bala, our 400 year old farmhouse is warm and welcoming. The views are spectacular. Animals abound and everyone, especially children, can take part in farm activities. Bedrooms have wash basins and tea-making facilities. The guest lounge has TV, books and games. Full central heating. Four our home-cooked meals we use best of local produce. All diets catered for. Ample parking. Riding, golf, water sports can be booked in advance. Brochure available.

Edward & Joan Best
Tel: 01678 530310
Fax: 01678 530310

B&B from £16pp, Dinner from £11, Rooms 2 twin, 1 family, No smoking, Children welcome, Pets restricted, Open all year except Christmas Day, Map Ref N

Frondderw Guest House, Stryd-y-Fron, Bala, Gwynedd LL23 7YD   **Nearest Road A494**

Frondderw is a 17th century period mansion quietly situated in its own grounds overlooking Bala town and Lake Tegid. There is a lounge, dining room and separate television lounge for guest's use. Accommodation comprises many en-suite bedrooms. All bedrooms have hot/cold water, central heating and tea/coffee making facilities. Good home cooking with vegetarian and special diets catered for given advance notice. Ample free car parking. Ideal centre for sightseeing in North/Mid Wales, walking, cycling and watersports. WTB 3 Crowns Commended. AA QQ.

Glynn & Wenda Jones
Tel: 01678 520301

B&B from £16, Dinner £10, Rooms 1 single en-suite, 2 twin (1 shower), 2 double (1 shower, 1 en-suite), 3 family (2 en-suite), Restricted smoking, Children welcome, No pets, Open March - end November, Map Ref O

Llwyndu Farmhouse Hotel, Llanaber, Barmouth, Gwynedd LL42 1RR   Nearest Road A496

Llwyndu Farmhouse is a delightful 16th century house which nestles in a spectacular location with panoramic views over Cardigan Bay, just north of Barmouth. Here Peter & Paula Thompson have created a very special place for you to stop and relax for a few days. A real historic farmhouse with inglenooks, oak beams, nooks and crannies. Seven very comfortable en-suite bedrooms, a fully licensed restaurant and imaginative cuisine by candlelight make a stay here one to remember. A very beautiful area to explore for more details ring Peter or Paula. WTB 3 Crowns Highly Commended. All leading guides.

Peter & Paula Thompson
Tel: 01341 280144
Fax: 01341 281236

B&B from £29pp, Dinner from £14.50, Rooms 1 twin, 4 double, 2 family, all en-suite, No smoking, Children welcome, Pets by arrangement, Open all year, Map Ref P

The White House, Llanfaglan, Caernarfon, Gwynedd LL54 5RA   Nearest Road A487

A comfortably appointed modern country house enjoying splendid views of the Menai Straits and Snowdonia. A haven for bird watchers and sea anglers. A swimming pool is available for guests. Caernarfon Golf Club is only 2 miles away. Access to The White House is via the A487 Caernarfon/Porthmadog, on leaving Caernarfon, across roundabout then turn right for Saron/Llanfaglan. Set mileometer to zero and proceed for 1.6 miles and turn right. The White House is on the left in half a mile, last house before the sea.

Beverley & Richard Bayles
Tel: 01286 673003

B&B from £18.50pp, Rooms 2 double, 2 twin, all with en-suite/private facilities, Pets by arrangement, Open March - November, Map Ref Q

Noddfa Hotel, Lower Road, Harlech, Gwynedd LL46 2UB   Nearest Road A496

Noddfa (place of safety) was protected by Harlech Castle in earlier times but was extensively rebuilt in 1850. The comfortable bedrooms are equipped with TV and tea/coffee making facilities. Noddfa is situated close to the castle within the Snowdonia National Park having splendid views of Snowdon and Tremadoc Bay. Near swimming pool, beach and theatre. Gillian and Eric are keen historians and will be pleased to explain the displayed mediaeval weapons or use the bows to give you a traditional archery lesson. A guided tour of Harlech Castle is a speciality.

Gillain & Eric Newton Davies
Tel: 01766 780043
Fax: 01766 781105

B&B from £18pp, Rooms 4 double, some en-suite, Restricted smoking, Children over 4, No pets, Open all year, Map Ref R

Y Wern, Llanfrothen, Penrhyndeudraeth, Gwynedd LL48 6LX   Nearest Road A4085, B4410

'Y Wern' is a 17th century stone built farmhouse situated in beautiful countryside within the Snowdonia National Park. 'Wern' abounds with oak beams and inglenook fireplaces, and the large comfortable bedrooms have delightful views and are equipped with beverage making facilities. An excellent centre for walking riding and well placed for beaches and attractions such as Portmerion, castles and the Ffestiniog Railway. Imaginative home cooked meals are served in the large oak beamed kitchen, truly the heart of a warm welcoming home.

Paddy & Tony Bayley
Tel/Fax: 01766 770556

B&B from £19pp, Dinner from £11.50, Rooms 3 twin, 2 double, all en-suite, No smoking, Children welcome, No pets, Open all year, Map Ref S

MONMOUTHSHIRE

The Wenallt, Abergavenny, Monmouthshire   **Nearest Road A465**

This historic 15th century longhouse, Wenallt nestles in the rolling hills of the Brecon Beacons described by some guests as the perfect peace and tranquillity. The small quiet hotel offers comfort, personal service and excellent home cooking. This ideal location for enjoying country walks, breathtaking views or just relax on the spacious lawns, if you happen to be budding artist or photographer then this is the ideal base with its panoramic views. En-suite rooms. Inglenook log fires. Restaurant licensed. AA, RAC & 3 Crowns Commended.

Mr Harris   **B&B from £18.50pp, Dinner from £12, Rooms 4 single, 1 twin, 5 double, 1**
Tel: 01873 830694   **family, all en-suite, Children & pets welcome, Open all year, Map Ref T**

Wye Barn, The Quay, Tintern, Monmouthshire NP6 6SZ   **Nearest Road A466**

Situated on the bank of the River Wye, and only 200 yards from Tintern Abbey, Wye Barn (a 450 year old converted bark house) offers comfort, style and good food. The spacious bedrooms are individually furnished and all overlook the River. Hot drink facilities and TV are provided in all bedrooms. No licence, but you are welcome to bring wine with you. Parking available adjacent to the pretty walled garden. Take your ease in a comfortable sitting room and admire the fine designer made furniture.

                          B&B from £20-£22pp, Dinner from £14, Rooms 1 single, 1 en-suite twin,
Judith Russill   **No smoking or pets, Children over 10, Open all year except Christmas,**
Tel: 01291 689456   **Map Ref U**

NEWPORT

The West Usk Lighthouse, St Brides, Wentloog, Newport NP1 9SF   **Nearest Road B4239, M4 J28**

Garde II listed, The West Usk is a real lighthouse built in 1821 to a unique design. Rooms are wedge shaped within a circular structure. The entrance hall is slate bedded and leads to a central stone spiral staircase and the internal collecting well! The views are panoramic from the roof patio. All the bedrooms are en-suite and have been individually furnished to include a king size waterbed and a 4 poster bed. Guest can try the flotation tank for deep and immediate relaxation. Most amenities are close by and there are many interesting places to visit in the area.

Frank & Danielle Sheahan
Tel: 01633 810126/815860   **B&B from £38pp, Dinner by arrangement only, Rooms 3 double with en-**
Fax: 01633 815582   **suite, No smoking, Pets by arrangement, Open all year, Map Ref V**

PEMBROKESHIRE

Plas Y Brodyr, Rhydwilym, Llandissilio, Clynderwen, Pembrokeshire SA66 7QH   Nearest Road A478

Our restful farmhouse will appeal to people seeking comfort and total relaxation. An ideal base for exploring Pembrokeshire and West Wales, walking and only a short, quiet drive to many sandy beaches and spectacular coastal path. Safe parking. Guests lounge with TV, attractive gardens with outstanding views of unspoilt countryside, wild flowers, birds and peace. At the end of the day, unwind by log fires in inglenook sitting room after delicious home cooking. WTB Farmhouse Award. Ring for colour brochure and local information.

Janet Pogson
Tel: 01437 563771
Fax: 01437 563294

B&B from £18pp, Dinner £15, Rooms 1 twin, 2 double (1 en-suite), No smoking or pets, Children welcome, Open Easter - End October, New Year, Map Ref W

Nolton Haven Farm, Nolton Haven, Haverfordwest, Pembrokeshire SA62 3NH   Nearest Road A487

The farmhouse is beside the sandy beach on a 200 acre mixed farm, with cattle, calves, and loads of Show ponies. It has a large TV lounge which is open to guests all day as are all the bedrooms. Single, double, and family rooms, two family rooms en-suite, 4 other bathrooms. Pets and children most welcome, baby sitting free of charge. 50 yards to the beach, 75 yards to the local Inn/restaurant. Pony trekking, surfing, fishing, excellent cliff walks, boating and canoeing are all available nearby. Riding holidays, and short breaks all year, a speciality.

Joyce Canton
Tel: 01437 710263
Fax: 01437 710263

B&B from £15pp, Rooms 1 single, 1 twin, 2 double, 3 family (2 en-suite), Children & pets welcome, Open all year except Boxing Day, Map Ref X

Grove Park Guest House, Pen-y-Bont, Newport, Pembrokeshire SA42 0LT   Nearest Road A487

Small friendly guest house situated on the edge of a coastal town at the foot of the Prewseli Hills, which are steeped in magic and mystery. 100 yards from Pembrokeshire coastal path and protected bird sanctuary. Excellent country, hill and coast walking nearby. Built in 1879 for a sea captain and his family, the house has been completely refurbished but still retains its original character. Most bedrooms are en-suite, all have colour TV and tea/coffee making facilities. Imaginative three course dinner menu. Vegetarians welcome. WTB 3 Crowns Highly Commended. Licensed.

Ann King & Malcolm Powell
Tel: 01239 820122

B&B from £19.50pp, Dinner from £14, Rooms 2 en-suite double, 1 twin, 1 double, No smoking, Children welcome, Open all year except Christmas & New Year, Map Ref Z

Primrose Cottage, Stammers Road, Saundersfoot, Pembrokeshire SA69 9HH   Nearest Road A478

Ours is a lovingly restored Pembrokeshire 'Cottage' that has grown over the years. We have 1 double bedrooms with en-suite facilities and 1 twin room with use of bathroom. Both have radios and tea/coffee making facilities. There's a dining room, separate lounge with TV, video etc. and a pleasant secluded back garden. We are 100 yards from village centre, beaches and harbour. The coastal and inland scenery is fabulous with many facilities and attractions as well as twenty two castles in the area. There must be something to please or intrigue, whatever your interest.

Malcolm & Jennifer Quinn
Tel: 01834 811080

B&B from £16.50pp, Rooms 1 twin, 1 en-suite double, No smoking, Children & pets welcome, Open January - November, Map Ref 1

Ramsey House, Lower Moor, St David's, Pembrokeshire SA62 6RP   Nearest Road A487

A first class WTB 4 star guest house catering exclusively for adults. Seven delightfully appointed en-suite bedrooms, some with sea view, all with remote control colour TV, hospitality tray, hair dryer and powerful electric shower. Award-winning dinners with Welsh emphasis featuring fresh local produce complemented by interesting, affordable wine list. Quiet location ideally situated for St David's Cathedral, Pembrokeshire Coast Path, beaches and attractions. Private parking. Dogs welcome, Dinner B&B £41-£45pppn. Stay 7 nights for the price of 6. RAC Highly Acclaimed. AA QQQQ Selected.

Mac & Sandra Thompson
Tel: 01437 720321
Fax: 01437 720025

B&B from £27pp, Dinner from £14, Rooms 3 twin, 4 double, all en-suite, No smoking or children, Pets welcome, Open all year, Map Ref 2

Fernley Lodge, Manorbier, Tenby, Pembrokeshire   Nearest Road B4585

Fernley Lodge is in the centre of the beautiful coastal village of Manorbier. The Pembrokeshire coastal path and superb beach, overlooked by the church and Norman castle are just a quarter of a mile away. The house is a wonderfully restored property, classically decorated with antique furnishings. All rooms have TV and tea making facilities. The guest's drawing room overlooking a croquet and tennis lawn is warmed by an open fire on cooler evenings.

Mrs Jane Cowper
Tel: 01834 871226

B&B from £19pp, Rooms 2 double, 1 en-suite family, No smoking, Children welcome, Pets by arrangement, Open all year, Map Ref 3

The Old Vicarage, Manorbier, Tenby, Pembrokeshire SA70 7TN   Nearest Road A4139

Situated in the village of Manorbier with its castle and beaches, the Old Vicarage offers gracious accommodation with glimpses of Barafundle Bay. Guests are free to enjoy the gardens or log fire in the drawing room. Both spacious bedrooms are furnished with antiques and have tea/coffee making facilities. For the more energetic the Pembrokeshire coastal path passes through the village. The old servant's quarters are available as a 2 bedroomed self-catering unit for longer stays. Irish ferries from Pembroke and Fishguard. Beaches a 5 minute walk. Absolutely no smoking.

Mrs Jill McHugh
Tel/Fax: 01834 871452

B&B from £20pp, Rooms 1 en-suite twin, 1 double with private facilities, No smoking, Children welcome, No pets, Open all year except Christmas Map Ref 3

Wychwood House, Penally, Tenby, Pembrokeshire SA70 7PE   Nearest Road A4139

Large country house offering sea views from some of its elegant and spacious bedrooms, some with large sun balcony and all with tea/coffee facilities and TV. Dine by candle light and relax and enjoy Lee's interesting and freshly cooked 4 courses menu of the day. Open fires in lounge and dining room. 2 miles south of Tenby, Penally lies a quarter of a mile off the A4139 and is situated between two full size golf courses. Nearby is an excellent beach, which you can walk along to the ancient walled town of Tenby. Boat trips are also available to visit the monastic Island of Caldey.

Lee & Mherly Ravenscroft
Tel: 01834 844387

B&B from £21pp, Dinner from £15.50, Rooms 3 double, 1 with 4 poster and private bathroom, 1 en-suite family, Restricted smoking, Pets by arrangement, Open all year, Map Ref 4

right, **The Old Rectory**, *Llansantffraed - see details on page 478*

POWYS

The Beacons Accommodation & Restaurant, 16 Bridge Street, Brecon, Powys LD3 8AH   **A40, A470**

Recently restored 17th/18th century house retaining many original features such as moulded ceilings, low doors, sloping floors, beams and fireplaces. Choose from a variety of well-appointed standard, en-suite or luxury period rooms. Enjoy a drink in the original meat cellar (complete with hooks) or relax in a comfortable armchair in front of the fire. Our Award winning chef will spoil you with outstanding cuisine freshly cooked to your order. Please ring Peter or Barbara Jackson for more information. Private car park and bike store.

Peter & Barbara Jackson
Tel: 01874 623339
Fax: 01874 623339

B&B from £18pp, Dinner from £9.95-£17.85, Rooms 1 single, 3 twin, 4 double, 4 family, most en-suite, Restricted smoking, Children & pets welcome, Open all year except Christmas, Map Ref 5

The Old Rectory, Llansantffraed, Brecon, Powys LD3 7YF   **Nearest Road A40**

see PHOTO on page 477

The Old Rectory dating from the 18th century, has been extended to form a home of character and charm. The back of the house faces south west with views of the mountains; the grounds run down to the River Usk. Conveniently situated for walking, horse riding or motoring in the Beacons and Black Mountains. The house is centrally heated with log fires in the winter and colour TV for guests use. Also self contained 1 bedroomed cottage, delightfully renovated - details available.

Mrs Margaret Howard
Tel: 01874 676240

B&B from £18pp, Dinner/Light suppers by arrangement, (wine can be brought in), Rooms 2 double, 1 twin, all en-suite, Restricted smoking, Open all year, Map Ref 6

Dolycoed, Talyllyn, Brecon, Powys LD3 7SY   **Nearest Road A40**

An attractive Edwardian house in mature gardens offering home comforts in a beautiful part of wales at the foot of the Brecon Beacons, 5 miles from Brecon. Directions to Dolycoed are: from Brecon A40/A470 take the A40 for Abergavenny, left onto the B4558 to Llangorse, turn right at the post office and next right, the house is on to right before the next 'T' junction.

Brian & Mary Cole
Tel: 01874 658666

B&B from £18pp, Rooms 1 twin, 1 double, disabled guests welcome, Open all year, Map Ref 6

Glangrwyney Court, Crickhowell, Powys NP8 1ES   **Nearest Road A40**

see PHOTO opposite

Glangrwyney Court is a Grade 2 Listed Georgian mansion set in four acres of garden, surrounded by parkland. The house is fully centrally heated with log fires in winter and all bedrooms have television and tea/coffee making facilities. The house is furnished with antiques and there is a residents lounge with television and video. Ample car parking is available and there is tennis, croquet and bowls. Golf and pony trekking can be arranged and hill walking in the Brecon Beacons National Park is only minutes away.

Mr & Mrs Warwick Jackson
Tel: 01873 811288
Fax: 01873 810317

B&B from £20pp, Rooms 1 single, 2 twin, 2 double, 1 family, all en-suite, Restricted smoking, Children & pets welcome, Open all year, Map Ref 7

*right, **Glangrwyney Court**, Crickhowell - see details above*

Guidfa House, Crossgates, Llandrindod Wells, Powys LD1 6RF   Nearest Road A44, A483

This stylish Georgian guest house has earned an enviable reputation for it's comfort, good food and service. It offers superior en-suite accommodation including a ground floor room. Relax in the elegant sitting room with its open log fireplace and discreet corner bar. Enjoy the imaginative meals prepared by 'Cordon Bleu' trained Anne accompanied by excellent wine list. Set in the very heart of Wales, 3 miles north of Llandrindod Wells. Guidfa House is an excellent base for touring the wonderful local countryside.

see PHOTO opposite

Tony & Anne Millan
Tel: 01597 851241
Fax: 01597 851875

B&B from £24pp, Dinner from £15.50, Rooms 2 single, 3 twin, 2 double, most en-suite, Restricted smoking, Children over 10, No pets, Open all year, Map Ref 8

Gelli-graean, Cwrt, Pennal, Machynlleth, Powys SY20 9LE   Nearest Road A493

Peaceful secluded 1700s farmhouse, safe flat parking. Glorious views, riverside strolls or energetic walks on hills behind the house from the back gate. Have complimentary tea and home made cakes in the garden beside the wildlife pool which attracts 46 species of birds or in front of the roaring fire in the inglenook fireplace. Spring and Autumn group activities for walking or photography with qualified instructors. Close to Centre for Alternative Technology, beach at Aberdovey. Special diets and the Michel Montignac method catered for. 3 nights inclusive Christmas package.

David & Monica Bashford
Tel/Fax: 01654 791219

B&B from £19.50-£23.50pp, Dinner from £14.50, Rooms 2 twin, 2 double, most en-suite, No smoking or pets, Children over 5, Open all year except Christmas & New Year, Map Ref 9

Little Brompton Farm, Montgomery, Powys SY15 6HY   Nearest Road B4385

Robert and Gaynor welcome you to this charming 17th century farmhouse on a working farm. The house has much original character with beautiful oak beams. Furnished with traditional antiques. Pretty bedrooms with en-suite or private bathroom enhanced by quality furnishings. TV. Home cooking a speciality (meals by arrangement). Offa's Dyke runs through the farm. Powis Castle and Llanfair Light Railway nearby. On the B4385, 2 miles east of the Georgian town of Montgomery. Come and relax in peaceful, stress free countryside. A warm welcome. WTB 3 Crown Highly Commended. AA 4Q Selected.

see PHOTO on page 482

Mrs G Bright
Tel/Fax: 01686 668371

B&B from £19pp, Dinner £10 by prior arrangement, Rooms 1 twin, 1 double, 1 family, all en-suite, No smoking, Children welcome, Pets by arrangement, Open all year, Map Ref 10

Dyffryn Farmhouse, Aberhafesp, Newtown, Powys SY16 3JD   Nearest Road B4568

Come and stay with us in our lovingly restored 17th century farmhouse. Set in the heart of a 200 acre working sheep and beef farm. There is an abundance of wildlife and flowers along the stream outside the door, with woodland and lakes nearby. Golf, fishing and glorious walks nearby. Luxury en-suite rooms with full central heating. Traditional farmhouse fare including vegetarian specialities and totally non smoking. Garden and banks of stream for guests to sit by. Come and enjoy life on a Welsh hill farm. You might want to stay! AA Premier Selected 5Q. WTB 3 Crowns Deluxe. EMail: daveandsue@clara.net

Dave & Sue Jones
Tel: 01686 688817
Fax: 01686 688324

B&B from £22pp, Dinner from £12, Rooms 1 twin, 2 double, 1 family, all en-suite, No smoking, Children welcome, No pets, Open all year except Christmas & New Year, Map Ref 13

*left, **Guidfa House,** Llandrindod Wells - see details above*

POWYS

Cambrian Cruisers, Ty Newydd, Pencelli, Brecon LD3 7LJ Nearest Road B4458, off A40

Our 18th century farmhouse is 3 miles south of Brecon, adjacent to the Monmouth and Brecon canal, with superb open views of the Brecon Beacons. Accommodation is in tastefully modernised and furnished rooms, with beamed ceilings. All are centrally heated, have en-suite facilities, colour television, and tea/coffee making facilities. Guests have their own entrance, and a conservatory lounge, with car parking in the farm courtyard. This is an excellent base for walking, riding, fishing, sailing, canoeing, cycling, including canal cruising, literally on the doorstep.

Nicola Atkins
Tel: 01874 665315
Fax: 01874 665315

B&B from £20pp, Rooms 1 twin, 2 double, 1 family, all en-suite, No smoking or pets, Children over 11, Open 1st March - 31st October, Map Ref 6

TORFAEN

Ty'r Ywen Farm, Lasgarn Lane, Mamhilad, via Trevethin, Pontypool NP4 8TT Nearest Road A472

A 16th century Welsh longhouse on a mountainside, with views down the Usk Valley and the Bristol Channel. Retaining many original features and modern comforts, 1 room with jacuzzi. From Pontypool town centre follow sign for Blaenavon, at roundabout turn right over river (sign Trevethin), take 2nd right at Yew Tree Inn, carry on for 1/4 mile to top of hill, turn right into Lasgarn Lane (sign Pontypool Golf Club), carry on for 1 mile to end of lane, through gate, turn right up concrete ramp. Proceed with care. http://freespace.virgin.net/susan.armitage/webpage.htm EMail: susan.armitage@virgin.net

Mrs Susan Armitage
Tel: 01495 785200
Fax: 01495785200

B&B from £20pp, Light supper, Rooms 3 double, (4 poster beds), 1 twin, all rooms en-suite, Children over 14, No smoking, Open all year except Christmas & New Year, Map Ref 11

VALE OF GLAMORGAN

Llanerch Vineyard, Hensol, Pendoylan, Vale of Glamorgan CF72 8JU Nearest Road M4 jct34

Recently featured on the BBC, TV "Holidays Out" programme, this beautifully converted and fully modernised farmhouse overlooks the six acre vineyard and the Vale of Glamorgan's rich farmland. All rooms are en-suite with central heating, tea-making facilities and TV's. Guests can tour the vineyard and winery, taste the award winning wines and follow trails through acres of protected farm woodland and lakes. Ideal location for touring South Wales, only fifteen minutes from Cardiff. Ample car parking. Golf, fishing and riding nearby. One of "Wales' great little places".

Peter & Diana Andrews
Tel: 01443 225877
Fax: 01443 225546

B&B from £22.50pppn, Rooms 2 twin, 1 double, all en-suite, No smoking or pets, Children welcome, Open all year except Christmas & New Year, Map Ref 12

left, **Little Brompton Farm,** *Montgomery - see details on page 481*

And since to look at things in bloom
Fifty springs are little room,
About the woodlands I will go
To see the cherry hung with snow.

A Shropshire Lad (1896) no. 2
A. E. Housman 1859-1936

the
Great British
Self Catering
Cottage GUIDE

includes
**CABINS
CASTLES
CHALETS
BUNGALOWS
CONVERTED BARNS
COTTAGES
FARMHOUSES
& TOWNHOUSES**

SECOND EDITION

COTTAGE MAP LOCATIONS
The Great British Self Catering Cottage Guide

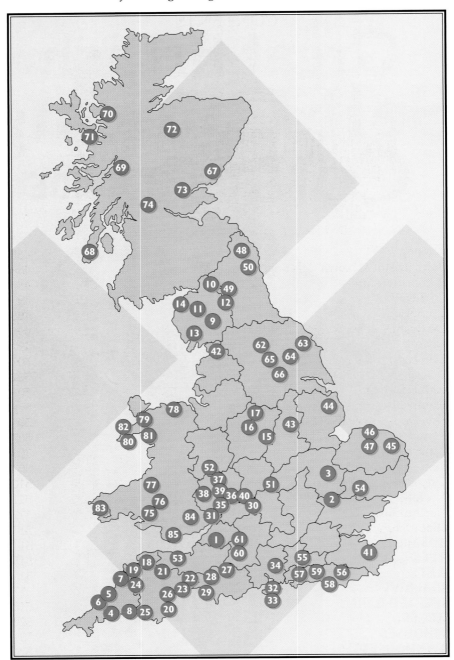

CONTENTS

Dad 'Jack, Tim, here's Mr Briggs to meet us'

❖❖❖

Cottages: Hideaways

A wide range of high quality cottages, farmhouses, country homes and apartments, many of period character, in rural and coastal settings and in historic towns throughout the heart of England, South, South East and South West. Short breaks available September to May. Phone or fax for our full free colour brochure giving descriptions. Alternatively you can visit our web site which has full descriptions and colour images of all our properties on www.hideaways.co.uk

110 - 120 cottages, sleeps 1-12, Price per week £166 low season, £1464 high season, Most cottages are available all year.

**Contact: Mr Pash, Hideaways, Chapel House, Berwick St John, Shaftesbury, Dorset SP7 0HQ
Tel: 01747 828000 (Brochure request) Tel: 01747 828170 (Reservations) Fax: 01747 829090
EMail: hideaways.cotts@virgin.net**

above, Hideaways

❖❖❖

The Great British Self Catering Cottage Guide

Cottage: Conygre Mews, Farmborough, Bath

Set in 2 acres of beautiful gardens, 7 miles from Bath and near Cotswolds, Stonehenge, Wells & Cheddar. 3 bedrooms, 2 bathrooms, former stables from 1710. Extremely comfortable, well equipped and tastefully decorated Rose and Wisteria clad facade with french windows opening onto patio, white plaster walls exposed stonework, beams, parquet flooring, persian rugs, country antiques and open fireplace. Barbecue, garden furniture. Ample parking.

1 cottage, sleeps 5/6, Price per week £300 low season, £450 high season, Children welcome, No pets, Available April - November, Map Ref 1

Contact: Jamie Blair Gould, Conygre House, Farmborough, Bath BA3 1AZ
Tel: 01761 470363 Fax: 01761 472995 EMail: papillon@Ibm.net

'Thats it my dear, welcome to Beech Farm'

❖❖❖

Cottage: Hill House Farm Cottage, 9 Main Street, Coveney, Ely, Cambridgeshire

A tasteful barn conversion in a farmyard. Furnished and decorated to a high quality in a peaceful location with open views of Ely Cathedral and the surrounding countryside. Situated three miles west of Ely, with easy access to Cambridge, Huntingdon and Newmarket.

1 cottage, sleeps 6, Price per week £180 low season, £350 high season, No smoking, Children from 8 years, No pets, Available all year, Map Ref 3

**Contact: Mrs Nix, Hill House
Farm, 9 Main Street, Coveney, Ely, Cambridgeshire CB6 2DJ
Tel: 01353 778369**

❖❖❖

Cottages: Whitensmere Farm Cottages, Ashdon, Saffron Walden, Essex

Converted 17th Century barns still retaining many original features. All cottages are extremely well equipped, with TV, video, microwaves, dishwashers, etc. 'The Brues' sleeps 8/10, 'Woodmore' sleeps 6/7 and 'Ladywell' 4/5. There is a games room and drying facilities, children play area and pets corner. Close to Cambridge and London only 1 hour. Heating by storage radiators and woodburners. Fresh flowers and welcome pack on arrival. 4 - 5 Keys Highly Commended. Brochure available.

3 cottages, sleeps 2-10, Price per week £200 low season, £700 high season, Children & dogs welcome, Available all year, Map Ref 2

**Contact: Mrs Ford, Whitensmere Farm, Ashdon, Saffron Walden, Essex CB10 2JQ
Tel: 01799 584244 Fax: 01799 584244**

❖❖❖

Please mention
THE GREAT BRITISH
SELF CATERING
COTTAGE GUIDE
when booking your accommodation

❖❖

Cottage: 3 Mowhay Cottages, Treveague Farm, Gorran, St Austell, Cornwall

This attractive cottage, part of a rural barn conversion on a working sheep farm, but only 15 minutes walk from Gorran Haven beach it is in an ideal situation for walking or days on the beach or exploring Cornwall. Well furnished with all modern conveniences including washing machine, microwave, TV and video. Heating, linen and towels inclusive. Garage and parking. Please 'phone for more details.

1 cottage, sleeps 4 + cot, Price per week £200 low season, £460 high season, No smoking, Children welcome, 1 dog welcome, Available from April - January, Map Ref 4

Contact: Mrs Lawrence, 3 Mowhay Cottages, Treveague Farm, Gorran, St Austell, Cornwall PL26 6NY
Tel: 01726 843197

❖❖

Cottages: Cant Cove, Cant Farm, Rock, near Wadebridge, Cornwall

Deluxe cottages set in 70 acres of private grounds, spectacular views of the Camel estuary and surrounding countryside. Open all year. Tastefully furnished and well equipped all in price includes full central heating and log fires for those special winter breaks. Free use of tennis court and golf practice area. Close to sandy beaches and beautiful North Cornwall coastline. Phone for full colour brochure.

6 cottages, sleeping 5-8, Price per week £265 low season, £1,570 high season, Children are welcome, No pets, Available Januray - December, Map Ref 5

Contact: Mr & Mrs Sleeman, The Cottage, Cant Farm, Rock, nr Wadebridge, Cornwall PL27 6RL
Tel: 01208 862841 Fax: 01208 862142

❖❖

Cottages: Houndapitt Farm Cottages, Sandymouth Bay, Bude, Cornwall

Set in 150 acres of farm land, 1 mile from a beautiful award winning beach and heritage coastline. This attractive development will sleep 2-9, in a high standard of accommodation. Ideal family holidays. Nearby indoor swimming pool. Free course fishing, large games room, adventure playground, Shetland pony rides, coastal walks, spectacular views. Central heating, electricity, bed linen and towels included. Featured in the Good Holiday Cottage Guide.

10 cottages, sleeping 2-9, Price per week from £100 low season, from £435 high season, Children welcome, No pets, Available all year, Map Ref 7

Contact: Mr & Mrs Heard, Houndapitt Farm Cottages, Sandymouth Bay, Bude, Cornwall EX23 9HW
Tel: 01288 355455

❖❖

❖❖

Cottages: Padstow Holiday Cottages,

Padstow Holiday Cottages welcomes you to the jewel of Cornwall. Each of our cottages is furnished to provide quality accommodation. All have modern amenities including washing machine, microwave, deep freeze, central heating. There is private parking and each has its own sunny patio garden. They are within a short walk of Padstow Harbour with its many local beaches, restaurants and country walks. Short breaks are available.

3 cottages, sleeps 2-6, Price per week £136 low season, £470 high season, Children welcome, No pets, Available all year, Map Ref 6

**Contact: Mr & Mrs Walker, 7 Hawthorn Close, St Columb Major, Cornwall TR9 6ST
Tel: 01841 533110**

❖❖

Cottages: Penvith Barns, St Martin By Looe, Cornwall

Penvith Cottages are Grade II listed set in superb countryside only a walk away from the wonderous coastal paths. Both cottages are furnished to a very high standard. The master bedroom have vaulted ceilings, toilet, wash basin, hair dryer and excellent quality duvets. Open plan kitchen lounge have dishwasher, washing machine, microwave, food mixers, etc. quality cutlery and crockery. Each cottage with private patio, barbecue, car parking. Easy access West Cornwall.

2 cottages, sleeps 4/5, Price per week £250 low season, £550 high season, No smoking, No children or pets, Available April - October, Map Ref 8

**Contact: Mrs M'Queen, Penvith Barns, St Martin By Looe, Cornwall PL13 1NZ
Tel: 01503 240772 Fax: 01503 240772 EMail: anne@penvith.demon.co.uk**

❖❖

Cottage: Polrudden Farm, Pentewan, St Austell, Cornwall

Clifftop fully equipped compact newly converted barn sleeps two plus put-u-up in lounge un-interupted, stunning sea and country views. Access to coastal path. Car parking and barbecue area. Private beach and local village beach 5 minutes walk. Good restaurants in village of Pentewan, 18 hole Golf Course and Sports Fitness Centre 2 miles. World famous Lost Gardens of Heligan 5 minutes. Woodland and country walks nearby.

1 cottage, sleeps 2-3, Price per week £150 low season, £300 high season, No smoking Children over 8, Well behaved pets are welcome, Available January - December, Map Ref 4

**Contact: Mrs Bainbridge, Polrudden Farm, Pentewan, St Austell, Cornwall PL26 6BJ
Tel: 01726 843213**

❖❖

❖❖

Cottage: 3 Swiss Villas, Vicarage Road, Ambleside, Cumbria

Victorian terrace house situated in centre of Ambleside (off main road). Convenient for shops, cinema, restaurants, parks, walks and the lake. Lovely views. Newly fitted kitchen and bathroom. Full central heating throughout. Private parking nearby or outside house (permit supplied). Main fuel costs and all bedding included.

1 house, sleeps 4-6, Price per week £190 low season, £380 high season, No smoking, Children over 13 welcome, Available January - December, Map Ref 9

**Contact: Mr Sowerbutts, 2 Swiss Villas, Vicarage Road, Ambleside, Cumbria LA22 9AE
Tel: 015394 32691**

❖❖

Cottage: Barn Cottage, Bassenthwaite, near Keswick, Cumbria

Tastefully converted stone built lakeland barn of character. Rural setting in peaceful Northern Lakes village at foot of Skiddaw. Excellent walking, cycling or just relaxing away from the crowds. Nearby village stream with ducks, lanes with wild flowers. Excellent pub nearby. Enjoy as taste of times gone by with modern comforts. Welcome basket on arrival. Price includes linen, towels, heating logs for wood burner and electricity. Short breaks available 1st November - 31st March.

1 cottage, sleeps 4 + cot, Price per week £200 low season, £300 high season, No smoking, Children welcome, No pets, Available all year, Map Ref 11

**Contact: Mrs Beaty, Willow Cottage, Bassenthwaite, Keswick, Cumbria CA12 4QP
Tel: 017687 76440**

❖❖

Cottages: Coniston Country Cottages, Little Arrow, Coniston, Cumbria

Quality cottages in superb surroundings. Each is individually and tastefully furnished to ensure you have a memorable holiday. All have off road parking. The cottages have easy access to lakes and mountains and offer free use of leisure club to relax at the end of the day.

9 cottages, sleeps 2-6, Price per week from £150 low season, £475 high season, No smoking, Children welcome, No pets, Available all year, Map Ref 13

**Contact: Mr Lupton, Coniston Country Cottages, Little Arrow, Coniston, Cumbria LA21 8AU
Tel: 015394 41114 Fax: 015394 41114**

❖❖

❖❖❖

Cottage: Manor Cottage, Caldbeck, Wigton, Cumbria

Relax in this unspoilt corner of lakeland. The 17th Century converted barn gives well equipped spacious accommodation. The picturesque village of Caldbeck (2 miles) has a pond, church, public house and sports facilities. Keswick is 30 minutes away with South Lakes, Scottish Borders and Hadrian's Wall within easy reach. Storage heaters, electric cooker, microwave, fridge, TV, small garden, patio, ample parking. Lovely walks from the door. ETB 3 Keys Highly Commended.

1 cottage, sleeps 2-3, Price per week £110 low season, £250 high season, No smoking, No pets, Available March - November, Map Ref 14

Contact: Mrs Wade, Manor Cottage, Caldbeck, Wigton, Cumbria CA7 8HA
Tel: 016974 78214

❖❖❖

Cottages: Milburn Grange Cottages, Milburn Grange, Knock, Appleby, Cumbria

Cosy quality cottages nestling in pretty hamlet at foot of Pennines with superb views. Some beamed, 4 poster beds, all are centrally heated, all have microwaves, colour TV and washing/drying facilities. Larger cottages have dishwasher. Enclosed garden, barbecue area, plenty of off road safe parking. Short breaks. Special couple rates. Excellent for walking, visiting Lakes (Ullswater 25 mins away), Yorkshire and Scotland. ETB 3-4 Key Commended.

7 cottages, sleeps 2-7 + cot, Price per week £140 low season, £380 high season, Children & pets welcome, Available all year, Map Ref 12

Contact: Mrs Burke, Milburn Grange, Knock, Appleby, Cumbria CA16 6DR
Tel: 017683 61867 Fax: 017683 61867

❖❖❖

Cottages: Old Farm Cottage & Barn Cottage, Bank End Farm, Roadhead, Bewcastle, Carlisle, Cumbria

All the privacy of commended cottages - but home cooking too! Meals and home cooking from the farmhouse if you wish. Central heating, electric blankets, dishwasher, fridge/freezer, microwave, video, open fire, utility room and more. Pretty garden. Attractive quiet countryside close to Scots Border. Good walking beside river or in forest, plenty of wildlife on our small hill sheep farm. Brochure/Photo available.

2 cottages, sleeps 2-6, Price per week £150 low season, £360 high season, Children & pets welcome, Available all year, Map Ref 10

Contact: Dorothy & Boy Downer, Bank End Farm, Roadhead, Bewcastle, Carlisle, Cumbria
CA6 6NU
Tel: 016977 48644 Fax: 016977 48644

❖❖❖

The Great British Self Catering Cottage Guide

❖❖❖

Cottages: Spinnery Cottage, Brantfell Road, Bowness-On-Windermere, Cumbria

Spinnery Cottage is only a few minutes walk from the centre of Bowness village and the lake front, yet is quiet and secluded. Converted from a 200 year old Spinnery, the apartments are warm, welcoming and maintained to a high standard. Kitchens are fully equipped. Safe car parking. All linen and bedding provided. Leisure club facilities nearby. A lovely way to spend your holiday in the Lake District.

4 flats, sleep 2-4, Price per week £175 low season, £290 high season, Smoking restricted, Children welcome, Pets by arrangement, Available all year, Map Ref 9

Contact: Mr Hood, Spinnery Cottage, Brantfell Rd, Bowness-on-Windermere, Cumbria LA23 3AE
Tel: 015394 44884 Fax: 015394 46565
EMail: Ray&barb@the-fairfield.co.uk

❖❖❖

'Here's a fresh loaf for your tea'

❖❖❖

❖❖❖

Cottages: Cruck Cottage & Graces Cottage, Wolfscote Grange, Hartington, near Buxton, Derbyshire

Cruck Cottage (as photograph) is an "ideal country hideaway" with no neighbours. Enjoy beautiful views of the Derbyshire dales and walk the picturesque Dove-Valley just below the cottage. Massive beams run throughout, cosy well equipped. TB Highly Commended. Sleeps 4. Grace's Cottage tucked away in the backwater of Hartington village. Immaculate cottage, open meadows behind lead to the dales. Pubs and shops available. Sleeps 4. Brochure 01298 84342.

2 cottages, sleeps 4, Price per week £140 low season, £300 high season, Children welcome, Pets welcome (charge made), Available all year, Map Ref 17

Contact: Mrs Gibbs, Wolfscote Grange, Hartington, near Buxton, Derbyshire SK17 0AX
Tel: 01298 84342

❖❖❖

Cottages: Honeysuckle & Brook Cottages, Park View Farm, Weston Underwood, Ashbourne, Derbyshire

Honeysuckle is a truly delightful peaceful country cottage with secluded garden set amidst lovely countryside. Beamed sitting room, antique furnishings, three pretty bedrooms one with romantic four poster bed. Brook is an attractive village cottage situated in the centre of Weston Underwood. Ideally situated for Alton Towers and the Peak District. Access to the working farm, see the cows milked and collect the eggs. ETB 4 Keys Commended.

2 cottages, sleeps 4-6, Price per week £150 low season, £400 high season, Children welcome, No pets, Available all year, Map Ref 15

Contact: Linda Adams, Park View Farm, Weston Underwood, Ashbourne, Derbyshire DE6 4PA
Tel: 01335 360352 Fax: 01335 360352

❖❖❖

Cottage: Rosewood Holiday Flats, Lower Berkhamsytch Farm, Bottom House, nr Leek, Staffordshire

Two delightful self-contained flats each with own private entrance in picturesque Staffordshire moorlands. Central to Alton Towers, Potteries and Peak District. Comfortably furnished with colour TV, carpeted throughout, microwave, laundry room with automatic washing machine, tumble dryer. Two pubs serving excellent food within walking distance. Little Chef nearby. Ample parking, patio, sitting area, children's play area. Heating, electricity and fresh linen inclusive. ETB Grading 3 Keys Commended.

2 flats, sleeps 6,7, Price per week £120 low season, £220 high season, Children & pets welcome, Available all year, Map Ref 16

Contact: Alwyn & Edith Mycock, Lower Berkhamsytch Farm, Bottom House, near Leek, Staffordshire ST13 7QP
Tel: 01538 308213 Fax: 01538 308213

❖❖❖

❖❖❖

Cottage: Cider Room Cottage, Hasland Farm, Membury, Axminster, Devon

Attractively converted thatched cider barn adjoining main 16th Century farmhouse overlooking old orchard and ponds. Surrounded by delightful countryside. Comfortable lounge, colour television, many beams exposed stonework. Well equipped galley kitchen all electric including microwave. Open plan staircase to double bedroom, twin bedroom and shower room. Night store heating. Parking in old cobbled yard. Many interesting places to visit. Linen. Evening meals available.

1 cottage, sleeps 4, Price per week £135, £270 high season, No smoking, Children welcome, Pets by arrangement, Available all year, Map Ref 22

**Contact: Pat & David Steele, Hasland Farm, Membury, Axminster, Devon EX13 7JF
Tel: 01404 881558 Fax: 01404 881834**

❖❖❖

Cottages: Glebe House Cottages Ltd, Bridgeruie, Holsworthy, Devon

Grade II listed Georgian estate with original Coach House, Stables and Barns beautifully converted into 7 well equipped, warm and comfortable cottages sleeping 2-8, with exposed beams, some four-poster beds and double spa baths. Set in 5 acres of tranquil countryside, but only 10 minutes drive from beaches. Games room, children's play area, cellar bar and restaurant with log fire. Superb home-cooked food. ETB 4 Keys Highly Commended.

7 cottages, sleep 2-8, Price per week £220 - £405 low season, £395 - £750 high season, Children welcome, No pets, Available all year, Map Ref 24

**Contact: James & Margaret Varley, Glebe House Cottages, Bridgerule, Holsworthy, Devon
EX22 7EW
Tel: 01288 381272**

❖❖❖

Cottages: Helpful Holidays, Devon

Helpful Holidays has cottages and houses all across some of England's most beautiful countryside. They range from snugs for two, grand hotels for great gatherings and simple cottages with roaring log fires. To see cottages close to beaches, on farm, on the moors and in the countryside all over the West Country, call 01647 433535 (24 Hours) for a free brochure.

450+ cottages, sleeping 2-30, Price per week £65 low season, £750 high season, Children & pets welcome, Available all year.

**Contact: Mr Bowater, Helpful Holidays, Coombe, Chagford, Devon TQ13 8QF
Tel: 01647 433593 Fax: 01647 433694 EMail: bowater@btinternet.com**

❖❖❖

❖❖

Cottages: Lower Waytown, Horns Cross, near Clovelly, Bideford, Devon

Within half mile coastal path this 17th century thatched Devon Longhouse has been lovingly restored to form 2 pretty cottages. Old world charm includes inglenooks, log-burners and beams. Furnished for every comfort, well equipped kitchens, maintained to high standards. Attractive courtyard setting with extensive grounds where black swans and ornamental waterfowl enjoy the ponds. Ideally located for exploring the spectacular coastline, Exmoor, picturesque Clovelly. Unspoilt coves nearby, sandy beaches 4 miles. Short breaks available. ETB 4 Keys Highly Commended.

2 cottages, sleeps 3-6 + cot, Price per week £200 low season, £540 high season, smoking restricted, Children welcome, No pets, Available all year, Map Ref 19

Contact: Mrs C May, Lower Waytown, Horns Cross, near Clovelly, Bideford, Devon EX39 5DN
Tel: 01237 451787 Fax: 01237 451787

❖❖

Cottages: Lufflands, Yettington, Budleigh Salterton, Devon

Country views from Barn cottage sleeping 6. Beamed, open-plan living area. Three bedrooms above. Stable Cottage sleeps 5. Open plan living area overlooking courtyard. Two bedrooms on one level. Suitable for wheelchairs. Both cottages comfortably furnished. Fully equipped with automatic washing machine, microwave, TV, fridge. Large garden, ample parking. Children welcome, excellent walking. Short drive to beaches. B&B accommodation in old farmhouse.

2 cottages, sleeps 5,6, Price per week £145 low season, £380 high season, No smoking, Children welcome, Pets by arrangement, Available all year, Map Ref 26

Contact: Colin & Brenda Goode, Lufflands, Yettington, Budleigh Salterton, Devon EX9 7BP
Tel: 01395 568422 Fax: 01395 568810 EMail: lufflands@compuserve.com

❖❖

Cottages: Mariners Cottage, Irsha Street, Appledore, Devon

Sea edge fishermans cottage: high tide comes up to garden wall. Extensive open sea and estuary views of ships, lighthouses, sandy island. Spacious cottages sleeps 6 in 3 bedrooms, second WC downstairs, modern kitchen, dining room, lounge, garden with garden furniture. Dog welcome. Colour TV washing machine. Fishing trips from quay, beach, waterside restaurants and pubs, cliff and coastal walks, stately homes, golf nearby. SAE please to K M Barnes, Boat Hyde, Northam, Bideford, Devon, EX39 1NX.

3 cottages, sleeps 6, Price per week £90 low season, £530 high season, Children & pets welcome, Available all year, Map Ref 18

Contact: Mr & Mrs K M Barnes, Boat Hyde, Northam, Bideford, North Devon EX39 1NX
Tel: 01237 473801

❖❖

❖❖❖

Cottages: Oldaport Farm Cottages, Modbury, Ivybridge, Devon

Four comfortable fully equipped cottages carefully converted from stone barns. Peaceful setting in beautiful South Hams Valley on historic 70 acres working sheep farm and miniature Shetland pony stud. There is an abundance of wildlife and many fascinating walks. The south coastal footpath and a sandy beach is nearby. Dartmouth just 8 miles away. Short breaks in low season. ETB 3 & 4 Keys Highly Commended.

4 cottages, sleeps 2-6, Price per week £149 - £231 low season, £288 - £441 high season, Children welcome, Dogs welcome in low and mid season, Available all year, Map Ref 25

**Contact: Miss Evans, Oldaport Farm Cottages, Modbury, Ivybridge, Devon PL21 0TG
Tel: 01548 830842 Fax: 01548 830998 EMail: cathy.evans@dial.pipex.com**

❖❖❖

Cottages: The Granary & Eeyore's Tail, Broome Court, Broomhill, Dartmouth, Devon

Broome Court is tucked into a hill facing south, overlooking three copses and surrounded by green undulating South Devon countryside rich in wildlife. Five minutes drive from the historic port of Dartmouth. One mile from Blackpool sands. Arrangements can be made for reduced fees at the Dartmouth Golf & Country Club. Both of our cottages are fully equipped with all mod cons. Please call for a brochure.

2 cottages, sleeps 2,4, Price per week £230 - £350 low season, £410 - £610 high season, No smoking, Children welcome, Pets by arrangement, Available all year, Map Ref 20

**Contact: Jan Bird & Tom Boughton Broome Court, Broomhill, Dartmouth, Devon TQ6 0LD
Tel: 01803 834275 Fax: 01803 833260**

❖❖❖

Cottage: The Pantiles, Thorn Cottage, Northleigh, near Colyton, Devon

"The Pantiles" nestles in the wooded lawned grounds of Thorn Cottage. Accommodation and furnishings are of a high standard and consist of a double bedroom, bathroom, dining/lounge with colour TV and fully equipped kitchen. Central heating and double glazing, a private entrance, parking and car port. Patio with barbecue and furniture. Northleigh has peace and tranquility, yet is just 15 minutes from the beaches and coastal resorts of Seaton, Beer, Branscombe and Sidmouth and the South West Coastal Path.

1 cottage, sleeps 2 adults, Price per week £150 low season, £225 high season, No smoking, No pets, No children, Available all year, Map Ref 23

**Contact: Anthony & Peggy Govey, Thorn Cottage, Northleigh, near Colyton, Devon EX13 6BN
Tel: 01404 871553**

❖❖❖

❖❖

Cottage: Whitefield Barton, Challacombe, Barnstaple, Devon

Extremely spacious characteristic accommodation in half of 16th Century farmhouse with modern luxuries. Tastefully furnished to a high standard. Warm cosy lounge with colour TV and video recorder. Well-equipped kitchen. Family and twin bedded rooms, bathroom/shower. Downstairs toilet, washing machine, private patio, barbecue, streamed garden, ample parking. Linen and electric inclusive. Peaceful surroundings with scenic walks and farm animals. Central for sandy beaches, moors, Lynton and Lynmouth.

1 cottage, sleeps 6, Price per week £100 low season, £360 high season, Children & pets welcome, Available May - December, Map Ref 21

**Contact: Rosemarie Kingdon, Whitefield Barton, Challacombe, Barnstaple, Devon EX31 4TU
Tel: 01598 763271**

❖❖

'Seven piglets!' 'No, eight, there's one underneath'

❖❖

❖❖❖

Cottages: Gorwell Farm, Abbotsbury, Weymouth, Dorset

Relax unwind and enjoy the peaceful surroundings of Gorwell Farm. A family dairy and sheep farm. Found in its own scenic wooded valley 2 miles from the coast. Comfortable well-equipped warm accommodation for any time of year. Log fires, dishwashers, microwaves, television, laundry facilities, cots and highchairs. Wonderful walks with views along the dramatic Dorset coastline and patchwork countryside. Short breaks available. Family holidays. Wildlife in abundance.

3 cottages, sleeps 2-10, Price per week £200 low season, £500 high season, No smoking, Children and pets welcome, Available all year, Map Ref 29

**Contact: Mary Pengelly, Gorwell Farm, Abbotsbury, Weymouth, Dorset DT3 4JX
Tel: 01305 871401 Fax: 01305 871441 EMail: gorwell.farm@wdi.co.uk**

❖❖❖

Cottage: Lamperts Farmhouse, 11 Dorchester Road, Sydling St Nicholas, Dorchester, Dorset

16th Century wing of Lamperts Farmhouse recently restored as a self-catering cottage for two people. Downstairs is the sitting room with colour TV. French window opening onto sheltered garden. Kitchen with electric cooker and fridge. Downstairs bathroom, up the winding stairs nestling under the eaves is the double bedroom. Full central heating. Guide books and maps provided. Car parking.

1 cottage, sleeps 2, Price per week £160 low season, £220 high season, Pets welcome, Available all year, Map Ref 28

**Contact: Rita Bown, Lamperts Farmhouse, 11 Dorchester Road, Sydling St Nicholas, Dorchester, Dorset DT2 9NU
Tel: 01300 341 790**

❖❖❖

Cottage: Mallard Lodge, Whistley Waters, Milton on Stour, Gillingham, Dorset

Mallard Lodge overlooks lakes in beautiful quiet location. Living room with kitchenette, double bedroom, bathroom downstairs. One twin bedroom, 2 single upstairs and WC. Double glazed, electric heating, microwave, 2 colour TV's, barbecue, garden chairs. Use of washing machine. 6 hectares gardens, woods, lakes, good trout and carp fishing. Excellent centre for National Trust visiting. One hour cities of Bath, Salisbury and coast. ETB 4 Keys commended.

1 cottage, sleeps 6, Price per week £170 low season, £420 high season, Children & dogs welcome, Available March - January, Map Ref 27

**Contact: Cleo Campbell, Whistley Waters, Milton on Stour, Gillingham, Dorset SP8 5PT
Tel: 01747 840666 Fax: 01747 840666**

❖❖❖

❖❖

Cottages: Whitensmere Farm Cottages, Ashdon, Saffron Walden, Essex

Converted 17th century barns still retaining many original features. All cottages are extremely well equipped, with TV, video, microwaves, dishwashers, etc. 'The Brues' sleeps 8/10, 'Woodmore' sleeps 6/7 and 'Ladywell' 4/5. There is a games room and drying facilities, children play area and pets corner. Close to Cambridge and London only 1 hour. Heating by storage radiators and woodburners. Fresh flowers and welcome pack on arrival. 4 - 5 Keys Highly Commended. Brochure available.

3 cottages, sleeps 2-10, Price per week £200 low season, £700 high season, Children & dogs welcome, Available all year, Map Ref 2

Contact: Mrs Ford, Whitensmere Farm, Ashdon, Saffron Walden, Essex CB10 2JQ
Tel: 01799 584244 Fax: 01799 584244

❖❖

'Now then boys, I dunno as you oughta be doing that!'

❖❖

❖❖

Cottages: Postlip House Cottages, Postlip House, Winchcombe, Gloucestershire

Beautifully appointed cottages set in seven acres of wooded grounds providing superb accommodation. Individual gas central heating, modern fitted kitchens, wedgwood china, silver, in fact everything for a relaxing country holiday and the ideal centre for touring the Cotswolds, Stratford and Oxford. Dinner if required prepared by proprietors and delivered to the cottages. ETB 4 Keys Highly Commended.

5 cottages, sleeps 2-6, Price per week £230 - £280 low season, £360 - £480 high season, Children & pets welcome, Available all year, Map Ref 30

**Contact: Mary & Paul Sparks, Postlip House, Winchcombe, Gloucestershire GL54 5AH
Tel/Fax: 01242 602390**

❖❖

Cottages: The 3 Cottages at Cinderhill House, Cider Cottage, Big Barn Cottage, Cinderhill Cottage, St Briavel's, Gloucestershire

3 separate stone built cottages in the grounds of 14th century house. All equipped and furnished to high standard; one has 2 en-suite bedrooms, one with four-poster bed and one is for the disabled. Very peaceful and beautiful location yet ideal for walking and touring. It is also possible to book in for dinner at the house which is open for very comfortable bed and breakfast. Short breaks available from £95.

3 cottages, sleeps 2-6, Price per week from £225 low season, from £410 high season, No smoking, Children and pets welcome, Available all year, Map Ref 31

**Contact: Gillie Peacock, Cinderhill House, St Briavels, Gloucestershire GL15 6RH
Tel: 01594 530 393 Fax: 01594 530 098**

❖❖

Cottage: Church End Cottage, Church Street, Willsersey, Worcestershire

Idyllic positioned period cottage with secluded walled garden. The end of the lane, overlooking the churchyard and hills beyond. Two bedrooms, bathroom, sitting and dining rooms, kitchen and vaulted garden room. Fully equipped "cooks" kitchen and microwave, washer/dryer, cooker, mixer etc. Log fires, colour TV, stereo, barbecue. All linen supplied, welcome grocery pack, cot and high chair. Great walking straight from the door. Sorry no pets.

1 cottage, sleeps 4 + cot, Price per week £300 low season, £495 high season, Children welcome, Available all year, Map Ref 40

**Contact: Mrs Beauvoisin, The Old Rectory, Church Street, Willersey, Worcestershire WR12 7PN
Tel: 01386 853729 Fax: 01386 858061 EMail: beauvoisin@btinternet.com**

❖❖

❖❖

Cottages: Beacon Hill Farm Cottages, Beacon Hill Lane, Exton, Southampton, Hampshire

Barn conversion comprising four self catering cottages. Tastefully furnished with beamed ceilings and galleried landings. One suitable for disabled with carer. Close to historic Winchester and Portsmouth and market towns Alresford and Petersfield. Ideal base for walkers (South Downs Way). TV, microwave, dishwasher, barbecue, garden furniture, small games area. Stunning location in the Meon Valley with magnificent panoramic views of surrounding farmland and valley.

4 cottages, sleeps 4-5, Price per week £300 low season, £450 high season, Children welcome, Pets by arrangement, Available all year, Map Ref 34

**Contact: Mrs C Dunford, The Farm Office, Manor Farm, Beacon Hill Lane, Exton,
Southampton, Hampshire SO32 3NW
Tel: 01730 829724 Fax: 01730 829833**

❖❖

Cottage: Orchard Edge, Undercliff Drive, St Lawrence, Ventnor, Isle of Wight

Orchard Edge is a pretty detached stone cottage. Newly renovated with a modern kitchen with electric cooker, microwave and fridge. No extra charge for heating. All linen provided plus cot and high chair. Also colour TV and video in lounge. The village of Niton is about 1/2 a mile away where you will find local shops, post office, doctors surgery, etc. Parking for 1 car outside cottage. Heating by storage heaters and open fire.

1 cottage, sleeps 4 + cot, Price per week £254 low season, £367 high season, No smoking, Children welcome, No pets, Available all year, Map Ref 33

**Contact: Heather Nolan, Little Orchard, Undercliff Drive, St Lawrence, Ventnor, Isle of Wight
PO38 1YA
Tel: 01983 731106**

❖❖

Cottage: Smugglers Barn, Ashlake Farm, Ashlake Farm Lane, Wootton Creek, Isle of Wight

Smugglers Barn forms part of 17th Century Ashlake Farmhouse and has been beautifully restored to create a delightful holiday home. Double bedroom on mezzanine floor overlooking living/dining area, with well-equipped kitchen and bathroom. TV, microwave, fridge, freezer, barbecue etc. Private terrace, field leading to waters edge. Jetty with dinghy. Central yet peaceful position.

1 cottage, sleeps 2-4, Price per week £125 low season, £425 high season, Smoking restricted, Pets by arrangement, Available all year, Map Ref 32

**Contact: Carol Pearce, Ashlake Farmhouse, Ashlake Farm Lane, Wootton Creek, Isle of Wight
PO33 4LF
Tel: 01983 882124 Fax: 01983 882124**

❖❖

❖❖❖

Cottage: Hartleton Lodge, Bromash, Ross-on-Wye, Herefordshire

4 miles from Ross-on-Wye. This former workman's cottage has been extended and recently refurbished to a high standard, offering all modern amenities including dishwasher, microwave, washing machine, dryer, TV and video. There is central heating throughout and a woodburner in the lounge. Situated next to a lake there are plenty of local walks and 2 golf courses nearby. Parking is plentiful.

1 cottage, sleeps 6, Price per week £300 low season, £450 high season, No smoking, Children welcome, Pets by arrangement, Available all year, Map Ref 35

Contact: Penny Smith, Mill Barn, Bromash, Ross-on-Wye, Herefordshire HR9 7SB
Tel: 01989 780300 Fax: 01989 780324

❖❖❖

Cottages: Hidelow House Cottages, Acton Beauchamp, Worcester, Worcestershire

Only 2 1/2 hours from London. Set in the grounds of a small country house in an area of Outstanding Natural Beauty. Near the Malvern Hills for walking. This is an idyllic place to unwind. Converted hop-barns, spacious studio apartment, sun-terrace, fish pool, waterfall, gardens, 4-poster beds, stunning views, log fires, central heating. Disabled persons cottage (Catergory 2 NAS). Also B&B, evening meals, taxi service. ETB 4 Keys Highly Commended. Central location.

4 cottages, sleeping 2-5 + cot, Price per week from £164 - £199 low season, from £311 - £419 high season, Children & pets welcome, Available all year, Map Ref 39

Contact: Pauline Diplock, Hidelow House, Acton Green, Acton Beauchamp, Worcester, Worcestershire WR6 5AH
Tel: 01886 884547 Fax: 01886 884060 EMail: hidelow@aol.com

❖❖❖

Cottage: Kilverts Cottage, Winforton Court, Winforton, Herefordshire

Relax in the beautiful Wye Valley at Kilverts Cottage in the grounds of 16th Century Winforton Court. Luxury accommodation with fitted kitchen, dishwasher and microwave. Elegant dining room, oak stairs to first floor with one twin, one double bedroom, bathroom, study area, large oak beamed lounge with colour TV. Breathtaking views to the Black Mountains. 3/4 acre gardens, garage and laundry room. Fishing available. Welcome hamper. All linen and electricity included.

1 cottage, sleeps 4 + cot, Price per week £200 low season, £320 high season, Children & pets welcome, Available all year, Map Ref 38

Contact: Jackie Kingdon, Winforton Court, Winforton, Herefordshire HR3 6EA
Tel/Fax: 01544 328498

❖❖❖

❖❖❖

Cottage: Mill House Flat, Woonton Court Farm, Leyster, Leominster, Herefordshire

A former cider house converted to a high standard of comfort. 4 Keys Commended. Sleeps 3-4. Central heated accommodation, large double room, small bedroom single or two children, kitchen, electric cooker, microwave, fridge, colour TV, linen provided. Electricity included, pay phone, washing machine/dryer. Patio, garden and parking. Freedom to walk on farm. Nature trail. Farm produce. Short breaks available from £95. Extra accommodation in farmhouse nearby.

1 flat, sleeps 3-4, Price per week from £160 low season, from £200 high season, No smoking, Children welcome, No pets, Available all year, Map Ref 37

Contact: Elizabeth Thomas, Woonton Court Farm, Leysters, Leominster, Herefordshire
HR6 0HL
Tel: 01568 750232 Fax: 01568 750232

❖❖❖

Cottages: The Cottages at Westwood House, Park Road, West Malvern, Worcestershire

Three individual cottages and spacious garden flat sleeping between 2 and 6, high on Elgar's Malvern Hills and providing the standards of a private home. National award-winners whose aim is to offer the most elegant and best equipped holiday accommodation for people who prefer to cater for themselves in private home comfort. Cleanliness, presentation and attention to detail are paramount. Owners resident.

3 cottages, 1 flat, sleeps 2 - 6, Price per week from £195 low season, £510 high season, Children welcome, No pets, Available all year, Map Ref 36

Contact: Mrs Wright, The Cottages at Westwood House, Park Road, West Malvern,
Worcestershire WR14 4DS
Tel: 01684 892308 Fax: 01684 892882 EMail: davidwright2@compuserve.com

❖❖❖

Cottages: The Swiss Cottage & Lime Cottage, Mill Cottage, Canon Frome, Ledbury, Herefordshire

The cottages are situated in beautiful 5-acre wooded grounds in a peaceful spot amid lovely countryside. The Swiss Cottage is on the banks of the River Frome overlooking a waterfall. Both are well equipped for two people. Excellent for wildlife including resident kingfishers. Well situated for the Malverns, Wye Valley and the Black Mountains. Bed and Breakfast also available in Mill Cottage-two en-suite rooms.

2 cottages, sleeps 2, Price per week £108 - £154 low season, £222 - £317 high season, No smoking, Children & pets by arrangement, Available all year, Map Ref 36

Contact: Julian & Lorna Rutherford, Mill Cottage, Canon Frome, Ledbury, Herefordshire
HR8 2TD
Tel: 01531 670506 Mobile: 0378 591899 EMail: julian.rutherford@virgin.net

❖❖❖

❖❖

Cottages: Haybarn & Garden Cottage, Walnut Tree Farm, Lynsore Bottom, Upper Hardres, Canterbury, Kent

Barn conversions to very high standard. Situated in 6 acres of sheep grazing pasture. The perfect escape for country lovers. 6 miles to Canterbury. 12 miles to coast. Horse riding, John Aspinals Zoo close by. All electric with wood burning stoves, microwave, washing machine, TV, steep stairs, use of family pool, garden, pretty villages, good pubs locally, safe parking.

2 cottages, sleeps 2-4, price per week £220 low season, £340 high season, No smoking, Children over 5, Available March - November, Map Ref 41

Contact: Sheila Wilton, Walnut Tree Farm, Lynsore Bottom, Upper Hardres, Canterbury, Kent CT4 6EG
Tel: 01227 709375

❖❖

'He's licking me - his tongue's all rough!'

❖❖

❖❖

Cottages: Mansergh Farmhouse Cottages, Borwick, Carnforth, Lancs

Unique cottages of quality and charm with lovely views across open countryside, sleeps 4/6, heated indoor swimming pool Easter/September, play area, games room. Each cottage has colour TV, gas central heating, microwave, washing machine, shared tumble dryer, patio, walled garden, barbecue, parking. Excellent for touring Lakes, Dales, Forest of Bowland, coastal regions of Morecambe, Silverdale, Flyde Coast. Superb location for touring. 4 Keys Commended ETB. Discounts available off season.

5 cottages, sleeps 4-6, Price per week from £243 low season, £434 high season, Children & pets welcome, Available all year, Map Ref 42

**Contact: Mrs Morphy, Mansergh Farmhouse, Borwick, Carnforth, Lancs LA6 1JS
Tel: 01524 732586**

above, Mansergh Farmhouse Cottages

❖❖

❖❖

Cottage: The Loft House, Criftin Farm, Epperstone, Nottinghamshire

17th Century granary on a working farm in the heart of Robin Hood country close to the historic towns of Southwell, Nottingham and all the stately homes around. Woodland walks around farm. 4 golf courses and water sports close by. Central heating, colour TV, washer/dryer. Two twin bedded rooms with own bathrooms. Heated swimming pool May - September. Snooker room. Barbecue in walled garden.

1 cottage, sleeps 4, Price per week £260 low season, £300 high season, Children welcome, Pets by arrangement, Available all year, Map Ref 43

Contact: Jenny Esam, Criftin Farm, Epperstone, Nottinghamshire NG14 6AT
Tel: 0115 9652039 Fax: 0115 9655490

❖❖

'Humbugs, Bull's Eye's & Sherbert - that's tuppence, my dear'

❖❖

❖❖❖

Cottages: The Old Farmhouse, Bramble and Hawthorn Cottages, Waingrove Farm Country Cottages, Fulstow, Louth, Lincolnshire

Highly Commended Award Winners in the England For Excellence Awards for the Self Catering Holiday of the Year by the East of England Tourist Board 1997. Open the door to a real country cottage - beautifully presented by caring owners. Relax in the gardens of our Old Farmhouse; sit under the shady barn in the courtyard to single storey Bramble and Hawthorn. 'Just Two' discounts.

3 cottages, sleeps 2-6, Price per week from £175 - £250 low season, £250 - £450 high season, Children over 10, No pets, Available all year, Map Ref 44

**Contact: Stephanie Smith, Waingrove Farm, Fulstow, Louth, Lincolnshire LN11 0XQ
Tel: 01507 363704 Fax: 01507 363704 EMail: stephanie.smith@lineone.net**

❖❖❖

'There! See him? A big one!'

❖❖❖

❖❖❖

Cottages: Clippesby Holidays, Clippesby, near Great Yarmouth, Norfolk

Family owned country park. Pine lodge, cottages and summer time apartments in spacious lawns and wooded glades. In summer there is tennis, swimming and more. In winter time the cottages have central heating and cosy log fires and lots of peace and quiet. Clippesby is in a great situation for exploring the Norfolk Coast and countryside.

22 cottages, sleeping 2-10, Price per week from £159 low season, £239 high season, Children & pets welcome, Available all year, Map Ref 45

Contact: Clippesby Holiday, Clippesby, near Great Yarmouth, Norfolk NR29 3BL
Tel: 01493 367800 Fax: 01493 367809 EMail: clippesby.hols@virgin.net

❖❖❖

Cottage: The Coach House, Rosedale Farm Guest House, Holt Road, Weybourne, Holt, Norfolk

Restored with many original features, the Coach House with luxury king-sized bedroom and twin bunkroom has ample space. "Shaker Style" kitchen with Suffolk pammets is well equipped with dishwasher, fridge/freezer, breakfast bar and stools. Sitting/dining area has large "Pine framed Futon" and colour TV. Only ten minutes walk to beach and coastal paths, Weybourne with its friendly village shop is an ideal base for holidays! All bed linen, towels and main services are included.

1 cottage, sleeps 4-6, Price per week from £180 low season to £320 high season, No smoking, Children Welcome, Small dogs welcome, Available all year, Map Ref 46

Contact: Charles & Pauline Lacoste, Rosedale Farm Guest House, Holt Road, Weybourne, Holt, Norfolk NR25 7ST
Tel: 01263 588778

❖❖❖

Cottages: Wood Farm Cottages, Edgefield, near Holt, Norfolk

Wood Farm is located outside the village down a long lane surrounded by trees and fields. The accommodation consists of 19th Century barns around a courtyard delightfully converted to provide eight well equipped cottages. Features include exposed flint, beams, woodburners, a four-poster bed, stereos and video players. Outside there is a superb play area which includes a zip wire and 1959 David Brown tractor. (Colour brochure available).

8 cottages, sleeping 2-6, Price per week £150 low season, £480 high season, Smoking restricted, Children welcome, Pets by arrangement, Available all year, Map Ref 47

Contact: Diana Elsby, Wood Farm, Plumstead Road, Edgefield, Melton Constable, Norfolk NR24 2AQ
Tel: 01263 587347 Fax: 01263 587347

❖❖❖

❖❖

Cottages: 1, 2 & 3 Cottages, Titlington Hall Farm, Alnwick, Northumberland

Our lovely cottages are situated in a quiet and beautiful area. They are spacious and well equipped with TV, fridge, microwave and washing machine, also tumble dryer and pay phone. Each cottage has parking at the front and an enclosed back garden. All linen, electricity and gas for central heating included in the rent. Can sleep families of ten, children welcome, Pets by arrangement.

3 cottages, sleeps 14, Price per week £165 - £195 low season, £265 - £295 high season, Children welcome, Pets by arrangement, Available all year, Map Ref 50

**Contact: John & Vera Purvis, Titlington Hall Farm, Alnwick, Northumberland NE66 2EB
Tel: 01665 578253 Fax: 01665 578253**

❖❖

Cottage: Middle Cottage, Farneyside, Ninebanks, Allendale, Northumberland

This comfortable stone built former lead miners' cottage stands in a quiet rural terrace enjoying magnificent views over the rolling countryside. Centrally heated by the multi-fuel stove and storage heaters. This cottage has two bedrooms sleeping 4 people. Well equipped with electric cooker, microwave, fridge, automatic washing machine, colour TV, video recorder, CD, radio cassette player and all bed linen provided.

1 cottage, sleeps 4, Price per week £170 low season, £210 high season, No smoking, Children welcome, No pets, Available all year, Map Ref 49

**Contact: Gillian Ford, Netherdale, Farneyside, Ninebanks, Allendale, Northumberland
NE47 8DB
Tel: 01434 345390**

❖❖

Cottage: The Old Smithy, Brackenside, Bowden, Berwick on Tweed, Northumberland

Splendid three bedroom conversion of the Old Smithy on our friendly working farm with stunning views of the Cheviots and Holy Island. Close to gentle woodland walks meandering by ponds and conservation areas. The Smithy provides superb accommodation with colour TV, central heating, washer/dryer and a wood burning stove in the original blacksmiths fireplace (all fuel free!). The Smithy has its own private walled garden.

1 cottage, sleeps 6, Price per week £190 low season, £440 high season, Children and pets welcome, Available all year, Map Ref 48

**Contact: John & Mary Barber, Brackenside, Bowsden, Berwick on Tweed, Northumberland
TD15 2TQ
Tel: 01289 388293**

❖❖

❖❖

Cottages: Cavaliers Cottage and The Old Dairy, Culworth Manor Cottages, Culworth, Banbury, Oxfordshire

Next to the owners historic 17th century Manor House on Culworth's peaceful Village Green, these two cottages offer wonderful rural country holidays. Four-poster bed, open fires, old oak beams, both superbly equipped with dishwashers, washing machines, microwaves. ETB 5 Keys Highly Commended. Pretty cottage gardens and charming old Herb garden with far reaching views. Oxford, the Cotswolds, Stratford upon Avon, Althorp and Warwick Castle are all close by.

2 cottages, sleeps 4 & 5, Price per week £225 low season, £575 high season, Children welcome, No pets, Available all year, Map Ref 51

**Contact: Richard & Beth Soar, The Manor House, Culworth, Banbury, Oxfordshire OX17 2BB
Tel: 01295 760099 Fax: 01295 760098 EMail: culworth_manor@compuserve.com**

above, Culworth Manor Cottages

❖❖

❖❖❖

Cottage: The Barn, Ryecroft, Richards' Castle, near Ludlow, Shropshire

Timbered cabin style radial roof barn with deck area and steps down to orchard. Rural area with panoramic views of the Welsh Borders. A superb relaxed atmosphere with wood burning stove and electric heating. Furnished and equipped to a high standard. Visit Ludlow fives miles away famous for its medieval castle. Explore the Shropshire Hills, Mid Wales or lovely walks from the door. ETB 3 Keys Commended.

1 cottage, sleeps 4-5, Price per week £160 low season, £360 high season, No smoking, Children welcome, No pets, Available all year, Map Ref 52

Contact: Peter & Sue Plant, Ryecroft, Richards' Castle, near Ludlow, Shropshire SY8 4EU
Tel: 01584 831 224 Fax: 01584 831 224

❖❖❖

'What about that big fish, Jack - would it bite?'

❖❖❖

❖❖❖

Cottages: Little Quarme Cottages, Wheddon Cross, Exmouth National Park,

Six stone cottages offering top quality, comfort and cleanliness in an idyllic peaceful location with outstanding panoramic rural views. Quality furnishings. Nicam TV, microwaves, etc. Lovely gardens. Many animals, pony rides. Non smoking. Ideally situated in the heart of Exmouth National Park. Farmhouse bed and breakfast also available. ETB 4 Keys Deluxe.

6 cottages, sleeps 2-6, Price per week £120 low season, £500 high season, No smoking, Children & pets welcome, Available all year, Map Ref 53

Contact: Tammy Cody-Boutcher, Little Quarme Cottages, Wheddon Cross, near Minehead, Somerset TA24 7EA
Tel/Fax: 01643 841249

❖❖❖

'Hey Tim, there's strawberries up here - let's pick em!'

❖❖❖

❖❖

Cottage: The Hatch, Pilgrims Lane, Cross Green, Hartest, Suffolk

Cottage is attached to main house but has its own entrance and patio/garden. Lovely views and very peaceful situation. Furnished with fine fabrics and antiques. Bed-sitting room, luxury bathroom and fully fitted kitchen. Guests may also use drawing room in main house. Warm and cosy in Winter. Delightful in Summer with double french windows, opening on to patio and barbecue area. Super walking country.

1 cottage, sleeps 2, Price per week £150 low season, £275 high season, No smoking, children or pets, Available all year, Map Ref 54

Contact: Mr & Mrs Oaten, The Hatch, Pilgrims Lane, Cross Green, Hartest, Suffolk IP29 4ED
Tel: 01284 830226 Fax: 01284 830226

above, The Hatch

❖❖

❖❖

Cottages: Badgerholt or Foxholme, Holmbury St. Mary, Dorking, Surrey

Two delightfully cosy single storey cottages, sympathetically converted from a Surrey barn forming a courtyard with the farmhouse. Fully carpeted, electric central heating, colour TV and linen (beds made up), commercial laundry room. Use of two acre farmhouse garden. Situated in picturesque quiet valley, ideal walking country, bird watching, woodland walk to conservation lake, convenient Wisley National Trust Properties in South East. Frequent trains to London and Dorking.

2 cottages, sleeps 2-4, Price per week from £150 - £230 low season, £200 - £300 high season, Children & pets welcome, Available all year, Map Ref 55

Contact: Gill Hill, Bulmer Farm, Holmbury St. Mary, Dorking, Surrey RH5 6LG
Tel: 01306 730210

❖❖

'He knows the way, doesn't he'

❖❖

SUSSEX
The Great British Self Catering Cottage Guide

❖❖❖

Cottages: Best of Brighton & Sussex Cottages Ltd, Sussex

We are a small agency offering good quality fully furnished houses, flats, cottages, studios and apartments in Brighton and Hove as well as in the country areas such as Alfriston, Lewes, Arundel, Storrington, Seaford, Rottingdean and Chichester. All personally inspected. 3 Keys Commended to 5 Keys Deluxe. Town centre, seafront and countryside locations. Short breaks available out of season. Lettings include linen and towels.

100 properties, sleeps 2-16, Price per week £170 low season, £2,000 high season, Children & pets welcome, Available all year, Map Ref 58

Contact: Richard Harris, Best of Brighton & Sussex Cottages Ltd, Horseshoe Cottage, Rottingdean, Sussex BN2 7HZ
Tel: 01273 308779 Fax: 01273 300266

❖❖❖

Cottages: Mill Pond Cottage, Pool House & Cider House, Duncton Mill House, Dye House Lane, Duncton, near Petworth, West Sussex

Enjoy the peace and tranquility of our unique downland setting. Accommodation within our small country estate and trout farm comprises three Grade II Listed cottages all with modern amenities, sleeping max. of two, four & five people. Fly fishing and tuition are available. Walk the South Downs Way or visit the many interesting places nearby, such as Chichester, Goodwood and Petworth. Venture further afield to London or Brighton. Guests can explore our woods, picnic in our old orchards or swim in the heated outdoor pool by arrangement.

3 cottages, sleeps 2, 4, 4-5, Price per week from £180 low season, £425 high season, Children & pets welcome, Available all year, Map Ref 57

Contact: Sheila Bishop, Duncton Mill House, Dye House Lane, Duncton, nr Petworth, West Sussex GU28 0LF
Tel: 01798 342294

❖❖❖

Cottages: Sliders Farm Barn & Cottage, Furners Green, Uckfield, East Sussex

Sliders Barn & Cottage are within a magnificent 16th Century barn. Peacefully situated down a country lane on edge of Ashdown Forest. Many famous properties, gardens and historic houses are within easy reach. Ardingly Showground 7 miles, London 45 minutes by train. Electricity, heating, linen, towels included, electric cooker, washing machine, dishwasher, fridge, pay phone, colour TV. Swimming Pool (Summer), tennis court and fishing lakes. Beautiful gardens.

2 cottages, sleeps 4, 4-5, Price per week £300 low season, £450 high season, Children welcome, Pets by arrangement, Available March - November, Map Ref 59

Contact: David & Jean Salmon, Sliders Farm, Furners Green, Uckfield, East Sussex TN22 3RT
Tel: 01825 790258 Fax: 01825 790258

❖❖❖

❖❖

Cottages: White Lion Farm Cottages, White Lion Farm, Shortgate, Lewes, East Sussex

Situated in the hamlet of Shortgate are two converted stables of a 16th Century coaching inn. Attractively decorated, fully equipped, TV, microwave, cooker, washing machine, fridge. Own patio. Set in 8 1/2 acres with 2 lakes, one stocked with carp for private fishing. Rural location. Convenient for coastal resorts, South Downs, Glyndebourne, Ashdown Forest, East Sussex National Golf Club and many other places of interest.

2 cottages, sleeps 4, 4, Price per week £150 low season, £275 high season, No smoking, Children welcome, No pets, Available all year, Map Ref 56

**Contact: Ivor and Diana Green, White Lion Farm, Shortgate, Lewes, East Sussex BN8 6JP
Tel: 01825 840288**

❖❖

Sliders Farm Barn & Cottage

❖❖

❖❖❖

Cottage: The Coach House, Sturford Mead Farm, Corsley, Warminster, Wiltshire

Converted from Longleat Estate, this 18th Century coach house is half way between Warminster and Frome, nestled under Cley Hill (National Trust). It is on the owners working farm, in an area of outstanding natural beauty. Accommodation offers lounge, dining room, kitchen, bathroom, 3 bedrooms. One with double, one twin and one single, all made up. Colour TV, microwave, dishwasher and freezer. Large fenced garden, garden furniture and barbecue.

1 cottage, sleeps 5/6, Price per week £200 low season, £300 high season, No smoking, Children welcome, No pets, Available all year, Map Ref 60

**Contact: Lynn Corp, Sturford Mead Farm, Corsley, Warminster, Wiltshire BA12 7QU
Tel: 01373 832213 Fax: 01373 832212**

❖❖❖

Cottage: The Dower House, Burghope Manor, Winsley, Bradford on Avon, Wiltshire

The Dower House is situated in the grounds of historic Burghope Manor, on the edge of Winsley village which overlooks the glorious Avon Valley, 5 miles from the city of Bath and 1 1/2 miles from Bradford-on-Avon. The Dower House has a large sitting room, an elegant dining room, fully equipped kitchen, downstairs cloakroom with shower, 3 double bedrooms each with bathrooms and showers. Front lawn, patio and garden to the rear, walled for complete privacy. Heating, linen and towels included

1 house, sleeps 6, Price per week £600, No pets, Available all year, Map Ref 61

**Contact: John Denning, The Dower House, Burghope Manor, Winsley, Bradford on Avon,
Wiltshire BA15 2LA
Tel: 01225 723557 Fax: 01225 723113**

❖❖❖

'How old am I, young man? I'll be ninety three come Michaelmas!'

❖❖❖

Cottage: Bream Cottage, 13 River Street, York, Yorkshire

Ideal family accommodation in quiet street, 50 yards from an attractive stretch of the river. Two en-suite bedrooms, one double, one with substantial bunk beds and regular single. Fitted kitchen with oven, microwave and washing machine, etc. Comfortable lounge with large colour TV. Seperate dining area. Central heating throughout. Car parking with permit supplied. 5 minutes pleasant walk to city centre tourist attractions. No smoking.

1 cottage, sleeps 5, Price per week £195 low season, £350 high season, No smoking, Children welcome, Available all year, Map Ref 64

Contact: Elsie Osterman, 20 Barbican Road, York, Yorkshire YO10 5AA
Tel: 01904 627617 Fax: 01904 647140
EMail: barbican@thenet.co.uk

❖❖❖

Cottages: Cedar Cottages, Keldholme, Kirkbymoorside, near Pickering, York & Laskill Farm, Hawnby, near Helmsley, Yorkshire

3 Listed old worlde cottages and 4 new barn conversions, all beautifully furnished, warm, clean and spacious. Gateway to England's finest National Park. Lots to do and see. York only 30 minutes. Peace and tranquility, personally supervised and well equipped. A walkers paradise. Linen included. Microwave, dishwasher, barbecue area, colour TV. Car parking. Garden and lots of garden furniture. All cottages with lots of character.

7 cottages, sleeping 2-6, Price per week from £100 low season, £560 high season, Children welcome, Available all year, Map Ref 63

Contact: Sue Smith, Laskill Farm Country House, Hawnby, near Helmsley, Yorkshire YO62 5NB
Tel: 01439 798 268 Fax: 01439 798 268

❖❖❖

Cottages: Cocksford Cottages, Cocksford, Stutton, Tadcaster, North Yorkshire

Attractively converted cottages in quiet picturesque valley. Ideal retreat, yet close to York and convenient to Leeds, Harrogate, Dales, Moors and coast. Warm and comfortably furnished with open fires and all modern conveniences. Sparrows Restaurant and Bar close by, adjoins Cocksford Golf Club.

2 cottages, sleeps 2 - 5-6, Price per week £150 low season, £350 high season, Children & pets welcome, Available all year, Map Ref 66

Contact: Sue Watkinson, Cocksford, Stutton, Tadcaster, North Yorkshire LS24 9NG
Tel: 01937 530344 or 01937 834253 Fax: 01937 834253

❖❖❖

❖❖

Cottages: Easthill House & Gardens, Easthill, Thornton-Le-Dale, North Yorkshire

Three Scandinavian style chalets, one cottage or choice of three luxury apartments sleeping 2-8. Set in 2 1/2 acres of landscaped gardens/woodland. Beautifully equipped and furnished to a very high standard. Grass tennis court, putting green, games room, play areas. ETB 3 - 4 Key Highly Commended. Short breaks available off season. Central for moors, coast, York and forestry. For brochure ring 01751 474561.

7 cottages, sleeping 2-8, Price per week £150 - £250 low season, £290 - £620 high season, Children welcome, No pets, Available all year, Map Ref 63

Contact: Jennie Green, Easthill, Wilton Road, Thorton-Le-Dale, North Yorkshire YO18 7QP
Tel: 01751 474561

❖❖

Cottages: Hobbits Hideaway, Stable Cottage
and Rue Crofts View, High Farm, Cropton, Pickering, North Yorkshire

Three delightful stone cottages thoughtfully and sympathetically converted from traditional farm buildings which offer a peaceful rural base to explore North Yorkshire Moors, Coast and York. Beautifully situated in own grounds on edge of quiet unspoilt village with open views over National Park. Extensive garden planted with trees, shrubs and roses. Barbecue available. ETB 5 Keys Highly Commended. Local inn has own brewery.

3 cottages, sleeping 2, 4, 6, Price per week from £120 - £150 low season, £310 - £475 high season, Children welcome, No pets, Available all year, Map Ref 63

Contact: Ruth Feaster, High Farm, Cropton, Pickering, North Yorkshire YO18 8HL
Tel: 01751 417461

❖❖

Cottages: Rains Farm, Allerston, Pickering, North Yorkshire

Five warm and comfortable recently converted barns. Furnished, decorated and equipped for luxury living. Very peaceful, magnificent views, relax and unwind and ease away the pressures of life in this idyllic rural retreat. Gaze on the ponies grazing in the paddocks. We are centrally situated for York, Pickering and Steam Railway, North Yorkshire Moors, Coast, Stately Homes, Castles and quaint villages. ETB 3 - 4 Keys Highly Commended.

5 cottages, sleeping 2-6, Price per week £160 low season, £425 high season, No smoking, Children & Pets welcome, Available all year , Map Ref 63

Contact: Jean & Lorraine Allanson, Rains Farm, Allerston, Pickering, North Yorkshire YO18 7PQ
Tel: 01723 859333 Fax: 01723 859333

❖❖

❖❖

Cottages: The Wasps Nest Holiday Cottages, Green Hammerton, Yorkshire

Four charmingly converted cottages in pretty gardens in a village between York and Harrogate. Ideally situated for exploring historic towns, ancient abbeys, stately homes and the Yorkshire Dales and Moors. We are inspected by the English Tourist Board and are graded 4 Keys (for facilities) and are Highly Commended. Please send for our colour brochure for a detailed description of our cottages and the area.

4 cottages, sleeps 1-5 + cot, Price per week £150 low season, £390 high season, Children & pets welcome, Available April - October, Map Ref 65

Contact: Mary Nixon, The Wasps Nest Holiday Cottages, Green Hammerton, Yorkshire YO5 8AE
Tel: 01423 330153 Fax: 01423 331204
EMail: waspsnest@phnixon.demon.co.uk

❖❖

Cottage: The Woodpeckers, Kirkby Malzeard, Ripon, North Yorkshire

Delightful stone cottage with original beams, very high standard of decoration and furnishings. ETB 3 Key Highly Commended. Sleeps 2. Open all year. Situated in village and ideal location for touring Yorkshire Dales and Moors. Fountains Abbey 4 miles, Ripon 6 miles, well equipped with cooker, microwave, colour TV. Central heating. Everything is included in price. Sorry no children or pets. Please phone 01765 658206 for brochure.

1 cottage, sleeps 2, Price per week £130 low season, £195 high season, No children or pets, Available all year, Map Ref 62

Contact: Mrs Drewery, The Woodpeckers, Kirkby Malzeard, Ripon, North Yorkshire HG4 3SE
Tel: 01765 658206

❖❖

Cottage: Green Loaning, 6 Castle Road, Thornton-Le-Dale, near Pickering, North Yorkshire

Situated in pretty village close to the North Yorkshire Moors Steam Railway. Fabulous detached bungalow with three toilets, two bathrooms, shower, colour TV's and Video, centrally heated, 5 telephones, magnificent conservatory, every conceivable extra. Well above your average holiday let. Secluded garden, garage and private parking for 3 cars. Village Green 2 minutes walk, 3 pubs which all do meals 7 days a week. Tourist Board Approved.

1 cottage, sleeps 8, Price per week £435 low season, £475 high season (fuel inclusive), Children welcome, No pets, Available all year, Map Ref 63

Contact: Frances Boardman, 10 Green Gables Close, Heald Green, Cheadle, Cheshire SK8 3QT
Tel: 0161 489 8505

❖❖

❖❖

Cottages: Purgavie Farm, Lintrathen, By Kirriemuir, Scotland

Escape the stress and relax in our Swedish loghouse or bungalow and enjoy the panoramic views of the lovely countryside. Explore the hills and see the wildlife or fish in Lintrathen Loch. Properties furnished to a high standard, dishwasher, shower, fridge/freezer, washer/dryer, pay phone, microwave. Garden. Parking. Open fires in bungalow. Glamis castle 10 miles. Dundee city of Discovery 26 miles. Scone Palace and Perth 30 miles.

2 cottages, sleeps 6, 4, Price per week £150 low season, £400 high season, Children & pets welcome, Available January - December, Map Ref 67

**Contact: Moira Clark, Purgavie Farm, Lintrathen, By Kirriemuir, Scotland DD8 5HZ
Tel: 01575 560213 Fax: 01575 560213**

❖❖

Cottages: Kilchrist Castle, Campbeltown, Argyll, Scotland

Six small, cosy, comfortably furnished, fully equipped cottages in Kilchrist Castle grounds, near Campbeltown and the famous Mull of Kintyre. Colour TV, microwave, bed linen (duvets) included. Towels for hire, but free for overseas visitors. All electric. Electricity by meter reading. Children welcome. Meet our Shetland Ponies. Close to Golf and sandy beaches. Featured in Good Holiday Cottage Guide. STB 2 Stars. Brochure on request. Contact Mrs Leonie Angus, Kilchrist Castle, Campbeltown, Argyll, Scotland, PA28 6PH.

6 cottages, sleeps 2-6, Price per week from £130 low season, £294 high season, Children & pets welcome, Available April - October, Map Ref 68

**Contact: Col & Mrs Angus, Kilchrist Castle, Campbeltown, Argyll, Scotland PA28 6PH
Tel: 01586 553210 Fax: 01586 551852 EMail: william.t.c.angus@btinternet.com**

❖❖

Cottages: 'Springwell Holiday Homes', Onich, Fort William, Inverness-shire, Scotland

Four cottages set in 17 acre private hillside, panoramic views overlooking Loch Linnhe into the Argyll-shire mountains. Fully equipped, fitted kitchens, microwaves, fridge/freezers, colour TV's, Baths, Showers, Central heating, all electricity and linen inclusive. Laundry. Ideal central position for touring the Highlands and Islands. Licensed hotels, shops, climbing, rambling, skiing within a short distance, ample parking facilities at all cottages. Small secluded rugged beach. Brochure.

4 cottages, sleeps 4, 6, Price per week from £180 - £285 low season, £300 - £380 high season, Children welcome, Pets by arrangement, Available all year, Map Ref 69

**Contact: William Murray, Springwell, Onich, Fort William, Inverness-shire, Scotland PH33 6RY
Tel: 01855 821257 Fax: 01855 821257**

❖❖

SCOTLAND
The Great British Self Catering Cottage Guide

❖❖

Cottages: Attadale Holiday Cottages, by Strathcarron, Ross-shire, Scotland

A mile from the sea on a private road, four well equipped and attractively furnished cottages. Beyond lies a 32,000 acre estate. A wilderness ideal for wildlife, birds, loch fishing and hill walking. Well placed for exploring Skye and the West Coast. No television but deer can be seen from the windows. Launderette at main house. Excellent restaurant 2 miles. STB 4 Star.

4 cottages, sleeps 4-8, Price per week from £225-£400, Children & pets welcome, Available March - November, Map Ref 70

Contact: Ray Bright, Attadale, Strathcarron, Ross-shire, Scotland IV54 8YX
Tel/Fax: 01520 722396

❖❖

Cottages: Clan Donald Cottages, Armadale, Sleat, Isle of Skye, Scotland

Superbly sited on a hillside, the log cottages enjoy breathtaking views across the sound of Sleat. Each has an open plan living room/dining room, kitchen, bathroom, double, twin and single bedroom. Each unit comes fully equipped with TV, VCR, telephone, cooker, dishwasher, microwave oven, fridge/freezer, washer dyer. Towels and linen. Electricity is included. There are no hidden extras. All STB 4 Star. Short breaks available.

6 cottages + 1 luxury suite, sleeps 4 - 6, Price per week £300 low season, £560 high season, Children welcome, Pets by arrangement, Available all year, Map Ref 71

Contact: Flora Maclean, Clan Donald Cottages, Armadale, Sleat, Isle of Skye IV45 8RS
Tel: 01471 844 305/227 Fax: 01471 844 275 EMail: office@cland.demon.co.uk

❖❖

High Range Holiday Lodges, Grampian Road, Aviemore, Inverness-shire, Scotland

Small private complex 500 yards from Aviemore centre. Under the personal supervision of the Vastano family for the past 22 years, where standards and style have been influenced by continuity and continental flair. One - three bedrooms providing all that is necessary for your comfort and well being. Magnificent views of the Cairngorm Mountains. Informal restaurant and café-bar, on site, highly renowned for it's excellent cuisine.

9 cottages, sleeps 2-6, Price per week from £200 low season, £500 high season, Children welcome, Pets by arrangement, Available all year, Map Ref 72

Contact: Mr & Mrs Vastano, High Range Holiday Chalets, Grampian Road, Aviemore,
Inverness-shire, Scotland PH22 1PT
Tel: 01479 810636 Fax: 01479 811322 EMail: highrange@enterprise.net

❖❖

❖❖❖

Cottage: Garden Flat, No 8 Marshall Place, Perth, Perthshire, Scotland

Luxury garden flat in charming Georgian terraced house overlooking a beautiful park. Central location. Ideally situated for touring and walking. Abundant golf opportunities nearby. Equipped to the highest of standards. Garden and garage. Sorry no smoking or pets.

1 cottage, sleeps 4, Price per week £200 low season, £400 high season, Children welcome, No pets, Available all year, Map Ref 73

Contact: Tricia Stiell, 5 Marshall Place, Perth, Perthshire PH2 8AH
Tel: 01738 447524 Fax: 01738 444056

❖❖❖

Cottage: Cnoc Famh, Balquhidder, Lochearnhead, Perthshire, Scotland

The cottage was completely refurbished in 1992, it is stone built, equipped to the highest standard, electric cooker, washing machine, dryer, TV, etc and wood burning fire. It is located between a small river and burn (stream), close to Balquhidder (no shops) and is surrounded by 7 acres of fields. This is Rob Roy country. Spectacular scenery, restaurants and shops, within easy driving distance. Free fishing on river and loch. Many local golf courses.

1 cottage, sleeps 6, Price per week £200 low season, £420 high season, Children welcome, Pets by arrangement, Available all year, Map Ref 74

Contact: Sandra Carter, Craigruie House, Balquhidder, Lochearnhead, Perthshire, Scotland
FK19 8PQ
Tel: 01877 384240 Fax: 01877 384240

❖❖❖

'Come on Billy Bull, you're too slow!'

❖❖

Cottages: Dryslwyn Fawr, Llanarthne, Carmarthenshire

Beautifully converted, fully fitted, peaceful cottages on 17th century farm situated by River Towy. In historic and picturesque valley near castles and close to the Brecon Beacons. Within easy reach of renowned Pembrokeshire coasts. Each cottage has a television, open fire or log burning stove, microwave, cooker and washing machine. With parking next to cottages. On site tennis court, croquet lawn, safe play area.

4 cottages, sleeps 2-6, Price per week £110 low season, £300 high season, Children welcome, Pets by arrangement, Available all year, Map Ref 75

**Contact: Monica French, Dryslwyn Fawr, Llanarthne, Carmarthenshire SA32 8JQ
Tel: 01558 668711 Fax: 01558 668711**

❖❖

Cottages: Maerdy Cottages, Taliaris, near Llandeilo, Carmarthenshire

Six beautiful cottages dating from the 16th century enjoy a tranquil setting amongst mature wooded gardens and stream in the lovely Talley Valley. Furnished with many antiques and well equipped throughout they are a warm welcoming and cosy retreat at any time of the year. WTB Grade 4 ensures unusual home comforts and essential facilities. Home cooking available from Mrs Jones nearby. Brochure on request.

6 cottages, sleeps 4-10, Price per week £195 low season, £750 high season, Children & pets welcome, Available all year , Map Ref 76

**Contact: Mrs Jones, The Annex, Dan Y Cefn, Manordeilo, Llandeilo, Carmarthenshire
SA19 7BD
Tel: 01550 777448 Fax: 01550 777067**

❖❖

Cottages: Hendy Pair & Ffosffald Isaf, Drefach, Llanybydder, Ceredigion

Two Grade 5 cottages, perfect for unwinding busy stressed lives. Set in glorious countryside against panoramic views of the Cambrian Hills. They are fully equipped for the discerning guest. Barbecues, croquet, swings, car parking, 186 acres to roam in. 20 minutes to coast and hills. Traditional home cooked meals by arrangement. Also farmhouse bed and breakfast. No pets. Free detailed and illustrated brochure available.

2 cottages, sleep 4,6, Price per week £170 low season, £320 high season, Children welcome, No pets, Available March - December, Map Ref 77

**Contact: Mary Thomas, Ffosffald Uchaf, Drefach, Llanybydder, Ceredigion SA40 9TA
Tel: 01570 434200**

❖❖

❖❖

Cottages: Bron-y-Wendon Holiday Cottages, Wern Road, Llanddulas, Colwyn Bay

Bron-y-Wendon is a farmhouse converted into luxurious, centrally heated cottages, offering the ultimate in self-catering accommodation. Facilities include satellite TV, dishwasher, microwave and games room. The beach is just 300 yards away and all cottages have sea views and are ideally situated for a sea side or exploring/activity holiday. Llandudno, Conway, Snowdonia and Chester are all within easy reach as are sports/leisure facilities. Open all year for holidays and short breaks. Colour brochure available.

5 cottages, sleeps 2-5+cot, Price per week £175 low season, £440 high season, Children & pets welcome, Available all year, Map Ref 78

Contact: Mrs Dent, Bron-y-Wendon Holiday Cottages, Wern Road, Llanddulas, Colwyn Bay LL22 8HG
Tel: 01492 512903 Fax: 01492 512903

❖❖

Cottages: Nant-y-Glyn Chalets, Cottages & Coach House, The Lodge, Nant-y-Glyn Road, Colwyn Bay,

Set in a picturesque, sheltered, valley, our high quality accommodation - chalets, cottages and a coach house - are in a tranquil setting and yet ideally situated for the town centre and beach. There are a range of facilities on offer including central heating, colour TV, microwave, washing machine, dishwasher, gardens, children's play area, car parking. Open all year for holidays and short breaks. Colour brochure available.

4 cottages, 7 chalets, 1 coach house, sleeps 2-9, Price per week from £85 low season, high season from £240, Children & pets welcome, Available all year, Map Ref 78

Contact: Mrs Dent, Nant-y-Glyn Chalets, Cottages & Coach House, The Lodge, Nant-y-Glyn Road, Colwyn Bay, LL29 7RD
Tel: 01492 512282 Fax: 01492 512903

❖❖

Apartments: Bryn Bras Castle, Llanrug, near Caernarfon

Welcome to beautiful Bryn Bras Castle - romantic apartments and elegant tower house within distinctive Romanesque castle, enjoying breathtaking scenery amid gentle Snowdonia foothills. Within easy reach of mountains, beaches, heritage, local restaurant/inns. Each fully self-contained, individual character, spacious, peaceful. Generously equipped from dishwasher to flowers. Central heating, hot water, linen inclusive. All highest grade. 32 acre gardens, woodlands, panoramic walks. Enjoy comfort, warmth and privacy in serene surroundings.

7 apartments, sleep 2-4, Price per week £300-£600. Short breaks available all year e.g from £120 for 2 persons for 2 nights. No young children or pets, Available all year, Map Ref 79

Contact: Mrs Marita Gray-Parry, Bryn Bras Castle, Llanrug, Caernarfon, North Wales LL55 4RE
Tel/Fax: 01286 870210

❖❖

❖❖

Cottages: Felin parc Cottages (Mill & Cottage), Tanlan, Llanfrothen, Penrhyndeudraeth, Gwynedd

Discover the idyllic stone and beamed 17th Century millhouse on River Croesor with own pool, falls, private waterfall valley near Snowdon, Portmeirion, Ffestiniog Miniature Railway. Charming Manager's cottage 100 yards distance overlooking ancient fording bridge and Cynicht Mountain. Both delightfully furnished, open fires, central heating, colour TV, fully modernised kitchens, bathrooms, microwaves, washing machines. Secluded river terraces with ample parking. Beaches, golf, fishing, good pubs all available locally.

2 cottages, sleeps 12 + 6, Price per week, from £175 low season, £250 high season, Children & pets welcome, Available all year, Map Ref 81

**Contact: Mr & Mrs Williams-Ellis, San Giovanni, 4 Sylvan Road, London SE19 2RX
Tel: 0181 653 3118**

❖❖

Cottages: Plas Y Bryn Chalet Park, Bontnewydd, Caernarfon, Gwynedd

Our small park is situated two miles from the historic town of Caernarfon. Set into a walled garden, it offers safety, seclusion and beautiful views of Snowdonia. It is ideally positioned for touring the area. Shop and village pub nearby. Accommodation has colour TV, fridge, gas cookers, shower or bath. We also offer caravans for rental.

13 cottages, sleeps 4 or 6, Price per week £75 low season, £265 high season, Children & pets welcome, Available all year, Map Ref 79

**Contact: Mr Livingston, Plas Y Bryn Chalet Park, Bontnewydd, Caernarfon, Gwynedd
LL54 7YE
Tel: 01286 672811**

❖❖

Cottages: Rhydolion, Llangian, Abersoch, Pwllheli, Gwynedd

Surrounded by a peaceful countryside setting and farm interest, but only three quarters of a mile from sandy beach. The charming 16th Century, farmhouse wing and ground floor cottage - 'Olde Worlde Charm' and modern comfort, beams, inglenook fireplace, attractive four poster bed in farmhouse. Microwave, dishwasher and laundry room. Ideal sailing, surfing, cycling, and good walks area. Out of season short breaks. Open March to January. Colour brochure. WTB Grade 5.

2 cottages, sleeps 6,7, Price per week £105 low season, £400 high season, Children welcome, Pets by arrangement, Available March - January, Map Ref 80

**Contact: Mrs Morris, Rhydolion, Llangian, Abersoch, Pwllheli, Gwynedd LL53 7LR
Tel/Fax: 01758 712342**

❖❖

❖❖❖

Cottages: Shaw's Holiday, Y Maes, Pwllheli, Gwynedd

Shaw's Holiday handle around 200 cottages, bungalows, houses, chalets and caravans in lovely North Wales. From a real former working windmill to a house built on the beach. Lleyn Peninsula, Snowdonia, Anglesey and all points between. Telephone for free full colour brochure and up to date availability or visit our website.

200 cottages, sleeps 1-35, Price per week £100 low season, £800 high season, Children & pets welcome, Available all year.

**Contact: Mr Shaw, Shaw's Holidays, Y Maes, Pwllheli, Gwynedd LL53 5HA
Tel: 01758 614422 Fax: 01758 613835
EMail: all@shaws-holiday.demon.co.uk**

❖❖❖

Cottages: Towyn Farm Holidays, Tudweiliog, Pwllheli, Gwynedd

A 150 acre beef and sheep farm with 1/2 mile of coastal frontage which includes the renown beach of Towyn, 200 yards from farmyard. Fully centrally heated for Autumn - Winter lets, also open fire. All beds made ready. Shop and hotel in village 10 minutes walk away. Golf 5 miles, Snowdon 25 miles, Caernarfon 25 miles. Excellent sailing, fishing and swimming imminent. Children welcomed and encouraged to help feed poultry, etc. Free baby sitting on request. Lawn garden with barbecue furniture.

2 cottages, sleeping 6, 7 + cots, Price per week £150 low season, £380 high season, Children welcome, Pets by arrangement. Available all year, Map Ref 82

**Contact: Owen, Towyn Farm, Tudweiliog, Pwllheli, Gwynedd, Wales LL53 8PD
Tel: 01758 770230**

❖❖❖

Cottages: Nolton Haven Farm Cottages, Nolton Haven, Haverfordwest, Pembrokeshire

Nolton Haven Farm Cottages, in the Pembrokeshire National Park. Situated beside Nolton Havens sandy beach which they overlook, these six stone slate and pine cottages, offer discerning guests the ideal situation to enjoy the superb Pembrokeshire coastline. The cottages are fully equipped with colour TV, microwave and fridge/freezer. 30 yards to the beach, 75 yards to the local inn restaurant, pony trekking, surfing, fishing, excellent cliff walks.

6 cottages, sleeping 4-6, Price per week £135 low season, £460 high season, Children & pets welcome, Available all year, Map Ref 83

**Contact: Jim Canton, Nolton Haven Farm Cottages, Nolton Haven, Haverfordwest,
Pembrokeshire SA62 3NH
Tel/Fax: 01437 710263**

❖❖❖

❖❖

Cottage: Old Vicarage Cottage, Llangorse, Brecon, Powys

Fully self contained semi detached cottage in lovely quiet location. A short walk from the shop and pubs. Facilities include colour TV, full central heating, fully equipped kitchen. Children and well behaved dogs welcome. Within easy walk of lake. Sailing, fishing, pony trekking, rope climbing can be enjoyed nearby. The cottage is prettily decorated and close carpeted. It is within the Brecon Beacons National Park.

1 cottage, sleeps 4, Price per week £125 low season, £260 high season, Children & well behaved dogs welcome, Available all year, Map Ref 84

Contact: Mrs Anderson, The Old Vicarage, Llangorse, Brecon, Powys LD3 7UB
Tel: 01874 658639

❖❖

Cottages: Vineyard Cottages, Llanerch Vineyard, Hensol, Pendoylan, Vale of Glamorgan

Converted from 19th Century farm buildings, Llanerch Cottages offer superb accommodation in an idyllic setting with six acres of vines and a further ten acres of conservation woodlands and lakes. 15 minutes from Cardiff and convenient for touring all South Wales. Rated 5 Dragons by the WTB, the highest accolade for quality, ambience and facilities which include washing machine, dishwasher, microwave, central heating, TV and telephone. Ample car parking.

2 cottages, sleeps 4 + 2, Price per week £230 low season, £500 high season, No smoking or pets, Children welcome, Available all year, Map Ref 85

Contact: Peter Andrews, Llanerch Vineyard, Hensol, Pendoylan, Vale of Glamorgan CF72 8JU
Tel: 01443 225877 Fax: 01443 225546

❖❖

'Goodbye Blossom, we'll come and see you again'

ART GALLERIES
& MUSEUMS
of Britain

A guide to many of the art galleries and museums in England, Scotland and Wales, available from all good bookshops from Spring 1999

NOTES

NOTES

NOTES

NOTES

NOTES

NOTES

NOTES

NOTES

NOTES

NOTES

NOTES

'See you again next year'

KGP PUBLISHING
Penrith, Cumbria, England